THE
MODERN
UZBEKS

STUDIES OF NATIONALITIES
Wayne S. Vucinich, General Editor

The Crimean Tatars
Alan Fisher

The Volga Tatars: A Profile in National Resilience
Azade-Ayşe Rorlich

The Making of the Georgian Nation
Ronald Grigor Suny

The Modern Uzbeks: From the Fourteenth Century to the Present;
A Cultural History
Edward A. Allworth

Estonia and the Estonians, second edition
Toivo U. Raun

The Azerbaijani Turks: Power and Identity under Russian Rule
Audrey L. Altstadt

The Latvians: A Short History
Andrejs Plakans

The Kazakhs, second edition
Martha Brill Olcott

Edward A. Allworth is Professor of Turco-Soviet Studies at Columbia University; he is head of the Center for the Study of Central Asia and the Division of Central Asian Studies, and director of the Program on Soviet Nationality Problems. Professor Allworth is the author, coauthor, or editor of twelve books about ethnic affairs in the USSR and the intellectual history of the Russian East. His works cover the press, literature, theater, and materials of formal education in Central Asia; his current research treats the publications of early twentieth-century reformists Abdalrauf Fitrat and Mahmud Khoja Behbudiy and their opponents in Central Asia.

THE
MODERN
UZBEKS

From the
Fourteenth Century
to the Present

A CULTURAL HISTORY

Edward A. Allworth

HOOVER INSTITUTION PRESS
Stanford University
Stanford, California

Hoover Institution Press Publication 373

First printing, 1990

04   10 9 8 7

Manufactured in the United States of America
The paper used in this publication meets the minimum requirements of American National Standard for Information Sciences—Permanence of Paper for Printed Library Materials, ANSI Z39.48–1984. ∞

Library of Congress Cataloging in Publication Data
Allworth, Edward A.
    The modern Uzbeks : from the fourteenth century to the present : a cultural history / Edward A. Allworth.
        p.   cm. — (Studies of nationalities in the USSR)
    Includes bibliographical references.
    ISBN 0-8179-8731-2 (alk. paper). —
    ISBN 0-8179-8732-0 (pbk.: alk. paper).
DK948.62.A45   1990
958'.7—dc20
                                              89-19899
                                                 CIP

Contents

Foreword

Uzbekistan is the Soviet Union's most important Muslim community, which in many ways serves as the model for other Muslim groups. It is of special economic significance for the Soviet Union that, after the United States and China, Uzbekistan is the world's largest producer of cotton. Uzbekistan has (1989 census), after the Russians (145,071,550) and the Ukrainians (44,135,989), the largest ethnic population (16,686,240) in the Soviet Union and is the fifth-largest Soviet republic (447,400 square kilometers), after the Russian Soviet Federative Socialist Republic, the Kazakh Soviet Socialist Republic (SSR), the Ukrainian SSR, and the Turkmen SSR. Although Uzbekistan's population is heterogeneous, more than 60 percent of its inhabitants are Uzbeks.

The origins of the Uzbeks constitute a complex question. Professor Allworth argues that the documentable roots of Uzbek history can be traced only to the late fourteenth century. He challenges the popular thesis of Soviet scholars that the beginnings of Uzbek society and politics go back to the ancient and medieval civilizations of Central Asia, such as Achemedia, Bactria, Sogdia, and Tokaria, the rule of Alexander of Macedonia, the Seleucids, and so on. For years, with official support and direction, Soviet scholars have given a great deal of attention to the study of the precursors of the Uzbeks in Central Asia and the Uzbek ethnogenesis. The uncovering of large quantities of fascinating archeological material on several earlier civilizations is truly impressive. But in the interpretations of these and other data the Soviet historians have relied heavily on Marxist doctrine, making extensive use of the ideological dictates of historical materialism and reading too broad and overgenerous meanings into the available historical sources.

According to Allworth, historians have found it difficult to distinguish Uzbek contributions to civilizations from those made by others in the region. At the end of the fifteenth century, large bodies of Uzbeks mixed with different people. The Uzbek ethnic heterogeneity nullified racial links and blood ties as effective bases for determining or studying group identity.

The dynamic population that some contemporary observers called *Uzbek* emerged amid a confusion of names from early fourteenth-century western Asia. Although the historians do agree that Tatar warriors made up the first conglomeration of people called *Uzbek*, Professor Allworth makes it abundantly clear that the belated appearance of documentary sources does not in any way detract from the intensity and richness of cultural, sociopolitical, and economic dynamics responsible for the emergence of the modern Uzbek nation.

Allworth concentrates on twentieth-century Uzbek history, but the earlier history receives considerable attention as well. This book, the first Western study of the sociocultural dynamics of Uzbek history written by a single author, offers a careful and insightful critique of Soviet historiography and its underlying philosophical and ideological commitments. Equally valuable and commendable are Professor Allworth's survey and assessment of Uzbek documents in Turkish, European, and American depositories. In the age of the cultural fermentation of *perestroika*, the work should attract much attention among Soviet historians in their search for historiographic models unburdened with ideological obligations.

Professor Allworth's criticism of the Soviet historical method is supported by a careful and critical examination of sources and by the logic of historical processes. In recent times Soviet historians—less critical of and more receptive to Allworth's views on Uzbek history—have begun to question the validity of the Soviet Marxist view of Central Asian history. Objective presentation of the historical past is what many Central Asian historians would like to have written, but could not. The era of openness has reduced the inhibition in Central Asian intellectuals over writing the truth in their books, and they have begun to look for models. Contemporary Soviet historians may not agree with everything in *The Modern Uzbeks*, but they will indubitably acknowledge its scholarship and accept many of its interpretations.

Uzbekistan is a veritable laboratory of changes and developments resulting from a clash between Russian and European culture on the one hand and Muslim society on the other, a conflict between differing religions, languages, and social customs. It is a testing ground for many Russian and Soviet policies, for the study of indigenous reformist movements and modernism, for the growth of the revolutionary movements, and for the never-ending struggle between traditionalism and secularism. From these experiences and struggle have emerged the successes of Soviet policy (education, industrialization) as well as its failures (lack of a genuine community, no sense of identity with the Soviet nation, and ethnoreligious antagonism).

The author's intimate knowledge of Uzbek history, especially its imperial Russian and Soviet periods, illuminates issues involving Uzbek relations with their rulers and the Uzbek response to challenges of Russification and modernization. The book touches many important questions, especially nationalism and religion. Before 1917 there was no consciousness among the Uzbeks of belonging to a modern, well-defined nation. Their nationalism was religious. The modernist, secular, native intelligentsia became conscious of a nation when they determined to achieve national independence. Stalin opposed this nationalism and pressed for an identity that would be "national in form, socialist in content." He fought the Jadids (the Uzbek reformists) and other nationalists, silenced them in the early 1930s, and extirpated them in the Stalinist purges of 1937–1938. The Soviets undertook to reform the Uzbek language so that it could better fit into a "broader socialist community." The Arabic script was first replaced by Roman and later by Cyrillic script. The Uzbeks resented the foreign script, the antireligious propaganda, the curtailment of religious education and press, and most measures that went against Islamic tradition. The Russification has made gains; but the Uzbek resistance has remained strong, and the tenacity of the Uzbek traditions has withstood the challenges to communist ideology and morals.

The official census indicates an increase in native Uzbek population in relation to the republic's Russian population, and native ethnic affiliation has become important in one's ability to advance in Uzbek society. This ethnic cliquishness of the Uzbeks and others has begun to show a negative side, breeding ethnic antagonism. Thus, the trend in Uzbekistan is toward nativization, not internationalization. The hope for the emergence of a new community of peoples—the Soviet nation—has proved an empty dream. Neither the policy of *sblizhenie* (drawing together) nor the policy of *sliianie* (fusion or merging) through intermarriage have succeeded.

The religious leaders have successfully replaced the concept of religious with the concept of national. As a religion Islam may have weakened, but not as a mark of ethnic and cultural identity. Islamic and Muslim practices are widespread in the rural as well as the urban communities. Professor Allworth offers cogent comments on the role of Islam as a spiritual force strengthening the Uzbek ethnic unity and enriching the substance and individuality of national culture.

The Uzbek achievements under Soviet rule are many. Widespread public education has nearly eliminated illiteracy. In addition to the well-developed system of elementary, secondary, and trade schools, Uzbekistan has two universities and a number of important scientific and cultural centers. Impressive progress has been achieved in the fields of publishing, radio, and television. Conditions of life have improved, and there have been substantial advances in economic and cultural developments.

After Stalin's death in 1953, restricted delegations of foreigners were allowed into Central Asia. In the 1950s, when the Soviet Union began to court Muslim states, the Uzbek SSR became a showcase of successful modernization and socialism to the Afro-Asian world. Soviet authors repeatedly stress the role of the Soviet Central Asian republics as "development models." Tashkent has been the site of major international meetings and conferences and a place for young specialists from African and Asian countries to come for study and training.

In Allworth's *The Modern Uzbeks*—a work thoroughly researched, well written, and insightful—we have at last a comprehensive and authoritative survey of the cultural history of the Uzbeks and Uzbekistan. No other U.S. historian has done so much to promote the study of Central Asia and the Soviet nationalities. For many years he has investigated and written on ethnic and nationality problems in the Soviet Union, with particular concentration on the peoples of Central Asia, their resistance to Russian and Soviet rule, and the impact of that rule on their society and culture.

WAYNE S. VUCINICH
Series Editor and Professor Emeritus
History Department, Stanford University

Preface

This study pursues a few modest aims, the broadest of which is laying a firm base for understanding the Central Asian saga. Helping students and scholars identify important new subjects for investigation should lead to more specialized knowledge of the Central Asia so strongly affected by Uzbek dynamism. These chapters mean to discover the dominant patterns of Central Asian thought represented by Uzbek history.

This is an appropriate time for a historical inquiry into the Uzbek situation because of the reinvigoration of Central Asia and an interest outside the USSR about Central Asia's nationality problems, as well as efforts of Soviet leaders to shape those nationalities. The Uzbeks, now turning toward modern life, are producing many Uzbek-language publications and providing new openings for travel to Central Asia. Few people in the West enjoyed such opportunities even ten years ago, evidenced by the useful but scant scholarship of the 1970s. The Marxist ideological burden carried by numerous Soviet writings about Uzbek cultural history has inhibited some non-Soviet scholarship but encouraged those outside the USSR to provide a different treatment of this important, fascinating group of people. Outsiders can now go beyond current international affairs into the ideas and motivations—the cultural and intellectual history—of this changing civilization.

Although primary sources include compilations of data, because Central Asians and their scribes (see Bibliography) emphasize the words and ideas of the region's thinkers, writers, oral poets, and leaders, this book provides many quotations from writings and speeches of indigenous people. Perceptive obser-

Edward A. Allworth (*far right*) with scholars of the Institute of Language and Literature, Academy of Science, Uzbekistan Soviet Socialist Republic in Tashkent. (*From left to right*) Jamal Kamal, poet and Senior Associate Scholar; Sadir Erkinov, Chief Scholarly Associate; Bakhtiyar Nazarov, Director; Salokhiddin Mamajanov, Division Chief; Matyakub Koshchanov, former Director, now Chief Scholarly Associate, Professor, and Corresponding Member, USSR Academy of Science.

vations by travelers to the region also raise important questions and prompt several major propositions in Chapter 1 that guide the train of thought.

Because of uncertainty about the survival of the Uzbek group in its traditional form, this inquiry explores how Uzbek group identity grew and sustained itself over long periods. This investigation suggests the historical meaning of that corporate identity to the people involved and to the region and how such group identity is related to a Central Asia that included several different cultural entities known variously as Bukhara, Khokand (Qoqan), Khwarazm (Khiva), Turkistan, or Uzbekistan. The study goes on to probe the effect of modern experience on the Uzbekness that is so crucial to effective group cohesion.

January 1987

Acknowledgments

Professors Richard N. Frye and Eden Naby originally suggested that readers interested in Central Asia required a new history of its indigenous prime movers, the Uzbeks. Uncovering elaborately camouflaged or submerged truths requires diligent effort and careful selectivity; the subtlety and depth of Turkistanian culture offer more attractions and substance for inquiry than a scholar could uncover in a hundred lifetimes. Encouraging me in this effort was Wayne S. Vucinich, Professor of East European History at Stanford University, whose steady moral support and infinite patience should inspire the treatment of every potential author.

This inquiry's efforts also depended on the efforts of others in the field. Clues to finding many of the rare publications, archives, manuscripts, and recollections that make up this cultural history came from the advice of colleagues and elders. In this respect, it gives genuine pleasure to mention a few who have helped supply or locate such valuable sources: Dr. Baymirza Hayit, Professor Aleksandr Bennigsen, Professor Zeki Velidi Togan, Professor Tahir Chaghatay, and Mr. Naim Oktem. Without their (surely Central Asian style of) generosity, this effort would have remained incomplete and less interesting.

Many students and friends have shared questions, observations, and advice over the years of gestation. They can only be acknowledged, not adequately repaid. Professor Pierre Cachia and Mr. Obeidullah Noorata, both giving instruction at Columbia University, listened and responded to questions about readings in the texts. The understanding of Professor Kathleen R. F. Burrill, the chair of the Department of Middle East Languages at Columbia University, made possible the completion of the final stages. Mr. Richard Wright of Bethesda, Maryland, responded most amiably to urgent appeals for help in locating essential primary materials. Graduate students at Columbia University delved for references and data; those not mentioned in the footnotes include the now Dr. Eli Lederhendler, Dr. Michael Klecheski, Bruce Cooper, the late instructor in Philosophy, Dr.-to-be Kenneth Nyirady, Dr. Timur Kocaoglu, and Reverend Judith Fleming. To them and many more, sincere thanks.

In Columbia University's libraries Dr. Eugene Sheehy, Eileen McIlvaine, Nina Lencek, Laura Binkowski Kunt, Diane Kelly Goon, Anita Lowry, Sara Spurgin, and their colleagues' advice was indispensable. Dr. Edward Kasinec, Dr. Svat Soucek, and Dr. Victor Koressar in the Slavonic Division of the New York Public Library and Ibrahim Pourhadi of the Near Eastern Section at the Library of Congress aided the work substantially. Linda Ferreira and Gary Hanks in Columbia University's Learning Center guided the author into the era of word processing. Christopher Brest prepared maps showing the location of the Uzbeks around 1400 and 1980, respectively.

A study grant as well as substantial research assistance from the Kennan Institute for Advanced Russian Study, Washington, D.C., and a grant from the Harriman Institute for Advanced Study of the Soviet Union, Columbia University, aided work in the libraries of Washington, D.C. Assistance from the Hoover Institution on War, Revolution and Peace at Stanford, California, materially furthered preparation of the manuscript.

The Central Asian proper names in this book appear without diacritical marks in the interest of economy and visual comfort. In endnotes and bibliography, transliterations comport with the system published in my *Nationalities of the Soviet East. . .* (1971), and I have prepared all original translations not attributed to others.

THE BASES OF UZBEK GROUP IDENTITY

PART ONE

1   Ideas of Community

Äytkän gäp atqan oq.
A word said is a shot fired.

Kob oylä, az soylä.
Think lots, say little.

(Uzbek sayings)*

Cultural history focuses on the ideas of the public at large, rather than those currents of thought that preoccupy highly educated elite. In this inquiry, two considerations make that prescription especially demanding. Until quite recently, Central Asians prized close-mouthed manhood (see the sayings at the beginning of this chapter). Furthermore, the nature of Central Asian politics over many centuries has discouraged free public discourse. Central Asia is not inarticulate, but a search for its voice often faces complex tasks and systemic resistance. In this research, diligence and good fortune were rewarded by finding witnesses and written sources. Attending to symbolic speech, savoring the works of creative writers and other intellectuals who speak for their community and strive to talk to all its members, and examining individual biography helps discover the region's salient values.

* Sher 'Ali Rozi, comp., *Ozbäk maqallari* (Moscow: SSSR Khälqlarining Märkäz Näshriyati, 1926), pp. 15, 39.

The situation in Central Asia confronts historians with the following questions: How will the creation of a corporate, retrospective nationality where none existed before affect people when it is politically motivated and applied and executed by outsiders? How long will it take an aggregate of people under alien laws, a superimposed group name, and an externally delineated territory to absorb the new identity to any significant degree?

Russian communist party officials perhaps meant to substantiate a pseudo-nationality, not a viable political Uzbek nationality when they established a Soviet Socialist Republic (SSR) named Uzbekistan. From the start they sharply distinguished between that administrative structure and the nationality itself. Apparently they meant the group formally designated Uzbek to restrain true patriotism while serving Soviet purposes in foreign and domestic policy. The people named Uzbek (designated by the founding of the Uzbekistan SSR in 1924–1925) understood these changes in Turkistanian life differently than the Soviet Russian politicians.

That divergence in understanding constitutes part of the problem confronting this inquiry. Uzbek writings and songs today infrequently celebrate the prowess of an Uzbek nationality; instead, they usually concern the administrative-territorial unit, Uzbekistan. Uzbeks did not measure out that unit on the map for themselves, which probably signifies something basic regarding their group identity. Contemporary evidence offers some arguments concerning the permanence (or transience) of modern, corporate Uzbek nationality ("nationality" and "ethnic" serve as adjectival synonyms here). Any contentions about its ethnic durability, however, become persuasive only when subjected to a thorough consideration of the extended preliminaries to the Uzbeks' current situation.

THE *MODERN* UZBEKS

This book uses the word *modern* to designate concepts more complex than the chronological distinctions between ancient, medieval, and recent times or the political and sociological categories that measure the extent of industrialization or education reached by a certain population. Instead, *modern* here carries one of two senses that coexist in acute tension in Central Asia. The first goes beyond economic or material cultural development to describe the arrival of a group at a shared frame of mind and outlook. In that usage, *modern* connotes collective self-awareness or superimposed group identity.

Many now believe the officially titled Uzbeks lent their name to the Uzbekistan SSR—a misunderstanding that probably signals some change in attitude about Uzbek group identity. This book evaluates sources that suggest a certain cluster of ideas around this grouphood, including a sense of self-reliance and responsibility, cultural diversity, independent thinking, and an increased understanding of the essential differences between tyranny and democracy. This advance beyond earlier dependency, self-pity, and patient accommodation to alien ideologies may allow the discovery of a new voice enunciating qualities and signals of Uzbek group maturity in the twentieth century.

The second usage of *modern* may owe something to a harsh streak in Central Asia's composite personality, which expresses itself in a contempt for the delicacy of civilization and diversity and in human cruelty. It deifies power and the mobilization of resources for selfish or ideological ends. This autocratic modernity emerged in Central Asia in the second quarter of the nineteenth century and continues throughout the region into the present period.

In what proportions do the Uzbek group exhibit the two kinds of modernity? The answer does not come easily. The two forms continue to exert countervailing effects on Uzbek ethnic group identity. The growing strain in this ambivalence in modernness illustrates within this regional struggle the universal rivalries between open and closed societies. Analyzing the opinions and feelings of Uzbeks for evidence of truly modern attainments should test a major thesis of this study: when Uzbeks make the choice, their Russian-sponsored nationality may not persist in the form so recently supplied.

This proposition sets a crucial task for anyone interpreting Central Asian cultural history. Each chapter of this book attempts to measure Uzbek progress, if any, toward *modern* life. The first part of the inquiry looks into seven aspects of group identity that the accumulations of centuries have ostensibly brought to the Uzbek population. Most significant in this respect are ideas about community, sovereignty (symbolized by foreign diplomacy), and group naming. In this case, leadership will probably prove indispensable to collective identity. Ideology and values in the most appropriate group language round out this understanding of group identity.

UZBEK HISTORY

The people now termed Soviet Uzbeks have a most complicated history and in cast of mind they appear to differ significantly from their predecessors. Why the Uzbeks have become the people they are can only be grasped through an understanding of their original nature and the great impact twentieth-century life has exerted on them. Old chronicles show the early Uzbeks actively engaged in relationships with surrounding tribes and aggregations, which affected their view of themselves and the world. The old interrelations shaped operative, practical distinctions between groups but, more important, conformed Uzbek outlook and thinking. This lateral interaction among Central Asian groups occurred much more frequently then than it does today. Some of those medieval contacts, seldom friendly but always influential, laid the groundwork for relations with non-Uzbeks far into the future.

Early Uzbek Interactions with Other Groups

Almost the first verifiable interactions of Uzbeks as a group with other tribes occurred in the area of Khwarazm. Then, as now, the middle of Khwarazm's territory lay in the delta of the Amu Darya (river) just south of the Aral Sea (see figure 1.1). By 1505, Khwarazm had become the Uzbeks' most powerful northern outpost. But more than a century before that, the establishment of Khwarazm tested the Uzbeks' military strength and the ability of a nomadic society to maintain a settlement.

Some Persian historians writing in the Middle Ages called the areas north of the Sir Darya Uzbek territory. Yet the Uzbeks of 1390–1420 often lacked hegemony in the eastern part of the Qipchaq Plains (*Däsht-i Qipchäq*). Formidable khans from the Golden Horde, based on the Volga River, contested for Khwarazm with Central Asian potentates. In those battles, the Uzbeks, at that time neither psychologically nor geographically true Central Asians, allied themselves with or were subject to rulers of the Golden Horde. Its Manghit amir, Idiku Bahadur (in Russian sources Yedigey), scourged Russia as well as Central Asia. Idiku Bahadur, a wily field commander and a power behind the throne of the Golden Horde from 1396 to 1411, brought Uzbek warriors into his fight over Khwarazm, among other battlefields. Uzbek participation against princes in Russia and against Timur's descendants in the Khwarazmian region colored the Uzbeks' image in Russian as well as Timurid memory.

By 1413 Timur's descendants had made Khwarazm their domain once again by driving out its governor, Idiku Bahadur's son, and his warriors, who probably included some Uzbeks. Two decades after Idiku Bahadur had passed violently from the scene, the Uzbeks under their own leadership invaded Urganch, the capital of Khwarazm. A courier brought that unpleasant news from the Qipchaq Plains to the Timurid capital, far to the south in Herat. A Timurid historian, Abdurrazzaq Samarqandiy (1413–1482), disapprovingly reported the event in his chronicle:

> Uzbek troops sprinkled the crown of their destiny with the ashes of perfidy and raised the dust of sedition . . . Listening to this news [about the Uzbek invasion] turned out to be painful and difficult for the stable mind [of Timurid ruler, Shahrukh]. He ordered several amirs to that territory, and these eminent amirs, displaying the signs of courage and bravery, attacked the Uzbek people and state [*ulus*], destroying and scattering all these insolent ones.

In fact, the conflict did not resolve itself quite that way. According to some later Central Asian historians, dampness and/or plague drove out the invading

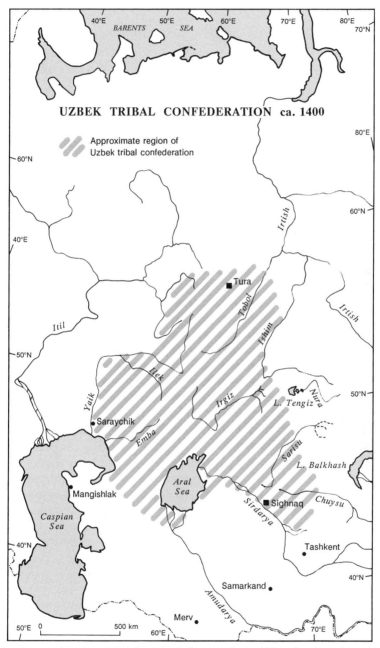

Figure 1.1 The first Uzbek homeland. Sources: B. A. Akhmedov, *Gosudarstvo kochevykh Uzbekov* (1965); *Hudud al-'Alam* trans. Minorsky (1970); W. Barthold, *Turkestan Down to the Mongol Invasion* trans. Gibb (1958).

Uzbeks, who were accustomed to the clean air and open spaces of the Qipchaq Plains. A modern interpretation suggests that the threat of strife in the plains drew the Uzbek forces back to protect their grazing lands. Regardless, the entry shows how the Uzbeks, by associating with antagonists to the Russian and Timurid thrones, acquired such a bad name. Although the Uzbeks evidently did not initiate the action, the negative epithets and attitudes expressed toward them in the account are the most consequential portion of this early record of Uzbek history.[1] Before many more decades had passed, the Uzbek name and the sight of characteristic Uzbek battle dress (see figure 1.2) scattered Timurid troops of Central Asia in fright.[2] In the early sixteenth century, Uzbeks once again received harsh words from their militant neighbors to the rear. Safavid historians in Persia colorfully chronicled battles between their forces and those they called miscreants and Uzbeks, Uzbeks and villains. The chroniclers registered the opinion that a victorious Central Asian Uzbek khan "throughout [Khurasan] raised the banner of oppression and injustice." That was a calculated insult, since justice was among the highest ideals of the Central Asian public and its monarchs. Their conception of justice included a belief that the ruler would deal fairly and responsibly with his subjects, good and bad, high and low. This popular view included deep admiration for the amir or khan's unwillingness to abuse his divinely bestowed authority.

Central Asian historians wrote of a good king's evenhandedness in meting out punishment, but no one dreamed of affording people the equality that characterizes newer thinking about a contractual relationship between leader and led. One recent definition of justice proposes that all "social primary goods—liberty and opportunity, income and wealth, and the bases of self-respect—are to be distributed equally unless an unequal distribution of any or all of these goods is to the advantage of the least favored."[3] Ideas such as distributive justice and complex equality have no relevance to the inherited Central Asian faith in the good ruler's justice, but they may connect with modern Uzbek aspirations for equality.[4]

In Khwarazm soon after its temporary conquest by the Uzbeks in 1431, aspects of these two versions of justice were at work. The Uzbek chieftain proudly rewarded his victorious warriors with gold and valuables from the rich treasury captured in Urganch. He demonstrated his idea of fairness not by giving each the same sum but by allowing officers and troopers to approach the door of the repository two by two and take away all they could carry in one trip. Here the Uzbek khan also acted fairly, relying on physical ability and sound judgment rather than exact equality. This idea might prove useful in late twentieth-century Central Asia when comparing medieval popular justice with what prevails in that area Russian authorities named Uzbekistan.[5]

As the early Uzbeks conglomerated and emerged into public view, they invited considerable verbal abuse. The specific charge of injustice leveled at

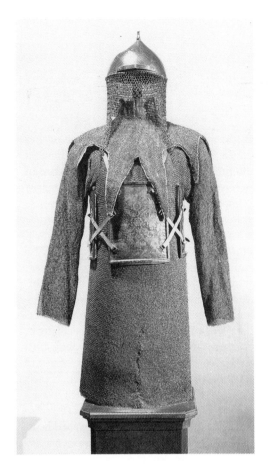

Figure 1.2 Uzbek ring mail shirt with helmet, Bukhara. Sammlung H. Moser-Charlottenfels No. MW917, Bernisches Historisches Museum, Switzerland.

these early Uzbeks by the Safavid historian arose out of the religious rivalry between Central Asia and Persia from the sixteenth century. Religious hostility alone, however, did not supply all the grounds for condemnation, for annalists also created attitudes.

In addition historians such as Mahmud ibn Wali, who dedicated his history to the governor of Balkh and later to the Ashtarkhanid dynasty's ruler, Nadir Muhammad, who ruled from 1642 to 1645, undoubtedly reflected the government's perception of the Uzbeks. In his *Bahr al-asrar fi manakib-i al-ahyar* (Sea of Secrets Concerning the Braveries of the Noble), composed 1634–40/41), ibn Wali, writing about the geography of Turkistan, added these remarks: "The people of this land in each era had a special name and nickname. Thus, from Tura ibn Yafas's time to the emergence of Mogul-Khan, people called the inhabitants of this land Turks." He explains that after the Mongols took power, all the tribes who inhabited the region were called Moguls. Then, "after the raising of Uzbek Khan's sovereign banner [over the Golden Horde] and to this day, the inhabitants of this land have been named Uzbeks." Abroad, however, people called all inhabitants of Turan, the area northeast of Iran, Turks. Once ibn Wali established that the Turks in Central Asia were the Uzbeks, he went on to characterize their nature: "This group is famed for bad nature, swiftness, audacity, and boldness."[6]

Thus, this seventeenth-century author deliberately distanced himself and his patron from the fearsome character and name of the Uzbeks, practicing a type of ethnic discrimination that often hardens its victims' defiant sense of identity. In this case, however, foreign hostility seemed to lessen the security of the Uzbek group name and image. That may have occurred partly because Uzbeks did not enter the scene until several strong powers—Ottomans, Safavids, Timurids, and Aqqoyunlu (White-Sheep Turkmens)—had established themselves in Central Asia or around its periphery.

If the Uzbeks as a whole projected an outlaw image among foreign rulers and historians, some in the tribe probably gloried in that fearsome reputation. But the socialization of a few Uzbek leaders made them want to be admired by their neighbors and peers. The unflattering image seemed to accompany their assumption of an imperial role in the Central Asian region. The incident in 1431 at Khwarazm, which Uzbeks briefly recaptured before withdrawing, and the language used to characterize it introduce another telling feature of group identity relating to the Central Asians. The written history of any era accords with the viewpoint of its writer or his sponsor. For perhaps one hundred years after their collective emergence in the 1380s, the Uzbeks evidently lacked their own literate historians. A few educated, ambitious Uzbek leaders learned from alien competitors that the compilation of histories conveyed contemporary glory and important status on the sovereigns who commissioned them. Later generations, including subjects, foreigners, scholars, and students, would judge a khan's stature on the basis of oral and written histories.

Beginning in the 1430s certain Uzbek khans, blessed with power, leadership, means, and the desire to have their stories told, began supporting learned emigrant scholars from Iran. Later in that century Fazlallah ibn Ruzbihan Isfahaniy (Khunji) (b. Shīrāz 1457, d. Central Asia sometime between 1521 and 1533), an eminent Persian Sunni historian, came to Samarkand. He had previously spent about four years in Azerbayjan at the court of the Turkmen Aqqoyunlu dynasty, where he wrote its annals. Isfahaniy entered the service of the Uzbeks' Shaybaniy Khan (r. 1500–1510) no earlier than 1503 and completed *Mihman namä-yi bukhara* (The Book of Bukhara's Guest), a highly respected history of that ruler's exploits and ideas, in 1509. After the khan perished in battle the following year, Isfahaniy also served Ubaydullah Khan (r. 1512–1539), a Shaybanid, for whom he composed a treatise on good government called *Suluk äl-muluk* (Rules for the Conduct of Sovereigns, 1514). It included an account of that khan's victory over Zahiriddin Muhammad Babur (r. Farghana 1494–1501, Kabul 1504–1530, Samarkand

1511–1512). Babur was the last Timurid prince to contend seriously with the Uzbeks in Central Asia; he bitterly disparaged them in every way.

Owing to their rarity and skill, these peripatetic scholars without tenure chronicled the Uzbeks as well as their rivals and opponents, thus expressing many values and ideas historically associated with the Uzbek tribes and dynasties. These authors composed in Farsi rather than in the Turkic language of the Uzbeks, which created not only a specific genre in regional historiography (that is, local history by outsiders) but conditioned the Uzbeks' view of themselves and recorded the epithets, few complimentary, that others applied to them. Because the dictates of the period reflected only refined opinion, those writing for the Central Asian khans sparingly applied the unqualified name Uzbek to their patrons. Isfahaniy found other formulations more comfortable: he referred to Uzbek-Shaybanids or employed complete circumlocutions.[7]

This noticeable reticence to employ the Uzbek designation added mystery to the Uzbeks' frightening public image throughout the cities of Central Asia and eastern Iran. The idiom of those serving the Shaybanid court combined with the invective of hostile historians to threaten the respectability, even the survival, of the Uzbek group name. Social and cultural pressures also threatened the name's use, positive or negative, into the twentieth century.

That complex circumstance challenges us to explore the vital but tenuous connections linking a name with its bearer group. Names have value for their bearers. The name *Uzbek* long ago lost its firm hold on the namesake group and may yet convey a new meaning. To verify the link between a self-name attached to a single living human group at different times in history demands analysis by onomastic methods. The connection may merely be that both exist in a certain time, not that the name and its group will linger in time and space indefinitely, unattached to the surrounding world, always conveying the same meaning.

It is possible that tribal and ethnic aggregations in Central Asia depend for survival on intangibles such as a group name outside the realm of economics or day-to-day politics. Group names alone, however, cannot cement individuals into a cohesive body. Group vitality requires that significant numbers of the society act on certain thoughts together. To do this, they must share a set of values and ideas that guide the group. The community's name helps focus on a group's shared beliefs, which are evidenced by its cultural development and accomplishments. At many stages in the Central Asian past, however, contemporary historians neither would nor probably could distinguish Uzbek contributions to civilization from those of others in the region.

In the present case, the Uzbek group, like many ethnic entities in the modern world, cannot reach into a distant past to anchor itself to an earlier counterpart. Both discontinuity with the past and insecure linkage between name and group complicate present Uzbek existence as well as the process of understanding this cultural phenomenon. The geographical distribution of people added to this complexity.

Changing Uzbek Territories and Symbols

After the major migration south at the end of the fifteenth century, large bodies of Uzbeks lived with different people, often distant kinsmen in Western Siberia, Turkistan, the khanates of Khwarazm and Qoqan plus the amirate of Bukhara, northern Afghanistan, and Khurasan. Except for Siberia (the western part of which fell within the Qipchaq Plains), conventional Central Asia today includes those areas, embracing approximately that space now designated by Soviet administration to include Kazakhstan and the area south of it reaching to the borders of Iran, Afghanistan, and the People's Republic of China. Reference to Central Asia, therefore, describes a region that extends far beyond the boundaries of the political-territorial unit first officially named Uzbekistan in the 1920s (see figure 15.1).

Turkistan's changeable location probably also destabilized the concept of homeland for the Uzbeks, for Turkistan, unlike Bukhara, Khwarazm, and Qoqan, did not designate some fairly definitive core zone. After the Middle Ages, Turkistan generally encompassed what was to become Russian Central Asia minus the Bukharan and Khwarazmian enclaves. Southern Central Asia comprised the region below Kazakhstan. Afghan Turkistan covered the strip of northern Afghanistan adjoining Soviet Central Asia. Eastern Turkistan lay entirely within what is now China, called Xinjiang by the Chinese. These place names, figuring in the vision of an Uzbek homeland, reappear throughout Central Asian intellectual history.

Although Uzbeks were widely dispersed and ethnically indistinct (and thus vaguely defined) they made aesthetic contributions to the culture throughout Central Asia. This lack of correspondence between tribal or ethnic group distribution and the boundaries imposed by politics have affected the group's sense of cohesion and self-understanding. Geographic and administrative delineations demand some attention in any determination of Uzbek group awareness; by themselves, however, these boundaries are too narrow to complete the search for this group's identity.

Over time, Central Asian group awareness and cohesion have seemed to depend on members attaching themselves, subconsciously and consciously, to certain labels, symbols, and values. These ideas and attitudes help define the group both for itself and for others. To some degree, external group attributes contribute to Central Asian identity when linked to labels, symbols, and values. (Writings about human value systems by modern sociologists help focus such an inquiry, though that methodology may better suit other purposes.)[8] These signs and beliefs (symbols and values) guided the group in medieval times as well as in the present. Even so, priorities changed and the constellations of values probably shifted when great alterations occurred in culture and society. Interpretations are sensitive to such alterations, subtle or drastic.

Authoritarian Modernity

Modern ways wrenched Central Asia when available military technology meshed with a new style of leadership. Guns had been known both in and out of the region for centuries, yet shortly before the mid-nineteenth century they suddenly received a domestic application that unbalanced the old system of equilibrium between rulers in the capital cities and peripheral tribal forces. A ruthless amir, Nasrullah-khan (1826–1860), succeeded in installing a small but regular, disciplined armed force in Bukhara's amirate. With help from Abdal Samad Tabrizi, an Iranian fugitive, he equipped and trained his troops with cannon cast and weapons made inside the amirate.[9] Employing Turkmens, he devastated Uzbek tribal power and fixed the surviving tribes on their pasturelands, away from the capital. This kept them in check but weakened the entire area's defenses against external assault. Exercising guile and power, the amir raised Bukhara over Qoqan and limited Khiva. Although he appeared to act like his medieval predecessors, his personal style, methods, and means displayed an important difference.

Amir Nasrullah-khan prepared Central Asia for one sort of modernity by reintroducing the idea of a totalitarian ruler without the traditional ameliorating qualities. Here was a man whose morals and ethics lacked any redeeming cultural or social features. He scorned religious life and the arts and avoided poetry writing. Notwithstanding some military and economic successes in the state of Bukhara, his contempt for public opinion of the future and his disdain for the plight of people in his domain caused both indigenous and foreign historians to judge him severely. An unjust ruler, according to them, spelled disaster for his people. Some even ascribed the ultimate fall of the Bukharan state to the ascent of Amir Nasrullah-khan to the throne.[10] That style of rule set the tone for a different type of Central Asian leader.

More important, Amir Nasrullah-khan also failed to prepare a successor who would build on the base of power accumulated at such cost by his tyrannical predecessor. Thus, the amir disrupted the old rhythmic counterpoint of Central Asian rule by which strongmen prepared the ground for and alternated with cultured patrons of religion, public well-being, and creative arts to benefit the society as a whole. That cycle, which began much earlier, characterized affairs in Khiva and Qoqan at the end of the eighteenth and beginning of the nineteenth centuries. In addition, Amir Nasrullah-khan strengthened the Turkmen and Iranian component in the military and government of Bukhara to the extent that the Uzbek-centered ethnic and linguistic equilibrium of the region was thrown out of balance. These conditions laid the foundation for the latest period of Uzbek group existence.

Given the present ideological limitations, how can an essentially new regrouping, such as the modernizing Uzbeks, fix a solid self-image? To derive a durable current image out of their imperial experience would seem to demand great creativity and resourcefulness. After four-and-a-half centuries of dominating others in the region, the Uzbeks were subordinated to another imperial power. This not merely altered their view of the world, it caused striking changes in attitudes toward society and leadership. Between 1863 and 1876, as Russian troops took authority away from local rulers all over southern and eastern Central Asia outside of Afghanistan and Kashgar, Uzbek political figures in government and society made unavoidable accommodations to the new circumstances. This did not by itself introduce abrupt political or technological change to the region, but it provided important elements of that process.

Traditional Uzbeks related to a chieftain with whom they felt a reciprocal set of obligations. This idea of authority as a compact between legitimate domination and subordination of groups forms a central thesis in some Western political thinking, and writings in that vein can inform modern authority as treated in this interpretation of Uzbek intellectual history. The main concern, however, must be with the ideas Uzbeks held and hold about authority and leadership, focusing on the structures of power as they become modernized.[11] That understanding of authority evolved in a heterogeneous human environment. The very notion of a place called Central Asia implies a mixture of people sharing common territory rather than a homogeneous ethnic homeland for one distinct nationality. That heterogeneity extended a tribal style of equality—in which all enjoyed access to the chief and shared a voice in decisions—to the interactions between whole confederations or states. Thus, a special relationship of heterogeneity to beliefs about authority appears to characterize the Uzbeks' specific culture.

This diversity within the group also nullifies racial links and blood ties as effective bases for determining or studying group identity in Central Asia. Thus, the officially sponsored Uzbek ethnic identity of the twentieth century, which seems inescapably impermanent, may stem from other important factors as well, such as indigenous leadership or its absence. Russian communist efforts to limit the leadership exercised by local ethnic groups contributes to uncertainties about the relatively brief Soviet Russian role in Central Asia, making it difficult to apply the restrictive definition of modernity to the Uzbek group. In addition, what is perhaps negatively modern includes an urban verbosity that, judging from the Uzbek sayings quoted at the beginning of this chapter, did not characterize the earlier tribal or present rural population. Among some city people—perhaps ideologists with ready access to the media—that garrulousness suggests a diminishing respect for the word as thought.

For cultural historians, another dilemma facing the Uzbek pseudo-sovereign polity is the intellectual consequence of a system that closes its eyes, ears, and mind to the competition of ideas. Conformity is the strongest threat to the intellectual independence of any group that willingly participates in someone else's closed system of thought. In the twentieth century, Uzbeks have the advantage of relating to their Islamic and recent Reformist legacies, as well as to a trickle of ideas from the noncommunist world—ideas their ideologists warn the Central Asians to beware of. Out of this diversity, Uzbek intellectual colloquy supports the group's spiritual health, which could be undermined if Uzbek thinking moves much further into the exclusive, dogmatic system promoted by Moscow's Soviet Russian leadership. A direct product of that ideological system is the necessity for its stewards to rewrite history.

In reading history, balanced Uzbek minds have to work around a misrepresentation concerning the significance of the Uzbek presence in Central Asia. Soviet ideologists acting as historians assert that the Uzbek migration into the region exerted no important impact on Central Asia or that the Uzbek coming produced regrettable consequences. Yet, in a Western interpretation, one hypothesis of Uzbek intellectual history proposes that the move by Shaybaniy Khan and his numerous tribesmen into southern Central Asia made a profound difference in the region's life from 1500 onward. Despite the bad reputation attributed to them by the Timurids and Safavids, Uzbeks, through the instruments of name, leadership style, values, attitudes, language, and other contributions, must have touched the imagination and sensibilities of the people and institutions of southern Central Asia. In time, the newcomers altered the mental picture the population held and registered for itself in the written record, including literature.

The reading of contemporary Uzbek histories leads to the conjecture that the triangular interrelationship between name, symbols and values, and concepts of leadership (sovereignty) structured the idea of supratribal, traditional Uzbek group identity. A great variety of mostly intangible group possessions—institutions, concepts, linkages—furnish both a foundation and a generator for group self-awareness. Communication within and without the Uzbek society, education, historiography, monuments and their locale, and systems of thought and ideology, all play a part. Ideas of homeland and attitudes toward politics carry great weight in the self-identity of confederations and nationalities. In the mesh of biography and the flights of literary imagination as well as in human style and manner, both the factual and the fantastic supply requisites for full-fledged group understanding. To an extent, each of these aspects of Uzbek group life contributes a necessary share to the formation of a durable corporate identity.

Those newer concepts cannot be disconnected from what came before. Beginning in the 1430s when the Uzbeks grasped a share of power in Central Asia, they held it with few lapses until the 1850s. It was only, however, for some decades before and after 1499–1500 (when they began to invest Mawaraun- nahr (Transoxiana), that this confederation knew the meaning of distinctive Uzbek political sovereignty, which created a basis for the symbols and attitudes that became a feature of Uzbek group identity. As a result of both early and late occurrences in the region, the grouping of people now living under the specific name Uzbek lacks recourse to any other genuine attributes of monoethnic independence or sovereignty established in recent centuries. If they possessed a leader or combination of leaders of their choice, they might assign true author- ity over the nationality's destiny to him or them. Lacking this, Uzbeks have relearned group vulnerability to political vicissitudes. They also have discovered that sovereignty as a separate force can represent weakness as well as strength in those complex factors supporting group self-awareness. Sovereignty's external signs as well as their internal meaning for the group similarly stand at risk.

2 Symbols and Values of Sovereignty

Hech qäydä padshahliq qäydichä yoqtur.

Nowhere is there anything like the bondage of sovereignty.

(Zahiriddin Muhammad Babur, 1528/29)[*]

The Central Asian view of a well-ordered world encompasses the striking contrasts prevalent in the region's array of formidable rulers. To reconcile these opposites, the Central Asian concept of history draws leadership models from at home and abroad, as well as from recorded and mythologized reality. By the time Uzbek multitudes migrated into southern Central Asia around 1500, such model leaders already dominated the nomads' imagination and historiography. These models generally represent two strongly conflicting currents of leadership—constructive and destructive.

From this dialectic emerged three giant symbolic figures: Alexander, Anushirwan, and Chinggis marked out ways of thinking and acting for later sovereigns. First and foremost to appear from that panoply of outsiders was Alexander the Great (r. 336–323 B.C.). Although the genuine Alexander set a heavily mailed foot in southern Sogdiana, Bactria, and Parthia—ancient Central Asia—in 330 B.C., myth depended not on that reality but on the ideals

---

[*] Zahriddin Muhammad Bäbar, *Bäbar namä* (London: Luzac & Co., 1905, repr. 1971), L349a, facsimile.

embodied in the image of such an admired monarch. Both educated and illiterate Central Asians esteemed yet another non-Muslim foreigner, Sasanian ruler Khusraw the First (r. 531–579), known widely in Central Asia as Anushirwan or Nushirwan, as an ideal prototype. He occupied that enviable position in the imagination even though he never set foot in Mawaraunnahr. His reputation for equitable treatment of his subjects was unparalleled. In later codes of behavior and literature, writers often referred to him simply as "The Just," without mentioning his given name or titles.[1]

JUSTICE AND EQUITY

Neither Alexander nor Anushirwan qualifies as a Central Asian although Anushirwan minted his Sasanian coins in Balkh, Herat, and Merv. But the authors in the tenth through the twelfth centuries who lauded them emanated from Khurasan, which is the fruitful southwestern part of Central Asia and one source of its intellectual and cultural inspiration. Alexander, in the role of perfect monarch, appeared in medieval codes of conduct for kings as well as in oral and written literature. With him emerge the lives and wisdom of Greek philosophers, notably Plato and Aristotle, whose quoted sayings often provided pointed lessons about virtue and justice in kings. In *Counsel for Kings*, for example, Muslim theologian Abu Hamid Muhammad al-Ghazali (1058–1111) ascribes numerous actions and sayings to Alexander the Great: "Alexander asked Aristotle whether courage or justice is higher. He answered, 'If the king has ruled justly, he will not need courage.'"

Those remarkable codes of princely values and behavior set down precepts and morals to guide the sovereign, including many discourses, anecdotes, or aphorisms devoted to the idea of justice. Guidebooks for good governance from that greater Central Asian area and late medieval age generally agreed that kingship came as a divine gift to a leader, not merely as an attribute of human ability or personality. Many passages in the holy *Qur'ân* (Koran) express that theme:

> Say: "O God, Master of the Kingdom,
> Thou exaltest whom Thou wilt,
> and Thou
> abasest whom Thou wilt; in Thy hand
> is the good; Thou art powerful
> over everything."[2]

In Central Asian understanding, with divine sanction came responsibility. Most authors of the medieval period indicated their values by pointing out the rulers' obligations. The earliest writing of this sort to appear in the Turki language came from the eastern part of Turkistan. In his *Qutadghu bilig* (Knowledge That Leads to Happiness, 1069/70), Yusuf Khas Hajib discusses the morality and values of good rulers:

> The foundation of kingship, the core of it, is based on righteousness
> The root of kingship is the road of righteousness.
> If the leader advances a just policy for the tribe, if he be right,
> The wishes and desires that he may want, he will find.[3]

Like Yusuf Khas Hajib's treatise concerning the way to felicity, al-Ghazali's *Nasihat äl-muluk* (Book of Counsel for Kings), written between 1105 and 1111, lays down as the first principle that a righteous exercise of authority by a king brings unsurpassed happiness to his domain. Failure in this respect incurs terrible torment. Al-Ghazali quotes God's apostle Muhammad as saying, "One day of just rule by an equitable Sultan is more meritorious than sixty (or seventy) years of continual worship."[4]

Few indigenous paragons balanced the extremes in political and social leadership during the history of the Middle Ages in Central Asia to emerge as great sovereigns. Of those who did, historians all recall the Samanid amir Abu Ibrahim Ismail ibn Ahmad al-Samani (r. 887–907), who changed an unstable situation in Bukhara into peace and security. According to a Bukharan historian writing in 943/944, Amir Ismail, "was indeed worthy and right for the padishahship. He was an intelligent, just, compassionate person, one possessing reason and prescience . . . he conducted affairs with justice and good ethics. Whoever might tyrannize people he would punish . . . In affairs of state he was always impartial."[5]

In his actions, Amir Ismail consistently adhered to a crucial principle not explicitly attributed to him by historian Narshakhiy. That trait distinguishes his style of leadership from those who followed an unrelenting authoritarian line. Forgiveness toward erring friend and relative or hostile foe characterized the amir's conduct and decisions. That quality governed the illustrious amir personally and ethically during his rule over the country of Bukhara for twenty years, Mawaraunnahr for seven, and Khurasan for seven.[6]

Amir Ismail's example lived on in the many books of advice for princes composed and circulated after his time. His austere mausoleum, which has been carefully restored and preserved in Bukhara, symbolizes his spartan asceticism. That personal austerity, admired by contemporaries and successors alike, was not miserliness—the amir gave vast amounts of booty and riches to others, keeping none for himself.[7]

Perhaps with Amir Ismail in mind, Abu Nasr al-Farabiy, a renowned

Central Asian and Arabic philosopher of the time (d. 950), reasoned that one of what he termed the twelve natural qualities essential in a perfect sovereign or imam must be fairness. Al-Farabiy, whose Turkic family lived near the Sir Darya, described the ideal king: "He should by nature be fond of justice and of just people and hate oppression and injustice and those who practice them, giving himself and others their due and urging people to act justly and showing pity to those who are oppressed by injustice."[8]

This philosopher eloquently articulates the strong aspirations expressed by generations of Bukharans, Khwarazmians, and others. In Mawaraunnahr, Turkistan, and Khurasan—the regions that gave Muslim Central Asia its settled, civilized identity—thoughtful leaders and poets affirmed the idea of beneficent and evenhanded leadership. The ideal of a just king thus received a mandate in both the popular and the erudite mind, and in the abstract, at least, the populations of those late medieval states were united throughout by a universal love for just rule.

GENEROSITY AND MODESTY

In addition, great generosity and magnanimity had very early earned unequivocal admiration among Central Asian thinkers as well as among the populace at large. Generosity repeatedly stirred praise from medieval authors, and their regard for that quality would impress modern Uzbeks to the extent that these Middle Age attitudes would re-emerge in the twentieth century. From the village of Yugnak, near Samarkand (some say Farghana or Turkistan), came the poet Ahmad binni Mahmud Yugnakiy in the late twelfth or early thirteenth century, who composed a long verse work, *Hibatul haqayiq* (A Gift of Truths). The poem was reissued, in part and in full, by the Uzbek press starting in the late 1950s and is now considered a monument of early Turkic literature, offering many pieces of advice bearing on all kinds of conduct. Prominent among these is generosity (*akhiliq*, in the Turkic language of his time): "If thou must praise, do praise the generous man" and "generosity, both the great and small will praise." Ahmad exhorted readers to shun stinginess.[9]

A current Uzbek saying phrases it this way: "If a generous person finds something, everyone will eat it, if a stingy one finds something, he'll cover it up and eat it alone."[10] Ahmad Yugnakiy also felt that the person wealthy enough to be generous had to guard against the sin of pride: "No one likes arrogance, neither the populace nor God himself," he wrote.[11] The proper counterparts to wealth, power, and position, Ahmad Yugnakiy believed, could be only *kamtarlik* (modesty) or humility.

Insistent practicality shaped public understanding of this idea's importance. Most people realized that intangible justice meant little in the absence of righteous actions on the part of the monarch. Therefore, educating present and future kings to ideals of justice and equity remained a constant goal of historians, thinkers, and politicians. It found expression in verbal folk art, as well as in the elevated verse of great creative writers. Some Central Asian oral art spoke the figurative and literal language of the nomadic Uzbeks, who created an abundant supply, in contrast to the rarity of written verse from the early Timurid poets and their predecessors. This popular literature offered hearers basic, clear-cut standards by which highly placed figures could measure or guide their decisions and behavior.

The heroic epic *Älpamish*—of great importance to the Uzbeks—repeatedly describes virtuous leaders locked in fierce combat with evil ones. Toward the end of a version of the epic recorded early in the twentieth century by Fazil Yoldash Oghli, the true leader of the Qonghirat (Uzbek) tribe returns from afar to oust a usurper and liberate his people from ignominy. In the process, medieval listeners, as well as readers centuries later, would understand several principles of kingship. Accretions to *Älpamish* since the early Middle Ages probably represent a mixture of old and new concepts about kingship and leaders' roles or conduct. The epic singer at the end of part five (of ten) in the epic depicts the generosity of Älpamish when he returns from hard campaigning:

> The noble one has come to his homeland, is overlord,
> How many animals does he slaughter, how much pilaf does he give?
> What does he do with the boundless wealth?
> When he pours, he does not stop.
> Daily, he holds this goat carcass contest [*kök bori*, in original].
> Daily, he keeps on giving prizes for winning at carcass-snatching.
> Those things Baysin's brave one did.[12]

These nurturing actions and leadership roles of a good chief contrast with the repressiveness, unfairness, and ugliness of an evil tyrant in the epic. Toward the climax of *Älpamish*, that villain, Ultantaz (Scabby Pate), reveals his true unjustness. Significantly, the Central Asian singer of the epic identifies Ultantaz as the half-breed of a despised Persian slave mother. The story portrays him as a usurping rascal who receives his comeuppance from Älpamish, the hero, who returns home after seven years' absence from an adventure in distant lands. As soon as Älpamish deals with this low-born tyrant, the folk poet sings:

> The fog of misfortune departs,
> So many of his enemies die . . . ,
> The khan of the Qonghirat really came.[13]

Innumerable variants of such lines echo throughout the ample oral art of the Uzbeks. In *Ahmäd wä Yusuf*, an epic from Khwarazm, the folk singer emphasizes that

> Their padishahs rule justly, regard all with the eye of impartiality
>
> . . . .
>
> Their open-handed inhabitants are like Hatem [an Eastern emblem for generosity], their commanders are like Bahram,
> On the day of battle like Rustam [two legendary heroes], the wars of young braves.[14]

Here, the popular literature lingers on the affirmative value of equity and impartiality, the folk concepts of justice.

In the real world, Mahmud of Ghazna (r. 998–1030), power of the Ghaznavid dynasty, stands as the model prince and native son admired secondmost, after Amir Ismail, in Central Asian writings. Although Mahmud forcibly dominated the southern reaches of the area—in 1016 including Samarkand, Bukhara, and, for a time, Khwarazm—kings' counselors ascribed to him idealized qualities of forgiveness, generosity, and charity. In a major dispute with his brother (another Amir Ismail) over the right to possess Ghazna, Mahmud and his forces won a pitched battle. Yet, "Amir Saif Addoulat [Mahmud's epithet], when his anger was appeased, the battle at an end, and the flame of war had gone down, forgave him [his brother] and received him under the guardianship of his protection and support, and forgot what was past." A contemporary chronicler of Mahmud and Mahmud's father's deeds and exploits asserted that

> Truly the sultan [Mahmud] was a man of perfect generosity and amiable disposition, with which virtues his royal garment was adorned and the robe of his intentions wonderfully embroidered . . . he proceeded according to that blessed proverb, that a wise king ought to act with such prudence that, in a state of anger, he should inflict injury upon a man in such a way as that, in a state of good humour, he may be able to repair the wrong.[15]

Mahmud learned to govern from his father, Sabuktigin, a Samanid slave, and "always loved to listen to the history of kings."[16] Learning from one's elders and from history meant enlightened leadership, though the preparation for responsibility was neither unusual nor new in Mahmud's time. Every early Central Asian sovereign and wazir of substance counseled heirs to thrones to read history and the biographies of famous men.

A special rhythm in the popular imagination that governed the choices of model potentates created asymmetrical patterns. Foreigners did not alternate with local chieftains; neither did all aliens come before or after indigenous rulers. If the public were going to consider an amir or khan truly just, they did so soon after his actual tenure on the throne. Popular opinion required a longer time to accept a foreign leader in this charmed circle; one outsider, Alexander the Great, preceded another, Anushirwan, by some eight centuries. Central Asia's own Amir Ismail found great, lasting favor relatively soon after his death. The same occurred with the indigenous Mahmud of Ghazna. Although he arrived in Central Asia only two hundred years after Mahmud of Ghazna, the foreign conqueror Chinggis Khan did not find general and durable popular favor there until much later.

IMPLACABILITY VERSUS FORBEARANCE

Chinggis (*ca.* 1167–1227), the famed Mongol khan who could neither read nor write, completes the trio of giant alien figures that, notwithstanding the tyranny of their rule or the drastic methods they used against or in Central Asia, captured the imagination of the Central Asian populace. Chinggis Khan and his sons' invading armies rapidly obliterated all resistance in the region between 1219 and 1223. Chinggis's style of leadership differed from that advocated in a Muslim "counsel for kings." He did not recognize forgiveness, piety, magnanimity, generosity, concern for ordinary people, or the general welfare, honesty, and other traits that constituted the Central Asian ideal. Under the early Mongol khans, ruthless effectiveness in battle, efficiency at the expense of human needs and values, and implacability toward rivals and enemies were the admired qualities. Accompanying these was an emphasis on strict obedience rather than persuasion or loyalty, a rigid, zealous belief in the Mongol khan's rightness rooted in heaven's mandate (which was also crucial to the Mongols' political legitimacy), an aristocratic view of society, and a tactical neutrality toward religion. Nowhere did Chinggis Khan emphasize the concept of generalized justice so treasured by Muslim Central Asians. The compelling undercurrent in the Central Asian concern for justice and the public, with its focus on a king's general esteem and good name, expressed a Central Asian Muslim attitude toward leadership. Chinggis Khan did not imagine himself a popular chieftain. Mongol organization and utterance reflected a hierarchical society that contrasted with the largely interactive Central Asian Islam. Maxims attributed to Chinggis and handed down by Central Asian historian and ruler Abul Ghazi Bahadur Khan (r. Khiva 1642–1663) reinforce the impression of Mongol stern responsibility and submission, not equality and fairness. Chinggis, according to Abul Ghazi, said that "whoever controls his own house well will most likely also control the country." A Mongol aristocracy rooted within family and tribe gave force to such attitudes and ensured ethnic homogeneity among the highest military ranks and the nobility. In this manner sovereignty attached itself to ethnicity in Chinggisid Central Asia.[17]

Amir Timur (b. 1336, r. 1370–1405), who prided himself on being a descendant of Chinggis Khan, is the last of the three great medieval Central Asian exemplar potentates before Uzbek hegemony. He at least partially followed the tradition of the region's indigenous leadership. The illiterate Timur made sure that he heard the works of historians in his native Turki tongue, or in Farsi, by establishing a *qissäkhan* (official reader) at court. His wide knowledge of history, which surprised eminent historians,[18] Timur used to exhort his subordinates. The *Institutes*, tentatively attributed to Timur, place historians ninth among the twelve valuable classes of men who

> rendered strong and permanent the basis and superstructure of my government . . . from these men I heard the lives of the prophets and the patriarchs, and the histories of ancient princes, and the events by which they arrived at the dignity of empire, and the causes of the declension of their fortunes.[19]

Like the two model Central Asian rulers that predated him, Amir Timur ranked justice and forbearance high in the techniques of a successful sovereign. Among his rules for the conduct of empire, the second (after a declaration that a sovereign's words and acts must be his own rather than his counselors) asserts that

> It is necessary to a king that he adhere to justice in all his actions, and that he receive into his service ministers who are just and virtuous . . . If the minister be unjust and cruel, it shall speedily come to pass that the edifice of his master's power and dominion shall be leveled with the earth.[20]

SYMBOLS AND MAGNANIMITY

Through his adherence to the pieties and established values of his era, as well as to the recognized symbols of sovereignty, Timur helped to convey his own and his predecessors' interpretations of the conventions of leadership. Three major symbols of authority constituted an irreducible constellation of signs for the independent ruler: the complete right to hold sacred services in his own name, the exclusive prerogative to mint money, and the sole power to rule and govern in his domain. Timur demonstrated that sovereignty meant power by his peremptory treatment of the "kings of Iran and Turan . . . [who] came to him and offered him gifts and presents, [and] stayed on the thresholds of servitude and slavery."[21] Sole right to rule a domain implied control over conduct of its external relations. Timur, along with earlier and later amirs and khans, actively exercised authority in the realm of foreign affairs, making it essentially a separate requisite of sovereignty.

Timur's thinking about kingship, however, deviated from earlier codes of princely behavior. This variation emerged not because his rules for kingship entirely lacked idealism but rather from the attitudes of the Mongols, whose reign intervened between the time of the old codes of kingship and the era of Central Asian revival under Timur. Thus, another important maxim called for strict obedience to the sovereign's commands, no matter what the consequences. Many of these rules resemble the axioms of a nomadic Mongol chieftain—Timur came from the plains and claimed Mongol lineage—more than the thinking of enlightened Central Asian monarchs from the ancient centers of Balkh, Nishapur, or Samarkand. That Central Asian inclination toward Mongol ideals would gain further momentum not in Timur's own dynasty—an opulent civilization stretching from Khwarazm to Herat and beyond—but in the decades following his death.

Not surprisingly, the stern code found intense expression in the open spaces outside the traditional capitals. The unsettled society in the realms of outer Central Asia chose peculiar rules of conduct and different goals and preoccupations. Envious of urban wealth and luxury but not the life-style, these horsemen and herders concentrated on getting and strengthening, not merely maintaining, themselves. The heroic mode, the mobile environment, and the detachment from surrounding people characterized the outlook of the plainsmen. The competing value systems created tension between migratory and settled people, but that tension, combining mores and attitudes of both arenas, contributed to the Uzbek nomads' rise to dominance over the urban south. That fundamental divergence, united with Central Asia's heterogeneity, posed questions for the people of the region that strongly affected their group identity.

VALUES AND BELIEFS

The first Uzbek leader to rise to prominence did so outside Central Asia less than three decades after Timur's death. Abul Khayr Khan (1412–1468), who shook the Qipchaq Plains with his thunder, represented a mixture of values, although he seemed to emphasize one side of the dichotomy. Among the qualities mentioned by one sixteenth-century historian are might, eminence, and magnanimity; another historian, sometime before 1590, stressed military prowess, political ruthlessness, fervent piety, breadth of vision, sagacity, grandeur, and generosity as the outstanding traits and qualities of the khan. Both writers enjoyed unusually free access to sons and grandsons of Abul Khayr Khan, for they served as counselors, as well as confidants, to Muhammad Shaybaniy Khan (1451–1510), ruler of Mawaraunnahr and

Khurasan; Suyunch Khoja Khan (d. 1524/25), ruler of Turkistan; and Abdal-Latif Khan (d. 1550/51), ruler of Samarkand—all sons or grandsons of Abul Khayr Khan. It is difficult to imagine any witnesses who could have more accurately recorded the testimony from these sources.[22]

These writers told of Abul Khayr Khan's triumph over Juchid tribal opponents in the plains at Ikri Tup. After the victory, the Uzbek khan followed a protocol of formal acts and moves incumbent on a royal person. He thanked the Lord for success in battle. Then he went to the Ordu Bazar in the valley of the Kengir River in what would become central Kazakhstan. (It once served Batu, the powerful Mongol khan [r. 1224–1256] in the northwest of Eurasia, as "the most august headquarters.")

> Ordu Bazar, which was the capital of the Qipchaq Plains and the glory of the sultans of the world, entered into the possession of the vicegerents of the court of the [Uzbek] khan, the refuge of the world. Here they pronounced the Friday Muslim prayer [in Abul Khayr Khan's name] and adorned the minting [of money] with the famed name and noble title of his highness the khaqan [Abul Khayr Khan].[23]

The khan also distributed robes of honor to commanders and dignitaries, invoking yet another royal ritual. Thus the khan exercised the right to the primary symbols of sovereignty for his Uzbek confederation in its chosen terrain.

All these attributes and forms of behavior seemed particularly suited to the nomadic chieftain. A friendly or official historian or biographer then, as in modern and postmodern Soviet times, could be expected to paint a postive picture of the political leader. Nevertheless, the traits the sixteenth-century authors emphasized specifically excluded, in Abul Khayr Khan's case, some qualities generally recognized as important in medieval guidebooks to regal conduct. Noticeably lacking in the excerpts and studies of primary sources from Abul Khayr Khan's era are any comments about his strong adherence to the principle of justice. Nor is anything reported about a sense of forgiveness or even the tolerance for imperfection advocated in Timur's *Institutes*.

A khan mirrored the tension in his society that pitted the great customary and religious force of obedience to authority against the ethical power of justice. Five hundred years before the Uzbek khans, thinkers in Central Asia had recorded the idea of royalty's embodying justice. The nomadic chieftains, persistently in touch with the civilization to the south, surely heard about this justice from the elders around Abul Khayr Khan's court or from the epic singers in their midst.

After piety, esteem for elders rated near the top of desirable behavior traits in the Qipchaq Plains. The histories often placed special emphasis on a leader's respect for not only his father but his mother. By extension, strong approval also went to the wives who mothered the khan's children. Those women not only continued the dynasty's unbroken line of sovereigns but in many instances brought strength and legitimacy to the dynasty from their own lineage. Numerous chronicles show Rabiya Sultan Begim playing just such a part in Central Asian history. This princess enjoyed the distinction, besides her political acumen, of being closely related to three of the most renowned leaders in eastern international affairs. She mothered two Shaybanid khans, Kochkunchi (r. 1510–1530) and Suyunch Khoja. Her talents earned her the special favor of her renowned grandfather, Amir Timur. After Rabiya Sultan Begim's brother murdered their father (Mirza Ulugh Beg, r. Samarkand 1409–1449), one of Timur's grandsons, the combative Mirza Abu Said (r. 1451–1469), married her to Abul Khayr Khan in 1451, thus making Rabiya Sultan Begim the fourth main wife, after women from the Burqut, Manghit, and Qonghirat Uzbek tribes, of this first great Uzbek khan. That arrangement created an important political alliance between her Timurid nobility and Uzbek tribal leaders.[24] Historian Masud bin Othman Kohistani (d. *ca.* 1590), in his *History of Abul Khayr Khan* (*ca.* 1544), expressed her sons' and other descendants' great reverence for Rabiya Sultan Begim: "The Shahina [who is] the supreme mother, cradle and most high counterpane, the Bilqis [Queen of Sheba] of the time, who was the esteemed wife of the khan of the country and the aunt, on the father's side, of the prince, arranged various diversions and kindnesses for the nephew." Her nephew Muhammad Jogiy (Juki) Mirza (d. 1463/64), Timurid prince and son of her brother Abd al-Latif Mirza (r. 1449–1450), took refuge in the Qipchaq Plains with Abul Khayr Khan, who gave Muhammad Jogiy Mirza the military support to seize Samarkand. A falling-out between Muhammad Jogiy Mirza and Bureke Sultan, the Uzbek-Kazak commander of that expedition, led to disaster after they scored some military gains in Mawaraunnahr against the Chaghatay tribe (*el*), as the historian called the Timurid forces. Rabiya Sultan Begim thus failed to achieve revenge against Abu Said Mirza, her brother's successor in Samarkand. Her experience illustrates the unstable nature of ideological or military alliances between the rival Uzbek and Timurid leaders and reflects the importance of the women among the Central Asian nobility in determinations of sovereignty.[25]

THE GOOD WINNER

On the basis of these records, Abul Khayr Khan could be seen as an excellent specimen of the Asian good winner, contrasting strikingly with the Western good loser of a later time. The Eastern good winner knew how to behave with friends and foes when he conquered. The role was not as clearly defined when he lost, for abject humility or principled defiance could suit the situation on the right occasion. The good winner knew that his supporters and troops had to be handsomely rewarded whenever possible. Abul Khayr Khan demonstrated this principle early in his career when, after seizing Khwarazm in 1431, he avoided subjecting Urganch to pillage by his nomadic tribesmen by opening the city's treasury in a limited way to each commander and warrior.[26]

This version of magnanimity lacked the noble touch of the Samanid model: Amir Ismail not only rewarded followers and generals, he preached and practiced deference and generosity to opponents as a guiding principle, not a tactical maneuver. Those emulating Abul Khayr Khan, therefore, added weight to the nomadic, Mongol side of Central Asia's heritage in this balance of values. Abul Khayr Khan's performance as a winner, according to the above-mentioned sources, lacked the conciliatory style—advocated by the medieval princes and their advisers—which spoke to the desire for stability and harmony rather than immediate revenge or temporary advantage. In this particular, Abul Khayr Khan brought to the developing Central Asian outlook more Mongol vindictiveness than Samanid restraint, more nomadic impatience than urban tolerance or civility.

Had Abul Khayr Khan's confederation of tribes remained in the expanses north of Central Asia, the influence of their attitudes toward authority and justice would no doubt have impressed neighboring areas to a degree; however, during the fifteenth century, repeated contacts between these nomads and the settled people south of them eventually became direct. In the meantime, the ferocity of the nomadic troops and commanders vented itself in actions large and small along the frontiers and at the very centers of Mawaraunnahr and colored the accepted practices in those areas. Likewise, the churning tribal mass of nomads could not remain entirely untouched by the standards of martial and civil etiquette displayed in settled Mawaraunnahr. For example, in 1464 the Timurids, as a gesture of goodwill, released Abul Khayr Khan's younger brother, Sayyid Yeke Sultan, held prisoner by the Timurids at Herat after being captured earlier near Khwarazm. The khans judged that the Qur'ân-reading "youth of excellent character and pure faith" was unsuited to become a successor to the powerful Uzbek chieftain and thus no threat to the Timurid dynasty.

The last important instance of reciprocal influence between these two forces occurred in 1467–1468 during Abul Khayr Khan's chieftainship. Sultan Husayn Mirza, future Timurid ruler of Herat (r. 1469–1506), when driven from Khwarazm by rivals, appeared at the nomads' headquarters in the plains north of the Sir Darya. The Uzbek court approved his plea for support in his fight against Timurid opponents, although they never supplied it because Abul Khayr Khan died in 1468.[27]

The abrupt disintegration of the Uzbek confederation upon Abul Khayr Khan's death reflected the failure of his principles and manner of governing to sustain loyalty and conditioned the dynastic pattern that followed. Although

Abul Khayr Khan ruled for 40 years, he did not secure the future, and his one-man dynasty virtually died with him. Despite Abul Khayr Khan's prowess as a tribal chieftain, his deficiencies as an inspirational leader caused succeeding generations to avoid memorializing him as a model for the ideal khan.

The marriage between Rabiya Sultan Begim and Abul Khayr Khan in the mid-fifteenth century seemed to add legitimacy to the Uzbek royal family. Surprisingly, toward the sunset of the Timurid era, that family alliance became somewhat of a detriment. For Uzbek purists the fusion of a Timurid branch into the Uzbek descent may have subtly tainted the partners and progeny of that union. Abul Khayr Khan's favorite grandson and political heir, Muhammad Shaybaniy, in selecting a pseudonym leapfrogged back over his Uzbek predecessors to adopt the name of one of Chinggis Khan's grandsons. He alternated that name with a term in the Chaghatay literary language for shepherd, *shāban* borrowed from Farsi, suggesting the image of guardian of the Uzbek tribal flock.[28] Chroniclers allude to the warriors and descendants of Muhammad Shaybaniy as Shaybanids, thus permanently inscribing that Mongol-Uzbek dynastic name in Central Asian history.

3 Names and Tribes

Ismi jismigä manänd.

Its name corresponds to its essence.

(Central Asian saying)*

Naming always possessed a quality of sacred mystery, perhaps magic, for Central Asians, beginning with folk beliefs. The *Qur'ânic* passage reinforced God's teaching Adam the names of everything, knowledge denied even to the angels. In the biblical version of this transmission, whatever the first man called something, that was its name. The potency of names continued to grow in the Muslim traditions, linking divinity with the capacity of the human mind to name creatures, people, things, and ideas. A Muslim tradition, quoted in Central Asia, is that God found Adam worthy of the name *al-mutakallim* (The Speaker), one of God's own beautiful names, thus "making man superior to all other creatures." (Central Asia's Timurid poet, Mir Ali Shir Nawaiy [1441–1501] referred to himself by the same epithet.)

In another Muslim tradition, "be it known that the name and the thing named are one, according to the truly orthodox people, so that Allah with all

* N. Jäbbaraw and J. Namazaw, "Ismi jismigä manänd kalkhaz (Bukhara abläst', Ghijduwan räyan, 'Gulistan' kalkhazi tärikhi)," in vol. 1, *Ozbekistan kalkhaz wä sawkhazläri tärikhi (Acherklär)* (Tashkent: "Ozbekistan" Näshriyati, 1969), p. 268.

His names is One." Interpreters asked, "did not the Prophet—upon whom be Allah's blessing and peace—say: "Verily, Allah has 99 names and whosoever recounts them will enter Paradise'?" Which meant that the prophet recommended the reciting of *tasmiya* (99 names), not that there are 99 gods. The interpreter carefully pointed out that in this case the name and the named are not the same, for "by whatever name you call him, he is Allah." As an example, the commentator argued that heat will not burn the mouth of a man because he says the word *fire,* for this is a matter of the *tasmiya* (naming) of the fire, not of the real fire.[1] That logic does not contradict the saying that introduces this chapter, for the interpreter shows that the name is not the same as what became named, whereas the saying points to a need for the name to be pertinent to the named.

The names held by sizable confederations of mobile tribes in medieval times carried great strength. Irrespective of their origin, such names remained so important that in tribal organization within Central Asia and surrounding areas the kinship of the group had to correspond to the self-name. To make it so, when significant outsiders became incorporated into the group, elders would devise a special genealogy to accommodate the new people to the name and the kinship identity. Pastoral nomads sometimes took the names of ancestors. Over time a name could go from one group of tribes to another. In contrast, although under one self-name, the complex of tribes making up a confederation changed when weaker groups dwindled and disappeared or when rebellious ones split off. Nonetheless, its name could and often did persist.

These developments indicate that continuity mattered. But in Central Asian history the exact makeup of the group was less important than the name of a sizable community in representing and sustaining a corporate identity. Moreover, that naming, and the group identity associated with it, have provided Central Asians with group ties more fundamental than any variant or competing ideologies, whether imperial, religious, or materialistic. Corporate names exert a powerful impact and play vital roles in Central Asian society; nameless groups have little or no place in a history of this area. The group's self-name was a designation that would exert lasting effects as a positive symbol and bond for an aggregate's identity.

TATAR OR UZBEK?

The dynamic confederation that foreigners called Uzbek emerged from early fourteenth-century northwestern Asia as a confusion of names. Contemporary observers, noting the comprehensive term in their histories, implied that the designation *Uzbek* served outsiders more than it identified the combination of individually named tribes to itself. Although the ambiguities in nomenclature may not have perturbed a tribesman at the time, they have perplexed his heirs ever since and created ambivalencies for later historians seeking to ascertain the origins and true identity of the modern Uzbek group.

Evidence now shows that Tatar warriors made up that first conglomeration of people called Uzbeks but does not show their point of origin. Their name, however, was the more important element, not their race or ethnicity. They were in fact Tatar tribesmen following the renowned Ghiyath ad-Din Muhammad Uzbek (Özbeg) Khan (r. 1312–1341), who was descended from Juchi, Chinggis Khan's son, through his grandson, Batu. Uzbek Khan, a Muslim proselytizer and one of the most powerful Golden Horde rulers, made his headquarters on the Volga River, thus centering his Uzbek territory astride the river, with the capital—Saray—below the westernmost bend in the lower reaches of that great stream (east of the river at longitude 46° east just above north latitude 48°). His prestige and a still-strong Mongol custom led the mobile Tatar troops that he commanded to take his name during his lifetime. In histories written then in Persian, references to *ozbekiyan* (Uzbeks) and to *ulus-i ozbek* (the country of the Uzbek) concern Uzbek Khan and his subjects.[2]

Elsewhere, the Uzbek tribal confederation appeared coincidentally with the Timur's rise to power in western Asia but remained largely outside both his jurisdiction and the bounds of Central Asia. Historians of the time and place (Ghiyas ad-Din ibn Human ad-Din Muhammad Khwand Amir, Masud bin 'Othman Kohistani, Muin ad-Din Natanzi, Abd ar-Razzak Samarqandi, Nizam ad-Din Shami, Sharaf ad-Din Ali Yazdi, and others[3]) situated these Uzbeks in what would now be western Siberia and upper Kazakhstan, putting this second Uzbek nucleus some 1,600 kilometers (1,000 miles) northeast of Saray in the 1380s. Uzbek as a corporate designation for the Turkic-Mongol tribes roaming above Central Asia and far from the Golden Horde capital probably appeared no earlier than the 1360s.

An understanding of this period requires an explanation of that twenty-year lapse between the death of Uzbek, the Tatar khan, and the eruption, far from his base, of an Uzbek-named group of tribes. The interval was probably sufficient for the designation and some of Uzbek khan's numerous Tatar tribes-men and their families to migrate up into the region of the Tobol River to coalesce around what became the Uzbek tribal center in Siberia, Chimgi Tura (Tumän / Tiumen'). A corresponding, temporary break in the use of that Uzbek label, however, may point to the possibility that the tribes along the Tobol borrowed or created their collective self-name independent of the deceased Uzbek khan and his horsemen. Nonetheless, shared kinship and designations as well as the general, supratribal name, seemed to connect these two centers. Between the 1360s and 1380s the eastern Qipchaq Plains—the domain of the White Horde—became known to historians in southern Central Asia as the Uzbek region. They called the chief of those nomads the Uzbek khan, not from the Golden Horde khan, but instead demonstrably separate from his specific existence.[4]

Obscure and limited sources detailing fourteenth-century developments have left students of the Uzbek question ambivalent about the origin of the group name. Several nineteenth- and early twentieth-century scholars and travelers followed authoritative chroniclers such as the Khivan khan, Abul Ghazi Bahadur (r. 1642–1663) in the view that Uzbeks borrowed their group name from the Golden Horde potentate Uzbek Khan. Abul Ghazi wrote, "After that [conversion of the Golden Horde to Islam by Uzbek Khan], they called the entire tribe [*il/el*] of Juchi the people of Uzbek and most assuredly will say so until the Judgment Day."[5]

Because many miles separate the two plausible locations for the origin of the Uzbek name and people, scholars have experienced great tension in attempting to reconcile the contradiction. As a result, several researchers in Europe and Russia looked for a solution in an etymological explanation of the name *Uzbek* that avoided links to either place. They offered the theory that the Turkic reflexive pronoun *öz* (self) had combined with the noble title *bek* to form *özbek*, a type of self-name common to various languages in tribal societies in and beyond Central Asia. That combination would mean, they reasoned, "his own master," "the nobleman himself," and the like.[6] Ingenious as this etymology may be, Abul Ghazi Bahadur Khan's understanding of his people's naming remains the most likely. Uzbek Khan's great repute as leader fed the Qipchaq tribesmen's inclination to name themselves after a khan. The horsemen who formed the Uzbek tribes differed little, if at all, from those in the Golden Horde, and Uzbek Khan's standing as the foremost Islamic guide among the Golden Horde thus made his name ideologically and spiritually attractive.

EPONYM

In practice, Central Asians related primarily to the living ruler—who embodied the multiethnic or supraethnic state—and identified with the dynasty that gave its name to the domain in which they lived. Consistent with what Abul Ghazi Bahadur Khan wrote, in northwestern Siberia Uzbeks considered themselves the subjects of Abul Khayr Khan, who united much of the Uzbek tribal confederation between 1428 and 1468. Except for raids that took them south, neither the Uzbeks nor their name planted themselves as any more than an occasional individual designation to the south of the Sir Darya river before the late fifteenth century. Khwand Amir called "Uzbek" troops (*sipah-i Ozbak*) the army of Timur's formidable enemy and sometime protégé, Toqtamish Oghlan (r. *ca*. 1378–1396), eventually khan of the White and Golden hordes of the old Mongol Empire. These troops were mainly situated considerably north of lower Central Asia.[7]

Some tribes (Khitay, Nayman, Qarluq, Uyghur, and others) roamed west along the banks of the Volga River and the plains bordering the Black Sea, appearing in northwestern Siberia in the fifteenth century, well before any Uzbek state came into being in Central Asia. Around Abul Khayr Sultan (b. 1412), the young Juchid prince descended from Shayban/Shiban, gathered, from tribes in the Golden Horde along the Volga, a number of powerful clan leaders: Shaykh Sufi Nayman, Aq Sufi Nayman, Qara Othman Nayman, Abeke Bahadur Khitay, Fuladak Bahadur Khitay, Kepek Biy Uyghur, Hasan Biy Uyghur, Abdal Malik Qarluq, and others.

Abul Khayr Sultan, when he became khan, headed a confederation that started with no fewer than 24 tribes, many with numerous subdivisions. (In alphabetical order, the original combination included the tribes Barak, Bayly, Durman, Imchi, Jat, Kenagas, Khitay, Kiyat, Kurlaut, Kushchi, Manghit, Ming, Nayman, Qarluq, Qonghirat, Tangut, Taymas, Tubay, Tuman, Ugrish-Nayman, Utarchi, Uyghur, Uyshun, and Yiyjan/Alman.[8]) Fourteen of these continued in the Uzbek tribes at least another one hundred years, according to local sources. A sixteenth-century roster, based on an earlier list, set at 92 the conventional number of *elatiyä* (nomadic Uzbek tribes). Of the original two dozen, some died out, split off, or merged with those who had separated from the Uzbeks. By actual count, the Uzbek confederation shared at least twenty tribal group names with the Uzbek-Kazak separatists out of that 92. Those held jointly included the Qirq, Jalayir, Qonghirat, Alchin, Argun, Nayman, Qipchaq, and thirteen others. Nevertheless, the separate migratory combinations lived on under the broader Uzbek or Uzbek-Kazak names, while the human composition as well as the tribal names under them altered repeatedly as the decades passed.[9]

Abul Khayr Sultan's own tribal affiliation evidenced intertribal connections as well as political maneuvers in the early Uzbek confederation in northwestern Siberia. He came from the Chin or Alchin tribe; his wife, Aghanaq Bigi, mother of his son Shah Budaq Sultan, from the Burqut tribe. Neither the Chin/Alchin nor the Burqut tribe figured in the 24 tribes that originally supported the sultan in northwestern Siberia. The Burqut governor of Chimgi Tura, the Siberian capital of the Uzbeks, brought his fellow tribesmen over to Abul Khayr Sultan's side for the saddle of an Uzbek khan. The sultan likewise married his son to Aq Quzi Begim, a Burqut woman. The young couple were the parents of Shahbakht, the Central Asian khan who, in the struggle for power within the Uzbek realm in the mid-1480s, built his support on five main tribes. Those did not include his family line but embraced the Durman, Ichki, Nayman,

Qoshchi, and Uyghur tribes. Genealogy and tribal affiliation in that nomadic environment thus controlled the destinies of men and their names.

In the standard lists of 92 nomadic Uzbek tribes, the Burqut ranked 47th in status, according to the nineteenth-century *Nasab namet-i ozbekiya* (Genealogy of the Uzbeks). Burquts had held a similar position in Akhsikenti's sixteenth-century list, but two later versions of the roster elevated the Burquts slightly. Thus, both earlier and later keepers of the tribal memory rated the Burqut's importance around the halfway point among Uzbek tribes, suggesting that Abul Khayr Sultan's prominent position in tribal affairs could have resulted in part from his tribe's modest status. A similar circumstance much later received just such an interpretation. During the selection in southern Central Asia of Ahmad Shah Durrani (1722–1772) as the founder and leader of independent Afghanistan in 1747, tribal status played a decisive role. His tribe, less controversial and contentious than those of any alternative candidate, made him an acceptable choice, according to the histories.[10]

When Uzbek tribal chieftains made seventeen-year-old Abul Khayr Sultan their khan in 1428/29, they called his realm *Däsht-i Qipchäq* (the Qipchaq Plains). Since the eleventh century, Qipchaq Plains had designated a vast tract stretching from the Dnieper River across the northern shores of the Black Sea eastward to the Irtysh River and Lake Balkhash down to Khwarazm and the lower reaches of the Sir Darya, where they connect with the Aral Sea. Within a hundred years, that concept shrank. A Central Asian historian described a Qipchaq Plains that ran eastward only from the lower Volga River to adjoin the Caspian Sea littoral and the Sir Darya. Thereafter, the new khan made great efforts to shift his headquarters from the frigid environment of Chimgi Tura to warmer climates in southern Central Asia.

During 1430–1431, invoking the precedent of his Juchid ancestors who had controlled Khwarazm, the khan led his tribesmen to reclaim that region. After conquering the city of Urganch, Abul Khayr Khan emulated cultured Central Asian potentates by assembling that city's eminent theologians and writers for literary and religious gatherings. Poets, including the renowned Sufi *shaykh*, (preceptor) Kamal ad-din Husayn Khwarazmiy (d. 1435/46), dedicated the customary verse commentaries and *qäsidäs* (panegyrics) to the khan. Notwithstanding the praise bestowed by literate Khwarazmians, a variety of threats (see chapter 1) compelled the khan to withdraw his forces from that corner of Central Asia. This delayed Uzbek expansion into Mawaraunnahr for some decades but did not destroy the urge for it.[11]

In 1446–1447, Abul Khayr Khan succeeded in going southeast beyond Khwarazm and securing new winter quarters. He chose as a capital for his nomadic tribes a district pivoting on the town of Sighnaq, just east of the middle Sir Darya, thus not only acquiring Turkistan territory but, more important, positioning the Uzbeks for their southward push. That shift of the Uzbek capital was termed by an eminent Russian historian "the most important event of his [Abul Khayr Khan's] reign for the subsequent history of the Uzbeks." Two years later, the Uzbeks crossed the river and raided the environs of Samarkand where, in the absence of Prince Ulugh Beg, emissaries from the city propitiated their forces. The tribes' success against the faltering Timurids, however, could not be converted into solidarity among the Uzbeks.

When concentrated, the Uzbek force that whirled across the Qipchaq Plains was able to overwhelm everything in its path. Nevertheless, events and obstacles in the second half of the fifteenth century nullified that drive almost entirely. The hostility of competing plainsmen from the region as well as from grazing lands farther east broke the strength of the Uzbek confederation. In addition, the death of the unifying ruler pointed up the importance of strong leadership for the nomads. Under these and attendant strains, the Uzbek confederation of tribes disintegrated and scattered, giving the Timurids another four decades of increasingly troubled hegemony in southern Central Asia.[12]

Fifteenth-century developments split the Uzbeks into three suborders (Siberian Uzbek, Uzbek-Shaybanid, and Uzbek-Kazak) and fragmented their earlier group identity and the specificity of their name. For historians such as Khwand Amir, however, those cleavages mattered little. He clearly states that *Uzbeks* served as troops in the northern Asia forces. Equally unambiguous remarks came from residents of the south, who acknowledged the name *Uzbek* by disowning it. Timurid inhabitants of Mawaraunnahr and Khurasan repeatedly fought against or made brief alliances with these *Uzbeks*. Abul Khayr Khan intervened decisively in a contest for Samarkand soon after the patricide of its viceroy, Sultan Ulugh Beg, in 1449. Uzbek warriors destroyed Sultan Abu Said's rival in 1451 in a great battle. Rewards for the Uzbek khan included "precious stones, fat steeds, fine garments, and a plethora of movable property" as well as a noble Timurid daughter in marriage. Yet another symbolic tie knotted them together when their descendants buried both the Timurid princess and her royal Uzbek husband in the grand mausoleum for the revered Muslim mystic of Central Asia, Khoja Ahmad Yassawiy (1103–1166). Amir Timur had ordered the structure built in the 1390s over that popular Turkistanian saint, whom the Uzbeks, Uzbek-Kazaks, and Timurids called *häzrät*.[13]

UZBEK AS A PEJORATIVE TERM

Royal intermarriages, interments, or tactical alliances could not obscure the facts of group membership. Although changing political fortunes forced many historians, artists, and writers to look for patrons outside their tribal or dynastic homes, in the written record the leader's group of origin remained obvious. The Timurid authors of Central Asia contrasted themselves to Uzbeks, usually in unequivocal, sometimes unflattering terms. Mir Ali Shir Nawaiy (1441–1501), Herat poet and Timurid statesman, in his long narrative poem, *Sädd-i Iskändäriy* (Alexander's Wall), completed in 1485, assigns Uzbek Moghul, Manghit Uzbek, and Kalmak warriors to the Eastern army opposing Alexander the Great, thus blending group names from periods millenia apart. He identifies them as mercenaries or foreign contingents contributing more than 100,000 soldiers to the 1.9 million host of Persian Shah Darius III (r. 336–323 B.C.). In his poem Nawaiy distinguished between the good and evil forces, characterizing Darius' command in these lines:

> And Darius, defender of the state,
>
> Directed troops against Alexander.
>
> Don't say troops, say a river of the bloodthirsty,
>
> Say the sea of destiny is more distinguishable than that mass is.[14]

The poet thus aligns Uzbeks with the losing (wrong) side in a titanic struggle between Darius' Oriental forces and the masses of *färängis* (Europeans), *rus* (Russians), *rumiys* (Greeks), and others from the West. The East lost that conflict in his poem but gained a popular legendary hero—Alexander the Great. At the same time, this casting in the poem's personae leaves no doubt that, in the poet's eyes, the Uzbeks differed from the forces of good.

In reality, among the accoutrements that equipped invading Uzbeks when they crossed into Mawaraunnahr, most portentous were their folk memory and supratribal group name. The folk epic *Älpamish* occupied an important place in their collective consciousness. Those versions of the poem that originated earlier than the Uzbek migration to Mawaraunnahr possess a broader, more general, identity than the later *Älpamish* epic typical of southern Central Asia. That identification of the hero and his people as Uzbeks must have been lacking before the main tribe of the epic—the Qonghirat—moved to Termez, near the northern Afghan frontier. The updating of the oral epic with respect to topography and place after these Uzbeks moved to Mawaraunnahr and beyond may give more important clues to chronology than the use of the Uzbek name.

The presence of scattered bands of Siberian Uzbeks inside Mawaraunnahr as early as *ca.* 1485–1490 is attested to by both Mir Ali Shir Nawaiy and Zahiriddin Muhammad Babur. From this preconquest inmigration as well as the large earlier hostile incursions, the Timurids learned to differentiate those outsiders from themselves, and to define Uzbek, both then and later.

Language played a part in this. The Uzbeks rode across a linguistic isogloss whose Turkic language differed noticeably from the language encountered in Mawaraunnahr. The Qipchaq dialect of the plains immediately differentiated the migrant speakers from Oghuz-influenced people around and in Khwarazm and from users of the Turki tongue prevalent in the Farghana Valley and eastern Turkistan. The fashionable urban Farsi-Tajik language from the Indo-European family—found in and around Bukhara, Samarkand, and Khojand—at first alienated the plains Uzbeks. People in the south spoke Turki, not Uzbek. Despite some general spiritual and linguistic links with the people of the south, the newcomers looked, sounded, acted, and thought in ways different from the Timurid population. Mir Ali Shir Nawaiy, the Timurid poet, saw them as members of separate tribes that he knew to be components of a vast *Turk ulusi* (Turkic race). He never confused his Timurid group and its literary language with theirs. Zahiriddin Muhammad Babur, writing about Andijan in the Farghana Valley, observed that

> Its people are Turkic. There is not a person in the city or its bazaar who does not know Turki. The speech of its people is right for the pen. That is the reason why the compositions of Mir Ali Shir Nawaiy are [written] with this tongue, despite the fact that he grew up in Herat.[15]

The diarist clearly distinguishes the Turki speakers from the Qipchaq-speaking Uzbeks. Ultimately, the Turki dialect and identity would prevail.

Shortly after Mir Ali Shir Nawaiy's time, Muhammad Salih Mirza, Timurid poet and historian, entered the service of Muhammad Shaybaniy Khan, the Uzbek conqueror of Central Asia. Notwithstanding his new affiliation, Muhammad Salih, too, makes clear his distinctness from the Uzbek people, who had by then fought their way into the Timurid state. In these couplets from his long, versified *Book of Shaybaniy* Muhammad Salih writes,

> They said [to me]: "Thou are of the Chaghatay [Timurid] people,
> In that very spot thou art of the Chaghatay group.
> Why didst thou become a friend of the Uzbek?
> Didst thou become a servant to [Shaybaniy] khan like this?

Here again, a Timurid intellectual distinguished his people from the Uzbeks.[16]

Zahiriddin Muhammad Babur, the Timurid perhaps most renowned in the West today (after Timur) wrote sorrowfully about a deep humiliation—expelling the invading Uzbeks from the Samarkand they had but recently occupied: "For almost 140 years Samarkand was the capital of our dynasty, indeed. What manner of alien, Uzbek enemy just now became [its] possessor? Once again, God gave [Timurids] the kingdom that slipped from our hands." Babur recorded his outrage in a diary entry for late 1500.

In his recollections about actions occurring at the end of 1506, with Uzbek forces driving southwest toward Herat, Babur makes a joke that could suggest an explanation for the group name Uzbek. Distancing himself and other Timurids from Uzbeks as well as from people who collaborated with Uzbeks, Babur commented (entry for 1507),

> The traitorous [Timurid] paymaster, Shah Mansur the sodomite, was at Andkhud. By dispatching people to Shaybaq Khan he seemingly sped up the khan's preparations [to invade Khurasan] somewhat. When the khan was approaching the vicinity of Andkhud, this sodomite, saying "I have sent a man to the Uzbek". . . took along gifts and tribute [for Shaybaniy]. When he went out [to present the gifts], it seems the masterless Uzbek [*bashsiz ozbek*] pounced on him from every direction.[17]

Babur's pun on *bashsiz* (headless / masterless) amusingly controverts the sense of "master of himself" implied in the formulation *ozbek*.

These statements from Mir Ali Shir Nawaiy, Muhammad Salih, and Zahiriddin Muhammad Babur help define the identity of the medieval Uzbeks by contrasting them with the people of the Timurid dynasty, giving rise to the following three observations. (1) Timurids differentiated themselves from and expressed enmity toward Uzbeks. (2) In other nomadic sectors, especially Turkistan, the Uzbek group name persisted as an intratribal and supratribal link, but in Mawaraunnahr and Turkistan, even after the Uzbek conquest, that name as a group designation played only a secondary political / cultural role in the era of powerful dynasts. (3) Group identity tied to the name Uzbek temporarily declined; however, in the presence of dynastic and tribal designations, the Uzbek designation retained sufficient power into the twentieth century to serve as a convenient negative epithet.

Thus, the Timurids knew these enemies and immigrants as a conglomerate of tribesmen, as Turks, and ultimately as Uzbeks. These identities and others would interrelate and complicate the question of Uzbek group identity for hundreds of years, as persistent competition appreciably weakened each designation. After the mass migration at the turn of the sixteenth century, Uzbeks planted their triumphant standards below the Sir Darya, but the renaming of Mawaraunnahr and its people remained unfinished. Historians sometimes treat this transfer of identity as though it happened overnight; in reality, an unsteady evolution in reidentification consumed the following ages.

This was a time in which Uzbek did not serve as the foremost name for human groups in Central Asian regions settled or controlled by the new forces from the north. Sixteenth-century historians, writing about the Abul Khayrids or Shaybanids, did not favor the term *Uzbeks* in their works. The author of *The History of Abul Khayr Khan*, completed before 1552, avoids the word entirely in the section devoted to the period of that khan. (See figure 3.1.) Likewise, *The Abdullah Story (The Story of the Shah's Fame)*, by a Bukharan historian writing in Farsi, freely employs the tribal designations Arghun, Durman, Jalayir, Kenagas, and the like, as well as, for the inhabitants of Bukhara, the names Turklär and Tajiklär (Turks and Tajiks). Abdullah Khan's troops he calls *ämirlär wä turklär* (Amirs and Turks), but nowhere does he directly call the people of the plains or of Mawaraunnahr Uzbeks.[18]

Other complementary, distinct strata of identity were not so crucial to group identity. Most societies carry multiple identities for different audiences almost continuously. Among the Uzbeks, these layers intermingled, interpenetrated, and exchanged degrees of visibility, audibility, and meaning over time. The mixture of names could affect ethnic group identity. The future of Turkistanian, Uzbek, and other group names remained uncertain but important. Local historians soon adapted the name Shaybanid as a kind of overall tribal title for the new, complex state and used it to distinguish between the divergent Uzbeks. Characterizing a battle between two of those groupings, a chronicler wrote, "Fire broke out and scorched patience and staunchness. The spear tied up the jaded body, and the straight arrow flew without missing. Uzbeks of the Kazak clan defended themselves against troops of Uzbek-Shaybanids, shooting from bows. The Uzbek-Shaybanids defeated them." Thus, out of the events around the turn of the sixteenth century came a dynasty who would dominate the region and whose title would affect group naming for another century and live in world history indefinitely.[19]

Much later a Central Asian writing the history of his region pointed out that the Uzbeks, when they emerged from the Qipchaq Plains and Turkistan to occupy areas to the south, brought with them *Ozbeklik* (the Uzbek character). This local historian followed that important observation with another: "The histories of precisely the present-day Uzbeks of Uzbekistan begin from this date. If Abul Khayr Khan is the founder of this [Uzbek] history, the one who inserts them practically and actively into history is Shaybaniy Khan." Thus, group name and Uzbek group character constituted the two essentials in this early sixteenth-century change affecting the identity of the Timurids, theretofore dominant in areas south of the Sir Darya. From the evidence, the supposed primacy of that Uzbek self-name, if it ever prevailed, quickly disappeared in Central Asia. By the turn of the seventeenth century, that disappearance seriously modified the historical integrity of the specific aggregate of people. The loss of a secure self-appellation influenced their future course tremendously, even though the change entailed sloughing off an ethnic group self-name rather than a sudden, fundamental metamorphosis in the physical composition of the group.

From this development twentieth-century scholars saw that Uzbek group identity had started off strongly in Mawaraunnahr in 1500. By 1600 the particular name had declined and lost power, and some tribal, dynastic, or regional alternative acquired precedence.[20] The facts suggest that corporate names, rather than human group aggregation or composition, had become the

Figure 3.1 Genealogy and Dates of Rule for the Shaybanid Khans

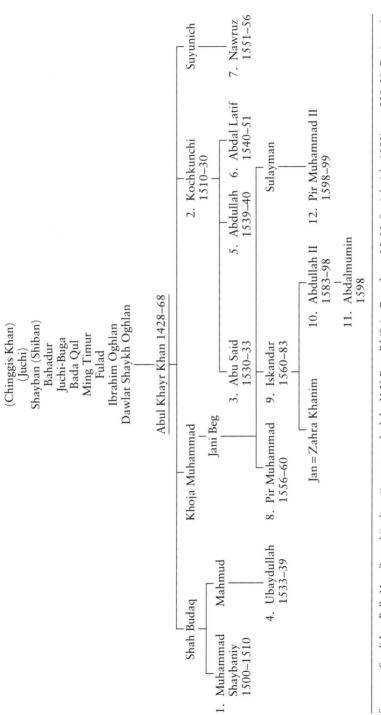

Sources: Stenli Len-Pul', *Musul'manskiia dinastii*, trans. and ed. by V. V. Bartol'd (Saint Petersburg: M. M. Stasiulevich, 1899), pp. 229–30; Boriway A. Akhmedov, *Gosudarstvo kochevykh Uzbekov* (Moscow: Izdatel'stvo Nauka, 1965), pp. 39, 42–48, 62–67, 103, 147.

predominant signal of supratribal identity. But were Central Asians ready for this larger form of belonging, of consensus?

In the second half of the sixteenth century the inhabitants of Bukhara, Abdullah Khan's (r. 1557–1598) Shaybanid capital, lacked an Uzbek identity. The prominent historian of the day, Hafiz Tanish ibn Mir Muhammad Bukhariy, described those people as *tajik wä turklär* (Tajiks and Turks). Not merely in the city but on the battlefield, he referred to common foot soldiers as *turk wä tajik piyadälär* (Turk and Tajik troops). Genealogists retained the collective epithet Uzbek as a convenient technical term for the tribes in Central Asia after the mass migration. In part that corporate terminology weakened because settlement and stability did not characterize the tribes during the early centuries following the move south. Besides the seasonal movements from winter to summer grazing lands and back, these tribes frequently shifted location, not always voluntarily. Such removals dispersed tribesmen but tended to spread their overall group name thinly and haphazardly throughout the scarcely populated, uncultivated pasturelands. The name *Uzbek* also failed to capture the towns. For that reason, as well as the hint of uncouthness it carried after the fifteenth century, the name aroused disdain among urban and other literate populations.

In its place, *Sart*, a term both local residents and outsiders felt suited the ethnic mixture of Central Asian urban areas, became prevalent. It embraced not merely townspeople, but the increasingly numerous settled populations, irrespective of origin or subgroup links.

While Uzbek languished at home as a corporate self-name in the sixteenth century, people abroad employed it emphatically and pejoratively, especially the foreign population that mattered most to the Central Asians—the people of neighboring Iran. Like their predecessors of the pen, Safavid historians Muhammad Masum and Muhammad Tahir-i Wahid continued to slur the Uzbeks in the chronicle started by Iskandar Munshi, *The World-Adorning History of Abbas*. The chroniclers referred to the troops of Khwarazmian prince Abul Ghazi Bahadur Khan, who opposed Iran in 1628, as "this horde of bandits," and persistently identified those enemies as Uzbeks.[21]

Yet another relationship served to put the Uzbek name in ill repute during those years. Under the Shaybanid dynasty, those who resisted or dissented from the Shaybanid khans at the center were referred to disparagingly by the sovereign's spokesmen as enemies of order and sacred law. Shaybanids applied the pejorative "Uzbek" to the whole category, as did Ashtarkhanid chroniclers from Bukhara to the authors of anarchy and disorder, thus continuing the contest between centralization and fragmentation. In the minds of most urban dwellers, government servants, and the religious establishment and literary intellectuals, that term classified no ethnic or linguistic group; it merely singled out a band of ignorant malcontents with destructive strength and no affirmative attributes. For nearly three centuries, Uzbek tribal recalcitrance made that supratribal name a troubling designation for the positive, decent people it had once described. The countervailing popular term *Sart* undermined Uzbek unity by reinforcing the division between settled and migratory Uzbeks. This terminological polarization accurately reflected the dilemma of social and political alignments facing the Central Asian leadership.

4 Leadership

Allahning räsuli. . . äytdi:
'Älbättä padshahlärning dilläri
tängrining yerdägi khäzinäsidir'

Certainly the souls of rulers are in the earthly treasury of the
Lord, said. . . Allah's messenger

(sacred Muslim tradition quoted by Hafiz Tanish ibn Mir
Muhammad Bukhariy, 1589)*

Fear of evil and a devastating decline in living conditions bred prayerful hope
and faith in Muslim Central Asians, who believed that outstanding rulers would
emerge in a prearranged cycle of leadership to bring better times. (Chapter 7,
"History," will examine details of this belief.) Uzbek history demonstrates that
failings and merits of earlier leaders may affect their descendants and suggests
several patterns of specific qualities relevant to their group identity.

Although few outsiders can name any past Uzbek leaders, some individual
Uzbeks did take the role of identifying the Uzbeks to themselves and the outside
world. Even before they came to Central Asia, the Uzbeks knew of the important real and mythical hero-kings of the region. However, their migratory life
plus their social and political structure demanded dynamic warrior chieftains.

---

* Hafiz Tänish ibn Mir Muhämmäd Bukhariy, *Äbdullä namä (Shäräfnamäyi shahiy)* (Tashkent:
Ozbekistan SSR "Fän" Näshriyati, 1969), L176b.

The distribution of power among numerous tribal heads and elders also required a khan to be a politician and conciliator. Habits of independence, harsh competitive egalitarianism, and decentralization called for an agile tactician.

ABUL KHAYR KHAN

In this light Abul Khayr Khan was a remarkable leader, although the earliest accounts of his prowess contrast with the ideal of the good king in Central Asia. Fazlallah ibn Ruzbihan Isfahaniy, a historian who served variously as secretary, counselor, and chronicler to five powerful chieftains and monarchs (Sultan Yaqub and his son Abul Fath Mirza Baysunqar, both Aqqoyunlu Turkmen rulers in Tabriz between 1487 and 1492; Sultan Husayn Mirza, famed Timurid sovereign, in Herat *ca.* 1504; Muhammad Shaybaniy Khan of the Uzbeks no earlier than 1503 and then in Samarkand, *ca.* 1507–1510; and Ubaydullah Khan, Shaybanid strongman, in Bukhara from 1512 to at least 1515), accumulated valuable experience in assessing the qualities of kings and the attitudes respected in regimes. Although Isfahaniy had no personal observation of Abul Khayr Khan—having arrived in the region decades after his death—the historian spoke with many persons, including the khan's grandson, who had known Abul Khayr Khan personally or had followed his advance at firsthand. In Isfahaniy's main work concerning Central Asian history, the author characterizes the khan in passages such as this one:

> None of the khans reached his might . . . He was an able padishah, shepherd of the flocks, and God-fearing. His highness . . . possessed an eminence among kings, because moral virtues achieved by no one [else prevailed] in his governance and reign . . . Abul Khayr Khan was distinguished among preceding and following kings especially by great magnanimity.[1]

The khan evidenced that trait, according to the author, when he refrained from occupying Samarkand in the mid-fifteenth century. The urban historian, however, may have misinterpreted the nomadic khan's motives, for Abul Khayr Khan exhibited no preference for settled life during his long sovereignty over the Uzbek confederation. The Chinggisid legacy that rejected city living survived intact in the Uzbek plainsmen. In addition, Abul Khayr Khan's forces scarcely possessed the resources for administering the populated, city-oriented society and economy of southern Central Asia.

Shahbakht was nearly five years old when Abul Khayr Khan, his powerful grandfather, made strategic mistakes that would forever affect the fortunes of the Uzbek group, for his unrelenting hostility toward unsubmissive Uzbeks turned their resentment into an irremediable breach. First, Abul Khayr Khan lost resourceful warrior-leaders like Sayidek or the brothers Ibak Khan and Bureke Sultan and their followers, who refused to migrate south with him to Sighnaq from northwestern Siberia. Several years later, around 1455, recalcitrant tribal leaders, including Giray and Jani Beg (1427–1488), fled with their people to escape Abul Khayr Khan's authority. They took refuge far to the east of Sighnaq in Moghulistan and before long became the Uzbeks' chief rivals in the region. The former Uzbek-Qazaqs, now known as Kazaks, fled southeast from traditional Uzbek territory and received asylum from Isan Bugha, khan of Moghulistan. He allotted them pastureland in the Chu and Talas valleys, just beyond the eastern Qipchaq Plains. There, they were said to have dwelt "in peace and content."

Abul Khayr Khan should have forseen their departure and its consequences. The people of the Qipchaq Plains, of Turkistan as well as of Mawaraunnahr and Khurasan, traditionally voted with their feet by moving away when a ruler's conduct made them despair. Although costly for the refugees, their flight depopulated an unhappy domain. This became an effective political referendum, for heavy-handed rulers in the Qipchaq Plains as well as in Central Asia lost manpower. Abul Khayr Khan's second fundamental error dismembered his painfully constructed tribal federation completely when he failed to protect his eastern flank. In 1457 Dzungarian Mongolians, in a rapid penetration of the Uzbek area, smashed the khan's forces in a bloody battle not far from Sighnaq and took one of his grandsons hostage. They forced the khan to abandon the battlefield and—in unnomadic behavior—hide behind the walls of Sighnaq. Fortunately for the Uzbeks, the Dzungarians, after plundering several Uzbek settlements and towns, proposed a treaty of peace. Procrastinating Uzbeks finally accepted, and the non-Muslim invaders withdrew eastward to their camping grounds. Guards held three-year-old Mahmud Bahadur Sultan (1454–1504) in the country of the Qalmaqs (as the Uzbeks called the Dzungarians) until he was ten. So impotent had the khan's authority become in the plains by 1464 that when the Dzungarians released young Mahmud Bahadur Sultan unharmed, some Uzbeks and Kazaks kidnapped and betrayed him. But a relative finally secured the youngster's return to his older brother, Shahbakht.[2]

These shocking blows, combined with the major defections of Uzbek tribes in the second half of the 1440s and in the 1450s, meant that when Abul Khayr Khan died in 1468, numbers of his tribes fled to join Giray and Jani Beg in the East, thus greatly enlarging the rival Uzbek-Kazak nucleus roaming beyond the Sir Darya. These two formidable Uzbek bodies never reconciled, thus losing the opportunities of unity and sustaining a fury usually observed only in civil wars, which their endless conflicts much resembled. Before long, the Uzbek-Kazaks discarded the first half of their name, permanently cutting themselves off from the parent Uzbek body. The difference in name has separated the two ever since, though their ethnic and physical makeup were the same. Those Uzbek tribes that had remained in northwestern Siberia rather than join Abul Khayr Khan in the vicinity of Sighnaq now coalesced around the family of Ibak Khan and his descendants. Centering themselves at the old Uzbek capital, Chimgi Tura (Tumen), they formed the Siberian khanate. This Uzbek state, maintaining close ties with Bukharan Central Asia, lasted through the sixteenth century until destroyed by Russian cossacks. Some Siberian Uzbeks continued to live in Siberia under Russian domination and without further Uzbek political identity. Thus, from the three-way split in the great Uzbek confederation, two large fragments—the Uzbek-Kazaks and the Siberian khanate—lost their supratribal Uzbek identity. Meanwhile, the main body formerly commanded by Abul Khayr Khan milled leaderless in the southeastern Qipchaq Plains and northwestern Turkistan.

MUHAMMAD SHAYBANIY KHAN

The formal, full name of the next leader to emerge was Abul Fath Muhammad Shaybaniy Khan (1451–1510), combining the Muslim *kunyä* (patronymic) with his *täkhällus* (pen name), derived from the Chinggisid dynast Shiban. Shahbakht ("Regal Fortune"), his pet name as a youngster (transformed into Shahibek or Shaybaq as he grew up), he evidently favored in later life as well. Two of his contemporary chroniclers evolved a pattern in selecting the right name form for Shahbakht. Both initially employed Shaybaniy or Shaybaniy Khan when mentioning him throughout the early years, but in 1500, his triumphal year of conquest, they prudently began to write Shaybaq/ Shaybak Khan.[3] (See figure 4.1 for a portrait of the mature Shaybaniy Khan.)

Shahbakht spent his youth, following the early death of his father and then of his grandfather, running for his life with his brother and a few guardian horsemen. This ordeal taught him cunning and survival skills in plains warfare, for a practical leader had to be effective. Abul Khayr Khan should have destroyed those in the rebellious faction, not forced them to flee. Their breakaway, however, demonstrated the strong force of individualism among the many major Uzbek tribes led by Shahbakht's grandfather and showed the difficulties of such an indomitable centralizing khan in the face of the individualism of his subgroup tribesmen.

From his grandfather and subsequent trainers Shahbakht learned the ferocious code of the plains handed down from Mongol times that taught him to deal implacably with enemies and potential adversaries and conveyed the importance of blood ties and ethnic kinship for nomadic survival. Chinggis Khan's martial legacy claimed divine right and heavenly origins for the rule. Opponents by definition, therefore, qualified as heretics, and as such were

Figure 4.1 Miniature painting of Shaybaniy Khan (1451–1510). The Metropolitan Museum of Art, The Cora Timken Burnett collection of Persian miniatures and other Persian art objects, bequest of Cora Timken Burnett, 1957.

marked for capital punishment. The Mongols furiously demonstrated this principle on the people of Turkistan and Mawaraunnahr. When the Khwarazmians destroyed a caravan of trader-ambassadors sent to Central Asia by the Mongols in 1219, Chinggis Khan is said to have declared, "How was my golden tether [bond of suzerainty] broken by the Sarta'ul [settled Central Asian but not yet Uzbek] people . . . I shall set forth against the Sarta'ul people:

> Avenging
> The avengement,

Requiting
the requital

of my hundred ambassadors." The political legacy of that chastisement has remained strong in the region's historical memory. The Chinggisids' outlook also abhorred the notion of popular leadership among subjects, for in Chinggisid times, Mongol aristocracy commanded the troops, served in the select guard, and held posts in the headquarters or tents of Chinggis, his four wives, or his nearest relatives. The documents reveal that "at that stage there was no democratic movement" in the mobile Mongol society, unlike the later Qipchaq Uzbeks. Thus, Chinggisid precepts made the nomadic existence not only preferable but obligatory by specifying that its princes live in the plains or mountains and keep away from settled regions.[4]

Shahbakht spent his early life mainly in the wide Qipchaq Plains outside of what had been the realm of Chaghatay Khan (d. 1242), another of Chinggis Khan's sons. The range allotted to Shiban (Chinggis Khan's grandson) by his father constituted only the northeastern portion of Juchi's territory. Thus, Shiban's domain lay east and southeast of the southern Urals. In summer it offered camping space between the Ural hills and the Ilek and Irgiz rivers. Wintering areas lay southward, in the upper parts of what is today Kazakhstan, approximately 52 degrees east longitude and 60 to 47 degrees north latitude, measuring about 3,610,000 square kilometers.[5] Encroaching civilization gradually contracted the extraordinary breadth of the Qipchaq Plains, a signal of change that would affect the nomads' territory and life. But Shahbakht's compelling hunger for his wide-open homeland, his sense of belonging to the plains, never left him nor did his ingrained desire to command the destinies of the entire original prairie from the Irtysh River to the Dniester. Shahbakht's Qipchaq Plains far surpassed the land of Shiban. Not long after Shahbakht emigrated from the Qipchaq Plains he described that expanse almost poetically:

> The Qipchaq Plains equals six hundred farsängs [if square, *ca.* 17,640,000 square kilometers: one farsäng = seven or eight kilometers] of land. The greater part of it is covered with rivers. The nightingale of reason lost its composure over the beauty of this country's flowers. Each of its trees is high as a lotus or as a beam reflected from the earth to seventh heaven.

Shahbakht Khan went on to describe the birches of the region from which, as a consequence of their hardness, people made fine carts and fashioned unwarped wheels, extremely durable and strong. He greatly admired birds of prey— hawks, white falcons, gerfalcons—that nested in those tall trees. From this attachment to this homeland he fervently praised the area's nature:

> It seems that the very essence of the world consists in delight, the abundance of blessings, the pleasantness of the climate and of the calm peace of the

Qipchaq Plains. In the springtime, days pass in the pleasing zephyr of a breeze as sweet-smelling as ambergis, and the nights in tranquility and freshness match a heavenly paradise . . . The tranquility and leisure of its inhabitants are greater than among all the descendants of Adam.

The khan termed the plains the world's most splendid flower garden. The historian who recorded this eulogy by the mature Shahbakht Khan declared that "all this is the domain of the Uzbek [*mämläkät-i ozbäk*]. What are the Qipchaq Plains? An extension of paradise."[6]

In this unspoiled natural wonderland, Shahbakht observed in dismay the spoiling of the Uzbek nobility. "The descendants of the khans [and of] the foremost sultans and of the influential nobles . . . wasted their exertions and efforts in large part on the gathering of wealth." He confessed that as he himself reached maturity, "I had absolutely no desire to accumulate herds of sheep." Instead, what fascinated Shahbakht were the habitat and habits of predatory birds. In his warm depiction of the plains he couples the phrase "hawks, white falcons, gerfalcons" with "the delights" and "blessings" of the tranquil countryside.[7]

A biographer of the time, noting Shahbakht's admiration for these birds of prey and his active engagement in falconry, wrote, "Each morning the falcon of resolve to conquer the world swooped in the hunt for land and water birds." Shahbakht, then, devoted his youthful energies to the passion and strategies of this regal hunt rather than the pattern of his kinsmen in getting rich.[8]

When a day's princely chase had brought down enough game, including deer, "men of learning, pious subjects, darwishes [itinerant Muslim religious men], *Qur'ân* reciters, and clergymen" gathered around Shahbakht for a royal feast. Those guests and companions were weighted on the side of religion and the Islamic faith more heavily than on the world of secular knowledge because Shahbakht's education emphasized adherence to the religious beliefs and rituals of Islam.[9] In Mawaraunnahr his religious attachment illustrated the difference between his kind of leadership and that of the urban-based sovereigns. Yunus (1415/16–1486/87), whose reign paralleled that of Shahbakht's grandfather, ruled as a powerful khan of nomadic Mogolistan, south-southeast of Lake Balkhash. Yet Yunus Khan, a man educated in both Persia and Mawaraunnahr, made his capital in Tashkent and thought that until his Mogols "settled down in cultivated countries and towns, they could never become true Musulmans."[10] This difference in religious fervor between the nomads of the East and the North did not seem to affect their leadership style, for they differed little in this respect. Perhaps the influence of the Buddhist and animist Kalmyks and other non-Muslims to the East, along with dispersal and mobility, limited the practice of Islam in Mogolistan.

Shahbakht's tutors did not limit his lessons for adult life and responsibility to religion and hunting. Besides his lyrical description of the native land, other evidence reveals that in his early youth Shahbakht absorbed far more than the stern code of his ancestor Chinggis Khan. He was exposed to education, to certain arts, and to a spiritual life. His grandfather ordered a commentary on the mystical, Persian-language *Mathnawi-i ma'nawi* of the famous Sufi poet Jalaloddin Rumi (1207–1273), who was born in Balkh.[11] Shahbakht's father, Shah Budaq Sultan, though he died very young, also valued knowledge. "He was an intelligent, learned royal prince," according to a historian of the Shaybanid epoch. Shah Budaq Sultan, in turn, put his appointed guardian, Atabek (Ateke) Shaykh Bek Uyghur, an elder of the Uzbeks' Uyghur tribe, in charge of Shahbakht, who continued under that tutelage in the Qipchaq Plains after his father's death.[12]

When Shahbakht's grandfather died in 1468, the Shaybanid amirs removed Shahbakht and his younger brother, Mahmud Bahadur-Sultan, from the care of Shaykh Bek Uyghur and entrusted the princes' further upbringing to Karachin Bahadur, who taught the boys the art of survival.[13] Within 80 days of when their uncle and protector fell to the rival Ibak Khan, Karachin Bahadur fled west with them to the Volga River. First they sought protection in Astrakhan but then, still pursued by enemies of Abul Khayr Khan's dynasty, escaped eastward with only a small guard, going again toward the Sir Darya. They wintered at Otrar, joined by the remainder of the Qoshchi tribe, which had helped them break out of Astrakhan. That body traditionally supplied guardians (*atäkäs*, *atabek*s) and foster brothers (*kükältash*es) to leaders descended from Shiban, but even that protection—together with that of a friendly Timurid, Sultan Ahmad Mirza—did not suffice.

The resident governor of Otrar, Muhammad Mazid Tarkhan, asked them to leave, which forced the young princes once more to become wanderers. Fleeing their late grandfather's archenemy, Giray Khan and his forces, it became apparent that Giray Khan and his allies meant to seize this opportunity to terminate the line of Uzbek leadership. At this juncture, Giray Khan's grandson, Irenchi Khan, killed Alike Sultan, one of Shahbakht's principal Shaybanid protectors. This attack exacerbated the enmity between the two Uzbek factions and widened the breach between Shahbakht's family and the separatist Uzbek-Kazak group. Under the circumstances, Shahbakht took flight anew, this time westward to Bukhara.[14]

To this desperate move into Bukhara, historians credit the origins of Shahbakht's deep early piety, aesthetic sensitivity, linguistic and artistic ability, calligraphic skill, and general education. Shahbakht, however, had attained full maturity before leaving Turkistan for Mawaraunnahr and Bukhara: in 1471 he would have reached his twentieth year. Thenceforth, his adult name, Abul Fath Muhammad Shaybaniy Khan, would date the turn in his career in history, though Shahbakht and its variants continued to be used by some people (see above). In the splendid Muslim educational and theological center of Bukhara, the chronicles say, he managed to study thoroughly the word of God, to acquire disciplined learning, and "to adorn himself with the garments of moral perfection and knowledge." He conversed with darwishes, ascetics, and scholars in both theoretical and practical discourse. His contact with ordinary and influential clergymen alike, historians asserted, gave him a clear understanding of the secrets of religion. Shaybaniy Khan's later conduct bears out the patterns formed during his young adulthood.[15]

Throughout his early life Shaybaniy Khan, despite his sometimes frenetic existence, was guided by religious tutors and counselors. Sources show that these came from the Khojagan (Naqshbandiya) Sufi order. While living in Bukhara under Timurid protection, "he assiduously occupied himself with his education," mainly under the tutelage of one of the best *Qur'ân* reciters of the time, Mawlana Muhammad Khitayi. Nithari, a late-sixteenth-century author, asserted that Shaybaniy Khan "mastered the *Qur'ân*." Bukharan shaykh Jamaladdin Azizan, a member of the Khojagan order, initially served as his Sufi guide. During the stay in Bukhara, Shaybaniy Khan also made a religious pilgrimage to the shrine for Khwajai Buzurg, where he met a grandson of Buzurg, Khwaja Nizam al-Din Mir Muhammad Naqshbandiy, whose disciple he may have become. Demonstrating his devotion, Shaybaniy Khan performed an extra *täjjähud* (voluntary prayer) after midnight in the shrine. However devout, he did not permit faith to curtail ambition. When Shaykh Azizan remonstrated with his pupil over his pretensions to grandeur, Shaybaniy Khan, according to Sufi sources, turned to another Bukharan, Shaykh Mansur, for guidance. Shaykh Mansur noted that "the Uzbek wants to be a padishah."[16]

As a result, Shaybaniy Khan's respect for learning and the arts, though not in the least superficial, took second place in his life after politics and kingship. He spent two years (*ca.* 1474–1475) under the protection of Bukhara's governor, Amir Abd al-Ali Tarkhan. Some six years before the full-scale Uzbek invasion of Mawaraunnahr, Zahiriddin Muhammad Babur lamented in his memoirs that the Timurid Abd al-Ali "was the reason for Shaybaniy Khan's advancing so much and for the ruin of such ancient dynasties [the Timurid branches]." Biographers of the time wrote that during this period Shaybaniy Khan busied himself equipping and preparing for combat, his heart full of emotion about the status of shahs and his mind on conquering the world "insofar as the abundance of important affairs and activities for conquest did not distract and obstruct [it] . . . the noble personage . . . rose to the highest point of cognition and penetration" in his education.[17]

Although much had preceded Shaybaniy Khan's first Bukharan experience, that Bukharan period affected him profoundly. Near the end of his active life, Shaybaniy Khan ordered Fazlallah ibn Ruzbihan Isfahaniy to compose a memoir and account of the khan's deeds. The sovereign felt a kinship with the learned Isfahaniy, a Sunnite refugee from religious persecution by Shiites in Iran. Isfahaniy quickly became counselor to the khan, who meant the volume as a gesture of gratitude for Bukhara's timely protection and hospitality three-and-a-half decades earlier. To match that intention, he named the memoirs (provisionally entitled *Travel Account of Bukhara*), as *Kitab-i mihman namä-yi bukhara* (The Book of Bukara's Guest).[18]

Shaybaniy Khan also had powerful memories of another refuge that followed his sojourn in Bukhara. When the khan said goodbye to that city, his party headed for the Qipchaq Plains. On the way, they reached the fortress town of Arquq, where a warm welcome met them and which became a temporary Turkistan base in Shaybaniy Khan's constant search for safety and a domain. Later, according to a contemporary poet and historian, the khan remembered that place and occasion with great feeling:

> This fort, Arquq, has the same significance for us as did the town of Yathrib [Medina] for the Prophet—may the very best blessings and peace be upon him—because the inhabitants of this fortress were the first persons who tied up the loins of life with the sash of zeal for creating our state, which grows with each day.

The khan proceeded to find parallels between his fortunes as refugee and the Prophet Muhammad's companions, for whom the people of Medina provided aid in desperate times. The khan declared that the Arquqites defied as heretics those who dared to oppose Shaybaniy Khan, God's chosen leader.[19] From Arquq, Shaybaniy Khan returned to the Qipchaq Plains at the urging of a courier from the Manghit leader Musa Mirza. Along with the Manghit warriors, the khan fought a pitched battle against the breakaway Uzbek tribes, under Qasim Sultan, and the troops of Burunduk Khan, grandson of Giray Khan and still Shaybaniy Khan's implacable opponent. Driving them off, Shaybaniy Khan and his brother Mahmud Bahadur-Sultan returned safely to Sighnaq in Turkistan, where another event took place that shaped Shaybaniy Khan's character and his education.

THE POWER OF POETRY

Escaping to Sighnaq from Otrar [the *wilayat* (province) of Muhammad Mazid Tarkhan], about 1475, earned Bek Ata Bahadur, for his bravery against Shaybaniy Khan's enemies in the terrain beyond Arquq, the epithet "a member of the tribe of Salor Kazan," a legendary Oghuz Turkic chieftain glorified in the folk epic *The Book of My Grandfather, Dede Qorqut*.[20] Bek Ata Bahadur, termed "one of God's friends," offered Shaybaniy Khan at Sighnaq or near it, in the Qipchaq Plains proper, a copy of the long poetic work *Iskändär namä* (The Alexander Story), completed in 1390 in Ottoman Turkish by Mawlana (Taj ud-Din) Ahmed (1334–1413).[21] Its author had served as secretary in the council of Sultan Bayazid I (1380–1402) in Anatolia, who was destroyed by Timur. A modern critic calls this Alexander Book "the first important secular poem of the Western Turks." Its 16,500 lines—the legendary story of Alexander the Great—touch on all branches of contemporary knowledge and use various events in the Alexander legend as sermon text. The author-poet finds allegories or parables in every scene and introduces scientific and learned discourse to summarize all known history. "His obvious purpose was to educate and to supply a guide for conduct."[22]

Because the poem came from a Sunni theologian of Istanbul who supposedly presented a verse *qasidä* (panegyric) to Timur and received his favor during the conqueror's campaign through Turkey in 1402, Mawlana Ahmed's didactic work would have in any case been well regarded in Turkistan and the Qipchaq Plains. More particular reasons, however, made it required reading for Shaybaniy Khan at this early stage in his adult career. History-conscious Central Asians knew of Alexander's ancient thrust into the region and of his legacy to the Greco-Bactrian kingdom. Numbers of Central Asian nobles claimed kinship with the ancient Greek commander. As late as the third quarter of the nineteenth century, "many of the petty princes in the mountain countries of the upper Oxus [Amu Darya] claim to be descended from him," wrote a U.S. eyewitness.[23]

Three themes seem to have struck the Shaybanid Uzbek field commander. (1) The discussions about science and history made the book a guide for everyday philosophy by exalting knowledge. (2) The poem showed Alexander to be beloved by his foreign subjects owing to the justice of his rule. (3) Most exciting for Shaybaniy Khan, various signs in Alexander's childhood pointed to his future greatness as the conqueror of both East and West.[24] A few words from the opening of the Alexander Story, "War emerged from the *däsht* [plains]," distilled the book's essence for Shaybaniy Khan by, according to the khan's fifteenth-century interpreter, "pointing to victories that will be obtained by someone from the plains." Being an acknowledged son of the Qipchaq Plains, Shaybaniy Khan made this "the reason for seeking the inherited domain and [his] desire to spread justice and beneficence around the entire world." He was driven, too, by the conviction that "Almighty Allah loves those of high designs and does not love low ones. [Thus,] despite an insignificance of wealth and power, pursuing high designs, [he] set out to conquer the world."[25]

Shaybaniy Khan carried the book with him during his campaigns and identified with the Alexander history and legend to the end of his days. One of his poet-biographers, Muhammad Salih, wrote, in 1505 or thereafter, a couplet in a versified history intended to please the khan:

They said this is Khan Shaybaniy,
Perhaps this is the second Alexander.[26]

Another biographer of the time devoted an entire panegyric to ranking Shaybaniy above the Greek conqueror. The famous model whom the Uzbek commander chose to emulate signified far more than temporary vanity or egotism. People saw Alexander the Great as a just sovereign, which harmonized with the Central Asian manuscripts of advice for rulers that Shahbakht would have discovered in the libraries of Bukhara. Justice was a quality that gave men the right to rule.[27] Kai Ka'us wrote in his practical *Mirror for Princes* (1082), well known throughout Central Asia in its Tajik and later Turki versions, "a just potentate [*adil padsha*] is the source of gladness for the universe. The despotic potentate [*zalim padsha*] is a flood of devastation for the world."[28]

Chinggis Khan and his Mongol descendants would have disagreed. Chinggis believed that his right to rule was absolute, through a dispensation from *kök* (sky). In that, his position vaguely resembled the Islamic persuasion, expressed in the holy books, about the divine origin of any right to kingship. Nor would the Muslim writers of counsels for good governance have cited Chinggis Khan's sayings and actions advocating religious tolerance to argue in favor of justice, equity, conciliation, or other Central Asian values.

In this regard, Shaybaniy Khan's actions often placed him in the middle of his Mongol legacy. In other acts and his writings, however, the Uzbek khan demonstrated devotion to Central Asian Muslim values by a stress on forgiveness, which contrasts not only with the Mongol code of behavior but with the ideas of a later time in the West. One way it was expressed in the Central Asian society of that temperament and era was that the warrior king be a good winner and show his greatness through forgiveness and magnanimity, as already referred to in connection with Abul Khayr Khan. The good loser, praising the victor, acknowledging sportsmanship in the contest, and the like—so valued elsewhere in idealistic times—earned no special respect in the late medieval Central Asian environment.

Shaybaniy Khan responded with forgiveness more than once when the eye of history was upon him and probably when it was not. Amir Muhammad Mazid Tarkhan, governor of the Otrar district in Turkistan, opposed Shaybaniy Khan with superior numbers when the khan's small force made a raid on nearby Yassi. In the fight, the khan's brother, Mahmud Bahadur-Sultan, knocked the amir from the saddle and captured him for the Uzbeks. "The khan forgave his sin and treated him well, because he [Shaybaniy Khan] had taken his [the Amir's] daughter to wife and because from previous times he was obligated to him for many services." Shaybaniy Khan had not forgotten the Amir's earlier succor in Turkistan, when the two young brothers fled Astrakhan for their lives from hostile Uzbek tribesmen. In his action he expressed more than simple gratitude.[29]

In an encounter in 1503, Shaybaniy Khan defeated and captured two formidable opponents from Mogolistan, Mahmud Khan and Sultan Ahmed Khan, sons of the great Chaghatay khan Yunus. Yunus Khan was the grandfather of Zahiriddin Muhammad Babur Padishah and the father of Mihr Nigar Khanim Chaghatay, whom Shaybaniy Khan married for a brief time after he captured Samarkand in 1500. An unfriendly historian of the time acknowledged that "Shahi Beg [Shaybaniy] Khan, observing the duties of the situation . . . having treated them both [the two captured khans] with respect, sent the khans into Moghulistan." That gesture reflected Shaybaniy Khan's Samanid heritage. Some five years later, when Sultan Mahmud Khan came into Shaybaniy Khan's hands again, however, the Uzbek leader said, "a second act of mercy would be the cause of the ruin of my kingdom," and in 1508 he caused Sultan Mahmud Khan and his offspring to die on the banks of the Khojand River (the Sir Darya). The Mogols of eastern Turkistan constituted dangerous rivals; thus Shaybaniy Khan's Samanid side (forgiveness) was overcome by his Chinggisid Mongol side (pragmatism).[30]

His subsequent meditation on these actions (*The Sea of Guidance*) reflects Central Asian distinctions between good and evil:

> O shepherd, even if thy enemy be the hero of the age,
> Perturbations will be lifted with good deeds.
> Thou didst not wrong the Timurid princes.
> The Lord surely will not wrong tribes who are good.
> Thy goodness with Yunus Khan's progeny was proper,
> For they acted wrongly and finally found retribution.

In these lines, the Shaybanid khan rationalized his ruthless dealings with hostile Timurid princes and some Chaghatay nobility by identifying himself as God's instrument. That did not entirely clear his conscience, however, for in the same composition, perhaps his last large literary work, he fervently advocated mercy to enemies:

> Do forgive, forgive, so that thy eternal reward from God be boundless.
> In the *Qur'ân* [42,38], God said "whoever forgives, his reward is with [God]" . . .
> If thou sparest the enemy who deserves killing, recite "and whoever saves a life
> In a sense has saved the lives of all men" [*Qur.* 5,35]—for thee, it is glad tidings.

> The vanguard of Islam's armed forces is that brave one
> Who, in a time of fury, will forgive, will smooth his brow.[31]

That explains why Shaybaniy Khan now avoided praising or expanding upon justice. The quality of justice attributed in the region's literature to Shaybaniy Khan's hero, Alexander the Great, might have urged the khan to glorify it; the khan's model, however, stood for secular justice. The Arabic word for justice (*'ädl*) appears only twice in these many couplets and refers to God's harsh judgment on earthly sins, not to equity in human affairs. The temporal justice of human leaders or judges was a symbol of sovereignty to which, temporarily at least, the lowly *shaban* (shepherd) of this panegyric to God and the Prophet Muhammad renounced a claim.[32]

The nature of the formal panegyric in Central Asia recognized, through praise, encomium, and eulogy, subordination to a higher power, temporal or spiritual. This could produce ritualistic, obligatory verse, rather than the intense, candid sentiments of Shaybaniy Khan's *Sea of Guidance*. The future of this literary form, therefore, would remain enmeshed with the complex network of Central Asian attitudes toward voluntary or unavoidable dependence.

In contrast with *Sea of Guidance*, pages from Shaybaniy Khan's other poetry—his *Diwan*—expose themes of the poet's secularity, with ideas of justice and self-praise prominent. It reads as if the khan perceived the dangers of absolutism in rulers like himself and thus extolls the rule of the khan's law, rather than the khan's temperament. In one short lyric *ghäzäl* he described his role as liberator of Astarabad and its region:

> In that same summertime, we left for Astarabad.
> Through justice and redress we greatly benefited this tribe.
>
> . . . .
>
> This Shabaniy, protecting the leaders of these tribes,
> Removing the cruelty and tyranny, we greatly redressed the people.[33]

The kind of just act claimed in those lines affects groups, areas, and religious conflict between Sunni and Shiite Central Asians. Shaybaniy characterizes these heterodox opponents as *temur oghlanlari täghäyyir qildi mädhhabin* (the offspring of Timur who altered the color of their sect), which probably meant that the Timurids around Astarabad had shifted from green to red head coverings when they changed from orthodox Islam to Shiism.[34] The liberation of Astarabad from Shiism by Shaybanid arms was exactly the sort of justice the medieval guides advocated, for they countenanced no religious flexibility within Islam. Here, the Mongols would have acted differently from Shaybaniy Khan, a true Sunni Muslim,[35] who believed that only the red-hatted heretics deserved the sword—the ideologically acceptable deserved justice.

Travelers in the area reported that Timurids and Safavids called Shaybaniy Khan "greenhead" (*yeshilbash*) whereas the Central Asians referred to the Safavid troops, largely Turkmens, as "redheads" (*qizil bashlär*). The tension between the green and the red soon evolved into a major conflict, with the episode at Astarabad exacerbating ethnic differences by reversing a tendency that had been growing under Timurids such as Zahiriddin Muhammad Babur toward greater accommodation between the largely Turkic Central Asians and the Turkmen-Iranian population to the southwest. When the Safavid ruler Ismail learned of the action around Astarabad, he saw it as a challenge to his sovereignty and to the faith of his people. A European visitor to the theater of conflict described the confrontation between those two powerful communities:

> [In] 1508, after making great preparations for war, he [Ismail Safaviy] advanced in person against the Tartar Leasilbas [Shaybaniy Khan], ruler of Samarcant, whose subjects are the Zagatai, otherwise called the Green Caftans (Sunnees). This chief was at that time on the frontier of Persia with a victorious army, having performed many feats of arms in the vicinity . . . By these conquests he had thrown all the East into the greatest alarm and particularly raised great apprehension in the Sofi [Ismail], who was an enemy of those of the Green Caftans. On this account he retired to Spaam [Ispahan] and encamped with his whole army, but the victorious Lasilbas [*sic*], in order to gain a pretext for coming to blows with the Suffaveans, demanded a free passage from Ismail, in order that he might pay his vows at Mecca . . . At length, by the intervention of some Tartar and Persian lords friendly to both, they concluded a peace between them.[36]

In this period, against both the hostile Uzbek-Kazaks east of the Sir Darya and the Timurids in southern Mawaraunnahr, Shaybaniy Khan brandished his ideological weapons. He called the Uzbek-Kazaks pagan sun worshippers, idolators, and enslavers of Muslims. According to him, they were worse than the *färängis* (Europeans) of the Christian West because, he said, they had fallen away from Islam, the true faith. Shaybaniy Khan invested great energy and military resources to exorcise that evil from Central Asia. He succeeded in destroying the government of the Timurid heretics but could not overcome his unbelieving brothers, the Uzbek-Kazaks. Their resolute opposition undermined Shaybanid strength in the exhausting campaigns during 1509. The khan soon after fell victim to the religious power he most hated, the Shiite Safavids, who routed the Sunni army and killed Shaybaniy Khan on the field of battle in Khurasan the following year. Thus, temporarily at least, the red triumphed over the green. Ideology had proved decisive again, as in early Muslim days, in Central Asian conflict.

LEGACY OF CONFLICT

A lasting legacy of Shaybaniy Khan to Central Asia was the ethno-religious clash in Khurasan. Central Asian rulers regarded the legacy as affirmative because the confrontation limited Shaybanid expansion and curtailed the assimilation of Iranian people and ideas, thus reinforcing the distinctiveness of Central Asia. That region had not been well-defined since the invasion of the Arabs in the eighth century that united Mawaraunnahr with the Islamic world. Major portions of Central Asia had come under the domination of various nomadic Turkic streams flowing across the area, as well as the Golden Horde in the fourteenth century, but it had not become a unified territory. In the fifteenth century Timurid rulers, led by Sultan Husayn Bayqara, embraced much of the then Iranian civilization and accepted Safavid intervention to defend against invaders from the northeast and southeast. The sixteenth-century approach of powerful Iranian enemies from the southwest, of invaders from Moghol India, and finally the persistent drive out of Russia outlined a territorial and cultural silhouette of Muslim Central Asia for the first time. Shaybanid leaders' successes and failures contributed to this coalescence of Central Asian self-understanding.

Thus the idea that a leader is not merely the product of events but may actively affect the course of history became deeply imbedded in Central Asian thought as early as medieval times. Speaking about a Samanid ruler's failure in the tenth century to recognize the merits of Alptigin, a Turkic slave who rose to lead the Samanid armies, a royal counselor wrote in 1086: "dynasties, kingdoms, and cities may at any time be dependent upon one man, and when that man is removed from his place, the dynasty crumbles, or the city is destroyed, or the country is thrown into confusion... When he [Alptigin] left Khurasan, fortune deserted the Samanid dynasty." This belief in the importance of specific leaders persisted until the twentieth century. If the idea has evolved into something less absolute, it is altered not so much in essentials as in the means available to individual leaders to affect their increasingly complex societies. For hundreds of years, beginning in the ninth and tenth centuries, attitudes toward leadership remained much the same in Khurasan, Mawaraunnahr, and Turkistan. The Uzbek influx modified the style and flavor somewhat, but people retained the image of Samanids and Chinggisids as sterling leaders. Change usually meant revival rather than innovation in this regard, a return to the supposedly purer behavior of the great models of the distant past.[37]

Shaybaniy Khan founded a remarkably powerful, durable dynasty, one that compared well politically and culturally with its immediate predecessors in Mawaraunnahr. Two relatives of the founder particularly embodied its strength: Ubaydullah Khan, nephew of Shaybaniy Khan, and Abdullah Khan, a great-great grandson of Abul Khayr Khan and third cousin of Shaybaniy Khan. Despite a few weak links in the genealogy, the Shaybanids gave Central Asia many extraordinary men and women.

Shaybanid history could lend credence to a belief in predestination. Several of the recorded Muslim *hädith* (verbal pronouncements handed down from the Prophet Muhammad) include the observation that "at the start of every hundred years a religious renewer will appear." Historians easily awarded the title of Islamic renewer for the eighth lunar century (A.H. 800 / A.D. 1398) to Timur, for his rule climaxed around that time. (Some Muslim clergymen applied the title of renewer to his pious son, Shahrukh [r. 1409–1447] in Herat.)[38]

A nineteenth-century Bukharan historian nominated the Timurid sultan Husayn Bayqara (r. 1470–1506, in Herat) as the Central Asian hundred-year renewer of the ninth Islamic century. In doing so he passed over Shaybaniy Khan, whereas Ahmad Mahdum Kalla Danish (1827–1897) designated the formidable Shaybanid khan Abdullah II as the renewer of the Muslim millenium beginning A.H. 1000 (A.D. 1591/1592). Ahmad Mahdum wrote, "[In] approximately each thousand-year and hundred-year history of the world, noble and godly persons appear from the powerful rulers and great scholars in each religion, and they renew it. They are called renewers of millenia and of a century." Thus the selection of Abdullah Khan II was much more significant than the nomination of Shaybaniy Khan because Abdullah would influence ensuing developments positively for at least the first half of his millenium.

This deterministic view of history attributes strong rhythms to the flow of human affairs, as powerful leaders alternate with weak ones to influence the cycles. Thoughtful Bukharans or Khivans expected regular fluctuation in the course of events, explained by variations of the planets and the conjunctions of planetary trajectories. Chronicles written in the time and place gave Timur the epithet *Sahibqiran* (Lord of the Fortunate Conjunction)—a label added to the Shaybanid conqueror's name. According to local astrologers, Shaybaniy Khan's nomads rose to power in Mawaraunnahr at the start of the ninth Islamic century owing to this positioning of the stars.

> Because a conjunction of Jupiter and Saturn occurs nearly every twenty years—which they call *'ulviin*—then at the appearance of the luck of Shaybaniy Khan in the fiery triangle, in the Zodiac of the Archer, in A.H. 908 [A.D. 1501/1502], a conjunction of planets of two levels took place, which signified the end of the epoch of Chaghatay and the onset of the epoch of the Uzbek.

Those predictable intersectings meant that, in affairs of state, descents would follow ascents. The Uzbeks, therefore, faced the future remembering the prophecy of their inevitable decline. The historian Ahmud Mahdum, with

Figure 4.2 Silver *tangas* of Shaybanid khans Shaybaniy 1508/9 and Ubaydullah 1533/34. Source: American Numismatic Society.

hindsight, forecast their fall in a quarter of a millenium, "for," he said, "by the laws of the stars, a historical epoch continues no longer than 250 years." That prediction gave them until about mid-eighteenth century to make their distinctive mark on Central Asia and the world, a moment when Uzbek tribes were politically and economically reasserting themselves over southern Central Asia.[39]

Shaybaniy Khan left behind more than ethnic strife and his genealogical legacy. He greatly admired the Timurid culture and openly praised its last important ruler, Sultan Husayn Bayqara, from whom he took Herat. Shaybaniy Khan borrowed many administrative practices from the Timurids, including striking coins like theirs (see figure 4.2); not only did he acquire some education from them but poets, historians, and his capital city, Samarkand, as well. Therefore, among his contributions to Central Asian history would be the reintroduction of Chinggisid attitudes that led to a different way of thinking and life. He married the plainsman's nomadic vigor, outlook, and style to the high civilization and religious tradition of Mawaraunnahr's urban centers, combining those two abundant streams from his own experience. Shaybaniy Khan spread that blend not only in Shaybanid Central Asia but abroad through the court's vigorous conduct of external affairs and encouragement of foreign trade. In turn, that outside world exerted some influence on developments in Central Asia.

5 Ideology and the Literature of Praise

Näfs-i kafir atïnï minip yürür men har taraf. 'Ajiz u miskin turur men.

Mounted on the horse of that Kafir, the Carnal Soul, I am carried around, hither and yon . . . powerless and miserable.

(Abul Fath Muhammad Shaybaniy Khan, imam of the age, 1508)*

Constructive mastery over others demanded self-control from the leader, according to conventional mores in medieval Mawaraunnahr. Absolute rulers who also wanted to be good governors first had to contend with external expectations. Although confessing to weaknesses, these pious warriors fought to achieve the unselfishness that wise men said ideal monarchs should display. This spiritual quest stemmed from the particular Islamic mysticism to which some subjected themselves, not the strict Muslim orthodoxy that formed them. In the internal war between good and evil the leaders fought against vice and avarice. Ultimately, however, ambition for high rank, arrogance, pride, and perhaps sensuality—all of which qualified as mortal sins for Sufis (practitioners of Islamic mysticism)—triumphed. A number of rulers, Sufi disciples, were

---

* Muhammad Shaybani, "'Bähru'l hudâ,' An Early Sixteenth Century Didactic Qasida in Chagatay," text and trans. by A. J. E. Bodrogligeti, *Ural-Altaische Jahrbücher*, no. 54 (1982):27, L11r.

expected to see any sort of self-discipline as a denial of God's power over oneself and to reject any notion about the wonderful nature of the heart because it signified engagement with the human rather than divine spirit. Popular concepts of right and wrong delineated a list of misfortunes or calamities that could stem from wrong faith or behavior. Thus the khans grew up steeped in a sense of Islamic Central Asian sin.[1]

CENTRAL ASIAN SIN

Any guilty turmoil suffered by a khan probably grew out of Sufi teachings. Those stringent rules, along with the socialization gained at their guardians' knees, guided the young princes' behavior and thinking into adulthood and offer a view of the society's value system. Each organized population with sufficient longevity as a voluntarily united group developed a particular complex of motivating ideals. The medieval Uzbek confederation was no exception; the khans' and amirs' piety and virtue constituted important symbols of sovereignty that ranked above such measures of effectiveness as safe streets or secure borders.

As a *Sunni* Muslim, the khan of the fifteenth century stoutly declared and acted against the major sins delineated by orthodox Islam. Nor does the record show that these orthodox Muslim khans sinned in other ways, such as disobeying parents or committing perjury.

The sins and errors of the fathers or forefathers may be visited on their children, but the good works of predeccessors cannot always benefit their political successor. That irony invites comparison between the actions of medieval ideologists and those of the late twentieth century whose deficiencies should lengthen Central Asian memories. Yet forgetful people accord passionate respect to certain ancestors, deeds, traditions, and monuments of the deep past, despite the fact that human evil appears to have stymied lasting good. Such a condition may have engendered the Central Asian spirit of hopeful melancholy that flavors human expression over the centuries. This same prevalence of evil also urged Central Asians to look to heroes and the *hädith* (sacred traditions) for guidance.[2] Many traditions about major and minor sins handed down from Muhammad's time are included in the authoritative edition of *hädith* compiled by Imam Muhammad ibn Ismail al-Bukhari (d. 870), illustrated with a series of parables. Like other Muslims, Central Asians knew this compilation either through seminary study or from a verbal transmission.

In Imam al-Bukhari's presentation, the cardinal Muslim sins number seven in one part, fewer in another. They bear little resemblance either to the "deadly" transgressions of the Christian churches (pride, avarice, lust, envy, gluttony, anger, and sloth) or to the ten biblical commandments. Islam's sins bear another strong ideological coloring.

The seven cardinal Muslim sins, beginning with the most serious, are (1) polytheism, (2) magic, (3) killing a person whom Allah has forbidden people to kill, except in the name of the law, (4) profiting from usury, (5) misappropriating the possessions of orphans, (6) fleeing from combat, and, finally, (7) bearing false witness against chaste, believing but careless women. According to al-Bukhari's compilation, certain Islamic traditions include the lesser sins of disobedience to parents and committing adultery with a neighbor's wife. Examples of traditions from Balkh and adjacent regions in Central Asia mention additional second-rank sins such as avarice and gluttony.

A current Soviet religious periodical tells an old story of the erudite Muslim traveler questioning a young theologian in Balkh at the time of Friday prayer. Asked the visitor, "What qualities may bring a person to downright baseness?" The young cleric answered with one word: "avidity" and went on to offer four rules to guide men on the path of truth: avoid consuming what is prohibited, do not lie, never harm or offend anyone, and repent repeatedly from the depths of your heart. These admonitions reflect both the systematic and the anecdotal commandments that guided the medieval Muslim's everyday conduct, be he amir or farmer. These same rules have survived to affect modern life.[3]

Central Asian authors of various sects had from the twelfth century, if not earlier, warned their readers and listeners away from sin. Khoja Ahmad Yassawiy, the darwish mystic from Yassa (near the present town of Turkistan), evidently wrote and declaimed fervent poems in his *Diwan-i hikmät* (Words of Wisdom) about the pitfalls confronting believers. Saintliness embodying the virtuous opposites received wide popular treatment in Nasiriddin b. Burhaniddin Rabghuziy's lengthy Central Asian Turkic-language prose composition, *Qisas ul-änbiyä* (Stories of the Prophets, 1310). Many other early Central Asian writings consider the sins and graces of evil and good men; one of the best-known is *Nahju'l färädis* (The Clear Paths of Paradise), possibly written by Mahmud b. Ali, a Khwarazmian author, around 1358. First, he relates the sacred history of the Prophet Muhammad, the four Imams, Fatima, the martyrs Hasan and Husayn, and the great legal authorities of Islam. The author then reviews the rites and duties of the religion. In the fourth part of his work he turns to the major sins ("evil deeds that remove men from God [*afät(lär)*]")—unlawful bloodshedding, harlotry, wine drinking, arrogance, slander, loving this world, hypocrisy through seeing and hearing, hatred, disdain and ignorance, persistent earthly desires. His medley of sins combines transgressions singled out in the sacred traditions along with Sufistic warnings against worldliness and other, less-than-cardinal, prohibitions against bad behavior. For the edification of his readers, he cited the suitable passage from the sacred tradition in Arabic, translated it into Central Asian Turkic, and followed with parables or tales from known scholars or from other sacred traditions. Mahmud b. Ali, if he was the author, set out to condemn evil, wrongful behavior and to teach virtue to the people of his region by making ethics readable.[4]

Against that background of codified transgressions, Shaybaniy Khan confessed himself a sinner (see the epigraph at the beginning of this chapter) and in his *Bāhru'l hudâ* (Sea of Guidance) earnestly, frequently begged God's forgiveness and grace. As a khan and field commander, the ethical, religious dilemmas of forgiveness and submission were much on his mind. The ideology of poverty, the importance of which the Prophet Muhammad emphasized, also became a leading article in the faith of Muslim Sufism. (The khan had experienced more than seven lean years after the Uzbek confederation shattered in 1468.) Alluding to another sort of deprivation, Shaybaniy Khan wrote, "Among the potentates, I alone, am a beggar," speaking of the simplicity of his existence, (which has been attested to), as well as his fidelity to the principles of Muslim and perhaps Sufi poverty. He also spoke of his abject nothingness before the Lord. This insistence on his role as subject, servant, and pleader for God's mercy showed throughout the eulogy from which these lines come.

PANEGYRICS

The poet khan conceived his *Sea of Guidance* a *qäsidä* (panegyric), in a traditional mode that required a degree of formality and precision not generally present in Central Asia's folk poetry. The elevated, ceremonial tone peculiar to a Central Asian *qäsidä* answered the khan's purposes as an expression of praise. The conventional panegyric's length ran between 20 to 99 couplets, but Shaybaniy Khan's expanded to 260. Rhyming *aa, ba, ca,* and so on requires an appropriate quantitative *arudh* meter (the poet used *ramal* in this one). For lyric verse or for rhymed couplets in narrative poetry, Central Asian poets often chose *ramal* meter. Its standard unit structure for a distich started with a long vowel followed by a short vowel and then two long vowels. After two further repetitions of that unit, the final unit contained long, short, long vowels, in that order ($-\cup--|-\cup--|-\cup--|-\cup-$). Shaybaniy Khan employed the form, considered relatively simple in poetics, for this panegyric and frequently in his one *diwan* (collection) of short verse.

Customarily, the Central Asia panegyric celebrated an important personage or occasion. In the *Sea of Guidance*, however, the poet first glorified Allah—the poem begins with the word *tängri* (Lord, borrowed through Mongolian) and ends with *khuda* (God, taken from Farsi).

Shaybaniy Khan also praised the Prophet Muhammad, devoting many more lines to him than to Allah. The subjects' sacred nature made inappropriate the customary lyrical opening, such as the one that begins the famed

Samanid Tajik "Mother of Wine," by Abu Abdullah Jafar ibn Muhammad Rudaki (*ca.* 850–940). Without an opening, the poet could not strictly adhere to the standard technique of employing a *gurezgah* (clever transition) to the main section of *mädh* (praise). *Sea of Guidance* has no opening of that kind at all, but two-thirds of the way along, a kind of modulation turns the work from lines exalting the Prophet to an extended series of couplets about the meaning of religious love, passages in the *Qur'ân*, and the Day of Judgment. Admonitions and moralisms follow that concern carnality and the importance of knowledge—spiritual and intellectual—and that give pious precepts. Near the end, as was traditional, the royal poet revealed his identity by including *shaban*, his *täkhällus* (pseudonym), and the name of the eulogy. Following the Arabic and Farsi models, he uttered a passionate final plea for generosity, begging the Lord to forgive his sins and invoking Allah's mercy on whoever heard or read his panegyric.

The most significant message in this eulogy is that because the poet is a khan, there is no patron to thank or *mamduh* (benefactor) to ask for favors, as usually appear at the end of this literary form. The nature of both subject and author make this work's general outline differ noticeably from convention, but the content—unremitting adoration for the objects of the panegyric—remains true to the genre. In that respect, Shaybaniy Khan set a pattern for the Uzbeks that would be sustained throughout the centuries. When he personalized his eulogy, as he did most of his known writings, the panegyric acquired particular significance. Filled with self-praise as well as self-abnegation, the panegyric written by this migrant from the Qipchaq Plains resonates with pre-Islamic, nomadic Arabic culture, as Shaybaniy praises his own forgiveness and his poetic prowess. Likewise, this poem's disregard for the formalities is a link to pre-Islamic tradition.[5]

Ideology threatens its adherents as well as its unbelievers. Abul Fath Muhammad Shaybaniy Khan, who about 1500 became commander of many devout Sunnis, was also a devout Sunni Muslim. For the zealot, this meant converting to Islam or destroying all heretics and unbelievers. In 1398, Timur carried the sword and torch of Islam to Delhi, future capital of Zahiriddin Muhammad Babur, and slaughtered myriad unbelievers in the name of what he deemed his faith. Shaybaniy Khan's impulse to ascend among the *shähidlär* (martyrs for the faith) by pursuing the same goal in a different place proved overpowering for himself and his immediate followers.[6]

Shah Ismail (1485–1524), a neighbor toward whom the outposts of the Shaybanid domain were quickly moving closer, revealed some traits startlingly similar to those of the khan. Ismail rapidly imbued the Safavid dynasty and its subjects with fervent Shiism. The settled population of Persia, like that of Mawaraunnahr, traditionally held to Sunna, but Shah Ismail, building on heterodox tendencies in Persia during the fifteenth century, converted them to

Shia through leadership and earnest proselyting. In this process he exploited and widened ethnic as well as sectarian cleavages. The shah, a poet like his Uzbek rival, composed patriotic verses in a Turkmen Turkic language that contained a considerable admixture of Central Asian Chaghatay. He also drew his main cavalry and many other fighting forces from Turkmen tribes, which tilted the balance of power within Central Asia. From the southwest, Turkmen warriors exerted great pressure on the Shaybanid Uzbek tribes of Mawaraun-nahr and Khurasan. Shah Ismail's propagandistic lines of verse, revealing a Sufistic masochism, also made his Shiite partisanship clear:

> I was on the gibbet with Mansur; with Abraham in the fire, and with Moses on Sinai.
>
> Come from the eve, celebrate the New Year, join the King.
>
> With discernment come to know the king. O *ghazis* (frontline warriors), prostrate yourselves.
>
> I wear a red crown, my charger is grey, I (lead a) mighty army.
>
> I have the virtues of the prophet Joseph (i.e., I am beautiful).
>
> I am Khata'i (The Sinner), my charger is sorrel; my words are sweeter than sugar,
>
> I have the essence of Murtada Ali (with whom God is pleased). I am the faith of the Shah [i.e., Imam Ali].

In his *Diwan*, the royal poet praised Ali—the Shiite model Imam—ahead of the Prophet Muhammad. Red crown alluded to the symbolic *qizil bash* (red head) garb worn by his Turkmens and allied Safavid soldiery.

Proximity played a fateful part in the lives of these two strongly opposed ideologists of Islam at the beginning of the sixteenth century in Khurasan. The devout Islamic mysticism professed by both leaders might have brought them together, but their ethnosectarianism put them fiercely in opposition to each other until the Shaybanids dynasty died out in Bukhara a century later. More than that, incompatibilities of character added a complicated personal twist to the confrontation between Muhammad Shaybaniy Khan and Shah Ismail Safaviy. Shaybaniy Khan openly excoriated himself for what he termed the urges of "that unbeliever, the Carnal Soul." In writing, he pleaded with God to forgive his weakness and urged readers of his poetry to understand him.[7]

Shah Ismail Safaviy, in contrast, adopted the pen name, *Khata'i* (The Sinner), as shown in the lines above. He meant to brand himself as humble and deficient in faith, a true Sufi, but the pseudonym suggested some realities of his life. European travelers to Persia reported details about Shah Ismail's personal habits that could have earned him his pseudonym. An anonymous merchant left these recollections of Ismail's behavior:

On his second arrival in Tauris [Tabrīz], Ismael committed a most disgraceful act, as he caused twelve of the most beautiful youths [boys] in the town to be taken to his palace of Astibisti for him to work his wicked will upon them and gave them away one by one to his lords for the same purpose; a short time previously he had caused ten children of respectable men to be seized in like manner.[8]

Ismail Safaviy's personal behavior greatly angered the pious Uzbek khan.

Throughout the sixteenth-century Shaybanid hegemony over southern Central Asia, the ferocious conflict between the Central Asian Sunnis and the Shiites of Iran continued. With the Ashtarkhanids, things changed. A diplomatic exchange between Istanbul and Bukhara around 1691 gave expression to the Central Asian desire to continue friendly relations with the Shiite country. Ottoman sultan Ahmed (r. 1691–1695) sent as ambassador to Bukhara his trusted Mustafa Chaush, who brought gifts including Arabian horses, precious stones, multicolored fabric, and other things suitable for a great sovereign. The Ottoman diplomat reached Bukhara at the same time as another embassy from Kashgar representing Muhammad Amin Khan. Ironically, both ambassadors requested military aid from sorely beset Subhanquli Khan to aid them in wars against unbelievers. In the Kashgar case, the envoy said that non-Muslim Kirgiz had taken control of Kashgar. Sultan Ahmed called on the Ashtarkhanid ruler to attack Shiite Persia in a war for the faith, arguing that the reputation of Mawaraunnahr and its countries was at stake. That territory—called "The Illustrious Land" where great savants, devout men, and shaykhs had dwelt together since ancient times—meant to Sultan Ahmed that

> you must bare the sword of faith and exercise all zeal and extreme effort for the triumph of the Prophet's law and the Muslim community. Order the Uzbek troops of your country so that, being with the victorious [Ottoman] troops as if with one body and soul, they might destroy these enemies of the faith and cleanse them from the nooks and crannies of the plain of Iraq [Sultan Ahmed's term for Persia].

Bukhara, weakened and beset by tribal conflict, was able to go neither east nor west to fight wars for the faith. Even if the Ashtarkhanid khan had possessed the military means to respond to the Ottoman invitation for another fight against Shiism, it is doubtful that he would have had the heart for a sectarian struggle with the Safavids. The climate of mutual restraint with Persia that his Bukharan predecessors so carefully created had not entirely dispersed.[9]

As late as the eighteenth century, Islam had the power to move Central Asians, commanding observance from low and high. Yadighar Khan of Khiva, after ascending to sovereignty in 1713, took a large suite with him on a *hajj* (pilgrimage) to Mecca and Medina. Perhaps no other ruling Uzbek monarch had carried out this obligation, for Shiite hostility in Persia had erected almost insurmountable obstacles to Central Asian Sunnites hoping to cross directly to the sacred shrines of Arabia. Thus, merely fulfilling his religious duty would be remarkable enough, but the khan also faced the threat of bandits along the way. During the return journey from the Muslim holy cities, a large crowd of Arabs blocked his party's route near Damascus, where the khan's voyage for spiritual felicity turned into a fight for his temporal existence. This skirmish his retinue won decisively. Subsequently, the governor of Baghdad honored Yadighar Khan with a royal feast and escorted the pilgrims onward. After passing through Astarabad, the Khivan travelers regained what a historian has called, in imitation of Balkh, Bukhara, and other city epithets, the Cupola of Islam—Khwarazm.[10]

In addition to the outright conflicts that exerted pressure on the believers and their institutions in Central Asia, political and cultural stagnation also became a prelude to change. Along with economic decline, increasing fragmentation in values, ideology, politics, and the arts gave sure evidence of social disintegration toward the end of the 1600s and the beginning of the 1700s. Popular Muslim mysticism led the ideological tendencies of both educated and illiterate. Other than mystic poetry, the arts suffered by comparison with earlier periods, and Uzbek tribes increasingly asserted their strength against enfeebled dynasts in Khiva, Bukhara, and Balkh (see figure 5.1). Leaders showed less and less resourcefulness and flexibility, leaning toward harshly defensive repression rather than tolerance or forgiveness.

MYSTICISM

A new religious voice in the form of mystical writings and recitations emerged in reaction to the narrow, fanatical rigidity among orthodox clergy of Bukhara, Khiva, Samarkand, and the other Central Asian religious centers and as a response to the growing chaos that accompanied the great decline of dynasties and institutions in Mawaraunnahr and all over the Muslim world. The inspiration for these new poetic tones did not come entirely from those negative developments, however. An indigenous creativity synthesized the insecure mood of the times with a language of feeling more immediate and passionate than compositions emulating the detached, intricate, and geometric perfections of medieval high-style literature, architecture, and music.

The self-denial central to Sufi verse offered hearers more than a rationale for their economic plight: Sufism's basic tenet, reaching back to the early ascetic khans and theologians, demanded personal poverty, which helped overcome the sinful wish for wealth. The mystics' rhymes and poems of spiritual ardor articulated feelings of religious passion, emotional calls for divine love, and forgiveness, which listeners and readers personally identified with. This revival

Figure 5.1 A rubbing from Manghit ruler Amir Shah Murad's (r. 1785–1800) modest tombstone, later destroyed on Soviet orders. *Epigrafika Vostoka* 7 (1953).

of an old, insistent sound in literature made it more humanly compelling than the elegantly formal patterns and rhythms of much Chaghatay and Farsi poetry.

For Central Asian Turkic people, this genre reached back to the twelfth-century *darwish* of the plains and patron saint of Central Asia, Khoja Ahmad Yassawiy, yet suited the despairing mood of early eighteenth-century Mawaraunnahr. For centuries, different versions of Yassawiy's *Diwan-i hikmät* (Book of Wisdom)—written out and amended or revised by many hands, often recopied, and finally lithographed and reprinted in numbers of places inside and outside Central Asia as late as the twentieth century—remained accessible to believers, in oral and written form. In one late printed version anachronistically embellished with a detailed preface, readers and listeners could learn the ten degrees of the *täriqät* (Sufi way): repentance, giving the hand to a *pir* (master) or preceptor, fearing God, hoping for God's grace, renouncing delights and desires of the flesh, performing service for the master, conversing by permission of the master, listening to his teachings, embracing asceticism, and adopting the hermetic life.[11] Discipline, denial, and asceticism put their mark on the Central Asian character as early as the Shaybanid century, in contrast to the opulence of the preceding Timurid era. Yassawiy's followers found in his *darwish* order a standard.

In the eighteenth century, a public reawakening to mysticism accompanied the tribalization of the dynastic leadership. At the extremes of the social and political scale, Sufi behavior and belief set a pattern that lasted out the century in Bukhara. Before this, Timurid poets had written mystic literature in abundance. Shaybaniy Khan composed a eulogy to Allah and the Prophet and wrote religious tracts. But the incantatory phenomenon—heard at both ends of the eighteenth century—contrasted with recognized medieval voices and in eerie tone resembled the Turkic writings of the sinful Khata'i. The later poets enunciated popular Central Asian (including Uzbek) sensations and attitudes as if in a state of delirium or ecstasy. The insistent, self-directed exhortation in their verse has an almost physical impact on the listener. Although the khans and mighty chieftains evoked awe, the *darwish* poets created ecstatic reverence. The popularity of this genre also derived from the Central Asians' love for obscuring motives and feelings, for camouflaging thoughts. They preferred indirection and hidden meaning over the explicit, and veiled metaphor and allegory in place of concrete statement. Subsurface meaning, with its special vocabularies, appealed to Central Asians. To some extent, mystic literature, with its complicated Sufi conceptions, presented an intellectual word game that had always been a popular folk play for Central Asians. Thus, the darwish poetry of the eighteenth century may have been the first mass Uzbek written literature to appear outside the established literary scheme.

SUFI ALLAH YAR

Its most prominent proponent, Sufi Allah Yar (d. 1721 or 1724), came from the Utarchi clan in the Khitay tribe of Uzbeks. Popular tradition has it that they buried his children, Muhammad Siddiq and Bibi Aysha, in the cemetery of Chankaymish village. People believe that the poet is interred in Vakhshivor, a village situated in the mountains west of Denaw (Denau), a town in southern Uzbekistan near the Tajikistan border (latitude 38° 20' north to longitude 67° 54' east) on the Sir Darya (river). Sufi Allah Yar—a native of Katta Qorghan, near Samarkand, who lived in Bukhara much of his life—was an illiterate Uzbek in a lesser amir's tribal service whom Shaykh Nawruz proselyted for the Naqshbandiy darwish order of Sufis, where he learned to read and write. Many of his works, prose and poetry in Farsi and Turkic, achieved great authority, reaching audiences not only in western Central Asia but in Tatarstan and eastern Turkistan. Clerical educators in Bukhara made his

Farsi-language work, *Mäslāk al-muttaqin* (The Path of the Believers) a required text in *mäktab* (religious primary school).[12]

Another of Sufi Allah Yar's religious works, *Thābat al-'ajizin* (Weakness of the Pious), became even more widely known than *Path of the Believers*. In Istanbul, Tashkent, Kashgar, and a number of other cities, copyists, printers, and lithographers reproduced it in uncounted editions, which were popular for introducing young people to the teachings of Islam. In Kazan, in 1735, a religious scholar translated the poet's work to Tatar and added a commentary in that language. His edition appeared in print in 1858 and probably at other times.[13] Sufi Allah Yar's enormous popularity belies Soviet ideological criticism aimed at showing Central Asians that he was merely a creature of the Bukharan throne. Although he held positions at the Ashtarkhanid court, the mystic poet reached out to all society and many countries. As if to underscore his universality, the poet took to the darwish road, renouncing the vanity of temporal life.

OTHER POETS

Three other accomplished poets—Nasafiy, Bedil, and Mashrab—expressed the mystical mood of Central Asia's troubled times. Mirabid Sayida Nasafiy (1637–1710), born in Qarshi (Nasaf), belonged, like Sufi Allah Yar, to Naqshbandiya (Khojagan), one of three great mystic Muslim brotherhoods of the region. Muhammad Bahauddin (d. 1389/90) of Bukhara, whose tomb people revere to this day, founded the order of Sufi darwishes in Central Asia. The other two, originating in medieval times, were the Qadiriya (Jahriya) order, associated with Khoja Ahmad Yassawiy of Turkistan (Yassa), and the Kubraviya order, founded by a famous Khwarazmian shaykh Najmuddin Kubra, who was martyred by the Mongols in the thirteenth century.[14]

Nasafiy wrote many panegyrics and narrative poems devoted to the founder of the Naqshbandiya, a darwish order, to the reigning sovereign, Ubaydullah Khan II (r. 1702–1711), as well as to crafts and craftsmen. His lyrical verses enjoyed great popularity. Called the greatest Central Asian Farsi-language poet of the seventeenth century, he also authored a versified historical chronicle about the Ashtarkhanid rulers' campaigns and other actions. A Bukharan historian praised the poet as follows:

Mullah Sayida was the refuge of beautiful expression, support of eloquence, weigher of the rarity of judgments, intellect of the pinnacle of penetration, exceptional sign of wit, declaimer of subtle works, chosen of the time as decorator of words, a penetrating critic, the prince on the throne of the poets of Bukhara.

True to the creed of poverty, this noble mind existed modestly in an attic over the mosque of Nadir Diwanbegi Tagay.[15]

Bedil

The writings and ideas of Mirza Abdal Qadir Bedil (1644–1721) exerted enormous influence upon Central Asian culture and literature, although he supposedly never lived in or visited the region. His family in Putna (Azimabad) was descended from Uzbeks who had evidently migrated to Hindustan much earlier. He, however, employed mainly the languages of his native country—Bengali, Urdu, Sanskrit, and Farsi, which he learned to speak and write at school. In the huge corpus of his writings, a Pakistani scholar identifies only 66 verses composed in Turki, which may have come down from his ancestors. His primary vehicle for reaching readers and listeners in Central Asian intellectual, Sufi circles was not Turki but Farsi.

Bedil's Hindustan—like Central Asia undergoing economic, social, and political disintegration—afforded the poet a spiritual and intellectual climate that caused him to create his poems in a common ideological language. Therefore, he communicated freely both linguistically and intellectually with his family's homeland. Although that harking back facilitated the exchange between him and his readers and listeners, it did not entirely account for the popularity he achieved in Central Asia, said to surpass by far the response in Persia or northern Hindustan.

Bedil intentionally created an unclear idiom in which to enunciate his zealous Sufism, using a scarcely legible Arabic script style called *shikasta*. In those dangerous decades, encoding the meaning of a literary composition protected the writer from official or critical reprisals. These methods of composition and his fertile imagination produced a literature so full of obscurities and possibilities for multiple interpretations that his intricate poems were regarded as wonderfully engaging puzzles. Both in Mawaraunnahr and Afghanistan admirers of the poet established a Bedilkhaniy cult, whose members discussed the poet's literary and philosophical writings.[16] Active interest in Bedil continued into the first decades of the twentieth century.

Mashrab

Bedil's studied vagueness left emotional, personal poetry to others, which is one reason people love the heartfelt verses of Babarahim Mashrab. Born in Andijan in 1657 (d. 1711), of the three poets, his memory is most alive. Starting at the age of fifteen, he served his religious mentor, Mullah Akhund Bazar, for ten years. No longer compatible with that arrangement, he was sent to Kashgar, where he served the renowned Ishan Appaqkhoja (d. 1695) seven more years.

(About 1873, to the memory of that eminent religious figure, the authorities built a mausoleum that became one of eastern Turkistan's most visited Islamic shrines.) After studying with the ishan, Mashrab also took up the calling of an itinerant Sufi darwish, traversing Central Asia, including Khurasan and India, and reaching an extensive public with his constant recitations and compositions in the region.

More important, a popular folk work in verse and prose entitled *Diwana-i mäshräb* (The Holy Fool, Mashrab) grew up based on him, parts of which may have come from the poet, whose name formed the core of that memorable composition. Innumerable people were attracted to its messages; everyone knew by heart some verses, which were handed on from one generation to the next. As late as the 1920s, the work remained "a composition without parallel among Central Asian Muslims," in the view of a Russian Orientalist. The composite work expounds an amazing tale of a Sufi and his pious inner meditations as well as his scandalously antisocial conduct.

> Every hour lodge in the soul the words: "Lord! I have harmed myself."
> And to sin I learned from pure Adam.
> Shedding bitter tears, screaming in desperation,
> And listening to God's commands, I learned from Moses.
> Leaving not one tiny needle in the world, he [Jesus] departed.
> The degrees of swallowing up the self in God I learned from Isa [Jesus].
> He [God] authorized and made Isa able to achieve the pulpit of truth.
> Inquiry I learned from the spirit of Jeremiah.
> How Soloman ascended the throne of the ages,
> I learned from Asaf, son of the spirit of Barachias [Solomon's uncle],
>   who many years burned with fear of the Lord's judgment.
> Fear of the last judgment I mastered from Yahya [Zachariah's son
>   John].
> I burn with compassion, completely desolated because of the dead
>   child.

In that work he declaims a typical Sufistic belief in denial:

> I clothed myself in indigence as in the garment of a king's dignity,
> and about nothing besides being swallowed up in God did I speak.
> To be proud of poverty I learned from Muhammad, son of Abdullah.

(According to tradition, Muhammad said "indigence is my pride.") The fervent outcry of the Sufi comes through in Mashrab's first-person lines:

> Suffering was granted me so that I would sob.
> Presented to God, I complained to the heavens.
> If my lamentations were heard, I would strike flint on steel;
> I would set afire heaven's house and destroy it.
> Save me, o brothers, from grief and agony.
> So that, by recollecting the Lord's name I might make my soul satisfied
>   and happy.
> If the beloved saw my condition, he would start to weep bitterly
> If I should reveal one dust speck of my grief.
> Mashrab is a man drowned in the sea of love.
> Sincerely, in the soul, must I sob before God.[17]

In other lyrical poetry attributed with assurance to this poet, these passionate sentiments repeat themselves, which substantiates the interpretation of *The Holy Fool, Mashrab* as a mirror of Mashrab's attitudes and utterances. One of his own *ghazals* (short lyric verses) declares in part,

> I saw thy face, became a holy fool,
> Became alien from my reason.
> Though I suffer torment on thy path,
> Perhaps I shall never turn back—I became bold.
> Being, in the world, the disgraced of the universe,
> I became notorious for good and evil.
> Wine of the river of Paradise I don't quite remember,
> From thy ruby lips I became intoxicated.
> I shut my eyes from thee once more,
> From everything drew away and became a libertine.
> In my dream I saw the candle of thy elegance,
> Circling 'round it, I became distraught.
> This body of mine died away for the wine of thy love,
> Both the cupbearer and the goblet did I become.
> One drop I was, drowned in the sea,
> I went into the oyster, became a pearl.
> When fire doesn't subside, it won't be glowing embers,
> With the fire of passion I became a cohabiter.
> Nothingness did I become in the dust,
> One particle I was, a thousand particles I became.
> In the flame of that face, existence became nonexistence,
> Soul entered soul; I became the soulmate.[18]

Mashrab's piety was unmistakable, but his eccentric orthodoxy offended the established ecclesiastics. His offensive utterances and public behavior are interpreted by specialists today as a reaction to unwanted worldly renown: "At once he strives against being the object of honor and respect. He tries to deflect any suspicion of the quality characteristic for him—saintliness, to obscure saintliness . . . he publicly does patently improper things that would leave no doubt that they emanate not from a saintly person." According to the version of his life inlcuded in *The Holy Fool, Mashrab*, the darwish, by contentiousness and through what Central Asian society considered indecent conduct, offended every male interlocutor with whom he interacted. (This conduct apparently worried women more than it offended them.) He began with his father, whom he went before after puberty without covering his private parts; he then alienated his first religious tutor, Mullah Akhund Bazar in Namangan, and Ishan Appaqkhoja in Kashgar. Afterward, by outrageous public behavior, he shocked the people of Yarkand, Khotan, Qulja, certainly Bukhara, and finally Balkh, which became the terminus of Mashrab's passionate journey and the place where he fell under the heavy fist of Mahmud Biy Ataliq, a Qattaghan tribal chieftain.

The stories of *The Holy Fool, Mashrab* sympathetically portray the end of his personal ordeal. Mashrab, riding a donkey and accompanied by his pupil Sarmast (The One Intoxicated by Religious Ecstasy), wanders from Namangan with Appaqkhoja's prophecy—that the restless Sufi poet must die at the hands of Balkh's ruler, Mahmud Biy, the Qattaghan—on his mind. Despite or perhaps because of this knowledge, Mashrab keeps his appointment in Balkh, for neither he nor any other true Sufi feared physical death. Mahmud Biy Ataliq gently, even respectfully, defers to the darwish, but royal forces compel the chieftain, against his will, to execute the conservative Bukharan clergys' *fetwa* (finding) of heresy against the poet. Mashrab's violent death provokes bitter mourning from the populace and retribution from a higher authority. Mahmud Biy, according to the story, dies within three days of the hanging, and history records that conspirators assassinated Mahmud Biy's Ashtarkhanid superior, Ubaydullah Khan, in that same year (1711).[19]

The mood of these poems and stories, even though some appear ribald and comic, is consistently grief stricken and full of suffering. Mashrab's Via Dolorosa leads him to destruction in both the desired Sufi spiritual sense and in the temporal sense; Mahmud Biy merely serves as the instrument. This somber, even sad, tone carries into general Central Asian expression a trait that identifies the poet with his readers and listeners in and of the region. As such, this literature affected the attitudes and style of expression there. In addition to ecstasy and grief, the Sufi poets transmitted something profound to their public.

POETS AS ENVOYS

Although listeners could identify these poets by tribe, birthplace, accent, appearance, and/or costume, such markers were of secondary importance; their mystical literature, a poetry of spiritual passion, hovered far above considerations of local attachment. Nor could the medium of poetic language serve a limiting purpose. These lyricists, like so many Central Asians, spoke a special idiom through two or three languages. In later terms they were Turkistanian or Bukharan or Ashtarkhanid Sufi artists, though they would not have asserted it. They proved their universality both by their poetic expression and by their indifference to a particular place. For them, the ideas of homeland or mother tongue signified nothing.

Part of people's fascination with the darwish and his words came from that lack of localism and the belief that a true darwish embodied the ideal of the good man in Islam—otherworldy, simple, generous, pure, plain but knightly in his magical folkway. Furthermore, these poets came from rural tribes rather than towns. Because of the poets' tribal, not necessarily linguistic, identity, these verses might be called Uzbek in the most limited, unethnic sense, rather than Chaghatay or Turki, even though the poets composed some of it in Farsi.

The wandering darwish poet relinquished close ties to family and place, but made himself a special visitor as he slowly crossed the territory of one *el* (tribe) after another. In practice, he arrived as an *elchi* (envoy) from the other worlds he touched, moving through rather than staying. Darwish poets functioned both culturally and spiritually as ambassadors whose paths over the Central Asian terrain united the many parts, turning the whole region into their spiritual domain.

6 Diplomacy

Qamugh ärdä ödhrüm yalavach käräk,
biliklig uqushlugh talu kädh yüräk.
Bayat qullarïnda äng ödhründüsi,
yalavachlar ärdi kishi ädhgüsi.

The envoy ought to be the choicest of mankind, wise, intelligent, and courageous. For God chose the very best of his Servants to be His envoys.

(Yusuf Khass Hajib, 1069/70)*

Diplomacy was a metaphor for sovereignty in Central Asia. Occasionally, Central Asian potentates abused visiting envoys, but generally these governments revered diplomacy because it validated their independent status. Diplomacy also, however, raised the problem of parity: how to compensate for inequality or lack of reciprocity between states. Insistence on equality often took the most trivial forms, including disagreements over modes of address or protocol. Central Asian rulers who participated in diplomatic exchanges aspired to recognition and permanence in their sovereign roles and wanted to impress the rulers they dealt with.

* Yusuf Khas Hajib, Qutadghu bilig (Tashkent: Ozbekistan SSR "Fän" Näshriyati, 1971), lines 2555–57, pp. 418–19.

Khans and amirs also usually wished to advance economic activity through trade, barter, customs duties, and export of valuable products or materials. Cities on caravan routes provided bazaars through which goods were distributed throughout the entire region. Most diplomatic missions from Central Asia engaged in trade unless they were under immediate military threat. Envoys often conducted trade on behalf of the ruler, for foreign commerce in the Uzbek era, as at other times, was essential to the public treasuries and private purses. There were also the granting of visas and searches by specialized procurement missions for scarce implements or luxuries to please the court. Purchases of small arms and artillery as gifts became an urgent duty of Central Asian ambassadors.

The Central Asian idea of diplomacy was probably influenced by the Chaghatay (later, Uzbek) word *elchilik* meaning "activity of a diplomat," as well as "familial relations, or relations among the tribe." The term *elchi* could also signify not only an envoy but the leader of the *el* (tribe). (Words ending in *-chi* in Central Asian Turkic languages designate the agent of an action or occupation.) Thus the peripatetic Sufi poets functioned as emissaries between the tribes (see chapter 5). An understanding of diplomacy that stemmed from tribal relations and from politics among kin absolved chieftains of the Qipchaq Plains from having to deal candidly with outsiders. Aliens could not qualify for the same treatment as family or tribal members. Diplomatic relations thus assumed a theatrical and deceptive mask.

Outside the family circle, especially in southern Central Asia, people used the Chaghatay word for diplomatic activity: *säfarat*. An individual envoy they called *säfir* or *räsul*. These terms, borrowed and assimilated from Arabic, lacked the personal or tribal flavor of *elchi*. They did, however, add religious weight to the designation, for the terminology not only came from Islam's sacred language but enjoyed special use in the holy *Qur'ân* and the traditions. *Räsul* meant not only envoy but apostle, even prophet sent by God, and became an epithet attached particularly to the Prophet Muhammad, who was also regularly referred to as *päyghämbär* (God's messenger), another Arabic term that designated an envoy in the holy books. The adaptation of these Arabic words to the field of Uzbek diplomacy communicated a sense of special respect for the function and persons in Central Asian diplomacy, although it did not activate the diplomatic immunity that might have prevented disgruntled potentates from mistreating envoys. Owing to that special aura and for a variety of practical reasons, however, ambassadors habitually received special attention from the rulers they visited.[1]

EARLY DIPLOMATIC ATTEMPTS

From around 1370 to about 1499 the nomadic aggregation's leaders focused on their extraordinarily demanding domestic affairs. External relations for them remained mostly in the Qipchaq Plains, Turkistan, Mawaraunnahr, and Khurasan—now Central Asia and northwestern Siberia. Diplomacy initiated by Uzbek tribal figures was transient in nature. When they began to orient their actions toward the Central Asian south, their temporary embassies repeatedly attempted to contact the rulers in Tashkent, Bukhara, Samarkand, and other centers. The first formal Uzbek diplomatic effort came from Ulugh Muhammad Khan in the Qipchaq Plains, who dispatched envoys to Timur's son and successor, Shahrukh (r. 1405–1447) at Herat in about 1421, most likely to request aid in Ulugh Muhammad's contest for leadership over the nomadic Uzbeks. Shortly before, his chief rival, Boraq Oghlan, had sought refuge in Samarkand, where he received help from its viceroy, Mirza Ulugh Beg (1394–1449). After returning to the plains, Boraq Oghlan, although at first to no avail, finally defeated Ulugh Muhammad in 1423 to take power briefly over the crystallizing Uzbek *ulus* (confederation), at which time he sent a highly placed Uzbek chieftain, Jumaduk, as his envoy to Mirza Ulugh Beg.

Jumaduk went through all the expected diplomatic protocol, presenting rich gifts to the Timurid prince and spending some days at court being honored and entertained. Mirza Ulugh Beg, according to a historian of that period, entrusted Jumaduk with valuable sabers, gold belts, silver harnesses, horses, money, a drum, and a banner of authority as gifts for his Uzbek khan. The Uzbek envoy returned to the plains with a special escort provided by the Samarkand viceroy. This attention reflected Timurid concern over relations with their volatile, dangerous neighbors.

Those fears were realized when Boraq Oghlan repaid Mirza Ulugh Beg's courtesies by administering a terrible military defeat to that Timurid prince and his troops in 1425–1426 near Sighnaq, close to the middle course of the Sir Darya. The Uzbek victory permanently damaged Mirza Ulugh Beg's reputation as a ruler and badly hurt the Timurid position in Central Asia. All Mawaraunnahr feared an imminent nomadic takeover, but the Uzbek triumph was brief. The winner perished in 1428/29, and young Abul Khayr Sultan rose to lead and dominate the Uzbeks, starting four decades of interaction with neighbors north, east, and south. A five-way competition involved the Uzbeks with Uzbek-Kazaks, Mogolistanians, Kalmyks, and Timurids.[2]

Uzbek-Timurid relations thus began as they would end 85 years later, with a mixture of repeated raids or outright military conflicts, occasional reciprocal protection, and sporadic, specifically motivated diplomacy. Of the three methods, diplomacy offered Uzbeks the opportunity to acquire new experience, technology, and ideas from the outside world.

Uzbek diplomats served their khans by projecting a brave image of the khan's power and by gauging the potential strength or resolve of opposing rulers. To this end, demonstrating resources, might, wealth, and the Central Asian idea of dignity or grandeur received first priority during diplomatic contacts. An early diplomatic effort, initiated by the Uzbeks in 1481 after the reign of Abul Khayr Khan, connected the Siberian khan Ibak, chieftain of the Uzbeks in Tumen, with Moscow. The fifteenth-century khans, eager to learn, personally questioned envoys about their masters' accomplishments and innovations, with testing a natural part of that style of diplomatic exchange.

DIPLOMATIC TESTS

When the Timurid Jani Beg Dulday of the Barlas clan governed Samarkand late in the fifteenth century, he tested a visiting Uzbek *elchi* (envoy) whom people considered an unusually strong physical specimen. A Timurid memoirist gleefully reported the incident as follows: "Jani Beg asked, 'Art thou a bull? If thou art a bull, be a bull, come on, let's wrestle.' However many difficulties this envoy might make, it wouldn't suffice; they wrestled, Jani Beg threw him. He was a manly person."[3]

Ghiyas ad-Din Muhammad ibn Khumamad-din Khwand Amir (*ca.* 1480–1535), a Timurid ambassador and courtier who contended with the patterns of history rather than with athletes, performed diplomatic duties for his government in Herat early in the sixteenth century. In 1506, as the Shaybanids pushed toward Khurasan, Sultan Husayn Bayqara dispatched Khwand Amir south to Qandahar in hope of gaining military support for the defense of Khurasan. A death in the family of the sultan caused that mission to return unfulfilled. In that same year, a fateful one for the Timurid dynasty, Khwand Amir attained high rank in the court; in the next year, after Shaybaniy Khan's troops seized Herat, Khwand Amir participated in working out conditions for surrendering the Timurid capital to the Uzbek khan.

The real test of Uzbek leadership and external relations lay ahead, when the nomads would become responsible for Central Asia's elaborate civilization and economic network. For the present, however, confederation leaders required a diplomacy that could help them get reorganized and stay established. For the mercurial nomads to understand and decide on the best long-range course to pursue in foreign affairs was not easy. Ambition overcame capacity, and instability thwarted many endeavors. When diplomacy was an element of a transitory military struggle, tribal chieftains could afford to ignore or slight those decisions, but, unlike those days when Uzbek nomads would retire to the distant plains and regroup or disregard a failure, they could not now avoid their new responsibility in settled Mawaraunnahr and Khurasan. They were to learn that lesson painfully not long after taking power, as well as the complications introduced into their affairs by inflexibly adhering to a set of strong social and political dogmas.

Preceding the final armed clash between the confessed sinner and the defiant sinner—Shaybaniy Khan and Shah Ismail—both with Central Asian troops, came the diplomatic tests. Tabriz made diplomatic overtures to Samarkand; according to convention, Ismail then dispatched an envoy to Shaybaniy Khan's court to inform the Uzbek ruler that Shah Ismail Safaviy now sat upon the throne of Persia. Gifts accompanied the polite official letter, which read,

> Hitherto the dust of dissension has never settled upon the skirts of our thoughts to such an extent as to raise a cloud of enmity. Let the path of fatherly conduct be observed on your side [Shaybaniy Khan in 1501 was turning 50, whereas Ismail would have been about 16], and on this side the bonds of filial relationship shall be established.

> Plant the tree of friendship: for its fruit will be the desire of your heart;
> Root up the sapling of enmity, which produces countless griefs.[4]

Shaybaniy Khan may have resented being addressed by the young shah, who spoke out without being spoken to; furthermore, everything the khan knew about Shah Ismail and his religious inclinations repelled him. Direct rivals—each became the founder of a dynasty and conqueror of an ancient civilization at nearly the same historical juncture—Shaybaniy Khan returned a bitingly sarcastic answer to the diplomatic note. Among other jibes, the undiplomatic Shaybanid message insulted the memory of Ismail's father and his wife and called the shah a Persian mendicant:

> Kings know the secrets of the business of the realm.
> Oh! Hafiz, thou beggar, sitting in the corner, do not complain.

Shaybaniy Khan accompanied this with the gift of a walking stick and a beggar's bowl, adding advice about ambition and kingship:

> He may clasp the bride of sovereignty firmly to his breast,
> Who dares to kiss her amid the clashing of keen swords.

This prompted a note from Shah Ismail, which read so provocatively that it caused Shaybaniy Khan, resting in Merv after hard campaigning, to order his armies mobilized and to depart ahead of them with small forces to meet his nemesis. To his small escort suite he announced, "to make war on Shah Ismail is a holy war and one of importance . . . We must be bold." In 1510, Safavid troops destroyed the khan and large numbers of his officers and men, driving the Shaybanids out of Herat and pushing their frontier far to the northeast.[5]

The parties to that series of contacts exchanged neither confidence nor new ideas. Diplomacy subjected to such impossible demands inevitably faltered.

The Uzbek khan meant to employ diplomacy in lieu of armed conflict to win submission; he failed to achieve either. The course of history would have been different if, in place of dogmatic, traditional rivalries, they had possessed new technology and ideas to offer one another or had understood the usefulness of an equitable peace. That would not come to these competitors for another hundred years.

FOREIGN ENVOYS

Into Central Asia shortly after the eminent Ottoman traveler, Sidi Ali Reis, left for Istanbul, came Anthony Jenkinson, a gun-carrying envoy and commercial agent from England and the Russian czar whose actions permanently affected the region's international relations. The Bukharan khan impressed Jenkinson favorably:

> The 26 day of the moneth [December 1558] I was commanded to come before the said king, to whom I presented the Emperour of Russia his letters, who interteined us most gently, and caused us to eate in his presence, and divers times he sent for me, and devised with me familiarly in his secret chamber, as well of the power of the Emperour, and the great Turke, as also of our countries, lawes, and religion, and caused us to shoote in handguns before him, and did himself practise the use thereof.
>
> But yet I must needs praise and commend this barbarous king, who immediately after my arrivall at Boghar [Bukhara], having understoode our trouble with the theeves, sent 100 men well armed, and gave them great charge not to returne before they had either slaine or taken the sayd theeves. Who according to their commission ranged the wildernes in such sort, that they met with the said company of theeves, and slew part, and part fledde, and foure they tooke and brought unto the king, and two of them were sore wounded in our skirmish with our gunnes: And after the king had sent for me to come to see them, he caused them all 4 to be hanged at his palace gate... to the example of others. And of such goods as were gotten againe, I had part restored me, and this good justice I found at his hands.[6]

Conventional diplomacy, however, was the important function of that mission. On the long return trip in 1559, the English-czarist envoy escorted diplomats from Central Asia to the Russian capital:

> There were in my company, and committed to my charge, two ambassadors, the one from the king of Boghar [Bukhara], the other from the king of Balke, and were sent unto the Emperor of Russia. And after having taried at Urgence [Urganch]... the second of Aprill we departed from thence, having foure more Ambassadors in our companie, sent from the king of Urgence [Khwarazm], and other Soltans, his brethren, unto the Emperor of Russia, with answere of such letters as I brought them... I promised most faithfully,

and swore by our law, that they should be well used in Rusland, and suffered to depart from thence againe in safetie, according as the Emperor had written also in his letters: for they somewhat doubted, because there had none gone out of Tartaria [Central Asia] into Russia, of long time before.[7]

A Russian orientalist points out that the initiative taken by the English merchants in this affair opened diplomatic relations between Russia and the Central Asian khanates. Until then, information about the region had come to Moscow through Noghay princes roaming the territory near the Volga. When Abdullah Khan heard his *elchilär* (envoys) were returning to Khwarazm, he dispatched a courier to the Khwarazmian khan Hajji Muhammad asking him to send on the envoys and their suite to Bukhara without delay. This contrasted with the usual protocol requiring layovers and entertainment in the city of Urganch.[8] Abdullah Khan's envoy and suite arrived in Bukhara from this Russia mission to great acclaim. The khan's contemporary biographer asserted that those diplomats enjoyed great success in their endeavor, for "no Central Asian khans had been successful in such a matter."

Advances in weaponry combined with reactivated diplomacy kept Central Asians attuned to developments in their geopolitical environment. This facing toward the outside world, so crucial for the progress of each state, continued throughout the Shaybanid era but did not yet include establishing permanent missions in foreign capitals, though envoys often found themselves waiting months, even years, for permission to return home. Consequently, those embassies were able to observe a great deal in the countires they visited. Abdullah Khan's court maintained contact with Russia after Anthony Jenkinson's visit. Fourteen Central Asian embassies were sent to Moscow during the second half of the sixteenth century, at least seven of which went from Bukhara and Khiva during the last fifteen years of Ivan IV's (Ivan the Terrible's) reign (1533–1584). Bukhara, the Shaybanid capital since the beginning of Ubaydullah Khan's rule, also engaged in exchanges with the Ottomans and Moghul India.

INTERNAL DIPLOMACY

Because authority remained decentralized, internal Central Asian affairs required the services of diplomats more frequently than did external matters. Delicate diplomatic negotiations between Bukhara and Tashkent in 1564 culminated in a harmonious meeting between the two heads of government. The cities of Andijan, Badakhshan, Samarkand, and Tashkent dispatched envoys to Abdullah Khan's court in 1573; during 1578 Abdullah Khan employed envoys to contact parties within the rebellious city of Samarkand. In the same year Mirza Pulad led an embassy from the Moghul shah Jalaluddin

Muhammad Akbar (r. 1556–1605) to Bukhara in response to a formal diplomatic initiative by Abdullah Khan the previous year. These exchanges concerned, among other things, the possibility of partitioning Khurasan and Qandahar between the two powers in Central and southern Asia, thus denying that area to Safavid Persia.[9]

In addition to political and trade questions, Central Asians now faced problems of ideology and diplomatic protocol, especially when confronted with devout Muslims from Mawaraunnahr and Turkistan who were endeavoring to complete obligatory religious pilgrimages. When Ismail Shah Safaviy solidified his regime and its official Shiite faith, Central Asian Sunnites could no longer safely cross Persia to reach their holy city, and when Russia conquered the Astrakhan khanate and its territory in 1556, it changed the world Central Asian Muslims believed in. The most powerful Shaybanid leader, Abdullah Khan, lacked the power to cut a path for his faithful through Persian territory to Mecca or to contest Russian control of the north Caspian passage via the Black Sea and Ottoman Turkish routes down to Arabia. His diplomats, therefore, were only sporadically successful in securing—from unsympathetic Russian officials—transit permits for religious believers eager to cross the czar's new dominions to reach the holy land. That anti-Muslim behavior by the Russians set a pattern that would continue for 400 years and more.

The czars accompanied this rejection of Central Asian Sunni religious petitions with additional displays of intolerance that affected the status of Bukhara and Khiva. The conquest of the Siberian Uzbek khanate (Bukhara's client) in 1583, further undermined the idea of equal relations between Russia and the sovereign states of Central Asia. Speaking for the feebleminded Czar Fyodor I Ivanovich (r. 1584–1598), Boris Godunov, a boyar and master of the royal horse, in 1589 reprimanded Abdullah Khan in writing for failing to adhere precisely to the lengthy royal title in addressing a diplomatic note to the Russian throne: "And thou Abdullah king, in future, correct thyself before our sovereign, our great sovereign Czar and grand prince Fedor Ivanovich of All Russia, and to our sovereign, to his czarist majesty, in future write in thy diplomatic notes with the full czarist appellation." Even though Bukhara was then at the height of its Shaybanid power and Moscow's house of Riurik was teetering on the brink of final collapse, Russian actions, diplomacy, and dispatches expressed disdain toward the Central Asians.[10] Regardless of the rhetoric, within a decade both the Central Asian and the Russian ruling dynasties would be overturned forever. Nevertheless, the Russians saw the balance between the two states tilting further in their favor, and Central Asian diplomacy reflected this evolution in relations between Russia and Bukhara.

Meanwhile, Khwarazm's Hajji Muhammad Khan (r. 1558–1602), whose subjects included numbers of Turkmens, tried to maintain friendly relations with the Safavids. He sent his son, Muhammad Quli Sultan, to the shah's court

and engaged in active diplomatic correspondence and exchange of embassies with Tabriz. In 1591, Hajji Muhammad Khan met the shah's deputy commander, Farhad Khan, at Bastam, where they royally entertained one another in tent camps outside the town, exchanged gifts, and "renewed a treaty" to aid one another against Abdullah Khan and his son.[11]

At the same time, the Russian court's foreign policy persistently gave preference to Persia over Central Asia. Throughout the seventeenth century and earlier, the Muscovite autocrats made sharp distinctions between Asian potentates. The czar acknowledged equality only with the shah of Persia and the great moghuls of Hindustan. In diplomatic records and correspondence, Moscow designated Central Asian khans as "governors, kings, or caretakers," whereas it referred to the Persian shah as "brother, majesty, and great sovereign." The preferences went beyond terminology, for Moscow's relations with Central Asia were largely restricted to trade in which Bukharans and others brought their goods to Russia. Those early Russian judgments about countries south of the czarist domain would put their imprint on foreign policy far into the future. The adamant Sunni militancy that guided Abdullah Khan and the earlier Shaybanid khans helped push Russia and Persia into an alliance against Central Asia. That equation retained residual force indefinitely, but the emergence of the new dynasty out of the ruins of the Shaybanids at the turn of the seventeenth century offered to alter that equilibrium in another direction.[12]

Although relations between Russia and Central Asia deteriorated, those with certain southern neighbors improved somewhat. The new Ashtarkhanid (Janid) dynasty came to power in Bukhara supported by the surviving Shaybanids. On the male side its successor kings descended from Orda, Chinggis Khan's grandson, and on the female from Shayban, another of Chinggis Khan's grandsons. Central Asia owed its new dynasty partly to the Russians, for it developed out of a line of rulers suddenly displaced from Astrakhan when Ivan IV took control of the mouth of the Volga River. The Shaybanid connection came through Abdullah Khan's sister, the daughter of Iskandar, who was married to Jan, a refugee from Astrakhan. The Ashtarkhanids, beginning with Imam Quli (r. 1608–1640), made themselves compatible with their Shiite neighbors, the Safavids of Persia, in a way the Shaybanids never contemplated. For instance, during Imam Quli Khan's rule he met a captured Persian prince, Murtaza Quli Khan, and graciously and humanely recalled ties of kinship. Imam Quli Khan not only "made peace with the Qizilbashes," according to the local account, but ordered "Uzbek troops" to lift their siege of Merv and return to Bukhara. His noble prisoner went on to become governor of Merv, and Imam Quli Khan returned to their homes many Mervis whom Abdullah Khan had forcibly resettled around his domain at the end of the sixteenth century. This conciliatory behavior virtually removed the two main barriers to Central Asian–Persian interrelations that had prevailed during the previous century, returning them to something approaching the state of affairs during the reign of the Timurids and their contemporaries in Persia.[13]

In this new peacetime, weapons systems and diplomacy ceased to be dual arms of the same offensive effort, and ideology (Islam) served to attract Muslims against an evermore visible common opponent, Christianizing Russia. With the sectarian friction abating in the Muslim relationship, contacts between Central Asia and Safavid Iran became cordial, almost benevolent, prepared for to some extent by the previous positive interaction between Khwarazm (Khiva) and Tabriz.

Bukharan and Khivan rulers continued to take the initiative in diplomatic activity between Central Asia and Russia in the seventeenth century. Of some 50 missions exchanged between the two areas during that one hundred years, Khiva sent 27, Bukhara 14, Balkh 2, and Russia only 7. Central Asians, wanting to increase trade, asked for certain embargoed goods, including armor, arms, knives, slaves, and gyrfalcons, and suggested that the Russians export fabric and other manufactures to Central Asia. Only a few political issues attracted attention. Khiva protested the violent behavior of Russian cossack communities along the Yaik River who attacked caravans and made raids deep into Khwarazmian territory. Central Asians repeatedly asked for czarist cooperation in counteracting martial conduct by the Kalmyks, who were supposedly subject to Moscow, against Kazakstan, Khiva, and Bukhara. The Russians, however, were preoccupied with repatriating a few hundred Russian captives held in the khanates.

Moscow's diplomats also collected intelligence about Central Asian arms and military capabilities. For example, Ambassador Ivan Fedot'ev in 1669 reported to his superiors that the Urganch (Khivan) khan had 15,000 troops but few firearms. The envoy also correctly estimated that Khiva's territory was relatively small and noticed that Khwarazm suffered from scarcity of provisions, absence of timber, and lack of wells and water. The ambassador also noted that, evidently owing to a shortage of precious metal, the khan was minting coins from brass, as would his successors as late as the twentieth century, and that Khiva's relations with Persia were soured because of bloody Khivan raids on Astarabad and Qarashar. In their diplomacy with respect to Russia, the Central Asian khans virtually ignored such economic and strategic factors.[14]

Diplomatic exchanges with Hindustan persisted, particularly from Balkh, whose governor, Nadir Muhammad, later ruled (1641–1645) in Bukhara. Central Asians also served as administrative and foreign service officials under the great moghuls in Hindustan at the courts of Shah Jahangir (r. 1605–1628) and Shah Jahan (r. 1628–1658). Fakhriddin Ahmad Bakhshi came from Balkh to Hindustan to work at the court for Shah Jahangir and headed a return embassy to Central Asia. His nickname, "Tärbiyätkhan," became the title of that position in Hindustan. Many gifts and envoys went back and forth between Agra and Balkh in 1632 and earlier. In 1637 the Moghuls intervened, at the invitation of Nadir Muhammad, to defend Balkh against the Uzbek tribes for two years. A historian serving the Balkh viceroy later recorded the aftermath to that action: "The writer of this history, proceeding to Hindustan as a diplomatic official, saw everywhere with his own eyes piles of bones of Hindustanis who had perished" when they fled from Balkh after the intervention ceased in 1639. Despite that standoff, diplomatic exchanges between the two countries occurred frequently throughout the century.

The animating spirit directing those heightened diplomatic exchanges seemed to be their common Sunni bond against Shiite Persians. The tolerance exhibited earlier by Moghul founder and former Timurid prince Zahiriddin Muhammad Babur toward the Shia had waned among his successors, who, a century later, more strongly remembered their blood ties with Turkic (Sunni) Central Asia. Nadir Muhammad, the Ashtarkhanid khan, also established close relations with Safavid Persia, again aimed against the Uzbek tribal chieftains. As a result, the Ashtarkhanids found themselves more and more at odds with their Central Asian population base. Although the Ashtarkhanids of Bukhara improved their foreign relations by being amicable, the situation became increasingly troubled at home.[15]

To their other rivals, the Khivan Uzbeks represented a complicated foe, for they maintained relations with the Safavids and kept themselves flexible in their redoubt near the delta of the Amu Darya. Abul Ghazi Bahadur Khan (r. 1642–1663), who fled Khwarazm to escape the fury of his hostile brothers, came back to Khiva about 1640 after a ten-year princely exile in Isfahan where he must have been exposed to the ideology and armaments of the Iranian forces. In his memoirs, Abul Ghazi details his first battle (after achieving hegemony in the Aral Sea region) for supremacy throughout the entire khanate.

In 1652 Abul Ghazi proposed, through an ambassador, that Bukhara employ whatever weapons and forces it possessed in an alliance against the troublesome Mongolian Kalmyks, who had been roaming both west and east of Khivan lands at least since the reign of the khan's father, Arab Muhammad (r. 1602–1623). The raids and continuing presence of those non-Muslims seriously disrupted life in Mawaraunnahr. Abul Ghazi Bahadur Khan dispatched Yadigar Inaq as an envoy to the court of Sayyid Abdul Aziz Khan (r. 1645–1680), the Ashtarkhanid ruler in Bukhara. That embassy retraced its steps when the Kalmyks retired. A sudden turn of events found the Kalmyks sending their own envoy to Abul Ghazi Bahadur Khan with a plea for peace. He had pursued them so relentlessly to the East that the Kalmyks faced certain destruction. The exchanges between Kalmyks and Khivans discovered a true diplomatic language. The Kalmyks acknowledged that they erred by crossing into Khivan territory, were responsible for it, and begged the khan's forgiveness.

His response, intentionally forgetful, was that because his ancestors and theirs had never become enemies and because they had trespassed on his country's lands by mistake, "he would pardon their sins." Giving the representatives gifts and granting estates, he accompanied them to their camp and came back to Khiva triumphantly.[16]

The khan exhibited perfect understanding of the Samanid Central Asian style of forgiveness in this altercation with the Kalmyks. Almost every conflict that followed ended in a direct attempt by the ruler of Khiva or Bukhara to form or strengthen the basis for amicable foreign relations.

RELATIONS WITH RUSSIA

For the small khanate of Khiva, as Khwarazm then called itself, diplomacy remained an important function of the sovereign. Active military and trade contacts between Khiva and Russia did not begin until after the mid-fifteenth century. Long after that, Khoja Muhammad Ashur Biy (hereafter and in most sources called simply Ashur Biy) entered the Russian empire's southern frontier as envoy from the court of Khiva's new khan. (See figure 6.1, engraving of Ashur Biy.) History especially noticed this new khan, Yadighar Khan (r. 1713–1714) who descended from Hajji Muhammad Bahadur II, because his death terminated the old line of Chinggisids, descended from Juchi, that had ruled in Khwarazm since the early sixteenth century. On arriving back in Khiva after his extended absence in Arabia, Yadighar Khan received a great shock, for a Karakalpak usurper, Ishim Sultan, sat on his throne. The ensuing civil war saw five terrible battles for control of Khiva's government. Yadighar Khan died early in 1714, and other Central Asians displaced the Karakalpak.[17]

Yadighar Khan's ambassador Ashur Biy, ignorant of these events, reached Astrakhan in 1713 on his way from Khiva to the Russian capital. His arrival caused no surprise—many Khivan envoys and traders had preceded him over the centuries—but an incidental comment he made and recommendations he later gave in Saint Petersburg precipitated an imperial reaction that influenced czarist attitudes toward Central Asia and shaped future relations between Russia and western Asia, especially Khiva.

The mission entrusted to Ashur Biy by his khan lay in the customary province of Central Asian diplomats. The newly enthroned Khivan potentate, identified by the ambassador as the grandson of Abul Ghazi Bahadur Khan and the son of Anusha Khan (r. Khiva 1664–1687), wished to inform Russia's Peter I that, "having returned from Hindustan a year earlier, on the fourteenth of Jumaziel [Jumada awwal A.H. 1124/A.D. 1712], I have assumed my father's place in the Khivan khanate, and I now rule the entire Khivan domain."[18]

Ambassador Ashur Biy reported that the enthronement had occurred.

Figure 6.1 Khoja Muhammad Ashur Biy, Khivan envoy to Peter the Great in Saint Petersburg, 1714. *Das Veranderte Russland* (1721).

Yadighar Khan promptly dispatched his envoy to Peter I with congratulations, evidently on the Russian victory over Sweden at Poltava in June 1709. Shortly after that triumph, Peter I narrowly escaped the disaster into which he had led Russian troops on the banks of the Pruth River in Turkish-controlled Moldavia in July 1711. That debacle, administered by Ottoman and Tatar armies, appeared to nudge him back and turn his attention toward the eastern frontier of his widening domain.[19]

Peter I, energetically looking for ways of expanding and enriching the empire, received Ashur Biy cordially and granted the khan's request for weapons—six small cannon, 139 kilograms of gunpowder, and 270 shot—to fight off the Karakalpaks. The Russians probably responded positively because the Karakalpaks were roaming widely enough to disturb Russian-held Bashkiria.

In return, Peter I made a request of his own—to verify the presence of gold in Khiva—to the Khivan khan through the envoy. During the months Ashur Biy was at the Russian court, two separate sources reported the existence of gold dust in the Amu Darya riverbed (incorrectly thought to be at Yarkand, in eastern Turkistan). Prince Matvey Gagarin, Russian *voivode* of Siberia, who had become closely acquainted with the ambassador from Khiva and who later died on the gallows for graft, conveyed one speculation about this to Peter I. Gagarin's information seemed all the more tantalizing because it reached him indirectly through Khoja Nefes, a Turkmen traveler in Astrakhan.

When asked about the existence of the precious metal in his land, Ashur Biy politely confirmed the presence of gold dust in the Amu Darya. He then suggested, through Prince Gagarin, that the Russian emperor construct a fort large enough for one thousand men at the old mouth of the Amu Darya, which fed into the Caspian Sea near or on the Krasnovodsk spit. (In fact, Ashur Biy was mistakenly referring to the Uzbay River, now judged to have dried up thousands of years earlier.) Such a stronghold would have established conventional Russian forces for the first time within a Central Asia that had not yet seen a single permanent Russian embassy.[20]

Nation-states, like compact ethnic groups, seem more introverted than heterogeneous polities. Communities focusing attention outward appear less concerned with self-preservation than ethnically homogeneous bodies, which greatly affects the historical profiles of both. Central Asia in the past usually arranged itself both politically and socially in composites that lacked great internal cohesion but actively involved their adjacent, even distant neighbors. After the seventeenth century, the Uzbek masters of old Bukhara, Khiva, and the new khanate of Qoqan (Khokand)—traditionally nomadic, then imperial—once more began to balance the pulls and pushes exerted by centralizing forces in contest with fragmentation.

To say that the Uzbeks of the eighteenth century belong to the modern era in any sense is difficult, but there is no doubt that the capitals of those three states had become fixed centers of trade and a more or less sedentary life-style by the early 1700s. Those developments affected not only the new leaders and their subjects but the many surrounding people related by religion, language, family, tribe, or racial commonality.

Like individuals, nearly every society in Central Asia lived in closer relations with some groups than with others, which meant more in one epoch than another. Such connections concentrated the focus of every society's outlook. In late medieval times in Central Asia, Khiva, from its position south-southwest of the Aral Sea, looked mainly north and west, especially in the thirteenth and fourteenth centuries, where the Juchid Mongols and then the Golden Horde combined Khwarazm with their domains along the Kama-Volga River axis. That tight link had parted, first under assaults by the Khwarazmians, then by Timur's armies before the beginning of the fifteenth century. Finally, Ivan IV's capture of Astrakhan just after the mid-sixteenth century completed the break, and Khiva moved again into closer interaction with the centers south and east of it as the political compass swung around without regard to geography. Nevertheless, the old Khwarazmian impulse to face toward the Volga River access route remained strong as the eighteenth century began and Russian frontiers west and east of the Caspian Sea rolled nearer to Central Asia.

In 1714 the Khivan ambassador let it be known that the Khivan khan would not oppose the destruction of dams reputedly constructed as a security measure by the Khivans to close off the flow of the great Amu Darya River along its ancient bed to the Caspian Sea. Nor, he remarked, would Khiva object to the diversion of the Amu Darya into its former Uzbay channel—branching off from Khwarazm, bypassing the Aral Sea inflow, to the Caspian Sea. Via this route Russian strategists dreamed of opening a river route from the sea to Khiva and beyond it to the south, thinking that such an engineering feat would immeasurably advance Peter I's search for wealth in Central Asia and on into India. That Petrine daydream powered extensive planning and investment in the East.

Ashur Biy, by diplomatically agreeing with the Russian delusion of abundant Central Asian gold, gave an impression of pliability—the stereotyped passivity attributed to Easterners. In this he performed a disservice to his homeland and to Khivan-Russian interaction by allowing Russians to develop the idea that copious gold dust awaited in an easily invaded Khiva populated with submissive Khivans. The ambassador's Central Asian courtesy and deference thus contributed to a Russian misapprehension that would produce unpleasant consequences for all. As a diplomat, Ashur Biy failed disastrously.

Peter I and his policymakers, to whom the gold rush became compelling, drew up an elaborate plan to send a large mission to Khiva. On May 29, 1714, the Russian sovereign announced that he would order to Khiva Prince Aleksandr Bekovich-Cherkasskii, an Asian officer in the imperial military, with an escort for the ostensible purpose of congratulating Yadighar Khan on his accession to the Khivan throne. As the Russian ukase stated it, the emperor also sent the young officer "for seeking out trade possibilities and making inquiries about the city of Irken [Yarkand], how far it is from the Caspian Sea and whether there may be some rivers from there or even if not from the place itself, at least coming near the Caspian." The degree of Russian attention to a coronation already past surprised the Central Asians, aroused their apprehensions, and revealed Russia's ignorance about the geography of Turkistan, its river systems, its climate, and the distances between cities.[21]

Uzbek and other Central Asian foreign relations in those centuries often included what might be called double diplomacy. Anthony Jenkinson had demonstrated third-party double diplomacy by serving British commercial interests, the Russian throne, and Central Asian governments in one mission. Russian authorities created no innovation therefore when they selected Ashur Biy to explore routes into Khiva and to discover the fabled Amu Darya gold. They simultaneously asked him to cater to their sovereign's whims by proceeding to India to acquire parrots and panthers for Peter I, which they probably intended to serve as a cover for an intelligence-gathering journey.[22] Thus the Khivan Ashur Biy learned that diplomacy in Russia lacked a national identity and a sense of high priority. That kind of haphazard diplomacy seemed to deny sovereignty more than to symbolize it.

Ashur Biy was appointed Russia's envoy and received imperial authority to leave Saint Petersburg in 1715. In March of that year he learned, through letters from two high officials—the Khivan ataliq Ishkar and Nazar Hajji, the inaq— that the situation had changed in the capital of Khwarazm:

> Now be informed that Yadighar Khan died and that the Khan Arang [Erenk, r. 1714–1715?] took his place. In the yurts and among the folk everywhere it is calm. If the younger brother does not manage to prevail, the elder one will reign . . . Travel at once to Khiva without fearing anything. No misfortune will occur.

Shir Ghazi Khan (r. 1715–1728), a Kazak born in Bukhara, then established a new line of Kazak rulers in Khiva that lasted more than half a century. Like a few nomadic princes before him (Shaybaniy Khan, his brother Mahmud Bahadur-Sultan, and Abul Ghazi Bahadur Khan, for example), he received an education in the urban *madrassahs* (seminaries). A later Khivan chronicler, judging this khan's standing and competence, said: "He was a lord of the fortunate planetary conjunction of this dynasty," which constituted high praise, for historians had applied the same epithet to Amir Timur and Abdullah Khan. This accession briefly reunited fragments of the old Uzbek-Kazak tribal confederation, for many Kazak as well as Uzbek, Turkmen, and Kalmyk tribes submitted to Shir Ghazi Khan. Even so, neither his thirteen-year reign in that salient of Central Asia nor the years of his Kazak successors on the Khivan throne could reverse the separation process begun some 300 years earlier. After the powerful Uzbek inaq Muhammad Amin drove out the last Kazak khan of Khiva around 1770, a new line of Uzbek rulers would hold Khiva's throne until the monarchy ended.[23]

Undismayed by the idea of Kazak royalty's sitting on Khiva's throne, Ashur

Biy departed homeward with his instructions and the heavy weapons, which were intended as gifts for Yadighar Khan. By the time the diplomat reached the lower Volga months later, however, news had come to Russia about the khan's death the previous year and the ensuing instability in Khiva's political affairs. Russian officials held Ashur Biy in Astrakhan, near the Volga's mouth. In one of his numerous recorded communications with Russian officials, the former Khivan-Russian envoy wrote to Astrakhan commandant Mikhail I. Chirikov on March 4, 1715, to remind the Russian of the imperial commission that had entrusted him to purchase exotic birds and animals in India. No response to that communication remains in the published archives. On November 1, 1715, Ashur Biy wrote in Turki to Commandant Chirikov again, requesting release:

> I came here at the command of the sovereign [Peter I] in order to proceed by the route required of me. But, because they killed the khan in Khiva, I delayed a bit . . . Now the khan is Shir Ghazi, from Bukhara. He knows and values me a thousand times more than Yadighar. Return the cannons to me, give me travel funds and send me off with a caravan . . . If you won't give permission, allot me support. [Host governments then customarily housed and fed visiting diplomats.][24]

Because Central Asian envoys personally represented the ruler who dispatched them on a mission rather than a government as a whole, Ashur Biy found himself no longer an accredited diplomat. Saint Petersburg could have sent an envoy to accompany Ashur Biy and thus continued the exchange at that level. However, the Russian government, engaged in preparing the enlarged mission of Prince Bekovich-Cherkasskii to Khiva, undoubtedly considered the Khivan ambassador an inconvenience and a security risk.[25]

KHIVAN MISSIONS

Two sizable armed Russian probes that had been set in motion by rumors of gold dust in Central Asian rivers ended badly. In 1715 the czar ordered the initial expedition (1,500–2,000 men and officers) north of Khiva beyond western Turkistan's easternmost edge down the Irtysh River toward Yarkand; it met disaster in the form of Kalmyk military resistance. Prince Bekovich-Cherkasskii's mission to Khiva ended in a debacle in August 1717 when, despite the Russians' superior firearms, Khivan tribesmen, through guile and patience, activated zealous antipathy to the Christian invaders and destroyed the 6,600-man invading force and its commander. A Khivan historian subsequently described the conflict as a religious war: "For defense, the khan assigned the Qonghirat ataliq Qul Muhammad and the Nayman inaq Amir 'Awaz with numberless troops. They concluded peace with Dawlat Giray

[Prince Bekovich-Cherkasskii] and under the pretext of hospitality sent the enemies of the sacred faith to the fires of hell." His upbringing in Russia and abroad evidently made the Kabardian prince forget what Chinggis Khan and Amir Timur taught Central Asians long before: wars won by deception save your army many casualties.

Although the Khivans decisively ended this combat in their favor, the victory gave the Uzbek-Kazaks and Turkmens premonitions of reprisal. Bukhara openly distanced itself from the Khivan action, and for the first time, southern Central Asians felt threatened by the growing power in Saint Petersburg and the invasions it might generate.[26]

Unquestionably, Central Asian diplomacy generated this apprehension. Feeble and unsystematic though it was, diplomacy informed the khans and amir in Khiva, Bukhara, and Qoqan about the very real threat of Russian military strength. All this combined to sour economic exchanges between the two regions for decades. Even worse, Russian disappointment contributed to growing exasperation; out of contempt, Peter I again ceased to treat Central Asians as diplomatic equals.

Ashur Biy wrote one last despairing message to Prince Gagarin on September 27, 1717:

> Twenty-five months they have kept me in Astrakhan, but by the ruler's [Peter I's] wish and your kindness, Mikhail Il'ich Chirikov [the Astrakhan commandant] has done much good for me. Mikhail Il'ich is an excellent person . . . You promised to send me your man, but I have lived on in Astrakhan and have seen no one. The rest, you know yourself. If through God's will both the sovereign and you, my well-wisher, will be alive and healthy, I still hope to be of service. My son bows deeply to you.

The court in Russia had only recently learned from Khiva of the annihilation of its expeditionary force, and no Russian official could then have permitted a Khivan envoy to leave imperial control. The emperor remained abroad. In that connection Ashur Biy's personal audiences with Peter I, who encouraged the expedition to Khivan territory, worked against the Khivan's gaining permission to depart from Astrakhan without or perhaps even with royal approval.[27]

Russian fury over the defeat by Khiva vented itself brutally against another diplomat, Ways Mambet (Aywaz Muhammad), Shir Ghazi Khan's new envoy to Russia, who arrived in Astrakhan in May of 1720 evidently expecting some form of diplomatic immunity. He brought a message explaining the events of 1717 from the Khivan standpoint; according to the diplomatic note, Khiva perceived Prince Bekovich-Cherkasskii not as the ambassador from Russia but as a cannon-firing invader, whom they must repulse or defeat. Many Khivans lost their lives in the battles, reported the khan's communication.

At the end of August the Russian College of Foreign Affairs sent a directive to Astrakhan ordering the governor to forward the Khivan envoy on to Saint Petersburg, treating him politely but as a prisoner. Brought to the College of Foreign Affairs at the beginning of 1721, the ministers interrogated and reviled him. They asked, "Why did you kill the innocent envoy of the sovereign, Prince Cherkasskii?" The Khivan envoy replied, "True, we did this, but he came to us not as an envoy but as an enemy; he built a city and stationed 8,000 troops there; then he approached us and, without proceeding to Khiva for fifteen days, killed our troops in a battle." The Russians then remarked, "Perhaps your khan is angry at you and sent you as a sacrifice so that you would be hung here for Prince Cherkasskii?" Aywaz Muhammad answered, "If you will, but the khan sent me with a declaration that he desires to be friends and to send away all the [Russian] captives [in Khiva]." The ministers said also, "We think that in no persuasion in the entire world is it possible to kill diplomats." They then incarcerated the Khivan ambassador in the fortress, where he soon died. When Shir Ghazi Khan received the Russian message reporting Aywaz Muhammad's demise, he stamped the note underfoot and left it for the children to play with.[28] These actions demonstrate the importance of diplomacy, unsystematic though it was, as late as the first decades in the eighteenth century: Russian as well as Khivan rulers regarded their ambassadors as extensions of dynastic sovereignty and took injuries to their envoys most personally and seriously.

The episode involving Ashur Biy at the Russian court and its aftermath accurately reflected the situation in and around Khiva, which, in the first half of the eighteenth century, was peculiarly representative of a seminomadic existence. There was a khanate, but its center did not always remain in the same place and never at a predictable moment. Its two poles—one around Khiva and the other northeastward on the Aral Sea near the mouth of the Sir Darya—repeatedly divided the people of Khwarazm. The elements making up the khanate related to one another in dynamic confusion, orbiting about an almost evanescent, insubstantial core that consisted mainly of ideas about descent from certain forebears.

In Khiva—virtual guerrilla territory throughout the seventeenth century under some strong leaders—stability by the end of the century seemed to vanish entirely in the searing heat of the endless desert under weak or temporary khans. The Khivan zone of polarization—it hardly qualified as an established area—further disintegrated. Like water evaporating from neglected canals and waterways, the Yadighar khans' power vanished and the state stagnated. A seminomadic or nomadic state cannot exist long in repose; its nature is action. In addition the Khivan conglomerate abruptly acquired an even greater diversity of population. Although Khiva was far away from any other substantial settlement (Bukhara was about 400 kilometers away, for instance), it was an oasis created by men husbanding scarce water resources and became a confluence of human streams as well. Early invaders had poured through the area many

qalmaq

times, but after the seventeenth century four more great nomadic currents flowed in upon Khiva. The Uzbeks' closest kin, the Uzbek-Kazaks, pushed into the region from the Qipchaq Plains to the east-northeast, and the Karakalpaks, nearly indistinguishable from the Kazaks, moved westward from the Sir Darya. Both these were fleeing ahead of another surge farther east. The Dzungarians, called Qalmaqs by the Khivans, had irrupted violently into this domain a hundred years earlier. Now pushed by China, many again thrust into the west.[29]

BUKHARAN *ELCHI* ~~Quli Bek~~ *Topchi Bashi*

While imperial Russia engaged in unrewarding conflict with hostile Khiva, Bukhara showed Peter I the receptive Central Asian diplomatic opening that suited his desires and pursued certain aims with the Russian court. Bukhara—vividly demonstrating the Central Asian tendency for political divisiveness—sent a senior diplomat to Saint Petersburg the very year that Khiva's tribesmen in deserts and villages fought against Prince Bekovich-Cherkasskii. The Bukharan *elchi* Quli Bek Topchi Bashi, as his name and titles show (*topchi* was a cannoneer; *topchibashi* probably served as chief of palace artillery) embodied two functions: he acted as envoy and as an expert on the military artillery that the Central Asians eagerly sought from imperial armories and cannon casters. Quli Bek, in his audience with Peter I on October 20, 1717, reported on the meetings he had held earlier that year with Prince Bekovich-Cherkasskii in the Astrakhan staging area before the disastrous Russian expedition to Khiva. The Bukharan ambassador said that he had warned the prince to beware of the Khivans and that the Kalmyks and Turkmens would resist on the side of the Khivans.[30]

The Russian court responded to Quli Bek Topchi Bashi's mission by appointing an outsider, rather than a Russian, to accompany the ambassador on his return journey to Bukhara. This suggests that the government could find no qualified Russian representative that would be acceptable to the Central Asians. Perhaps Saint Petersburg dared not risk dispatching a Russian diplomat into a zone where he might fall hostage to the Khivans, but it also illustrates the tenuous connection between ethnic identity, sovereignty, and diplomacy.

Peter I sent a well-educated Italian, Florio Beneveni, to Bukhara with instructions to gather military and diplomatic intelligence and to conclude a defensive alliance against all mutual enemies, especially the Khivans. Among other specifics, he ordered Beneveni to determine how many forts, troops, and cannon Bukhara could field and where they were emplaced. The emperor also instructed his envoy to offer Abul Fayz Khan (r. 1711–1747) a special Russian guard troop and to discover all he could about the gold-bearing rivers in the Khivan khanate.

The Bukharan and Russian envoys must have become well acquainted, for they waited more than a year in Shamakha for an end to Bukharan-Persian hostilities. In November 1721 they finally arrived in Bukhara, where tension between the Uzbek tribes and the Ashtarkhanid throne prevented Beneveni from accomplishing most of his aims. His three-year stay virtually converted his visit into a resident embassy; nevertheless, he could not conclude the mutual defense treaty proposed by Saint Petersburg. While in Bukhara, Florio Beneveni secretly sent and received messages outside the khanate. In one of them the Khivan throne invited him to appear, but because he could not obtain the necessary exit visa from the Bukharans, he secretly fled to Khiva in April 1725. In August, after an audience with Shir Ghazi Khan, Beneveni left that place clandestinely and made his way through unhospitable terrain to the coastal settlement of Gur'ev at the mouth of the Yaik (subsequently Ural) River, across to Astrakhan and north to Saint Petersburg.

His report, delivered to the Russian court after a seven-year absence, was a detailed survey of mineral wealth and gold-bearing sand from the Amu Darya and Gokcha rivers. The ambassador urged the imperial government to attack at once both the chaotic amirate of Bukhara and the hostile Khivan khanate. Imperial preoccupation with internal affairs after the death of Peter I in January 1725 and the protective geography surrounding Khiva and Bukhara saved the Central Asian states from an immediate Russian siege.[31] The Central Asians' actions became more circumspect, the only indication that they sensed the true proximity of the growing menace from the north. At the same time, they paid too little heed to the rejuvenated Iranian military, powered by firearms and Central Asian Turkmen horsemen. Bukhara soon capitulated, but others mistook their remote locations for strength.

In combat during 1740, Khiva refused to submit to the invading Nadir Shah, though it had been invited to do so with semblance of honor in a long diplomatic note addressed to Ilbars Khan (1728–1740) from Nadir Shah in 1739. In a patronizing tone, that message recounted what the Persian shah regarded as Ilbars Khan's many military offenses against Khurasan. It sermonized in verse against obstinacy and threatened punishment if the Khivan khan did not submit. This so enraged Ilbars Khan that he forgot the lesson of Shaybaniy Khan's fatal exchange with Ismail Shah 200 years before and lost the diplomatic contest when he was provoked into rash action by an insulting letter. Ilbars Khan impetuously commanded his men to kill the shah's envoy along with the two escorting Juybar Khojas (religious representatives from Bukhara's Abul Fayz Khan). As a Bukharan historian later acknowledged, almost paraphrasing the Russians' complaint about Khiva's earlier treatment of Prince Bekovich-Cherkasskii: "That manner of conduct is authorized by no religious denomination." Khiva's premier nineteenth-century chronicler, Shir Muhammad bin Amir Awaz Biy Mirab al-Munis (d. 1829), evidently found the cause and details of that lethal incident too painful to record in his history of the khanate.[32]

Retribution sailed toward the Khivan fortress town of Fitnak (Pitnäk) on the left bank of the Amu Darya, as Nadir Shah used the river to transport his heavy and light artillery. The shah moved the two parts of his expeditionary force to the khanate in late 1739, and the armies first collided around Fitnak. For the Central Asians, it became a holy war against Shiites:

> However many unbelievers they killed with ferocious zeal, lacking cleverness they could not decide how they must proceed. Finally, the Muslims [Central Asians] suffered defeat and, not being in a condition to remain in Hazarasp [on which they had fallen back], fortified themselves in the town of Khanqa. Nadir Shah pursued them and besieged that fortress. The troops of Islam [Central Asians] fought well, but suffered defeat.

Khanqa surrendered after Nadir Shah promised to pardon Ilbars Khan. When the Khivan leaders came under the shah's control, however, he executed twenty Khwarazmian amirs as well as Ilbars Khan and Ish Muhammad Biy, the Khivan *inaq* (prime minister). The shah justified this treachery with the Khivans' murder of his ambassadors.

These events caused the mutual perceptions among Central Asia, Iran, and Russia to change fundamentally. Russia became increasingly exasperated and scornful toward the amirs and khans. Central Asians suffered great ambivalence, becoming increasingly nervous while growing more involved with Russia. That anxiety added to the introversion already generated by an again militant Iran and the sectarian block it constituted on the southwest. Afghanistan under the Persians and their new Afghan dynasty cut away another previously open southern frontier. To the East reigned unfriendly and unconquerable nomadic Kazak brothers.

Ashtarkhanid diplomats continually came and went, yet the rulers could not understand that they—southern Central Asia's most long-lived dynasty since the advent of the Uzbeks—had led the region to catastrophe. Ineffective leadership drastically reduced prestige and power, which shrank the size of the domains and stimulated a psychology of introversion and vainglory. The decline offered Central Asians convincing proof that a polity's failure to keep in intelligent tune with the larger world could lead to cultural, political, and economic atrophy. Central Asia, into the eighteenth century surrounded by decaying Islamic societies and institutions, took its lower-than-average status for normal. As late as the 1730s it subsisted on fantasies of grandeur from a more glorious past.[33]

CONFLICT BETWEEN OLD AND NEW MODERNITY

PART TWO

7 History

Historians in Central Asia rationalized their creating new works by arguing that
no such history yet existed in the language. Annalists of several outstanding
histories included lines explaining why and for whom they intended their work.
Yet seemingly none meditated on the importance of recording and interpreting
the pattern of actual events. The creators of Muslim historiography went on the
assumption that such writing must serve didactic purposes. Interpretation
leaned toward edification.

From the beginning of Muslim historical writing, its authors made royalty
not only the subject but the object of that form of education. "The knowledge of
genealogy and *akhbar* (history) belongs to the sciences of kings and important
persons. Only noble souls aspire to it, and small minds do not want it," wrote
one of the fathers of the discipline. As a consequence of its central place in the
training and thought of royalty and large minds, history writing, like other
branches of knowledge in medieval Islam, developed elaborate theories and

* Voltaire, "Of the Method or Manner of Writing History, and of Style," in *A Philosophical
Dictionary*, sect. 4 (London: John and Henry L. Hunt, 1824), p. 70.

guidelines. Because Islamic historiography stressed the concrete factual element, it concentrated on separate events and characterizations. The historian omitted inquiry into subtle links and underlying causes. Reliable information depended as much upon an authoritative, unbroken succession of transmitters as it did on primary sources. This atomizing of history into discrete items of information gave the writing an episodic form that continued into the twentieth century.[1]

ROYAL HISTORIANS

Early Central Asian writers supplied models for what would become a well-established convention. Muhammad bin Khavendshah bin Mahmud Mirkhwand (Mirkhond) (1432–1498), a Timurid historian already cited here, addressed his work to a small circle of Timurids for a specific purpose. His work, which went on to serve a great many people in numbers of languages both inside and outside of Central Asia, was given its lasting authority by the quality of the exposition and the author's intimate connection with the leading politicians and intellectuals of the region.

Mirkhwand wrote his large manuscript in Farsi rather than in the Turki of the Timurids or in the Qipchaq of the numerous, fast-approaching Uzbeks. Ironically, the author dedicated this Farsi-language history to its commissioner, Mir Ali Shir Nawaiy, who volubly championed using the Turki language. Both fashion and necessity explain this paradox. These historians—erudite, skilled in narrative as well as verse, and often philosophical men of the world—offered the khans and amirs valuable service and educated counsel. Being outsiders to the dynasty or the tribes, certain perspectives of their eyes and minds were useful to Central Asian patrons, who accepted Farsi-language writings because most Central Asian rulers of that time could understand and even write the language. More important, in this respect as in many others, the leaders followed the fashion set by Amir Timur and the glittering courts of his descendants, who also used Farsi.

Mirkhwand's work, *Rawzat us-safa* (The Garden of Purity), spells out the uses of history and the qualities historians should embody. The principal reason for such writings, he declared, could only be "because world affairs depend on their [rulers'] option and consideration, as well as good and evil acts committed." Rulers have greater need of historical knowledge than others, he believed. The historian emphasized that rulers study history to

> strive to act justly, to govern mildly, to make their kingdom permanent. When monarchs become impressed with the happy consequences of magnanimity, as portrayed in the characters of some former sovereigns, and contemplate

the effects, intense pleasure takes hold of their minds, and they become desirous of surpassing the good reputations of their predecessors.

Mir Ali Shir Nawaiy set forth similar ideas in his book of ethics, *Mähbub äl-qulüb* (The Heart's Darling, 1500/1501). Mirkhwand also felt that reading historical narratives, even those parts that might be fictitious, refreshes the mind. Above all, history gives knowledge, guidance, help in learning to make critical distinctions, and the power "to ascertain from events of former times the causes of prosperity and distress, of happiness and calamity." Such writers reminded Central Asian royalty (and subsequently lesser readers) of those precepts common in older Muslim historiography.

To accomplish such aims, Mirkhwand thought a historian must be unbiased in religion (though of the orthodox sect), objective, without exaggeration, direct and open (with clear, easy style), honest, and pious.[2] Ideas about the didactic function of history, already long known, lived vigorously in the Central Asian tradition on the eve of the Uzbek takeover.

Zahiriddin Muhammad Babur certainly knew this convention when he wrote *Memoirs of Babur* in Turki. In 1506 he added a few lines that emphasized an aim different from that of his contemporary Mirkhwand. Babur Shah's principles were more personal:

> I do not write this in order to complain [about those who have not shown the courtesy and generosity I gave them]. I have written the plain truth. I do not record this in order to convey my worth. I set down just what happened. In this history I was determined that the truth come out in everything, and that each action be noted exactly as it happened.

Furthermore, he asserted that by necessity he had written whatever was known about good or evil, whether it touched father, elder brother, relative, or stranger. "I set down their virtues and faults," he wrote. Babur Shah's text—full of criticism as well as of praise—does not claim to benefit others or establish models for guidance. In his evaluations of rulers and leaders, however, he establishes the basis for his positive or negative criticisms. In that sense, using an elaborate form of diary, he has written a history worth the king's reading.[3]

Writing a few decades later than Babur Shah, Mirza Muhammad Haydar (1499–1551), a prince of the Dughlat tribe of Chaghatays whose native language must have been Turki, composed his major work in Farsi, a mark, he would have believed, of his refinement. Although he later became ruler of Kashmir, Mirza Haydar earned renown mainly for his *Tärikh-i räshidi* (History of Rashid, 1541–1544) in which he outlines his historical method and his motive. He began the history with the reign of Tughluk Timur Khan (1348–1362) because, he said, previous authors had thoroughly covered the foregoing periods. He tells the reader that,

Notwithstanding my ignorance and want of skill, I felt my duty to undertake this difficult task. For much time has already passed since the khakans of the Moghuls were driven [eastward] from the towns of the civilized world and have had to content themselves with dwellings in the desert. On this account, they have written no history themselves but base their ancestral records upon oral tradition. At this present date [A.H. 951/A.D. 1544], there remains not one among them who knows these traditions, and my boldness in attempting this difficult work is due to the consideration that, did I not make the venture, the story of the Moghul Khakans would be obliterated from the pages of the world's history.

Further along, Mirza Haydar inserts a paragraph that sounds like a mixture between Babur Shah's declared methodology for his *Memoirs* and Mirkhwand's rationalization for writing *The Garden of Purity*. Mirza Haydar writes about "the practice of historians" to record everything, worthy or unworthy, good or bad, "to reproduce all facts without discrimination, in order that they may leave behind them a record of the people of this world. Thus all men in power, as well as others, reading their histories, may profit by their advice."[4] Nationalist historians of the nineteenth and twentieth centuries would make comparable claims for their works.

Khiva's Abul Ghazi Bahadur Khan (r. 1642–1663) reconnected this sequence of royal Central Asian historians, which had been detoured by a preference for lyric versification during the Shaybanid era. The khan, in the final year of his life feeling the need to correct mistakes in earlier works and to fill the gap between Abdullah Khan's time and his own (some 65 years), set about writing Khwarazm's history. He did this, he asserts in his *Shäjärä-i turk* (Genealogy of the Turks, 1663), because, through neglect and inability, no one had completed such a work. The khan-historian forthrightly claimed: "At this time no one has more knowledge than this pauper [the khan] of the names of the padishahs who were in Arabistan, Iran, Turan, and Mogholistan and of the amirs and sultans from Adam's age up to my day." Why did he compose *Genealogy of the Turks* in Turki rather than Farsi, in which he rightfully claimed full competence? He does not say but hints that in the surrounding countries, no one has his capacity to write such a history except possibly the scholars in Persia and Hindustan, which implies that he felt the need in Central Asia for a record in the language and style of his own region.

Referring to eighteen manuscripts for background and his memory of events recounted to him, he composed the section covering the period from Shaybaniy Khan to his own time. Not only the khan's erudition but the old custom of preserving oral history served him well, judging from reading his *Genealogy of the Turks*. In both literature and history, the habit of cultivating a long memory prevailed among high and low, especially in seminomadic domains. The royal author goes on to relate a further motive for his effort: "From

Adam's era to this time God knows the number of histories that have been composed, but no padishah and amir and no wise savant had composed his own history as he should." Later on the khan, feeling decrepitude undermining him, resolved to complete the work if he could, for, "From my heart I said if I stop ahead of time, there is not a person like me by whom the book can be composed. From Yadighar Khan up to the poor pauper [himself], no one knows our society, a person of an alien country does not know this; among our own people, there is not a single person who knows." Abul Ghazi Bahadur Khan's premonition proved correct: his health did not grant him time to finish the history. His warlike son and successor, Anusha Khan, added just a few lines in which, after a few notes, he acknowledged his failure to carry out this promise to his father.[5]

Usually the khans wrote with confidence, authority, and only minor self-praise. Consequently their style lacked the nearly obligatory effusive flattery of histories composed by underlings. Thus, these accomplished royal historians succeeded both in intellectual-aesthetic leadership and in dynastic politics and earned the acclaim of the ages. Cycles in Central Asian history raised powerful leaders in periods of triumph and after disaster, but too often the rhythm of events replaced strong men with weaker ones.

HISTORIOGRAPHY OF THE DECLINE

After Abul Ghazi Bahadur Khan's era in Khwarazm came the Ashtarkhanids' not entirely unrelated decline in Bukhara with its accompanying historiography of dynastic decay. Several authors wrote extensive annals detailing the unnatural deaths of five ruling khans and princely heirs—the last real or potential sovereigns of the dynasty's line. Although the authors entitled these works *The History of Muqim Khan*, *The Story of Ubaydullah*, and the like, their great detail as well as their interpretation concluded on one theme: the rulers and heirs to the throne of Bukhara could not rise to the demands of those perilous times. At Balkh, Ubaydullah Khan II's (r. 1702–1711) nephew (Subhanquli Khan's grandson) Muqim Khan, in 1702 rebelled against Bukhara to enthrone himself. Like many enemies of Bukhara, he died in 1707 at age 30 at the hands of the khanate's Uzbek tribal field general and, in this case, royal executioner Mahmud Biy Qataghan, ataliq. Writing about that regicide, Muqim Khan's scribe and historian characterized Mahmud Biy's appearance and motive for killing royalty thus: "The damned Mahmud Biy, whose loathsome appearance and vile look was on everyone's tongue, out of malice of heart desired to immortalize his dishonor on the pages of history and to the day of Judgment became the target for everyone's arrows of condemnation." That assumption by the court historian about the verdict of history on a man's worth continued a principle expressed by the chroniclers of the region from the earliest days of the Uzbeks and before. Above all, assumed the public and the writers of histories, a leader meant to leave behind him a good name.

The author of *The Story of Ubaydullah* blamed Ubaydullah Khan II's failure to accomplish this on insufficient self-discipline and a weak will. Ubaydullah Khan, in this interpretation, ignored good counsel and mistakenly associated with and brought into the court men of low origin and character. The dissatisfied courtiers and Uzbek amirs conspired to have a Kalmyk assassinate him (thus alleviating their religious and ethnic guilt) and seat his brother, Abul Fayz, on the uneasy Ashtarkhanid seat of authority. In turn, the heirs of that potentate died by violence soon afterward. The historiography of dynastic decay in these histories, like the annals devoted to triumphant sovereigns, related an edifying story for the benefit of noble minds. No prince with ambition to rule in Central Asia could mistake their message about needing piety, competence, self-discipline, and strong will to face down the Uzbek tribes.[6]

Southern Central Asia's revival under the driving, new tribal dynasties peaked around the turn of the nineteenth century. The new age of advancement and power lasted about half a century, from the 1770s to 1825. Dynamic leaders—energetic, intelligent, and educated—swept most troubles away in what they believed to be a return to old virtues and values. Following in the wake of the Ming chieftain Narbuta Biy in Qoqan came his able sons, Alim Khan (r. 1798–1810) and Umar Khan (r. 1810–1822). The documents do not show whether either died a natural death, though Umar Khan earned tremendous public approval for his conciliatory style of rule, Qoqan's flourishing economy, and the elegant literate culture around his court. Without question, they advanced the Qoqan khanate's political fortunes and made a mark in Central Asian history and on international relations involving Chinese, Russians, and Hindustanis.

In Bukhara, Amir Haydar Tora (r. 1800–1826) could not match his coevals in the Ming dynasty of Qoqan. For the Bukharan amirate, any progress in the new century came from earlier momentum. On his accession to the throne in Bukhara, Haydar Tora, the son of Amir Shah Murad, received the Bukharan domain in Mawaraunnahr plus Turkmen lands including the Murghab Valley, again a large part of Afghan Turkistan, as well as the town and vicinity of Turkistan in the north. His subjects at the outset numbered approximately 2.5 million. During his rule, however, the amir's territory shrank, while the Qoqan khanate's lands grew, sometimes at the amir's expense.

Haydar Tora's letters to his nephew Said Ahmad Khoja in the provincial posts of the amirate revealed that another problem was the ongoing unsatisfactory interactions with the Uzbek tribes. Writing in 1803 he cordially instructed his sister's son to draft sizable auxiliary contingents from certain tribes—Saray, 200; Manghit, 600; Kurama (a mixed group), 300; Aymaq (another mixed nomadic group), 400; Arabs, 150; Qonghirats, 1,000—for the defense of Shahr-i Sabz. In 1815 he warned his nephew again that "the season for migration of the nomadic tribes to summer pastures has arrived. Migration by them into the Shahr-i Sabz pastures must be prohibited... If they are in need of a greater amount of pasture, let them go in the direction of Hissar. Be beforehand in this matter." The amir's tenure ultimately deteriorated into old patterns of conflict with the Khitay-Qipchaq and other contentious Uzbek tribes. As a consequence, Amir Haydar Tora's relatively long time on the throne could not be called an entirely happy or successful reign. In cultural developments this negative pattern reflected itself in attitudes toward learning and history.[7]

Visitors to the amirate during Amir Haydar Tora's time found scholasticism dominating the *madrassahs* (seminaries) of Bukhara. Although the amirate supported at least 150 of these institutions[8] before the mid-nineteenth century, they had little influence in shaping a favorable attitude toward education. Most Bukharans could not read or write. Tajik merchants, however, sent their sons to school to acquire skills for success in trade, but Uzbek scorn for Tajiks sharply restricted their employment and indirectly reflected Uzbek tribal disdain for education. This prejudice was demonstrated in religious practice, for very seldom did Tajiks become high clergymen. In fields of higher learning, regardless of group affiliation, astronomy was mixed with astrology, and even the most educated men could not read a map or boast a good grasp of geography. When confronted with the cartography of travelers from Russia, no one, up to the highest officials, was curious or understood the significance of maps. Bukharan rejection of those modernizing and, at that stage, westernizing, instruments for conveying knowledge underscored the deteriorating status of true learning in the amirate.

History writing and study suffered commensurately. Mullah Ibadullah and Mullah Muhammad Sharif did write what an eminent Russian scholar called a unique, interesting *Tärikh-i ämir häydär* (History of Amir Haydar). Muhammad Ya'qub ibn Muhammad Daniyal Biy left a manuscript, *Gulshän äl-muluk* (The Rosegarden of the Kings, 1876), valuable for its treatment of the late eighteenth and early nineteenth centuries. There was, however, nothing like the thorough coverage of dynastic history produced in the late seventeenth and early eighteenth centuries for Bukhara. Notwithstanding the rich historical literature already possessed by Mawaraunnahr, cultural blight among the population early in the nineteenth century seemed to limit historical awareness severely.[9]

A measure of that intellectual turn could be seen in the fascination of people with legends and uninformed tales about Alexander the Great (Iskandar Dhul-qarnain). In 1820 a foreign traveler listened to a mullah obliged by the amir to read the Alexander story in public. Although the Bukharan's story reached a number of listeners, the visitor found that the man knew virtually nothing about the *actual* history. He could answer no questions about Alexander's route through Sogdiana or where the fortresses were that he captured in Central Asia. *'Ilm-i tawarikh* (the study of history) could not progress in Bukhara, said the observer, because "stern mullahs considered it either as useless or, worse, a profane occupation. Laymen read it only for amusement." Medieval Arabic madrassahs avoided the field of history, but standard Central Asian madrassah curricula in the first half of the nineteenth century, and perhaps even earlier, included it, though it may not have been taught regularly. From the story of the traveler, it is not surprising that among the basic texts used in the madrassah's course of history the student in nineteenth century Bukhara would face *Tarikh-i iskandariya* (The History of Alexander) by an unnamed author, along with Ibn Khalkan's Arabic biographies. The curriculum likewise included *Tarikh-i jihan qusha* (History of the World Conqueror), possibly the Farsi-language monument to Chinggis Khan and his empire, written by Ala ad-Din Ata Malik Juvaini (1226–1283), though later authors also composed other histories under that heading.[10]

Amir Haydar reversed his father's harsh policy regarding clergymen and started treating them with such deference and generosity that their numbers in the city of Bukhara rapidly grew to more than 2,000 from the few supported by Shah Murad after his drastic purge of the mullahs and *mudarris* (seminary teachers). The clergymen developed extensive popular support among an uneducated, fanatic populace. A Russian visitor to Amir Haydar's court regarded that swift growth in numbers of clergy as inimical to government interests not only because of the burden upon the state treasury but because they could oppose the decisions of the amir. A Bukharan historian noticed that the amir, after devoting some ten years of study to the madrassah curriculum, held classes for 400–500 mullahs, instructing them eight or nine hours a day.

With his heavy schedule of religious studies and teaching, the amir could not stimulate the intellectual life of the state or effectively direct the country's economic welfare or day-to-day foreign and domestic political affairs. The situation was inviting to the Khwarazmian leader Iltuzar Khan and his Turkmen troops, who repeatedly penetrated Bukhara's frontier from the north, plundering and enslaving the settled families. According to a local historian, in two or three years the Khwarazmians made off with from 40,000 to 50,000 families from Bukhara—some 200,000 people.[11] Besides depopulating Bukhara, Khwarazm dealt additional blows to the Bukharan economy when in the 1820s Bukhara lost the Urganch trade, which reduced customs duties to a third of that taken in during the previous period. Transit caravans, because of Khwarazmian and Kazak attacks on them, could no longer travel safely in and out Bukhara from north, east, or west, and most ceased trying.[12]

CHRONICLE OF AN UNJUST AMIR

Amir Haydar's son, Nasrullah Bahadur-Khan (r. 1826–1860, see figure 7.1), captured Bukhara's throne from rivals and held it firmly for an unusually long and stormy time. His reign, remarkable for its savagery and perversion, also saw the creation of a new military machine. In 1840 the amir murdered his commander of palace artillery, Ayaz Topchibashi, and his chief minister, Muhammad Hakim Qushbegi, to clear the way for an attack on the *sipahi* (irregular military forces). The amir employed a Turkmen named Rahim Birdi, who hated the Bukharan Uzbeks deeply, to drive the existing military out of the service or butcher them; the amir then proceeded to introduce a regular army. This arch intriguer of Bukhara then brought in a notorious outsider—Naib Abdul Samat, said to be a native of Tabriz and a criminal adventurer who had served in India and Afghanistan—to complete this revolution. Abdul Samat cast eleven cannon and two mortars and trained 1,000 *särbaz* (regular troops); in the autumn of 1841 the amir took those troops and 30,000 Uzbeks into the field against Qoqan's forces in small forts where Abdul Samat's artillery decided the contests. In 1842 Amir Nasrullah pushed on to distraught Qoqan, took the city, executed Muhammad Ali Khan and Umar Khan's widow, Nadira Hanim, and briefly made himself ruler of all southern Central Asia outside of Khwarazm and Afghanistan.

The amir's wars ruined Qoqan and nearly stopped the Bukharan cultural development that had revived so promisingly at the turn of the nineteenth century. Universally hated and feared, he was also regarded by his subjects with contempt for the vicious treatment of his relatives and for his harem of boys and men whom he capriciously rotated into high office. Bukharans particularly loathed the amir for his reliance on people they considered outsiders, notably Tajiks and foreigners, to man the government and quell the rebelliousness of the Uzbek tribes. Only under extreme necessity did he associate with clergy and scholars. The amir, like his father, enforced the rules of the Shariat (Muslim religious law), appointing strict *muhtäsib* (inspectors) everywhere so that "the sounds of flutes and drums scarcely reached beyond the gateways [of private dwellings]"—the historian's observation of the joylessness and misery that characterized Bukhara. These policies and actions demoralized the country, disrupted life, and weakened institutions in Central Asia. To Amir Nasrullah goes a good part of the credit for Bukhara's loss of independence to the invading Russians in 1868 and Qoqan's dissolution in 1876. Historians understood it very well.

A young man who for years was a close associate of Qoqan's Umar Khan became one of Central Asia's most important nineteenth-century historians.

امیر نصر الله بهادر خان

Figure 7.1 Contemporary lithograph (1843) of Nasrullah
Bahadur-Khan (r. 1826–60), Manghit amir of Bukhara.
Khanikoff, *Bokhara: Its Amir and Its People* (1845).

Muhammad Hakimkhan (1806–*ca.* 1845 or later) evidently received his initial
education at court and later took advanced training in Egypt and in a Bukharan
madrassah. His special education and association with the khan was a result of
his origin in the royal family. Historians knew his mother, Aftab Ayim (Umar
Khan's sister), for her strength of character and her royal lineage as a daughter
of Qoqan's khan Narbuta Biy (r. 1770–1800), which made Muhammad
Hakimkhan a grandson of one khan and the nephew of another. These relationships offered him exceptional opportunities to observe the khanate closely.

As a by-product of his status came many personal dealings, not entirely friendly, with Umar Khan's successor, Muhammad Ali (Madali) Khan (r. 1822–1842), from whose control in his native city of Qoqan Muhammad Hakimkhan had to flee. His experience widened through contacts with Russia's Alexander I (1801–1825), Iran's Fath Ali Shah (r. 1797–1834), Bukhara's Amir Nasrullah Bahadur-Khan (r. 1826–1860), and others. He also made a pilgrimage to Mecca and traveled across Iran (dangerous for a Sunni) on his way back to Central Asia.

From this rich exposure to governments and civilizations he brought perspectives that gave his work, *Muntäkhäb ät-täwarikh* (Selected from the Histories, *ca.* 1843–1845), unusual authority and value for the study of Central Asian developments.[13] His extraordinary opportunity to observe events in southern Central Asia from both the Bukharan and the Qoqanian sides brought to Muhammad Hakimkhan's writing more than the laudable royal dispassion and lack of eulogy. He functioned as a synthesizer, reaching beyond the narrow constraints exercised by strictly local or dynastic historiography on its authors. His open eyes and mind conveyed to readers an understanding of much that put the Central Asian states increasingly at risk. In his and others' treatment, Muhammad Ali Khan is credited with turning the flourishing country of Qoqan into a troubled state shuddering as much from acute internal strife as from repeated hard military blows delivered by Bukhara. Thereafter, in none of the relatively short reigns of his successors up to the termination of the khanate by Russian arms in 1876 could the tormented Qoqan state recover the equanimity it had known under Narbuta Biy, Alim Khan, and especially Umar Khan.

Muhammad Ali Khan was like Amir Nasrullah Bahadur-Khan of Bukhara—a modernizer who drastically changed the character of khanship in Central Asia and the attitudes toward such leadership among the public. This contribution to the modernization of Central Asia was more than showing the people another unjust amir or khan, for they had seen many. Muhammad Ali and Nasrullah Bahadur-Khan appeared simultaneously at a time when people's hope and faith in the sovereign needed reward; instead, these rulers proffered a spectacle of despair.

Yet to philosophical historians Amir Nasrullah was an imperfect specimen of a bad king, for he widened the domains of the state and strengthened his hold on the government. His gestures toward religion attracted approval from high clergy. He fixed most Uzbek tribal leadership to their tribal lands, which reduced their threat to central rule but at the same time greatly increased the vulnerability of the periphery to outside incursions. These policies, invariably involving violence and intimidation, validated the popular notion that an evil ruler makes his people ill and that human affairs remain beyond earthly justice. One Bukharan historian, who characterized Shah Murad as "the sinless Amir" and Amir Haydar Tora as "learned, generous, and just," wrote that "[Amir Nasrullah Bahadur] was a cruel, bloodthirsty sovereign; he took nothing and no one into account." Another, the amir's contemporary, judged him even more harshly, concluding that his 35-year rule represented Bukhara's fall: "after 1834, a decline began in affairs of religion and state."

Amir Nasrullah's most negative legacy may have been his son Muzaffar, the next amir, who joined stupidity and stubbornness to his father's cruelty. In defense of Amir Nasrullah, the record shows that he designated one of his grandsons heir to the throne, for he had noticed that "perversity predominated in [Muzaffar's] nature." Muzaffar, like Amir Nasrullah, murdered the designated heir and seized the throne. These dynastic brutalities, new in the Manghit succession, added black marks to the esteem in which the public hoped to hold its ruler. By word of mouth they learned that Amir Muzaffar had chosen the moment when Russian Christians were besieging Tashkent in 1865 to unleash the fury of his artillery to break down the walls of Muslim Qoqan.

Some Bukharans wondered if Amir Muzaffar was the real offspring of the Manghit royal line. One elder, referring to the amir's debaucheries, said to the Bukharan historian Ahmad Danish (1827–1897): "I think that our amir [Muzaffar] is not the son of Amir Nasrullah. Probably, his father was a dancer or clown. A person of noble origin would not give himself up to these sinful and stupid fancies." This widening cleavage between the ruler and ruled would express itself in indifference toward infidel Christians pouring down on Islamic Bukhara.

History may regard Muhammad Ali Khan, Amir Nasrullah Bahadur-Khan, and Amir Muzaffar as Central Asia's first indigenous rulers to become modern in that they were incapable of beneficially adapting or employing new technology or knowledge. Contemporaries considered them personally despicable, unethical, geopolitically introverted, devoid of historical understanding or human consideration, essentially uncultured, and ruthlessly ideological.[14] Personalities alone could not account for this failure in the tradition of Central Asian leadership. The insularity of previous decades that blinded amirs and khans to new possibilities and limitations in both domestic affairs and external relations seemed the true source of these deficient potentates. The phenomenon, however, went beyond capabilities into the crucial realm of character, with the weak or vicious personality stemming from the narrow fanaticism and ignorance of the people responsible for educating the royal princes.

KHWARAZM'S NEW HISTORIES

During the time Khiva, Bukhara's longtime rival in the Amu Darya delta, was helping to strangle the Bukharan prosperity developed with such effort by Shah Murad, an authoritarian Khwarazmian khan was encouraging constructive new cultural growth at home. Under Muhammad Rahim Khan (r. 1806–1825), royally sponsored history writing became again a sign of sovereignty, as it had been in the time of Shaybaniy Khan, Abdullah Khan, and some Ashtarkhanids. A Russian intelligence officer who visited the khanate in 1819 discovered the Khwarazmians enjoying a lively, varied cultural life, including evenings composing verses, reading books, relating stories, performing music, hearing epic narratives and playing chess—a game commonly played in Khiva. A host entertained the visitor with spirited conversation, stories, and a recounting of Eastern history, which "[he] related . . . with passion, mixing into his stories fitting verses from the best poets." The outsider also noticed that the khan strictly prohibited drinking spirits and smoking *bäng* (hemp), thus upholding the Shariat. The ban also may have encouraged clear thinking among the court annalists: "Khivan scholars busy themselves greatly with a knowledge of the ancient history of the East and are quite learned in it. But unfortunately, into it everywhere they mix fables which obscure the truth."[15]

This more recent historiography contrasted with that of the late Ashtarkhanid period as well as the following Manghit era, when each chronicle expressed the apologetic tone of melancholy obituary rather than the affirmative mood with which historians surrounded effective rulers. Central Asian historiography showed winning dynasties or groups recalling their joys and forgetting their sins. In a more positive vein, Khwarazm's court historian, Shir Muhammad ibn Amir Awaz Biy Mirab al-Munis (1778–1829), started a chronicle that would run for more than a century under a succession of authors. He called his work *Firdäws äl-iqbal* (The Paradisiac Garden of Happiness). Readers also knew it under the title *Iqbal namä* (Book of Happiness). Like Abul Ghazi Bahadur Khan and other historians before him, Munis acknowledged the difficulties of writing a complete history:

> So far as my strength allowed, I researched, clarified, and wrote about the events which took place in that period [from the end of Abul Ghazi Bahadur Khan's history as extended briefly by Anusha Khan up to 1665]. But I did not succeed in clarifying the time when many events occurred. Therefore, writing the history of this period extended over a long time.[16]

Munis's nephew, Erniyaz Bek oghli Muhammad Riza Mirab Agahiy (1809–1874), carried on Munis's chronicle from 1813 to the end of Muhammad Rahim Khan's reign in 1825. First an apprentice and a continuer of Munis, Agahiy soon earned a name for himself as a prodigious historian and poet. His various titles carried Khwarazm's history forward almost to the time of his death. In addition, with Agahiy's command of both Farsi and Turki, he translated into the Turki of his region several histories, including parts of that by Mirkhwand and "The History of Nadir" (*Tärikhi nadiriy*) about Nadir Shah, by

Mahdiy Astrabadiy bin Muhammad Nasir, and a number of works about ethics.

Agahiy's chronicles' strength is in their continuity. His annals reached 1872, one year before the last pre-Soviet Russian invasion of Khwarazm, and covered a 49-year period during which five successive khans ruled independently, including the first seven sovereign years of Sayyid Muhammad Rahim II (r. 1865–1910). In the manuscript of his *Gulshän-i däwlät* (Rosegarden of the State), which covered the reign of Sayyid Muhammad Khan (r. 1856–1865), the author commented about this long effort and its aim: "Let it be known to those who read and those who study this book closely that for years on end in my turn I . . . was overjoyed when writing the history of Khwarazm."[17]

When Munis and Agahiy joined historians Otemish Hajji, Abul Ghazi Bahadur Khan, and Mullah Babajan Sanai, they paved the way for one more important Khwarazmian historian in this sequence, Muhammad Yusuf ibn Babajanbek Bayaniy (1859–1923). Because Bayaniy could rightfully claim Khwarazm's Iltuzar Khan as his great-great-grandfather, he also belongs in the select category of historians with royal blood. Like most well-educated Central Asians, he mastered more than one art and skill. He studied medicine and was considered an accomplished calligrapher and musician by contemporaries. *Diwan-i bäyaniy* (Bayaniy's Book of Poetry) came out in both manuscript and lithographed form. Bayaniy used his knowledge of Central Asian languages to translate at least four major histories into what he called Chighatay Turki (Central Asian Turkic) including Ali bin Muhammad al-Hirawiy Binaiy's *Shäybaniy namä* (Story of Shaybaniy) and Abu Ja'far Muhammad bin Jarir at-Tabariy's general history, *Tärikh-i täbäriy* (Tabariy's History).

Bayaniy's two original histories of Khwarazm repeated the period covered by his immediate predecessors—from the late seventeenth century to 1873—and then supplemented them up to 1914. Extending the custom of court-sponsored historiography one last time, Khwarazm's penultimate khan, Asfandiyar (r. 1910–1918), ordered the writing of Bayaniy's major work, *Shäjärä-i khwaräzmshahiy* (Genealogy of the Khwarazmshahs). In his own chronicle, Bayaniy reported on Khwarazm as a state that had once more become the focus of an international power struggle. Both Bayaniy and his predecessors recorded Khwarazm's active diplomatic life nearly every year. Among the ambassadors who came and went during the rule of Allah Quli Khan (r. 1825–1842), Agahiy noted in particular an envoy who arrived with a warning: "From Hindustan exactly in that 1840th year, on January 15, the English ambassador named Häybät Sahib (James Abbott) was honored to kiss the [khan's] threshold." According to Bayaniy's chronicle, in a conversation with the khan Abbott predicted—fairly accurately as it turned out—that the Russians would take over Khwarazm within 50 years and suggested that the khan seek British protection. Allah Quli Khan rejected the proposal, declaring that no one knew who would be here in 50 years and that "now we shall not give our state [*yurt*] to anyone. Let those who come after us do whatever they may wish." Ambassador Abbott's account of this exchange corresponds to the local historian's entries. Despite Abbott's lack of success in persuading the khan to make defensive alliances, he learned, during his dozen or more audiences with Allah Quli Khan, that his Farsi language served him poorly at the Khwarazmian court, where Turki predominated. He also found that the khan considered his twenty badly mounted, venerable brass cannons to represent formidable armament, which told the ambassador that Khwarazm understood nothing of developments in Europe or Russia and thus stood no chance against a more technologically up-to-date enemy. Without outside help, the khanate seemed doomed. James Abbott also records that Allah Quli Khan expressed a lively curiosity about contemporary armaments, shipping, telegraph, and similar developments in Europe and England.[18]

Allah Quli Khan's successors zealously defended Khwarazm's isolation as well as alien ideas and techniques. In spite of the great efforts made by Muhammad Amin Khan (r. 1845–1855), his country failed to stabilize its domestic affairs and was thus unprepared to stop the oncoming invasion from the north. It was internal weakness, not the overpowering strength of the Russians, that produced an attitude of resignation, even detachment, in the khanate.

The literate civilization in Khwarazm began to revive again under the khans after the mid-nineteenth century. As before, this improvement owed its impetus to the court. Sayyid Muhammad Rahim Khan II's biographers wrote that he possessed great skill in Turki poetics—under the pen name Firuz—and in Central Asian music. The khan patronized the arts, collecting a circle of accomplished artists, writers, and calligraphers. When Bayaniy was just fifteen years old, newly subordinated Khwarazm acquired its first modern innovation relevant to the profession of letters, when in 1874 Sayyid Muhammad Rahim Khan II empowered a Persian craftsman to lithograph pamphlets and books in Khwarazm and to train Central Asian lithographers. No indigenous lithographic or printing facilities appeared before then in southern Central Asia.

One of the first such local *basmächi* (printers) was Atajan Abdal oghli (1856–?), only a few years Bayaniy's senior. Atajan's royal lithographic establishment reproduced books of poetry from local historian Munis, writings from Mir Ali Shir Nawaiy, and the verses of the khan. Reports say that the lithographers also issued some chronicles by Munis and Agahiy—the court historians. In 1983 in Tashkent's Institute of Manuscripts the author of this study examined a rare copy of a large Turki-language anthology of poetry by court poets, including the khan, entitled *Mäjmuätush shu'ära* (Assembly of Poets), compiled by poet and musicologist Ahmadjan Ali oghli Tabibiy (d. 1910) on the khan's instructions. A calligrapher wrote out the verses in an elegant Arabic script, and Khiva's official lithographer reproduced the thick edition cleanly and clearly on good, durable paper. Because Bayaniy did not begin composing his *History of the Khwarazmshahs* until 1911, he was too late to appear in the special editions of Muhammad Rahim Khan II's lithographer. The craftsman evidently ceased to issue publications for the court after that khan's death in 1910. Although the Khivan lithography shop stimulated the imagination of intellectuals around the khan and later cultural historians, it issued few books during its 36 years. It did, however, insert into conservative Central Asia a forward-looking technology that could reach a popular audience. By speeding up the techniques of publishing all sorts of writings, it symbolized and accelerated cultural changes badly needed at that time.[19]

The manuscripts of most of Agahiy's histories have gone from Khwarazm into the collections of the Russian Oriental Institute in Leningrad. Neither the second of Bayaniy's histories, *Khwārāzm tārikhi* (History of Khwarazm), nor the first has yet appeared in print in a definitive text or translation. In the case of Bayaniy's later history, that delay in issuing a standard edition may be because the final eight chapters of the work, probably treating the first half century of Russian domination, have not yet come to light. Fortunately, the existing leaves of *History of Khwarazm* carry remarks by the author that place him in the mainstream of history writers in the region who profess objectivity but leave readers unaware of his broader, philosophical outlook:

> There is one requisite for writing a book of history. One must, without showing partiality, write about the historical events and set forth with veracity the events that occurred. If they are not set forth with veracity, its words will not be acceptable to one single man. Therefore, I write with an understandable, simple language, so that the majority may benefit from my own written work.[20]

MYSTICISM REVIVES

Bayaniy's credo of stylistic clarity contrasted sharply with the rhetoric and diction of certain mystical literary schools of his time, particularly the style of Bukhara and Samarkand. That eighteenth-century mysticism carried through into the nineteenth century. Scholars and ideologists retained strong interest in the popular mystical poetry. Further testimony to its impact comes in the amir of Bukhara's decree at the end of the nineteenth century that banned the mystical writings in Mirza Abdul Qadir Bedil's works, calling them atheistic because of their deviation from orthodox writings.[21]

The intensified mysticism in Central Asian Islam expressed itself in another, more drastic fashion before the end of the nineteenth century. At Andijan a charismatic *ishan* (Muslim instructor), Muhammad Ali Khalfa, called Dukchi

Ishan (1856–1898), became a disciple of a Sufi master, made the pilgrimage to Mecca, and attracted great attention in several subregions with his preaching and pious deeds. Eventually he achieved a reputation for holiness, and people contributed to his efforts. He built religious structures, planted shade trees, and, in a poignant gesture, assembled books he could not read, owing to his illiteracy, into a library. In 1898 he embarked with hundreds of his irregular forces on what he termed a holy war against the foreigners in his country—the Farghana Valley. He was hanged on a Russian gallows, and several dozen Central Asians and Russians lost their lives in this outbreak of religious fury and vindictive Russian retaliation.[22]

These feeble reversions to mysticism in the last years of the nineteenth century were a continuation of an old strain of intense belief lingering in both educated and uneducated people. Perplexed Central Asians, now subordinated to Russian generals and bureaucrats in all their political and economic life, saw their institutions and practices of the past, like their technology, as badly out of order and antiquated. This created an ambivalence toward sources of knowledge and understanding that was reflected in the histories of the period and that generated some entirely fresh sprouts in the garden of Central Asian thought. Almost exactly at the turn of the twentieth century, Muslims of Bukhara, Khiva, and the former Qoqan khanate initiated a search for new ways to relate to their backward situation and to the larger world. They began an undertaking in self-enlightenment that would exert long-term effects in the region.

8 Education

'Ilmsiz, ittifaqsiz millätlärning yashayä almasligi tabi'ydur.

Uneducated, disunified communities naturally cannot survive.

(Hajji Muin ibn Shukrullah, 1913)*

The men of Central Asia who dared reconsider the predicament of their people differed in one fundamental respect from those internally governed by fixed habit and rigid tradition: they could look beyond the present arrangements without trepidation to new ways of improvement. To change could save the culture; to reform meant to improve. Ultraconservative officials and clerics could not imagine that they might benefit from the notions of these cultural-social thinkers. Officialdom surrounding the amirs, czars, and khans failed to grasp the idea that transforming contemporary ways and structures did not mean a total change of identity but its renewal. The rulers and their administrators reacted harshly to these moderate efforts and, in so doing, caused a conflict between revival and retrogression. They failed to understand that the Reformists offered the best chance Central Asia might have to retain and improve its Muslim civilization and heterogeneous polities.

Dispersed and diverse, indigenous Muslim *Jädidlär* (reformists, hereafter, Jadids, Innovators, or Reformists) began making an impact in Bukhara, Khiva,

---

* Hajji Mu'in ibn-i Shukrullah, "Istiqbal qäyghusi," *Ayinä*, no. 2 (November 2, 1913):10.

and Turkistan during the first years of the twentieth century. News of events in Azerbaijan, Tatarstan, Afghanistan, Egypt, Iran, and Turkey, as well as the intrusion of Russians into Central Asian life, stimulated constructive responses among indigenous occupational groups, especially those outside the well-established and economically benefited nucleus. The Jadids became active in the Russian governor-generalship of Turkistan, the Khivan khanate, and the Bukharan amirate almost simultaneously. To halt the cultural and social retreat that Central Asia had experienced for so long and to urge the public forward in a new direction, Jadid leaders undertook to popularize several important reforms.

For the indigenous population of the region, they created or adapted six instruments for their purposes: reformist education, historiography, literature, press and publishing, religion, and theater with accompanying drama. These did not appear to unfold according to any coordinated local plan or effort, and some certainly occurred through the intervention of outsiders. All, however, would have an impact on Central Asian civilization.

Muslim Innovators centered in Samarkand, Khiva, Bukhara, Tashkent, and several other ancient cities of Central Asia farther east grappled at the beginning of the twentieth century with a multitude of tasks. In their efforts to bring Central Asia up to date, they demanded a re-evaluation and improvement in ethics, faith, legal justice, public health, the status of women, and additional social and cultural fields.

Living an an area that had recently fallen almost entirely under the rule of a single foreign power, the populace of the region lost an autonomy that dated, with a few short interruptions, from at least the fourteenth century. Certain of the Innovators thus realized that none of their issues could affect them more fundamentally than communal identity. Thus, at the prime of the Jadid drive (around 1913–1916) came what may have been its most significant, long-range intellectual development: adopting terminology for the area in which they and their potential constituency lived. They called it Turkistan, using the term to encompass all southern Central Asia outside the remaining two Russian protectorates and occasionally including those as well. For these Innovators, as well as for much of the public, one powerful determinant shaped the concept of community: their understanding of what had gone before.

Literary innovation—in genres, forms, subjects, language, style, and medium—began to crowd out old-fashioned, stylized writings. The profound interest in community identity that emerged came about not solely in the new thinking about Central Asian historiography but in the schoolbooks and literature of its new era. Of the six reforms, the new education started earliest, lived longest, and probably exerted the most lasting effect on the Central Asian population. To influence the situation as a whole, however, one of the first intellectual endeavors focused on creating a modern Turkistanian historiography.

HISTORIOGRAPHY

Some educated Central Asians at the turn of the twentieth century began to look at history writing as a way of creating a historical awareness similar to that of more advanced nations. Leading Jadids, such as Hajji Muin ibn Shukrullah of Samarkand, understood, as he wrote in the epigraph to this chapter, that a community without a sense of history has no basis for vitality. The Reformists believed that historians must interpret their documents and oral heritage to show readers and listeners how to identify themselves, once more adopting the traditional Central Asian idea of a didactic purpose in history writing. Such an assignment implied not the traditional approach of dynastic Islamic or world history writers or the glorification of the ruler, but rather the general education of the populace. This changed viewpoint, one of the sure signs of the new times, emerged from the intellectual cluster around Mahmud Khoja Behbudiy (1874–1919) in Samarkand and related the role of historical awareness to a new sort of polity. This shift of thought came about logically in Samarkand or Andijan, where no indigenous dynasty still applied hegemony and tradition to their train of thought, and, where in Saint Petersburg, the czar uttered alien ideas in a foreign tongue. In Jadid thinking, history began to conjoin with a community of people, not with the khan. That reorientation altered the outlook of the new men fundamentally and set the framework for all their theories and actions.

One version of Turkistan's past came down through oral tradition, up to then still strong in the largely illiterate society, along with written chronicles or histories circulating through the private libraries of the region. The question then arose whether such sources could sufficiently nourish the quest for re-vitalization. At best those writings could begin to satisfy the needs of the new, forward-looking men; at worst, reliance on the old sources could impose obstacles and rigidities that might hamper the drive for a modern way of life. Between 1903 and 1914 several conventional Central Asian historians completed chronicles about the region's eventful experience. Chapter 7 of this book, "History," discusses the chronicles of the Manghit and Qonghirat dynasties that Mirza Abdal Azim Sami and Muhammad Yusuf Bayaniy completed in the early twentieth century.

An additional chronicle came from Mullah Alim Makhdum Hajji, Central Asian editor of the Russians' Turki-language government bulletin *Turkistan wilayätining gäziti*, printed in Tashkent beginning in 1870. He succeeded in serially issuing his *Tä'rikh-i turkistan* (History of Turkistan) on the bulletin's pages in 1908, 1909, 1910, 1914, and 1915. He subsequently assembled the parts and supplemented them with new chapters to form a separate history of what he called Turkistan, including Bukhara, Khiva, and Qoqan. Mullah Alim

Makhdum Hajji shared the Jadid opinion that other (conservative) Turkistanians, including the literate, regarded history books or manuscripts with suspicion, sensing, probably correctly, that such books conveyed dangerous ideas. Secular knowledge threatened many in the predominately *qadimiy* (conservative) population across Central Asia.

Mullah Alim Makhdum Hajji's further service to education consisted of offering his history when everyone except the Jadids seemed frozen by the cold stare of the established Muslim orthodox *'uläma* (clergy). Writing a useful, accurate history book presented a challenging task to Mullah Alim Makhdum Hajji, who held the local editor's position in the Russian governor-general's Turki-language bulletin, but certain of his motives resembled those energizing the Jadids. He argued, evidently against Muslim conservatives, that the third of three aspects of God's Word, as conveyed in the *Qur'ân* through the Prophet Muhammad, concerned the community of ancestors. This meant, the editor said, "to call into being a discipline or field of knowledge for [recording] the situation and information of the ancients." The majority of nationalities and people and all informed persons accept the advantages of *ilm-i täwarikh* (the field of history), he wrote:

> They especially make extreme efforts to preserve the memory of past tribes and clans of the nationalities [*tuwa'if*] of Turks and Uzbeks; but our [uninformed] Turkistanian Sarts [settled Turkic and Iranian-speaking people mainly in towns of southern Central Asia], giving little importance to history, hardly know their forefathers two or three generations back [in contrast to the customary seven or nine generations], and do not in the least know the narrations and events that occur in their times.[1]

Entreating his readers to forgive his deficiencies as a historian, the author, paraphrasing the famed royal history by Abul Ghazi Bahadur Khan of the seventeenth century, remarked that he composed his work in "a simple, ordinary Chaghatay Turki language [*Chighatay turk tilidä*]." Mullah Alim Makhdum Hajji begs "our Turkistanian brothers" to ponder the great positive changes that he said had taken place in Turkistan since the Russian conquest of Tashkent in 1865. He adds, in Arabic language, "success depends upon Allah."[2]

Despite his demonstrative piety the bulletin's indigenous editor failed to receive acceptance from the Reformists, probably because of his remarks praising the Russian power but also because he served the colonial regime. Educated Central Asians who allied themselves too closely with official or individual Russians in the region generally suffered ostracism by the Muslim community. Other examples of this shunning in the educational and literary fields included Sattarkhan Abdalghafar-oghli (1843–1901), who around 1867 became acquainted with Russians in Chimkent and began to serve them in a token program called Russian-Native schooling. Furthermore, he affected Russian dress, furnished his home partly in Russian style, and in other ways set aside Central Asian tradition. Observers noticed that he lost employment and hope for the future because "he had broken his natural links with his co-religionists . . . many Muslims censured Sattar Khan . . . for having left his own people."

In addition, the local Russians, who too often came to Central Asia as an escape from difficulties in Russia proper, frequently spoiled the situation by bad behavior and venality for Turkistanians. A U.S. diplomat visiting the region in 1873 obtained a copy of a report written by a Russian officer high in the military government that oversaw the Russians' conquests. The unnamed officer wrote that the officer corps was "the true scourge" ruining the Russian reputation. The army of this region, he declared "served[d] as a refuge for the scum of military society . . . most of the functionaries of our administration have been distinguished by their bad character." Scandal and corruption among military and civilian Russian colonialists grew to such an extent that the imperial government initiated a formal investigation and ultimately recommended drastic changes.

Observers later said that the colonial administration "grouped around itself the dregs of the native society." The presence of such poor specimens of the Russian population in association with outcasts from Central Asian society affronted the Turkistanians subject to them and added to the alienation between militant Muslim and Christian communities.[3] Evidently, the Jadids judged Mullah Alim Makhdum Hajji's *History of Turkistan* to be tainted by his links to the Russian regime in Central Asia, for they pursued a Jadid historiography as if this contemporary chronicler and his work did not exist.

Western Turkistan in the early 1900s remained a region vividly conscious of its splendid legacy, however vague and distant, and its people full of reverence for saints and heroes of earlier centuries. Yet the status of history itself—as an intellectual discipline, a record of the ages, or a popular written form—continued precarious. This was not because of a lack of technological advancement or a decline of civilization from its heights centuries earlier but because the centers of discourse and learning strongly felt the grip of an anti-intellectualism that originated in ideological constriction and evolved into pure ignorance and fear. The Jadids of the southern cities now set about breaking the grasp of that unthinking present on the minds of their countrymen and reintroducing them to the affirmative accomplishments of their elevated predecessors.

Prejudice against enlightenment can be expected when religious fanatics and benighted autocracy team up or unite in one ruler, such as Bukhara's Amir Nasrullah Bahadur-Khan in the mid-nineteenth century. After 1900, however, such animus against learning seemed strangely incongruous in light of the changed situation and the elaborate historical record preserved in Turkistan's

Figure 8.1 Photo of Mahmud Khoja Behbudiy (1874–1919), leading Samarkand Reformist. Miyan Buzruk-Salihov, *Ozbek teatr tarikhi uchun materiyallar* (1935).

vast manuscript collections. Both indigenous and foreign scholars appeared aware that these rich funds of knowledge existed, but religious conservatives zealously opposed both writing new histories and using older works.

Mahmud Khoja Behbudiy (see figure 8.1) led the Jadid move to disprove the conservatives' charges that history writing could only serve profane and pointless purposes by arguing that both the sacred book and the traditions of the Prophet Muhammad countenanced acceptance of the lessons of history. Mahmud Khoja pointed out that verses in the holy *Qur'ân* provide many passages regarding historical *khäbär* (information) and *qissä* (expositions) concerning the past:

> In a series of verses, God Almighty's prophets set forth the exposition and situation of historicity and of the events of the tribes of Islam. And they certainly elucidated the exposition and the historical situation and events of the most important tribes [*qawm*] and people [*khälq*] and of the most important men, as well.[4]

Mahmud Khoja also cited an annalist expounding the *'ilm-i tä'rikh* (discipline of history) who noted that history and historical information make up nearly a quarter of the *Qur'ân*. The Jadid leader went on to remind Turkistanians that "these expositions set forth by the Lord God and the Holy Ones of the Almighty constitute the essence and basis for the discipline of history, and they also order us Muslims to study past history as well as the narrations yet to be composed." Later analysts have also referred to the historicity of Islam's sacred book, citing, for example, the Prophet's dealings with the chieftains and Noah's responses to his chieftains in Sura 11:31. Passages in the *Qur'ân* about Alexander the Great also would have been compelling reading for Central Asians.[5]

A second step in the Reformist's effort to elevate the status of history in twentieth-century Turkistan made an open attack on the anti-intellectualism of the established clergy: "Unfortunately . . . some people speak without thinking, calling the study of history and geography a transgression [*bid'ät*]? And a sin [*gunah*]." Such an attitude, Mahmud Khoja Behbudiy pointed out, would leave people woefully uninformed and could lead to disgraceful errors, such as the embarrassing incident that occurred during a *Qur'ân* conference in Samarkand Mahmud Khoja attended around 1907. There, a self-styled scholar, a *murid* (disciple) of the most important, learned *ishan* (religious teacher) and an *imam* (pastor) for a large neighborhood of 200 houses, publicly asked: "Ishan . . . were there commentaries [to the *Qur'ân*] during the Prophet's time?" Astonished, Behbudiy reminded his readers that the writing of such commentaries began several centuries after the Prophet's day. The pious Jadid concluded from the episode that "precisely this failure to study history is a sin."[6] Mahmud Khoja's story of this *mullah* (clergyman) who was not a *mullah* (learned man) seemed doubly ironic because Turkistanian Innovators as well knew that history and geography held a place in the curricula of Muslim higher educational institutions.

Continuing his argument against the conservative opponents of history writing, Mahmud Khoja Behbudiy alluded to the princely behavioral guides so prevalent in earlier Central Asian letters. The motives for meeting this particular religious obligation included, according to the Jadid author, the need for people to study and know history "in order to live in the [present] world, to become intelligent, to be perfected and just. History study is imperative for the padishah, wazir, government official, and politician." Another Jadid author spelled out an additional set of reasons for writing history, rather than merely reading it. Having its own written *milliy* (national) history, he wrote, typified the progressive society and constituted such a community's initial move toward modernity.

> If the time for making the first step on the way toward knowing our national history has not yet come, at the very least we must constantly be preparing to set out on that precise route. If we Turkistanians, giving importance to our national history beginning right from this very day, start undertaking study and research, of course, little by little, complete works of that sort will appear.[7]

An unidentified local author, surely a Jadid judging from his remarks, wrote in 1914 in one of the primary Jadid journals about "The Need for a History of Turkistan" and corroborated their awareness of historical sources and criticized the prevailing indifference toward them:

> We Turkistanians are completely uninformed about the situation of our deceased forefathers as well as the historicity [*tä'rikhiyyä*] of Turkistanian events. For, an ordered and beneficial, perfect work written with fresh research about the history of Turkistan has still not come into being. True, such a historian still has not emerged from among the Turkic sons, and in this respect, because the Turkic offspring have become black sheep [unworthy] we do not have a true son.

The author went on to caution readers not to rationalize Turkistan's lack of a new written history. With regret, he meditated on Central Asia's self-imposed ignorance, declaring that

> We have our history. How many books of history have surely been written in the Turki, Farsi, and Arabic languages about the occurrences and situation of Turkistan and the Turks in former centuries. . . Probably we all remain uninformed about the majority of such history books, but even if we become informed about some of them, we place no importance upon publishing and printing them.[8]

Central Asia possessed rich sources of historical information. Scholars Aleksandr L. Kun, Petro I. Lerch, Eugene Schuyler, Arminius Vámbéry, and others traveled to Turkistan, Bukhara, and Khiva from Europe, Russia, or America late in the nineteenth century to obtain manuscripts in the region's bazaars, from individuals, and from confiscated libraries. Jadid leaders knew that Russians and Europeans were buying and exporting their manuscripts. Reports from Ahmad Zeki Velidi (later, Togan) (1890–1970), a young Turkic scholar who came to the cities of Farghana Valley in 1913, also alerted them to the extent of the dispersion of their materials. The Society for Archeology, History and Ethnography of Kazan University commissioned this enterprising researcher and future Bashkir leader to survey manuscript collections en route to and in the centers of the former Qoqan khanate; the next summer the Russian Committee for the Study of Central and East Asia of the Imperial Academy of Science dispatched him to Bukhara for a similar purpose. During an interview in 1967 with the author of this book, Professor Togan said that he had met with Turkistanian Jadids, including Mahmud Khoja Behbudiy, during those field trips to Central Asia. Professor Togan established close contact with the Samarkand and Farghana Jadids, and his extensive findings, combined with his enthusiasm, disciplined knowledge about Turkic history, and non-Christian direction, made a strong impact. The Turkic framework he offered for historical investigation differed greatly from their accustomed dynastic approach and moved toward the idea of some ethnic division not yet applied in Central Asian thinking about history.

At about that same time, the eminent Crimean Tatar reformist Ismail Bey Gaspirali (1851–1914) visited Central Asia again, and reinforced the ideas of the local Jadids in respect to education, history, and language. He delivered persistently the message that advancement lay through modern learning. His newspaper, *Tärjüman*, exerted great influence on open-minded, literate Central Asians, who made up 20 percent of *Tärjüman*'s 1,000 subscribers.[9]

From Afghanistan beginning in 1911, the newspaper *Siraj ul-akhbar*, in an Iranian language, argued in Turkistan for Asian self-reliance and assertion. Other periodicals in accessible languages that came into the region from Egypt, India, and Turkey conveyed messages about social renovation and ethnic pride. The growing Jadid numbers converged around the belief that Central Asia must modernize and rejoin the greater Middle East, especially the Islamic world. Modernization meant revitalizing the practice of Islam as the basic ideology of the land, ending the dominance of the ignorant, bigoted clerics, and informing the public about the outside world and the possibilities for ending social, economic, and political backwardness in Central Asia. Most of all, modernization signified rearing the younger generation with a new, enlightened unsuperstitious way of viewing their land within the larger universe of people and states. These aims, using new historiography along with many other instruments, brought the local Reformists into conflict with Central Asian officials and established clergy.

A newspaper reader about this time asked the editor of a Jadid newspaper, *Säda-i turkistan*, who would actually write Turkistan's national history. The response: "In our opinion, writing such a history as this will be an extremely difficult task; at present its fullfillment seems to be beyond our capacities." As a consequence, said the editor, Turkistanians placed their hopes on *yash mu'ärrikhimiz* (our young annalist), Ahmad Zeki Velidi Afandi (a person already seen as acquainted with Turkistan's history). That endorsement of the youthful Bashkir historian underscored the acceptibility of the Turkic approach as well as Turkistanian receptivity to having an outsider perform vital cultural service for Central Asia. Ahmad Zeki Velidi had earned Turkistanian confidence through his visits to Central Asia but gained even more from his first book, *Turkic and Tatar History* (1912), which he also published. That study, printed in Tatar in the Arabic script familiar to Turkistanians, included a map of the Great Turko-Mongol Qaghanate of the thirteenth century, the sketched map included Central Asia, and appendixes gave extracts of several medieval alphabets that scribes had employed to copy *Qutadghu bilig* (Knowledge that Leads to Happiness), the Central Asian guide to good government and ethics written by

Yusuf Khas Hajib in eastern Turkistan. Ahmad Zeki Velidi tied Turkistanians to Tatars and Bashkirs to Bukharans in his history, which went up to the sixteenth-century Russian invasions of Kazan and Astrakhan. The Jadids of Turkistan acknowledged that no one of their Reformist persuasion in the region could write such a history with the needed point of view, which came as a painful revelation to their colleagues and journal readers.[10]

The Muslim educational system to some extent created that deficiency. The standard *mäktäb* (primary school) of the region, which excluded historical study from its lessons, occasioned no dismay among the educated public. Jadid leaders felt distressed that their own institutions, the *usul-i jädid* (New Method) schools, drew criticism from conservatives because they included history. In reality, pupils in most New Method schools read only religious treatises such as *Tä'rikh-i islam* (The History of Islam), *Tä'rikh-i muqäddäs* (Sacred History) by Shakirjan Rahimiy, or the anonymous *Tärikh-i änbiya* (History of the Prophets), perhaps a popularization of the medieval work by Rabghuziy and studied no secular history. In time certain Jadid schools, like that of Munawwar Qari Abdurashid Khan-oghli (1880–1933) in Tashkent as well as the reformist madrassah,[11] introduced the history of the Turks and some geography.

That secular history received relatively little attention in traditional institutions and scarcely more in the New Method schools did not mean that open-minded scholars in Turkistan lacked awareness of these important fields and their interconnections. Relating history to geography, a learned Jadid commented, "In order to understand history well, one must have geography, too. History will explain a certain event; geography, however, will describe the place where that particular event occurred and the influences that brought it about. That is, history and geography are like a container and its contents."[12] The same author went on to detail his understanding of the various subdivisions under geography—mathematics, natural science, mineralogy, botany, history, and politics—and to recognize a unity between astronomy and geography. Beyond this, he asserted, a person must have a knowledge of geography to understand the four *'änasir* (elements)—fire, air, water, and earth—the climate, the chemical makeup of the atmosphere, chemistry, and meteorology, all of which he referred to as branches of the science of *'ilm-i hikmät* (temporal wisdom). Relating history to the entire range of secular knowledge, he went on to say that studying geography, which encompassed the sciences pertaining to earth and sky, was not only canonically legal but in earlier times had been the subject of Muslim books and those sciences taught in the madrassahs. The present lack of science, equipment, or experiment in the madrassahs, according to the Jadid author, made the contemporary pursuit of temporal knowledge akin to "cook[ing] some pilaw without fire or kettle."[13]

These trends in Jadid thought not only meant directional change in historiography but signified the end of a long isolation from the new developments overtaking Egypt, Turkey, and India. This secular ecumenism derived only in part from the Russian conquest; the press, relatively rapid travel, and other communications contributed frequency and velocity to the process. Urban Central Asians now made contact with a non-Muslim, technically more advanced and organized society and war machine that enforced an alien system of regulations and military controls and dampened local armed feuds and political conflicts in Turkistan, including the outbreaks between Khiva and Bukhara. Surcease from internal strife gave men time to think of positive matters.

Russian military governors, entering only superficially into the social and cultural life of Turkistanians and hardly at all into most people's daily existence, helped freeze cultural and religious expression into their contemporary mode. Russian officials preferred preserving tradition to welcoming innovation; they encouraged new gestures and thoughts for Bukhara and Khiva but regarded reform with hostility in czarist Turkistan.

Regardless of Russian conservatism, the civilization's larger needs had impressed themselves on the Reformists. How, they asked, can we respond to those problems of backwardness? Adopting revamped school curricula and new techniques of instruction meant preparing fresh teaching material. To extend education to adults and adolescents and to create an alternative to the old, narrow public opinion that existed along the thin literate stratum of Central Asian society, Central Asian Jadids experimented with a public press, whose publications represented the area's first privately published local newspapers and journals. These early reforms—new schools, modern schoolbooks, and newspapers—reached some of the target population but left several issues and audiences unaddressed.

NEW AND OLD SCHOOLING

Jadid initiatives had two goals in education—accelerating training and countering old school enrollments. Shortly following the Russian annexation of Turkistan, Russian missionaries and officials began offering schooling to Turkistanian youngsters in a hybrid Russian-Native school. One opened in Chimkent in 1874, as was said earlier, and in time the network and admissions expanded considerably. By 1907, 83 such institutions taught 2,700 local boys.[14]

Before Central Asian Jadid New Method schools appeared in Turkistan (toward the end of the nineteenth century), in Samarkand oblast alone, in the school year 1887, 2,013 standard mäktäb (primary schools) and madrassahs (seminaries) enrolled 23,410 boys and 109 girls. Besides the 1,755 primary schools, the Russians operated four Russian-Native schools for 48 children and twelve Jewish schools taught 317 pupils. Furthermore, Russian officials vigorously objected to Central Asians acquiring secondary education in Russian institutions: "In my view," wrote Nikolai I. Ilminskii, missionary and education specialist, "Kirgiz [meaning Kazaks] and Sarts [that is, settled Turkistanians] should absolutely not be attracted and admitted to the secondary school . . . for the Sarts, Kirgiz [*sic*], Buryats, and Kalmyks the simple, primary, but sound, substantial Russian education is much more useful." In a secret communication to Konstantin P. Pobiedonostsev, archconservative attorney general of the Russian Orthodox Synod of Russia, Nikolai Ilminskii wrote that Ismail Bey Gaspirali, in Bakhchisaray, Crimea, used all possible efforts to spread Muslim enlightenment, to dye Muslim ideals with European enlightenment, to unite and solidify all Muslims in Russia, and to establish Ottoman Turkish as a common language for all Turkic people in Russia. "It means," wrote missionary Ilminskii, "that Gaspirali and company want to bring European education to the Tatars [and presumably to Turkistanians], but by no means via Russia."[15]

By 1916 the number of old-style primary schools in Samarkand oblast had grown to 3,210, and the number of seminaries, to 196. Russian-Native schools increased to nineteen in the oblast by 1910. If the numbers of pupils and students for each school remained constant, by 1916 close to 40,000 pupils were attending the Muslim institutions of Samarkand oblast alone—an average of eleven to twelve children in each school (population growth probably increased enrollments somewhat).

To counter the proselyting trend and to overcome the inertia standard in most Muslim classwork, Turkistan Jadids opened schools of their own and converted a few standard Muslim schools to the New Method. They had a precedent for this in Ismail Bey Gaspirali, the great Crimean Tatar Reformist, who personally founded one of the earliest Tatar New Method schools in Samarkand in 1893. In Andijan at factories and cotton gins, Tatars organized New Method schools no later than 1897 with Tatar instructors for both Tatar and Turkistanian boys.[16]

Central Asians accorded great reverence to learning; building on the Tatar example, that spirit quickly spread the promising New Method in the region. In 1900 young Munawwar Qari Abdurashid Khan-oghli (hereafter, Munawwar Qari) became the first Turkistanian to open a New Method school in Tashkent in the Russian quarter. The same year, a Jadid school appeared in Pustinduzan, near the capital of the Bukharan amirate. Because of local religious opposition, it did not function very long.[17] Mahmud Khoja Behbudiy and a close Jadid associate, Abduqadir Shukur-oghli Shakuriy (1875–1943), established New Method schools in Samarkand as early as 1904 in Behbudiy's house. (Shakuriy opened one by himself in 1901.)[18] Operated on a monthly tuition charge of two or three *som* (rubles) from each pupil, the New Schools would open only to close soon afterward.[19]

Around 1914, the people of Tashkent funded fifteen Jadid schools with 24 teachers and 1,230 pupils, an average of 50 pupils per teacher and 82 per school. Half of those instructors received training in the six-year New Method Shaykhantawr madrassah founded by Munawwar Qari. Seventy-three New Method schools gave instruction in the Farghana, Samarkand, and Sir Darya oblasts between 1910 and 1915. At least six of these admitted only girls. Such efforts also took place outside Russian-controlled Turkistan. Between 1908 and 1913 four, and by 1917 up to ten, such primary schools for boys opened in the Bukharan amirate and Khivan khanate, respectively. Czarist administrators, worried about the secularism of these outposts of new thinking, had by 1917 recorded the existence of 74 New Method schools in the same Turkistanian districts. These figures show the relative stability of the network during imperial Russia's tumultous years of change and its entry into World War I.

Some of these modest institutions gave schooling to considerable numbers of children. In Qoqan, one enrolled 145 pupils, another 85, and a third 80. Abduqadir Shakuriy taught 117 pupils in his Samarkand classroom. When the czarist Count and Senator Konstantin K. Pahlen made an official inspection of institutions in Central Asia in 1908, he found four such schools in Samarkand accommodating more than 200 children. Not underestimating the potential of the reformed schooling, he reported that

> the New Method schools . . . deserve the most serious attention . . . the Reformists of Muslim life even strive to take the (regular) schools into their hands. By proper organization of instruction and matters of administration, they strive to create strong, enlightened warriors for the [Reformist] ideals. In one memorandum of a New Method school teacher it says, "the school is the foundation for creating a unified state in the future."[20]

For that reason and others startling to him, Nikolai P. Ostroumov (1846–1930), a Russian missionary director of the Turkistan Teachers' Seminary and Tashkent Men's Gymnasium for local Russians, attacked the New Method schools in print. (Ostroumov also served as editor in chief of the governor-general's Turki-language bulletin.) At about the same time, Turkistan military governor-general P. I. Mishchenko (served May 2, 1908, to March 17, 1909) identified, among people he called the "natives" of the region, three subversive intellectual currents: anti-Christian ideas of liberation, brewing social change, and reformist ideas filtering in from the Tatars and Turks. State inspectors objected to the use of publications imported from Turkey or uncensored local publications in the schools. After the czar dismissed General Mishchenko from his post for corruption, the new Slavic governor-general of Turkistan, A. V. Samsonov who served May 1909 to August 1914, reported to Saint Petersburg in rhetoric surprisingly similar to the polemics of Soviet politicians: "along with the teachings of these [secular] subjects in these New Method schools . . . goes the propagation of ideas of openly separatist and narrow national character.

And if such schools are left to themselves they will in future become hotbeds not only of pan-Islamism but also of pan-Turkism and pan-Asianism." Two decades later these notions would fan dangerous paranoia among the ideologists of Moscow's political leadership.

Judging from Reformist schoolbooks and curricula, that observation appears exaggerated. General Samsonov felt that the revolutions of young Turks and young Persians had turned the heads of the promising young people in Central Asia. Cooler Russian officials discounted the notion that Jadid schools offered a danger. The superintendent of public schools in Sir Darya oblast, including Tashkent, wrote "I find nothing pernicious in their [New Method schools] existence."[21]

Records show that large numbers of old method primary schools functioned in the Sir Darya and Farghana oblasts of Turkistan, as they did in Bukhara and Khiva. A Soviet researcher estimated the ratio between the populations of pre-1917 old and New Method school pupils at twelve to one, which puts the number of Jadid school children at between 8,000 to 10,000. There were, however, about 6,000 schools occupied in old method instruction in the four oblasts of Turkistan compared with about 100 New Method institutions. Each Jadid school, therefore, taught many more children than did the old *mäktäb*. Given these enrollments, Jadid instruction must have reached many thousands of Turkistanian children between 1900 and 1928.[22]

Several senior Uzbek authors and intellectuals who became prominent in the Soviet establishment have acknowledged the start they received from New Method schools. An alienated Qoqan poet, Hamza Hakim Zada Niyaziy (1889–1929), attended one of the early Jadid schools in Qoqan after 1901. As Tashkent youngsters, Abdurahim A. Ghayratiy (b. 1902 or 1905–1976), Ghafur Ghulam (1903–1966), Rahmatullah Ataqoziyew Uyghun (b. 1905) and Musa Tashmuhammad-oghli Aybek (1905-1968), among the most prominent, and others who later declined to acknowledge it, benefited from the Jadid system of education. In it, they learned firsthand the prevalent methods of literary exhortation and admonition.[23]

SCHOOLBOOKS

During the Jadid period literature, owing to its capacity to teach and entertain simultaneously, became the preferred medium for conveying the Reformist message both inside and outside the school. This procedure accorded with previous practices in Central Asian education, but the message and selection of readings greatly differed. Poems and tales came into the New Method schoolbooks, along with informative essays.

Ädib-i thani (Second Teacher, *ca.* 1903), an early Jadid textbook in Turki, written by Munawwar Qari, demonstrated the departure from standard parochial schoolbooks, as did *Ädib-i äuwäl* (First Teacher, ca. 1901), which taught first-graders the alphabet and its sounds and conveys today much about the Jadids' ethical priorities. Qari's 44-page booklet, *Second Teacher*, which sold for fifteen *tiyin* (cents)—much less than a ruble—moved, in its first seventeen pages, from a brief pious invocation and a discussion of being Muslim to lessons dealing with reading and writing (see figure 8.2). These gave way to the *Akhlaqi därslär* (Moral Lessons) about the child's relation to mother and father and went on to a short story entitled *Bir anäning baläsighä muhäbbäti* (A Mother's Love for Her Child). The edifying tale cautioned children to revere and appreciate their mothers.[24]

Fänniy därslär (Science Lessons) instructed pupils in telling time, complete with a sketch of a pocket watch, and months of the year in three languages: Arabic, Russian and *rumchä* (Turkish). Then the boys and girls learned about the centuries and saw sketches of a steam locomotive and a steamboat. They learned the four seasons of the year, the days of the week in Arabic, Farsi, and Turkish but not Turki, for children knew the Farsi names in Turkistan. The author then offered another Moral Lesson about telling lies and about truth. Another tale demonstrated the lesson with a story about two boys playing at school who broke a clock. When asked who broke the clock, one admitted the truth, for he was a "truth-telling boy." The other blamed his playmate, showing himself to be a liar. A man praised the truth-teller and scolded the liar. Nothing could make the lesson clearer or simpler.[25]

The author included another story about a cruel padishah urged by a darwish to stop living as the best means to prevent further sinning, thus sparing both himself and his subjects more indignities. Under this guidance, the bad padishah corrected himself, "withdrawing his hand from tyranny." This tale presented pupils with the idea of a just king and the notion of redemption and improvement of a bad leader by a quick-witted holy man. This parable gave way to six illustrated pages of animals, fish, and insects and then went on to another Moral Lesson about the *Tärbiyäli balä* (Trained Child) devoted mainly to proper behavior, attitudes, speech, and respect for important people. In this way, *Second Teacher* approached one aim of Jadid education: preparing civil as well as competent people. Geography, state and government, and morality received similar treatment.

A brief story about Iskandar Dhul Qarnain (Alexander the Great) and a *dewanä* (holy fool) who resembled the popular eighteenth-century Mashrab illustrated that renowned potentates display weakness before the smallest of creatures. In the story Alexander the Great could not command flies to stop annoying and biting the *dewanä*'s face and hands. This tale also taught a lesson in humility.[26]

Munawwar Qari supplemented the two final, brief but enlightening tales

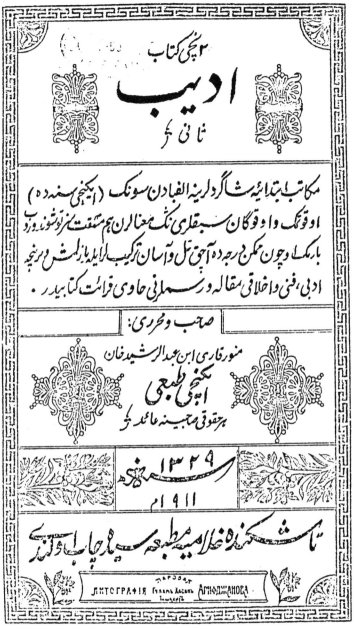

Figure 8.2 Cover on Munawwar Qari's Reformist schoolbook *Second Teacher* (1911, 2d ed.).

with a line or two pointing out the *hissä* (moral). One story, *Ikki yoldash* (Two Comrades), told of a fleet, young companion who abandoned his slow, older friend when a bear rushed at them. The old man saved himself by lying still, letting the bear sniff around his head, and walk away. When the young man came out of hiding, he joked: "Oh friend, what did the bear whisper in your ear?" His companion answered: "It whispered, 'After this, never try to be a comrade to a person who suddenly abandons thee at a helpless moment like this.'" The booklet's conclusion offers rhymed couplets that are easily memorized and signed with the writer's name.[27]

Entertaining, edifying booklets like the *Second Teacher* poured into the New Method schools and bookstalls of Central Asia from Jadid authors. Munawwar Qari prepared, besides primers and readers, schoolbooks for religious instruction: *Hawa'ij-i diniyyä* (Requisites of Religion, 1910), with 36 pages; *Hisab* (1915), with 120 pages, for arithmetic, a radical innovation in Muslim education; *Yer yuzi* (1913), 49 pages, for geography; and additional titles, usually reprinted more than once. The prolific Jadid leader, Mahmud Khoja Behbudiy, wrote at least eight practical textbooks. Stressing the necessity for instructing Turkistanian children about their place on earth, he prepared schoolbooks entitled *Mädkhäl jäghrafiya* (Introductory Geography, 1905), 88 pages and *Mukhtäsär jäghrafiya-i 'umumiy: Asiya qit'äsi* (Abridged General Geography: The Continent of Asia, 1906), 99 pages. He wrote popular primers for beginners and religious booklets such as *Mukhtäsär tä'rikh-i islam* (Abridged History of Islam, 1909), 38 pages.[28] Others known for writing and lithographing Jadid schoolbooks and teaching in New Method schools included the Tashkent intellectual, Abdullah Awlaniy (1878–1934) and Bukharan seminary graduate Sadriddin Ayniy (1878–1954).

The more versatile authors offered a larger range of subjects in their texts, but all declared themselves pious. Many schoolbooks appeared in both Turki and Farsi editions, for Bukharan, Khivan, and Turkistanian schools functioned bilingually. Hamza Hakim Zada Niyaziy's booklet *Yengil ädäbiyat* (Easy Reading, 1914), twelve leaves, gave, in 45 lessons, brief versified stories calling on the young to study and be modest, honest, and devout. The simple, rhyming lines that open lesson one as usual treated religious themes: *Khuda birdur bi sherik / Olmas hich daim tirik* (God is one, without rival / Deathless, ever vital).[29]

From the beginning of the century, elementary textbooks prepared by Turkistanian authors combined with others from Tatars, Turks, Persians, and Azerbaijanians to supply basic needs in Reformist schooling. The variegated offerings by many authors supplemented by uncoordinated publishing in dispersed and distant places created what might have become chaos in the New Method schools. But, although there was no rigid system, the books, the ideas conveyed in them, and the teachers remained surprisingly uniform, even though most of the schools operated independently. That independence may have provided teachers, parents, and children with their most precious instruction.

For the same reasons and because the early authors followed relatively few models, the subjects, too, received similar even if not identical treatment. Jadids worked for practical results. In 1906, an early reformist newspaper quoted Munawwar Qari as speaking out against the old schools' rote learning and their choice of incomprehensible texts for grade-school children: "If we put a reader into the pupil's hands instead of Fuzuli's works, the teaching of dogma instead of Nawaiy, an arithmetic book in place of Bedil, practical knowledge instead of Hafiz, it will yield great benefits, and the pupil will become a true Muslim."[30]

Munawwar Qari understood the need to give children comprehensible readings for their age group, rather than inflicting on them the complex Eastern medieval and late medieval Turkic and Iranian mystic poets. Throughout Central Asian towns, children in the standard curriculum confronted, besides the four Turkic and Farsi poets that Qari named, later mystic poets Sufi Allah Yar, Babarahim Mashrab, and others. Without extended years of schooling few pupils could become truly literate under the old system; nevertheless, in the twentieth century the old grade schools still assigned those difficult, obscure texts starting in the earliest classes. Strikingly literate individuals did emerge from that Muslim educational method, but the system failed to produce a generally literate society in modern Central Asia.[31]

The curriculum in New Method schools offered reading, writing in Turki or Farsi, arithmetic, some natural history, geography, and, always, strong attention to the religion of Islam. Munawwar Qari's six-year program of weekly lessons in the Tashkent New Method primary school in 1911 offered a fairly broad education compared with the standard orthodox curriculum. Each pupil spent eleven hours on religious subjects, using Munawwar Qari's Muslim catechism in Turki, *Requisites of Religion*; passages in the *Qur'ân*; legendary episodes from the life of the Prophet Muhammad using Shakirjan Rahimiy's textbook *Tärikh-i muqäddäs* (Sacred History); and finally the rules of expressive *Qur'ân* reading in the Jadid schoolbook *Täjwid*.[32]

Pupils spent nine additional hours a week studying and copying moral lessons, supplemented by precepts for courtesy and decorum. They devoted four of those nine hours to reading Munawwar Qari's *Second Teacher*, surveyed above. An hour went to Sufi Allah Yar's mystical eighteenth-century poems, no doubt in Farsi/Tajik. Each pupil spent 2 hours on arithmetic, 2 hours on geography, and 1 hour on natural history, which altogether added up to 25 hours of classroom instruction, not an insignificant weekly exposure for young primary school pupils. A fourth-grade class in another Tashkent New Method school (Mirzajan-oghli's) offered 30 hours of classes, using much of the same instructional material.[33]

At a more advanced level, the Jadid madrassahs conducted a broad program with both secular and religious content. Munawwar Qari ran one in Tashkent called the *Namuniyä* (Model) seminary that trained some prominent intellectuals of the Soviet period. When the future poet and novelist Musa Tashmuhammadaw Aybek studied there, the curriculum presented (1) religious doctrine, (2) sacred traditions, (3) history of Islamic doctrine, (4) Arabic grammar, (5) legal inheritance rights, (6) arithmetic, (7) world geography, (8) history of Islam, (9) sacred history, and (10) orthography of Arabic and Turkic writing. Representatives of the various Muslim groups in the Russian empire strove to standardize a curriculum for their New Schools by adopting guidelines resembling the instruction of Munawwar Qari and his fellow teachers.[34] This instruction aimed not so much at prolonging the contemporary structure of employment and society as it did to preparing it for alteration. Jadid teachers intended these programs to make the ordinary child, probably from illiterate parents, into a person who would be proficient anywhere in the society.

Mahmud Khoja (Behbudiy was a pen name) and Munawwar Qari came from modest homes, as did most Reformists. Mahmud Khoja's devout, poor parents lived just outside Samarkand when he was born. People revered his father, a mosque teacher and trainer for boys learning to repeat the *Qur'ân* from memory (*qari*), because he devoted heart and soul to helping the poor. Given that background, the son's lifelong drive to elevate poor, illiterate Turkistanians to a better life cannot startle anyone. Educated in standard Muslim schools, Mahmud Khoja completed his madrassah training in 1894 at the age of twenty, rapid progress for a student of that time. Like his compatriots, the future Jadid leader mastered Arabic and Farsi in addition to his native Turki. Unlike many, he also taught himself Russian. After madrassah he married, had a family, and sent his son to Russian-Native School, where he could learn Russian and some secular subjects. During this time, Mahmud Khoja worked at starvation wages as a scribe for a provincial judge, studied for the law in Bukhara, and started developing a Muslim law practice, which gave him greater economic freedom. The rising Reformist traveled extensively, making his first trip to Russia in 1907, where he visited Saint Petersburg, stopping in Orenburg, Kazan, Ufa, and Tashkent along the way. Later he would travel extensively through the outer Middle East, including Cairo, Damascus, İstanbul, and other cities. In addition to his many contributions to the reform drive, this active Jadid opened the first free library and reading room in Turkistan for Turki speakers. The collection of books and journals that he assembled for this reading room grew to become the largest of its kind and was posthumously awarded his name in Soviet Turkistan.[35]

Munawwar Qari's career differed little from that of Mahmud Khoja Behbudiy. Born in Tashkent, he lost his father and, along with two orphaned uncles, received primary schooling from his mother, Khasiyat Atin, an educated, literary woman. He took more training from Othman Qari to become a proficient *Qur'ân* reciter, then entered a Bukharan madrassah in 1898. Lack of money forced him to return to Tashkent to become a mosque teacher in the Daekhan quarter. He traveled to Turkey for additional education and, when in Central Asia, enlightened himself further by reading the foreign press, such as *Tärjüman*, from the Crimea. Like most educated Turkistanians, he wrote poetry, little of which evidently went into print. His abilities and vigorous efforts in New Method education, journalism, and other activities brought him respect in Turkistan culminating in a leading position in the Ministry of Education from 1922 to 1925 for the Turkistan region.[36]

Comparable biographical profiles should be sketched for the many Reformists who lacked the prominence and authority of these two leaders, for neither these two nor very many others have received appropriate treatment in recent Central Asian scholarship of the USSR. Abdalrauf Fitrat, Hajji Muin ibn Shukrullah, Sadriddin Ayniy, Abdullah Awlaniy, Hamza Hakimzada Niyaziy, Mominjan Muhammadjan-oghli, Fayzullah Khoja, and hundreds of others from that period played lesser but constructive roles in the Jadid effort.[37] Generally, these Innovators came from cities and small towns, not rural areas. Most of them emerged from the lower-middle economic strata of the population, including students in the Muslim seminaries, scribes and clerks, small shopkeepers, bottom-level bureaucrats, and clergymen. However, a few farmers, well-to-do merchants, and more highly placed figures in the religious hierarchy and state gave support and some guidance. Social class alone did not categorize these Reformists.

Sadriddin Ayniy, in a history of the early twentieth century, spoke of the Jadids as high-principled people with an awareness of the world and with a young outlook, regardless of sect, ethnic origin, or occupation. He said that their members included many from the clergy, the public at large, the soldiery, the seminarians, and people of status, including men of commerce and the constabulary. As he termed it, a common urge to oppose evil, tyranny, corruption, ignorance, fanaticism, and intrigue of the rulers, governors, and judges united the Jadids.[38]

The efforts of such men revolutionized primary schooling in Turkistan. Although the quantity of new books lithographed and numbers of readers remained relatively small compared with the quantity of pupils or texts found in regular elementary classrooms, their content differed drastically from anything assigned by old schools. To say that old institutions outnumbered New Method schools amounted to a gross understatement; yet these modest institutions made a huge impact on Central Asian society, especially on the entrenched clergy at all levels. Even a small number of New Method schools frightened them in Bukhara and in Turkistan, just as they did most Russian officials. The establishment's anxiety became obvious when the Russian authorities in Turkistan closed more than 50 New Method schools during the 1910/11 school year and when, on January 1, 1911, New Method schools in Qoqan employing Tatar teachers became the target of an order that discriminated between ethnic groups. The authorities denied individuals from non-Turkistanian Turkic or Iranian communities permission to teach local Turkistanian children and compelled the New Method schools to teach Russian or close down. The amir of Bukhara, in the 1913/14 school season, closed all New Method schools known in the amirate; Jadid schools then shifted to other towns in the amirate, including Karki and Shahr-i Sabz. Throughout Turkistan and Bukhara, officials denied legal permissions required to open the New Method schools. The five New Method schools organized in the Khivan khanate at Yangi Urganch, Khiva city, Qonghirat, and Gurlen from 1905 to 1911 led a precarious existence because of extreme conservative opposition.[39]

The insignificant but growing number of Jadid schools plainly bothered the authorities, but what the instructors said in those classrooms seemed to disturb officials and old-fashioned mullahs even more. Although control undoubtedly constituted the basic conflict, content in these new institutions became the overt public issue. The Reformists intended to draw the culture of the region into a new shape. Conservatives at all levels adamantly opposed the alteration of the cultural institutions or expressions.

The New Method school textbooks, though vague, specified new forms of geographic and ethnic identity as well. At the time, such imprecision could be expected, for European notions about nationality and nation remained alien to Central Asia. The Reformist press, created by the same men who opened the New Method schools and wrote the schoolbooks, gave much attention to communal and territorial identity for the population. But group identity by no means preoccupied the thoughts of Jadids, for other problems seemed more pressing. At least a portion of the Central Asian public, however, began to engage in sustained discussions concerning the emerging human group framework within which it would be appropriate to institute a new social and cultural orientation.

9 Culture and Religion

The falcons were extraordinarily well trained, the best-educated beings in all of Bokhara, humans not excepted.

(Andrew D. Kalmykow, Russian political agent, 1901–*ca.* 1914)*

Religious reform did not so much alter the traditional Islam of conservative Central Asia as slowly displace it. Some members of the community drew away into a revived, cleansed, loosely related congregation. A few religious leaders expressed the new views in polemics printed in pamphlets and the young medium of the press. Literary innovations—genres, forms, subjects, language, style, and medium—began to crowd out old-fashioned, stylized writings. The second phase of reform startled Central Asia with its political turn and in one instance radically changed for a short time the form of government and in another extracted important political concessions from an existing ruler. (An analysis of the intellectual impact of these developments will come in chapter 10, "Politics.") Although the Reformists exerted themselves to their utmost, most outsiders remained only dimly aware of the importance Jadid reform would have in the region. On the Jadid side of the controversy between the old ways and the new, clergymen led the reform movement.

---

* Andrew D. Kalmykow, *Memoirs of a Russian Diplomat. Outposts of the Empire, 1893–1917* (New Haven: Yale University Press, 1971), p. 202.

Mahmud Khoja Behbudiy became known as Mufti to his countrymen, meaning that they could turn to him for authoritative interpretations of Islamic law. His circle in Samarkand consisted of clergymen, parochial educators, and theologians. In Tashkent, Munawwar Qari, as his title (*qari*) indicated, came out of *Qur'ân* school to serve as an *ishan* (teacher at the mosque). The writings of these leaders and their associates reveal their deep piety and devotion to reviving the great constructive forces of Islam in Central Asia. The confessional schools and the seminaries educated the senior and junior Reformists, preparing them with a background that combined religious reform with features of fundamental revival. The Reformists believed strongly that the teachings of Islam demanded that they improve and defend the faith. Their foremost effort, as chapter 8, "Education," has already shown, entailed banishing ignorance by seeking to spread knowledge in place of blind dogmatism, which required elevating and extending the general education of the public. The New Schools performed that obligation for those whom the Jadid teachers could reach and influenced many of the standard schools to modify curricula and teaching techniques in the New Method direction. Those successes brought down conservative attacks.

The most basic charge against the New Method schools centered on two irrational fears about religion: that the Reformists would turn their pupils into infidels and that Islam could suffer permanent harm from these new ideas. In both the Russian and the Central Asian governments under which the Reformists conducted their educational efforts, the rulers remained wholly identified with the state religion and its clerical hierarchy. The establishment's opposition to change increased the Innovators' problems immensely.

Government and clerical authorities had grounds for their apprehension. The most moderate spokesmen for the new tendency in Central Asia linked the reforming of schools and seminaries to their hope "to achieve progress . . . in order to have our own rulers, doctors, and learned people." Jadid backers among well-to-do merchants recognized economic viability, lively trade, and independent productivity as the bases for progressive development. Besides publishing the newspaper *Tujjar*, these men supported a few existing Jadid schools, opened new ones, and lent social support to the Reformist movement in Central Asia.[1] Growing stronger as the years unfolded, Jadids often spoke of "the benefits of knowledge" to be gained through the New Method schools: "An intelligentsia is a necessity for us Turkistanians just like fire and water are. We especially require people who have a commercial education."[2]

Despite the considerable religious teaching in New Method schools, conservative Muslim spokesmen such as Mullah Abdurazzaq called them harmful, antireligious, and against the state. The old school adherents further branded the New Method schools' young pupils, along with their parents and teachers, *kafirlär* (unbelievers). Established clergymen declared that the Jadid schools deviated from Muslim methods. Conservatives specifically abhorred the phonetic method of teaching language and scriptures instead of rote memorization and uncomprehending recitation. They also objected to including such subjects as arithmetic, geography, and especially natural science, which they believed contradicted the Muslim outlook.[3]

Jadid polemics embodied several aspects of the new religious feeling, especially what they regarded as the pervasive corruption and sinful behavior of entrenched clergymen. Like others before them, the Central Asian religious Reformists knew that general respect and concern for Islam decreased as clerical venality and immorality grew. Jamal al-Din al-Afghani (1838–1897), who came from outside the Russian-dominated part of Turkistan and whose preachings reached Turkistanians by word of mouth and through the press, put the responsibility for Islam's decline and the duty to reform it on Muslims, blaming not only the obscurantism of the clergy but the unenlightened leadership of governments.[4]

The dilapidated state of theological schooling in Central Asia often portrayed in Jadid tracts prompted Reformists to advocate other strong measures to strengthen the faith. Mahmud Khoja Behbudiy focused on several reforms in the pages of his journal, *Ayinä*, where he persistently attacked the personal and social abuses condemned under Islam. Of these, pederasty and alcohol consumption stood out, but religious impurity or sinning concerned Mahmud Khoja Behbudiy even more. Feeling that the ecclesiastical system needed total overhaul, he reasoned that first priority should go to developing new, well-trained clergymen and theologians. Because Bukhara, Khiva, Tashkent, and other centers could not meet that challenge, in early 1908 he proposed sending promising students to Cairo and Istanbul for advanced training. "When the religious scholars come back from Egypt, and the secular scholars return from Saint Petersburg, it will be a basis for the flourishing of our religion and our [*millät*] community on earth and in the hereafter."[5] He reiterated this thought in various media.

THE DISPUTE

In Central Asia an eloquent young Jadid, Abdalrauf Rashid-oghli Fitrat (1886–1938), became Mahmud Khoja Behbudiy's protégé after proving himself an extraordinary graduate of the Bukharan madrassahs. Fitrat spoke out vigorously against the decadence of the religious establishment and its supineness in the face of tremendous problems in Central Asia. His first widely known writing, *Munazarä* (The Dispute, 1909), initially appeared as a Farsi / Tajik pamphlet in Istanbul, where Bukharan Jadids had sent him for further study. This polemic targeted Bukharan readers, but it sounded tones significant to any Muslim audience concerned with self-preservation and improvement. A prominent Samarkand Jadid soon translated *The Dispute* into Turki, making it accessible to all Turkic-language readers. That translation carried an appended short review of the work by Mahmud Khoja Behbudiy, reprinted from the czarist *Turkistan wilayätining gäziti*, in which he chided Abdalrauf Fitrat for not advocating Russian-language training for Central Asian children. The translation, which appeared in Tashkent in 1913, circulated throughout Central Asia, including Bukhara, unlike the Istanbul version.[6]

To make his religious and cultural points, Abdalrauf Fitrat used a traditional Central Asian and Middle Eastern style of imaginary travel account in dialogue form. Set in Hindustan, it pits a visiting European against a Bukharan madrassah teacher on his way to Mecca for a religious pilgrimage. The content and flavor of *The Dispute*—insistent didacticism and repetitive argument rather than brilliant wit and literary flair—aim at persuading by reason and familiar example rather than by literary invention. Nevertheless, the fictional altercation and the topics arising from it certainly differed from conventional *munazarä*s (dialogues), which usually involved a donkey quarreling with a horse, a bow arguing with an arrow, or hashish disputing with opium.[7]

This author exposed the willful ignorance underlying the Bukharan clergy's misreading of the *Qur'ân* and *hädith* (sacred traditions). Says his Bukharan teacher in the dialogue, "if everyone were to strive for knowledge, of course work would remain unfinished and the world would be ruined." The European rejoins, "if the spread of sciences and education harmed the world, the Prophet would not have said in the Tradition . . . 'Knowledge is the glory of this world and the honor of the next' . . . Unfortunately, you of the Muslim nation [*ta'ifä*] wandered off very far from science." Fitrat's foreigner went on to argue that Europeans had looked into the *Qur'ân* and benefited enormously from just one reading of it. "But you Muslims, remaining unmindful of your *Qur'ân*, of the results of its laws' felicity, without sharing in the content of its pieces of sacred information and guidance according to wisdom and law, you plunged into this very well of ignorance-decline-abasement."[8]

Fitrat designated corruption as the second sin. In *The Dispute* the Bukharan seminary teacher tells how the chief judge recommends individuals to the amir for appointments as muftis, scholars, teachers, and the like. Thus according to the Bukharan pilgrim, anyone who profusely praised the judge would receive certification as a teacher or mufti, regardless of his abilities or qualifications.[9]

Monetary gain ensued when the newly appointed mufti or teacher began to deal with the public. Anyone with a problem concerning Muslim law would get an opinion from someone familiar with it and then take that opinion to a certified mufti and receive a legal document. The mufti would charge from 2 to 500 *tängä*s (a silver coin worth fifteen kopecks) to stamp it with his seal. The

Bukharan traveler naively explained to the European that to stamp a legal document without receiving a fee would denigrate religious law, a blasphemy.[10]

Abdalrauf Fitrat wrote another fictional travel account, *Tales of a Hindu Traveler*, which was originally published in Farsi and translated into Russian by Mahmud Khoja Behbudiy to educate Russian readers about Central Asia's cultural predicament. In it, the author created a visitor to the Bukhara of his own day who observed and heard evidence from reliable witnesses about the flagrant abuse of *waqf* (philanthropic foundations') income. Madrassah teachers and staff stole all the money left in trust to support students and maintain the facilities. They then extorted additional fees from the students. The condition of the buildings deteriorated, and the process of education came to a virtual halt.

The Hindu Traveler also witnessed Muslim justice in a wife-beating case. Although the wife withdrew her charge, the chief judge would not unblock the legal impasse until he extorted a payment of 2,000 *tängäs* from her, which she paid to forestall the judge's sending the abusive husband to prison and leaving her without any support or protection. This and many other scenes in *Tales of a Hindu Traveler* reflected how the abuse of religious law or practice affected the economics of everyday life in Bukhara. The tract's dialogues portray the rigidity and misuse of position by clergymen as principle causes of economic decline in the city of Bukhara, Qarshi, and elsewhere in the amirate.[11]

In the four main deviations from true religion pointed out by Abdalrauf Fitrat, next comes wanton disregard of Islamic strictures that ban usury and avoiding alms payments to the poor. He also reminds readers that tradition forbids committing adultery, drinking alcohol, and engaging in pederasty— laying before his readers a modern list of Central Asian sins reminiscent of but not identical to the medieval seven or ten.[12] Personal dissoluteness and extortion broke the commandments but were not the worst offenses, for Fitrat identified the worst as first, Bukharan believers who relied on saintly miracles to support them. In this argument, the Bukharan seminary teacher declared that Bukhara had a protector in Bahauddin Naqshband (d. 1389/90), whose tomb drew pilgrims to Bukhara's environs by the thousands. The European remonstrated, saying that relying on miracles of the saint signified laziness and cowardice that could be neither legally nor intellectually justified. (This passage about Bahauddin evidently offended conservative clergy in Tashkent, for in the Turki edition either the translator or the censors deleted it entirely, along with other sections.) The second kind of irresponsibility pointed out by Abdalrauf Fitrat was the clergyman's rejection of science and modern technology, making impossible the most important duty confronting Muslims in the contemporary situation: defending Bukhara and Islam from encroachments by infidels.[13]

When Muhammad Abduh (1849–1905), the leading Reformist in Muslim

Egypt, became grand mufti of Egypt by imperial decree in 1899, he issued *fatwas* (rulings) that permitted Muslims to dress in European style, to eat food prepared by Christians and Jews, to bank money, and to draw interest; his opponents accused him of heresy and sectarianism. Like Muhammad Abduh, Mufti Mahmud Khoja Behbudiy worked tirelessly to disabuse his countrymen of the confusing or erroneous rules laid down by leading conservative clergymen. In 1915, however, old-style Muslims denounced Mufti Mahmud Khoja Behbudiy as an infidel in Central Asia for ruling that Islam's believers might eat food prepared by Christians.[14]

Hair splitting and relying on rules of etiquette characterized the reactions to Jadid reform. A group of very conservative mullahs from the old schools sponsored a Tashkent journal named (oddly) *al-Islah* (The Reform, 1915–1918) that defended the traditional positions against any sort of monetary banking and questioned the acceptability of European and Russian perfume and of listening to music or singing and the like. Jadid tolerance toward relaxed personal dress or financial arrangements did not, however, extend to religious practices; here, Jadid religious thinkers called for greater strictness. In 1903 Mahmud Khoja Behbudiy wrote a strong criticism of certain ishans and mullahs who distorted Islamic dogma in their *risalä*s (tracts). Primitive craftsmen's guild tracts, for example, gave the right to a local religious guide instead of the prophets of the past—Adam, Noah, Abraham, and Muhammad—to pronounce the *täkbir* (glorification). Mufti Behbudiy called on scholars and muftis to re-examine such tracts and to restore the orthodox Islamic treatment of sacred questions prescribed in the *Shäri'ät* (Muslim Law Code). He also urged artisans to repent their religious errors and cease infractions of Muslim law.[15]

A broad solution to religious decline, inconsistent rulings, and arbitrariness by judges in religious courts as well as individual backsliding would come, it seemed to Mahmud Khoja Behbudiy and his allies, through organization and supervision. Seizing the opportunity, he drew up a plan to establish a single, overall ecclesiastical board for Muslim religious affairs in Turkistan. When Count Konstantin K. Pahlen arrived in Turkistan during 1908–1909 to inspect the Russian administration, Mahmud Khoja Behbudiy delivered the plan to him as well as to the Muslim caucus in the Imperial State Duma. Receiving no response, Mahmud Khoja Behbudiy appealed directly to the clergy for religious reform:

> The clergy, writers, and thinkers of each community [*millät*] set out the subsequent path for their community and give it advice; for the reform of the community's morals, they give people in the mosques admonitions; they teach, in the schools and seminaries, the knowledge and science required in this world and that [next] one; with books and newspapers they conduct discussions and conversations for the sake of the community's affairs.[16]

In these times every thought and action by Central Asian Reformists and conservatives alike bore the stamp of Islam. No responsible person advocated atheism or conversion to another faith. The activity of ethical persuasion thus reached outside the field of religious practice, ritual, and observance. Beyond the walls of mosque and *mäktäb*, newspapers, periodicals, and a new sort of literature communicated the Jadid message to the literate core of Central Asian society.

Reformist theater and drama (the area's only new, indigenous stage art), which they explained as a *janli surät* (living picture), deeply influenced both illiterate and lettered Turkistanians. (It arrived later in Bukhara and Khiva.) The press came to Central Asia in 1906, and drama and new theater, in 1911–1913. Conservative Muslim antipathy to and Russian suspicion of these local innovations greatly complicated and delayed the introduction of these media and arts to the indigenous population. Once they began to function in the towns and villages, however, they spread rapidly with powerful impact. Unlike their experience with public education, the Jadids faced little direct competition and could apply the two media for their own purposes.

THEATER

Sin preoccupied Reformist writings and speech, testifying to the new thought's close ties with traditional ethics and religion, and the Jadids included it in new plays. Their theatrical instinct proved sound, for sinners make engrossing images on the stage. For the Jadid, sin embraced religious and social default, personal conduct, and motive. Avoidance of Islamic prescriptions for daily conduct enraged the men of old ways, the Qadimgi, most. Over everyone whom the Qadimgi castigated hung the medieval list of capital and lesser sins. The Jadids usually brought those traditional commandments into their dramas indirectly, but the horror over serious transgressions added power to the presentation. The greatest offense against mankind, Jadid playwrights and performers demonstrated, was to betray the splendid opportunity offered by a benevolent deity to act positively, to do good for society and the world. Drama placed more emphasis on action than on thought.

The main task of Jadid plays was to show a problem or illustrate wrong ideas about a situation—defining and forecasting disaster that would result from the specified trouble. In the Reformist scheme of things, an authoritative spokesman, an elder or educated clergyman, would argue against making that particular error. (This approach to literature and theater denied the inevitability of predicted consequences.) Then would come an admonition, probably from another right-thinking personage (perhaps a Jadid), to act or to avoid acting in certain ways to prevent the threatened disaster. The dramatist then showed cause and consequence—dire punishment following at once on wrong behavior or thinking resulting in human loss. Ignorance, allied with impiety and disrespect for positive values or for elders, led to drinking alcohol, whoring, pederasty, thieving, wife abuse, and even murder. The basic Jadid message declared that all these crimes represented the disintegration of social order and creativenesss because of the pervasive backwardness of the population. In the end, the play pointed out that moral, sometimes sermonizing about the failure of one character to take action that would have prevented catastrophe. This homily, coming after the predicted disaster, reinforced the opening prophecies and reinstated the force of inevitability as a moral issue confronting Turkistanians.

Up to late 1917 Jadid playwrights did not accept the notion that men were not perfectible, which gave even their most gloomy themes an optimistic nuance or turn that later playwrights from the region seldom, if ever, capture on stage. In the Jadid period, correct thinking—the true ideology—materialized on stage as the sole means to ward off destruction. In the early plays, Turkistan's new intellectuals expressed twentieth-century values with little ambiguity. Players embodied virtues and vices on the stage—virtues by Jadid-like individuals, vices in the wilfully ignorant and errant. Tragedy, by Jadid definition, differed from the usual modern understanding of the word in European culture.

The initial play from a Turkistanian dramatist, *Pädärkush* (The Patricide, 1911) by Mahmud Khoja Behbudiy, carried the label *milliy birinchi faji'ä* (first tragedy of the community).[17] Dramatist Behbudiy's troupe premiered this work in Samarkand on January 15, 1914, to a house jammed with 370 people. The audience saw not only the wages of religious and personal sin but the consequences of failing to take action. The play portrayed idle youth gone astray, but the destruction of a family left the real imprint in the minds and feelings of the audience. Another troupe opened *The Patricide* in Tashkent on February 27, 1914, and it continued to attract crowds all across Turkistan. Copies of the drama sold for twelve *tiyin* (pennies).[18]

Russian censorship prevented Turkistanian authors from writing openly about the colonial dilemma of Central Asian society. Poets and playwrights in Bukhara and Khiva, unable to ignore the power of the authorities to censor literature, turned to symbolic or Aesopian devices to convey a significance beyond or below surface meanings. Their specialized vocabulary and semantic nuance also drew on the immensely popular, mystical Sufi poetry of the Central Asian past, a genre that made an art of multiple meanings.

The Patricide, Mahmud Khoja Behbudiy's only published drama, employed an even larger literary and dramatic double entendre. The plot involves three members of the Rich family and a young servant in a fatal confrontation with six members of the underworld—three outsiders and three Turkistanians. A police officer and the teen-age son of the family move in and out of that underworld, with beer, sex, and money becoming the immediate motives for burglary and the father's murder by his son's surrogate. In the last scene of the drama a long speech by a teacher points out that the son's terrible crime destroyed this small family and canceled the son's potential to carry on the name of Rich, shoulder responsibility, or pass along a positive legacy to his descendants. The son carelessly broke the genealogical connection, so important to all Central Asians, between past and present. Such is the story of the drama.

At a broader level, this somber tale about twentieth-century Turkistan shadowed the literature and thinking of all serious writers in the period because it seemed to presage the end of the Turkistan Muslim community. In that respect the criminal who struck the mortal blow in act 3 could take only partial blame for this tragedy because in the 1900s, the thinking went, to permit even one of Turkistan's young people to grow up in such an unpious, incompetent and lazy fashion counted as nothing less than criminal negligence. Nothing seemed more pressing in the Jadid assessment than finding able, educated, modern people of faith to save the community from total dissolution, which appeared inescapable under the existing system of governance, religious practice, and cultural backwardness. The tragedy in *The Patricide* stemmed from the child's murder of its parent—an analogy for the destruction of spiritual belief along with that of the physical leader and the country. In this respect, Reformist theater preached a sermon of communal salvation through enlightenment guided by purified religion.[19]

From the short (six-year) life of the Jadid theater, no fewer than 25 plays remain. Like *The Patricide*, a number of them enjoyed repeated presentation by all-male troupes, amateur and semiprofessional, in the larger towns throughout Turkistan. Some also appeared briefly in Bukhara, though they may not have played in Khiva—the evidence remains inconclusive. Whether excellent or not according to critical standards, the popular Jadid plays single-mindedly advanced the leading Reformist ideas. The canon thus serves as a paradigm of important Reformist themes. Nusratullah Qudratullah wrote *Toy* (The Circumcision Ceremony) in 1913 to expose extravagance by showing the destructive effects of the custom, common in Turkistan then and later, of spending beyond the family's means on weddings, funerals, and other rituals. In this play, a conservative Muslim teacher, for personal gain, insidiously encourages a father to waste all his financial resources on a circumcision ceremony. A Jadid-like character inveighs against such profligacy unsuccessfully. The overspending later bankrupts the father and sends him to prison. (A Russian Turkologist, well-versed in Turkistan life, commented that the playwright composed this four-act play very successfully.)

Abdullah Badriy's *Juwanmärg* (Prematurely Dead, 1914) aimed at the problem of women's inequality by dramatizing the melancholy fate of a wife and young daughter cruelly manipulated and finally destroyed by a brutal husband who threatened the girl with marriage to an undesired mate. The same dramatist's one-act piece *Ähmaq* (The Fool, 1915) dealt with ignorant provincialism in a comic way by showing a bragging, narrow-minded village huckster who claimed to be a descendant of the caliph but displayed no distinction but miserliness.[20]

Educator and journalist Hajji Muin ibn Shukrullah created five plays in 1916 that ranged across a spectrum of Reformist subjects: women's inequality, poor traditional schooling, drug addiction, pederasty, and the New Schooling. His one-act play *Koknari* (The Addict), amusingly presents life in the lower depths of Turkistan society, where narcotics and quail fighting preoccupy the boy-chasing, disheveled, filthy male near-residents of a local tea house. Only one issue angrily arouses these addicts from their stupor: the rumor that a few Turkistanian young people were learning to speak Russian and going to Russian schools. In this comedy, those living at the bottom of Central Asian society embodied conservative fears of Russification. Another departure in the dramaturgy of this author compared the New Method schools with the old. Shukrullah's three-act play *Eski mäktäb, yängi mäktäb* (Old School, New School, 1916) portrayed 35-year-old Kamil-bay, a progressive partisan of the New Method schools, as a careful, serious, quite educated personage. According to a Central Asian scholar who studied the drama, "[Kamil-bay] is a far-seeing politician who understands perfectly that the time has come when [only] the community to which knowledge is not alien and which possesses well-developed professions can be considered to play the most important role." Kamil-bay's aim is to save the Islamic community of Turkistan by acquiring secular knowledge. Purely religious education could not accomplish this, in the playwright's view. The conflict centers on Kamil-bay and Mullah Achildi, a nervous, fanatic instructor in an old school. This play, perhaps more than any other Jadid drama, pointed out the need for progressive men of action (politicians) to forward Jadid causes. The New Method schoolteacher turns up in this cast of characters but does not assume the most important place in the play. (See figure 9.1 for communist reaction to Shukrullah's play.)

After Samarkand led the way with its gloomy, macabre, and edifying plays, in 1915 Abdullah Qadiriy (1894–1939) in Tashkent, wrote *Bäkhtsiz kuyaw* (Unlucky Bridegroom), and Hamza Hakim Zada Niyaziy (1889–1929) in Qoqan wrote *Zähärli häyat* (A Poisoned Life). These dramas concentrated on the serious family problems caused by Islamic customs of multiple and arranged marriages. These two dramatists—depicting the fatal consequences arising from great human unhappiness within the family—advocated Jadid-style reforms by allowing free choice to all partners.[21]

Abdullah Awlaniy, poet, actor, and theater circle organizer, contributed a pair of plays—*Finäk/Pinäk* (Somnolence, 1915) and *Adwakatlik asanmi?* (Is

Figure 9.1 Communists lampoon playwright Hajji Muin Shukrullah Oghli as ink spiller in attack on reformists. *Mushtum*, no. 24, December 28, 1924.

Being a Lawyer Easy? 1916)—that laughed at the difference between the old and new ways, especially the sloth and inaction of current traditional life. They touched on gambling and narcotics and ended with the difficulties of a Turkistanian educated abroad who could not alleviate misery in his homeland because the illiteracy and ignorance of his countrymen made it impossible to communicate new methods and means for improvement.[22]

Jadid priorities for meeting the needs of Turkistan society underwent fairly rapid adjustment. Thus, in 1917 when Abdalrauf Fitrat composed his first two dramas—*Beggijan* and *Muqäddäs qan* (Sacred Blood)—he focused the audience's attention on the most recent bright spot in Central Asian history. People gave the affectionate name Beggijan to Bukhara's Manghit amir, Shah Murad, (r. 1785–1800), in his time. He became a renewer and almost a sacred hero in popular myth and historical chronicles. He succeeded because of his ascetic piety, his ruthless fight against Bukhara's enemies, and his rejection of wealth.[23] In the theater, emphasis on such a person directed attention to successful Central Asian leadership and the political community that had once flourished in the region. In this respect, these plays by Abdalrauf Fitrat reverberated with the sonority of Mahmud Khoja Behbudiy's drama *The Patricide*.

Local and government press reports make clear that this new medium had a strong, extensive, sometimes negative impact on the region. Conservative clergy deemed Jadid theater Satan's work and banned performances, just as they had proscribed folk players and skits appearing within their territorial jurisdiction. These religious leaders feared that the theater and cinema, both new to Turkistan, would lead Muslim women astray. (That apprehension meant that women were seeing the Turkistanian stage works even if they could not take roles in performances.) Both the ends (to purify religion and to educate the Turkistanian public with Reformist ideas) and the means (these "frivolous diversions") offended the old-fashioned clerics and laymen and shook the Russian Orthodox missionaries and military governors as well. Furthermore, the proceeds from these theatricals benefited the New Method schools and organizations such as the Tashkent Benevolent Association, which was formed to further Jadid activities.[24]

NEWSPAPERS AND PERIODICALS

Information about the New Method schools and the innovations in drama and theater came from the equally new Jadid press. Among the 23 newspapers and journals published or written before November 7, 1917, by Central Asian Jadids to express their ideas, the most influential included *Sämärqänd* (1913) and *Ayinä* (Samarkand, 1913–1915), both edited by Mahmud Khoja Behbudiy, and *Säda-i Turkistan* (Tashkent, 1914–1917), edited by Ubaydullah Khoja and Asadullah Khoja-oghli. Readers also favored *Bukhara-i shärif* (Bukhara, 1912), edited by Ayaseddin Mirbedel, and *El bayraghi* (Qoqan, 1917), edited by the erudite Ashur Ali Zahiriy. Quite a few of these newspapers carried articles in Farsi as well as in Turki. Sources for the history of the Reformist press reveal no Jadid newspapers or journals issued in Khiva, although other reforms advanced rapidly there before 1920. This omission seems odd because Khiva had introduced the first indigenous lithography to the region, but conservative opposition rejected Jadid ideas vehemently in the oasis and may have succeeded in stifling efforts to publish.[25]

Slogans for the Jadid periodicals of those years rarely expressed religious nuances but referred instead to issues vital to the Reformists and to the public they sought to reach. These slogans extended far beyond the religious underpinning of the Reformist movement, but the content of the periodicals continued to forward Jadid principles of religious reform. The new journal *Yurt* (Qoqan, June 1917–) which, like a number of Jadid newspapers and magazines, began to appear after the overthrow of the czar, expressed its philosophy with the alliterative slogan *Hurriyat, Musawat, 'Adalat* (Liberty, Equality, Justice). Its editor, Ashur Ali Zahiriy (d. *ca.* 1937), characterized the journal as a weekly political, social, historical, and literary magazine, thus linking the familiar ideas of its slogan with the practical affairs of the region. In Tashkent three months earlier, Munawwar Qari had begun editing the new journal *Najat*, which, like the publication headed by Ashur Ali Zahiriy, was contributed to by a cosmopolitan group from various communities of the region. *Najat*, too, adopted the slogan Equality, Liberty, Justice, placing Equality first, perhaps because the journal emanated from the capital of the governor-general of Turkistan, where Central Asians felt and saw the presence of powerful outsiders more immediately than in Qoqan.[26]

Like the pamphleteers and playwrights, Reformist journalists denounced drug, alcohol and tobacco use, sexual abuse of children, institutionalized homosexuality, adultery, prostitution, inequality of women, and profligate spending for funerals, wedding celebrations, and entertainments. The Jadid press also came out against war, social and moral degradation, laziness, self-ishness, lack of ambition, disunity in the community, and backwardness in the homeland. They particularly attacked superstition in an attempt to separate fantasy from true Islamic religious belief. Thus they opposed everything that was wrong with Central Asian society except its political stagnation, a subject the Russians censored in nearly all Jadid serial publications, for most emanated from the Russian-Turkistan section of Central Asia.

The three spheres in which the Jadid press advocated reforms not surpris-ingly accorded with the main lines of Reformist thinking: purifying religion and self, revolutionizing education, and perfecting reformed social institutions and practices. From the beginning, Reformist papers and magazines also made it their responsibility to inform readers about the population and geography of the world, international affairs and incidents, and mankind's history and accomplishments. They also reported technological inventions that appeared in the West and reported normal news. With the onset of World War I, they focused their attention on the Russian-Turkish conflict. Editors gave preference to the East and to cultural figures and events connected with Afghanistan, Egypt, Syria, and India, frequently reviewing periodicals and books in Arabic, Tatar, Turkish, or Urdu. Thus one important role of the Jadid press, though their editors may have regarded it as secondary, was to bring public awareness into the twentieth century. These newspapers, informing readers about the vastly different existence experienced elsewhere by both coreligionists and non-Muslims, graphically brought home to Central Asians how their community differed from others, despite the religious bonds that united Islamic countries in western Asia. In this manner the Reformist press paved the way for an evolution in local thinking about group identity.

Jadid newspapers and magazines addressed group, communal, and ter-ritorial identity in articles about history, geography, and religion. The jour-nalists wrote about the *wäzifa* (obligation) to work for the welfare and unity of the *millät* (community) of Muslims of Turkistan and thus all of Turkistan. A survey of Reformist periodicals and newspapers revealed that "the Jadid press habitually saw the community's being 'devoured by others' because of the lack of knowledge, lack of unity, and absence of compassion." Mahmud Khoja Behbudiy's *Sämärqänd* newspaper scolded Turkistanians who studied in Russian schools because "you don't grieve over the community."[27] The Samarkand *Ayinä*, like other Reformist journals, frequently directed its readers' attention to various aspects of the community's significance and life. Writers argued against accepting names for the community from outsiders, such as the Tatar habit of calling settled Turkistanians "Sarts." They equally detested the same Russian practice but could not with impunity criticize it in print. Tatars here served as substitutes for the Russians. *Ayinä*'s writers, discussing the most-needed reforms, specified forward-looking clergymen as the persons best suited to implementing those reforms, which reflected the fact that the Reformist drive depended a great deal on men in the religious professions. The very notion and way of reforming the community provoked controversy, for partisans of the *qädimgilär* (old ways) still demanded blind faith and could not visualize the improvement of Islam through intelligent reform. Critics attacked both the Jadid press and the conservative journal *al-Islah* for failing to advance and glorify Islam and to serve the religious community adequately.[28]

Neither school textbooks nor the press in the twentieth century could avoid specifying some geographic and ethnic identity, as well as religious community. A Jadid schoolbook explained to children that "our homeland [*wätän*] is the Turkistan country [*mämläkät*] and our government is the government of Russia." Another primary schoolbook—describing the community's membership in a larger ideological universe—listed Muslims of the world, including several subgroups from Central Asia, in this order, mixing categories of tribe, ethnic group, and place of residence or occupation: Sart, Qazaq, Qirghiz, Turkmen, Qipchaq, Tekka, and Taranchi. The book does not mention the names Qaraqalpaq, Tajik, Turkistan, Uyghur, or Uzbek.[29] Religious community remained paramount.

OPPOSITION

The Jadid press deserves credit for moving the public discussion beyond parochialism and for bringing a new concept of group identity to Turkistanians. The newspapers thus awakened Turkistanians to broader political consciousness. Although the Reformist serial publications experienced severe censorship, like all other press under the Russians, they created and represented a new kind of community, a reading public. Russian officials refused permits to Reformists who desired to publish periodicals and withdrew licenses on an individual basis. In response, Jadids changed the names and editors of their press and reapplied for official sanction under new journalistic flags. By arbitrarily stopping all of the indigenous Turkistanian presses between 1908 and 1913, except around 1912, Russian administrators, amir, and khan persuaded the new intelligentsia that it had lost something. To the Innovators, such repression deprived people of open communication both among themselves and with and from the larger world. The parallel closing of New Method schools by the same arbitrary authorities reinforced this Jadid understanding of events; these deprivations influenced public opinion more powerfully than the modest Jadid institutions, unmolested, could have by themselves. For the Jadid leadership, the harsh measures and opposition from Russian, amirate, and khanate missionaries and highly placed religious officials helped them convert Jadid reform from a cultural effort into quasi-political resistance against dual repression.

10 Politics

First: [We act to] grant all our people freedom of speech,
freedom of thought, freedom of association; to annul preda-
toriness and tyranny once and for all

(*Manifesto* of the amir of Bukhara, March 2, 1918)*

There was a small band of ruffianly Bokharan subjects, most of
whom had been forced to leave the country, who styled themselves "The Young Bukharan Party"

(F. M. Bailey, 1919)**

Innovations in cultural institutions prepared the ground for new thinking in
other fields. A few years after the height of the Jadid period, a Reformist in
Bukhara declared that the New Method schools, though harassed and feeble,
had helped to pressure the government to change its treatment of people. "I
personally remember very well how our friends, parents, and children gathered
under one pretext or another in the schools of Osman Khoja-Oghli [1878–
1968] and [Abdul Wahid] Burkhan-oghli. Very timidly at first, and then openly,

---

* Faizulla Khodzhaev, "Manifest emira," in *K istorii revoliutsii v Bukhare* (Tashkent: Uzbekskoe
Gosudarstvennoe Izdatel'stvo, 1926), p. 49.
** F. M. Bailey, "A Visit to Bokhara in 1919," *The Geographical Journal*, no. 1 (January 1921):
75.

we began to work in them against the amir personally and against his government."

Fayzullah Khoja (1896–1938), that young Bukharan Jadid, cited the closing of newspapers and of the Maarifat Bookstore by the authorities during 1914–1915 as specific events that further mobilized Jadid sentiment against the political regime and galvanized the Reformist circle. As early as 1909, during the crisis over opening New Method schools in Bukhara, conservatives had declared that the New Method schooling "contradicts the spirit of the Shari'at. In the first year, pupils begin to read newspapers [a truly remarkable achievement in literacy!], in the second they demand freedom, and in the third they dethrone his highness and put him in prison." In fact, Jadids strove to rehabilitate the old order by introducing modern thinking and values but until pushed to the extreme did not advocate overthrowing the ruler.

THE DUMA

Reformists responded enthusiastically to the potential for change offered by the establishment of the Russiawide state Duma, instituted by political events in Saint Petersburg in 1906 and 1907. That deliberative body gave some seats to Turkistan until the Russian ruler revised the rules and disenfranchised the provinces of Central Asia, among others, on June 3, 1907. The newspaper *Tujjar* stressed the Jadid's policy of participating in Russian institutions and giving fealty to the Russian state. With an admonition to the ruler reminiscent of writings in the medieval counsels for kings, *Tujjar* printed an article saying in part: "We must send deputies to the Duma. Our Czar is just and merciful. He will not turn away with empty hands deputies sent in the name of ten million Turkistanian Muslims." The Jadids strove to make the Russian czar into a just king.[1]

Elections to the Russiawide state Duma aroused political party activity that drew the Jadids in. Reformists found nothing strange in allying themselves with two very different organizations. Among the 26 political parties with deputies in the first state Duma, Turkistan's moderate Muslims had the most in common with the Russiawide Muslim Ittifaq party and the Russian Constitutional Democrats. One Jadid rejected alliance with the Russian Monarchists' party, judging it responsible for keeping Russia's Muslims backward in culture and economy. "Along with this," he wrote, "the Monarchists' party is serving as an obstacle between the people and the Czar and [the fact that] it has inflicted every kind of evil thing on the populace is and has been the reason for the terrible spectacle of the autocracy." The Jadid leader advocated following "the program of the Muslim bloc in economic, ideological, and scientific questions and the program of the Cadets [Constitutional Democrats] in political questions." He rejected leftist platforms, observing that "these parties are striving for liquidation of private property and classes, and for collectivizing economic resources. . . The most important thing is this: in the socialist parties' programs the planks speaking about private property, the individual and the family are harmful and contrary to the Shari'at."[2]

The Cadet party's call for creating a constitutional monarchy to replace the autocracy appealed to Turkistanian Jadids, who believed that this would permit them direct access to the Russian ruler for the first time rather than through the local administrators. In 1910 several political developments suggested hope for change to Central Asian Reformists. Internal tensions in both the Bukharan amirate and the Khivan khanate pressed those governments to ameliorate conditions for their subjects. Imperial Russia, embarrassed by their backwardness, also urged reforms on the Central Asian dynasties. With the accession of a new ruling amir and khan to each throne late in that year, came the opportunity. The new rulers—Sayyid Asfandiyar Khan (r. 1910–1918) in Khiva and Sayyid Mir Muhammad Alim Khan (r. 1910–1920) in Bukhara—promptly proclaimed their intention to institute certain reforms. Khiva's Asfandiyar Khan agreed to adopt most economic and public health improvements proposed by a Russian government commission. He promised in his manifesto "always to be a fair judge, to do away with ancient procedures that are hard and burdensome for our people, and to take measures so that prosperity, well-being, and justice will reign amongst our people and that agriculture and trade will flourish."[3] This declaration revived the old idea of the ruler's accepting responsibility for the well-being of all his people.

From the throne, the new amir in Bukhara issued, on December 30, 1910, his first *Färman-i humayun* (royal manifesto) to an assembly of dignitaries, Bukharan nobles, and Russian diplomats. The document read as follows: "We most sincerely wish for calm and peace among the people, and we shall strive, with God Almighty's help, for the happiness of the subjects [*rä'iyä*] and the permanence of the state [*yurt*]." Following that sentence, a spokesman, Mirza Urganjiy, read out some specific commands regarding land grants and regular compensation for high officials in place of billeting and service payments that burdened the population. Evidently, the amir communicated nothing more definite about reform.[4]

Neither ruler's statement accorded the Reformists any recognition, but the messages and their tone of conciliation encouraged the Bukharan Jadids, but not the young Khivan Jadids, who modeled themselves after the Young Turks of the Ottoman state. The Jadids' 1910 Reform Plan called for putting the system of government administration in order and retaining the khanate structure but, as in Bukhara, transferring officials to stated salaries rather than permitting them to make exactions from the public at will. The Jadids demanded new public schools and similar cultural institutions, state land reform and use, taxes to provide equitable distribution of scarce water, and regulation of the wonderful but much abused system of *waqf* (philanthropic foundations).[5]

The year 1910, then, marked the beginning of even more persistent efforts by the Jadids to alter the political situation in Central Asia and thus improve cultural and social arrangements and status for the local people. The triple opponent by now they could clearly identify: the Russian, Bukharan, and Khivan administrators and the practices of government but neither the persons of the rulers nor the political institutions (thrones) of the three political units.

The developing political process left its casualties, for the Jadids' opposition—frightened, desperate and authoritarian, like all such states, medieval or modern—quickly resorted to violence. The Jadids, however, made nonviolence a guiding principle in all their efforts, for it accorded completely with their system of values. No responsible Reformist leader called for physical measures against Russians or Muslim conservatives, and many Jadid positions take on meaning by reference to that pervasive underlying rule. Besides their rejection of violence on moral and ethical grounds, the leading Reformists possessed a sophisticated, subtle grasp of the realities of the Central Asian Muslim situation. The practical Jadids saw that a major disruption of any sort, whether from the right or the left, would endanger the growth of freedom and independence and, as a consequence, appreciated the risk inherent in allowing their members to move toward physical confrontations. Public education and private persuasion, the Jadids felt, would in time surely improve the condition of all Central Asians without the destruction of human life and the economy that would come through forcible revolution. Deploring both violent acts and words, they urged alienated, impatient Jadids like Hamza Hakim Zada Niyaziy to temper the bellicose language of their literary works.[6]

THE LABOR DRAFT

An example of this careful approach to crisis occurred in 1916, when the Russian government began conscripting Central Asians to provide support services to the Russian army during World War I. Until then, Saint Petersburg had avoided calling up Turkistanians for involuntary duty in the armed forces. Important Jadids—Munawwar Qari from Tashkent, Pehlivan Niyaz from Khiva, Osman Khoja-oghli from Bukhara, Qari Kamil from Jizzakh and Abidjan Bek from Qoqan—met at Samarkand in the house of Mahmud Khoja Behbudiy in May 1916 and decided to undertake measures to prevent, if possible, the drafting of Turkistanians into Russian military uniforms. They hoped to forestall it legally and through protest demonstrations; when both tactics failed, they attempted to monitor the process and prevent abuses. Despite their efforts, the situation exploded into riots and mob action, during which gunmen killed both Russian colonists and Turkistanians.[7]

Following the Russian conscription decree dated June 25, 1916, an incident of shooting and killing occurred in Jizzakh Uezd on July 13, 1916, and a general uprising broke out in Central Asia. This large-scale resentment, although partly directed at excesses of Russian colonization, mostly aimed at the military labor draft, which seemed to Turkistanians to betray Russian promises not to force Central Asians into military service of any kind. The insurrection, focused against Russian troops, administrators, settlers, and their Turkistanian agents, spread rapidly and reached far. Russian detachments suppressed the protest quickly and with much bloodshed. Russian officials blamed Turkistanians for the violence. That outcome vindicated the Jadid position against violent action, for Turkistan suffered the consequences of resorting to physical measures against the Russian regime. After conscription became a fact of Turkistan life, the Jadids sought public assistance to support conscripted Turkistanian youths working in difficult circumstances behind the lines during World War I. After the beginning of the worst repression of the uprising by Russian units, *Ghäyrät* (Energy), a Jadid organization located in Qoqan's old city, entered the picture. Referred to as *Yash särtlär* (Young Sarts) by Russian administrators, its members invited Tevkelev and Aleksander F. Kerenskii (1881–1970), the future Russian prime minister, as deputies of the Russian state Duma, to inspect those areas of Turkistan affected by the insurrection and its savage suppression, which continued to take the lives and property of many Turkistanians even after mid-August 1916. In reprisal, Russian colonists and cossacks attacked and killed hundreds of the largely unarmed, innocent so-called Sarts—men, women, and children.[8]

That experience shook the Turkistanian population and, by emphasizing its differences from the Russians, forced Turkistanians to reconsider their relationship to the imperial power. Central Asian Reformists had envisioned a constitutional monarchy in which a largely ceremonial ruler would replace the hereditary Russian autocrat. (In this the Central Asian Jadids differed from Reformists in the greater Middle East; Muhammad Abduh and Jamal al-Din al-Afghani had insisted that only an enlightened despot could improve the lives of Muslims in western Asia.)

Jadid spokesmen had called for cooperating with the Russian state and leadership, for learning the Russian language, and for supporting Russia against Germany in World War I and worked for stability in government and realistic relations with the dominant military forces of Russia. Under the conditions of growing political awareness and hope, Jadids, along with commitment to Russia, strove to strengthen Central Asian society by establishing indigenous institutions and committees to carry out contemporary social and administrative functions and to plan for the future.

In 1913 several Samarkand Reformists cautiously joined forces with Farghana Jadids and the visiting Turkic scholar and future Bashkir commander Ahmad Zeki Velidi (Togan) to lay a foundation for political action. In Qoqan the following year a group gathered around one of the new journals agreed on three general guiding principles consistent with Reformist aims: equality between Central Asians and Russians under taxation and law, priority for land allotment to Central Asians over Russian immigrants to the region, and modern education and training for all. Societies like Ghäyrät, mentioned above, became active in Qoqan from around 1910 on. In 1909 *Bukhara Ta'mim-i Mä'arif-i Jämi'yät-i Khäyriyäsi* (The Bukharan Benevolent Society for Universal Education) in Istanbul and in 1910 *Tärbiyä-i ätfal* (The Society for the Education of Youth) in Bukhara started exercising many cultural and social functions. Along with schools, press, and theater, as well as new libraries and bookstores, these organizations supplied a new structure for a society whose older cultural and social mainstays showed signs of crumbling swiftly into dusty debris.[9]

The activities of these organizations, combined with conservative pressures, compelled Jadids to define their position and seek out ways to better the situation of Central Asians. The Reformists first decided to identify and reaffirm the principles of a rejuvenated Islam as their chosen ideology, having already insisted on a nonviolent road toward their many goals. Their ends and means would soon be codified through the political evolution in Russia in 1917 to something closer to democracy when Russia's last Romanov lost his throne to the new provisional government on March 2, 1917. Central Asian Jadids, like moderates in Russia, faced a political choice. In all three parts of southern Central Asia, Innovators set about building on those structures and precedents to shape the future of their people without again yielding decisions to outsiders. Promptly, in March, reform-minded Turkistanians gathered in a *Shora-i islamiyyä* (Council of Islam). Aware that they could not proceed alone, the Jadids joined with conservative Muslims in a crucial attempt to achieve Central Asian self-determination. Within a few weeks, some 350 delegates from the two factions met in Tashkent to create *Musulman märkaziy shorasi* (Central Council of Muslims), popularly called *Milliy märkäz* (National Center). The delegations included Azerbaijanians and Tatars as well as Turkmens and other Central Asians. Munawwar Qari, Mahmud Khoja Behbudiy, the Kazak Mustafa Choqay-oghli, and additional prominent Reformists also joined the Milliy märkäz and spoke of establishing a Turkistan *Olkä Mäjlisi* (Territorial Assembly) in the future.

The key question in those discussions, which ran from April 16 to April 23, 1917, focused on choosing autonomy, federation, or both for Central Asia. In this context, they broadened the term *Turkistan* to include Bukhara, Khiva, and Kazakstan. Some Tashkent Jadids were ambivalent about supporting federation for an independent Turkistan, even though it would be in a reconstituted and hypothetically democratic Russian state. Samarkand's delegates and some allies stood firm for autonomy within federation, saying, "If we pass up the propitious moment, when we wish to achieve autonomy in the future we shall have to spill a great deal of blood and bear heavy losses."[10] Under these plans lay the assumption that the new Russian provisional government, led by Aleksander F. Kerenskii, would get control over the increasingly violent Russian political action being inflicted on Central Asia.

In their corner of the region, the Young Bukharans' decade of efforts to produce governmental reforms now found an outlet. On the Muslim day of worship, *Jumadi ussani* 28, A.H.1335 (Friday, March 17, 1917), Amir Sayyid Alim Khan held an audience at which his *Qazi kälan* (chief justice) read out in Farsi eight paragraphs of short *Färman* (manifesto) that bore a marked resemblance to the proposals submitted to the throne by the Jadids in 1910. In this 1917 document, the amir proposed reorganizing the administration of the amirate, forming a state treasury separate from his own, and putting officials on a regular payroll to keep them from wilfully remunerating themselves at the expense of the populace. Other provisions included establishing a printing and publishing facility that would issue schoolbooks and information bulletins and, above all, establishing an advisory council whose makeup and purpose the manifesto sketched as follows:

> For the reform and progress of the capital, I desire that they select from among the entire community [*millät*], itself, clear-minded and advisory people who reside in the capital, and that they form an assembly. For the peace and benefit of our subjects located in the capital, let it take action, endeavoring and striving for ordering and protecting the welfare of the capital.[11]

Some two hundred notables assembled to receive the manifesto including dignitaries and favorites of the court, especially the highly placed clerical supporters, as well as two Jadid clergymen from Bukhara and Samarkand, one of whom was Mahmud Khoja Behbudiy. The court admitted a few members of the *Samarkandskii Sovet Rabochikh i Soldatskikh Deputatov* (Samarkand Council of Workers and Soldiers' Deputies), representatives of a similar council in Kagan (the Russian town in the Bukharan amirate), and members of the Russian diplomatic mission in Bukhara. An eyewitness, Bukharan Jadid Fayzullah Khoja, invited through the influence of his uncle, an official, reported that, as senior Jadid leader (then age 43), Mahmud Khoja Behbudiy gave the congratulatory response to the throne after the formal reading of the manifesto, which underscored the importance of the Reformists in bringing about these changes.[12]

Under the guidance of the Russian resident diplomat in Bukhara who drafted the amir's manifesto in consultation with the amir's court, the proclamation received advance approval in Petrograd (Saint Petersburg). In addition to petitioning for these changes, the Young Bukharan Jadids pressed the ruler to adopt a constitution as another step toward democracy and to discharge several ultraconservative high officials of the amirate. When the amir delivered his manifesto, he responded to those Reformist pleas and Russian pressure by replacing the right-wing chief justice Burkhanitdin with the Tajik man of letters and partisan of reform Sharifjan Mahdum (Sadr Ziya, 1865–1931).[13] The amir also named Abdusamad Khoja as the new *Ra'is* (Moralskeeper), warning him and the new chief justice through *Qushbegi* (Prime Minister) Nasrullah, a comparatively moderate official, to keep their distance from the Jadids to avoid tainting themselves with the Reformist ideology so repugnant to conservatives. This caution notwithstanding, the conservative reaction would soon put all three Bukharan appointees out of office.[14]

The Young Bukharan leaders met at the house of Ahmad Naim Nusratullabek, a younger member of the group, in the afternoon of the day the amir proclaimed his reforms. To put the manifesto's provisions into practice, some thought, required an immediate public manifestation on their part, but others disagreed. The more moderate Young Bukharan chiefs—Abdul Wakhit Burkhan-oghli, chairman of the group; Muhitdin Rafaat, and Musa Saidjan-oghli in its guiding committee; as well as Sadriddin Ayniy and Ahmadjan Makhsum outside it—opposed the activists Abdalrauf Fitrat, Osman Khoja, and Fayzullah Khoja, who strongly favored taking to the streets to show support for the changes. Mahmud Khoja Behbudiy, Qazi Haydarbek, and others at the meeting urged moderation. To resolve the stalemate, Mahmud Khoja Behbudiy; Bah Mullakhan-oghli; Mirza Ghulam, the Resident's interpreter; and Fayzullah Khoja, according to the latter's recollection, met with the Russian Resident. His blunt advice, as well as that of the new, moderate prime minister of the Bukharan amirate, was not to hold the parade. Mirza Muhitdin Mansur-oghli, a senior Reformist, urged them to desist. The next morning, however, Fayzullah Khoja deceived leaders of the Young Bukharan committee concerning these negative counsels and actively proceeded to organize a street parade. In this he revealed an arbitrariness and inability to accept advice that promised to cloud his judgment in situations to come.

When officials in Karki and other small towns in the amirate announced the news about the amir's proclamation, the Jadids there staged small parades. In Bukhara, organizers picked a spot near the Shirkat-Barakat store under the dome of the passage to the main bazaar, the usual place for the chiefs and active members of the Young Bukharan party to rendezvous. About 150 people gathered. The demonstration started between 8 and 9 A.M. at that rallying point. As Ahmad Naim Nusratullabek (see figure 10.1) another Jadid participant in the Bukharan action, speaking to the author of this study much later, remembered it:

Figure 10.1 Ahmad Naim Nusratullahbek, Reformist
activist and Young Bukharan, *ca.* 1922. Archive of
Naim Oktem, Istanbul.

The youths gathered in our house. Then we decided to have a demonstration.
We said that the young people should walk to the Ark [citadel], you know, the
amir had the Ark. We decided to go there to thank the amir of Bukhara.
Fayzullah Khoja was there, Mirza Abdul Wakhit Burkhan-oghli was there,
Abdalrauf Fitrat was there. Well, we prepared banners, you know. We made
those banners saying "Long Live the Amir of Bukhara." We had banners
saying [the same thing] in Farsi, *'Zindä bad Amir Bukhara'*. We were preparing these in Fitrat's house. Well, we made those banners. The youths were
carrying the banners. All of us carrying them. We were shouting *Hurriyät,
ädalät, musawat* (Freedom, Justice, Equality), and we arrived at the Läb-i
Hawuz, this large basin in Bukhara. There were several ponds in Bukhara but
this was the largest, called Läb-i Hawuz. This, of course is not Turki, it is
Farsi. It means the pond of the Diwanbegi. In front of the pond was a large
area where people gathered for prayers and all that.

Ahmet Naim Nusratullabek went on to describe how he marshalled the young Jadids in preparation for the march:

> Music, well no, we didn't have music. But, in order to march in unison we wanted to sing a tune, a freedom song. Well at that time, here, in Turkey in the schools, there was this march,
>
> > O fatherland, [*vatan*], O compassionate land
> > Be glad and youthful today.
>
> And then "To the land of the Ottoman." But I replaced that phrase with "To the land of Turan." This march song was, however, a bit long. I taught it to them. [sings] But to my amazement, then people, old-fashioned, I mean, these people who hadn't learned anything like this before, they learned it so fast. Singing this, we moved to the Ark, toward the Ark.

He said that because the streets were narrow and people were throwing flowers from the roofs, it was really, really very excitiing. Everybody was proud.

> And then we arrived there. When we came near the Ark, two cavalrymen on their horses, the amir's officials, appeared. They said, in a stern voice, "halt, halt." We stopped, Mirza Abdul Wakhit Burkhan-oghli looked at me, I looked at him. Fayzullah Khoja and others called "What happened?" We were told that the amir of Bukhara had sent the cavalrymen to stop us from marching there, for the square of the Ark was as white as snow with the turbans of the conservative mullahs. Had we gone there, the mullahs would have slaughtered us.

The Young Bukharan told how they escaped as the crowd scattered and the demonstrators dispersed. His family was well known, and therefore people were respectful toward him. But they were cursing the others, calling them fools, infidels, and the like. He came home. His brother also returned.

> What would we do then? People—some people gathered outside the house, and they were shouting about how somebody was flogged upon the amir's orders, how another person was imprisoned, how yet another was put into the dungeon, and so forth. We were afraid. What could we do? I pondered awhile and then said to my brother, "If we go out wearing our robe [*chapan*], and so on, it would not be appropriate. Let's wear a suit like this and wear a fur fez on our heads. Both of us... Let's leave in the evening; at night. Together."

Although momentarily at liberty, they did not escape the police dragnet.

In Bukhara the street parade that had started so jauntily the morning after the amir's proclamation revealed the young Reformists' vulnerability in the face of conservative fury. The New Method schools, the Reformist principles, and the changes in direction in the amir's manifesto had thoroughly aroused the old-fashioned clerics. Provoked by what they regarded as insulting disrespect toward the pillars of Bukhara's sacred faith, they whipped thousands of ignorant Bukharans into a rage. All the marchers received threats and abuse; crowds stoned and attacked some who tried to hide, and the demonstration wildly dispersed. Police imprisoned up to 30 Jadids, including Ahmad Naim Nusratullabek, his friend Ziyauddin Makhzum, Hajji Mirbaba Muhsin-Zada, Atakhoja-Oghli, Yusuf-Zada, Mirza Sahbaba, Mirza Abu Fayaz, Mirza Ahmad, Mirza Nazrullah Abdulghafur the memoirist, historian Sadriddin Ayniy, and Abdurasul Abdullah-Zada. Severe floggings killed Mirza Nazrullah Abdulghafur and caused serious injury to Hajji Mirbaba Muhsin-Zada and Sadriddin Ayniy.[15]

Shortly afterward, a second Reformist attempt to soften the reaction by contacting the amir turned into another debacle. A delegation of Jadids including Mirza Abdul Wakhit Burkhan-oghli, Mirza Muhitdin Mansur-oghli, and Fayzullah Khoja almost lost their freedom and their lives in the Ark and had to be extricated by the Russian Resident's cossacks from the amir's citadel. From these experiences, most Jadids received a sobering political education. The Young Bukharan leadership fled back to New Bukhara (the Russian Kagan) and on to Samarkand, Tashkent, and intervening places.

Fayzullah Khoja later attempted to rationalize all that had taken place by blaming racial prejudice and political adversaries. Jews, Lezgins, Persians, and Turkic Central Asians had participated in the parade, and, Khoja said, "It was particularly the presence of these national minorities in the demonstration that outraged the fanatic orthodox partisans of Islam." That emphasis on ethnicity most likely represents a backward projection of later attitudes rather than an accurate assessment at the time. Other eyewitnesses did not mention that ethnic conflict had exacerbated the Bukharan events of March 18, 1917.[16]

Fayzullah Khoja's published recollections of these events never showed any sympathy for his injured and terrorized associates or any personal responsibility for the horrifying violence, even though he could be regarded as the instigator of events that not only destroyed the Young Bukharan cultural movement within Bukhara but caused great suffering and death for some Jadids. His offhand attribution to social causes of consequences that he might have prevented, points to the callous split between ethical principles and public behavior that typified him and some other ideological politicians. Deceptiveness to colleagues, manipulative opportunism in dangerous circumstances, and lack of long-range vision would soon make him a Central Asian leader most suitable to the Russian authorities in Moscow.

Bukhara's official reforms thus stopped before they started, and violent interactions made the Russian provisional government seem Central Asia's savior. Such events and the outrages that followed publicly measured the

Bukharan Manghit dynasty against civilized, twentieth-century conduct. The new element was an intellectually articulate alternative to the extreme conservatism of the amir's officials; the Jadid values, programs and mediums now available spread understanding of them among many people. The ruler's resolute negativism and backwardness threw Reformist ideas into sharp relief. He obstinately refused to learn from the Jadids who, like good advisers in the past, wanted to show him the way. Had he listened, he might have earned the respect of his subjects and saved the state. One Bukharan Jadid leader confirmed this when he declared, "Not the slightest doubt can exist about the tremendous significance of the Jadid schools in preparing the way for the revolution. This is absolutely indisputable." By Jadid schools he meant not only the fragile institutions themselves but the Reformist ideas that motivated them and that they propounded.[17]

In Khiva the Jadids enjoyed their greatest political success, although, at first glance, history would not seem to bear this out. The human resources for the movement seemed feeble. The uprising in Saint Petersburg that shook the empire in 1905 soon stimulated formation of a Young Khivan cluster of Innovators, much as in Bukhara, from civil servants, lower clergymen, artisans, and small traders. But Khiva's Jadids concentrated in the khanate's few, closely proximate small towns. The few New Method schools helped Reformists maintain contact. The Khwarazmian settlement area, compact by comparison with Turkistan and Bukhara, made communicating ideas and carrying on activity less problematic. From the north—Crimean and Kazan Tatarstan—into Khiva came the Reformist press. The Khwarazmian intelligentsia thoroughly understood Reformist ideas. The Reformists were shocked by the assassination of the reform-minded, moderate *wazir* (prime minister) Islam Khoja, in August 1912, by political opponents within the khanate's court. Nevertheless, by 1917, Reformists had prepared the ground well for political reform, and early in that year the Young Khivans began to push for their goals in the Khwarazmian oasis.[18]

Khwarazmian Reformists, like the other Jadids of southern Central Asia, preferred peaceful persuasion through constitutional government to force. To achieve this, they assembled clergymen, judges, elders, traders, and guild craftsmen of Khiva, along with some Russian officers, and allied themselves with a Council of Russian Soldiers' Deputies. The chief khanate official, Husayn-Beg Matmurad-oghli, son of a previous conservative prime minister who died in 1901, went with the Young Khivans to the khan's palace to seek reforms. There, on April 15, 1917, Husayn-Beg Matmurad-oghli addressed Asfandiyar Khan (r. 1910–1918) as follows: "My magnanimous khan. Thy subjects who have come before thee pray that thou grant them freedom according to the Sharī'at." He handed over the manifesto that had been composed for the court by the Young Khivans. The text included provisions for a constitutional monarchy headed by the khan, for a *Mäjlis* (Chamber of Deputies), and for a *Nazirlär* (Council of Ministers) to limit the khan's power. It also called for a treasury to control state finances, for the Mäjlis to reform water distribution, for New Method schools to open alongside the old primary schools, and for building railways and postal-telegraph systems. The khan signed it on the spot. A gathering of notables ratified the document in the capital of the khanate on April 17, 1917, scarcely a month after the collapse of the Russian throne.[19]

The manifesto read like the list of Jadid reforms it was. On the day it was signed by the khan, the Young Khivans issued an Appeal to the People welcoming the Khan's reforms. Sounding as much like an internal, Reformist admonition for its own members as a public announcement, the Jadids' appeal, using the traditional word *millät* for community, revealed their concept of a modern nationality: heterogeneous, encompassing the entire community undivided by ethnic or class stratification, and permeated with a spirit of Muslim equality and brotherhood.

> Khivans, taking advantage of the great act of freedom, must awaken their people from the age-old slumber of oppression and illiteracy. If this is not accomplished now, then other people will again enslave our community and use us as their servants, as it was in the old times... Where agreement is lacking, the community will never grow and develop. Away with enmity within the country and the community! The first step in the attainment of equality is to bring knowledge.[20]

Within their circle, Young Khivans greeted the manifesto with joy. The first session of the Mäjlis took place on April 20, 1917, with the participation of 30 deputies, joined subsequently by seven Turkmen tribal leaders. That assembly selected as chairman Muhammad Kerim Baba Akhun from Gurlan, northeast of Khiva and Urganch, and author of the Young Khivan Appeal to the People. Husayn-Beg Matmurad-oghli became head of the Nazirlär. Not long afterward, while a delegation headed by Muhammad Kerim Baba Akhun Salim-oghli visited Tashkent to obtain weapons to arm the new Khwarazmian government, a military coup in Khiva, authorized by the khan, ousted and arrested the main Jadid leaders, including Husayn-Beg Matmurad-oghli. Khwarazm's conservatives denounced the Young Khivans as apostates, just as the Bukharan reactionaries had declared their Jadids to be unbelievers. In Khiva, the conservative upper clergy, landed nobility, and high government officials took over the Mäjlis. This setback notwithstanding, Baba Akhun Salim-oghli and other Khivans carried on lively interactions with the Council of Islam in Turkistan, with the Kazak leader Mustafa Chokay-uli, and with the Afghanistan consul in Khiva. Although geographically isolated, by means of these channels the Khivan Jadids remained in close communication with fellow Reformists throughout Central Asia.[21]

Nor did the Jadid style of language remain the exclusive property of the Reformists. In Central Asia before late 1924, spokesmen for the new government of Khwarazm (formerly Khiva) employed very similar rhetoric because Jadid influence exerted strong political impact there even before the coup in Russia. At the Second Khwarazmian Congress of Councils, convened from May 15 to May 23, 1921, a report on the nationality question remarked that the Khwarazmian overthrow of Khan Sayyid Abdullah (r. 1918–1920) had been "just." In an unwitting paraphrase of Reformist rhetoric, the report styled the overthrowers as partisans of "justice and humaneness" and called on politicians "to elect just, honest individuals" to the Central Executive Committee and to the local councils to root out ethnic hostility by driving out "our backwardness and ignorance."[22]

Although the Young Khivan Reformist government lasted but two months, it evidenced the potential of the Jadid drive and gave notice to Central Asian conservatives, Russian overlords, and colonialists that an indigenous political current, however gentle, already flowed against them. Events in Khwarazm like those in Bukhara in the same period, showed that the small Jadid numbers, notwithstanding their moral and social strength, in the short run would have difficulty dealing with the violence of extremist political opponents. In both Central Asian states, the leaders, trying to gain time for putting Jadid reforms into practice, found themselves dependent on outsiders for protection against the dangerous forces deployed around the dynastic rulers.[23]

In part that happened because Young Khivans and Young Bukharans could not quickly develop wide support in their countries for their ideas. In Turkistan, Reformists labored endlessly to spread their attitudes and influence among all segments of the population. Central Asians who had served as rear echelon labor draftees with the Russian army during World War I came together with tanners, builders, craftsmen, and other working people of old Samarkand in June 1917; a new organization brought in teahouse operators, small tradesmen, and the unwealthy intelligentsia. The several thousand people that gathered at the square of the Shah-i Zinda mausoleums formed an organization called *Ittifaq* (Unity), initially, at least, directed and influenced by Jadids. By autumn of that same year, Reformist initiatives led to political expression in Turkistan that conveyed a peculiarly Central Asian ethnoideological coloration. In September 1917 a new umbrella organization came into being that pulled together various societies and groups for concerted action. The *Turk adämi märkäziyyat* (Turkic Self-Determination Society) grew up in Tashkent with the added participation of Azerbaijanians. In September, the society issued a short-lived newspaper, *Turk eli* (The Turkic People), edited by Shakirjan Rahimiy and others. Jadids also founded the Ghäyrät Library, part of the Jadid *Ghäyrät* (Energy) Association, which had been established some years earlier and which became increasingly important in these developments.[24] The newspaper that it launched in September 1917—*El bäyraghi* (The People's [or Tribe's] Banner)—first spoke for the *Shorä-i islamiyya* (Council of Islam). Later, it became a local paper representing striking Reformist political efforts centered on Qoqan. This newspaper, along with *Turk eli* and *Turk sözi*, supported the Reformist political effort impending in Qoqan. *El bäyraghi*, according to Soviet historians, became the official outlet for the soon-to-be-formed independent Turkistan government and turned into the most important newspaper in Qoqan under the joint editorship of the future Soviet Central Asian scholars and historians Ashur Ali Zahiriy (d. *ca.* 1937) and Bolat Saliyif (1882–1937), both Turkistanians, and some Tatar authors. Demonstrating yet again the characteristic heterogeneity in Central Asia's society and its Reformist ranks, it also showed that Turkistan enjoyed a widespread, talented network of educated men devoted to improving the fortunes of their country through reforms in all aspects of life, from artistic to political.[25]

Tashkent, in the former Qoqan khanate and the Russian colonial hub, became increasingly inhospitable for Reformist efforts. In October 1917, the Turkistanian and Jadid leadership of the *Olkä Musulmanlär Märkäzi* (Territorial Muslim Center) shifted its locus of political action from Tashkent to Qoqan. There, lacking a ruler of their own, they began forming a free, indigenous nation for all Central Asians. The organizers named the new creation *Turkistan Äwtanam Hukumäti* (Turkistan Autonomous Government), which earned fame as the *Qoqan Äwtanamiyäsi* (Qoqan Autonomy). The Kazak whom delegates elected president of that new Turkistanian state, Mustafa Choqay-oghli, remembered the intense feeling generated by that historic moment:

> It stays in my memory as if it were today, the decision of the congress regarding Independent Turkistan [*Turkistan Mukhtariyäti*]. All members seemed to meet it with extraordinary enthusiasm. When they read the decision, all members of the congress appeared to listen closely. When the reading of the decision ended, they applauded with shouts of Long Live Independent Turkistan! [*Yashasin mukhtar Turkistan!*]. A good many persons, non-Muslims and local Jews, wept for joy. And they embraced one another as brothers and congratulated each other.[26]

The congress focused on more than strong emotions, as in both words and deeds the leadership and delegates made clear their commitment to ethnic neutrality and the ideal of independence and sovereignty for Turkistan. In delegations to this unprecedented, extraordinarily multiethnic undertaking in twentieth-century Central Asia, Kazaks and other nomads joined the settled people of southern Central Asia. At meetings in Samarkand and Qoqan, Jadids spoke of their determination to prevent the small foreign minority (of Russians) in Central Asia from deciding the future of "the Muslim majority." They became more outspoken during the Fourth Extraordinary Territorial Muslim Congress, held at Qoqan between November 25 and 27, 1917, when autonomy and territorial integrity overshadowed other topics on the agenda. A Reformist leader declared: "We shall resist with all our hearts anyone who wants to partition our land and property. Essentially, autonomy is created for preserving land, property, and religion.[27]

The interpenetration, cooperation, and interaction of Jadid efforts in the three southern Central Asian political units—Bukhara, Khwarazm, and Turkistan—illustrated this supraethnic outlook that testified to a Jadid propensity and capacity for social and political organization overlapping the bounds of divisive substrata. That viewpoint freed their drive from any strict nationality orientation and complemented the Reformists' guiding principle against violence. Likewise, it explained their dislike for revolution, for the advocates of that strategy made it synonymous with force and violence.

Repeated frustration of Jadid aims in the period from 1916 to the fall of 1917 forced them to search for a more effective strategy, which may explain the late, rather brief appeal of the Turkists, who tried to generate enthusiasm for racial solidarity in answer to the ostensible Slavic (Christian) unity against Turkic and Iranian Muslims. Within Russia's borders, regional identity continued to hold sway over the political imagination of southern Central Asia. The Jadids, unrevolutionary rather than counter revolutionary, did not believe in violent overthrow of ideological opponents. Persuasion and alteration became their watchwords. The Reformist position against violence vindicated those who recalled the Young Bukharan and Young Khivan crises in April–June 1917, when some of them emulated provocative leftist Russian tactics. Throughout the Bukharan turmoil in the spring of 1917, Young Bukharan leaders such as Mirza Abdul Wakhit Burkhan-oghli, Fazmitdin Makhsum, and Mirza Muhitdin Mansur-oghli resolutely opposed both public protest and armed action and insisted instead on legal dissent. Young Bukharan Ahmad Naim Nusratullabek told how even peaceful gestures made publicly in old Bukhara converted the process of reform and steady persuasion into physical reaction and its ensuing excesses. Besides establishing a modern model for peaceful change in Central Asia, Jadids made their media and organizations forums for lively intellectual and ideological discussion of real issues. In this respect, readers of history may regard the Jadid period as the region's first and, up to the late 1980s, the last, modern era of open interaction and lively public discussion among Central Asians concerning controversial cultural, social, and political issues.[28]

When the Jadids revived and modernized the old positive Central Asian values, they gave more to posterity than all the techniques and activities they brought into isolated Central Asia. Going into November 1917, however, no objective observer could doubt that the Jadid momentum in cultural as well as political fields would influence coming developments. Jadids renewed the principles of altruism and generosity for the public good in societies that had in great part grown so selfish that they could no longer defend against foreign manipulation or local abuse.

The Turkistan Autonomous Government (Qoqan Autonomy), born of Reformist parents December 10–11, 1917, became Central Asia's second (after Khiva, earlier in the same year) twentieth-century independent, indigenous state. Its premature death the following year before the muzzles of Russian guns would transform a political style that had offered a peaceable environment for debate into a theater prone to conflict.[29]

11 Homeland

Yeridän äyrilgän yetti yil yighlär,
Elidän äyrilgän olgunchä yighlär.

Anyone parted from his land will weep seven years;
whoever is parted from his tribe will weep until he dies.

(Turkistan saying)*

For Turkistanians, the disappearance of the Russian throne in March 1917 introduced a time of great hope and happy anticipation. All over southern Central Asia Reformists worked to establish a more democratic framework of cultural and social institutions to be provided by representative government. The region's first move toward independence occurred at Qoqan between December 1917 and February 1918. Russian armed destruction mercilessly squelched more than this embryonic experiment in Turkistanian self-determination; the violence provoked more conflict, betraying the Jadid promise of orderly alteration and among the young, in particular, stirred a new militance.

Turkistanian politicians then found in the fourteenth-century Amir Timur a strong appeal to imaginative patriotism. Twentieth-century Central Asians,

---

* M. Äfzälaw, S. Ibrahimaw, and S. Khudaybergänaw, comps., *Ozbek khälq mäqalläri*, 2d ed. (Tashkent: OzSSR Däwlät Bädiiy Ädäbiyat Näshriyati, 1960), p. 19.

hoping to participate in a new society, in 1919 organized *Timur todäsi* (Timur's Band). Authorities did not outlaw membership in the group, in part because a former, much-respected Turkish officer headed it. Around the same time, young Bukharan Jadids circulated political leaflets appealing to "Dear Brothers, Famed Sons of Timur!" Abdalrauf Fitrat, the prominent Jadid author and politician, wrote a historical drama entitled *Timurning saghanasi* (Timur's Mausoleum) in 1918. (Curiously, for a time the play remained in the repertory of the Karl Marx Troupe when it returned to Tashkent in 1918.) Relying on the authority of the medieval conqueror, the play portrays an appeal from the drama's modern hero, "a son of the Turkic ethnic group" and "frontier guard for Turan," to the ghost of the conqueror. In one speech before Amir Timur's tomb in Samarkand the Turkic son declaims:

> My sovereign! A son of the oppressed and plundered Turkic ethnic group, badly wounded in the dust, has come to thee to plea for aid! To thee with a complaint came the frontier guard of Turan, whose gardens are destroyed, whose flowers wound round and unintentionally silenced the nightingales. . . the Uzbek is crushed, the Kazak dead from hunger—rise up, my sovereign!

In each appeal to the Timurid dynast to restore Turkistan's greatness, modern Central Asians saw the obvious political as well as regional symbolism. An outside observer commented a few years later that Turkistanians considered themselves the direct descendants of Timur's legacy and "renewers of Timur's Turkic empire." This would not be the last time that modern Central Asians turned to the memory of Amir Timur for reassurance.[1]

THE QORBASHIS' RESISTANCE

When the Russian military snuffed out the peaceable Qoqan Autonomy, there began an extended period of armed resistance to the Soviet Russians all over the region by Central Asian irregular forces led by warriors who called themselves Qorbashis. Despite the great provocation by Russian troops, the Qorbashis' breaking the rule of nonviolence confounded the pacific expectations of Jadid leaders.

By 1920 violent clashes had spread to Khiva and Bukhara, with Russian guns ending once more the existence of feeble indigenous states and installing new governments against a background of Russian military action and guerrilla warfare. Disconcerted Turkistanian intellectuals found their ideals tested and their ability to function constructively severely constrained, as Russian functionaries in Turkistan quickly instituted rigid new ideological guidelines and restrictions on free expression in place of the old ones. In both Bukhara and

Khiva, Jadid leadership for a short time directed governmental affairs. In the chaos surrounding the turnover of governments occasioned by the Bolshevik coup against the government in Russia in November 1917 and destruction of the dynasties in the khanate and amirate, not every channel of communication immediately came under effective communist censorship or control.

Reformists and like-minded people knew from experience with previous autocratic regimes how to employ publishing, schools, the press, theater, and public and private assemblies to convey their message. Now, however, they altered their tactics and the content of that message to meet the new situation. Many Jadids and their followers helped staff the region's new, Soviet-directed institutions in the expectation that this regime, despite its roots in violence, would occasion the freedom for which they strove. Ambiguous public announcements from the Russian headquarters at first led many local intellectuals to believe that Turkistan would find genuine self-expression in a Soviet-style government.

As the Qorbashis—vilified as Basmachis by the propagandists—fought against the new communist regime, their leaders evolved a new form of government in Turkistan. Foreign scholarship devotes too little analysis to reliable documents of this important resistance movement, principally because in the West there are few primary sources in Central Asian languages.[2] Neither do Soviet publications provide dependable treatment of the subject, though the documentation must be available in Soviet archives. Nevertheless, accessible evidence shows that at the height of the Qorbashi movement's operations in southern Turkistan, its leaders spoke of their fighters as *mujahidlär* (warriors for the faith) and disseminated its political and cultural aims to the people of the region. (So distasteful is the memory of this Qorbashi episode in Central Asian history to Soviet ideologists that communist editors removed the word *mujahid* from their recent large Uzbek dictionaries, though earlier Uzbek lexicons carried the entry.) This Qorbashi program grew out of an extraordinary meeting of resistance leaders in Samarkand City, April 15–20, 1922—the second *qurultay* (Conference) of Turkistan Muslims. Qorbashis from Farghana and Samarkand as well as delegations (around fifteen) of young fighters from Bukhara, Khwarazm, Transcaspia, and the Kazak district of Akmolla (Akmolinsk) gathered to consider the future organization of their territory. (Sher-Muhammad Bek had led the armed fight for a provisional Turkistanian government from May 3, 1920, up to that time.[3]) The Qorbashis' strength was based on the Lokay, Qarluq, Qonghirat, Durman, and other Uzbek tribes as well as numbers of non-Uzbeks fighting against Russian troops.

The conference announced plans for a new entity that would include all Turkistan, embracing the south as well as Turkmenistan and Kazak Yetti Suw (Semirechie) territory. The name these leaders proposed for their future state— *Turkistan Turk Mustaqil Islam Jomhoriyäti* (Turkistan Turkic Independent Islamic Republic)—embodied the Turkistanian ideal of Central Asian unity. In addition to erecting modern administrative structures, they proposed representative congresses to assure ethnic minorities the right to their own locations, occupations, use of mother tongues, and free adherence to religious sects. The conference also called for encouraging foreign trade and protecting private property. Disdaining these affirmative political efforts by the Qorbashis, the Soviet gendarmerie captured Bahram-Bek and Qari Kamil, Qorbashi chiefs of the Samarkand district, and shot and beheaded the two guerrilla chiefs; Kamil, a schoolteacher from Samarkand City; and many others. The savagery that typified the repression came to light when, in September 1922, the organizers of a regional communist party conference in Tashkent displayed the two severed Uzbek heads as trophies. Emigrant sources reported that this throwback to the methods of Amir Timur was not an isolated instance. Jadid leaders could not welcome either the cause or the effect of this resort to arms in Turkistan. One interpretation suggests that the Jadids and Qorbashis saw the dilemma of Turkistan differently and thus disagreed over how to overcome the Russians' brutal use of arms. According to this understanding, the Qorbashis despised the Jadids as pro-Russian; Soviet statements accused the Jadids of supporting the Qorbashis.

Town and country certainly saw the problem differently, but these disagreements probably amounted to matters of degree rather than to substance. Until a deeper study with better sources can be made of the Qorbashi fight and its links to Turkistanian, Bukharan, and Khivan society, the history of this connection between indigenous segments of the population will remain unclear. Jadid writings such as those by Abdalrauf Fitrat and Abdulhamid Sulayman Cholpan suggest that these Jadids strongly empathized with the general aim (liberation) of the Qorbashis if not with their specific motivations (restoration of the amirate, traditional Muslim schooling, and the like).[4]

STRUGGLE FOR GROUP IDENTITY

In the battleground of ideas, where devoted Turkistanians fought against alien ideologists, several themes captured the agenda for intellectual debate. By the nature of the situation in southern Central Asia—still divided into three heterogeneous political and cultural units—modernizers no longer focused entirely on institutional change within a protective state framework. Assuming that they would see positive developments in schooling and the like, they extended the range of reorganization far beyond such concrete structures, thinking about who they were and the contemporary limits of their particular universe. At the start of the twentieth century, intellectual leaders in southern Central Asia seldom found the subject of group identity compellingly interesting, but after the czarist government disintegrated in March 1917, they began grappling with the question of group identity not merely for immediate political reasons but for basic cultural and intellectual ones. Their attempts to find themselves entered several forums, including the periodical press.

When local newspapers and journals first appeared in Turkistan in 1905, they could easily ignore this issue. Now the Reformists—the most active indigenous users of the new media—came to grips in their press with the crucial matter of group naming, which defined cultural constituencies and homeland. After 1917 corporate names again took on great significance, and nothing but logic appeared to restrict their selection. But tension would soon grow between these leaders and their people over two contradictory types of group names. Were Central Asians going to link themselves to their region as a whole or divide themselves up according to some narrower principle? To the extent that the selection of a name remained in Central Asian hands, the chosen designation would most likely encompass the heterogeneity of population that characterized the region and had done so for centuries.

Around 1900, people in southern Central Asia still defined themselves broadly and loosely, finding it difficult to accept tight definitions. In particular the eponym *Ozbek* (Russian *Uzbek*) proved uncertain. One Slavic author, who had links to Russian Orthodox missionaries, advanced the opinion that the name *Ozbek* should apply comprehensively, not merely to one group: "In Turkistan territory, it is accepted that those Turkic people are called 'Ozbek' who hold the middle ground between Kazaks [whom he incorrectly called *Kirgiz*] and the Sarts." In modern Central Asia, people named *Sart* did not migrate but settled down, usually in a southern village or town, and spoke a language they called *Turki*. The designation *Sart* also included urbanites of Iranian stock who had adopted Turki as their main language. To complicate matters further, when the Slavic invaders came to the region around the mid-nineteenth century, they indiscriminately alluded to all southern Central Asians as Sarts if they could not readily identify them as nomadic Kazaks or Turkmens.[5]

In the case of *Ozbek*, that appellation gave way to the more flexible *Sart* centuries before 1900, though the two did not coincide. *Sart* retained its primacy in much of settled life and therefore in reported speech and records until the czarist invasion of the 1850s. Russian adoption of the term *Sart* fixed it even more strongly in both publication and the vernacular of Central Asia. The application of this name to all Central Asians in the south by the foreign infidel conqueror, however, seemed to distort and taint it irredeemably. Not only the occupying Russians but the Uzbeks' medieval kin and strongest Central Asian rivals, the Kazaks, uttered *Sart* in tones that displeased its bearers immensely. One folk etymology explained Sart as a merging of the two Turkic words *sari(qh)* (yellow) and *it* (dog). (A "yellow dog" was a pejorative resembling the identical insult heard in the colorful English of the southern United States.) The noted modern Kazak poet Ibray (Abay) Qunanbay-uli (1845–1904) described in his *Ghaqliyya* (Reasonings) a second Kazak derivation for Sart matching the first with its pointed offensiveness:

> Our Kazaks, encountering Ozbeks, would call them Sarts and make fun of them, saying: "Oh, you so and so's, skirted, gibberish-speaking people; sweet-smiling but abusive behind the smile; oh, you Sarts!" In our language, you see, *sart-surt* means loud sound, jabber, gabble, and *sart* means jabbered, gabbled, roared. That's how we joked over our neighbors . . . If we ran into Russians, we poked fun at them behind their backs, considering them unbridled, credulous people.[6]

Sart also enjoyed official recognition. An early Soviet Russian proclamation (November 24, 1917), signed by Vladimir I. Lenin and Iosif V. Stalin after the Bolshevik coup, referred to Turkistan's Sarts, not Uzbeks. In their appeal To All the Toiling Muslims of Russia and the East, the two politicians addressed "Tatars of the Volga and Crimea, Kirgiz [that is Kazaks], and Sarts of Siberia and Turkistan, Turks and Tatars [Azerbaijanians] of the Transcaucasus, Chechens and Mountain people of the Caucasus; all those whose mosques and prayerhouses were destroyed, whose beliefs and customs were trampled by the czars and oppressors of Russia!" Most of the Soviet documents in the early years after November 1917 continued to employ the term *Sart*, not *Uzbek*.[7]

Whether on the tongue of a Russian colonist or Kazak competitor, Sart survived into the 1920s as an ethnic epithet. An eminent Russian linguist, Evgenii D. Polivanov (1891–1938)—later expelled from the communist party and killed in a Soviet prison for his intellectual independence—reported in the mid-1920s that "In reality, three terms imbued with a spirit of [Russian] colonialism still live on among the uncultured part of the Russian population in the [Central Asian] territory [and] regrettably are aimed at Uzbeks. The three are *Sart, Sartishka,* and *zver* ["beast," in Russian]." Turkistanians also reported the use of such slurs as the untranslatable *sartuqan/sartugan*, which Russians had applied to southern Central Asians even earlier.[8]

Humanists of Central Asia could thus not avoid pondering the question of their group naming. A Marxist-trained local historian wrote of an *"ozbek wäqti"* (Uzbek era) that he said began in Central Asia during the first years of the sixteenth century and continued up to his time (1920s), reflecting the fact that the Uzbeks had an epoch but not a distinct geographic area or population. Another local historiographer writing in the 1920s declared, after substantial research, that "The name [*ism*] 'Ozbek' lost its old grandeur and scope in the recent centuries and has been thoroughly preserved only in the deserts of Khwarazm and of some other districts." In contrast he noted that the name Sart possessed historical status along with clear meaning and now enjoyed such general usage that everyone in southern Central Asia recognized it and that serious consequences resulted from the Uzbek's group name declining "to entirely meaningless status in the last few centuries." One serious result of that fall: the lack of strong monoethnic identity particularly retarded the emergence of a specifically "Uzbek" culture and education in modern times. His testimony gave reliable, firsthand proof that as late as the start of the 1920s no unified, self-confident Uzbek aggregate existed.[9] Documentation from the Turkistan Jadids substantiated the observation.

This evidence explains why some subgroups of Central Asia, later categorized by Soviet politicians as nationalities, still lacked a single, persuasive secondary (ethnic) identity as late as in the third decade of the twentieth century. The people destined to be renamed spread across the extensive territory called Turkistan, Bukhara, or Khwarazm whose various inhabitants' life patterns and language differed from one another. Several dialects within the Turkic tongue distinguished Chimkent, Farghana, Khiva, Samarkand, and Tashkent, but only at Khiva did cultural and language boundaries coincide.

According to the report published in 1925 by the Russiawide Academy of Sciences Commission for Studying the Tribal Makeup of the Population of Russia and Adjoining Countries, "Uzbeks could not conceive of the same sort of unified and distinct ethnic group for themselves as the [nonurban] Kazaks, Kirgiz, or Turkmens." The commissioners found Uzbek cultural-linguistic boundaries "extremely diffuse." One great portion of the group, the Turkified Iranian inhabitants—referred to as Uzbeks by some and as Sarts by the Kazaks—"had nowhere created a particular ethnic identification for itself." Data collectors, instructed to ignore the term *Sart* for the farming census of 1917 in Central Asia, lumped Turkified Tajiks together under the heading *Uzbek*. This methodology magnified the problem of counting either classification accurately and further confused information relating to the vaguely defined groups.[10]

TERRITORIAL IDENTITY

Clarifying this ambiguity remained irrelevant in the short-lived, supraethnic Turkistan Autonomous Government (TAG) based in Qoqan, which acquired a complexion prescribed by the Jadid newspaper, *Säda-i Turkistan* (Voice of Turkistan) (April 1914–May 8, 1917). TAG combined many subgroups of Turkistan and thereby united the heterogeneous region under the selfname *Turkistan* for the first time in history. Usage had located old Turkistan elsewhere and given it another dimension, derived from no self-incorporation. Contributors to *Säda-i Turkistan* included some of the most illustrious thinkers and leaders of the region from the Reformist generations: Munawwar Qari, Abdullah Awlaniy, Abdulhamid Sulayman Cholpan, Mullah Sayyid Ahmad

Wasli, Hajji Muin ibn Shukrullah, Shakirjan Rahimiy, Ubaydullah Khoja (one of its chief editors), Said Ahmad Khoja Siddiqiy, Hamza Hakim Zada Niyaziy, and others who, by their participation, signaled support for the new aggregate identity.

The newspaper drew large numbers of public-spirited individuals and intellectuals from what it called the *millät* (community), meaning Turkistan. A succeeding newspaper, also published in Tashkent, took a similar name *Ulugh Turkistan* (Great Turkistan), in April 1917, but its outlook differed significantly. *Ulugh Turkistan*, dominated and edited by Tatars from Kazan, offered a remarkable extension in the idea and compass of the appropriate framework in which to secure unity, as evidenced by its sponsorship, audience, and linguistic media—Kazak, Turkistanian, and Tatar. By the newspaper's definition, then, all the subregions and Turkic people of Tatarstan and of Central Asia, including Kazakstan and eastern (Chinese) Turkistan, except those of the Transcaspian region, were partners in this Great Turkistan. The newspaper editors felt the Turkistan they represented and addressed to be an ideological or racial concept rather than a fixed geographic, ethnic entity[11] and that this Turkistan conveyed a Tatar world view, not a local focus. In this journalistic usage the name no longer stood simply for part or even all of Central Asia but reflected a political thrust at cross-purposes with any drive felt by Samarkand or Tashkent Turkistanians to refine a notion of homeland and group name peculiar to the people of southern Central Asia. This Tatar concept created tension between Tatar and Turkistanian interests, but it advanced no idea of any specific ethnic subgroups in Central Asia and no measure of a homeland by conventional limits. In delineating Turkistan from that vantage point, ideas remained more important than territorial limits. The extent and human identity of this Turkistan remained vague well into the period of upheaval that began in March 1917.

The first modern attempt to indigenize a Turkistan identity in political terms ended less than three months after the leaders in Qoqan established the TAG, although the name had already acquired popularity and currency in southern Central Asia. A Turkistan committee, appointed April 7, 1917, by the provisional government of Russia, now matched to some degree a Turkistan Territorial Council of Workers and Soldiers' Deputies that held its first congress there April 7–15, 1917. When the provisional government in Petrograd in 1917 and, thereafter, the new regime in Moscow in 1918 moved to reorganize the administration in southern Central Asia, the general popularity and currency of the Turkistan name induced the country's political leadership to employ it for the territorial unit.

The editors of *Ulugh Turkistan* perceived the threat implicit in these manipulations of Central Asian affairs. One of the paper's writers commented:

> When it comes to the country [*olkä*] of Turkistan, the situation is totally different, of course, because the ethnic group [*khälq*] found in it is 98 percent

Muslim... The [Russian] soldiers and laborers located in Turkistan...
mean to go on administering the entire country themselves. Clearly, Turkistan's Muslims will not agree to this proposition, in which two or three
percent govern the remainder.[12]

In that respect, Russian political actions solidified Turkistanian consciousness
by contrasting Central Asian Muslims to Slavic non-Muslims as the political
infighting began.

A new Autonomous Turkistan Republic (ATR), set up on April 30, 1918,
by the Soviet Russian regime, proved more durable than the unlucky TAG. This
new ATR temporarily bore the name Federative Soviet Republic of Turkistan;
Soviet authorities later renamed it the Turkistan Autonomous Soviet Socialist
Republic (TASSR). From the outset, the ATR struggled with the ethnic principle—an intangible, invisible opponent—in addition to the dictatorial leadership of the Russian Socialist Federated Soviet Republic (RSFSR), which was
unfriendly to ATR almost from the start.

The principle of monoethnicity aimed to reduce or neutralize the influence
in Turkistan of any heterogeneous entity, tribe, or ethnic group that possessed
large numbers and stretched throughout the region. The new political managers
tried to concentrate certain dispersed groups into relatively compact bases. As
early as 1920, perhaps even 1918, some Russian ideologists advocated establishing monoethnic administrative units in southern Central Asia in place of the
multiethnic blends of ages past and of the contemporary TASSR. That being
inexpedient as open policy at the time, they forwarded the idea through a
Turkkomissia (Turkistan Commission) dispatched from Moscow and other
devices. The Turkistan Commission, appointed in Moscow by Vladimir I.
Lenin October 3, 1919, consisted mainly of Russians and served directly under
the Russiawide Central Executive Committee and Council of People's Commissars of the RSFSR. Acting quickly, it set in motion the measures needed to
segregate subgroups in Central Asia. No later than January 15, 1920, the
commission made the decision

> to acknowledge as necessary the administrative regrouping of Turkistan
> according to the ethnographic and economic circumstances of the territory.
> Also required is to outline the following groupings: Turkmens (of Trans-
> caspia), Uzbek-Tajiks (Samarkand, Farghana and part of Sir Darya Oblast'),
> Kirgiz [that is, Kazaks] (part of Sir Darya Oblast', Amu Darya Otdel and
> Semirechenskaia Oblast').

That quick decision of the Turkistan Commission did not then apply to
Bukhara (see figure 11.1) or Khwarazm, for they still remained independent
states, though greatly influenced by Russia. The decision was approved by the
RSFSR government, making doubly plain the Russian source and base of the

commission's authority. These actions converted this naming ethnic subgroups into an unavoidable political principle.[13]

In Tashkent, capital of the ATR and its subordinate centers during this period, the government established a Turkistan Commissariat for Nationalities' Affairs, directly responsible to Stalin's Russiawide Commissariat for Nationalities' Affairs in Moscow. The Turkistan commissariat opened a series of ethnic departments in 1918–1919, including Armenian, Dungan, Jewish, Kazak, Russian, Tajik, Uzbek, and three others. Moreover, sizable Turkistanian towns such as Jizzakh and Samarkand established corresponding subdepartments in this network.

From then on the administration of the ATR worked to focus and raise the subgroups' ethnocentricity rather than continue their integration. This divisive activity evidently helped to introduce the subgroup segregation of the population, but it also provoked the Turkistan commissariat's dissolution in October 1919, decided on by irate delegates to the Eighth Congress of the Councils of the ATR, October 1–2, 1919. Referring to "the internationalist slogans of the Soviet government," the congress resolved that "there cannot be any talk about separate institutions that set the goal for themselves of defending separate subgroups [narodnosti]." In the same period, the fact that Ishtirakiyun, the chief communist party press outlet of the ATR, came out, as it claimed, "in the Sart language" (meaning the Turki tongue of the southern oases), suggested that the main force in domestic affairs of the ATR was not ethnically impartial but rather served the interests of the Sarts, however defined, whom demographic evidence proved to constitute most of the relatively small reading public for the paper as well as much of the population at large.[14]

The method adopted by Russian politicians to disintegrate the ATR, as well as the Bukharan and Khwarazmian political complexes, entailed stripping away its outer circumference until they exposed the old human nucleus of the political organism. Moscow's agents tried to make these actions appear as if they had occurred on local initiative, or at least that is how such moves have been interpreted and presented in official histories. First, on August 26, 1920, the Central Executive Committee and Council of People's Commissars of the RSFSR issued a decree in which they proposed combining the territory where Kazaks lived, both inside and outside the ATR, though this unity had probably never existed in nature. This gerrymandering ostensibly responded to Kazak group appeals like the one dated September 1918, said to come from Manghishlaq tribesmen. Another communication, dated June 1920, allegedly came from Adaev, Tabin, and other Kazak nomads demanding the Manghishlaq uezd and two volosts in Krasnovodsk uezd as part of a new Qirghizistan (properly, Kazakstan) Autonomous Socialist Soviet Republic (QASSR). In January 1921, the political managers called together what they termed a congress of poor Kazaks and Kirgiz living in the ATR; led by visiting communist party leaders,

Figure 11.1 Leaders, banners, and slogans of the Bukhara People's Conciliar Republic in Congress, August 1921. Front and center, seated, Fayzullah Khoja, to his left, Abdu Qadir Muhitdinov, next left, Osman Khoja Oghli (future president of the Republic), to Fayzullah Khoja's right, Qari Yoldash Polatov. Archive of Dr. Timur Kocaoglu.

the congress adopted a resolution favoring the shift of these Kazaks of the ATR, and their lands, into the Qirghizistan ASSR.[15] When that QASSR came into existence, the September 1, 1920, decree of the Russiawide Central Executive Committee transferred Manghishlaq *uezd* from the ATR to the new unit, which still left many Kazaks and their pastures within the ATR. Moscow encouraged Qirghizistan officials to pursue vigorously gaining control over those additional people and territories within the ATR.[16]

In April 1922 a conference in Moscow of representatives from the ATR, QASSR, and, presumably, the RSFSR debated turning over the Sir Darya and Yetti Suw (Semirechie) oblasts of the ATR to the QASSR. Meanwhile, following the Ninth Congress of Councils of the ATR, September 19–25, 1920, the government, under the Central Executive Committee of the ATR, opened separate subgroup sections that differed markedly from the subsections in the old Turkistan ASSR Commissariat for Nationalities' Affairs. This time, these subdivisions functioned directly under the TASSR executive body, who staffed them with Kazaks, Turkmens, and Uzbeks. In August 1921 the government marked out a Turkmen Autonomous Oblast within the ATR, thus making another move toward merging politically disparate lands inhabited by Turkmens into a single Central Asian Turkmen unit.[17]

While the politicians maneuvered, intellectuals and figures in the creative arts in the ATR started efforts that hinted at the end of an older era and outlined a modern framework. Reconciling the broad concept of Turkistan on which their generation had grown up with the use of such cultural subdivisions as "Kazak" and "Uzbek," they allocated different functions between the two classifications, a precursor for which had appeared in the Reformist press before World War I. In his influential journal *Ayinä*, Mahmud Khoja Behbudiy drew careful distinctions among local and outside Reformists and languages. Reporting activities within the then new theater of Turkistan that involved Turkic visitors, the editors used phrases such as "Uzbek and Tatar youths and progressives."[18] Ordinarily, *Ayinä* never spoke of ethnic subgroups in its pages, referring only to Turkistan people and the Turki language. When foreigners came into the picture, even those who might qualify as linguistic or racial kinsmen of Central Asians, the Turkistanian editors made clear distinctions between themselves and the outsiders. When the parties to an endeavor in Samarkand or Tashkent came entirely from among Turkistanians, they uniformly omitted further journalistic subgroup designation.

LITERARY AND LINGUISTIC IDENTITY

For several more years Turkistan spelled place, territory, history, statehood, and people. The designations Kazak, Turkmen, Uzbek, and the like seemed to refer to literature, language, and subordinate ethnicity and remained disconnected from government, nation, and politics. There were still those, however, who linked Turkistan tightly with their language and literature. At the First Countrywide Uzbek Language and Orthographic Congress, January 1921, Sayyid Ali Osmani, an invited Tashkent specialist, quoted an appropriate verse by the Turkistan Reformist Abdullah Awlaniy. In part, it read:

> Awake, o community [*Uyghan millät!*], which senses dawn's approach
> when the sky is turning light for our Turkistan . . .
> Our glorious Turkistan, that lost the sun of its freedom, its fame and
> nobility, and remained oppressed, disgraced.[19]

Here was a Turkistan patriot's literary call to homeland and country. Osmani, during the same congress, declared, "Our Turkistanians [*Turkistanlilär*] used to love verse very much in earlier times," attaching the popular comprehensive territorial name Turkistan to its inhabitants as well.

Participants in the congress, however, found complete agreement regarding these issues of place and people elusive. This lack of unanimity persisted, even though organizers had called the meetings to standardize terminology, orthography, and grammar in the language. It remained for Shahid Ahmad, commissar for education of the ATR, like Osmani from Tashkent, to express the political direction behind this cultural meeting. In his speech Shahid Ahmad responded to reports and comments from Osmani and Abdalrauf Fitrat—the Bukharan poet and politician who then headed in Tashkent the influential literary society, Chaghatay Gurungi—by including such terms as *ozbek khälqi* (Uzbek ethnic group), *ozbek ädäbiyati* (Uzbek literature), *ozbek eli* (Uzbek tribe/populace). At the same time, he acknowledged the lack of a distinct Uzbek art and culture into the early 1920s and the difficulties such a hiatus entailed for anything other than an arbitrary definition of group identity. He also rejected as ineffectual the old call from Ismail Bey Gaspirali, the deceased Crimean Tatar Reformist and Gaspirali's Reformist followers in Turkistan, to treat all Turkic people of Russia as one cultural and political body.[20]

Uncertainty over the choice of written language for the ATR continued, for many teachers felt that the Uzbek dialect was only a hearthside tongue that schoolchildren might use in the first two or three grades and that they should supplant this household Uzbek language with *umumi turk tili* (the common Turkic language), which closely followed Ottoman Turkish of the period.[21] Mir Mashriq Yunus-oghli Elbek (1898–1939), an outstanding young "Uzbek" poet of the early 1920s, demonstrated in his verse this two-tiered language arrangement. In his first short poem, "Language," which appeared in *Yash ozbek shairläri* (Young Uzbek Poets, 1922), probably the earliest book of contemporary verse entitled Uzbek, Elbek wrote,

Sing and sing on in sad unison, understand!

Who are those who sell out the Turki tongue?!

Shan't I be abashed if I fling from this land

This tongue that ever sings like a nightingale?!

Shall I not comprehend, I who forever abuse, abuse

The soulful Turki, sweeter than honey?![22]

In these lines the poet, alluding to country and populace without reference to specific place, links them to the Turki tongue that he finds delicious. As he writes in his Turki idiom, he never calls it Uzbek. Further illustrating this mixture of identities, in the same special volume a second young poet offers 'Ozbek qizi' ichun (For an Ozbek Girl), dated August 1920, Baku, and composed not in Turki but in, as he labels it, 'Uthmanlichä (Ottoman Turkish).[23]

Had he composed that verse at home in Andijan, he probably would have regarded the conceit and thus the maiden's identity differently. Despite the titles of these two verses, neither in language nor in content can these poetic selections remove the traditional subgroup ethnic ambiguity so characteristic of Turkistan. Nor do any other poems in the same collection try to accomplish that aim.

Although ethnically neutral under its covers, Young Uzbek Poets' title and most of its literary language represented a genuine innovation in twentieth-century Turkistan and the path that authorities of the ATR would follow in the early 1920s toward delineating language groups and their names. But these new cultural practices left the problem of place strikingly indefinite, for this and similar publications lacked any reference to territory other than Turkistan. Omission of the place names Ozbekistan or Tajikistan in such publications seems consistent with the ideas about group and territorial labeling that prevailed among the literati of the region. This 104-page book of Uzbek verse—although an anthology compiled in the name of a historical tribal confederation within the ATR—was no threat to the ATR or its heterogeneity. Nor does the writing of these young "Uzbek" poets suggest that they harbored a dream of administrative or social separateness and segregation of their language group.

Elbek's poetic devotion to what he called turk tili (Turki language) in the early 1920s echoed public attitudes. The Section for Public Instruction of the ATR had offered a resolution in March 1919 at the Special Seventh Congress of Councils of the ATR that spoke of Turki schools, Turki script, men of Turki origin, Turki language, and the like in the most positive terms. Moreover, the resolution specified that "a Central Asian Turk must head the Commissariat of Education of the ATR or be its first deputy commissar." The statement went on to assert that "they [the Turki people] are full of understanding about the needs of their supraethnic group" and that productivity in the work of the commissariat demanded that "Turki" leaders stand at the top in the capital of the ATR as well as in subordinate sections and towns. The congress delegates attested that the term *Turki* would designate the fundamental population in Turkistan.[24] According to the folk wisdom expressed at the beginning of this chapter, however, if circumstances forced individuals to choose between community and homeland, they would turn to human rather than geographic attachment, though they might prefer to sustain both.

Turkistanians, Bukharans, and Khwarazmians also began to see themselves (again) in a context that reached beyond the Turkic family. Spokesmen in Moscow as well as in Central Asia frequently referred to an even larger Asian association. This gesture toward Eastern affinities beyond Central Asian frontiers occurred early in the life of the heterogeneous autonomous and people's republics, as Moscow sought to employ these groups in its external propaganda and ideological indoctrination. During the Congress of the Peoples of the East, held in Baku in 1920 with the enthusiastic participation of Central Asians and other Middle Easterners, many delegates voiced community with foreign Asia. A new poet from Turkistan composed verses about the *Shärq* (East), tracing its old complexities common to Turkistan and lands beyond. Politicians from Russia and Central Asia projected the region's new role as that of "revolutionary beacon," "outpost of revolution," and "magnet" for the other people of Asia. Linking the RSFSR's and then USSR's domestic East with foreign Asia soon became a prominent theme of the new regime in Moscow.[25]

The puzzle for Central Asians (who normally avoided using the name *Central Asia*) lay less in selecting and defining any extensive relationships than in contemplating and designating the fractions that made up Turkistan. Neighbors and kin do not invariably provide the most objective evidence for judging the worth, popularity, or importance of their friends and families. In naming, however, neighbors' attitudes, when offered with or without malice, can inform the question. Such a gesture by a prominent Turkistanian politician and journal editor told much about the thinking among communist party officials regarding group names. In the course of analyzing Turkistan's political situation in March 1922, Nadhir Toraqol-uli (1892–1939) quoted a contemporary non-Soviet newspaper report from Riga, Latvia, to the effect that "Muslim businessmen and Turkmen, Tajik and Sart (?) *mullahs* (educated men) are becoming dissatisfied with the policy adhered to by the Conciliar government and are agitating against the government."[26] That parenthetical question mark inserted by Toraqol-uli, a Kazak, reveals his discomfort with the name *Sart*, for he knew well enough what the name signified. As an ATR communist party leader, he understood as early as spring 1922 that the label *Sart* retained no promise in Moscow's political plans for Central Asia. Two likely possibilities for naming remained.

Toraqol-uli, a Kazak, edited all and wrote much of the principal "Uzbek-language" political affairs periodical, *Inqilab* (Revolution), designated by the Central Committee of the communist party as its leading journal for the ATR. Toraqol-uli thus symbolized the continuing Asian ethnic heterogeneity in the ATR's internal arrangements. Ingrained Russian habit, however, inexorably drove the Soviet political machine in Central Asia, and elsewhere in the USSR, away from that organic mixture toward a hybrid homogeneity by distinguishing the local communities from one another but uniting each with the Russians.

12 Disintegration

Milliy jomhoriyätlärgä bolish aldida shundä shashilishdukki
ozimizning qaysi millätdän ikänimizni bilmäy aldiq.

Before the partition into nationality republics, we got so com-
pletely befuddled that we couldn't figure out which of the
nationalities we ourselves might belong to.

(*Mushtum*, satirical Turkistan magazine, 1924)*

Alien voices other than Russian sounded often during the 1920s in connection with Turkistanian cultural change. Abdalrahman Saadi, a Kazan Tatar scholar in Central Asia, occupied himself with the linguistic development and classification for the region. In his opinion, by late 1922 Turkistan's culture had moved past the era of the supraethnic Chighatay (Chaghatay) literary language, which had lasted from the fifteenth century until the beginning of the twentieth into what he and others called *Chighatay-Uzbek*. In his analysis, after czarist Russia fell, the ideology as well as the economy changed in Turkistan, and in consequence "a new vital name, Uzbek language and Uzbek literature, gained the day over Chaghatay." Calling this a victory, he attributed it to the rise of young Uzbek poets and authors beginning at the end of the old Russian regime in March 1917. Saadi claimed that these young writers displayed a completely

* *Mushtum*, no. 11 (October 3, 1924):8.

different, fresh language, style, intonation, meter, mood, and literary content that seemed in keeping with the new name. He listed as representative "revolutionary poets and authors" Abdalrauf Fitrat, Abdulhamid Sulayman Cholpan, Mir Mashriq Yunus-oghli Elbek, Shakir Sulayman, Mahmud Khadi-oghli Batu, and Ghulam Zafariy, most of whom had actively engaged in the Reformist or Turkistan movements, or both, in literature and the press.

KAZAN TATAR TUTELAGE

Saadi's argument in one respect seems implausible, for it would mean that a new Turkistanian cultural and intellectual core, small but dynamic, had suddenly arisen in late 1922 writing what its members called *Uzbek poetry and prose* in what he termed *Uzbek language*—though they did not insist on this. This development might constitute the laying of a cultural base on which to establish ethnic group identity, but no specific political framework stood around it.[1] Professor Saadi's Tatar background conditioned him to think in terms of monoethnicity, and his thesis continued the convenient distinction between geographic-political-administrative necessities and those aspects of Central Asian life more particular to given groups of people; but the concepts of Turkistanian poets came from another direction.

These young Central Asian literary intellectuals cautiously starting to publicize the name Uzbek in print embodied not so much a political vision as a cultural one. Struggling with the encumbrances and conformity clamped on all poets and authors by the rigid traditional literary forms and other conventions in old Turkistan, their principal aspiration in declaring themselves "young Uzbek poets" lay in the desire to modernize and match the experimental Azerbaijanian and Turkish writers who had long before sensed the changes taking place in literature and language in Europe. This opportunity to throw off the dominance of the old Arabic *arudh* (meter) and the clichés of subject matter in the omnipresent lyric forms like the *ghazal* had to be seized if Turkistanian writers wanted to catch up with the aesthetic progress of other Middle Eastern countries. Beneath these questions of form lay the underpinnings of values and attitudes.

Although this "Uzbek" literary movement proved convenient for communist politicians, scholars must seek its origins outside the political developments of Turkistan in the period after 1917. Professor Saadi's proclamation of a new age in Turkistan letters did not, even if true, guarantee a positive influence on cultural affairs in the region. Among outsiders, the Kazan Tatars, more than any related group, aroused the resentment of southern Central Asians, and the Tatars, in turn, disdained Turkistanian life and achievements, infuriating intellectuals in Turkistan. Ghazi Yonis (Yunus) Muhammad-oghli (*ca.* 1887–1937), a Turkistanian writer and cultural figure, charged Tatar authors with distorting Turkistan's history. Their willful misstatements, he felt, fashioned a chain of incorrect impressions and inference to which succeeding authors, adopting the Tatar version of Turkistanian history, would innocently add. Such treatment of the Turkistanian legacy, Ghazi Yonis reported, earned the Kazan Tatars Turkistan's lasting aversion.

This animosity became hatred when coupled with the Kazan Tatar identity (the same antipathy did not extend to the Crimean Tatars). Although linguistic kinship links Kazan Tatars with the Central Asian Turkic people, Turkistanians in the twentieth century and earlier regarded Kazan Tatars with suspicion because they laced their language with Russianisms and because their activity in Central Asia convinced Bukharans and Turkistanians, with some cause, that Tatars served as proxies or agents for their Russian masters. Ghazi Yonis called Tatars "the latest generation to obstruct Turkistan's progress."[2] His identification of Kazan Tatars with Turkistan's Slavic conquerors indicates how group hostility enhances the sensitivity of populations to the difference between insiders and outsiders yet imperfectly defines their image and perimeters. Kazan Tatar unpopularity in Turkistan suggests that disparagement and name-calling like that practiced by such well-defined outsiders as the Kazaks, Russians, and Kazan Tatars consisted more of a long-term contest for group survival than an enunciation of petty differences, which still did not explain the vacillation in the Turkistanian's preferences for self-names.

The feelings already alluded to about the term *Sart* did not represent the only ambivalence in the larger Turkistan community, for Uzbek also sometimes fell short of being a good name. A folk saying among early twentieth-century Sarts—"Uzbek! Watch what you say when you call your neighbor *thief*!"— meant you are not immune from the same sort of accusation. The Sart fared better in sayings common to his own group: "If a Sart gets rich, he builds a new roof; if a Kazak gets rich, he marries a new wife." In other words, Sarts characteristically act providently, Kazaks recklessly.[3]

As late as 1920 or 1922 uncertainty persisted concerning the designation *Uzbek* in general communication; otherwise, the Uzbek name would have shown up in the flags of the rapid growing Reformist press, in the new stage works of Turkistan before 1918, or in the widely circulated Soviet-sponsored newspapers and theater. Indifference to Uzbek as a heading showed itself in both the Turkic and the Slavic written languages in Central Asia at least until 1925. Editors of newspapers and bulletins, communist or noncommunist, chose for their press the most wide-ranging, symbolic names available, selecting flags with larger territorial extent or supraethnic meaning. Drama and theater of that era, so important to the education of illiterate Turkistan, introduced plays entitled *Turkistan tabibi* (Turkistan Doctor) by Mannan Majidov Uyghur, *Turkistan khanlighi* (Turkistan Khanate) by Mannan Ramiz, and *Turkistan* by

Ziya Said, but nothing in the record shows an indigenous play with a title using the subgroup name *Uzbek* or *Tajik* during that period. Also, starting in 1917 or before, in addition to *Säda-i Turkistan* and *Ulugh Turkistan*, newspapers appeared under the flags *Turan* (Land of the Turk), *Turk eli* (Turki Tribe), and *Shora-i Islam* (Council of Islam). *Turk sözi* (The Turki Word) came out in 1918, and in Russian *Turkestanskaia pravda* (Turkistan Truth) continued in the pattern.[4]

Like *Qizil bäyraq* (Red Banner) in 1920, the new intellectual journal issued by the ATR's Commissariat for Education, *Bilim ochaghi* (The Source of Knowledge), which started in 1922, employed an even more general and unethnic flag. On the masthead for issue number one, the magazine declared itself to be printed in Uzbek. Numbers two/three omitted the stipulation altogether, signaling that this periodical, printed in a modified Arabic script that tended to obscure linguistic differentiation among Turkic dialects, could not qualify as an Uzbek house organ in the ATR in the early 1920s.[5]

During the years immediately following the Russian czar's deposition in March 1917, the Marxist politicians and press introduced a very different rhetoric into public expression. They spoke about congresses, about classes, and about nationalities and workers in strong ideological terms. That accent on changed rhetoric soon increased Central Asian sensitivity to the importance of cultural and political meaning in public discourse.

How strongly Turkistanians felt about the symbolism carried by press flags and other titles became apparent when another change occurred in the flag of the newspaper *Qizil bayraq* (Red Banner), with its alien Marxist heading. That paper was the main press outlet in a local language for the communist party of Turkistan. In September 1922 the editors adopted the name *Turkistan* for the flag, surely to evoke a strong historical, cultural sense of identity among readers and those who heard it read aloud. Usmankhan Ishan Khoja, editor of this new *Turkistan* and two other first-rank serials, wrote in a lead article about the instability in contemporary Central Asian subgroup identities: "The formerly enslaved ethnic groups [*khälqlär*] have neither sufficient awareness nor adequate customs. Thus, our overriding concern for the present is to raise consciousness . . . and achieve the goal [of providing that awareness and custom]."[6] Usmankhan Ishan Khoja thus clearly determined to unite the community of Turkistan under that name through use of the media. To fix a group identity in which both intellectuals and illiterates could recognize themselves evidently posed the immediate challenge.

A second author addressed the crucial question of naming in the same issue of that paper:

> Denominating each thing by its name is an inescapable law . . . We think that the name of this newspaper, *Turkistan*, will give reminders frequently about

all of Turkistan's needs. We hope that our government . . . will also give broad scope to translating the truth into reality, despite the fact that the truth will seem bitter [this paraphrases the popular Arabic saying in which the prophet exhorts his followers to speak the truth even though it be bitter] . . . We trust that public-spirited young people . . . of Turkistan will make use of this newspaper and put forward their demands.[7]

The writer alluded to and underlined the *Qur'ânic* teaching about Adam's divine knowledge of God-given names and invited the younger generation's press to create public opinion favorable to cohesiveness around both the Turkistan name and the polity. With these admonitions the editorial related Islamic belief and tradition to a place and proper group name to enhance popular support through the new media. That press outlet remained important to Turkistanian intelligentsia even after drastic change supplanted the Jadid reform movement.

IDENTITY OF THE NEW STATE

Speaking to and for Turkistanian readers in 1922, journalists in the communist press, like their noncommunist predecessors, stressed the broadest common identity possible among their people, area, and communications media, thus attaining the high point for that assertion of choice in modern Turkistan. Following the short-lived independence of the Autonomous Provisional Government of Turkistan in late 1917–early 1918, local leaders and intellectuals became aware of what self-determination meant and how a group must pursue it. They also knew that Turkistan had a formidable history and territory in its favor and that no other group or territorial designation promised more for the future. In the race between outside political manipulation of the region and self-determination by its indigenous people, proponents of each still expressed their fundamental differences fairly guardedly.

In this drive for a state identity, Turkistan struggled against a peculiar handicap that its opponents moved to capitalize on: Turkistan made up only one large part of southern Central Asia, and events affecting group identity would soon have an impact on the people of the ATR that they could not ignore. After the gestures toward subgroup acknowledgment that Soviet politicians made to Karakalpaks, Kazaks, and Turkmens in the three heterogeneous states of southern Central Asia in the early 1920s, in 1922 public conflicts flared over the disagreements between Russian-sponsored advocates of monoethnicity in each subunit and those who wanted heterogeneity everywhere: segregation versus independent overall community. This polarization was especially pronounced in the Bukharan and Khwarazmian People's Conciliar Republics (BPCR and KhwPCR).

By August 1923, policymakers had arranged a near symmetry among the three governments of southern Central Asia in population subgroup align-ments. The KhwPCR and the BPCR declared that, through their Central Executive committees, they would establish special Turkmen and Kazak de-partments of quasi-autonomous oblasts within their own territory. By October 1923 Bukhara had also carved a semiautonomous Turkmen oblast of Charjoy and Karki *wilayäts* (provinces) out of itself.[8] Thus, the units in southern Central Asia had created the organization and structure necessary for segregating from Turkistan the many Kazaks and all the Turkmens of the ATR, two of the most dynamic and sizable nomadic populations of the region.

In the midst of the Russian-directed drive toward segregation, the au-thorities in Moscow and their deputies in Central Asia openly scolded Bukhara's leadership in August 1922 for what they labeled *ethnic discrimination*. People must have been perplexed then when officials declared: "So far, Fayzullah [Khoja] has selected people to work on the basis of kinship and nepotism . . . a secretary of the Bukharan CP must remain independent of nationality. He must likewise reject an ethnic Council of Ministers. Ministers must be outside nationality."[9] The Bukharan leader evidently brought only members of his own Turki-speaking clan into the government of the BPCR. No action could express more clearly a devotion to the principle of monoethnicity, but the outsiders thought otherwise.

ACTIONS AGAINST INTEGRATION

Elsewhere in Central Asia Moscow acted against integration through the local Khwarazmian branch of the communist party. The Russians made accusations of nationalism against those indigenous leaders who at-tempted to maintain the heterogeneity of the KhwPCR. In November 1921 communist authorities had ousted as "bourgeois nationalists" Central Asians including Ata Makhsum Madrahim-oghli, M. Timur Khoja Ibniyamin-oghli, and M. B. Rahman-oghli, respectively the chairman of the KhwPCR's Central Executive Committee, the chairman of its Council of Ministers, and the opera-tions chief of the Central Executive Committee, three of that government's highest officials. The outsiders also sharply criticized a minister in the BPCR for his assertion that a sovereign state must have its own army, railroads, technical specialists—that such a state required real independence.

Russian authorities thus added to their list of nationalist crimes any effort to support or seek the heterogeneous state's independence. They fired several top officials of the Bukharan government and expelled them to Turkistan in the summer of 1923 for dissenting from such Russian prescriptions for Central Asia. Bukharan ministers Abdalrauf Fitrat, Nazrullah-Khoja, Muhiddin Amin-oghli, and others lost their posts in this Russian-sponsored purge.[10]

Another part of Moscow's campaign against Central Asian self-determination was the argument that subgroup dispersion accounted for the difficulties and evils of societies. An ethnic population's compactness, they asserted, equated with a positive mode of life. This concept of human society exalted the inward orientation of people by elevating the sanctity of ethnic subgroup names. Russia tried to impose this attitude on those outside as well as those inside its empire. Central Asia, which lay within Russia's military control, thus became a prime target for rearrangement according to the Russian model of limited group self-identity combined with ethnic subgroup homogeneity. By this logic Russian deputies in Central Asian centers could say that ethnic dispersion encouraged bourgeois nationalism in heterogeneous states like the BPCR and KhwPCR.

One Soviet Russian argument ran that predominant bourgeois nationalists in a given political unit could infringe on the interests of other nationalities. This manner of thinking led to actions in the BPCR on the part of Fayzullah Khoja's group and in the KhwPCR on the part of the group around Palwan Niyaz Yusup. Yusup had served as *rä'is* (president) of the first KhwPCR government in the early 1920s after leading the Young Khivan Party under the last Qonghirat government. In Bukhara Fayzullah Khoja, by then a communist leader, claimed in 1924 that "existing political borders of the republics of Central Asia (Turkistan, Bukhara, etc.) are artificial. These borders," he declared, "unjustly tear apart each of the tribes [*elät*] that lives in those republics." He described consequences of that dispersion as an "artifically contrived hostility between the ethnic groups [*khälqlär*] of Central Asia." By implication he blamed czarist leaders for creating that dispersion and said that it fostered an enmity that both the amir of Bukhara and the czar of Russia had earlier exploited.[11]

Communist officials, brandishing accusations of creating ethnic conflict, beat down Central Asian efforts to form new heterogeneous states based on existing relationships among local subgroups. The political authorities blamed Central Asians with independent ideas for exacerbating ethnic tensions in the region. *Ethnic tension* became a code phrase to condemn any local government initiative outside Russian-controlled structures. Ahmad Zeki Velidi (Togan), an eyewitness to the events in Turkistan and other areas in Central Asia during the early 1920s, commented that, in fact, he and others worked effectively for a time in Khwarazm to keep ethnic relations harmonious. Togan, who was head of the Bashkir Revolutionary Committee in 1919–1920 and also participated in Central Asian events, said "But the Russians knew that to stir up Turkmen-Uzbek hostility [in Khwarazm] worked to their own advantage."[12]

There is no doubt that Russia and its Central Asian agents after 1917 fostered Turkmen and Kazak antipathy to continued cooperation and coexistence with Uzbeks in the same political-administrative units, as seen by the persistent efforts from the beginning of the 1920s of anti-Uzbek politicians and policymakers in Moscow and Central Asia. Playing on ethnic prejudice by

convening exclusive congresses of illiterate Kazak day laborers and farm workers as well as similar groups in Turkistan and Khwarazm, they incited hundreds
of these individuals—who possessed no information about the larger cultural
and political issues surrounding ethnic affairs in Central Asia—to enmity
toward the group now designated as Uzbeks. The imposition of the name thus
quickly fostered ethnic conflict. In these political actions, the authorities tied the
idea of achieving group civil and personal rights to instituting specific ethnic
subgroup segregation throughout the region.

Aside from the official explanations (helping the economy and hindering
ethnic discrimination) advanced for segregating subgroups in Central Asia,
several important motives and numerous consequences came into play. Sarts,
Tajiks, and Uzbeks, perhaps less than any other people in the region except the
true Kirgiz, lacked feelings of group exclusiveness and cohesion, and this
cosmopolitan outlook did not appear merely among town dwellers. From
different parts of Central Asia came reports that members of the population
innocently misidentified themselves on a large enough scale that exact ethnic
distinctions and lines required endless clarification. Into this vacuum in ethnic
policies moved Lenin's deputies, whose mission consisted in large part of
neutralizing the dangerous potence of these Uzbeks by isolating them from
other Central Asians.

ANTI-UZBEK POLICIES

The segregation drive thus concealed an anti-Turkistan policy that
in turn masked the anti-Uzbek goal in both cultural and political spheres in
which Uzbeks had played a dominant part throughout much of southern
Central Asia. To the Russians, the Uzbeks' tribal and dynastic legacy constituted a three-way threat. (1) They stretched across much of settled Central
Asia in sufficient numbers to participate in the culture and society of the entire
southern territory. (See figure 15.1). (2) If they continued to engage in politics of
the areas they inhabited, the Uzbeks would carry a strong potential for influence in local affairs. (3) More than any other part of the Central Asian
population, the Uzbeks exerted a pull of ethnic assimilation on others that
expanded the Uzbek population and enhanced their reach in nearly every field.
This process, which had proceeded for centuries without conscious effort or
emphasis, occurred notably in the heterogeneous towns and villages. The
Uzbeks were in the best position to unite the various subgroups because they
dominated most of the educational and cultural system of the old cities.
Through their active trading economy and the great spiritual energy of their
clergy, Uzbek influence went far beyond their home areas.

These factors seemed to challenge the Russian sense of mission and colonialist thrust in ways that became very important during the decade following March 1917, when the ideas and policies of the Russian Social Democratic Workers' party relating to nationalities as enunciated by Lenin and Stalin became the guidelines for the new Soviet Russian government. Moscow's leaders felt that lessening Uzbek influence would make it easier to manage the Central Asian region and would rapidly increase their control over people of all groups. Thus, segregating the Uzbeks became the cornerstone of the Soviet drive to divide Central Asians into six administrative units instead of the three that previously existed. Evidence attributes the immediate rationale for the timing and decision to segregate Central Asia to Stalin, who from his eminence at the pinnacle of the communist party (he recently [1922] had risen to become general secretary to the RKP(b) Central Committee), organized one of the political purges for which the Soviet regime and the communist party became notorious. In a speech to the participants at the Fourth Conference of the Central Committee of the RKP(b) with Executives of the Nationality Republics and Oblasts, June 10, 1923, the communist chief denounced an array of non-Slavic, Eastern party leaders including Central Asians such as Akmal Ikramov (1898–1937), who represented the communist party of Turkistan, because they argued that in post-1917 Soviet Turkistan only "the signboard had been changed." Stalin aimed his heaviest guns at Mir Sayid Sultan Galiyev (1880–1939?), a Kazan Tatar politician who had promoted unification of all the Muslim and/or Turkic populations of the East, including Central Asia, in a socialist aggregate distinct from Russia and the European sectors of communism. The salvo climaxed assaults on Sultan Galiyev by the Tatar press and led to his ejection from the RKP(b). A prominent Central Asian leader said that the denunciation of Sultan Galiyev set off an even stronger attack on Eastern Soviet communists generally by central communist party authorities who resented resistance to their reductive doctrine in the controversy over heterogeneous as against homogeneous organization of the non-European, non-Slavic populace. This offensive directly affected the Central Asian conflict between local segregationists and the more numerous indigenous aggregationists.[13]

In 1923 Stalin demonstrated his guile again when he came out against broad supraethnic federations in Central Asia that tended to unify a refractory, culturally related population. Having overseen the establishment, December 13, 1922, of the Transcaucasus Socialist Federated Soviet Republic, which encompassed Stalin's own country with others culturally unrelated, meant that the authorities could tolerate uniting unlike cultural units that they were reasonably certain would retain their distinctiveness. They could not, however, accept the idea of pulling together close kinsmen already united by language families and religion. Sultan Galiyev's plans certainly embraced Central Asia's Turkic Muslims, and the general secretary's action against Galiyev may have sent a signal that he would no longer permit talk about racial-religious groupings in the communist party. If the decision to segregate subgroups of Central Asia stemmed from this affair, it added another example of interference in Central Asian developments by Moscow. Either way, the timing signified less than the tendency toward ethnic segregation that gathered momentum in the RSFSR and Central Asia.

Central Asians who opposed the principle of ethnic separation maintained that the existing states of the region had been historically formed, that the combination of Turkic subgroups created a higher-level unity, and that Islam joined the population closely together. To deflect these claims, Moscow's representatives in the three Central Asian republics answered with a kind of European-based Marxist formula modified by Stalin's categorizing and defining the modern nationality (*natsiia*, as he called it). Fayzullah Khoja declared that rather than what he designated as the tribal/racial origin of a *khälq* (ethnic group), economic interests, language, and conditions of daily life should guide the unifying of people. He wrote, "The reason for nationality [*milliy*] unity does not at all times go on being tribal oneness. A tribe [*qäbilä*] is not a nationality [*millät*]."[14] Advancing that Marxist argument, he pushed for a definition of nationality that depended on the external features prescribed by Stalin rather than the expression of group choice that grew out of values and attitudes rooted in the group's shared experience.

By insisting that ethnic groups could not be joined if their bases of daily life profoundly differed, Fayzullah Khoja seemed opposed to assembling the scattered branches of any one subgroup. Despite ethnic links, groups differed from one another when they lived long in detached communities of other nationalities. If he followed the Soviet logic here, he meant that one could not expect economic development and social compatibility in a state of mixed ethnicity. (The evidence against this proposition in the European and American experience of the nineteenth century did not dismay Fayzullah Khoja, for his model came from underdeveloped Russia and the Middle East.) He professed to believe that culturally and economically undeveloped ethnic subgroups with varying outlook cannot coexist constructively in the same state. None of the polemic faced the fact that ethnic subgroups in this century snap at each other's throats *within* their country's borders, and the Bukhara, Khwarazm, and Turkistan of that day were no different. Moreover, members of the group soon to be labeled *Uzbek* expressed distaste for political, cultural, and geographic dismemberment.

Three documented examples (in addition to those already noted that occurred during 1920–1922) reveal the widespread, diverse resistance to ethnic segregation that appeared most consistently in areas predominantly inhabited by those known as Sarts or Uzbeks.

Late in 1923 an outburst in the southeast corner of the Turkistan ASSR over threats to divide up Central Asia came when delegates from the ethnically heterogeneous Farghana oblast to the Twelfth Congress of Councils of the Turkistan ASSR, held January 1–8, 1924, pressed for creating an "autonomous Farghana" political unit to encompass the densely populated Farghana Valley. They appealed directly to the Turkistan communist party chiefs as well as to the headquarters of the Central Asian Bureau of the Central Committee, RKP(b). After the congress, the bureau responded,

> It is a mistake to raise for discussion the question of "separating Farghana in present-day conditions and making it into an autonomous oblast" in the form advocated by the Farghana comrades. That is because it is imperative that the oblasts proceed via the route shown in the decisions of the Eighth, Tenth, and Twelfth Congresses of the Party [RKP(b)] for dividing up [*äjrätish*] nationality territories.[15]

That disapproval concerns the secondary political reasons (communist party policies that demanded monoethnic units for the strenuous drive to impose ethnic segregation) but not necessarily the primary one (to undercut potential integrative Uzbek power in the region).

This rejection failed to deflect Farghana's energies, for six months later Qoqan newspapers advanced another idea for Central Asian reorganization. Instead of acquiescing to Russian-controlled ethnic segregation and lines of command, Qoqandians proposed to make their own city the capital of a planned *milliy jomhoriyät* (nationality republic) because "the Uzbek khans' capital that happened to be located in Turkistan has remained constantly in Qoqan right up to the present."[16] Qoqan, unlike Bukhara and Tashkent, lay beyond the main urban concentrations of Tajiks, Russians, and other non-Turkistanians in an area with a strong sentiment for independence and often (1850s, 1876, 1898, 1917–1918, 1919–) known for resisting Russian military and political moves. This logical proposal failed very likely because establishing an Uzbek union republic in a concentrated Turkistanian Uzbek area would strengthen the unit through its cohesive ethnic homogeneity. From Moscow's standpoint, Iranized Samarkand or Russianized Tashkent evidently looked like more tractable locations for politically administering a new territorial subdivision.

In March 1924 a second and more serious nonviolent confrontation took place over ethnic segregation, this time in Khwarazm. The Executive Bureau of the Central Committee of the KhwCP formally decided against ethnically partitioning their country. Little Khwarazm thus again defended against Russian encroachment as it had so many times in earlier centuries, and in 1924 it again held off its opponent. In Moscow the Politburo of the Central Committee RKP(b) on June 12, 1924, confirmed preserving the Khwarazmian republic as the sole heterogeneous entity in Central Asia. Between that date and July 26, 1924, however, purges and other pressures caused the Central Executive Committee of the KhwCP to rescind its earlier decision (now termed *mistaken*) and to abjectly request that the higher authorities in Moscow reconsider its case. The Russian Central Committee's Politburo at once shifted the Khwarazm republic into the category of those units about to be subdivided in the name of ethnic parity and homogeneity.[17]

Both these incidents (the autonomous Farghana oblast, probably the final Turkistanian effort to save heterogeneous Central Asian polity, and the Khwarazmian resistance) involved Central Asian branches of the Russiawide communist party. A third, noncommunist dissatisfaction with the Russian solution to Central Asian supraethnicity flared up in a Turki-language region northeast of Tashkent, in Chimkent *uezd*, and deep in the Amu Darya delta at Chimbay, near the Aral Sea. Residents in those places feared the destruction of their culture by a segregation that would give Kazaks and Karakalpaks jurisdiction over their exposed salients. Communist organizers denounced these resisters as nationalist-deviationists, class enemies, and the like, employing much greater severity than they had with the erring communist comrades of Farghana and Khwarazm.[18]

STRUGGLE FOR TASHKENT

One of the greatest conflicts over the prospect of segregation arose in August–September 1924 over the disposition of the oasis of Tashkent, both town and district. In this disagreement the Kazaks, who stimulated the awareness of distinctiveness among the Uzbeks, may have done a greater service for Moscow than almost anything the central Soviet authorities attempted (unless they deliberately provoked this conflict). The Kazaks had controlled Tashkent for some years during the mid-eighteenth century, and in the early 1920s Tashkent served as a Kazak center.[19] One new borderline that the planners now sketched to demark the Kazak unit from the Sart/Uzbek unit fell very near Tashkent City, to which the Kazaks passionately advanced their claim. This border dispute inflamed a patriotic group spirit among the oasis Sart population, whose rivalry with the Kazaks was fierce and long. The Kazaks dominated the district of Tashkent outside the town, but there were fewer of them in Tashkent City than Sarts. When Kazak spokesmen, sensing a rebuff, as an alternative urged Russian authorities to constitute several rural Kazak subunits in the district, the executives refused on the grounds of economic dislocation. The Kazaks fought at all levels against a settlement that would give Sarts both the Tashkent district and the city in the partition. However it worked out, this decision would provide one more source of bitterness between ethnic subgroups that the existing heterogeneous dispositions could avoid. The Karakalpaks and other groups brought new border grievances to the Central

Executive Committee of the RSFSR's Eleventh Convocation in late 1924 but received no satisfaction.[20]

This friction—a result of the laying down of unprecedented borders to divide a population that had long symbiotically existed as an integral cultural, social, and economic aggregate—apparently stimulated new waves of Central Asian ethnocentrism. From that time onward, the communist party and government in Moscow have persistently denounced any integrative tendencies in the region as nationalism.

Part of the local resentment toward outside interference in Central Asian affairs arose from the jealousy provoked by the Russians' playing off one group against another. A contemporary analyst observed that "the project for ethnic segregation emanates from Bukhara," thus signaling the channel through which the RKP(b) leadership in Moscow elected to manage the segregation so that it would seem like a local initiative.[21] Open, formal steps to divide Central Asia into ethnically qualified administrative units started with a finding by the Central Committee of the Bukhara Communist Party (CPB) on February 25, 1924, that declared the time to be ripe for partitioning Central Asia on an ethnic basis. Fayzullah Khoja's theses respecting the setting up of what he called *Uzbekistan* received a kind of sanction from the CPB on that date. The Central Asian Bureau of the Central Committee of the RKP(b) on April 28, 1924, also called for dividing the region according to ethnic-territorial features of the population and the region. Political imperatives carried the plans of the Russian-based Turkistan commission through to completion. In Bukhara's next move, on September 20, 1924, the Fifth Bukharawide *Qurultay* (Congress) of Councils resolved that

> although the majority of the population's makeup of Central Asian oblasts historically, in fact, belongs to the Turkic nationality, in the course of its history the population split into tribes distinguished by way of life, daily existence, and economic situation. Constant clashes, wars, and antagonism compel us to regard these tribes as separate, independent nationalities . . . [the congress] finds it imperative to put the life and destiny of all nationalities in their own hands [and] for this reason to create an Uzbek republic.[22]

This Bukharawide Congress of Councils, though alluding to differences in life-style and economic position, defined nationalities largely by the conflicts between them, which seemed a peculiarly Russian interpretation of intergroup affairs. This definition reflected the violence introduced into the region by the Russians and their proxies as a solution to Central Asian problems at the climax of the Jadid era of moderation.

Into the wording of that same resolution came the stubbornness of history, for those references hinted at some disquiet among local leaders over the rationalization that had been formulated to justify the scission of Central Asia's population. During that Fifth Bukharawide Congress of Councils, Fayzullah Khoja addressed the assemblage at length about the final decision it would take to alter Bukhara's and, with it, all Central Asia's pattern of existence. He called the change "turning the most important and significant page of the East's own history."[23]

Although Khoja occasionally referred to history as merely a "passage of time," in 1924, in another polemic favoring the segregation of Central Asian groups, he equated the dismemberment of Turkistan and the other two political entities with "a tremendous revolution for political life" and wrote, "The idea of the pan-Turkists [about unification of the entire Central Asian Turkic population] remains a flight of fantasy... Nationality delimitation now rectified history's mistakes."[24] Yet the Bukharan politician dismissed the "pan-Islamists" and "pan-Turkists" for failing to meet *tärikh täqazasi* (history's imperative) in the nationality question, and, without attempting a Central Asian approach, he agreed with Stalin that a nationality was a *tärikhdän wujudgä kelgän* (historically formed) entity.[25] History's imperative, as Khoja understood it, led surely and naturally to ethnic segregation in political, economic, and social organization, a notion that came from his mentors in Stalinist Marxism. The general public in Bukhara, Khwarazm, and Turkistan held quite a different understanding of history, as the chapters about history and culture have shown. One of Khoja's Russian advisers asserted in 1924 that, in connection with current developments in the region, the Orientalist historians of Russia simply could not read their sources properly. "They could not search out the necessary preconditions for nationality in history," he wrote.[26]

Marxist theoreticians then decided that nationalities must come into being among the populations according to a chronology of economic changes. These ideas had become codified in Stalin's writings, which by 1924, the year of Lenin's death, had started to acquire the status of scripture. Bolsheviks and everyone dominated by them or who followed them had to accept the claim that history inevitably leads to ethnic segregation. New Central Asian communists generally repeated such dogma without embellishment. Inconvenient contradictions or inconsistencies in actual history thus became targets for Marxist attack.

Nevertheless, until very late in the deliberations over partition, some Turkistanians remained unconvinced that the political leaders and social guides knew the history and society of southern Central Asia well enough to come to an informed decision about its human groupings. Certain commentators referred cuttingly to that brand of history as *ta'rikh-ma'rikh* (mystery history) and asked pointed questions in public about group origins, the chronology of group names, ethnic tensions, the variety of designations for Iranians in Central Asia, the status in Turkistan of Russian colonialism, the status of the Tatars, and dividing the land. Tashkent's new satirical magazine, *Mushtum*, ordinarily quick to offer a tart rejoinder to dissenting opinion, instead published open comments—like the one heading this chapter—about the confusion in group identities caused by changing government and political party policies. Doubters concerned with that list of questions received feeble sarcasm from *Mushtum*'s editors: "Nothing had been revealed about the nationality question [*milliyat mäsäläsi*] in the great star [*äkhtär-i käbirdä*]." When the editors tried to provide a serious answer, they showed such extreme caution—warranted by Soviet Russian political severity—that their response sounded like another joke: "After a dictionary about the nationality question has been published, it is our intention to give a suitable answer," showing the journalists' uncertainty over the position they should take on the eve of the great partition in Central Asia.[27]

Mushtum came out as an adjunct to the main political-social bulletin (often called a newspaper but hardly qualifying for that term) of the communist party Central Committee of Turkistan, the communist party Tashkent City Committee, and the Central Executive Committee of the Councils of the Turkistan ASSR. The newspaper briefly served the same function for the Organizational Bureau of the CP(b)Uz and Revolutionary Committee of Uzbekistan. The idea that such sponsors would countenance the publication of competing points of view on such a politically charged subject reflects the lack of total acceptance in Turkistan of that principle of ethnic partition.

Even more dramatic than words of doubt were a series of bold cartoons printed in *Mushtum* testifying to the impossibility of fairly segregating the various groups living intertwined in southern Central Asia. In September, October, and November of 1924, Turkistanian readers were confronted by these bold jibes on the pages of their humor magazine. A scornful caricature of the Kazak Maghjan Jumabay-uli showed him insisting in poetry that Kazaks require independence from the remainder of Central Asia for their welfare. A full-page sketch (see figure 12.1) depicted large scissors clipping (partitioning) the map of Central Asia while two sober-faced men filled in blanks for identity on questionnaires. The Sart-looking gentleman wrote down *Qazaq* (Kazak); the man opposite him, dressed in Kazak costume, put down *Ozbek*. On the cover of the November issue appeared a cartoon joking about the racial and nationality identity of a Tajik, with one man asking another why he had put colored makeup on his face. The answer: "So I can be a real Tajik." (See figure 12.2).[28]

In 1926 the entire literate population of Uzbeks amounted to 149,000, less than 3.8 percent of all Uzbeks in proposed Uzbekistan. Only a minute percentage of the educated people, like the "young Uzbek poets" already mentioned, could read or write the name *Uzbek* or discuss the Uzbek language in public meetings. In a limited circle the name acquired currency as a cultural label, but virtually no printed source in Turki from southern Central Asia in the 1920s

ملتى جومهوربيهنـلهرگه بولغ ألـهبدا شونهه داشبلشبوككر.
ئوزبهرنك خايسى مللهتدهن ىبگهنمزنى بلمهى خالدبز.

Figure 12.1 Ethnic confusion in the partition of Central Asia. As scissors cut the map, man on left in Kazak costume writes *Uzbek* on a blank form. The Tajik-appearing man on right declares *Kazak* on a questionnaire. *Mushtum*, journal no. 11, October 3, 1924.

Figure 12.2 Figures with un-Uzbek-looking profiles consider ethnic choice in mountainous Tajikistan. Man on left has darkened his face, but second man says, "From your fair skin and black eyes, you belong precisely to the Tajik nationality. Why be an Uzbek?" *Mushtum*, no. 17, October 28, 1924.

wrote of a political community, much less a territorial reservation for Uzbek people.

Something like the legislating of a Central Asian group name occurred to the Uzbeks' close kinsmen, the Taranchis, the Qashqarliqs, and their relations. As late as June 1921, Soviet organizers steered a congress of "Dzungar and Altishaar toilers" in Tashkent to adopt the designation *Uyghur* as a general name for the Taranchis and other settled people living both in the RSFSR and in Chinese Turkistan (Xinjiang). In the 1930s, as the Russian presence increased in Western China, the Uyghur name spread to embrace those Eastern Turkistanians.[29] The Russians never held a plebiscite among the population of Central Asia and called no popular referendum to select the group name most desired by the Taranchis or the Sarts for the 1920s. The authorities arbitrarily selected dead or dying medieval designations and conferred them on the people of the region by political decree.

END OF TURKISTAN'S POLITICAL-CULTURAL SYMBIOSIS

Within ten days of the Bukharan congress's action, the Fifth Khwarazmwide Congress of Councils also adopted a resolution releasing its Uzbeks, Turkmens, and Karakalpaks to form their own ethnic units. A joint meeting of the Bukhara, Khwarazm, and Turkistan branches of the RKP(b) Central Committee on October 11, 1924, seconded these motions. On October 27, 1924, the Eleventh Convocation of the Central Executive Committee of the USSR, at its second session in Moscow, sanctioned the change. Not until May 11, 1925, did the Twelfth Russiawide Congress of Councils formally approve dismemberment of the TASSR, citing the principle of self-determination and the "will of the toiling masses."[30]

Along with the many mass meetings held during 1924 to point the public in the new direction for Central Asian affairs, a flurry of activity toward the end of that year completed the preparations for ethnic separation. In contrast to the spontaneous opposition of Chimkent, Khwarazm, and Farghana, the action of the Politburo of the Central Committee of the RKP(b) in Moscow on October 11, 1924, decreeing ethnic separateness in Central Asian organization and administration, did not surprise any politician in the three parts of the region. Thus, fundamental changes in the cultural, social, and political life of all Central Asians initiated and ordered by the communist hierarchs in Moscow received a formal stamp of approval from the government of the RSFSR. The Russian leadership created no Central Asian government competent enough to determine its own destiny. The elaborate routine to give the appearance of local initiative only made a show of sovereignty in public and on the record. Superficially imitating genuine popular government, it supplied a semblance of legitimacy to a newly contrived political structure. That edifice could not stand on its own any more than could the dynasties of the Manghits, Mings, and Qonghirats in the face of the light force applied by Russian arms. Instituting the name *Uzbek* as a defining concept in twentieth-century Soviet affairs could not have happened without determined Russian insistence on ethnic segregation.[31]

The Soviet authorities' multiple decisions, sanctions, and jurisdictions authorizing partition confused the lines of command as well as exactly when the new administrative-territorial unit of Uzbekistan came into existence. Seemingly, the authorities never brought a new Uzbek ethnic community, as such, officially into being. The two did not coincide. In order to remove some of these uncertainties, the *Märkäziy Ijraiyä Kamiteti* (Central Executive Committee) of the Uzbekistan Soviet Socialist Republic (UzSSR) (in Uzbek, *Ozbekistan Ijtima'i Shoralär Jumhoriyäti* [OzIShJ]), decreed, on December 12, 1925, that Uzbeks would celebrate the founding of the OzIShJ thereafter on December 5, 1924. On that date the *Inqilabiy-Kamitet—Inqkam* (Revolutionary Committee) of the OzIShJ ostensibly took provisional responsibility for the new entity. Officially, the OzIShJ did not declare itself in existence until the authorities called the First Constituent Congress of Councils of the UzSSR in Bukhara between February 13 and 17, 1925. At that meeting Fayzullah Khoja and the other leaders announced that the new OzIShJ would willingly enter into the Soviet Union as one of the seven union republics (Ukraine, Belorussia, Georgia, Azerbaijan, Armenia, and Turkmenia were the other six), technically equal but actually subordinate to the ruling RSFSR.[32]

After the political reorganization came reports from various parts of Central Asia that members of the population could not avoid innocently misidentifying themselves, just as *Mushtum* had predicted they would. For example, many farmers in Bukhara still could not say whether they should call themselves Uzbek or Kazak. One observer remarked that in 1925, at the time of the First Communist Party Congress of the UzSSR, February 6–12, the townspeople lacked what the rural dwellers strongly possessed—a sense of subgroup identity:

> There is no distinction of nationality in the workers. One must call their nation the nation of the proletariat of the world. In the farmers, though, such is not the case. For farmers, nationality traits pass on and on through the years, generations, and centuries. That way, it [the process] forms a human being who has special traits. They [farmers] are continually set off [from others] by those very peculiarities.[33]

That recollection stressed the contrast in ethnic attachment between town and country people but did not affirm that rural dwellers saw themselves as what the officials administratively termed Uzbeks. In the newly organized Tajik administrative unit within the UzSSR—the Tajik ASSR, established in October 1924 even before the final partition of Central Asia—the few educated Central Asians keenly felt the need to take ethnically sustaining measures. Sadriddin Ayniy, the former bilingual Bukharan reformist, suddenly became a Tajik patriot. He compiled his anthology, *Namunai adabiyati tojik* (Specimens of Tajik Literature) *300–1200 hijri* in 1925, as he wrote, to "benefit the nationality policy of the Party" and to oppose the efforts of Turki speakers to sustain the fruitful old Tajik-Sart-Uzbek symbiosis in Central Asia.[34]

Many could not adapt as quickly as Ayniy to the Soviet prescriptions. Had the choice of identity remained with the Turkistanians, Bukharans, and Khwarazmians, their three heterogeneous states would likely have continued to develop their supraethnic identity. If the region had retained the popular name *Turkistan* in the south as a broad, unifying administrative and territorial designation, subsequent development of group identity in much of Central Asia would have taken a very different course. *Turkistan* remained the foremost communist newspaper's flag as well as the eponym for the TASSR, at least until December 4, 1924, although political events had rapidly begun draining practical effect and cultural or ethnic content from the self-name many months before that.[35]

On December 4, 1924, then, the designation *Turkistan* vanished from the press and as an official group or territorial-administrative title in Central Asia. For decades Stalin's censors treated it as a forbidden political concept or name. A small town in Kazakhstan and a village in the Khwarazm oblast of the UzSSR have, however, quietly preserved the place name, and military authorities still apply the czarist name *Turkistan* to the *Turkistan Härbiy Akrugi* (Military District) encompassing much of southern Central Asia, a command headed by a succession of Slavic generals.[36] The loss of the name *Turkistan* represented more than a change of designation—it deprived Central Asians of the prerogative to determine their own identity. The Russian insistence on instituting ethnic compartmentalization did not mean to benefit the people of the South, as some Soviet histories claim, but, besides neutralizing the Uzbeks, to validate Marxist theories of nationality development. The Russians also wanted to establish themselves and their presumed ethnic homogeneity, which they believed admirable, as the sole model of ethnopolitical development for the East, both domestic and foreign.

Renaming played an important part in the disintegration of the previously composite Turko-Iranian complex so characteristic of Central Asia and delivered a devastating blow to the concept of group self. One contemporary Central Asian scholar recorded that the authorities reached their decision in favor of the Uzbek name not by finding a consensus among those most directly concerned but by consulting the opinions of outsiders, who adamantly rejected Turkistan. "The Soviet government, in order to focus on an ethnic group [*khälq*] with a great homeland [*diyar*] and huge country, to lead it to a new life, put forward the name [*ism*] 'Uzbek.'"[37]

The shock to the Central Asian intelligentsia from the anti-intellectual direction of these events added to their earlier dismay over their dashed hopes for independence from foreign domination. Many intellectuals returned to Islamic mysticism to escape unpleasant ideological reality. Against the background of political tension exacerbated by armed conflict between the Russian troops and Central Asia's Qorbashi resistance movement, Mirza Abdulqadir Bedil (1644–1721) again became a subject of popular as well as scholarly interest, especially in southern Central Asia, including Afghanistan, where libraries and collectors preserved many of his works in manuscript form. Well-known poets and other writers of the Turki language in the twentieth century "assiduously studied and esteemed" Bedil's eighteenth-century Farsi-language works. In 1924 the Central Asian Jadid author Abdalrauf Fitrat published a one-scene dialogue entitled simply *Bedil* that portrayed "Bedilkhaniy" assemblies, popular in earlier decades, using extensive quotations in Farsi in this otherwise Turkic text. One character in the dialogue remarks that the assembly will have two parts, the second of which is *Bedilkhanliq* (Bedil Admiration Session) because "Bedil is the greatest poet of the East." In twentieth-century Central Asia, such a Bedil-like composition employed a kind of double-talk to circumvent Russian and other ideological censors. Bedil used this same technique in his era for getting around spying bureaucrats and the holders of autocratic power with cunningly disguised free speech to communicate with Sufi believers. Central Asians, including the Turki speakers, emulated Bedil's style of Farsi diction.[38]

Enlightened Turkistanians sought an acceptable new intellectual base as place deserted them. In the end, however, the change of name affected the situation much more profoundly than the territorial realignment, for it broke a crucial link between self and group and group and outside world. Turkistan had existed in many shapes and sizes over the centuries, and its human group relied on recorded or generational memory and surviving monuments, both physical and spiritual, to recapture and maintain a sufficient sense of group identity. To these monuments the thinkers and writers now turned for nourishing attachment.

13 Monuments or Trophies

> *Khwarazm . . . was . . . the dwelling-place of the celebrities of*
> *mankind; . . . its environs were receptacles for the rarities of the*
> *time; its mansions were resplendent with every kind of lofty*
> *idea.*
>
> (Ala-ad-Din Ata-Malik Juvaini, *ca.* 1252–1260)*

A group's monuments help to sustain it in its struggle for self-identity. Trophies, in contrast, tell a group who it is not and who the others are. Trophies taken from a group by outsiders signal defeat and contempt. After 1924 the monumental evidence of Central Asia's great cultural and political past anchored the Uzbekistan population in an identity that no longer coincided with ideological reality. For many, the years beginning with 1925 brought a persistent disorientation that one generation's lifetime could never fully dispel. The Uzbekistan Soviet Socialist Republic (UzSSR) began its existence as a theoretical framework into which the politicians of Moscow expected the leaders in Samarkand and the other principal cities to fit appropriate content. Those responsible for responding to Russian policies within this union republic faced severe difficulties. The situation displayed the complexity of an archeological dig that reveals innumerable strata that intricately leak into one another.

---

* 'Ala-ad-Din 'Ata-Malik Juvaini, *The History of the World Conqueror*, vol. 1, trans. John Andrew Boyle (Manchester, Eng.: Manchester University Press, 1958), p. 123.

Very early the Central Executive Committee and Council of People's Commissars that made up the subordinated government of the UzSSR—mirroring the central government in Moscow—resolved to preserve historic monuments located within the union republic's borders. From the beginning, however, even the best-motivated, most-informed leader could not distinguish Uzbek monuments from others within the vast Central Asian accumulation, which led people to avoid making decisions entirely or to take cautious, safe actions that might escape censure. Executives of the UzSSR therefore decided to carry out the provisions for preserving such structures that they had enacted on March 27, 1923, during the former Turkistan republic (TASSR), then in disrepute. Following those provisions solved the problem of decisionmaking but could hardly contribute sound guidelines for determining which monuments qualified as Uzbek and why. Nor could they enlighten citizens of the new UzSSR about which contemporary connection they should attach to given edifices.

The list appended to the TASSR decree illustrates the dilemma, including without distinction both medieval and late nineteenth-century buildings from various dynasties and states with nothing peculiarly ethnic in their architecture or adornment. Out of hundreds of structures in the former Bukharan amirate only twenty were named for Central Asian protection and repair, including the early tenth-century mausoleum of Amir Ismail Samaniy; the Kalan Minaret (1127–1129) (see figure 13.1); ten madrassahs ordered built by several rulers including the Timurid prince Ulugh Beg (1417), the Shaybanid khan Ubaydullah (1535), the Shaybanid khan Abdullah (1566, 1588), and Nadir Muhammad Diwanbegi (1622); the eighteenth-century citadel, eleven city gates, and the main square of Bukhara; a mosque near the city; palaces; and the like.[1]

These monuments, probably singled out for their prestige and aesthetic importance, characterized Central Asian history—Islamic, linguistically and ethnically mixed, a blend of styles, and a variety of political patrons. The law to maintain these structures did not guarantee equal treatment to them or the thousands of others now under the control of a government openly hostile to the Islamic thought and values reflected in these works of art and architecture. USSR policies toward historiography showed that old buildings commissioned by leaders who had lost favor in Soviet interpretations of history suffered neglect while others received attention and perhaps better care.

That imperfect system of preservation came into play because the Soviet regime found private foundations incompatible with state capitalism. For centuries Central Asian philanthropists, like those in other Muslim regions, had set up income-producing foundations in perpetuity to construct, maintain, and provide personnel for bridges, caravansaries, hostels, madrassahs, mosques, and other public works. These philanthropic foundations flourished under a concept and institution entitled *wäqf*, which Soviet authorities attacked from

Figure 13.1 Bukhara's 170-foot Kalan Minaret (1127) in the early 1920s was designated a protected monument by the Turkistan Autonomous Soviet Socialist Republic. Photo: Uzbekistan Society for Friendship Abroad.

the start of the Bolshevik takeover. First these authorities employed out-and-out confiscation, later, economic regulation, and finally they abolished the existence of such philanthropies entirely. Between 1922, when the TASSR issued strict guidelines for their operation, and 1930, when the state made them illegal, *wäqf* properties underwent persistent attack because they and the institutions that financed them embodied not only independence from Moscow but the deepest traditions and values of Islam.

These philanthropies contradicted Marxist doctrines regarding non-governmental property; furthermore, the atheistic communists could not abide Islam's active presence in the society, a feeling that gained strength from deep-seated Russian Christian prejudices against Muslim practices and institutions. Opposition to everything the *wäqf* represented increased along with the great ethnic contempt—discussed in chapter 10, "Politics"—that ordinary Russians expressed toward Sarts. This happened during the 1920s when ideologists glorified the attitudes of the most uneducated, narrow-minded working man while reimposing Russian hegemony over the region. Russian eradication of the Islamic *wäqf* destroyed thousands of Central Asian institutions inside the borders of Uzbekistan, which terminated the previous social or religious function of nearly all monumental structures as well as the wherewithal to keep them presentable as objects of art for group admiration and identity.[2]

TROPHIES

Russian suppression of Central Asian religious institutions in the Soviet period supplemented the Russian neglect and confiscation of czarist years. In addition to the problems of regulation or preservation, Central Asians lived with a continuing legacy of deprivation, which they suffered along with other Asian countries invaded by Western and Eastern European colonial powers. From the earliest days of the Russian invasion, the occupation authorities and their subordinates had taken away thousands of Central Asian objects, of all sizes and kinds, as trophies or plunder that they shipped to Saint Petersburg or Moscow. At the time of the conquest of Khiva in 1873, for example, though the Russians preserved the khanate as a partly independent protectorate, they stole many significant symbols. General K. P. von Kaufman (r. 1867–1882), the first Russian military governor of Turkistan based in Tashkent, plundered the movable symbols of sovereignty as well as the records of intellectual life and history from Central Asia. According to a participant in the plundering,

> Many of our public collections and museums, thanks to von Kaufman, were enriched with the most precious objects . . . and . . . a huge quantity of Arabic, Persian, Central Asian, and other Eastern manuscripts. In the Aziatskii Muzei of our Academy of Science there is also a mass of precious manuscripts received from Central Asia; an abundance of gold and silver jewelry and equestrian ornaments, money and the seal of the Khivan khans grace the collections of the Tsarskosel'skii Arsenal.

In 1873, General von Kaufman, after leading the Russian invasion of Khiva, seized the silver throne of the Khivan khans and sent it to Moscow, where it became part of the collection of the Oruzheinaia Palata in the Kremlin. The general delegated these actions to Aleksandr Ludovich Kun (1840–1888), a half-Armenian Christian graduate of the Oriental Faculty, Saint Petersburg University, who accompanied the invading Russian armies into Khiva and reported on his confiscations:

> Externally, the throne very much reminds one of our very old Czarist thrones. It is made of wood covered with very thin silver leaf, on which are impressed patterns of a Persian character. The cushion on the throne was covered with hide. On a high back of the throne an ornamental silver panel is located with the inscription "In the time of Muhammad Rahim, Khwarazm Shah, in H1231 [A.D. 1816], in Khiva, the handiwork of the unworthy Muhammad."

Orientalist Kun goes on to detail the actual process of looting the Khivan royal palace:

> While K. P. von Kaufman rested on the terrace, I, looking over this part of the palace, noticed this throne in the reception hall. . . Reporting about what I had seen to K. P. von Kaufman, I got permission from him at once to take the throne and all the books and papers from the library.[3]

Asked about how the Khivans reacted to the removal of their throne, Kun responded that he attributed their impassivity to ignorance of its significance or indifference to losing this remarkable, historic symbol of Khwarazm's sovereignty that dated back to the early decades of the ruling Qonghirat dynasty. Kun also took from the Khan's palace one of the precious manuscripts, the monarch's own copy of the history *Firdaws al-iqbal* (*A Paradisaic Garden of Happiness*), commissioned early in the nineteenth century by successive khans from the chroniclers Munis and Agahiy. (See chapter 7, "History.")[4]

Religious objects also attracted the attention of Russian collectors. In 1873 an American diplomat visiting the mausoleum of Khoja Ahmad Yassawiy, a patron saint of the Uzbeks and Kazaks, closely examined the large bronze water vessel; around the outside of the 50-gallon vessel artisans inscribed several lines of Arabic that read "the Highest and Almighty God said, 'Do ye place those bearing water to pilgrims and [those] visiting the sacred temple.'" Completed, that verse from sura 9, verse 19, of the *Qur'ân*, reads "on the same level with him who believeth in God." At the end of that inscription was a reference to making the tank for Amir Timur, who ordered the building of the mausoleum, and the blessing "May God prolong his reign!" followed by a credit to the craftsman: "the work of the servant, striving Godward, Abul-aziz, son of the master Sheref-uddin, native of Tabriz." Metalworkers cast the large container in Karnak, a settlement 25 kilometers north of the town of Turkistan. The mosque within the huge mausoleum, observed the American diplomat, "is considered the holiest in all Central Asia." A recent extensive photographic study of the mausoleum by a

Kazak author reports that, in 1898, subsequent to the diplomat's learned scrutiny of the place, the Russians demolished the adjoining mausoleum of Rabiya Sultan Begim, Abul Khayr Khan's wife, to use its bricks for official czarist buildings.

The fact that Abul Khayr Khan's contemporaries also buried him at the mausoleum gave the site extraordinary historical meaning for Uzbeks. Describing the same water vessel noticed earlier by the American diplomat, the modern Kazak author said it weighed two tons and could contain 60 pails of slightly sweetened water, asserted to have curative powers, that clergymen administered to believers after Friday prayers. The bronze water tank once sat in the mausoleum surrounded by ten tall spears, each with a horse's tail attached, decorated with bronze tips, half-moons, or inscriptions. The Kazak art historian noted that the sacramental vessel now makes up part of the state Hermitage Museum collection in Leningrad. The Russians evidently also broke loose the great inscribed seal of the mausoleum and sent it to a Russian museum.[5]

Some educated Russians deplored these desecrations, but their protests had little effect on the Russians in Central Asia or in Saint Petersburg. From Samarkand General von Kaufman obtained a famed old Qufic *Qur'ān*—the "*Qur'ān* of Uthman," the third Islamic caliph (644–656)—which the general sent on to the minister of Public Education in Saint Petersburg with the advice and assistance of the Orientalist Kun. Although some people criticized this confiscation, Russian personnel said the Turkistanians cared little for the holy book and could not even read it. Muslims, however, felt very strongly about the loss of this sacred volume, which they believed was marked with drops of blood from Uthman himself. To placate the ire of Central Asians and other Muslims, the Soviet regime, on December 9, 1917, ordered this *Qur'ān*—then held in the Petrograd Library—restored to "a congress of Muslims." (Uzbekistan could not receive the book at that date because the unit did not yet exist.) The Russians also removed Timur's tombstone from Samarkand to Moscow. Muslims knew it as a sacred stone that for centuries had served as the ceremonial object on which high officials crowned their khans or amirs. When the Soviet authorities transported this carved *kök tash* (blue-green stone) back to Central Asia, a large ceremony drew approving public response from Uzbeks and other Central Asian writers.

In czarist times and in Soviet days, amateur and professional archeologists tore inscriptions from the walls of historic buildings, demolished old cemeteries of Bukhara containing historic and royal tombstones including that of Amir Shah Murad (r.1785–1800), after 1929, and chopped inscriptions from mountainsides in the wilds. A message carved in April 1391 into the stony Ulu Tagh mountainside near the Karsakpay mines noted the crossing of Amir Timur and his 200,000 men in pursuit of Tokhtamish Khan, a ruler of the Golden Horde from 1378 to 1395. In 1936 that historic fragment of stone found its way into the state Hermitage Museum in Leningrad. Between 1932 and 1936, when people discovered a 23-foot frieze dating back to the first and second centuries A.D. at Ayrtam on the right bank of the Amu Darya eight miles above Termez, it went not to the learned institutions of Uzbekistan but to the same Hermitage Museum, where it remains. Notwithstanding some criticism by czarist Russian intellectuals of such methods, few instances of similar public expression have been published since 1925. Many other instances of authorized looting could be cited, but these better-known examples of Uzbekistan's archeological and cultural losses suggest the great number of such occurrences and give shape to the continuing pattern of a Russian policy seemingly meant to deprive Central Asians of their most significant symbolic monuments—ancient, medieval, and modern.[6]

NEW SYMBOLS OF DEPENDENCE

In 1923, Moscow finally denied the governments in Bukhara and elsewhere permission to issue their own money. From then on, the money of Soviet Russia, printed almost entirely in Russian and circulated in the name of the USSR, officially supplanted local coinage and currency in Central Asia. Pre-1925, the three sectors of the region had each issued unique, instantly recognizable kinds of paper money and some coins that carried their banners and state seals. These they lost entirely. After the partition of Central Asia the authorities contrived two new official symbols for the UzSSR—a union republic flag and seal. On the red banner in gold letters near the pole at upper left appeared the initials Oz. I. Sh. J. in Arabic letters. Below that, evidently as a reminder to Uzbeks of their subordinate status, came Uz. S. S. R. in Cyrillic letters. A close resemblance to the other union republic symbols in the USSR, not distinctiveness, characterized these two new symbols.[7]

The same sort of official ruling designated Samarkand as the first UzSSR capital city. Located near the geographical center of the union republic, that town offered reasonable access to the Bukharan and Khwarazmian populations, which observers said lagged behind Turkistan in all phases of development, including cultural affairs. One of the first centers of radical thought in Central Asia and perhaps the primary focus of Reformist ideas, Samarkand also offered the purest kind of indigenous, Muslim site from which to project Moscow's foreign policy message to the outer Muslim world. This choice of location thus avoided the appearance of continued Russian colonialism that the selection of Tashkent, with its recent history as headquarters for the Russian military governor and its large Russian population, would have made inevitable. Samarkand's architectural beauty testified to the power of Islam, long before Amir Timur's day, to create significant art in Central Asia that could have become the nexus uniting traditional and modern Uzbek identity. The shift of the UzSSR capital out of Samarkand within six years negated that close association by relocating the heart of Uzbek ideological and cultural life in the Russian-dominated town of Tashkent, which displayed relatively few notable Islamic monuments and institutions.[8]

Before that time, Turkistanians, as well as the inhabitants of the other political units in Central Asia, considered most ethnic distinctions unimportant in art and religion. The multiethnic group of intellectuals that coalesced around Abdalrauf Fitrat in Tashkent in 1918 after his flight from the violence in Bukhara called itself by the supraethnic name *Chaghatay Gurungi* (Chaghatay Conversation Circle), and, along with other lively discussion groups, functioned outside communist cultural institutions. Before the political authorities terminated its existence in 1922, the Chaghatay Conversation Circle made progress in educating Turkistanian students about the written history and the Turki (Chaghatay) literary monuments of the past. Many Central Asian intellectuals of the 1920s rejected the Russian plan to divide up Central Asia by ethnic subgroups, a disagreement that continued to provoke dissension in Uzbekistan after 1924. By a peculiar logic ideologists aimed a standard charge of being *millätchilär* (nationalists) against intellectuals who opposed ethnic segregation. The intellectuals' ideas about group and regional names became primary targets of the party spokesmen.

In recasting Central Asian history, Russian ideologist-scholars, publicists, and their followers undermined the meaning and importance of group naming by denying group names to the people and thus directly interfering with Turkistanians' own self-designation. This occurred in spite of or because of the Soviet practice and theory that persuasively demonstrated their ideologists' opinion that names for groups, places, areas, and topographical features have great significance in education and propaganda. The propagandists did not so surely grasp the idea that names of groups and individuals bear deep, essential relationships to their most basic spiritual identity. Soviet theorists show striking inconsistency in this respect.

During the partition of Central Asia and the maneuvering that preceded it between 1923 and 1925, officials ascribed little importance to the traditional names of regions and groups in Central Asia. When Turkistan, Bukhara, and Khwarazm gave way to their Sovietized successors, the authorities of the period ignored the psychological and cultural costs to the population of that abrupt, arbitrary change in group identity. They allotted very few months to people for preparing and executing the drastic change from names used for decades or even centuries and conveyed their disrespect for the traditional names of groups, institutions, places, or terrain features in Central Asia. Leninabad, Frunze, and Stalinabad replaced the age-old Khojand, Pishpek, and Dushanbe in southern Central Asia. The larger, historic cities of Uzbekistan escaped this mistreatment because they possessed too much fame and history and too many inhabitants to permit Soviet ideologists to tamper with their names.

Late in 1926 administrators introduced a law that redistricted the territory of Uzbekistan. Instead of the seven *wilayäts* divided into 23 *tomäns* and 241 *kent jayi*s that the UzSSR inherited, they subdivided the land and people into ten *okrug*s split into 87 *rayon*s, which converted the division types from Central Asian into Russian. Those who ordered this regionalization did not give foreign designations to a single one of the ten new okrugs or to the more than seven dozen rayons, naming them instead Khwarazm, Bukhara, Orta Zarafshan, Samarkand, Tashkent, Khojand, Qoqan, Andijan, Surkhan Darya, and Qashqa Darya. Among the rayons and villages listed in this redistricting law appeared some old tribal names, such as Manghit rayon in Khwarazm okrug and Durmancha and Qurama-Qipchaq villages in Andijan okrug. A great many more old tribal names appeared on the sketch maps such as the locations for Qipchaq and Khitay villages in Khwarazm okrug, Katta-Ming in Orta Zarafshan okrug, and probably hundreds of others.

This sample shows that people traveling the roads of Uzbekistan at that time would have recognized the place names as their own. These vital and concrete toponyms sounded with the intimate tones of Central Asia's cultural life. As the bureaucrats went about drawing up new laws and maps, real tribal life continued in Uzbekistan. In the new Qashqa Darya unit, beyond the okrug center at the town of Behbudiy (formerly Qarshi, renamed for the Turkistanian Jadid leader martyred in 1919), people of the Qonghirat tribe occupied the southeastern portion of Qashqa Darya okrug as well as the rayon of Tangi Kharam and parts of the rayons of Baysun and Shirabad abutting it in Surkhan Darya okrug. In Tangi Kharam rayon, the 1,604 households of the tribe, divided into five clans, made up about 23 percent of the rayon's homesteads, most of whom customarily migrated with the seasons to the foothills of the mountains toward their own winter quarters, moving an average of 110 kilometers. In Samarkand okrug's Yangi Qazan Ariq rayon, Manghit tribesmen constituted the main population group. Down in the Danau rayon of Surkhan Darya okrug, the predominant Uzbeks consisted mainly of the Yuz (Juz) tribe with its clans the Qaratamghali and Turkmens plus the Durman tribe and some Qonghirats. The numerous Uzbek tribes like the Qipchaqs of Baliqchi rayon in Andijan okrug and Qipchaqs of Andijan's Narin rayon formed substantial percentages of the families in those and other districts. From surveys officials learned that a great many Uzbeks continued to retain a strong tribal identity after the partition of Central Asia.[9]

For that and other reasons, the UzSSR's local leadership felt it urgent to popularize the new name now decreed for their people and administrative-territorial unit. The *Inqkäm—Inqilabiy kämitet* (Revolutionary Committee) of Uzbekistan served some two and a half months as an interim government for the emerging union republic. This Revolutionary Committee went out of existence at the First Constituent Congress of the Ozbekistan I.Sh.J. that began February 13, 1925. Before the union republic government supplanted the Inqkam, however, that provisional committee expressed the sense of vibrant ethnocentrism stimulated by the partition of Central Asia.

To begin with, in the formal Appeal to Uzbekistan's Working People, the Inqkam's chairman, Fayzullah Khoja, spoke glowingly about the new *Ozbek jomhoriyäti* (Uzbek republic) as a republic of and for Uzbeks. Here, he committed a bad blunder, in the view of higher authorities, for the appeal expressed a complete misconception about the degree of correspondence that the political authorities in Russia meant to institute between his ethnic group and the administrative-territorial unit of the USSR adopting the group's name. The mirage of a true Uzbek republic that Khoja and his comrades thought they saw in 1924 and early 1925 quickly dissipated when they found that Uzbekistan served as a name but did not specify a place or population identified exclusively with the eponymous group. Fayzullah Khoja and the others could not publicly name the unit in their Turki language as "Uzbek republic" but had to learn the right designation, Ozbekistan I.Sh.J., an ethnically indifferent, neutral label meant to distance the territorial name from the ethnic eponym.

UZBEKIFYING UZBEKISTAN

After this lesson and as a partial recompense, the Inqkam began Uzbekifying the activity and personnel of government—then largely in the hands of outsiders—by making the "Uzbek" language mandatory in the bureaucracy to distinguish insiders from outsiders[10] and bringing into effect official segregation. This action, termed *yerlilashdirish* (localizing/indigenizing) or *ishlarni ozbek tilida yorgozish* (conducting business in Uzbek) meant that the language of administration and government had to change and that Russians and other outsiders working in Central Asia's civil service would have to gain command of written and spoken Uzbek or resign. More significant still, the measure prescribed installing indigenous personnel rather than outsiders in state, public, cooperative, economic, and other specialized institutions. Theoretically, *milliylashdirish* (nationalization) of the main organizations and employers in the new union republic should have reduced the colonialist heritage that had left a preponderance of non–Central Asians holding responsible positions throughout the principal towns and settlements. In practice, displacing even a fraction of the Russians, Ukrainians, European Jews, and other Soviet westerners from key posts in Central Asia took a long time. On March 1, 1928, statisticians found that the proportion of what they now defined as Uzbek personnel in the chief organizations of Uzbekistan had reached 23.5

percent. By September 1, 1930, that percentage had slipped to 22.6, though the Central Committees of CPUz, the Central Asian Bureau of the Unionwide communist party and the Central Executive Committee of Uzbekistan had all resolved to Uzbekify establishments and agencies at 100 percent by that date. The situation led a frustrated Samarkand communist leader to comment that "Uzbekification goes on among us in such a way that Uzbeks and coachmen-Uzbeks sit at the head of institutions; one rides, the other drives, and Russians direct the work. Is this really Uzbekification? Isn't this colonialism on the Russian side?"

Overnight, the manipulation of political organizations in Central Asia appeared to create a fresh basis upon which to reduce local Russian dominance. Most educated Turkistanians had not sought the new name, but when, late in 1925, the benefits of being Uzbek remained intangible, the obvious inequities in employment produced a new kind of ethnic irritability.[11]

About a year after Russian authorities founded the UzSSR, the cultural leaders of that new unit called intellectuals together for their first formal meeting under the union republic's aegis. In 1920, Stalin, the RSFSR People's Commissar for Nationalities' Affairs, had urged his comrades throughout the country to draw the local intelligentsia into Soviet activity:

> It would be unwise, even harmful...to reject these even so infinitesimal groups of local *intelligent*s [the Russian form of specifying the individual] who would perhaps even wish to serve the public but could not do this, perhaps because as noncommunists they consider themselves enveloped in an atmosphere of distrust and they fear the possibility of repression.

The intellectuals attending the gathering in 1926 surprised the proletarian regime's chairmen and secretaries of the UzSSR by openly debating the organization of the assembly itself as well as the subjects on the agenda. The intellectuals evidently anticipated hearing free discussion about important issues and acted on that assumption. The unhappiness of Uzbekistan's communist leaders with this unexpectedly democratic turn of affairs seemingly prevented publication of the full proceedings from this first conference. Brief reports in the press and some prompt reactions by the authorities made a few of the disagreements public. They deserve discussion here. The *Birinchi Ziyalilär Qurultayi* (First Conference of Intelligentsia) (not intellectuals) began in Samarkand February 20, 1926 (possibly 1927—sources disagree concerning the exact date). Politicians opposed to the democratically minded intellectuals denounced them as counterrevolutionaries and nationalists because they opposed efforts to discriminate between categories of intellectuals at the conference. These intellectuals also resisted efforts to put teachers of the UzSSR under the communist party and the councils (Soviets) and rejected the slogans put before the conference that read Unite Knowledge and Labor, End Illiteracy, The Political Proletariat Is the Basis for Culture, Take the Direct Road to Communism, and Fighting against the Nationalists. They worked hard to prevent the communist politicians from, as they put it, dividing intellectuals into bourgeois and proletarian. The UzSSR's communist politicians, believers in class stratification, faced intellectuals who refused to give up the idea, unacceptable to the communists, of preserving "a single Uzbek intellectual community." Even more shocking to the union republic's communist leadership, these intellectuals did not understand that the officials could not permit anyone to disagree with the *firqä yolbashchilighi* (party leadership) or with the approved conciliar intelligentsia. The flustered officials complained that the intellectuals had not learned that party unity demanded their following, not questioning or resisting. The intellectuals had yet to grasp the dogma of communist infallibility.

Besides these procedural matters, Uzbek intellectuals also disagreed with much of the substance on the conference agenda. News reports indicate that the conference "took on a political tinge" because the intellectuals strove for the *ghayä* (idea) of preserving and deepening their influence in the press and the schools. "Preparing ever more strongly," news stories noted, "they [the intellectuals] entered seriously into the task of fighting for [the minds of] the young people." The leaders began to define sinning in a new way, and, like the moralskeepers of Islam before them, they threatened real punishment and damnation for infractions. Communist leaders in the UzSSR (and elsewhere) could not face the sort of ideological competition that had nurtured the Jadid movement. Official UzSSR thinking in the initial stages of formal Uzbekhood showed the inflexibility that characterized Marxists in the USSR.[12] Perhaps in response to the disagreement, the new governors of the region acted arbitrarily and irascibly toward the governed. Instead of showing traditional Central Asian conciliation, they treated as a transgression any sort of independent thinking by the citizenry, especially among the communists.

In every aspect of public life, the leadership began to threaten dissenters with physical retaliation. Consequently, when the UzSSR's first secretary of the communist party offered the following comment during the Second Congress of the CPUz in November 1925, intellectuals had to take it very seriously: "Because of the fact that these comrades acknowledged their own mistakes openly before the party, we all shall consider their repenting with their pure hearts 'satisfactory' for the purpose of forgiving their sins [*gunahlär*]." These words hinted at the violence to come against the independent thinkers in Uzbekistan's social, cultural, and political life.[13]

Communist party policy aimed at undermining another symbol and unifier of Central Asian civilization came into effect in the fall of 1926 when the UzSSR government directed Uzbek leaders to begin introducing, throughout the rayons and centers of the union republic, the New Uzbek (romanized) Alphabet. The law provided for appointing and financially supporting a central committee that would replace the modified and traditional Arabic alphabet with one they called Latin. Central Asians, like most Muslims in that period, regarded Arabic as fundamental and sacred to their culture, owing to its association with the written form of the *Qur'ân* and other holy texts central to Islamic beliefs. Although nothing had yet changed the writing system of Central Asia, this development further stirred Uzbek apprehensions respecting the new government.[14]

To ensure that Uzbeks preserved, read, printed, and performed only approved literature from the past, the UzSSR authorities, within two years of the union republic's inauguration, issued decrees setting strict limits to such things as the performance repertoire in public entertainment. The UzSSR government established a Main Committee for Supervising the Repertoire in March 1927 that furthered the censorship already formally initiated by the UzSSR Council of People's Commissars on July 15, 1925. This new decree gave three officers in Uzbekistan, none of them necessarily or probably Uzbek, responsibility for prior censorship. These officers were (1) a chairman appointed by the office for literary control, *Uzglavlit*, (For Protection of State Secrets), (2) a member of the main political education agency, and (3) a member of the Committee for State Security (GPU—secret police), a forerunner of the KGB. The UzSSR government required this committee to give permission for each performance of every dramatic, musical, or cinematic work, including circuses and folk theatricals. Moreover, the government ordered the committee to compile and publish periodic lists of approved and prohibited works and delegated punitive powers to the committee to summon rulebreakers before the criminal authorities. In smaller towns, these duties fell on the respective inspectors for press affairs or rayon political education agencies. Officials directed the UzSSR Ministry of Education to issue instructions for implementing this decree to all concerned. That comprehensive set of rules made it virtually impossible for theaters to show Jadid or Middle Eastern plays or for folk singers to perform Central Asian epics because the usual Muslim content of most Jadid or traditional literature offended the censors. This decree complemented equally restrictive regulations governing literary publishing.[15]

The rule makers meant to prevent clashes of ideas like those that highlighted the First Conference of Intellectuals of the UzSSR, for neither on stage nor the printed page could communist leaders tolerate ideological dissent. They organized a Second Conference of Intellectuals, to meet October 2–3, 1927, but beforehand called preparatory conferences in cities outside Samarkand. The one in Farghana—that okrug's first conference of intellectuals—heard a Russian (rather than an Uzbek) named Aleksandrof set forth "The Immediate Tasks of the Intelligentsia in the Field of the Ideological Struggle." The choice of the speaker as well as the subject told listeners that the communist party considered local Uzbeks unfit to bring Uzbek intellectuals into line. Aleksandrof spoke repeatedly about the "toiling intelligentsia," who seemed to be semiliterate or literate working men, as distinguished from the troublesome traditional intellectuals. He accused those nonconformists of educating their children in the old schools or *Qur'ân* schools, thus "poisoning the young juveniles' minds with every sort of religious prejudice and nonsense." Reports added that this conference "expressed scorn for such persons in a stern warning" and that "remnants of the old Jadids, abjuring the training of Moscow and Leningrad . . . sent young juveniles to places like Istanbul, which are gripped by pan-Turkism." Ideologists continued to disseminate the fiction of a supposedly dangerous pan-Turkism for decades.

After publicizing the likelihood of unpleasant consequences from continued disagreement with communist directives, the conference outlined what it termed the chief priorities and duties for intellectuals: (1) to work against ideology alien to the poor proletariat, (2) to use science against religious superstition, (3) to emancipate Eastern women, (4) to advance Soviet government and party measures in the fields of education and culture, and (5) "to unite toiling conciliar intellectuals under the leadership [*rähbärlik*] of the communist party in the ideological struggle, rooting out religious prejudice that has poisoned the humanity of workers in general."[16]

REMODELING THE TEMPLE OF LEARNING

Before the Second Conference of Intellectuals, UzSSR leaders announced an agenda that showed this meeting would address only those themes decided on in advance by party officials. The conference would first investigate the work that intellectuals had accomplished so far and give more strength to this sector in the political struggle. The agenda then listed such matters as the tenth anniversary of the Bolshevik coup, the emancipation of Eastern women, the ideological struggle, the fight against imperialism, the communist party's cultural leadership, the conversion from the Arabic to the Roman alphabet, an increase in the numbers of worker-peasant reporters in the Red press (to replace those who had grown up in Jadid journalism), and the like. That ominous first item on the agenda—looking into the previous conferences—probably represented the only subject not unanimously agreed on. The conference adopted extreme ideological positions in the field of education that would affect Uzbek schooling such as paragraph six of the conference decisions, "The old schools are unsuitable for the present way of life and are remnants of the ignorance that obstructs our cultural improvement. For this reason, the conference categorically demands their elimination in the near future. It is considered emphatically imperative not to permit the reformed primary schools to continue."

This marked the end of old and New Method Muslim educational institutions in Central Asia. Political authorities undermined Muslim schools by refusing to pay the teachers and confiscating the *wäqf* endowments that had supported them. Despite Soviet economic inadequacy, which forced the closing of virtually all Soviet schools in Central Asia, fanatic communist leaders' antireligious doctrines could not permit the network of Muslim schools to continue functioning, even though Soviet schools had not yet replaced them. During the first Five-Year Plan (1928–1932), the Soviet government confiscated the assets of Muslim philanthropies, dissolved the remaining endowments, and sternly enforced what the regime called "separation of church and school." In 1925, Rahim Inoghamaw, the Uzbek commissar for education, reported to the First Uzbekwide Congress of Councils of Workers, Farmers, and Red Army Deputies of the UzSSR that formal schooling still trained less than 1 percent of the union republic's young people. A consequence of the Soviet dogmatism that destroyed traditional and reformed Central Asian schools could be seen in literacy figures published by the Central Asian Economic Council in 1931. Of people in the age group 16 to 40—the most educated broad adult cohort—only 27.3 percent were literate in the UzSSR by 1930, thirteen years after the Bolshevik takeover in Turkistan, and only 12.2 percent of the women in that bracket could read and write. Nonetheless, the Second Conference for the Cultural Advancement and Upbringing of Workers, as they now designated the Conference of Intellectuals, moved to ostracize intellectuals who argued at the conference against closing existing Central Asian schools. Akmal Ikramov, a leading UzSSR communist politician speaking elsewhere about the accomplishments of that conference, revealed that Central Asian communism really had no place for intellectuals:

> Into this nonparty conference dropped one of those people who talks everywhere against Soviet authority, and another one—roughly the very same type, one of the recognized poets—had written a few rhymes. When they appeared at the conference, people said to them: "Among the laboring Uzbek intelligentsia there is no place for people who are against Soviet authority, against the laboring masses," and both men were expelled with unanimous agreement. This is how we solve the nationality problem.

Coercion and exercise of authoritarian control became the ways in which Soviet politicians managed Uzbekistan's affairs. By late 1927 the UzSSR branch of the communist party abandoned tolerance entirely and determined that it wanted no independent minds in its intelligentsia. To isolate those intellectuals whose views differed from the authorities seemed more desirable to the politicians than exploiting their abilities. The communist party leadership took this path even though the UzSSR suffered from a shortage of capable, educated persons to help operate the educational system and other arms of the pervasive governmental structure. The new leadership put Soviet Marxist ideology ahead of common sense and educating Uzbek children.[17]

In the latter part of the 1920s a concerted anti-intellectualism came to Uzbekistan with the Russian version of Marxist proletarian internationalism. Within the learned community of Central Asia, even in this unlikely atmosphere, serious scholars again addressed bringing to the public's attention the great heritage of Central Asian art, history, and literature by preparing for publication several volumes of articles and texts.

Russian Orientalists such as Aleksandr A. Semenov (1873–1958) played a crucial role in this effort, for they knew the civilization of Central Asia and could serve in place of Uzbeks, whom the ideological authorities evidently disqualified from such efforts. For example, early in his career, Professor Semenov took an interest in Mir Ali Shir Nawaiy's creativity that resulted in Semenov's first published article and short translation about the medieval poet. Not until much later, however, did another of his works about Mir Ali Shir appear in print because the chronology depended on a nonacademic calendar over which he had no authority. Dr. Semenov's first article and translation commemorated the 500th anniversary of Mir Ali Shir's birth, 17 Ramazan A.H. 1344 (February A.D. 1926). Several additional memorial volumes appeared in the Soviet East outside Uzbekistan, for all Central Asia and other Turkic areas considered Mir Ali Shir their legacy. Three books appeared in Baku, one in Ashkhabad. The Turkmen cultural leader and poet Ahmad Qul-Muhamedov (189?–1933?) translated and edited Mir Ali Shir's *Muhakamät al-lughätäyin* (Debate of the Languages, 1499) into Turkmen for its first Soviet publication (1925). The Azerbaijanian volumes *Nawaiy*, '*Ali Shir Nawaiy*, and *Husayn Bayqara diwani* presented texts and studies of Timurid-era language and literature prepared by the Azerbaijanian scholars Ismail Hikmat and Mirza M. Ibrahimi and the Crimean Tatar Bekir W. Chobanzada (1893–1937).[18] One of those edited by Professor Chobanzada reproduced Mir Ali Shir's *Wäqfiyä* (Muslim Philanthropy, 1926) just when Russian authorities were forcing that benevolent tradition out of existence in Central Asia and made the scholar vulnerable to communist party retaliation. Politicians purged him and Dr. Aleksandr Samoilovich, two of many good minds from the outside contributing much to knowledge of Central Asian culture, for nonconformity and killed them in 1937–1938. For political reasons posthumous bibliographies of Professor Chobanzada's scholarly works ignore his edition of *Wäqfiya*.[19]

In his role as a Central Asian Islamic classicist, Professor Abdalrauf Fitrat wrote the main work in Uzbekistan dedicated to the quincentenary celebration of Mir Ali Shir's birthdate on the Muslim (lunar) calendar. In 1926 Professor Fitrat published a minor journal article entitled "About Nawaiy's Farsi Poetic

Art and His Farsi Diwan,"[20] and in the same year published his edition of the *Diwan* (Collection of Poems) by Husayn Bayqara, Mir Ali Shir's onetime schoolmate and Timurid sovereign. The central Academy of Science of the USSR decided to issue a volume devoted "to the Turki poet, Mir-Ali-Shir Nevai" in the autumn of 1926. When the book came out in Russian two years later, the contributions, edited by academician Vasiliy V. Bartold (1869–1930), included Bartold's long essay about Mir Ali Shir's political activity. Other authors and reviewers included some of Russia's most eminent Turkologists and Orientalists of the time: Samoilovich, Yevgeniy E. Bertels (1890–1957), and Aleksandr A. Romaskevich (1885–1942). No Central Asian authors participated.[21]

These academic commemorations dedicated to Mir Ali Shir and his monuments of literary and religious works showed that serious scholars regarded the achievements of the Timurid poet and official as a patrimony of both Central Asia and the outer Muslim Middle East. The long gap between academician Semenov's first publication about Mir Ali Shir and his second work in 1938 gave evidence of the rising ideological tension in Central Asia over the interpretation and adoption of the cultural legacy. Central to the controversy was Professor Fitrat's anthology *Specimens of the Oldest Turkic Literature* (1927), which properly treated the famed eleventh-century dialect dictionary and anthology by Mahmud of Kashgar as a general Turkic legacy. Professor Fitrat's presentation denied that scholars must divide the Central Asian culture and people into ethnic subidentities. Professor Fitrat's next compendium (*Specimens of Uzbek Literature*, 1928) aroused even greater consternation among UzSSR and other Central Asian ideologists, for he devoted most of its 319 pages to the writings of Mir Ali Shir and other Chaghatay (Turki) authors and poets of Timurid times.[22]

Communist ideologists criticized the texts because they suggested the universality of Central Asia's literary monuments and also outraged proletarians who could not stomach the Islamic mysticism, outright religiosity, lyrical imaginings, and magical fantasies of poets such as Mir Ali Shir and Sultan Husayn Bayqara. Ideologists finally termed those presentations of early literature *nationalistic*, meaning un-Soviet. This Chaghatayism became a severe political charge against Professor Fitrat and like-minded Central Asians. The 500th anniversary commemoration of Mir Ali Shir's birthday passed quietly for the public; within the intellectual community, however, the events of 1926–1928 aroused a furor that intensified and turned increasingly vicious in the ensuing decade. Although this fight involved semantic differences over the meaning of Chaghatay and other charged adjectives, it focused on genuine intellectual issues such as free possession and use of the cultural heritage as opposed to severely limited access to that legacy through the strict ideological interpretation supplied by Marxists. The intellectuals striving for free study of the Central Asian civilization found themselves in an increasingly perilous position. When Marxist ideologists could not prevail in reasoned argument, they employed force to resolve the question the way they preconceived it.

Signposts of a less-tangible sort than town markers or communist party ostracism guided Central Asian groups through the unstable 1920s. People in a society's past may enrich a civilization like the sun and rain and leave their influence in the cultural accretion for later generations. Attitudes toward such a person continually evolve; at times his former existence serves no later purpose, at others, he is crucial to a concept of group self. Among Central Asia's wealth of poets, people remember Mir Ali Shir Nawaiy for his elegant lines of lyric and narrative verse. By the twentieth century, however, his elaborate diction and lexicon posed great difficulties for ordinary readers as well as for learned ones, but Mir Ali Shir still stood as a towering monument to Central Asian culture. When Professor Fitrat claimed Mir Ali Shir in 1928 for Uzbek literature, the unimaginative, uninformed proletarian critics—then in their heyday in Central Asia—could not grasp the significance of their contemporary's vision and responded, like most reactionaries, with loathing and revulsion. They could not tolerate those new ideas advanced by Professor Fitrat that identified the great Timurid writer affirmatively and directly with UzSSR culture.

During and after the academic commemoration for Mir Ali Shir in 1926, the main UzSSR state association for mobilizing intellectuals to serve communist party purposes—the Uzbekistan Union of Soviet Writers (UzUSW)—expressed its official attitude toward Central Asian culture during meetings in 1934–1935. Rahmat Majidi (1906–197?), chairman of both the Uzbek Committee in the UzUSW and the Organizational Committee for the UzSSR branch of the unionwide state-controlled Writers' Union, denounced and harassed intellectuals opposed to total communist ideological interpretation of Central Asian culture. In a speech before the First Congress of the Union of Soviet Writers in Moscow in 1934, Majidi, among other things, accused writers and allied intellectuals who had participated in previous writers' circles of the crime of "trying to make Chaghatay literature the basis of Uzbek Soviet literature." Considering his forum, Uzbek intellectuals could not ignore Majidi's political accusations, for Stalin's lethal reign of terror had already made itself felt in Central Asia and elsewhere in the USSR.[23]

Scholars, writers, and other Uzbek intellectuals retreated into activities they hoped would shield them from the recriminations of Rahmat Majidi and similar ideologists. Some intellectuals concentrated on bibliographic research, others devoted themselves to translating, and some scholars turned to studying medieval sources relating to property rights and other economic subjects. Professor Fitrat prepared, in collaboration with a Russian scholar, perhaps as his last published scholarly work, an annotated collection of rare sixteenth-century documents from the Qadi of Urgut. He made an unlucky choice. To begin with, the small booklet emphasized the Shaybanid period and its tribal symbols—two topics threatening to the authorities. Furthermore, several of the documents selected by the two authors related not merely to local economic agreements or disagreements but to transactions involving Russians. Documents 15 and 17 detail the freeing of two slaves by their Central Asian masters. In the first, a Mawlana Qadim ibn Khoja Aziz freed absolutely a person described as "his own Russian slave of medium build, brunette, with sound body, age about 60, named Yusuf." In the second case, Khoja Mumin ibn Khoja Muhammad Husayn freed unconditionally "one of his slave women, a Russian, with a white face, with slightly grown eyebrows, of middle height, with sound body, approximately 70 years old, by the name of Aq-Qiz [White Girl]." The presence of Russian captives in the Central Asian states had inflamed public opinion in Russia against the Khivan khan and other Central Asian rulers in the nineteenth century and served as a prelude to the Russian invasion. In Professor Fitrat's day, ideological critics used nearly any pretext to damage intellectuals in the eyes of the Russian secret police and political purgers; Fitrat's essay may have added weight to the case accumulating against him.[24]

Throughout 1936 and probably 1937, communist ideologists continued to label any reverence for the splendid Chaghatay literary heritage as nationalism. Harboring any ideas unacceptable to authoritarian Russian and UzSSR political figures could result in arrest and imprisonment. In 1938 and 1939 Professor Fitrat and many of his colleagues were put to death by the secret police for defending their convictions about the Central Asian literary identity. More would follow and others had gone the same way before them.

In a manner of speaking, the communist party and its secret policemen displayed the heads of Professor Fitrat and his companions as trophies to triumphant communism along with those of the Uzbek politicians such as Fayzullah Khoja and Akmal Ikramov. Subsequent apologias have tried to blame this barbarism on the psychopathology of Stalin, but in Central Asia executioners loyal to the communist system committed these atrocities. (Until the mid-1980s, like-minded politicians continued to deny a full posthumous exoneration of Abdalrauf Fitrat.) The ideological functionaries who executed those indigenous political leaders also, around 1938, did away with a number of other Uzbeks in responsible positions for embodying the eponym for Uzbekistan.[25]

ABRIDGING LITERARY MONUMENTS

After that disaster wiped out the foremost figures in Uzbek society and culture, reconstructing an upper stratum for Uzbek intellectual society began. In late 1938, the officially planned and guided rehabilitation of medieval

Central Asian literature—personified by Mir Ali Shir Nawaiy—aimed at a longer-range goal than simply reviving a narrow, controlled intellectual life in the UzSSR. The turnabout, the first step toward a more important goal, entailed a major rewriting of Uzbek history. Mir Ali Shir's legacy served as both an instrument and a test case. Whichever way things developed in the troubled atmosphere created by Soviet Russian policies, the case of Mir Ali Shir would be a harbinger of things to come. That mainly non-Central Asian tutors rather than Uzbek scholars and researchers initiated this revision of policy and intellectual history has great meaning.

Communist political solutions to intellectual problems not only did violence to the extraordinary writings of medieval Central Asians but invariably involved coercion and force against strong-minded men and women who refused to abandon conscience and submit to ideological pressure. This communist inhumanity matched the feats of the most aberrant rulers such as Nadir Shah, Amir Nasrullah Bahadur-Khan, and Lt. General Mikhail G. Cherniaev (1828–1898; r. Turkistan as governor-general, 1882–1884), who had scarred the history of modern Central Asia.

The ideological authorities and their tame intelligentsia in the UzSSR seemed bent on outraging the memory of Professor Fitrat, who headed whole rosters of murdered Uzbek cultural leaders, but to achieve this revenge they executed a nearly complete turnabout in their attitude toward the Central Asian Chaghatay heritage. Thus in 1938 the authorities appointed a multiethnic committee to arrange new celebrations for the 500th anniversary of Mir Ali Shir's birthday. This time, by dating it according to Russia's Christian (solar) calendar rather than Mir Ali Shir's Muslim one, they selected 1941 as his Soviet-style quincentennial year. Under the auspices of the Jubilee Committee for Ali Shir Nawaiy headed by A. Abdurahmanov, the leading UzSSR Uzbek government official and chairman of the Council of People's Commissars, a group of Russian and Central Asian scholars and writers put together a new volume devoted to Mir Ali Shir Nawaiy. By not entitling it something concerning Chaghatay or Central Asian Turki writing, but *Father of Uzbek Literature* (1940), they adhered to the political directives guiding the adaptation of medieval literature. Chairman Abdurahmanov gave a state seal of approval to the volume by signing the introduction. In his opening statement the official called the jubilee for Mir Ali Shir "a triumph of Leninist-Stalinist nationality policy" but omitted acknowledging the harrowing path the Uzbeks had trod to reacquire portions of their Central Asian cultural legacy. Abdurahmanov remarked that previous scholars could not correctly evaluate and understand Mir Ali Shir Nawaiy and labeled as enemies those intellectuals "who had declared Nawaiy's art to be 'heresy' and 'trash.'" Other contributors to the 223-page book—including Russian academicians Evgeniy Bertels, Aleksandr K. Borovkov (1904–1962), Aleksandr Semenov, and Central Asians Hadi Zarif,

Yunus Latif, Hamid Alimjan, and Uyghun—dealt carefully with the subject of their study or simply translated the poet and his contemporaries.[26]

This directed effort aimed at the Uzbek understanding of both recent and medieval Central Asian history. The great Chaghatay poet Mir Ali Shir needed no glorification by the Soviet regime's propaganda, but his stature compelled Soviet officials to return him to the canon of acceptable Central Asian literary history. This official campaign also served to set up the systematic activity needed to occupy the remnants of Uzbekistan's literary and historiographical establishment. Thus these preparations for celebrating anew Mir Ali Shir's birthdate became a token restitution of the Central Asian cultural heritage denied to the Uzbeks from 1928 to 1938 by Russian communist ideologists and their local deputies. More practically, the rehabilitation of Mir Ali Shir Nawaiy as a pillar of Soviet Central Asian culture demonstrated a procedure that would serve as a model in the methodology of communist literary-historical evaluation. That assessment ideologically screened works and either rejected them entirely or expurgated them so that Uzbekistan's publishers could safely reproduce or popularize the remnants. The technique provided a doctrinaire reinterpretation of those selected writings to make them acceptable to the political authorities.[27]

Following this system, they could print many great compositions by Mir Ali Shir by cutting out sections that might offend the sensibilities of Marxist atheists or purists. In preparing Mir Ali Shir's narrative and philosophical poem *Alexander's Wall* for publication, editors deleted many stanzas from the opening sections because the Timurid author, as customary, devoted them to praising Allah and the Prophet Muhammad. They followed this same procedure (though acknowledging some of the abridgements) when they removed most of the first four chapters from the medieval *Qabus-namä: Mirror for Princes* for Uzbek readers. Innumerable examples of Soviet editors' applying retrospective censorship to the best of Central Asian literature and history occupy the world's library shelves.[28]

This drastic change meant that articles about Mir Ali Shir—now usually designated by his pen name, Nawaiy (which expressed proletarian reluctance to using his noble title Mir, short for Amir)—suddenly reappeared in the press of the region. In 1938 the ideologists, to rid themselves of the term *Chaghatay*, prescribed *Old Uzbek*, though this attributive badly distorted the literary history of the region. Without quite calling Nawaiy an Uzbek, Academician Aleksandr A. Semenov, for example, wrote that "Nawaiy [is] the most outstanding creator of the literary Uzbek language [and] belongs among the most famed founders of the Uzbek language and Uzbek literature." Academician Semenov wrote several articles on that theme during 1939 and 1940: one appeared in the Russian-language Tashkent literary journal *Literature and Art of Uzbekistan* and another, in the communist *Pravda Vostoka*, in Russian. Thereafter he published only two brief writings about the Chaghatay poet, one in 1945 and one in 1946. Otherwise, Professor Semenov left this touchy argument over Mir Ali Shir's group identity alone.

The Tatar teacher Abdurrahman Saadi felt less restrained than academician Semenov in revising literary history. In 1938 Professor Saadi declared Mir Ali Shir "the great poet of the Uzbek people" and said that "Nawaiy created the Uzbek literary language" but avoided referring to Nawaiy directly as "an Uzbek." Satti Husayn, an Uzbek journalist, playwright, and dogmatic critic, skillfully switched from opponent to proponent of the Chaghatay heritage. Before 1938 he helped lead the fatal attacks on writers such as Abdulhamid Sulayman Cholpan, whom he and others called nationalists for favoring Chaghatayism. After 1938, however, Satti Husayn exhibited no qualms over embracing Mir Ali Shir Nawaiy as "the greatest" and a full-fledged Uzbek poet.[29] These turnabouts in cultural understanding and history undermined serious inquiry and distorted informed discussion.

Soviet Central Asian political authorities took Uzbekistan's cultural heritage over an extremely costly, convoluted route between 1922 and 1941 only to arrive at approximately where they started. That maneuver, however, sharply limited the accessible heritage, replaced the leading Central Asian intellectuals with a compliant cultural establishment, and terrorized the populace. That seems to have been the aim of the entire effort, but it did not end there. More ideological reinterpretations of all past thinking and art accompanied the development of what the authorities hoped would become a truly Sovietized Uzbek intelligentsia.

14 Genealogy

Ozgä elning sultani bolgunchä,
oz elingning chopani bol!

Rather than becoming sultan of another tribe,
be a shepherd of thy own!

(Central Asian proverb)*

Events in the late 1920s and 1930s proved to communist party leaders that they could not persuade many of Central Asia's traditional intellectuals to discard their values or ways of thinking in favor of Marxist dogma. To alter people's thinking about their group identity, then, the ideologists of the UzSSR, going beyond changing the ethnic name and filtering the cultural heritage, modified the meaning of the name they had applied to the group by revising its history. To accomplish this, they altered the systems of writing and teaching as well as the subjects of instruction. They redirected both children's and adults' education to create a new and different pool of selectively educated people in Uzbekistan.

Intellectuals—persons who examine their own thoughts—define themselves by independence of mind and association as well as catholicity of knowledge and outlook. This *äqlli adäm/intellektualnyi chelovek* differed remarkably

---

* M. Äfzälaw, S. Ibrahimaw, and S. Khudaybergänaw, comps., *Ozbek khälq mäqalläri* (Tashkent: OzSSR Däwlät Bädiiy Ädäbiyat Näshriyati, 1960), p. 20.

from the citizen desired by the new leadership. To distinguish the new from the old, the ideologists referred to the new as an *intelligent* in the Russian version of that European term, which translated into the Uzbek word *ziyali*. By communist design this individual lacked the breadth and depth of Central Asia's old intellectual.

The classically educated men of the Jadid period sought to prepare a new type of educated person who could use communications skills of all kinds and engage in the modern schooling and other activities but who lacked the profound knowledge or insight that characterized his conventionally well-educated predecessor. The Soviet version of this intelligentsia embodied those limitations but in addition followed the directions of others rather than thinking for himself. He became the model *ziyali/intelligent* for the new era in Central Asia. Into this impressionable new man the communist cultural leaders of the UzSSR began putting their specialized understanding of the group name *Uzbek*. For this important effort local officials took their lead from Russian ideologists, who held a special view toward group naming.

Others believe that human group names have extraordinary significance for the persons included in such bodies, lying at the very root of individual attachment to a group. But denominations for the groups, as such, serve an even more crucial function. Wrenched from his group, an individual retains the strongest sense of its importance. The trauma becomes even more devastating for the group that is deprived of its own self-designation. Such a group ceases to exist in history and international society and eludes the grasp of its own former members. Voluntarily discarding a group self-name becomes nearly impossible because its members require its preservation. Central Asian emigrants from the 1920s and 1930s fervently clung to *Turkistanian* as their group's primary identification; *Uzbek*, *Karakalpak*, or *Kazak* commanded only perfunctory loyalty. Changes in names of political entities, states, subordinate units, and the like, in contrast, have import for the individual affected but give an external meaning to the ethnic identity system unless the state name coincides with the ethnic group designation.

The intimate, synchronic connection between name and group must be vital, for although an ethnic group in peaceful times changes almost completely every few generations, the persistent denomination of such an ethnic group holds its power, even though the makeup of the aggregation actually bearing the name differs from the original group (see figure 14.1). The viability of the group name overlaps the outgoing and incoming membership, embracing the gradual alteration in the population with its potent symbolism.

What would happen if the group suddenly lost or gained huge numbers of members or if a crisis extinguished the living name? A hypothetical example shows the singularity of the group's name. If, on the demise of ethnic group A, community B, after a considerable period of time, should adopt group A's de-

Figure 14.1 The Last Indigenous Rulers of Southern Central Asia

UZBEK TRIBAL DYNASTIES 1710–1920

Manghit (Bukhara)		Qonghirat (Khiva)		Ming (Qoqan)	
Muhammad Rahim	1753–1758	Ishmed Biy	1717–1763	Shahrukh	ca. 1710–1721
Daniyal Biy	1758–1785	Muhammad Amin Inaq	1763–1790	Abdalrahim	1721–1734
Shah Murad	1785–1800	Awaz Inaq	1790–1804	Abdalkarim	1734–1750
Haydar Tora	1800–1826	Iltuzar	1804–1806	Irdana Biy	1751–1770
Husayn	1826	Muhammad Rahim I	1806–1825	Narbota Biy	1770–1798
Umar	1826	Allah Quli	1825–1842	Alim Khan	1798–1810
Nasrullahkhan	1826–1860	Rahim Quli	1842–1845	Umar Khan	1810–1822
Muzaffar al-Din	1860–1885	Muhammad Amin	1845–1855	Muhammad Ali (Madali)	1822–1842
Abdalahad	1885–1910	Sayyid Muhammad	1856–1864	Shir Ali	1842–1845
Mir Muhammad Alim	1910–1920	Muhammad Rahim II	1865–1910	Khudayar	1845–1858
		Asfandiyar	1910–1918	Malla	1858–1862
		Sayyid Abdullah	1918–1920	Shah Murad	1862
				Khudayar (2d reign)	1862–1863
				Sayyid Sultan	1863–1865
				Khudayar (3d reign)	1866–1875
				Nasiraddin	1875–1876

SOURCES: S. V. Bakhrushin, V. Ia. Nepomnin, V. A. Shishkin, eds., *Istoriia narodov Uzbekistana*, vol. 2 (Tashkent: Izdatel'stvo Akademii Nauk UzSSR, 1947), pp. 459–63; Stenli Len-Pul', *Musul'manskiia dinastii*, trans. and ed. V. V. Bartol'd (Saint Petersburg: M. M. Stasiulevich, 1899), pp. 233–37; V. A. Romodin, "Nekotorye istochniki po istorii Fergany i kokandskogo khanstva (XVI–XIX v.v.) v rukopisnykh sobraniiakh Leningrada," *Trudy dvadtsat piatogo mezhdunarodnogo kongressa Vostokovedov, Moskva 9–16 avgusta, 1960*, vol. 3 (Moscow: Izdatel'stvo Vostochnoi Literatury, 1963), p. 65; M. G. Wahabaw, W. Ya. Nepomnin, T. N. Qariniyazaw, eds., *Ozbekistan SSR tärikhi* vol. 1, book 2 (Tashkent: Ozbekistan SSR Fänlär Äkädemiyäsi Näshriyati, 1957), pp. 448–60; S. V. Zhukovskii, *Snosheniia Rossii s Bukharoi i Khivoi za poslednee trekhsotletie* (Petrograd: Trudy Obshchestva Russkikh Orientalistov, No. 2, 1915), pp. 200–202.

nomination, nothing would transfer the intimate linkage between group A's elders and its name to group B, the newly named group. This fresh cluster of humans could now begin to pass on an accumulated history and ethnicity to its successors even though holding the same name as the now defunct group A. Thus, theoretically, names can regenerate but cannot become more than homonyms, for they convey different meanings. The selection of group A's name by another, subsequent human community—group B, disconnected from group A and its designation—would not, therefore, constitute a furtherance of the group identity considered here. Nor would this happenstance prolong the history of group A; groups A and B would remain distinct. Unbroken continuity, however tenuous, within one evolving group under the same name provides the key connection between past and present. Members of A and B could share neither experience nor devotion to the same group. These relationships demonstrate that continuity of name, not continuation of physiological type, sustains the ethnic group.

RACIALIST THEORY

Around 1940 Russian cultural supervisors directing the program to reorient Central Asian group identity began still another phase in their revision of group history and identity. This started in 1938 (see chapter 13, "Monuments or Trophies") with the UzSSR state committee working to rehabilitate Mir Ali Shir (Nawaiy) and some of his writings. For such theoretical ideologists, this radical endeavor grounded itself in racialist (based on race) theories. (A perversion of such ideas had gained notoriety around the world owing to efforts made by the National Socialist German Workers' Party [Nazi] regime in Germany, which advanced the notion that certain races of people are distinguishable from and superior to others.) Then, as now, the practical definition of race lacked precision. Proponents of the racialist theory of Central Asian Uzbek history began with the premise that an ethnic group (in Uzbek, *khälq*, Russian *narod*) or nationality's identity is determined by its physical human composition. This comes about, assumed the ideologists, not through a group's own volition or choice but by the very corporeality of its members, something they would refer to as an objective identifying feature of the group. These theorists held that circumstances surrounding the formation of a certain ethnic group must be such that the merging of unlikes would produce a unique aggregate through an "ethnogenetic" (Russian, *narodoobrazuiushchii*) process.

"The Uzbek ethnic group," such Russian writers emphasized, "was composed both of representatives of the white European races . . . and representatives of the yellow, Mongolian races." These theorists cited language, culture, history, and physical aspect/appearance as evidence. These same ideologists proved, they thought, that the twentieth-century Uzbeks constituted a great human conglomeration and that observers could, by sight, distinguish their predecessors from other Central Asians.[1] In this hypothetical development, geographic site took second place only to blood relationship. Ethnogenesis mainly analyzed and explained people occupying a given piece of territory. These Russian scholars thought that immigrants, invaders, emigrants, and refugees could affect the process of ethnogenesis, but the theories made land the core, centering on the region in which the group under scrutiny lived at the time of the theorizing, in this instance, Uzbekistan around 1940. That fixation on current geographic location required that those advancing this argument search for retrospective proof on the same piece of territory.

Out of this grew the proposition's second weakness or fallacy, that of projecting backward. To validate the scheme, "land of the Uzbek"—*Ozbek-i stan* (Uzbekistan)—had to exist from time immemorial. Presumably, the multitudes of people whose lives could have touched that territory at one time or another contributed to the makeup of the eponymous ethnic group that occupied it in 1940. Racialist theorists proposed that the natural human physical amalgam determined the ethnic identity of Central Asia at least until the conquest by Russian armies and perhaps afterward. Furthermore, the racialists, when realigning group genealogies by time, encountered an era in which they could not avoid discussing and designating the groups that they had co-opted. The Russian scholars were obliged to say that the people from whom the Uzbeks mainly derived at that time were "the whole Turkic population" of what later became Uzbekistan.[2] The term *Old Uzbek*, by this logic, had to be applied to "the entire Turkic past" of what officials in 1940 called *Uzbekistan*. That arbitrary exclusion of the considerable Iranian component—so characteristic and the mixture so definitive of the Central Asian population since antiquity— seemed to undermine even the racialists' explanation for Uzbek ethnogenesis. Selectivity remained true to their line of reasoning, however.

Besides pointing to blood ties and designating limited territory, some racialists claimed that language family and sublanguage—whether they functioned through a living tongue or a literary medium—would identify the group in question. Again, the theorists pointed to the Turkic linguistic family, where they evinced some lack of conviction by using the awkward formulation "old and new Uzbek." Had they been as sure as they claimed, simply using "Uzbek" for that span should have been adequate. This dual terminology became a means to avoid applying such recognized terms as Turki, Chaghatay, or Qipchaq at appropriate periods to link the twelfth century with the twentieth through "that same unbroken line of development." This technique did not seek a language terminology (they could choose existing terms) but pre-emptively maneuvered to remove ideologically dangerous traces from names that connoted Central Asian connections too old and too broad to harmonize with the

Russian Marxist theory of Uzbek existence. Beyond that, the ideologists needed to effect certain political and linguistic manipulation to make the hypotheses even roughly fit the realities.[3]

These ideological steps in the language field preceded by two decades the public campaign to reinterpret and rename Mir Ali Shir Nawaiy's legacy to Central Asia but seem to relate to it. When the communist policy to partition Central Asia necessitated the invention of a modern Uzbekistan in Central Asia to replace the Turkistan, Bukhara, and Khiva of the mid-1920s, Russian cultural officials looked for a logical language base. They soon would standardize the Soviet Uzbek language for its writers on the basis of what specialists conceived to be the cleanest, most distinctive, most Uzbek version of the tongue. At the time, they could hear that language spoken in the villages and the countryside geographically somewhat removed from Tajik and other Iranian concentrations. Isoglosses enclosing pure Uzbek speakers existed in the small towns of Chimkent, Mankent, Qan, Qarabulaq, and Turkistan, north of Tashkent as well as the great tribal areas spreading south of Samarkand to include Kitab, Shirabad, and Kelif. Although the numerous Qipchaq-Uzbek speakers covered a great area, in this competition another dialect—one employed in the densely populated Farghana Valley, Tashkent, Jizzakh, and Bukhara—prevailed. Against Uzbek wishes, the authorities transferred Uzbek places north of Tashkent into the Kazakhstan Autonomous Soviet Socialist Republic (KazASSR) in 1924–1925.

At first officials dealing with the UzSSR chose to generalize those vowel-harmonized dialects of the language known under the Turkic subfamily heading as Qipchaq-Uzbek. Morphologically similar to other dialects, the spoken Qipchaq-Uzbek language differed most noticeably in the pronunciation of certain consonants: for example, initial hard *j* instead of *y*, *jigit* rather than *yigit* (young man). Soviet cultural politicians soon shifted the language focus away from the linguistic anchor in the communities of southwest Kazakhstan and southern Uzbekistan. In changing their position the ideologists established the Iranized, unharmonized Tashkent dialect as the official language base and altered the Romanized alphabet that represented the vowel-harmonized language. Because the unharmonized language used fewer vowels and therefore needed fewer vowel signs in the alphabet, in 1935, cultural managers removed four letters standing for the matching vowel sounds (in Uzbek alphabetical order) *ä, ö, ü, ï*, counterparts of *a, o, u, i*.[4] Although this alteration probably originated in a drive to recenter the UzSSR's political affairs in Tashkent rather than Samarkand, educated Uzbeks could not have mistaken its consequences. Reducing the number of vowels in the language would differentiate Uzbek from other Turkic languages—Uyghur, Turkmen, Turkish, Kazak, and Azerbaijanian as well as additional languages in the extensive family that retained vowel harmony. That shift in language base also severed another connection with the

Qipchaq-Uzbek (Abul Khayrid and Shaybanid) past that contributed to the historical identity of the modern Uzbeks.

Not every Russian specialist subscribing to the racialist explanation for modern Uzbek identity unconditionally accepted all three parts of the theoretical linkage—blood kinship genealogy, fixed territorial limitation, and the "unbroken line" of language development. Some placed the era when the Uzbek language formed between A.D. 500 and A.D. 1200 yet admitted that instead of an unbroken line, "at the base of [the Uzbek]. . . lay various languages of these [northern Central Asia] tribes. Into these, ancient Scythian-Iranian elements considerably admixed." The language line, according to this interpretation, not only broke off at times but became polyglot.[5] These rather minor differences over tracing Uzbek language back to A.D. 900 or earlier, however, caused no major disunity among Soviet specialists.

But not all Russian scholars of that period yielded completely to ideological pressure on these points. Professor Aleksandr A. Semenov, a senior Russian scholar of those years who was widely known for his many works about Central Asian history, told his readers not to confuse the real Uzbek name with its application in the 1940s. He noted that "the designation 'Uzbeks' is at the present time conferred upon the ethnic group of the USSR that was formed on part of the territory of Mawaraunnahr that went into the makeup of the Uzbekistan SSR." That is, Central Asians should not mistake the ideological revision in the usage of the Uzbek name under way at that time for historical actuality. Professor Semenov also felt that historians could not project the name back in time beyond the sixteenth century for southern Central Asia (notice the title of his chapter devoted to this subject: "The Forming of the Uzbek [nomadic] State and Conquest of Mawaraunnahr by the Uzbeks"). Otherwise, his presentation parallels the line laid down as early as 1941 by Professor Aleksandr Iu. Iakubovskii (1886–1953).[6]

In the field of literary history some serious scholars also rejected the ideological framework of Professor Iakubovskii's tract about Uzbek ethnogenesis and refused to change what they called the "historical terminology" for Chaghatay Timurid authors to make it accord with the ideologists' much later redefinition of the name *Uzbek*. Generally, the somewhat younger ideologists in the field of Central Asian studies promptly adopted the new formula. But senior researchers like Professors Sergei Ye. Malov (1880–1957) and Semenov held to their intellectual position under what must have been heavy pressure to conform to the official political approach.[7]

Regardless of a few scholars' firm stands, the silencing of intellectual disunity increased with respect to the racialist designation of Uzbek. Starting around 1938 the ideologists linked the components of their theory to the reinterpretation of the Chaghatay heritage, created in good part by Timurid authors with their inclusive definition of Uzbek. They began calling the Timurids—Mir Ali Shir Nawaiy, Zahiriddin Muhammad Babur, and many others—Uzbek authors and leaders. They showed less enthusiasm for such Timurid authors as Sultan Husayn Bayqara because those sultans and khans stood out as medieval rulers who happened to write poetry. The ideologists wanted to de-emphasize the political side of figures in the new Soviet literary histories by concentrating on their writings rather than their statecraft. Thus the Timurid figures selected for the new Uzbek identity turned out to be the very men defeated and humiliated by the Uzbeks—Mirza Ulugh Beg, Zahiriddin Muhammad Babur, and the like. This revision of history seemingly meant to countermand earlier Uzbek military success.

In his tract on the theory of Uzbek ethnogenesis, Professor Iakubovskii declared that a particular ethnic group's name does not have to be connected with its history. He asserted that group names lack primary importance and that historians might separate them from the bearer group for the convenience of historiographers and ideologists pursuing a certain order in history. The rhetoric that Professor Iakubovskii employed in writing about Uzbek ethnogenesis has some interest. In setting forth his position, the ideologist's idiom resembled the repetitive, heavy style of one-man dialogue used endlessly in Soviet political discourse, especially Stalin's ponderous disquisitions. Contemporaneous with the historian's exposition, Stalin's prose very likely provided the model for this dogmatic, repeatedly menacing phraseology, witness the closing sentence in Professor Iakubovskii's pamphlet about Uzbek ethnogenesis:

> Having overcome the purely formalistic [logical or intellectual] considerations relating to the origin of the name "Uzbeks," does not what was set forth above give one the right to designate the entire Turkic past on the territory of Uzbekistan prior to the sixteenth century with the term "Old Uzbek?" It seems to me that it does.[8]

That categorical statement does not fit into the usual fashion of Soviet scholarly publishing. To begin with, it appeared under the sponsorship of the Nawaiy Jubilee Committee, which functioned directly under the Council of People's Commissars, UzSSR. That backing provides testimony enough, if the content of the booklet does not suffice, to tie this conclusion to the ideological redirection of the Chaghatay heritage into Uzbek channels. These nineteen pages, published by Uzbekistan's most authoritative state academic agency of that day—the Uzbekistan Branch of the Academy of Sciences (UzFAN), in Tashkent—carried no reference footnotes or bibliography, which revealed them to be less a scholar's investigation than an ideologist's directive. Placing "Prof." before Iakubovskii's name on the title page confirmed the sponsors' intention to convey the message's authority to uninformed readers so that they would take it seriously. Because the pamphlet came from a Russian and circulated in the

Russian language it gained further ideological weight. The essay also accorded with the practice, common among pre-1920 Central Asian tract writers, of presenting the reader with a set of arbitrary arguments without documents or other recognized sources to back them up.

Every circumstance connected with Professor Iakubovskii's tract—its substance, its issuance, and its form—suggests that this constituted an official policy statement, and that it exerted an impact commensurate with its authority. This same individual touched on the subject again, some ten years later, in an even more threatening tone. He issued it in the approved official history of Uzbekistan (although it covered the ancient to late medieval period mainly preceding the existence of the Uzbeks) through the newly formed publishing house of the Academy of Science, UzSSR, along with the first volume, which came out three years after the second. Three non–Central Asians, including Professor Iakubovskii, authored volume 1, entitled *History of the Ethnic Groups of Uzbekistan* (1947). Iakubovskii reiterated his assertions of the 1941 pamphlet and declared anyone who disagreed with his understanding of Uzbek history to be worse than misguided:

> It was not very long ago that in the historiography of Central Asia there prevailed, as a heritage of bourgeois discipline, the naive and primitive view that the Uzbeks were an immigrant nationality. . . Now, this naive point of view, having nothing in common with discipline, and also politically pernicious, is abandoned entirely.[9]

He also repeated his racialist thesis that the history of an ethnic group often begins earlier than the history of its self-name and again attempted to detach people from their self-name. Trying to diminish the significance of self-naming altogether, he implied that the signal physical essence of a Central Asian group must go on through the centuries and endless population mixing still mystically carrying the anatomic germ of its identity. But the author asserts that the name and memory by which that group knows itself and by which history remembers it does not have a primary role in sustaining the group's identity.

Why would Russian cultural officials in the late 1930s and thereafter prefer such a controversial, unconvincing, even radical interpretation of Central Asian history and reject findings of the great Russian historians of Central Asia such as Vasiliy V. Bartold? Why should a professional Marxist teacher, his official sponsors, and his followers in the field of study assume such a categorical stance based on discredited theories of race in an intellectual sphere? A posthumous biographical sketch of Professor Iakubovskii's academic life offers the beginning of an answer in saying that the polemical aims of Professor Iakubovskii's tract regarding ethnogenesis of the Uzbek group and a similar pamphlet were meant "to refute the antischolarly views held by those partial to the 'theories' of pan-Turkism and pan-Iranism."[10]

Traditional supraethnic and other universalist beliefs rooted in religious community, language subfamily, ethnic kinship, and a sense of regionalism without doubt interested a part of the Central Asian population. But propagandists conjured up "pan-Islamic," "pan-Turkic," and sometimes "pan-Mongolian" specters for years, in keeping with the excesses of Stalin's era. This style of polemic reached its highest pitch during the terrible political purges that by 1941 had barely run their course. Professor Iakubovskii's essay may have deferred to dangerous code words such as "pan-Iranism," for he minimized the Iranian element in the Uzbek cultural makeup. But none of the "pan-ethnic" perils purportedly facing the Soviet state turned out to be much more than fanciful imaginings. Nevertheless, when used by a powerful political party, a paranoid party general secretary, and his willing collaborators, they could destroy men and ideas. In retrospect, the new intellectuals of Central Asia would regard the contribution by Professor Iakubovskii, who died about two weeks after Stalin, not only as a vocal Stalinist propagation of fictive dangers but as a polemic that endangered the educated populace. In clearing the way for Soviet-style unanimity around Marxist-Leninist internationalism, such efforts exerted strong pressure on writers, teachers, and students—the core of Central Asian intellectual strength.

This pamphlet about Uzbek ethnogenesis succeeded less in distinguishing Uzbeks from other Central Asians than in synchronically relating the Turkic inhabitants of the region, a kind of methodological "pan-Turkism." Other ideologists had earlier undertaken the controversial job of directly and forcefully segregating various Central Asian subgroups (see chapter 13). To beat on the subject again with the same dogma (the unnaturalness of ethnic heterogeneity in Central Asian society) merely whipped a dead camel. This goal differed from arguments for physically separating ethnic groups, though it went equally far in interpreting their history and identity.

Professor Iakubovskii's tract, although outdated, evidently retained some purpose, for three decades later the Academy of Science, UzSSR, gave it a posthumous reprinting and a new preface written by two non-Uzbek authors. That republication suggests that some ideological authorities in the UzSSR sensed a diminution among Uzbeks in the agreement about their origins that the Russian scholar laid down so forcibly in the tense times following the great political purges. Uzbek and other intellectuals had undergone repression on political charges over issues encapsulated in this tract.[11]

This revision of Central Asian history, reinforced by Marxist speculations, reached out from two ingrained Russian prejudices: first, deep loathing for nomadism and nomads, whom Russians have long considered inferior people with third-rate social systems; second, unrequited hatred and hunger for revenge against the Asiatic descendants of the Turko-Mongol Golden Horde that dominated and humiliated the Russians long after the thirteenth-century

Mongol conquerors of Russia gave way to their successors. The Russian memory—preserved through epic songs and church chronicles of the Abul Khayrid (Shaybanid) Uzbeks roaming wide areas of northwestern Siberia during the fourteenth and fifteenth centuries—offered an opportunity to inflict on the social and ethnic protoenemy both ideological punishment and physical discipline. To deny recognition to that original Uzbek force in Central Asia's life and civilization, following Professor Iakubovskii's line historians had to disregard or at least diminish the importance of the arrival of these numerous large Uzbek tribes in Mawaraunnahr around the end of the fifteenth century.

REHABILITATING TIMUR

This could only be achieved by regarding the actual Uzbek impact on Central Asia as unimportant and the attachment of the Uzbek name to a significant portion of it as incidental. Accomplishing this revision involved posthumously renaming the contemporary rivals and opponents of the Uzbeks—the Timurids—as Uzbeks. That directive required the cultural ideologists for Central Asia to accept the famed conqueror Amir Timur and his attainments as positive features in Uzbek historiography. That rehabilitation of Amir Timur and the Timurids helped the revisionists de-emphasize the accomplishments and genealogy of the sixteenth-century Shaybanids and the closely related seventeenth-century Ashtarkhanids.

Professor Iakubovskii quickly regularized and coordinated the previously negative Soviet treatment of Amir Timur with the new ideological requirements for a Stalinist historiography in a long contribution that appeared in the Russian journal *Questions of History* five years after his pamphlet prescribing the political treatment of what he called Uzbek history. Reviewing Amir Timur's ruthless military saga and biography from many studies prepared by others as well as from sources contemporary with Timur, the Russian historiographer found many positive sides to Amir Timur, including the fact that Amir Timur knew well the nomadic and the settled, agricultural milieu as well as town life. Amir Timur spoke both Turki and Farsi from childhood and savored the history that he heard. Professor Iakubovskii spoke approvingly about Timur's talents as a chess player, as a lawgiver, and as a builder of great architectural structures. Most of all, the Russian historian admired Amir Timur's political shrewdness; as a strategist and commander in chief, Amir Timur seized no land from Tokhtamish Khan (r.1376–91, 1395–96) (the territory the Golden Horde conquered from Russia) but rather strove to weaken Juchi's Ulus to reduce the threat of the Golden Horde to the Timurid state. Amir Timur's blows against the Golden Horde and Tokhtamish Khan, acknowledged Professor Iakubovskii, proved useful not only for Central Asia but for Russia as well. The

Central Asian ruler achieved this indirectly through relieving pressure that the Tatars applied to the Muscovites and other Slavic principalities. The professor spoke especially positively about Amir Timur's ability to consolidate and centralize the Central Asian state (another approved theme, centralization of a state, in Soviet historiography). These actions accorded with the self-congratulatory view of Soviet Muscovites, who only recently had forced together again most of the disintegrating multiethnic Russian empire:

> Timur's activities in Central Asia...had no small positive aspects in the sphere of ending feudal disturbances and fragmentation, for one thing, and of massive building activity, for another. Karl Marx, not accidentally in his "Chronological Lists," speaking about Timur, as it were stresses this contradiction: "He gave his new kingdom state structure and laws, making a great contrast with those beastly and inhuman sorts of destruction which the Tatar [*sic*] hordes committed at his order."

At the same time, this historiographer tried to disconnect Amir Timur from Chinggis Khan's Mongols, even though Amir Timur's historians persistently reiterated such a connection in his genealogy. (An affirmative interpretation of Chinggis Khan's decisive role in Central Asian history remained and remains unpalatable to Soviet Russian historians owing to Russia's long subjection [*ca.* 1238–1480] to the Mongol descendants of Chinggis Khan.) Professor Iakubovskii's principal arguments against the link between the two conquerors seemed to rest on Timur's not naming himself a khan but an amir and the lack of reference to putative ties on the pages of histories commissioned by other rulers or composed independently by Persian chroniclers.[12] Considering the independent nature of Amir Timur and the intense dislike for him felt by rival potentates, those lapses seem less than persuasive.

Professor Iakubovskii also rejects the genealogy inscribed on Timur's tombstone by order of the amir's own grandson, Ulugh Beg, that aligns Amir Timur with Chinggis Khan through Tumenay, a common ancestor. A twentieth-century Bashkir scholar in Turkey, however, subsequently determined, through long study of Mongol genealogies, that Chinggis Khan and Amir Timur did indeed share a common ancestor, which if accurate, gave the amir the right to call himself a Chinggisid. Such links with Chinggis Khan retained surprising power and often accounted for respect shown those links by foreigners and countrymen.[13]

Those ideological reinterpretations of Timurid history exerted a great impact on the group identity sensed by mid-twentieth century Uzbeks. Nineteen forty-six, the year in which Professor Iakubovskii published his detailed rehabilitation of Amir Timur in the historiography of Central Asia, marks the beginning of the full-scale Timurid conversion to Uzbekhood. Until that time, cautious Russian ideologists had restricted their attention to the cultural, artistic, and literary magnificence of selected Timurids (Mir Ali Shir Nawaiy, Zahiriddin Muhammad Babur, the historian Mirkhwand, and the like) whom they contrasted with the Uzbek conquerors of the late fifteenth century. By accepting Amir Timur, who had defeated those Uzbeks of the Qipchaq Plains, the Russian ideologists achieved three goals. (1) For the first time since the Stalinist purges in Uzbekistan, they could introduce a mainly political Timurid figure with tremendous prestige and notoriety throughout the world into the approved canon for Soviet Central Asian history. (2) They dampened any enthusiasm in Uzbek readers of late fourteenth-century history for the role of their real Uzbek ancestors (through Urus Khan and Tokhtamish's forces with the Golden Horde) in combating and dominating Russian principalities. The fact that Amir Timur placed in his campaign suite a small number of Uzbek princes, such as Koirichak Oghlan, one of Urus Khan's sons, and detachments of Uzbek braves only reinforced the ideologists' intent to obscure the distinctions between Timurids and Uzbeks of that era and thereafter.

(3) The revision put up another barrier against any strong intrusion by Shaybaniy Khan, his Uzbeks, and the dynasty he founded at the start of the sixteenth century into the historiography of Soviet Uzbekistan. Coincidentally, perhaps soon after this presentation by Professor Iakubovskii, the UzSSR Academy of Science issued the Russian-language *History of the Ethnic Groups of Uzbekistan* (vol. 2, 1947). Focusing as it did on Shaybaniy Khan and the Uzbeks of the fifteenth and sixteenth centuries, it underwent a devastating attack from the ideologists, especially Professor Iakubovskii. The publishers hastily withdrew the book and within a decade issued a new multivolume *History of the Uzbek SSR* (1955–1957), which offered the corrected ideological interpretation of Timurid-Uzbek history, to replace the censored version. The new title also emphasized the postpartition territorial identity preferred by Russian ideologists rather than the traditional group identity of the Uzbeks.[14]

The politicians of the UzSSR spoke directly to the historians of Uzbekistan about their ideological direction. In early 1952 A. I. Niyazov, CPUz Central Committee secretary, publicly criticized individual scholars for their "unscientific, confused" presentations of Uzbek origins. Taking his cue from Moscow, Secretary Niyazov demanded that Uzbek historians not minimize what he referred to as the benefits accruing from the Russian conquest and occupation of southern Central Asia. Attacking the UzSSR Academy of Science for publishing works that committed such errors, the CPUz secretary specifically condemned *History of the Ethnic Groups of Uzbekistan* (1947, 1951) with familiar rhetoric: "Serious deficiencies occurred in elucidating questions of the history of the ethnic groups of Uzbekistan. . . Idealizing the feudal [*sic*] past inescapably leads to strengthening bourgeois nationalism. In the conditions of the East it frequently takes the form, as comrade Stalin indicated, of pan-Islamism and pan-Turkism."[15]

Nevertheless, half a century after the Turkistanians of the Jadid period honored Amir Timur's mystique, one of the most prominent Soviet Uzbek academicians of this second half-century and a Central Asian, Professor Ibrahim M. Muminov (1908–1974), prepared a thorough re-evaluation of the medieval leader. At the start of his analysis, Professor Muminov acknowledged the work done by Professor Iakubovskii as a "correct" Marxist approach to writing about the conqueror and brought forward several additional arguments for Amir Timur as a constructive figure in Central Asian and European history. These included the amir's talent as a military organizer and commander, his benevolence and patronage for scholars, his admiration for erudition and fine poetry, his dynamic personality and physique, his honesty, his constant concern for the good of the state under the slogan "truth is justice" or *rost-i drusti* (truth is order), and his protection of commerce, including the caravan trade along the Silk Road, as well as the development of agriculture. Professor Muminov especially praised Amir Timur's sense of discipline, honor, and dignity; his firm opposition to drinking alcohol; and his repeated efforts to engage Central Asia's leaders in action, thought, and art to discuss the country's administration and well-being.

Professor Muminov delivered his report to at least 46 members of the Presidium of the Academy of Science of the UzSSR on June 5, 1968. His thesis helped pave the way for celebrations in 1969 to commemorate the 2,500th anniversary of Samarkand, Amir Timur's capital city and the jewel of his empire. A popular edition of the report, issued separately in Uzbek and in Russian, cited the main histories touching Timurid accomplishments but largely ignored the matter of the amir's ethnic identity or his ostensible Uzbekness.[16]

Outside Central Asia, this repopularization of Amir Timur provoked a few sharp criticisms that attempted to counter the positive image in the accounts written by Professor Muminov, by the authoritative noncommunist Russian scholar Vasiliy V. Bartold, and by Professor Iakubovskii. This criticism also rejected the notion that Amir Timur's actions benefited Russia and Europe. Although debunking the Central Asian ruler by insisting on a close similarity between the amir and Chinggis Khan, this Russian critic attempted to detach Amir Timur from Central Asia's cultural development. The same criticism carefully avoided identifying Amir Timur with the Uzbek name or Uzbek nomadic society. Without specifying the name or the society, the critic called the fifteenth-century Juchid (Uzbek) irruption into Mawaraunnahr a regression into primitive life that caused a decline in the region.[17] Had this outburst carried the force of the 1938 ideological criticism that launched the rehabilitation of the Timurids, the result could have again drastically disrupted Uzbek historiography, for it amounted to a return to the pre–World War II line regarding Amir Timur and the medieval Uzbeks. The stern criticism in the 1970s noticeably lacked the coercive power of the frightening strictures of the 1930s so that despite the combative tone of this conventional (negative) interpretation in Moscow's main historical journal, Amir Timur soon received further sympathetic attention from Central Asia. Raim H. Farhadiy (b. 1942), a young Samarkand-born poet of Uzbekistan who composed his poem in Russian, conveyed a sense of grudging pity for the dying conqueror's final separation from his native Zarafshan Valley. These lines come from his fifteen-stanza "Tamerlane" (1975):

> Death's grasping claws
> Fiercely tore him, now conscious of but
> Homing without pause
> And nothing more.

> Steam rising from bright snow.
> Night set in, thickening . . .
> "Medic from Kashgar,
> Servant low . . .
> No help with anything."

> . . . "Hurry!" choking, rasped
> The master, in ebbing hours.
> Hurry! Where the Zarafshan runs
> Through valleys frothed with flowers.

> Go home!—to weeping river sand.
> Go home!—to fiery occident,
> To healing herbs, to springs, and
> Go home! Push on.
> To Samarkand!

> He knew that
> Above, unlimited
> Was foreign, empty firmament.
> The people he had conquered,
> Would never once lament.

> Hundreds of towns he seized,
> Half a world enslaving,
> But the land where he was sired,
> Still, as before—
> Not grand, not trifling.

Hoarse, Timur beseeching,

By mighty suite surrounded.

Otrar.

The final crossing.

In a strange land he expired.[18]

Nothing in the poem hints that Amir Timur might be an Uzbek, but more than a few vivid lines tell readers that the amir remains a paramount figure in the Central Asian imagination. The dilemma raised by ideological criticism remains: How to adopt the Timurid accomplishments as Uzbek without accepting Amir Timur? Central Asian historians, unable to confront this difficulty squarely, leave gaps and ambiguities in their interpretation of Central Asian documents, including monuments and writings by famous men.

Regardless of the historical realities, Uzbeks today, like Afghans and other Central Asians, properly claim Amir Timur and the Timurids as a significant segment of their medieval heritage. Among Uzbek intellectuals, thoughts about his example for present-day Central Asia remain unpublishable. The emphasis on the official category "Uzbek" makes this persistent contradiction awkward to purists, who know and remember Uzbek genealogies. But to the extent that they do not strictly exercise, visualize, or fuse the "Uzbek" identity with a Central Asia–wide or Turkistanian (that is, supra- or multiethnic) past, that Timurid background can remain compatible with the Uzbek present. The partition of southern Central Asia in the mid-1920s and the reinterpretation of Uzbek history beginning around 1938 introduced ambiguities into the historiography as well as into popular understanding. These uncertainties regarding group identity have not disappeared.

Only Soviet political control gives today's Uzbeks the exclusive claim to the Timurid statesmen, generals, artists, writers, and thinkers inside the USSR. The ideologists enforce that monopoly by denying other Soviet nationalities the possibility of considering public figures from the Timurid era as part of their heritage. The territorial definition of nationality enforces that exclusiveness. Whoever invented the idea of granting one ethnic subgroup exclusive access to a general predecessor or ancestor such as Amir Timur or Babur Padishah had great daring but not historical verity on his side. Among less-educated Uzbeks that allocation could not fail to be popular, but in reality they held no exclusive right to the Timurid civilization. Soviet politicians can prevent neither the Uyghurs of Eastern Turkistan nor the Afghans of Herat, Kabul, and Mazar-i Sharif from claiming Mir Ali Shir Nawaiy, Zahiriddin Muhammad Babur, and Sultan Husayn Bayqara—all buried on Afghan Central Asian soil. The cultural basis for Central Asian—some would say Turkistanian—unity remained patent to most educated people in the great region. Its intellectuals reserved final judgment respecting their cultural identity, and perhaps their attendant ethnic group identity as well. Such unspoken reservations would continue until developments could move past the stage of automatic responses to temporary ideological rulings and proceed on to human group orientation and the act of self-identification. How deeply those 50 or 60 years of official Uzbekhood penetrate should become clear in individual profiles and cultural institutions of the second half of the twentieth century.

15 Intelligentsia

*The main hero . . . is an upright human being, a tall, commu-
nist believer* [e'tiqadli]. *. . . . No contradictory matter can ever
enter his mind.*

(Nurali Qabul, *Don't Be Late for Living*, 1984)*

After the early 1950s, cultural historians and literary scholars struggled less
diligently to sustain the delicate equilibrium between the reacquisition of full
access to the Central Asian heritage and the ideological requirements of Uzbek
group definition. In the post-Stalin era parts of the civilization began to move
again after the long paralysis of thought. The intellectuals managed in this
period to shift the mode of thinking from entirely negative to somewhat
positive. Emerging from an era largely typified by prohibitions or anathemas,
highly educated Central Asians now began exploring the frontiers of permissi-
ble inquiry. Tacitly regrouping, they embarked on a period of affirmatively
contributing to the intellectual life of their people. The official agenda sounded
repetitious and routine, but intellectuals evolved ideas of their own once again.
A period of rebuilding ethnic group confidence set in that would amplify the
range of thought narrowed by ideologists during the decades 1925–1955.

The first gathering of Uzbekistan's intelligentsia organized after World War

---

* Yoldash Salijanaw, "Bash mäqsäd. Bähs," *Ozbekistan ädäbiyati wä sän'äti*, March 1, 1985,
p. 3.

II by UzSSR authorities adopted an agenda listing only one topic, couched in familiar Soviet phraseology: "The historic decisions of the XXth Congress of the CPSU and the tasks of Uzbekistan's intelligentsia." That prosaic heading camouflaged coming discussions of a most uncommon subject. Sharaf R. Rashidov (1917–1983), then chairman, Presidium, UzSSR Supreme Council, opened the congress. All rose to hear musicians play and sing the UzSSR "Anthem," which fulsomely praised Stalin. Departing from the earlier practice of naming the dictator and his close associates individually, this gathering agreed by acclamation to designate as an honorary presidium, without specifying names, all Central Committee members of the CPSU along with official representatives from other Central Asian union republics and the Transcaucasus and visitors from the People's Republic of China, India, Egypt, and North Korea.

Delegates heard misinformation about their past from a prominent visiting Russian A. M. Rumiantsev, editor of the Moscow journal *Kommunist*, who sat among at least 25 non-Uzbeks (not counting the honorary Presidium members) in the 80-person Presidium. He congratulated the assembled intelligentsia by informing them that they were participants in "the first congress of intelligentsia of Uzbekistan. But this congress is not only the first republic one," he said, "it is the very first in the USSR," thus expunging the record of two Uzbekistan congresses held in 1926–1927. That incident characterized Soviet treatment of history, seriously afflicting all Central Asian historiography in the Soviet period. Organizers in 1956 judged that nothing should remind party members about that history because those earlier meetings—a colorful diversity of opinions and views—contradicted the communist party outlook. The authorities also needed this memory lapse because Russian ideologists had not yet returned the deceased Akmal I. Ikramov, the chief CPUz leader and a figure in previous congresses, to acceptance.[1]

Despite the false premises and the doctrinaire framework, this assemblage marked a shift in cultural policy toward the indigenous heroes and leaders of the past. The congress, called from October 11 to 13, 1956, in Tashkent, demonstrated that at least some important figures in Uzbek or Turkistan life must retain a place in Uzbek history. It also showed that power wielders might not again be allowed to remove individuals physically from the society simply because they displeased officials. That unspoken guideline made it possible for communist leaders to acknowledge that tyranny could and did inflict gross injustices in Central Asia. Leaders could willfully err and others call them to account. This retribution would not come in the classical or religious pattern but cloaked in Russian Marxist morality. Thus the ideologists now spoke not about murder or justice but of the "vulgar" denunciations that destroyed the fallen leaders and purged writers of the 1920s and 1930s.[2]

In the end, this concept of the leadership's responsibility somewhat resembled the general sense of duty that traditional Central Asian authors had always underscored in their writings. But in this period the reaffirmation remained implicit; the communist party leaders left unexamined a leader's obligations to his people for his acts and to his state for the consequences of those policies and actions. The old notion of a khan's *jäwabgärlik* (accountability) that underlay the codes of princely behavior and that advisers to kings often explicitly pronounced sounded no echo in Soviet Central Asian life. Ordinary persons often heard exhortations about their duties and responsibilities, but leaders merely seemed required to survive the political infighting of the authoritarian Soviet regime. In this era, Central Asian leaders received no formal direction or counsel from the public, answering only to those above them in the hierarchy.

EXONERATING SOME NATIONALISTS

The October 1956 congress reactivated the series of congresses that had broken off after the stormy gatherings of the second half of the 1920s. This time the intellectuals, who excited the earlier meetings with their arguments and reasoned opposition, remained silent, for the communist party had intimidated those few it had not put to death. As its principal work, the congress set about restoring the status of the dead and the few survivors of political repression, although publicly no one ever brought to account the criminals or the system that perpetrated the crimes against Uzbekistan's former cultural leaders. Those returned to acceptance included both intellectuals and creative artists, as well as scholars, critics, and political figures. This reversal in the UzSSR followed Moscow in exonerating some victims of the politicians of previous decades and quickened efforts to include in studies, literature, and published history the roles in history of many important figures. Writers, thinkers, and rulers of the past whose names disappeared because of official censorship now began to reappear. Among those Uzbeks, congress speakers suggested re-evaluating the young politician Akmal I. Ikramov and a number of others. Fayzullah Khoja went unmentioned. Murdered by the oligarchy under Stalin's orders in 1938, Ikramov and Khoja had served as the foremost Uzbeks in the government and the communist party of Uzbekistan from 1925 through 1937. The authorities charged them, and nearly all Uzbek cultural and political leaders of that time, with "nationalism."

To a significant degree, genuine nationalism constituted a challenge to authority in a state that denied the right to self-determination. Ideologists described such nationalism as heretical to the faith of Marxism-Leninism-Stalinism. By claiming nationhood and thus putting in question the legitimacy of the oligarchs in the USSR capital, true Uzbek nationalists would have raised objections to the hegemony of the Moscow-centered communist party and the Soviet government, both staffed at the top mainly by Russians. The rehabilitations showed, however, that the Soviet punitive judiciary that had lodged charges against those leading Uzbeks either grossly exaggerated or completely falsified the accusations. An unjust, irresponsible regime had placed power in the hands of men unacquainted with justice or humanity. The attitudes expressed by that communist rule and its terrible propensities to torment and destroy would appear similar from the viewpoint either of such bad rulers or of those they injured. The victims could wish for better.

During the congress the main speaker, Nuritdin A. Muhitdinov (b. 1917), First Secretary, Central Committee, CPUz, concentrated on the Twentieth Congress of the CPSU, held seven months earlier. His speech for the first time revealed openly to Uzbekistan's intelligentsia Stalin's fall from grace. The carefully edited stenographic report reads almost as if it had but insignificant, routine importance. No one who lived in Uzbekistan or who understood the tremendous impact of that liberation could read those lines indifferently. Uzbekistan's CP first secretary then turned to the matter of exonerations. Among the intellectuals who had innocently perished, he mentioned only Abdullah Qadiriy (1894–1939), the noncommunist Uzbek novelist from Tashkent. Like that of many leading Uzbek intellectuals, his death date came within the fatal three-year range, 1937–1939, of extreme official lawlessness in Uzbekistan.

In 1956 many politicians still opposed the condemnation of Stalin or the rehabilitation of his party's political victims, and this proposal by First Secretary Muhitdinov seemed a cautious trial effort. In selecting Abdullah Qadiriy the anti-Stalinists chose an important symbol, for his three-volume *Otkän kunlär* (Days Gone By, 1922–1926), a historical novel about Qoqan, qualified him as the first Uzbek-language novelist. As a young Jadid (before 1917) he published stories, poems, and a Reformist play. In the Uzbekistan period, Qadiriy contributed to the satirical Uzbek magazine *Mushtum* and other periodicals and wrote and published two additional novels. In vindicating him, the revivalists would pave the way for many others to return, alive or dead, to contemporary Uzbek culture.

Although Qadiriy represented the best of Reformist schooling and point of view, his posthumous exoneration failed to restore the Jadid movement to political or cultural acceptability. From the 1920s on, Central Asian ideologists, taking their cues from Russian communist party guides, slandered the Jadid movement in every conceivable respect because it originated, with Crimean Tatar help, among Central Asians in Turkistan and the protectorates of Bukhara and Khiva and gave the people of the region an indigenous point of reference for real modernization. Russian ideologists preferred to contrast a benighted amirate or khanate with the "inspirational" properties of the November 1917 coup and the subsequent changes in the Soviet Russian regime. The Jadids made this comparison awkward because they offered Central Asians new models for cultural life and understanding.

The historians' official accounts of the 1940s–1960s blanketly condemned the Jadid phenomenon, labeling it pan-Islamic, pan-Turkic, bourgeois, anti-socialist, and the like. That treatment, regardless of its inconsistencies and inaccuracies, succeeded in denying Uzbeks the right to regard their Jadid predecessors in a positive light, thus effectively continuing the Jadid movement in the proscribed category of enemies of the Central Asian people.

Nevertheless, the political-cultural authorities restored a number of Bukharan and Turkistanian Reformists to respectability, including Abdullah Awlaniy, Sadriddin Ayniy, Batu, Mir Mashriq Elbek, Abdalrauf Fitrat (partially), Fayzullah Khoja, Hamza Hakim Zada Niyaziy, and Qadiriy. But ideologists have avoided the implication that the movement in which those men played important parts should accompany its rehabilitated members onto the pages of new literature and history. One standard presentation of the Jadid drive for reforms published in the 1970s continued (contradictorily) to call the movement a pan-Islamic, pan-Turkic (in that order), nationalist drive. The article named Mahmud Khoja Behbudiy and Munawwar Qari as the main Reformist leaders without mentioning any others. Nowhere have the two men been affirmatively restored to Central Asian history. Nonetheless, the very existence of a long entry about the Jadid movement and its leaders in the recent edition of the UzSSR encyclopedia gave evidence of an advance over the Stalinist publishers, even though the encyclopedia generally slighted entries and details about this important twentieth-century development in Central Asian cultural history.[3]

During the Congress of Intelligentsia, First Secretary Muhitdinov went on to reclaim much of Uzbek epic poetry, including the oral epic *Älpamïsh*, which ideological critics had earlier condemned for containing Muslim motifs and thoughts about ideal kings. The CPUz first secretary also brought back to favor the *mäqam*, a large, intricate form of indigenous classical music. Ideologists had earlier anathematized such indigenous music because its sponsors included the royalty of Central Asia.

In the political arena, Muhitdinov's address, subtitled "The International Upbringing of the Toilers," resurrected politicians who had perished in communist party purges. He named fourteen men "unjustly accused of nationalism" and then singled out four middle- to lower-level administrators and journalists that he said shared blame for the political and ideological excesses of the past.

That token condemnation told the intelligentsia at the congress that no one would make high officials, the ideology, or the political system responsible for the terrible events of the 1930s and that their society would experience only partial, gradual release from the political grip of dictatorial forces in the communist party. Evidently they feared that the destructive political tyranny might return at any time. Readers could infer this from an entry in the Uzbek-language *History of the Uzbekistan SSR* (1958). In the several terse paragraphs devoted to this important congress, the historians passed over Stalin's fall and the exoneration of Uzbek intellectuals and politicians. Reading that official source, students would gain no inkling about the most dramatic event shaping intellectual life subsequent to the purges of the 1930s.[4]

The congress also gave concrete numbers for the "intelligentsia of Uzbekistan" in the second half of the twentieth century. Its membership resembled the makeup of the educated population of Turkistan before the partition of 1924–1925 in its ethnic heterogeneity. Of the 1,196 delegates, Slavs constituted 31.25 percent (Russians, 27.6 percent), indigenous Central Asians about 60 percent (Uzbeks, just over 51 percent), and the rest from Tatarstan and the Transcaucasus. Those numbers do not correspond to the proportions in the UzSSR population for the census year 1959 (Slavs, 14.7 percent [Russians, 13.5 percent]; Central Asians, 74.2 percent [Uzbeks, 62.2 percent]; Crimean and Kazan Tatars, 5.5 percent; Azerbaijanians 0.5 percent; and the remainder, Armenians, Jews, Mordvins, Bashkirs, and Germans).

But the delegations' ethnic distribution may have matched more closely categories of employment in the union republic. Communist party officials selected the delegates from meetings in government offices, learned institutions, educational institutions, implement and tractor stations, state and public farms, and the like. Some 337 of the delegates (more than 28 percent) had never finished college or gone beyond secondary school. Uzbek women held 186 seats (15.5 percent), though they constituted more than 50 percent of the population. The delegates represented the following occupations: academic and research personnel, 323; teachers at levels from grade school to college, 274; technical specialists in industry and agriculture, 249; party and government bureaucrats and journalists, 173; medical doctors, 108; artists and theater personnel, 52; writers, 17.

The few creative artists and writers that attended the congress emphasized the functional nature of the UzSSR intelligentsia, as defined by the party organizers. Thus the creative intelligentsia made up a small portion of the "people engaged in mental labor," as the bureaucrats termed them. In data from the 1959 UzSSR census record, writers, artists, university and college professors, composers, and scientists of Uzbekistan (by no means all of them Uzbeks) added up to 17,938, slightly more than 4 percent of the Soviet category of intelligentsia. Such classifications hardly match the more general description given earlier by Lenin, who defined the intelligentsia as a group "more conscientious than all, more decisive than all, and more precise than all," which pictured an action-oriented, dull-sounding category of unthinking implementers whose exact vocation meant nothing.[5]

On the last day of the congress, the CPUz press carried parts of First Secretary Muhitdinov's lengthy opening report in which he stressed the need to end the long isolation of Uzbekistan's institutions from those of the outside world. "Unfortunately," he commented, "we inform people in the foreign East very poorly about our achievements. Broadcasts from Tashkent Radio, often sound grey, boring. . . In turn, the workers of our republics. . . are inadequately acquainted with the life of the Eastern people. This must be corrected."[6]

His admonition—to face the union republic's intelligentsia and public outward more than it had under the self-preoccupation enforced by Stalin's restrictiveness—came at a time when Nikita S. Khrushchev, CPSU first secretary (1953–1964), and other Soviet leaders, including Uzbekistan's Muhitdinov, challenged the People's Republic of China for popularity in the East. Soviet political figures cultivated diplomatic relations with Egypt, India, Indonesia, Pakistan, and other countries of Asia and Africa. That theme would become one of the principal subjects in the report to the next congress of UzSSR intelligentsia.

MOBILIZING THE ELITE

Sharaf R. Rashidov, in 1957 still chairman of the Presidium, Supreme Council UzSSR, replaced Nuritdin Muhitdinov as chairman of the Congress of Intelligentsia. Muhitdinov advanced to one of the positions of secretary, Central Committee, CPSU, and became a full member of its Presidium (in Moscow) in December 1957. In Rashidov's address to what officials called the Second (in reality, the Fourth) Congress of Uzbekistan's Intelligentsia, December 11–12, 1959, he spoke enthusiastically about the international contacts of the union republic. Since 1956, according to his summary, they had held a Soviet Union–wide Congress of Orientalists involving foreign participants and foreigners had joined in a scientific session on seeding and cotton growing. An international film festival for countries of Asia and Africa, with representatives from ten foreign countries, met in Tashkent, as did a seminar for public health leaders from various countries, a seminar concerning cooperatives for more than ten Asian and African countries, an Asian international chess tournament, and an Asian and African writers' conference with delegates from 50 states.

The congress chairman declared that "the 'spirit of Tashkent' came to life during this writers' conference and became the symbol of the fight by Asia and Africa's cultural leaders for peace, friendship, and progress." He added that 1,750 representatives of Uzbekistan (not necessarily Uzbeks) from a population of more than 8.1 million in 1959 had, since 1956, visited dozens of foreign countries in delegations or as tourists. Outsiders might judge these as modest efforts, but they represented a crucial change from passivity to activity in international affairs and cracked the door, after three decades of introversion, for Uzbeks to see people and cultures other than their own.[7] The formal nature of these events notwithstanding, that emphasis on external affairs greatly altered the outlook and thinking of Uzbekistan's well-educated stratum and helped them re-establish their natural cultural connections in the larger world.

Certain nuances in the keynote address for this Second Congress had not been heard three years earlier. Rashidov, himself a novelist, twice distinguished the Uzbek *narod* (ethnic group) from the general population of Uzbekistan. (Since 1925, leaders had rarely employed that form of address for their own nationality.) In addition, the congress chairman, referring to the ideals of communism that must be ingrained in a Soviet citizen of the UzSSR, characterized them as having "a spirit of lofty culture." Aside from such fleeting remarks, this Second Congress of Uzbekistan's Intelligentsia lacked the excitement of the previous one, for it considered nothing comparable to the news in 1956 about the exoneration of abused Uzbek intellectuals.

Nevertheless, UzSSR Supreme Council Chairman Rashidov reminded the delegates that the political repression practiced by the communist party from the 1920s to 1950s had damaged the culture of Uzbekistan. What he called "a nihilistic approach to the spiritual wealth of the ethnic group" had caused Uzbek literature, music, and historiography to suffer. He noted that ideological critics had proscribed medieval Central Asian writings as mystical and antipopular "merely because traces of religious motifs had a place in them." This comment loosened scholars and teachers from the straitjackets that dogmatic critics had tied them in for years. But in the same speech, congress chairman Rashidov emphasized that everyone in the congress must work persistently and resolutely against religion. "The fight with religious prejudices demands an effort from all our intelligentsia that is persistent, stubborn, and profoundly thought out." He called on all learned establishments to give full attention to the history and theory of atheism and to produce effective antireligious writings for Central Asians. Finally, he pointed out that less than 50 percent of Uzbekistan's school teachers had received a college education. He insisted that universities and institutes must improve teacher training so that instruction in all subjects would move up from the "feeble level" it then occupied.[8]

Proceedings of the Second Congress probably seemed tedious to the delegates because, taking on the style of communist party congresses, they were largely hortatory, not decisive. Such meetings became poor theater in that they gave a formal presentation of official guidelines without participation by the assemblage. The arrangements resembled those for 1956, although fewer people (1,140) participated. Uzbeks constituted a somewhat larger percentage of the total (56.1 percent) than before, and Russians considerably smaller (18.9 percent) (see figure 15.1). As a counterweight to that decrease, 370 delegates came from party, government, and economic sectors, more than doubling their 1956 contingent. Writers and performing artists also increased, to 77. It appears that organizers had reduced the numbers of technicians and educators to enlarge the numbers of politicians and creative intelligentsia. The admissions committee calculated that, as in 1956, an outstanding majority of delegates could claim a part or full college education. (A partial college education could consist of a few courses.)

Toward the end of his address, Rashidov offered his characterization of the UzSSR "intelligent": "[He]...must possess the best qualities of the leading workers and farmers: proletarian purposefulness and persistence, principled in ideas, selfless devotion to party and Motherland, limitless loyalty to the great ideas of Marxism-Leninism, and with all [his] strength must fight for the purity and complete triumph of socialist ideology." To this description he appended what he termed *deep internationalism*, an idealized trait especially damaging to subgroup self-identity. The CPUz leader thus considered a person whom the Soviet system had ethnically neutered the true "intelligent" of Uzbekistan.

As a positive example of internationalism, he mentioned the close links between Uzbeks and Tajiks, who built canals together and shared many cultural links. Recently, he said, the Supreme Soviet of the UzSSR decided to transfer 50,500 hectares (124,786 acres) of UzSSR land "to the fraternal Tajik ethnic group" (significantly, not to the TajSSR). He reminded listeners that the UzSSR had earlier transferred the huge Bostandik section of Uzbekistan to the Kazak SSR. He called those acts, which reduced the UzSSR's acreage, "brilliant examples of socialist internationalism." Such border changes could not have occurred without the consent and no doubt initiative of the Moscow authorities. Such cooperation between ethnic subgroups within Central Asia very much resembled the supervised actions under the Turkistan ASSR, Bukhara Kh. Sh. J., and Khwarazm Kh. Sh. J. during the first half of the 1920s.

IRANIAN AND TURKIC MELDING

The old Uzbek-Tajik linkage, although colored with ages of ambivalence, remained strong in the 1950s, regardless of Soviet attempts to enforce a separation. Under whatever slogans, these interactions suggested the communal ties still uniting indigenous Central Asia.[9] Invective concerning Uzbek biological identity leaned on alleged racial differences between Turkic and Iranian people. But Uzbekistan's historians and anthropologists of the late 1960s designated as a distinct race the population inhabiting what the conquering Arabs later called Mawaraunnahr:

[Research has shown] very substantial closeness between contemporary Uzbek[s] and the Tajik ethnic groups who belonged, basically, to the so-

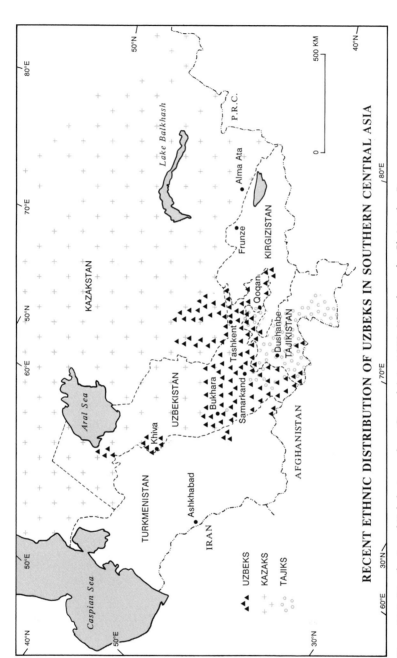

Figure 15.1 Distribution of Uzbeks in southern Central Asia. Map drawn by Christopher Brest.

RECENT ETHNIC DISTRIBUTION OF UZBEKS IN SOUTHERN CENTRAL ASIA

Caspian Sea

Aral Sea

Lake Balkhash

KAZAKSTAN

TURKMENISTAN

UZBEKISTAN

KIRGIZISTAN

TAJIKISTAN

AFGHANISTAN

IRAN

P.R.C.

Ashkhabad

Khiva

Bukhara

Samarkand

Tashkent

Qoqan

Dushanbe

Frunze

Alma Ata

UZBEKS
KAZAKS
TAJIKS

0   500 KM

40°N
50°N
30°N
40°N
50°N
30°N
50°E
60°E
70°E
80°E
50°E
60°E
70°E
80°E

called Europoid race of the Central Asian intrariverine region . . . The difference between these two ethnic groups comes down to the fact that an insignificant percentage of elements from another—Mongoloid—race, to which Turkis and Mongols belonged, was deposited on the Europoid base of the Uzbek population.

The Central Asian anthropologist went on to assert that the physical type of the Uzbeks came closer not to Turkic-language ethnic groups with predominantly Mongoloid features, like the Kazaks and Kirgiz, but to the Iranian-language Tajiks. She observed that "the history of those people closely intertwined with the history of the contemporary Uzbek *narod* (ethnic group)."[10]

Although recognizing the fallacy of segregating Uzbeks and Tajiks by physical type, these historians continued to project the Uzbeks back into prehistory, thus separating the identification of the Uzbek group from the symbolism and signal meaning of its nomenclature. In this formulation, the official view defined Uzbeks as those physical human atoms assembled on the territory of Mawaraunnahr and what had recently become known as Uzbekistan. This teaching denied the importance of chronology and self-identity and argued that, in keeping with Marxism-Leninism's tenets about nationalities, the Uzbek subgroup came together over a long period on the territory of Central Asia.

In contrast to the interpretation of these developments in chapter 7 of this book, they maintained that

> the Uzbek subgroup [*narodnost'*] is composed not of the fairly recently arrived nomadic "Uzbeks" of the fifteenth century of the Qipchaq Plains, but of the ancient inhabitants of Sogdiana, Farghana, and Khwarazm. From the most distant times they led a settled life and were occupied with cultivating the soil. [The Uzbek group was composed] as well of nomadic tribes who lived as neighbors with the settled population of the oases.[11]

This presentation of Uzbek naming and origins continued, as it had in the 1940s, to deny the significance of the Uzbek name in favor of the biological identification of people with territory, which ideological historians seemed to require to sustain adherence to the name *Uzbek* in a segment of Central Asian society. That hardly appeared necessary for the very young, raised from the beginning as Uzbeks. Older, less-educated Central Asians might still have harbored memories of the times when they gave allegiance to names other than Uzbek. For them, time would also take care of the ambivalence. Educated men and women remain uncertain, for most know that communist party ideologists supplied the Uzbek name, despite its role in the heritage, in much the same way they promoted many other changes and slogans that have appeared in the region since 1920. As late as the mid-1970s country people—the conservators of group identity—still lived among reminders of the tribal past in the place names throughout rural and village areas.

In a list of populated locations in a toponymic, regional survey of the mid-1970s, the proportion of foreign, usually Slavic, names for Uzbek towns and villages rose dramatically over what it had been earlier. (See the analysis of this phenomenon in chapter 13, "Monuments or Trophies.") Whereas virtually no alien nomenclature could be seen in the mid-1920s, fifteen villages in Samarkand oblast, UzSSR, now bore the name Kalinin, after the deceased Soviet politician Mikhail I. Kalinin (1875–1946), the titular head of state under both Lenin and Stalin. Eighteen villages in Khwarazm oblast had acquired the name Kirov, from Stalin's murdered Russian comrade and probably his victim, Sergei M. Kirov (1888–1934).[12] These samples show that the imposition of foreign names, begun in earnest during the 1930s in Uzbekistan, had advanced rapidly by the post–World War II period. Yet traditional designations for minor settlements and towns survived in a great many locations, and, more significantly, names derived from tribal genealogies hung on tenaciously into this same period, despite the opinion of Soviet anthropologists that tribes had lost their meaning in Central Asia.

In 1975 villages in Andijan oblast bearing tribal names included Baliqchi, Nayman (twice), and Uyghur; Baliqchi also designated a rayon. In Bukhara oblast, Dorman appeared twice as a village name along with Jankeldi, Alchin, Chandir (twice), and Qonghirat. Farghana oblast had the villages Jalayir, Naymanbostan, Uyrat, and Qonghirat. Khwarazm oblast retained the village names Kenagas, Nayman, Qataghan, Uyghur (twice), Chandirqiyat, Yuqari Dorman, Qiyat, and Qataghan. Namangan oblast included a Nayman village. Qashqa Darya oblast listed villages called Kat, Uyshun, Khitay, Qataghan, and Qutchi. Samarkand oblast included Joiryät (Juiret?), Kattaming, Misit, Chimbay, Qangli, and Qonghirat villages. Surkhan Darya oblast included a Jalayir village, a Yurchi, and Qarluq. In Tashkent oblast remained the villages of Arghinchi, Telaw, Chighatay, Qiyat, and Qarakhitay. Within the Karakalpak ASSR of the UzSSR, travelers could find towns named Nukus, Qonghirat, and Chimbay and villages called Kenagas, Naymanqol, Khitay, Qipchaq, and Qirq Qiz. Subordinate towns included Chimbay, Qonghirat, and Manghit and rayons with the same names. People called another settlement Aq Manghit. Those names derived from the tribal experience that renaming with foreign designations now obscured. As an example, compilers of the 1975 list omitted five villages from Andijan oblast that they showed during 1954—Saray, Arghin, Qirghiz, Dorman, and Qipchaq Qorghan.[13] Expunging those living place names from the map paralleled denying the existence of earlier cultural figures in the region's history and ignoring the culpability of its contemporary politicians for misdeeds.

DRAMAS

In 1960 those crimes against the Uzbek cultural and social leadership, fortunately for the Central Asian public, elicited pertinent statements about the problems of leadership and responsibility from two well-known playwrights of Uzbekistan. In a variety of media—stage, print, and recording—these plays reached a wide audience.

The two-part drama, *Iman* (Faith, 1960), written by Izzat Sultan (b. 1910), came out first. A play about uncompromising honesty and dishonesty in an academic family, it exposes a moral dilemma and gives unstinting approval to the hero, "who devotes his own effort, entire existence, and life to society" to the extent that he cannot save his only son from disgrace.

Dostlär (Friends), the three-act drama written by Rahmatullah A. Uyghun (b. 1905) in 1961, comes even more to the point. Uyghun, an undissenting, old-fashioned supporter of the regime, treats the aftermath of the false denunciations of the 1930s but skirts any inquiry into the system that made such false accusations so common and so devastating. The drama brings a victim back to his *kolkhoz* (public farm) to work after serving part of his wrongful sentence. (Probably the timely death of Stalin reduced it from full term.) Punitive sentences, in literary treatment, represent tests of endurance and faith rather than corrective measures. The returning farmer encounters both enemies and well-wishers and, through wordy dialogue with virtually no action, shows an environment that nurtures suspicion, enmity, and vindictive injustice, in which intrigues inevitably work against honest men and enrich evil ones. Defining virtue and sin as less than absolute ethical opposites, the drama simply portrays the destructive consequences of bad character. None of the cast considers the larger causes of the dilemma facing that farm community. The dramatist uses the farm as a microcosm of Uzbekistan's society to depict the local excesses encouraged by communist coercion. The playwright worked cautiously, but his statement of the ethical problem earned stage performance of the play and elicited pointed criticism.

Dostlär also offered a few observations about leadership that recall the Samanid ideal king's doctrine and practice of conciliation. Good leadership could save and return to righteousness erring but willing farm laborers, as the party organization's secretary, Kamal (the name means perfection), reminded the reinstated chairman of the farm, Haydar (the name means the strong lion and was the surname of Caliph Ali). By itself, unforgiving sternness against mistakes would benefit neither the errant member nor the farm community, Kamal pointed out.[14]

In the opening and closing scenes of *Dostlär*, dialogue between the good, but not perfect, characters concerns ethical judgment. In an early scene,

Qarasach speaks about her ex-husband—the victimized Haydar—now returned from disgrace. When false accusations sent him to prison for twenty years, people said to her, "If he were not a sinner, would they have imprisoned him? May the scoundrel's face wither away!" In despair, she forsook Haydar and married his friend and rival Qochqar (the name means the ram). Qarasach describes Kamal, Haydar, and Qochqar as the closest of *dostlär* (friends), thus providing the first of several layers of meaning for the play's title. In act 2 Haydar assures Qochqar that he does not blame him for marrying Qarasach, repeatedly denying that Qochqar incurred any *äyb* (guilt) or committed a *gunah* (sin). The guilt, Haydar says, rests with that damned error that he made in managing the farm earlier. Qochqar, in turn, blames himself for not supporting his friend more strongly against the false denunciations. In the face of these provocations, the strongest condemnation the wronged man can make is that "Those were touchy times."

From this dialogue the audience learns that Haydar spent five *begunah* (faultless) years in prison before release. The dialogue never hints at the reason for the commutation of the twenty-year sentence, however, and Stalin's name goes unmentioned. (Alexander I. Solzhenitsyn describes such reprieves in his case and many others shortly after the dictator's death.) Haydar, quietly speaking of *märdlik* (manliness), delivers the key line in the play as he proposes the very Russian notion that one must not succumb to despair or revengefulness despite mistreatment and injustice. Certainly, the two women in the drama come off wretchedly because they persistently exhibit what the author portrays as female (unmanly) behavior. These speeches advanced to an Uzbek audience the alien notion, fashioned from the outlook of a Russian nation inured to endless abuse, that to bear unwarranted punishment without bitterness shows strength of character. In emphasizing this tenet in the communist party's behavioral canon, playwright Uyghun perhaps inadvertently elucidated one of the basic incompatibilities between Uzbek and Russian values.[15]

Although playgoers at the end hear forceful lines about sin, guilt, *uzr soräsh* (forgiveness), and *iqrar bolish* (confession), the final episode in the play mainly conveys the notion of communist manliness. In Uyghun's play, a true man may not hold a grudge against those who victimized him, even though they ruin his reputation, his marriage, and years of his life. Nor may he hold the Soviet political system accountable for his personal loss; it remained untouchable if not infallible. Haydar reveals this self-denial and mildness in all his relationships. His friend Qochqar gives a positive rendering of such manliness. At the end of the play he confesses:

> I came today to open my heart and to speak. Let no one undergo the torment that I experienced during those two months. . . The sins that were committed, inability to confess the guilt one was constantly aware of, unfounded

suspicions concerning friends, the isolation greatly oppressed me . . . No my friend . . . I have sinned greatly.

Qochqar admits that he gathered evil men around him, yielded to their flattery, gave in to pride, and overlooked the theft of public farm property. At the end of his self-condemnation he promises: "I shall go and tell all of it! I shall conceal nothing! I'll not shift responsibility from my neck for any kind of sin! Whatever truth and justice [*ädalät*] require, I am ready for it!"[16] Qochqar speaks not to any larger sense of fairness or equity but about the justice peculiar to the Soviet system of ideology or belief. In it, judging from this example and others, victims must expiate sins committed against them by politicians.

The director/producer of a provincial Uzbek theater performing in the small Tajikistan center, Now (Nau), populated mainly by Uzbeks, found this play appropriate to the situation of the people in that farming community, whom he was well acquainted with. The director selected *Dostlär* as the major new production of 1973 for his troupe and managed, with the cooperation and encouragement of the playwright, to insert new lyrics by Uyghun and music from a professional composer to make the production into a musical drama. (Audiences of the region favored musicals over ordinary drama.) Following its premiere performance at the end of December, the local authorities, led by the party first secretary of the rayon committee, Now rayon, suppressed it. According to the director, who has since moved to the West:

> This [situation in the drama] seemed as similar as two drops of water are to the life of *kolkhoz* farmers of Now rayon. This is exactly what so frightened the leaders of Now, the first and second secretaries of the *Raykom* of the party. So, the presentation was removed from the repertoire of the theatre. Abdurashidov, head of the Division of Agitation and Propaganda of Now *Raykom* of the party, summoned me to him and told me off very thoroughly for being self-willed and warned me: "Hereafter, you shall put on only those plays which we suggest to you."[17]

In closing *Dostlär* the politicians meant to stifle discussion about injustice and to maintain the arbitrary conduct and manipulation throughout the Central Asian rural and urban scene, a side effect of their power to blackmail individuals with threats of official reprisal. The interplay between right and wrong among public farm workers in the scenes of this play came as close as Uzbek audiences and readers could get to an open discussion of justice. Limited as it was, Uyghun's play and comparable writings from others opened the door for the first time in years to public examination of the authoritarian ethic.

RASHIDOV'S ROLES

Intellectuals as well as "mental workers" and the public, despite the obvious abuses of power, still considered leaders symbolically and practically important. In the political arena Sharaf R. Rashidov stood foremost among living Uzbeks beginning around 1960 and became the CPSU's choice for the CPUz position. Had the authorities put his selection to a vote he might not have received a mandate; a long-dead, non-Uzbek Timurid probably would have won because the Uzbeks knew little (and that negative) about their own Shaybanids. Nevertheless, the higher politicians demanded that Rashidov act like a man of his people, even though no one could tell clearly who those people were. First Secretary Rashidov, by the age of 22, before graduating from the Philological Faculty of Samarkand University in 1941, had chosen to concentrate on becoming the total communist party man, which, in Uzbekistan, placed him in an even smaller, more exclusive category than in many other parts of the Soviet Union.

Party membership in Uzbekistan in 1939, when Rashidov entered the party, totaled just 35,087; of those, Uzbeks made up 47 percent, with Russians, Kazaks, Tatars, and Ukrainians supplying the majority. Uzbeks numbered 4,068,960 in the UzSSR, according to an estimate based on the 1939 Soviet census, which meant that Uzbek party members made up only .004 percent of the Uzbek population, not allowing for age differentials (not available for the year) that statistically could have disqualified the large percentage yet to reach adulthood and therefore reduced the numbers eligible for party membership by reason of age.[18]

Party membership made less difference than it had when the political authorities organized another Congress of Uzbekistan's Intelligentsia, January 26–28, 1962. Managers selected as its principal theme a discussion of the decisions of the Twenty-second Congress of the CPSU, which was held October 1961. The Third (Fifth) Congress of Uzbekistan's Intelligentsia gave even less attention to intellectual and more to political matters than the previous gatherings. According to the report about the makeup of those attending, "Of the congress delegates, the most important participants in the building of communism are the 357 persons [13 fewer than in 1959] who are leaders in the work of the party, the Soviet government, and the economy." As politicians' numbers fell, women's representation and writing-acting-cultural affairs people rose to 385 and 153, respectively, out of the 1,150 total.

These rigidly structured congresses heard numerous and varied speakers: for example, the Russian chief of the Political Board, Military Council, Turkistan Military *Okrug* (District); the Uzbek chairman of the Uzbekistan Theater Society's Board; and the first secretary of the Karakalpak oblast committee. Each of the dozens of speeches briefly referred to some local economic or cultural effort and, in the old Central Asian way, included glowing words of praise for the leadership and the party's policies. Preoccupation with saying the right things about the official agenda ruled out any real intellectual questions.[19]

In the first of this second series of congresses of Uzbekistan's intelligentsia, the Soviet style of political rehabilitation entailed speaking of the former leader's or writer's being free of hostile intent, of his not being a criminal. Not a word, however, was said about the physical suffering of innocent victims or the emotional trauma and economic deprivation of his family and associates. Blaming the cruelties of the regime entirely on the personal excesses of Stalin, the ideologists undertook no move toward fixing responsibility in Uzbekistan, partly because the persons ultimately accountable owed their political positions to the party that sponsored the meetings.

Rashidov once again served as chairman of this Third Congress of UzSSR Intelligentsia. His term in office (March 14, 1959–October 30, 1983) lasted longer than that of any previous Uzbek leader since Bukharan amir Abdalahad (r. 1885–1910) and Khwarazmian khan Sayyid Muhammad Rahim II (r. 1865–1910). Among previous communist party chiefs, Akmal Ikramov perhaps stayed longest at the top, December 1929–September 1937. The tenure of these three men terminated in death, with Secretary Ikramov being forcibly removed and then executed.

Higher authorities had installed Rashidov as first secretary, CPUz, in place of Sabir K. Kamalov, the fourth incumbent since 1955 and the twentieth since the beginning. A Russian, V. I. Ivanov, first held the position beginning his tenure on February 13, 1925.[20] Unlike the tenure of Secretary Ikramov, Rashidov's first secretaryship corresponded with a period of relative cultural and political stability in the UzSSR. After the turbulence of the previous decades, this interlude of calm must have seemed an accomplishment unmatched by any preceding period. Uzbeks could judge the significance of First Secretary Rashidov's stewardship and his leadership against a variety of scales— cultural, artistic, social, economic, and political. When a leader remained in position for so long, people had a strong tendency to identify him with the period and place. To what degree and how positively or negatively Rashidov might be linked with events and developments in Uzbekistan after March 1959 posed a crucial question for the Uzbeks. Part of the question reflected the leadership tradition of Central Asia related to popular values and attitudes and part depended on outside interference in Uzbekistan's affairs.

First Secretary Rashidov's background, education, experience, and style of action helped in such an evaluation, although few personal details appeared in the public record. His first fourteen years evidently made him ambitious for recognition. A poor boy from small-town Jizzakh, he went through junior high school and a teachers' training school there. In 1934 he joined the Young Communist League and in 1935 finished his secondary vocational education. He taught high school and soon began working in the local press. (It was while serving as executive secretary and then associate editor of the Samarkand oblast paper *Lenin yoli* from 1937 to 1941 that he joined the communist party.) Simultaneously, he studied in the university in Samarkand, where he composed his first poems (which showed that he possessed some of the outlook of traditional Central Asian youths, most of whom in earlier days found poetry writing to be the mark of an educated man). In 1944 Rashidov returned from World War II as a wounded veteran from service in the political section. The authorities selected him as secretary of the Samarkand Oblast Communist Party Committee. Beginning in 1947 he served as executive editor for *Qizil Ozbekistan*, the principal CPUz press outlet for the entire union republic, his first important republicwide position. He wrote war poems that went into his collection *Qährim* (My Fury) in 1945 and contributed articles to the Soviet press in Moscow as well as Tashkent. A first short novel *Ghaliblär* (The Victors), a political tract about farm irrigation, he published in 1951. In July 1949 political authorities chose Rashidov as chairman of the Union of Writers of Uzbekistan, a post that he held not too happily only until 1950.

In May 1950 communist party personnel directors made him chairman of the Presidium, Uzbekistan SSR Supreme Council, a position he held until he became CPUz first secretary. In 1956 he published a short novella *Käshmir qoshighi* (Song of Kashmir), a retelling of a fairy story he heard in Srinagar while on a diplomatic goodwill mission for the USSR in 1955. He soon completed two novels, *Borandän kuchli* (Stronger than the Storm, 1958), again about farm work, and *Qudrätli tolqin* (Mighty Wave, 1964), concerning events during World War II in the rear echelons. The writer-politician revised and expanded his book *Ghaliblär* in a version that appeared in 1972. Russian emigrants who had considerable contact with First Secretary Rashidov in Uzbekistan claimed later that they had helped him revise these large works. Author Rashidov acknowledged the rewriting of his fiction—a common procedure under Soviet ideological evaluation—but not the role of any ghostwriters. His main personal literary effort, therefore, ended before 1964. In addition to his many articles and speeches, the outside world knew First Secretary Rashidov for a book of political publicity translated into English as *Banner of Friendship* (trans. 1969) (see chapter 17, "Tradition").[21]

While politician-Rashidov rose in the hierarchy, author-Rashidov decreased his literary output. The two directions of his personality intersected when, in 1961, Nikita S. Khrushchev appointed him alternate member to the Politburo, CPSU Central Committee, to be filled concurrently with his UzSSR position. Regardless of Rashidov's tenuous claims to literary respect, on his death in the autumn of 1983, more than one UzSSR writer expressed fears to this author (who was in Tashkent at the time) that the first secretary's demise would inflict a painful blow to Uzbek authors and poets, who regarded Rashidov as an ally and protector.

AGAINST ANTI-INTELLECTUALISM

Events occurring after the new regime replaced the first secretary proved them right, for many Uzbeks lost important posts, and even before Rashidov's death many changes had occurred in the staffing of the UzSSR literary institution. A U.S. analyst points out that specific efforts to maintain ideological orthodoxy in Uzbek literature accompanied these shifts. The selection of the doctrinaire writer Sarwar A. Azimaw (b.Jizzakh 1923) to replace Kamil Yashin (b.Andijan 1909) as first secretary to the board, Uzbekistan Writers' Union, November 1, 1980, seemed connected with the more general shakeup among cultural managers of the UzSSR between 1981 and 1983.[22]

Beneath the surface of these structural formalities, however, a fresher and less dogmatic current had begun to run in Uzbek life, and communist party politicians and literary ideologists could not entirely prevent this divergence. The new intellectuals could not long support their yearning for interest or invention on a diet of dry sloganeering. For one thing, their attitude toward political leadership stayed more realistic than the fantastic view then being promoted by the communist party. First Secretary Rashidov and other ideologists had repeatedly employed the phrase "triumph of the communist party" to credit and praise the party's policies for its self-assigned functions. Intellectuals edged around such expressions and the mindlessness behind them.

One example of literary rethinking occurred in the late 1960s. An Uzbek literary scholar carefully reassessed an early panegyric written by the Timurid poet Mir Ali Shir Nawaiy in 1469. In the late 1930s, when the ideologists converted Mir Ali Shir into an "old Uzbek" writer, they likewise felt obliged to transform the medieval author into a proletarian poet who could not have praised a king. They accomplished this by disregarding large segments of his writings: for example, they overlooked a *qäsidä* (panegyric) composed by Mir Ali Shir called "*Hiläliyä*" (The One with the Face of a New Moon). The poet personally declaimed it at the celebration for the enthroning of Timurid Sultan Husayn Bayqara (r.1469–1506) on April 14, 1469, dedicating it to the sultan, himself an accomplished composer of Chaghatay verse. Mir Ali Shir structured the panegyric in the traditional Central Asian form of 89 or 90 couplets, with an opening, a transition, a passage of praise, and the poet's self-identification along with pleas for blessings and rewards. In it Mir Ali Shir Nawaiy wrote figuratively about a poetic contest and then proceeded to eulogize Sultan Husayn Bayqara as the new, just king whose ascent to rule resembled a sunrise that turned bleak night into happy day.

According to the Uzbek scholar conducting the re-evaluation, twentieth-century Uzbek ideologists tried to read the panegyric as a class-oriented tendentious poem:

Nawaiy is relating to us in it the sad fate of the populace and the ravaging and dismemberment of the country. He calls on Sultan Husayn Bayqara to create a centralized state and for political unification of the country. He expresses indignation against the dark forces of reaction and those persons who inflicted social evil.

In the *qäsidä*, according to political criticism, the poet intended to make socially significant statements.[23]

The poet put none of that in his panegyric, said the later Uzbek scholar re-evaluating the *qäsidä*. Rather, in the one-third that comprised the eulogy proper, he characterized Sultan Husayn Bayqara as a just, powerful, and merciful *darwish*-ruler. In taking to task the ideological critics, the scholar insisted on a closer reading and more careful interpretation in place of the habitual over-simplification and outright anti-intellectualism employed by the ideologists. Scholars necessarily exercised great delicacy in turning back established communist positions on sensitive subjects like this one that involved praise of rulers and an officially glorified literary figure.

Wahid Y. Zahidaw (1914–1983), who published the panegyric written by Mir Ali Shir Nawaiy for the first time in Cyrillic letters, entitled his text "A Newly Discovered Literary Work of Nawaiy." Dr. Zahidaw or the journal editors most likely labeled it a new find to mislead Russian ideologists concerning the identity of this genre and to return the work to acceptance, for Central Asian and Russian scholarly communities had known about this panegyric for decades with literate Turkistanians having read it for centuries. It may have taken an act of courage for Wahid Y. Zahidaw to publish it in 1957 because this *qäsidä* fit the qualifications of works—and modern Central Asians who studied them—seen as undesirable by ideological critics in Central Asia until Stalin was desacralized in 1956. Both Dr. Zahidaw and the scholar who revised that evaluation of the poem twelve years afterward merited praise for pushing back the curtain of political censorship even that limited distance.[24]

One further re-evaluation in another field of thought around the same time suggested a pattern in this quiet undercurrent of change. During the 30 years from 1925 until 1955, communist party policy demanded that everyone avoid evidence or assertions that countered official Soviet claims about separation of ethnic subgroups in Central Asia. The arguments of ideological historians attempting to follow those directives concerning the racial origins of Uzbeks forced them to take strange positions on the identity of Central Asians generally. One such ethnogenist wrote about what he called the Aryan antecedents of the Uzbeks and about "alien blood" separating Iranian and Turkic "races" deep in the Uzbek past, long before anyone had recorded the name "Uzbek" or the existence of the Uzbek confederation in fifteenth-century Siberia.[25]

The tribal names lingering throughout Uzbekistan revealed a continuity in Central Asian life as well as bases from which an indigenous population could recognize itself and its traditions. In the Soviet Union, decision makers for the most part selected and applied names for political reasons. For instance, following the public exposure of a few crimes charged to the dead Stalin in 1956, important centers in Uzbekistan dropped the pseudonym of the discredited dictator. At the same time, a great many places still answered to the assumed name of the deceased, nearly deified Lenin. The assault on Uzbekistan's place-names appeared intended to overcome any symbolic value peculiar to Central Asia and to undermine the visual, verbal, and historical identity of Uzbekistan's Central Asian past that traditional place-names help sustain. By substituting Soviet formulations, the authorities introduced some discontinuity; yet the vital cultural groups showed great resilience, intuitively shifting their constellation of group supports when they needed to. Educated, thoughtful Uzbeks and other Central Asians inundated with foreign place names, mainly Slavic, and deprived of true indigenous leadership would look to other means for communicating symbols and values to nourish their people's imagination and spirit.

16 Communication

*The village library is playing a tremendous role in training
young people in the spirit of communist ideals [ideällär], in
shaping the new social relations in them, in mastering magnanimous feelings.*

(*Ozbekistan mädäniyäti*, 1980)*

The constellation of values shared in a society, it is worth repeating, provides the
basic key to nationality identity. Over time the values serving as the gyroscope
for southern Turkistan's population have altered only subtly. Because the largely
youthful population of the 1980s experienced none of the drastic strains of the
pre-1956 era, they can recall few fundamental changes. How much reference
does today's Uzbek make, consciously or unconsciously, to the traditional
values of the society, and how strongly do those values influence group life? To
answer these questions would require an awareness of those traditional values
and what force they carry, as well as the means and channels of communication
that bring them into the new times. Once the world sees the scheme of such
values, it can perceive how they have adapted to the present ethical system.
Some "communist morality" already may have penetrated the value system of
the new Uzbek nationality. The changes that affected all of Central Asia after

---

* "Qishlaq kutubkhanäsi," *Ozbekistan mädäniyäti*, February 26, 1980, p. 1.

the mid-1950s succeeded great alterations in spiritual and material life style of the previous decades.

Russia's conquest of southern Central Asia between the 1850s and 1880s affected the region's urban upper levels of society but change at first touched indigenous life instrumentally, not substantially. No single importation influenced Central Asian intellectual and cultural development more than the new modes of communication. Printing and its products—especially the newspaper or government bulletin, the telegraph, and, later, the telephone—accompanied the czarist administration into Transoxiana to supplement the process of lithography adopted by the Khivan protectorate in 1874.[1] The railroads, which added faster mail and travel service, soon reached from Krasnovodsk on the Caspian Sea, with regular shipping links across to Baku and other capitals of the Transcaucasus, as far east as Samarkand, Tashkent, and, by 1899, to Andijan in the Farghana Valley.[2]

Those instruments of change—provided from Western Europe for and by Russian administrators—soon entered the existence of indigenous Central Asians. The newly introduced technology began replacing the popular word-of-mouth network. In the early 1900s, New Method schools and theater preserved and channeled human intercommunication. When radio, airplanes, and television came to Central Asia, they accelerated the transfer of ideas, values, and people. Central Asia's growing cultural and social complexity, together with its expanding population after World War II, have multiplied the application of those mediums without improving the dissemination of public information. The wordprocessor had scarcely made an impression there by the mid-1980s, but the freedom in public thought implicit in person-to-person relays had shrunk.

CENSORSHIP

One notable feature of the years since the ethnic partition of Central Asia has been the institutionalization of increasingly effective censorship. A pervasive, redundant apparatus of editors, committees, and party censors of media, organizations, and the postal service practices both prescriptive and corrective censorship. Recent visitors to Central Asia tell of Soviet citizens working in the censorship system remarking that they are mainly concerned with efficiency. Censors strive to read incoming and outgoing mail so that it reaches its destination without too much delay. That acknowledgment of the censors' role shows the lack of sensitivity to the rights of privacy or free speech in a state that claims democracy as its own.

Under strict ideological censorship the modern Uzbek intellectuals thus confront two intricately connected problems: How or what to think about their group's condition, and how to express those thoughts. Because the present concept of nationality came to Uzbeks but recently, the dilemma is fairly new. Earlier, Islam guided everything, and around 1900 the Jadid reform of social and cultural thought offered some correction of abuses. Since 1924, Marxism, Stalinism, and Leninism have rigidly steered public attitudes. But, late in the century, the times and an awareness of the world at large through education and international communication seem to have ameliorated the effect of those strictures. Given the absence of a wealth of *samizdat* (unofficial publications) from Uzbeks (though a great deal of such material continued to come from the Crimean Tatars of Uzbekistan during the 1960s to 1980s), avenues into the real opinions or ideas of Uzbek spokesmen that might represent the collective Uzbek consciousness remained limited. Perhaps literature must serve as the only medium that can consistently offer promise for authentic understanding.

Attitudes reveal themselves in history writing, in critical essays, and in social analyses as well as in other nonfiction compositions, regardless of the attempts by government and party censors to control every expression of views. But good literature cannot retain its authority or readers unless the writing speaks in a true, believable voice. Censors can prevent publication or broadcast, but they cannot excise every idea from imaginative prose or poetry, for they permeate all good artistic creations. Therefore both the substantial numbers of such writings and the wide range of publishers have greatly extended the possibilities for conveying subtle Uzbek expression.

PUBLISHING AND TRANSLATING

In the 1950s the authorities organized book publishing in the UzSSR under four major structures. The largest—the administration in the State Committee for Publishing of the Uzbekistan SSR—oversees five publishing houses (1) literature and art (Ghafur Ghulam namidägi Ädäbiyat wä Sän'ät Näshriyati), (2) medicine (Meditsina), (3) social science (Ozbekistan), (4) precollege education (Oqituwchi), and (5), for the Autonomous SSR, (Qaraqalpaghistan). Second in size of output ranks the Academy of Science publishing house, Fan; third, the Communist Youth League agencies' outlet Yash Gwardiya; and fourth, the UzSSR Central Committee of the CP's news bulletin and magazine publishing house. In 1970 the authorities arranged to have a number of peripheral organizations publish as much as 30 percent of the UzSSR's books.[3] After 1979, they added the encyclopedia publisher Ozbekistan Sawet Entsiklapediyasi.

In addition, between 1979 and 1981, fourteen literary journals in all languages came out each year in the UzSSR—an annual average of more than 44.5 million copies during those three years, thus circulating about three copies of literary journals for each man, woman, and child every year in some language of the UzSSR.[4] In 1982 and 1983, however, the number of journals dropped by more than half, to six each year, and the quantity of issues printed decreased as well.[5] Uzbekistan's population now received only about 1.1 journal copy per person annually. This abrupt decrease might have resulted from an economy or efficiency measure, but it succeeded in diminishing the amount of available reading matter that conveyed intellectually stimulating ideas and liberating feelings. The pattern in publishing books of fiction, drama, and poetry failed to undergo a comparable alteration, which suggests that only journal literature had expanded beyond the extent judged suitable by the authorities. Statistics from no other Central Asian union republics reflected a comparable sharp drop in numbers of literary journals or copies of them issued in the same period, but each SSR experienced some curtailment in such publishing after 1981.

Published books and pamphlets of Uzbek literature (drama, fiction, and verse), in all languages including Russian, between 1979 and 1983 averaged 238 titles in 6.58 million copies each year. Within that period, both numbers showed a trend upward, perhaps in keeping with the population increase.[6] Americans visiting the bookstores of Uzbekistan as well as Moscow during the period confirmed that such shops offered multiple copies of a broad range of literary titles in the local languages—Crimean Tatar, Tajik, Uyghur, and Uzbek—for purchase at reasonable prices. Of the literary volumes, an appreciable proportion consisted of works translated from non-Uzbek Soviet and foreign languages. Translations made up more than 28 percent of the Uzbek-language books and pamphlets and a surprising 48 percent of the copies in all subjects published between 1979 and 1983.[7]

Soviet translators had rendered a prodigious amount of foreign literature— 9,500 English-language fiction and poetry titles and more than 6,900 French titles—into Soviet literature during the years 1918–1982.[8] Some of these surely found their way into Uzbek and other Central Asian languages and brought their viewpoint to Soviet Central Asian readers.

Soviet authorities often chose local languages such as Uzbek when publishing foreign works in translation, which seems to confirm that local language remains a functional communications medium with which to reach the big population of Uzbeks. At first glance, this practice of the decision makers appears contradictory, for census reports claim that nearly 50 percent of the Uzbeks in the USSR in 1979 spoke fluent Russian.[9] Such easy command of the main non–Central Asian language, however, evidently did not coincide with the Uzbeks' preference for their own written literary language. Thus among groups like the Uzbeks, indigenous-language publications reached more of the intended audience than Russian-language publications, notwithstanding the promotion of Russian as the language of interethnic communication in the USSR. Extensive translating and publishing of literature into Central Asian tongues showed that Central Asian readers had, as in the centuries before 1924, started to become partners in the writing, circulating, and reading of world literature and no longer limited themselves to communist or domestic writings. This tendency released Uzbek readers and writers from some of the rigorous constraints and isolation of the three decades after 1924.

To what extent original poetry, fiction, and drama continued to reflect that influence became apparent in literature of the 1970s and 1980s from Central Asian authors. From the standpoint of ethnic group identity, traits in earlier writings held more significance than borrowed or unsolicited writings. Central Asian, not specifically Uzbek, literary history reaches back at least to the ninth century A.D. From the eleventh century onward trilingual written literature supplemented Central Asians' powerful oral traditions as well as their elegant written poetry and prose. That they treasured and preserved much of it to the present time suggests what a comprehensive means of communication Central Asian literature remains. Complemented by its extensive historiography (see chapter 7, "History"), the verse and plain writing reveal attitudes, values, and, of course, interests from the earlier days that fit into late twentieth-century imaginative writing, giving further evidence of the universality of that literary articulation and suggesting continuities and discontinuities. Finally, a certain configuration in the old Central Asian values imbedded in the newest writing testifies to the latest version of literary identity among the Uzbeks in Uzbekistan.

Spokesmen for Marxism declared its basic incompatibility with such values. Karl Marx and Friedrich Engels rejected what they termed "moralistic categories" in their call for a ruthless exercise of power to deal with the troublesome nationality question of Eastern Europe. Specifically dismissing justice, liberality, freedom, equality, humanity, independence, and like qualities, they asserted that such things "prove absolutely nothing in historical and political questions,"[10] thus consigning ethical literature to the garbage bin. In genuine democracies, public opinion about justice, equality, and independence carry weight in resolving social or political problems, but Uzbekistan's government or communist party leadership in the late twentieth century did not demonstrate any great affection for these exact "moralistic categories." Although the authorities seem bent on ignoring or redefining basic values out of recognition, they have begun to emphasize categories of conduct that bear some social relation to them.

COMPETING MORAL CODES

When the third program of the CPSU first appeared in 1961, it asserted that twelve "principles" should make up the "moral code of whoever advances communism," the seventh and ninth of which cited general attitudes and values. Someone who advances communism, said the code's seventh paragraph, should embody "honesty and truthfulness, moral purity, modesty, and unpretentiousness in social and private life." Paragraph nine, mixing general with Soviet specifications, expected the individual to display "an uncompromising attitude toward injustice, parasitism [a specialized Soviet concept with ideological-political but not ethical significance], dishonesty, careerism [another term carrying specific Soviet nuances], and money-grubbing." These two exhausted the selection of positive and negative generalities in the "Moral Code of the Advancer of Communism," for Marxist and other ideological semantics colored the other ten precepts.

The communist code, then, defined as moral what the authorities believed would advance communism and as immoral what they thought weakened communism's power: this made official acts by communist party leaders moral as well as political and said party general secretaries would lead the country and the world to its moral goal. This approach to Soviet politics precluded moral or ethical evaluations of Soviet policy, for such practices would amount to questioning dogma and doctrine. Thus many of the values of "communist morality" enunciated in that version of the CPSU program remained incompatible with those traditionally held by Central Asians and probably other Soviet citizens.[11]

A variant of that program, issued by the CPSU in the spring of 1986, differed in two respects from the 1961 version: the list of formal, numbered commandments disappeared, and the editors presented their ideas more humanely. The 1986 text spoke about justness, nobility, "common human moral values and standards of conduct," and, moving away from Marx and Engels, cited moralistic categories such as liberty, social equality and the values of happiness and peace. The passage against selfishness lauds dignity, honesty, simplicity, and modesty and emphasizes creative, enthusiastic participation in the country's life. Its precepts relate directly to "a resolute struggle for communist ideals," which remain unspecified.[12]

In these two lists of beliefs and principles of good behavior observers cannot find the personal and ideological traits associated with the religion and culture of Islam that characterized the Uzbeks depicted in twentieth-century oral literature and writings. Communist and Muslim morality diverge significantly from each other and from Central Asian values. The extent and nature of that divergence suggests a certain constellation in Central Asian and Uzbekistan beliefs. The events of 1956, for example, liberated scholars and public figures from Stalin's opinions about "nation" and allowed them to re-examine the definitions of "nation" and related concepts. The idea of "national character" came under repeated scrutiny. Such discussions centered in the academic world within the field called "philosophy" in the USSR.

Before the Russian idea of nation faded from the foreground of ideological discussion, a rising public figure of Uzbekistan began addressing the concept of Uzbek national character. Said Sh. Shermuhamedaw (b. Qaraqol rayon, Bukhara oblast 1930), by 1961 became deputy director in the Institute for Philosophy and Law, UzSSR Academy of Science and head of its Division of Ethics and Esthetics, located in the city of Tashkent, like most offices in the UzSSR Academy of Science.[13]

In 1961 Shermuhamedaw, who would later become minister of education for Uzbekistan as well as a professor, published the ten basic traits he believed defined the nature of the Uzbek ethnic group, first acknowledging that five of his choices might be found in ethnic groups everywhere: patriotism, heroism, amicability, humanitarianism, and industriousness. Collectivism, he observed in harmony with the official ideology, made up part of the psychic composition of every Soviet ethnic group, but he judged especially notable among Uzbeks their hospitality, courtesy, and love of children, along with musicality and poetic nature.[14]

Shermuhamedaw recognized that these contemporary attributes, including collectivism, came out of the long Central Asian history rather than from recent developments. Notwithstanding this, he took a controversial position (for the West, not the USSR) when he declared that traits of national character change as the socioeconomic conditions in a nationality's existence alter.[15] Arguing heatedly with some "bourgeois ethnographers" of the past who called Sarts cowardly, hypocritical, servile, and the like, he implied that every Central Asian, especially Uzbek-speaking Tajiks and Uzbeks, had the same (good) character.[16] Shermuhamedaw criticized Europeans who listened to the prejudices of local Russian officials or concluded after short journeys through Central Asia that all Turkistanians were alike and that the few they encountered typified the entire population.

From the mid-1920s on, ethnic slurs and negative judgments akin to those heard in the nineteenth century entered into everyday expression among both ordinary and educated Russians stationed or settled in Central Asian towns.[17] Those epithets demonstrate the danger of generalizing from the outside about national character on the basis of limited observation. Even though ethnic slurs and judgments speak to group and class antagonisms, they delineate national character negatively, if at all. Thus, the future minister of education for Uzbekistan offered an interesting set of traits with which to begin an inquiry into Uzbek national character. The five traits Shermuhamedaw ascribed especially to Uzbek national character (hospitality, courtesy, love of children, musicality, and poetic nature), together with the five he attributed to all ethnic groups, are external or physical, thus differing from ideas preoccupying most serious imaginative writers. Rather than embodying values, these ten traits describe natural gifts or social habits. The attitudes, behavior, and judgments of modern Uzbeks could reflect the values guiding those traits, but basic values exist separately and originate elsewhere. Several values central to the ethical system of Central Asians have concerned them for centuries. Consistent with Soviet mores, categories relating to behavior and performance—in Western social science sometimes termed *instrumental values*—receive persistent treatment in the controlled Soviet press, probably because the fundamental values exist either locked within the Central Asian mind and psyche, out of the ideologists' reach, or should remain the province of the leadership.

The instrumental values referred to regularly in the Uzbek press included *mäs'uliyät* (responsibility), *burch* (duty), *mäjburiyät* (obligation), *hälallik* (honesty), and *kämtärlik* (modesty). Admonitory statements advancing these concepts prodded listeners and readers to carry out directives and prescriptions from the authorities obediently and in good grace. The difference between this set of key values and those provided by Shermuhamedaw is that his relate entirely to interpersonal and personal qualities in Uzbek life. These instrumental values regulate character from the outside by setting social standards that present-day moralskeepers, similar to the earlier *rä'islär* of Islamic Central Asia, must monitor. During the eighteenth and nineteenth centuries those officials had tried to regulate behavior and usually failed miserably. Their ineffectiveness impugned the leadership's notion that it could punitively inculcate ethical behavior rather than inspiring it by example.

In today's Central Asia, traditional thinking about correct conduct reappeared quietly in various forms and media, often in writings that portray the character of a good person. Under the heading, "Our Elders' Wisdom," one author reminded readers in an evening newspaper of the 1970s that "the most intelligent person is the one that can master his/her own passion . . . the most stupid man is one who goes wherever his passion leads."[18] Besides pointing out proper behavior, hints from the elders related to ways of thinking:

> Four things are welcome: knowledge [*ilm*], gentleness [*hilm*, *mulayimlik*], fairness [*ädalät*] and self-control [*ozni tutish*]. If everyone has knowledge, he will do good and there will be no place for badness [*yamanlik*] in his existence. If everyone is gentle, he will be healthy. If everyone masters himself, his reputation will not be weakened . . . Everything you look at, observe with the eye of fairness.[19]

Although newspapers printed old sayings like those far less frequently than paraphrases of the official code of communist morality, pupils and students at all grade levels, along with general readers, could not avoid the omnipresent quotations from earlier thinkers and writers. Abu Nasr ibn Muhammad Farabiy (873–950), born near the confluence of the Arys River with the Sir Darya, began his learning in Shash (Tashkent), Samarkand, and Bukhara, ultimately finding fame in Baghdad and the West as a philosopher. Late twentieth-century admonitors often quoted Farabiy, who was not an Uzbek, to

Uzbeks for their ethical improvement: "The eminent philosopher, Farabiy, stressed that a human's beauty, his spiritual wealth, will be manifested in ethical respects: 'Just as the maturity of a tree is measured by its fruit, all the qualities of a human being will be summed up by his ethics.'"[20]

Such references to wisdom of the past gave tradition a stronger voice in late twentieth-century Central Asia than it had in the first half of the century. The return of traditional ethics suggested a broadening of minds, perhaps an acceptance of some diversity in outlook. But ideologists presented those attitudes as dated samples from quaint, old-fashioned thinking, not as revivifying values. Scholars and other thoughtful people, in the decades before 1928 and after 1956, repossessed portions of the great medieval legacy of Central Asia's extensive ethical literature, including such early histories as Narshakhi's *History of Bukhara* (943), printed in Uzbek translation from the 1960s on[21] and often referred to by moralists interested in the region's wisdom.

Ahmad binni Mahmud Yugnakiy's writings (late twelfth–early thirteenth century) also elucidated a notable ethical system for his countrymen.[22] Yugnakiy, a medieval Central Asian philosopher, counterposed *kämtärlik* (modesty or humility) to wealth, power, and position. In an Uzbek elaboration of the *Kammunizm quruwchisining akhlaq kadeksi* (communist moral code), modesty ranked first as the suitable antithesis to *mäghrurlik* (pride). Modesty likewise stood at the top of the list of aspects of *äkhlaqiy gozällik* (ethical beauty). Mirzakalan Ismailiy (b. 1908), the translator and novelist (*Färghanä tang atqunchä* [Farghana before Dawn], a trilogy, 1958–1968), also composed popular tracts: *Man's Beauty* (1969), *A Narrative of Humanity* (1972), and others. According to reviewers, these works discussed beauty, civility, good breeding, *äkhlaq* (ethics), love and family, and humanity. "The publicist, guided by people's primordial customs and habits and by contemporary moral standards, strives to get to the bottom of the matter," which makes explicit the truth, often ignored in Soviet times, that a contemporary Central Asian's roots reach far into a deep ethical foundation.[23] Popular sayings such as *Kämtärgä kämal, mänmängä zäwal* (Perfection to the modest, destruction to the egotist), reflect these same views.[24]

Teachers emphasized modesty to Uzbekistan schoolchildren of the 1980s and gave it a special definition: "When we say 'modest,' first of all an industrious, polite, quiet individual comes before our eyes. A modest person respects those older than himself. The modest individual dresses simply and neatly; he will not be flamboyant." Underneath that admonition lay the fear, often caricatured in the Uzbek press, that the outré dress and rude manner affected by Western hippies and other social or cultural rebels would conquer Uzbekistan.[25] Explicit rules for good conduct constantly bombarded Uzbek children and other impressionable persons from every conceivable direction and medium, including admonitions from earlier centuries: *Yamandän yäkhshilik kutmä!* (Don't expect good from evil!) and *Yaman yoldashdän täyaq yäkhshi* (A beating with a cudgel is better than an evil companion).[26]

SOCIAL PROBLEMS

Readers learned what the ideologists labeled bad behavior from newspapers and magazines, mainly in local papers not distributed beyond the issuing city or rayon. Object lessons concerning parental indifference or carelessness in properly raising children frequently received coverage. For instance, under the heading "Don't Lose Thy Honor," the evening paper of Tashkent City related the history of a family that failed to inculcate good behavior in its son, Bahriddin. His downward path started at school, where he showed unchecked disobedience in minor ways and began to steal. By the time he was thirteen, his thievery had gone beyond rabbits to watches, money, and other valuables. Before long, heavy drinking added to his (Muslim?) sins, and a serious, violent crime against another boy was the consequence. In reference to the mother's lament, a journalist wrote, "Although such heartless occurrences often happened and regularly, too, in the life of her son, this was the most heinous of them, the most evil." Ineffectual upbringing thus received all the blame for the downfall of this adolescent male, including his disobedience, truancy, theft, drunkenness, and violent crime in what the official journalist described as a *bolgan waqea* (actual case).

A major report about the distress experienced by parents of such youngsters, published in the main cultural weekly of Uzbekistan, prompted letters from all over the UzSSR. Further essays on the subject followed over a period of months in 1980. The authors emphasized two aspects of the problem: the primary role of mothers, rather than fathers, in bringing up children and the consequent anxiety of the mothers over their children's delinquency. Simultaneously, commentators blamed parents for failures in childrearing and for neglecting to shield the youngsters from evil companions—who were, no doubt, also children of comparable age. In this way the press exculpated public establishments, the government, the system, and, most notably, the authoritative party moralists from sins of omission and commission in the rearing of the younger generation.

An outpouring of responses to editors of *Uzbekistan's Literature and Art*, the main newspaper for current Uzbek opinion, datelined Qashqa Darya, Bukhara, Tortkol (Karakalpak ASSR), Ghuzar, Samarkand, and a number of other towns of the region confirmed that concern. What caused this extraordinary expression of general distress? No self-aware, orderly society regards a breakdown in acceptable behavioral or ethical standards among its young people complacently, of course, and Central Asians had always prided themselves on the decorum of their boys and girls. The crisis among the new generation shocked people all the more because glowing promises and utopian predictions accompanied the new morality. No one had expected this negative turn of events, which cast a shadow on the omniscience attributed to the new social and political managers still holding office in Uzbekistan after six decades.

Mashrab Babayew (b. 1941), an Uzbek poet and playwright born in the Payariq rayon, Samarkand oblast, entered the public discussion in the SSR's Uzbek-language press respecting values seemingly discarded by the young. The author stressed what he saw as the incongruity of juvenile delinquency in present-day Central Asia and held fast the dream that societal perfection would come true in all Soviet regions. Yet he recounted a telltale episode that belied his expectations. On Nawayiy Kochasi, one of Tashkent's main boulevards, Babayew encountered young performers entertaining passersby with their skill on the extremely high stilts renowned in Central Asian folk theater. Their dexterity on the poles impressed him far less than the troupe members carrying the *darbazlär* (stiltwalkers) on their shoulders and approaching spectators for *bäkhshish* (money). Even more telling than this plea for money, wrote the poet, was the short Muslim prayer or *fatihä* (blessing) that, on receipt of a gratuity, they would utter for the donor; "they would carry out this [religious] task as if it were their very favorite occupation," he noticed. Gloomily summing up the meaning of this episode, Babayew insisted that "because their [the delinquents' and the street performers'] nature is absolutely contrary to the nature of our society," these unhappy people could not number more than a few and would not exist in the future. The ensuing discussion and several sharp replies by other authors and journalists did not remove the impression of disappointment among them, which shook the confidence of the regions' ideologists in the effectiveness of communist moral re-education in the region. None of these journalistic discussions, however, lamented the fact that if dramatist Babayew had his way the disappearance of colorful street performances from folk theatricals would deprive Central Asia of yet another customary cultural expression.[27]

Like the Jadids in the 1900–1920 period, a breed of reformists (*islahatchi*, not Jadids) in the late twentieth century, powerless in politics, concentrated on social abuses. The habit of smoking tobacco, traditionally prohibited under Islam, came under attack. An assistant professor in the Farghana State Teachers' Institute blamed the omnipresent cigarette smoking by young children in the schoolyards of Uzbekistan on universal indifference by their instructors. First reform the teachers, he advised, then address their pupils. A senior educator of Uzbekistan commented to this author in the 1980s that the most serious problem confronting primary and secondary schooling in the UzSSR consisted of keeping pre-college-age youngsters free of trouble outside of class. (That difficulty obviously related to urban children, whose living conditions did not demand the abundant chores assigned to rural youngsters.)[28]

Patterns in juvenile delinquency reflect problems around the world. Central Asia, notwithstanding its ethical system and a social organization that purported to remove the social causes of crime, continued to exhibit those same strains whose precedents both Jadids and foreigners alluded to in the beginning of the twentieth century among the urban Central Asian population. Thus one colonial observer early in the century in Central Asia speculated that "The negative aspect of any [foreign] civilization always is assimilated better and faster [than the positive aspects] by the ordinary people, and it produces the most melancholy consequences." In Turkistan the seamy side of civilization manifested itself in "Russian drunkenness," an abuse unknown as public behavior before the arrival of Russian models. Worse, according to some commentators, the spread of drunkenness among the Sarts owed its speed to the *märjä* (Russian woman, from the Tatar version of Mar'ia), who enticed men to taverns and solicited in the open heterosexual prostitution unknown under Islam in Central Asia before the Russian colonization.[29]

The worst Central Asian vice, in the view of outsiders, remained *liwatagarchilik* (male homosexuality with minors, pederasty). Those outsiders reported that urban Sart men had practiced it in organized form to a pronounced degree before 1920 and that pederasty prevailed among Tajiks, especially in Samarkand, Bukhara, and Khojand, and was spreading among Russians as well.[30] In the second half of the twentieth century pederasty (also known as *bächchäwazlik*) continued to be a touchy subject in Central Asia. In 1929 laws made it a crime in Uzbekistan; these laws remained on the statute books at least as late as the 1970s and could result in a man's imprisonment for five to eight years. Critics severely attacked as "a vile book," a history published in 1948 about the practice of organized pederasty in Uzbekistan. A pronounced degree of sensitivity to this sin continued to prevail among officials. In the authoritative dictionary of Uzbek prepared by the prominent Russian scholar and academician Konstantin K. Iudakhin from the vocabulary of the local press and literature in 1925, he defined *bächchäwazlik* as "a passion for boys" or "active pederasty"; major Uzbek dictionaries issued in 1981 omit the reference to *bächchäwazlik* altogether.

Under the influence of sexual prudery instituted by Stalin in the early 1930s, ideologists found intolerable not only the offense of male homosexuality but open reference to it as well. The fact that few public references or allusions to male and female homosexuality appear in Uzbek fiction or journalism in the late twentieth century measures the degree of this squeamishness. Soviet publishers thus avoid reflecting the social reality of Central Asia and other regions in the USSR (all fifteen SSRs had passed laws against male homosexuality in any form). Avoiding artistic and nonfictional references to the practice implied that public officials clung to the belief that they could ideologically exorcise widespread sexual practices in Central Asia.[31]

Uzbek stage productions dramatized the question of homosexuality in original plays written and performed between 1911 and the 1920s. That generation of Uzbeks also heard about modern ideas of justice from the Jadid teachers and journalists. Few of the ten "evil deeds that remove men from God" (discussed earlier) outlined and illustrated in "The Clear Paths of Paradise" in the fourteenth century exerted ethical force in Central Asia after 1950. But some laws, attitudes, and values still reflected Islam's traditional seven *käbirä gunah* (mortal sins). Even so, the priorities had changed, and the values dominating intellectuals' public meditations or writings sprang from concerns with fairness, responsibility, and equity. Because those codes of morality persisted in the creative literature of the Uzbeks and other Central Asians, cultural leaders had reason to believe that the same subjects concerned the general public as well.[32]

JUSTICE, RESPONSIBILITY, AND DUTY

From these commentaries an important distinction emerged. *Ädl* meant "justice," its derivative, *ädalät*, "equity," *adil*, "just," and *insaf*, "fairness" as used by the Timurid Central Asian writer Mir Ali Shir Nawaiy in the second half of the fifteenth century. He applied those terms to rulers, viziers, merchants, judges, and religious leaders that others depended on and whom he expected to act justly. To others, remote from affecting the public good, Mir Ali Shir Nawaiy assigned a different set of necessary qualities.[33] The late twentieth-century usage of "justice" and related terminology resembled its medieval counterpart but skewed the sense of those crucial words. In Central Asia justice had become selective; the word *ädalät* might look and sound the same but an invisible qualifier negated its force in the case of unbelievers (in communism). That restriction affected the semantic system to the extent that essayists or journalists in the Uzbek press rarely addressed the idea of absolute and social justice or its function in their society. Soviet ideology defined traditional justice out of Central Asian existence, except as a legal concept, and tied its opposite (injustice) to the Uzbek past or to the contemporary situation in foreign, noncommunist countries.

Nevertheless, readers of Uzbekistan's press were interested in foreign concepts of justice. Thinkers from ancient Greece and Rome to nineteenth-century Europe reached educators through the pages of the UzSSR *Teachers' Gazette* in mid-1981, which quoted Cicero, Democritus, Helvetius, Voltaire, Rousseau, Spenser and a number of others. Adam Smith's maxim "For men to love justice, it is imperative to show them constantly the consequences of injustice" in an Uzbek paraphrase would puzzle Central Asians readers today, for by ideological definition injustice cannot exist in communist Central Asia. (Adam Smith's wisdom could signify that, lacking examples of its opposite, Central Asians under Soviet Marxism could not learn to love justice.) Fortunately for the equilibrium in Uzbek ethical life, a sufficiently recent, adequate memory or demonstration of injustice evidently survived. Some poets and dramatists of Uzbekistan occasionally referred to a sense of justice in their verse and plays.[34]

More than the popular idea of justice, a thirst for the three H's—*hälallik* (honesty), *häqqoylik* (candor), and *häqiqät* (truth)—was revealed in the educational press. Newspapers offered Uzbek translations favoring all three in the words of many wise men, from Kai Ka'us ibn Iskandar, the eleventh-century Ziyarid ruler renowned in Central Asia and the world for composing *Qabusnama* (Mirror for Princes) to William Shakespeare, Miguel de Cervantes, and Benjamin Franklin. Kai Ka'us, for instance, said, "There is nothing more shameful than calling a statement 'truth' whose falsity is known from the start," or, as Thomas Paine said, through the Uzbek, "The unbending nature of truth is such that it demands and desires only one thing—its right to come freely into the world."[35]

This serious probing for truth and its corollaries continued in Uzbek literature of the twentieth century's second half, especially in those writings of men and women ideologically molded before Nikita S. Khrushchev commenced the public disgrace of Stalin. Lines in the drama *Iman* (Faith, 1960), by Dr. Izzat Sultan (b. 1910), mentioned earlier, exemplify this specialized outlook. Critics characterized the protagonist, Professor Yoldash Kamilaw, not so much as a man who knew right from wrong and could distinguish bad from good but as a man "who understands communist morality as his own faith . . . In whatever circumstances, he keeps his conscience clear. He wants this lofty morality to be the supreme law, the faith for everyone." A dishonest man walks among the characters, but in a class conflict the author showed more concern for the professor's unblemished social image than for the consequences of an artificial confrontation between ideological conformity and dishonesty. That choice limited the effectiveness of this didactic play because it insisted on an ideological rather than a universal interpretation of honesty. In spite of that weakness, the play exerted a strong pull on audiences whose knowledge of corruption in their own society seemed to create a terrible yearning for integrity in their heroes.[36]

Kamil Yashen (b. 1909), another much-published, prominent Uzbek writer, also advocated an ideological version of ethics in all his writing, both fictional and scholarly. In addition to the evidence in the literary works themselves, Yashen declared in public and in interviews his

profound belief that every single writer must be a journalist and propagandist, without a doubt. This is Soviet literature's oldest and best tradition . . . A writer—if he is a true writer—must not always sit quietly in a room and merely go on writing. The time for that is not now. Today's writer is, of course, a public figure, as well.

Responsibility now served as a wide net in which everything from a suitable vocabulary to political duties might be caught and displayed. Another doctrinaire literary figure, Ramz Babajan (b. 1921), who held the post of secretary of the board for the state-sponsored Union of Uzbekistan's Writers until replaced by Sarwar Azimaw, also adhered to that view. In Babajan's report to a regular plenum of that official organization of writers on January 29, 1980, he declared that writers must take political stands in their public life; Yashen seconded him. Many other literary figures held personal values and convictions firmly, judging from their written works. Yet their conception of honesty and kindred values seemed more absolute, less relative, and freer of ideological bias.[37]

Yashen spoke here not only about relative honesty but about ideological duty. *Burch* and *mäjburiyät* (duty and obligation) along with *mäs'uliyät* (responsibility) or *jäwabqärlik* (accountability) occurred persistently in the speeches and writings of authority figures in the UzSSR. Sharaf R. Rashidov, the late first secretary of the CPUz, detailed the important *wazifälär* (assignments) of Uzbekistan's social scientists: "In order to understand questions of social development and the real problems of a developed socialist society thoroughly and theoretically, scholars must keep trying to learn and generalize the communist party's leading role," thus making social science an official duty akin to military service. Similar remarks about "duty" appeared in connection with nearly every vocation, almost invariably from unproductive segments of the political system, such as party spokesmen or ideologists who directed their remarks to the productive parts of Uzbek society: educators, directors of farms or factories, and persons farther down the scale of authority.

Umarjan Ismailaw, a playwright purged from the State Union of Soviet Writers and chastised during the 1930s, since his exoneration in the 1980s has worked as a press correspondent on education, among other subjects. Writing in the *Teachers' Gazette* (press outlet of the UzSSR Ministry of Education and of the republic's state-run Committee for the Union of Higher School and Learned Institutions' Employees), Ismailaw lauded M. Bazaraw, a teacher of Uzbek language and literature in the Aybek Primary School, along with four others for "faithfully approaching their own duties [*burchlär*] and conscientiously working on the responsibility for the tasks assigned to them [together with] the 3,126 different teachers [who] have been working in the general education primary schools of [Tashkent's Kiraw] rayon."[38] The epigraph to this chapter concerning the laudable quality of *himmät* (magnanimity) here acquires a sense of the unremitting self-denial desired in the educated population of Central Asia.

Such a concept of public duty implied a notion of presumed malfeasance.

In the new prescriptions for responsibility, writers of the 1980s began to sound like their Jadid predecessors. An interviewer quoted Kamil Yashen as saying that the writer must propagandize and publicize the slogans of the communist party. Other authors believed that the Central Asian writer had to expose the country's social ills. Official sins now regarded with the greatest opprobrium by Soviet ideologists included *paräkhorlik* (bribery), *byurakrätlik* (bureaucratism), *ichi-qarälik* (perfidy and hostility), *ighwagärlik* (troublemaking), *ämälpärästlik* (office seeking), and *illätlär* (inadequacies). Those abuses, which related entirely to the behavior of officials within the establishment, existed apart from the more universal set of values held by Central Asians generally, and delimited a particular category of individuals and abuses.[39]

Thus a canon of official sins for that era came into being that stood more in the foreground than the Islamic sins of the fourteenth to sixteenth centuries. The communist ideologists' list of sins probably seemed trivial to members of the population remote from the political bureaucracy, for bribe taking, for instance, only affected persons with position and power to dispense services, favors, or scarce goods and lacked the transcending force of those universal transgressions that had been ingrained in the values of the society. Nevertheless, when officials focused on perfidy or office seeking, a considerable part of the urban bureaucracy in Uzbekistan saw these attitudes or acts as sinful. A small fraction of the Uzbek population remembered that not many decades earlier both innocent and guilty persons accused of ideological and political sins suffered terrible punishment from the communist party and its secret police. Consistent with past behavior, officials responded to Uzbek corruption by blaming the communicators more than the sinful or the system.

Yashlik, the relatively new Uzbek youth magazine, printed in its numbers 9–10 for 1985 a story entitled *"Kongil kozi"* (The Soul's Eye) by Emin Usman. Editors headlined the literary criticism of this moral tale "A Sense of Duty and Responsibility," noting that senior Communists of Uzbekistan recently condemned contemporary literature because, they said, it lacked positive model heroes for young people to admire (an old official complaint about modern Uzbek prose and poetry). The tale portrays former schoolmates Wali-Aka and Karim Jamalawich as moral opposites. The story reveals the character of the good man, Wali-Aka (the name could mean "saintly elder brother"), by showing his protective attitude toward nature. The evil onetime schoolmate, Karim Jamalawich, abuses and shows contempt for the environment. The Russian patronymic ending *-awich* also suggests alienness. (From the 1960s to the 1980s, at least, naming people with true Central Asian appellations rather than adopting Russified forms of names for them had become a subtle tendency in Uzbek society.)

The story, however, depends less on such nuances than on direct characterization. Karim Jamalawich, an egotistical, unfeeling, base individual, competes with Wali-Aka for the same Uzbek girl. Analysts like Emin Usman, seeking a plausible way to explain how this immoral, unethical adult could have grown up in the Soviet era, blamed the villain's genes: Jamalawich's father likewise displayed evil (capitalistic) traits. "The swindling and egotism present in the character of the father also were transmitted to Karim." But "Wali-Aka is an unselfish human being who devotes his whole existence to service for the homeland [*wätän*], to the concerns of people of the home territory [*el-yurt*]." This cliché of Soviet fiction removed the necessity of confronting an unpleasant truth—the existence of evil products from the utopian communist society—by ascribing it to a legacy from the past. Once another decade had passed, however, this literary device or political polemic would outlive its usefulness by any normal life span. How then could serious critics explain Uzbekistan's normal social gamut that ranged from saintly to devilish?[40]

CENTRAL ASIAN DUALITY

The authorities wanted to rationalize present social failures by referring to a set of everyone's official sins against responsibility to the five-year plan and to the party as separate from the more homely values: attachment to family, adherence to ethics, civility in behavior, and the expression of love. The need for two styles—public and private—suggests a double standard, a painful separation between the inner and outer life of Central Asians and especially poets, teachers, journalists, public politicians, and social leaders in the late twentieth century. These communicators symbolized the dichotomy dividing Marxist-Leninist political-ideological thinking from the internalized ethical standards of Central Asian intellectuals and their constituencies, and much of the fiction and drama of the region reflected this tension. In the press, public standards attracted more attention than private ones. For example, critics spoke of "weaknesses" that could be remedied if young authors applied to their work a trinity of principles—*mehnät, mäharät, mäs'uliyät* (labor, mastery, responsibility)—that were remote from either personal or aesthetic judgment. New writers and their editors, critics said, had a responsibility to make "every line of verse, every word substantial, profound; it should become brightly portentous."

Young people furnished the target for much advice. Ideologists cautioned nearly six hundred youthful amateur performers participating in a festival, for instance, that they "had a responsibility" to avoid too much imitation in their presentations of music and theatricals: "Where there is a drive [to perform, a sense of] responsibility, too, must be strong." Vocabulary also had to come from appropriate sources. Critics counseled Nartokhta Qilichew, a new author, that his straining to find Uzbek words to replace perfectly useful Russian terms loaned to the Uzbek vocabulary, "served no esthetic purpose" in *Mo'jiza*, his new collection of stories. Qilichew heard that he had a "responsibility" to retain the Russian *telefon trubkäsi* (telephone receiver) rather than supply *dästäk* (handle/ lever), an Uzbek term earlier borrowed from Farsi/Tajik. He made the same mistake, said a critic, in selecting the Uzbek *kursi* (armchair) loaned from Arabic, in place of the Russian *kreslo*.[41] A recent short analysis, however, reveals that Uzbek-language writing since the mid-1960s has decreased its employment of Russian or European words and increased its Central Asian vocabulary (Turkic and Arabic).[42]

Regardless of age, local practice generally divides Uzbekistan's writers into five main groups of ethnically named sections within the state-regulated Union of Writers of the UzSSR, which accomplished its latest stage when it established a section for the small group of Uyghur writers in Uzbekistan (Uyghur Ädäbiyati Sektsiyäsi) at the end of February 1980 (no Tajik section was mentioned, though at least a few authors and poets must exist among the 448,000 Tajiks, numbers much larger than the Uyghurs who lived in the UzSSR by 1979). Adults writing in the UzSSR's five recognized literary languages— Crimean Tatar, Karakalpak, Russian, Uyghur, and Uzbek—heard exhortations to be ideological in content: "Let us grasp profoundly the responsibility for the noble assignments which the CP and Government have made our obligation," counseled the literary managers in messages about what they called "literary responsibility."[43]

One aspect of such responsibility obliged writers to pay attention to the officially recognized sins. Not forgetting the recent political persecution of dissidents, journalists demonstrated their perception of the new sins through techniques of writing, choice of language, and selection of stories to report. In the mid-1980s in the main Uzbek-language cultural newspaper of Uzbekistan, readers learned lessons from reviews of selected stories and books. In a culture like Central Asia's, which is subject to a strong, insistent official direction, gradations that seemed to exist in ethical positions could not express themselves publicly. A great divide between the official and the unofficial or personal systems of values and attitudes characterized the culture and the thinking of the population in Uzbekistan. Those attempting to exploit the system leaned toward the official outlook, whereas people merely trying to remain out of trouble with the authorities anchored themselves to a private set of values and ethics. This situation differed from the one five centuries ago, when the values, ethics, and ideology of the society could hardly be distinguished from one another so unified were they, which constitutes one of the major differences between sixteenth-century Uzbek thinking and the mentality identifying people bearing the same name toward the end of the twentieth century. That great duality may have affected nationality group identity in a significant manner.

17 Tradition

Shashilish shäytanning ishi.

Haste is the Devil's trait.

(Central Asian saying)*

The detailed Soviet model of ethnic organization has so far produced inconclusive results in Central Asia. This new group identity seemed to require long exercise before it could become comprehensive and well established, demanding further examination and experience in the region. This monoethnic cultural and social arrangement also required a drastic readjustment in that environment. Insiders (Central Asians) and outsiders (Russians and other foreigners) would have to watch carefully the actual dimension, shape, and significance the new forms might assume and the effect monoethnicity would have on Central Asian subgroup identity.

The vital ethnic group cohesion that enlivens the European style of nationality grows out of several forces operating in fluid interrelation and equilibrium, including dynamic symbols, communication, shared values, and causative direction. Earlier, dynasty and divine guidance made the leader the most important of such forces in Central Asia. After the turn of the twentieth century, while notions about popular sovereignty and supraethnic nationality

---

* Quoted by Obeidullah Noorata, July 5, 1987, in Massapequa, New York.

awareness circulated in Central Asia, the polity required a chief who could symbolize, even personify, the corporate identity of the nation(ality) and whose values would coincide and harmonize with those of his variegated people.

The authoritarian Soviet system of politics and government partially defined modern Central Asian leaders after 1924. Even so, to be consistent with Soviet policies concerning nationality and the imperatives of the developing world, people needed to identify closely with their leaders much more than did eighteenth-century Khivans under Kazak khans. Correspondence between the ethnic identity of the leader and an important number and segment of his subjects or countrymen has been standard in Central Asia since Shaybaniy Khan brought the Uzbeks south. Subsequently, only conquerors from outside Central Asia had briefly broken that rule until the Russian czars, succeeded by Russian communist party secretaries, placed themselves over some Turkistanians. The pattern in the twentieth century varied, but outsiders often ruled over parts of Uzbek society between 1925 and 1985. This lack of congruence in the day of nation-building would have subtle effects on the idea of nationality and on the individuals who made up the nationality group.

Such a collective identity depends on the shared values and attitudes of ethnic group members. People recognized a Turkistanian early in the twentieth century by his demeanor, dress, style of speech and gait, and actions. In the late twentieth century, some of these traits remained, suggesting that the older personal identity that contributes to group awareness might yet persist.

PROPER CONDUCT

Central Asians also obtained, around the turn of the century, some minute rules of etiquette. Muhammad Sadiq's *Ädäb-us salihin* (Decorum of the Righteous), published in Istanbul and well-known in Tashkent, prescribed in detail the correct conduct for men in any private and public situation. A tract lithographed in Ottoman Turkey that found ready response in Central Asia confirmed the existence of a community of mores embracing the large Sunnite regions of the Islamic world. The level of society interested in proper manners was aligned around the middle stratum, who emulated royalty, whereas the more common people, ordinarily courteous and hospitable, seemed unconcerned with those special rules of conduct.

Two modes of behavior, seen particularly among urbanites in southern Central Asia at the end of the nineteenth century, made a strong impression on foreigner observers and contributed to the local person's personal vision. The first, dignity, then stood above all other desirable traits among Central Asians. Whether on horse, camel, or foot, dignity required men to adopt a deliberate pace: "Haste is the Devil's trait." A Russian resident observed that a deliberate gait had become so important in the court of Khiva that officials there had achieved a fluid, pedestrian locomotion by moving their feet almost imperceptibly. In Central Asia, beyond the khanate and amirate courts, men self-consciously imitated the courtiers.

> The Sarts, particularly the more eminent ones (qadis, imams, muftis, and the like) and the rich men among them, are distinguished by smoothness and slowness of movement; they hold themselves with great dignity and importance, and in spite of a liveliness of character, avoid any urgency which is not recommended by the Shari'at.[1]

Deliberateness in walking and riding found a natural counterpart in careful speech: anyone who talked and laughed too much or too fast could not remain dignified. (See the sayings at the start of chapter 1.) Thus the second mode of behavior remarked by outsiders—the customary gathering of men for social or intellectual conversation, called a *bāzm*—demonstrated these manners. With an understanding of diplomacy that would instruct international negotiators, the Central Asian politesse demanded that individuals in such a gathering sit in a circle, so that all faced one another, making all places of equal rank. Social arbiters also preferred the circle because it resembled one of the letters spelling the name Allah, the final *ah*, in Arabic: ه . No one sat in the midst of that circle, but an honored guest or eminent person would sit in the *tor*, the most desirable place, facing the entrance to the room.

Uzbek scholars invited this author to meet with 25 members of a learned institution in a modern office building in Tashkent. The host seated the author in a seat opposite to and facing the single entrance to the medium-sized room. The senior scholar sat just to the right of the visitor, also facing the doorway; another senior and elevated person specially invited to attend the meeting sat immediately to the author's left. These courtesies spoke of traditional Central Asian hospitality to guests but also replicated a protocol long followed in southern Central Asia.[2]

Muhammad Sadiq's etiquette book prescribed modest conduct in an assemblage, sitting civilly without disturbing or brushing against anyone. Early in the century members of such a circle called out to God intermittently with the expression "O, Lord" or enunciated one of the many beautiful names of Allah: *al-Hai* (the Living One), *al-Badi'* (the Incomparable), and the like. Pious Muslim expressions emphasized the common religious ties already uniting most Turkistanians. If there are communist echoes of similar ideological reverence, perhaps to Marx or Lenin, this visitor to both Russia and Uzbekistan in the 1980s never heard them voiced during small meetings in the presence of foreign noncommunists.[3]

PERSONAL NAMES AND PATRONYMICS

Personal names, even more than given names in other societies, served as verbal signals of individual identity among Central Asians. In the absence of surnames, Central Asians chose their fathers' and grandfathers' given names for their sons, calling them "the son of" by attaching the patronymic sign: the possessed Turkic word *-oqhli* (*-qizi* for "daughter of") or the Tajik suffix *-zadä* and sometimes the separate Arabic *ibn/bin*. Turkistanian names come largely from Arabic epithets for Allah such as *ar-Rahim* (the Compassionate), and *al-Mu'min* (the Faithful). Distinguishing between the numerous Abdurrahmans or Rahims required more than patronymics. Some individuals traced their genealogy from the Prophet Muhammad and added the title Sayyid, or—if descended from one of the four Imams (Abu Bakr, 'Umar, Othman, or 'Ali)—Khoja to their own and their father's name. Anyone completing the pilgrimage to Mecca affixed the epithet Hajji. Literate men called themselves Mullah, or if they worked as scribes, Mirza. People knew ecclesiastical judges as Qadhi (kazi), and military platoon and company commanders as Ellikbashi, Yuzbashi, and the like. A facial feature or habit could bestow a nickname like *Chotir* (pock-face). A leading Turkistanian Jadid playwright, known in the literature as Hajji Muin Shukrullah-oghli, called himself Hajji Muin ibn Shukrullah (the pilgrim Muin, son of Shukrullah).[4] Writers could create and shape their names because the pen name had centuries of history behind it in Central Asia, just as those now discarding Russian endings from their names have tradition on their side. But the ordinary person still must justify his deviation from the socially sanctioned Russian patronymic.

Of the 86 literary figures listed in *Writers of Soviet Uzbekistan* (1959), only Hamza Hakimzada Niyaziy, Fazil Yoldash-Oghli, and Ergash Jumanbulbul-Oghli, three men who had been dead for decades, retained the older name forms. The more than three hundred authors and critics presented in a later edition (1977) of the handbook revealed only a single person designated by a traditional patronymic form: Eshref Shemsi-Zade, a Crimean Tatar whose entire nationality the Russians exiled in May 1944 to the Urals and Central Asia. It had become the fashion in the 1920s–1950s, encouraged by Russocentric ideologists, for adults to discard their inherited patronymic form and to change their children's names as well.

The Russian male/female patronymics *-aw/-awnä/-awä*, regularly applied to Uzbek last names after 1924, had begun slowly to disappear by the 1960s, a trend particularly noticeable among authors and other intellectuals. Of the 26 poets featured in the Uzbek-language volume *Anthology of Uzbek Poetry* (1962), only four, two of them women, still employed the Russian *-aw/*

-awnä/-awä. The other 85 percent registered no patronymics at all or listed only their pen names.

The rosters for the UzSSR showed that in 1959 there were three women writers (3.48 percent of those listed as writers), two of whom omitted the Russian *-awä* patronymic. By 1977, the percentage of Turkic and Iranian women writers in the UzSSR had more than doubled, to 7.33 percent. Again only 2 of those 22 women rejected the Slavic patronymic. In 1984 the proportion of women to men rose to 21.24:78.76, 7 out of 58 whose professional names lacked Slavic patronymics. Central Asian women in the intellectual life of the UzSSR fell far below parity with men but increased their position during those 25 years. Also, far more women than men cling to identification with their fathers, signified by their use of Russian patronymics. Because Uzbekistan's writers could not or would not return to the true Central Asian patronymic signs, they relied on borrowed forms. Among women, this choice may have indicated a wish for protection: Turkistanian custom had for centuries emphasized such paternalism. Should that protection explain the patterns among women intellectuals, it would show the strength of another old tradition.

Avoiding the patronymic posed a problem for a good portion of all UzSSR writers in the 1980s. Compilers of the directory to the UzSSR's living writers in 1984 listed around three hundred names of authors and poets, those Central Asians with Turkic or Iranian names who did not attach the Russian patronymic amounting to about 50 percent including a number who had used it earlier. Since the first appearance of the register in 1959, the Turkic or Iranian writers of the UzSSR had shown no new direction in adding or ignoring the Russian patronymic. Again in 1984 as in 1977, none of the Uzbek writers retained the traditional Central Asian *-oghli, -zadä,* or *-qizi* as a patronymic but did reflect the Russian-language forms of the names. Had all three sources, instead of only one, appeared in Uzbek, the proportion of intellectuals employing the Russian patronymic might have decreased. For instance, an author who called himself Ismailov in Russian used the form Ismail in Uzbek or another Central Asian language. Russian-language editors, disregarding local or individual preference, automatically added *-aw/-awnä/-awä* endings to make the names conform to Russian usage. In the end, educated people showed no active increase in using the Slavic patronymic, which indicates that parents in at least half the instances named their children without a patronymic. If that pattern continued, it could further discourage genealogical memory among Uzbeks and their kinsmen, but that would not happen so long as children persisted in using their father's name as a last name, with or without a patronymic. In the late twentieth century this constituted a minor loss but not an insignificant one in the evolving process of sustaining contemporary group identity.[5]

These layers of identity in a person helped visitors and residents recognize a local man. When mingling with countrymen, he named himself by specifying the hometown, such as *Toytepalik*, if he were a native of Toytepa (a small town 39 kilometers south-southeast of Tashkent).⁶ Journeying outside the immediate area but still in Central Asia or the greater Middle East, he again "came from Toytepa." With foreigners from China, Europe, India, or Russia, he enlarged his perimeter, becoming a *Turkistanlik* or a *Farghanalik* person. When the occasion demanded it, he distinguished his religious allegiance from theirs by referring to himself as a *Musulmanlik*.

Because societies interact with their individual members—that is, members interact with each other—intellectual leaders in southern Turkistan seldom found the subject of ethnic group identity compelling at the start of the twentieth century.⁷ The nationality group definition said by Marxists and others to depend on the objective factors of economy, literary language, territory, and cultural/psychological makeup, however, relates to such external group recognition. But to hold that opinion is to agree that those four factors stand behind the spiritual unity that constitutes communal identity. Although they are in some sense interdependent, the reverse is more likely true, for it is internal cohesion, a sense of common identity and purpose, that concerns the feelings, signs, and symbols motivating people to share a corporate identity and that anchors the group in place and represents it to itself as well as others. An idea of homeland and of a central, significant place within it begin the conception of group awareness.

CITY EPITHETS AND STATUS

Thus Turkistanians lavished an unusual amount of affection on their towns, attributing to them qualities that expressed attachment and added color and character to the places. "Mughal and Turkic hordes call Samarkand 'Fat Town,' [*simizkänd*]," according to a memoirist of the fifteenth and sixteenth centuries, because fertile, irrigated lands surrounded it. Shaybanid historians designated Samarkand as *Firdäws nishan Sämärqänd* or *Sämärqänd behesht manänd* (Paradisaical Samarkand). Balkh and also Bukhara acquired the nickname *Qubbät ul-Islam* (Cupola of Islam) for their great piety. In the first decades of the 1900s, people knew Bukhara as *Bukhara-yi Shärif* (the Noble Bukhara). In 1980 Bukharan poet Jamal Kamal revived that evocative epithet for his city in a short verse entitled "Fakhirä," following a medieval historian who had written,

> In one of the Muslim traditions [*hadith*] Bukhara is called Fakhirä... Gabriel, the go-between, said: "In the lands of the East there is a country they call Khurasan. On the day of resurrection from the dead three of its cities will be adorned with rubies, pearls and coral. They will shine. Around these cities

will be angels for praise and glory"... The Prophet—may Allah bless him and greet him—asked: "O Gabriel, call out the names of these cities." Gabriel said: "The first in Arabic they call Qasimiyya, in Farsi, Washgird; the second in Arabic they call Samranat, in Farsi, Samarkand; the third in Arabic Fakhirä, in Farsi, Bukhara." The Prophet asked: "Why do they call it Fakhirä?" Gabriel said: "Because on the day of resurrection from the dead it will pride itself among all cities by the number of martyrs for the faith." The Prophet said: "Allah bless the ones in Fakhirä and purify their hearts in piety and multiply their deeds and acts with good for my people."[8]

People called Termez "City of Men" and Balkh "The Mother of Cities," and Hissar became "Jolly Hissar." Qoqan, known in the nineteenth century as *Qoqan-i lätif* (Enchanting Qoqan), in the twentieth bore still another pleasant epithet from the Uzbek writer, Temur Fättah (b. 1910), who wrote about himself: "I was born in a weaver's family in 1910 in Qoqan, which was called the city of poets [*shairlär shähri*]."

The vitality of city nicknames diminished when people ceased to revere certain towns as unique, special places to live. Modern cultural homogenization as well as political naming and Soviet bureaucratization removed the distinctive flavor of these towns, and time reduced the old urban character. Nevertheless, as Kamal's poetic interest reveals, younger Uzbeks began to show sensitivity to the personalities of cities and their meaning for the inhabitants' group attachment.[9]

Before 1925, however, those cities and their special names symbolized much more than personal nostalgia. Both intellectually and politically they represented *mustäqillik* (sovereignty) at various times in their history. Four attributes—capital city, coinage, naming in Friday prayers, and conduct of foreign affairs—consistently denoted the supremacy of a particular ruler and his domain in Central Asia. In this respect, Samarkand played a significant part in modern Central Asian history. Samarkand had served as the center for the renowned court of Timur until 1405, when political necessity forced his son, Shahrukh (r. *ca.* 1409–1447), to make his seat in Khurasan, at Herat, which subsequently became the jewel of the Timurid dynasty. Although Shaybaniy Khan later captured Herat, he treasured Samarkand and organized his capital there, returning it to authority in his regime. The Shaybanids following him preferred Bukhara, making it once again, as in Samanid times, the great Central Asian center of politics, religion, and learning. When the Russians conquered southern Central Asia just after the mid-nineteenth century, they picked Tashkent for their base and avoided the old capitals with their firm Central Asian identity. This confirmed a pattern: New rulers wishing to enhance their prestige through links with the past selected the great old capitals for their government seats. Newcomers intending to break such a precedent deliberately established a new town (like the Ming dynasty did in Qoqan for their khanate in the eighteenth century) or selected a city whose contemporary situation served military and administrative purposes without burdensome historical encumbrances (as the Russians did in choosing Tashkent in 1865).

In the twentieth century, after the lapse of czarist Russian control, southern Central Asia possessed several potential capital cities. When the Soviet government partitioned the region into monoethnically named administrative-territorial units, Uzbekistan considered the three recent khanate and amirate capitals, Bukhara, Khiva, and Qoqan, but rejected them because they had recently functioned as traditional political centers. Tashkent bore a bad name among local inhabitants because it had been the colonial headquarters of Russian governor-generals. Samarkand had become the Jadid center for renewal between 1900 and 1924 and still displayed the stunning visible monuments of Amir Timur and his countrymen. Thus almost by default the authorities chose Samarkand as the center for a politically dependent, new entity—the Uzbekistan Soviet Socialist Republic (UzSSR). On March 6, 1925, several months after the partition and the creation of the new union republic, higher authorities permitted the constituent republic's Central Executive Committee to declare Samarkand the UzSSR capital.

The physical transfer from the Russian colonial base began on March 24 and ended on April 1, 1925, although the UzSSR's Central Executive Committee's chairman, the illiterate Yoldash Akhunbaba-oghli (1885–1943), and the UzSSR's Council of People's Commissars' chairman, Fayzullah Khoja, did not arrive at the Samarkand railway station until the next day. These heads of the UzSSR government, after crossing what they called the local *Qizil Mäydän* (red square), immediately left that new, Russian part of town: "Their cortège stopped at the Registan, where state trade union members, Qoshchi poor people's organizations, young communists, and crowds were massed. An indigenous orchestra perched on top of an old Timurid mosque [*sic*] played a salute." When they had completed this ceremonial visit to the old town, the government members returned to the Russian section to meet on red square with the chairman of the provincial Executive Committee, who handed a silver key to the gate of the main government building to chairman Akhunbaba-oghli. They also declared April 4 an UzSSR holiday. The key and the declaration of a national holiday symbolized the beginning of Uzbekistan's new status of subordination. Samarkand, however, lost its position as capital city on September 30, 1930, and the government moved back to Tashkent, thus replacing the Uzbek-Tajik environment of Samarkand with the Russian presence in Tashkent.[10] Neither the key to the city of Samarkand nor the April 4 commemoration date received any attention sixty years later.

NEW SIGNS OF AUTARCHY

The new capital, recently the political center of the dismembered Turkistan ASSR, now became little more than a conduit for instructions from

Moscow, the political core of the increasingly centralized Soviet state. People thus turned to an idealized homeland, an alternative symbol possessing special appeal to the Uzbek imagination. Shaybanid historian Fazlallah ibn Ruzbihan Isfahaniy had described the *mämläkät* (country) of the early Uzbeks, when they were nomads, as "an extension of paradise. Its fields and plains surpass the gardens of [Qur'anic] Irem." Isfahaniy attributed to Shaybaniy Khan the statement that "the nightingale of reason lost its composure over the beauty of this country's flowers." The idea of beauty in nature's open air connected the Uzbek to his place from that time forward, though he gradually became more and more settled and distant from the wilderness and plains. This may partly explain the urban Uzbek's passion in the twentieth century for traditional housing with its central courtyard garden and living area shaded by fruit trees.[11]

Late in the twentieth century this respect for home continued to sound in the popular sayings circulating in Uzbekistan: *Anä yurting altin beshiging* (Thy motherland is thy golden cradle); *Kishi yurtidä shah bolgunchä, oz yurtingdä gäda bol!* (Rather than becoming the shah in someone else's land, be a pauper in thine own); written verse earnestly praised the Uzbek homeland in terms unexpected in that late period:

> Thou art my shelter, my fatherland,
> Thou art my flower garden, my motherland.
> . . . Thou art my honey sugar, my sweet,
> Thou art my homeland, my Samarkand!

These poetic sentiments contrasted sharply with the attitudes toward "homeland" in the primary school curriculum. Schoolbooks prescribed as the *wätän* (homeland) for an Uzbek first grader the unified, integral, sacred USSR and conveying that idea, "the noble duty facing public educators" to create automatic Soviet patriotism rather than attachment to Uzbekistan. Teachers wanted pupils to assimilate the following ideas about *Wätän* with a capital W:

1. The place where a human being has been born and grown up is his *Wätän.*
2. A human being exists in harmony, love and concern with the individuals who live in his own *Wätän.*
3. A human being loves his own *Wätän*, defends it from enemies.
4. Our *Wätän* is wide, limitless, its riches abundant.
5. In our *Wätän*, different *khälqlär* (ethnic groups) live freely, happily, peacefully.
6. Our *Wätän* has become well off as a result of the work of the Leninist generation, that is, the work of Soviet individuals.

7. Our *Wätän* defends peace.
8. Our *Wätän* is called the Soviet Union.[12]

The Uzbek *anä yurt*, uncapitalized, specified Uzbekistan, whereas *Anä Wätän* designated the Soviet Union, which removed some of the confusion about which homeland might be meant in journalism, literature, or song. Ramz Babajan (b. 1921), a Tashkent poet and chairman of the Wätän Society of the UzSSR, which aimed to keep in contact with Central Asians outside the USSR, traveled often to New York City and other concentrations of Turkistanian emigrants. He carefully distinguished the Uzbekistan homeland (*Wätän*) from the Soviet *Rodina*, which preserved the capability of addressing the immediate homeland in speech and verse as seen in recent Uzbek literature and journalism.[13]

A ruler, besides siting his place of government in the beloved homeland, had the right to coin money and to place his name on every *dirhäm*, *tängä*, or *tillä*. Shaybaniy Khan during his decade of sovereignty (1500–1510) over southern Central Asia, including the large territory of what is now northern Afghanistan and northeastern Iran, minted his silver *tängä* coins (see figure 4.2) in Bukhara, Herat, Mashhad, and other towns throughout the domain. The sovereign prerogative of issuing money remained effective for centuries in Bukhara, continuing even after the amir fled in 1920 and new regimes supervened. But a year and a half before the dissolution of conciliar Bukhara in late 1924, Russia removed from its leaders the right to issue separate, unique paper money. (Newly minted Bukharan coins had stopped appearing there after 1920.) Following dissolution of the conciliar republics, neither the new local leadership nor the UzSSR had any right to mint coinage or print money. Since its very formation, Soviet Uzbekistan had lacked that important traditional symbol of sovereignty. Soviet currency made one gesture to its Central Asian and other nationalities: each banknote, though printed in Russian, showed the denomination in each of fourteen eponymous nationality alphabets and languages of the union republics, including Uzbek.[14]

Religious recognition of sovereignty, shown when the designated Muslim cleric pronounced the ruler's name during the Friday *khutbä* (liturgical prayer) in the mosques of his domain, in turn disappeared. Several decades after the Russian army destroyed the Qoqan khanate and deposed its last khan (1876), indigenous Reformists continued to insist on the symbolic importance of the *khutbä*, not as the pious recognition of a royal sovereign but expressing another kind of sovereignty. Turki-language Jadid newspapers such as *The Voice of Farghana*, with Ashur Ali Zahiriy as editor in chief, persistently advanced the demand that the imam deliver that prayer in Turkistanian rather than in Arabic, the language of mosque services. This reform mixed a standard Jadid technique—disseminating knowledge and ideas through the medium most accessible to the public—with an acknowledgment of the relationship, only then emerging in southern Central Asia, between vernacular language and the population's corporate identity,[15] thus making the community's chosen language a symbol of its legitimacy.

The conventional *khutbä* had constituted a third vital sign of hegemony but one that became null after atheistic Russian dictators took over Central Asia. A public ceremony such as the one held for the new UzSSR on Samarkand's red square in early April 1925 became the secular substitute for the *khutbä*. The new counterpart, no longer necessarily or publicly repeated on Fridays, took place during closed meetings of the ruling inner circle of the UzSSR and the communist party.

Previously the ruling prince caused historians to write about his exploits or encouraged poets to compose verses in his honor to ensure that literate contemporaries acknowledge his position in the political and social arrangements and left dynastic and genealogical documents recording his sovereignty for subsequent khans and amirs to refer to and for chroniclers to build on in their annals. Uzbekistan's authoritarian political organization continued that practice, creating untold pages and copies of reports, which may surpass the medieval chronicles in ambiguity and unreliability, of what it termed its victories in the twentieth century.

One ideological register of UzSSR political events emerged under the new circumstances as a carefully edited, censored version of a stenographic report of communist party congresses. After the Soviet Russian government partitioned Central Asia, the new Uzbekistan remained without a unified official UzSSR capital city for several months; the UzSSR's political leadership therefore conducted urgent business from various convenient locations. It arranged the First (Organizational) Congress of the Communist Party of Uzbekistan from February 6 to 12, 1925, in the city of Bukhara, hometown of Fayzullah Khoja, the incoming head of government (chairman, Council of the UzSSR People's Commissars). Outside the USSR, it is difficult to find a full report of that organizational congress. But for the *Ozbekistan Kammonist (balshäwik)lär firqäsining IInchi qurultayi* (Second Congress), which ran from November 22 to 30, 1925, the Central Committee of the CPUz in Samarkand used the First Uzbekistan State Publishing House in Tashkent to issue 797 copies of a 481-page report printed in the contemporary Uzbek Arabic script. That restricted circulation reflected Russian ideas that political discussion must be privileged information and confirmed how few literate Uzbeks then belonged to the party. This account of the Second Congress of the CPUz made an interesting contribution to ethnic group identity when it distinguished speeches given in Uzbek from those translated into Uzbek and noticed that all of the Uzbek orations had to be interpreted into Russian, evidently to keep Russian outsiders abreast of congress discussion. In the record, published entirely in Uzbek, speakers repeatedly alluded to Samarkand, then the new capital of the UzSSR. The transcript also showed that Russian speechmakers and organizers, starting with Uzbekistan's highest official, CPUz First Secretary V. I. Ivanov, dominated the proceedings. (Moscow had selected the Russian Ivanov for the post at the end of the First Congress of the CPUz, in February 1925.) Under the circumstances and disregarding the language of the congress record, it would exaggerate to call the congress document a true symbol of Uzbek sovereignty or identity.

Fifty-six years and eighteen CPUz congresses later, things had not significantly altered from the standpoint of symbolic sovereignty. Only careful searching could discover any Uzbek language in the 523 Russian-language pages of a recent congress record, this time issued in 10,000 copies. One instance, however, did occur in the stenographic report of the short Twentieth Congress of the CPUz, held February 3–5, 1981. During the second session, the evening of February 3, boys and girls from the communist party children's and young people's organizations—*Pianer* (Young Pioneers) and *Kamsamal* (Communist Youth League)—greeted the congress in Uzbek with rhymed verses:

> These days in Tashkent, the city of friendship and peace
> Are the days of our chieftains, the communists.
> To all the representatives who came to the gathering
> Salutations from fervent young people!
>
> . . . .
>
> Live on, my dear countrymen,
> O tireless strong arm,
> Live on, Uzbekistan,
> Land of the Brave.

The record did not name the language in this Uzbek passage or another short one in Karakalpak, and nobody quoted in the report used the ethnic attributive "Uzbek." This avoidance of ethnic group identification could not be mistaken for the indifference to ethnic group specificity so noticeable in many pre-twentieth century historical manuscripts. Times and situations differed profoundly. Communist party authorities obscured the ethnic identity of members and groups in their internationalist ranks to forestall sectional alliances among nationalities that might counterbalance the overrepresentation of Russians in the CPUz.[16]

As traditional symbols faded away, what officials designated as the Uzbek language, along with homeland, became significant marks of group identity. By 1979, 98.82 percent of Uzbeks in the UzSSR still claimed Uzbek as their language of nationality; the percentage for Uzbeks living throughout the USSR fell only slightly below that: 98.54 percent (12,273,845 individuals). Those two percentages had declined slightly since 1970 when there were 98.88 percent in the UzSSR and 99.65 percent in the entire USSR (9,070,748 persons). Losses that small could not undermine the power of the Uzbek language as an ethnic identifier.[17] Whether more drastic falling away could affect Soviet Uzbek group identity would depend on a complex of factors in addition to language identity.

DIPLOMACY

Conducting diplomacy and other foreign affairs between the ruler's khanate and friendly or hostile countries constituted the fourth practical but symbolic royal function. Diplomacy, like the dedicated histories, demonstrated an independent political identity and was a form of communication that delineated the self of a state or of a nationality.

In the second and third decades of the twentieth century the authorities introduced some diplomatic practices that differed from those in semi-independent Bukhara and Khiva in foreign affairs. Beginning in 1918 Central Asians started participating in the service of the several young *jomhoriyätlär* (republics) in the region. No longer representatives of a royal person, these diplomats performed political and cultural functions that would have been incomprehensible to the envoys of previous centuries. Starting in 1919, a crucial moment in Central Asian international affairs, Abdullah Awlaniy (1878–1934), the madrassah-educated Jadid poet, journalist, and playwright from Tashkent, became deputy political agent and then consul in Muslim Afghanistan, where, with his knowledge of Islam and Central Asian languages and membership in the communist party, he represented the Turkistan Autonomous Soviet Socialist Republic (TASSR) a bit more than a year. Awlaniy's striking combination of skills and identities corresponded closely to the heterogeneity that characterized the Turkistan of his day.

The Bukharan author Sadriddin Ayniy (1878–1954) held a sinecure in a diplomatic mission outside Bukhara. A Jadid poet, schoolteacher, and, later, amateur Tajik scholar, vivid memoirist, and derivative novelist, he recorded in his short autobiography:

> I had not gone to Bukhara for a long time [since being imprisoned and flogged in 1917 at the amir's orders]. I had not participated directly in the affairs of the Bukhara People's Conciliar Republic Government. However, because of that, I did not want to be separated from it completely. In this climate of opinion, it was possible to create a bad impression on others regarding the Bukharan revolution.

To avoid that, in 1921 Ayniy became a consultant for the Bukharan consulate in Samarkand (in the TASSR). "However," he acknowledged, "there was neither such a [diplomatic] staff there nor required duties. As before, my basic task remained entirely press and literary work." An earlier version of Ayniy's biography said that he worked from 1921 to 1925 in the Samarkand *wäkalätkhanä* (consulate) of the Bukhara Kh.Sh.J. In September 1920, an envoy from the Khwarazm People's Conciliar Republic went to Moscow officially to notify Lenin about the founding of that Jadid-dominated regime south of the Aral Sea. According to a witness, the envoy, Baba Akhun Muhammad Salim-oghli, received congratulations from Lenin, who said, "Khwarazm is the first country in the East that has carried out a [socialist] revolution."

Awlaniy's contemporary—the Bukharan Abdalrauf Rashid-oghli Fitrat, another madrassah-trained Muslim scholar and master of Central Asian languages—also played a role in Bukhara's international relations. Fitrat, a leading Young Bukharan Jadid strategist who had traveled widely in the Middle East and worked as an official at the Afghan consulate in Tashkent before the fall of the Bukharan amirate in late 1920, conducted important cultural and political activities in Samarkand and Tashkent, two centers of Reformist strength in the Turkistan ASSR. He held several ministerial posts in the Bukhara People's Conciliar Republic between 1921 and 1923, including the position of *Täshqi Ishlär Naziri* (minister of foreign affairs) in 1922–1923.[18] In 1919 Fitrat issued a long analysis of Asian politics that favored the position of the *Rossiyä Shoralar Hukumäti* (Russian SFSR) over the policies of western European powers then dominating Egypt, India, and Iran. His understanding of international affairs strongly resembled that enunciated 30 years earlier by the Crimean Tatar Reformist leader Ismail Bey Gaspirali.[19] Because Soviet politicians could not trust Fitrat to adhere unthinkingly to an ideological position, Bukharan and Russian communists forced him out of the foreign and other ministries on June 25, 1923, and banished him from the Bukhara People's Conciliar Republic.

The justification for manning diplomatic facilities connecting parts of Central Asia with each other or with Russia disappeared early in 1925 when the political realignments consolidated the territory of Samarkand, Bukhara, and Khiva (capital of Khwarazm) into one Uzbekistan. With the demise of separate powers to conduct foreign affairs vanished the last formal right symbolizing Central Asian sovereignty and independent identity.[20]

The superior, highly educated men who conducted their conciliar and autonomous republics' foreign relations brought an idealistic, broad vision of a new Central Asia to their diplomatic work. Judging from the writings of Abdullah Awlaniy and Abdalrauf Fitrat, it was the image of a free, independent Bukhara, Khwarazm, and Turkistan that motivated them to leave their libraries, beloved poetry, theaters, and schools to go into local and international politics.

Political changes in Central Asia after 1922 drastically affected the region's symbols of sovereignty and identity. The Bukhara People's Conciliar Republic, however, retained its medieval capital, with its political leaders coming mainly from the people of the country. Thanks to the treaty relationship with Moscow, Bukharans also retained some say in foreign relations, and in place of the Friday prayer sanction they acquired both formal meetings and a separate official constitution that was copied in part from the one devised for the Russian Socialist Federated Soviet Republic (RSFSR) in 1918. Bukhara's political leaders shaped their constitution to the particular interests of the conciliar republic by referring to the Bukharan people as a whole rather than to selected strata within the population, thus ignoring the class differentiation admired by Russian communists and asserting the existence of a Bukharan nationality. In Article 2 the statute speaks of "government control passing into the hands of the Bukharan ethnic group [khälq] upon the fall of the power of the Amir [in 1920]." An equally striking provision refers, in Article 26, to the requirement that "legislation issued by the Republic must not contradict the bases of Islam." In addition to these particularities and the very existence of the document, a state flag offered another symbol for the modern Bukharan republic.

Additional usages and practices signified the separate Bukharan identity.[21] In 1927, three years after the Russian authorities dissolved the Bukharan, Khwarazmian, and Turkistanian republics, statutes adapted from RSFSR models came out under the heading "Qanun [Statute]: Fundamental [Constitution] of the Uzbekistan Socialist Soviet Republic." Besides those reproduced in the law register, the government published only 1,500 copies in Uzbek and 750 in Russian. This Qanun, which came out in the capital city of Samarkand, provided, in Article 112, for the first of a trio of formal signs of UzSSR identity. First came the new coat of arms—golden sunbeams and a silver hammer and sickle with crossed descending handles encircled by a wreath of wheat bundles on the right and cotton bush branches with blossoms and bolls on the left against a white background. A red ribbon showed the Uzbek initials Oz. I. Sh. J. (Ozbekistan Ijtima'i Shoralar Jumhoriyati [Uzbekistan Republic of Socialist Councils]) and the Russian letters, UzSSR. To the right on the heads of wheat the design includes in Tajik: J. Sh. I. Oz. (Jumhuriyati Shorahai Ijtimai Ozbekistan). At the top, between the tips of the wheat heads and the twigs of the cotton plant rises a five-pointed red star with gold outlining. The following inscription, in Uzbek on the right and Tajik on the left, "Proletarians of the entire world, unite!," encircles the entire coat of arms. The same message shows in Russian at the bottom (see figure 17.1).

Uzbek- and Russian-language editions of the Uzbekistan constitution published in 1927 did not refer to the Tajik wording on these emblems and deleted Article 69, whose provisions prohibited anyone from altering the territory of the Tajikistan Autonomous Soviet Socialist Republic (Tajikistan Mukhtariyätlik Ijtima'i Shoralar Jumhoriyäti) without Taj. M. I. Sh. J. (TajSSR) agreement. Did these inconsistencies hint that Moscow's leaders soon meant to change the status of the TajASSR? On October 16, 1929, they separated the Tajik ASSR

Figure 17.1 Official seal, Uzbekistan SSR. *Natsional'naia gosudarstvennost' soiuznykh respublik*, 1968.

from Uzbekistan and promoted it to SSR, striking again at Uzbek territorial identity. This metamorphosis of Soviet Tajikistan nearly severed the principal surface communication routes that connected Qoqan, Andijan, and the Farghana Valley with the western part of what was now UzSSR territory. This occurred when Russian politicians permitted the TajSSR to take into its borders from Uzbekistan the venerable city of Khojand (from 1936, Leninabad) and surrounding lands.

These documents proposed no Tajik or Russian wording for the flag, the other official symbol of sovereignty. Article 113 of the constitution called for a UzSSR flag with a rectangular red field, in the left corner of which by the staff at the top they wrote in gold, the Uzbek letters Oz. I. Sh. J., just as in the coat of arms. Article 114 designated Samarkand the capital city of the UzSSR, completing the three formal identifying symbols with which the new union republic started out.[22]

Diplomacy also changed. In motivation and educational attainments, the Bukharan, Khwarazmian, and Turkistanian diplomats, such as Awlaniy and Fitrat, of the 1920s far outranked the Central Asians who followed them into the field of foreign relations after the mid-twentieth century. The new diplomat—denied the direct expression of his Uzbek nationality in domestic politics and outside the confines of his homeland—represented not the UzSSR but the Soviet Union. Nevertheless, the Soviet leadership exploited the Central Asian diplomat's appearance and racial identity, including a residual tie with Islam denied domestically, in assignments abroad. At the United Nations and its branches or in foreign capitals Moscow used the Central Asian to advance Russian aims in Muslim and other Eastern countries. Unlike the envoys of the Bukhara or Khwarazm People's Conciliar Republics in the 1920s, Central Asian diplomats of the late twentieth century may well have been persona non grata in their native Uzbekistan.

Nuritdin A. Muhitdinov (b. 1917), an Uzbek combat veteran of the Red Army in World War II and a party member since 1941, projected the Soviet Union's "Asianness" during his missions to independent Eastern countries such as India and Indonesia in the course of a dangerously visible career in Soviet politics. Chapter 15, "Intelligentsia," noted that he rose near the top of the UzSSR and USSR hierarchies in the 1950s and 1960s (chairman, Uzbekistan Council of Ministers, 1951–1955; first secretary, CPUz, 1955–1957, ultimately, secretary and Presidium member Central Committee CPSU, 1957–1961, preceded by appointments to many other positions). In February 1968, however, Russian authorities exiled him from the USSR by naming him ambassador to Syria not long after Syria's disastrous war with Israel. The USSR Ministry of Foreign Affairs kept him in Damascus as the chief Soviet diplomat until April 1979, his tenure covering another military conflict involving Egypt, Israel, and Syria and intense Soviet involvement in the Middle East.[23]

Writers of the first Uzbekistan constitution (1927) assigned the UzSSR no right to conduct diplomacy on its own behalf. During World War II, as a defensive and conciliatory measure, fearful USSR politicians added that right to other prerogatives said to be possessed by the union republics. In the 1980s, the Presidium of the Supreme Council, UzSSR, channeled the union republic's mainly ceremonial activity in foreign relations through the UzSSR *Täshqi Ishlär Ministrligi* (Ministry of Foreign Affairs). The new UzSSR constitution (1978) repeated the sovereign provisions printed in earlier versions of the statute. These articles, essentially unrealized, assert that the Presidium, UzSSR Supreme Council, has the right "to appoint and recall diplomatic representatives of the UzSSR in foreign states" and "to accept credentials and letters of recall of accredited diplomatic representatives of foreign states" (Articles 30z, 30i, 1937 amended through June 5, 1948; 1960). The later law added the right of the UzSSR Supreme Council to ratify or reject international agreements and "to appoint and invite for its own purposes diplomatic representatives to international organizations" (Article 112, paragraphs 13–15, 1978). Although the right of a union republic to conduct its foreign affairs remained one merely on paper during and after World War II, the position of UzSSR foreign minister stayed occupied—theoretically according sovereign rights and expressing Uzbekistan's peculiar corporate identity.

On March 31, 1985, USSR political authorities approved the appointment of Rafik N. Nishanov (b. 1926) as UzSSR foreign minister. By choosing a prominent Uzbek politician active in the Soviet diplomatic service, they appeared to link nationality, the Soviet version of domestic union republic sovereignty, and foreign affairs representation. Nevertheless, Nishanov's previous career in Uzbekistan raised questions about his suitability and effectiveness as symbol of Uzbek group identity and sovereignty and suggested that, as of old in that region, ethics and values could influence the relationship between chief and followers in Central Asia and thus reflect the actual validity of a given nationality. Nishanov's career in politics began promisingly. He moved from regional department posts to become, by 1963, secretary and Presidium member of the Central Committee, CPUz. Simultaneously, he became a Presidium member in the UzSSR Supreme Council and chairman of the Executive Committee of the City of Tashkent. By mid-1969, as a deputy from the UzSSR, Nishanov chaired the Legislative Proposals Commission of the Council of Nationalities, USSR Supreme Council, in Moscow. In that position he reported on changes to corrective labor legislation, including a statute on pretrial imprisonment, for the USSR and the union republics. It appeared that his rise would continue yet within a year, Soviet politicians removed this prominent Uzbek from his many positions and appointed him USSR ambassador to the southern Asian countries of Sri Lanka and the Maldives. Emigrant sources reported that Nishanov had allegedly used his position in the Tashkent City government, where he served as a kind of mayor, to extort large financial payoffs from persons desperate to find housing in the Tashkent area.[24] If true, this politician could not claim the respect of his constituency or receive the admiration from his public and political entourage that Central Asian sovereigns had always desired. Politics probably motivated his temporary demotion, for just as abruptly Nishanov rose to a much higher political post as CPUz first secretary after the death and disgrace of Sharaf R. Rashidov, the quick retirement of Rashidov's successor, Usmankhojayew, in Tashkent, and the ascent of Mikhail S. Gorbachev to power in Moscow.

The USSR has used Article 112 of the UzSSR constitution to authorize dispatching Central Asians to sessions and meetings abroad that it considered useful for its policies. Dr. Rais A. Tuzmuhammadov served as an Uzbek specialist in international legal affairs in the USSR's Institute of World Economy and International Relations, Academy of Science. One of his published works, a study of national sovereignty, connects it only tangentially with nationality group identity:

> National sovereignty arises as an aggregate of a nation's [*natsiia*] (ethnic group's—*narod's*) rights to the free selection of a social and political system, to integrated territory, economic independence, to respect for its customs, culture, national honor, and dignity, to full equality with other nations and ethnic groups and for other rights realized and preserved in conditions of genuine democracy on routes to social progress in the interest of the general population and with the aims of strengthening peace on earth, friendship, and rapprochement of ethnic groups.

By avoiding the political independence entailed in sovereign acts and by concentrating on how national sovereignty emerges, the scholar skirted the

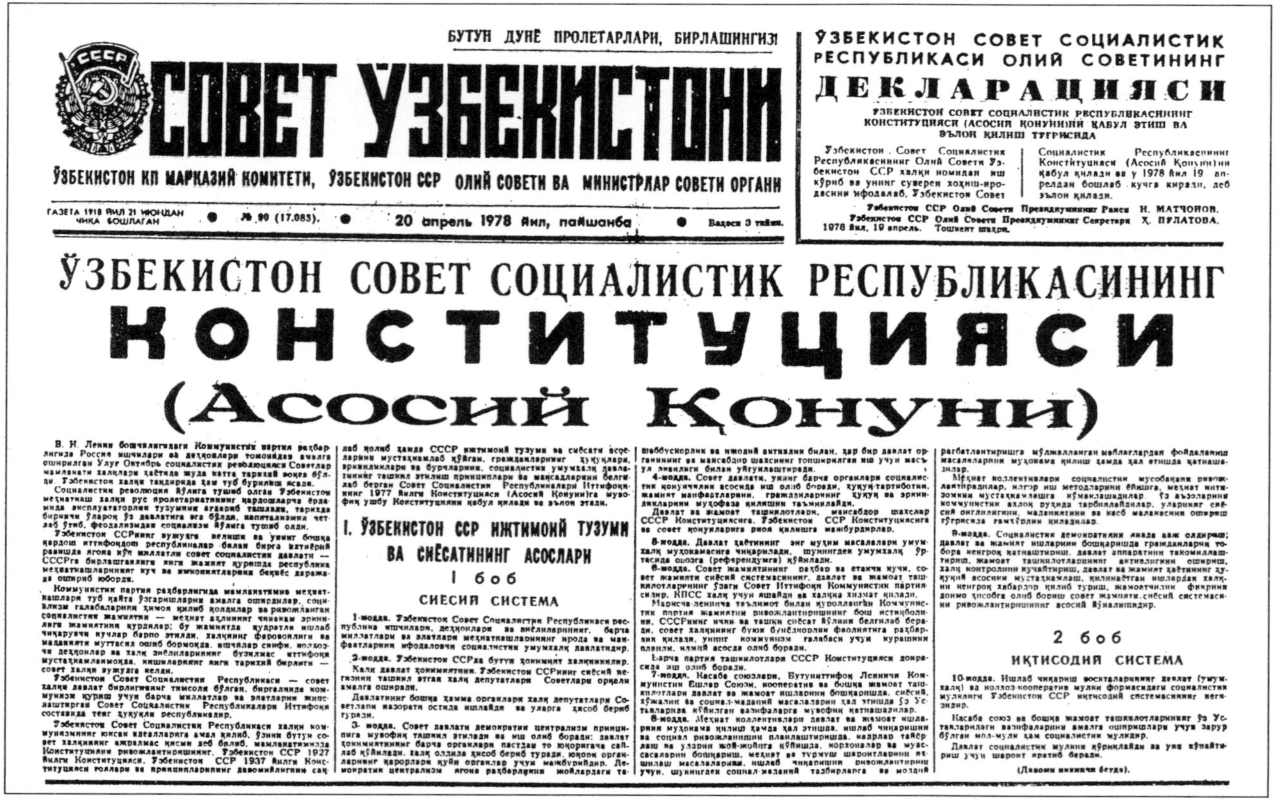

БУТУН ДУНЁ ПРОЛЕТАРЛАРИ, БИРЛАШИНГИЗ!

СОВЕТ ЎЗБЕКИСТОНИ

ЎЗБЕКИСТОН КП МАРКАЗИЙ КОМИТЕТИ, ЎЗБЕКИСТОН ССР ОЛИЙ СОВЕТИ ВА МИНИСТРЛАР СОВЕТИ ОРГАНИ

ГАЗЕТА 1918 ЙИЛ 21 ИЮНДАН ЧИҚА БОШЛАГАН • № 90 (17.083). • 20 апрель 1978 йил, пайшанба • Баҳоси 3 тийин.

ЎЗБЕКИСТОН СОВЕТ СОЦИАЛИСТИК РЕСПУБЛИКАСИ ОЛИЙ СОВЕТИНИНГ

ДЕКЛАРАЦИЯСИ

ЎЗБЕКИСТОН СОВЕТ СОЦИАЛИСТИК РЕСПУБЛИКАСИНИНГ КОНСТИТУЦИЯСИ (АСОСИЙ ҚОНУНИ)НИ ҚАБУЛ ЭТИШ ВА ЪЭЛОН ҚИЛИШ ТЎҒРИСИДА

Ўзбекистон Совет Социалистик Республикасининг Олий Совети Ўзбекистон ССР халқи номидан иш кўриб ва унинг суверен ҳоҳиш-иродасини ифодалаб, Ўзбекистон Совет Социалистик Республикасининг Конституцияси (Асосий Қонуни)ни қабул қилади ва у 1978 йил 19 апрелдан бошлаб кучга киради, деб эълон қилади.

Ўзбекистон ССР Олий Совети Президиумининг Раиси Н. МАТЧОНОВ.
Ўзбекистон ССР Олий Совети Президиумининг Секретари Ҳ. ПУЛАТОВА.
1978 йил, 19 апрель. Тошкент шаҳри.

ЎЗБЕКИСТОН СОВЕТ СОЦИАЛИСТИК РЕСПУБЛИКАСИНИНГ КОНСТИТУЦИЯСИ (Асосий Қонуни)

I. ЎЗБЕКИСТОН ССР ИЖТИМОИЙ ТУЗУМИ ВА СИЁСАТИНИНГ АСОСЛАРИ

I боб

СИЁСИЙ СИСТЕМА

2 боб

ИҚТИСОДИЙ СИСТЕМА

(Давоми иккинчи бетда).

Figure 17.2 New constitution for the Uzbekistan SSR. *Sawet Ozbekistani*, April 20, 1978.

basic question of how to act without interfering in the nationality's name and interest. A polity characterized by a definition of national sovereignty limited to certain political systems and essentially passive would scarcely be able to project any identifying national image. Dr. Tuzmuhammadov, who resided in Moscow, often represented the USSR, rather than his Central Asian homeland, abroad. As a Soviet delegate to the Afro-Asian People's Solidarity Organization (AAPSO), headquartered in Cairo, he attended its sessions around the world. On one occasion, beginning June 12, 1978, in New York City, Dr. Tuzmuhammadov served on AAPSO's six-man delegation to the U.N. General Assembly's Tenth Special Session that was devoted to the Soviet foreign policy aim of promoting disarmament in noncommunist countries without comparable divestment in the USSR. The other AAPSO delegates came from Iraq, Cyprus, Angola, Sri Lanka, and Egypt; thus the Uzbek Soviet diplomat found himself identified with a collective Asia outside the USSR but with an ethnically, regionally ambiguous Soviet Union inside it. Neither alignment assisted Central Asia or Uzbekistan to realize a rounded group image particular to itself.[25]

The 1978 UzSSR constitution (see figure 17.2) revealed an addition as well as several changes to these symbols. Tashkent had become the UzSSR capital city. The name of the statute had been changed to *Ozbekistan Sawet Satsiälistik Respublikäsining Kanstitutsiyäsi (Äsasiy Qanuni)*, adopting Russian or European words in place of most of its former Central Asian wording. The authors of the constitution also added an official anthem (*gimn*—the Russian spelling of "hymn") for the first time. On April 20, 1978, the day after the UzSSR Supreme Council announced its acceptance of the new Uzbekistan constitution, the Presidium decreed that the UzSSR would from that date on have a *däwlät gimni* (state song), as sanctioned by Article 180 of the constitution. The day the Supreme Soviet published the statutes, the official bulletins printed the words (by Temur Fattah, modified by Turab Tola) and music (by Mutal Burkhanaw) for the new anthem. The previous (1947) version of the song, never mentioned in the Uzbekistan constitutions, opened with "In the land of the Councils" and went on to declaim, in the refrain, "Thou art my radiant motherland in the East, seek perfection." Unlike the 1978 official third verse, which credited communism and the Soviet banner with leading them forward, the older anthem attributed progress to learning: "With the ray of knowledge and science our path is bright." The earlier anthem fawned on Stalin, saying that he had shown them the road to *azadlik* (freedom), a term used in the same way in the next redaction of the anthem. Because the USSR's Politburo had downgraded Party Secretary Stalin, for more than twenty years people could not sing the words of Uzbekistan's anthem; the *Uzbek Soviet Encyclopedia* (1972) printed the music but omitted the lyrics. The later rendition substituted Lenin's name for Stalin's in two verses. Thus the first verse reads,

Greetings, Russian people, our great elder brother,
Greetings, our immortal wise leader, darling Lenin.
The freedom road You showed us,
In the land of the Councils, the Uzbek found glory.

In that official song group identity took on descriptive forms, with the authors employing the personal ethnic attributive "Uzbek" in a verse of the song and the territorial place-name Uzbekistan once in its refrain. The 1978 anthem referred to the councils in two verses plus the refrain and mentioned communism and Russian people in the same two verses. The lyricist, perhaps hinting its temporary existence, omitted the union republic name, UzSSR, from the song. The lines repeatedly characterized the homeland, without ever employing the word *wätän*, as *serquyash olkä* (a sun-drenched land), and referred to *tupraghing khäzinä* (thy soil is a treasury). The earlier anthem conveyed sensory images of the Uzbeks' country somewhat more evocatively than did the newer one, which also avoided suggesting particular passion for the Uzbek ethnic group's place, accomplishments, or history and focused on the dual subordination of Uzbekistan to the Russians and their USSR. In that regard, the song held scant intrinsic value for distinguishing the Uzbeks from others; but as a trapping of Soviet-style SSR sovereignty, it offered another formal symbol of identity and as such, might help to focus modern Uzbek group self-awareness.[26]

Uzbek intellectuals regarded those formal symbols of group identity without great enthusiasm. While UzSSR party and government officials guided people through the formal ritual of accepting the document and the prescribed symbols, local scholars asked for more solid proof of group identity. As late as 1977, three Uzbek historians called on their educated countrymen to look into what ideologists termed Uzbek group ethnogenesis. "One of the primary duties in the field of ethnographic research," they acknowledged, "was interdisciplinary learning about the ethnogenesis of the Uzbek ethnic group [*khälq*]." Other Uzbek scholars continued to examine Central Asia's intricate human past, endeavoring to relate the much earlier tribal proliferations to the racial or ethnic makeup of present-day Uzbeks.[27] They could do this only by bringing together with ethnographers people in the fields of history, archeology, anthropology, linguistics, literature, art, and the like. Thus the special Soviet version of Uzbek history and ethnic origin had not yet found firm footing, an acknowledgment that Uzbek group identity remained unsatisfactory from a scholar's and perhaps even an ideologist's standpoint. The new research, by the very nature of the disciplines from which the authorities drew scholars, could not avoid considering the many intangibles in the human biographies, attitudes, and thoughts of the people they called Uzbek.

18 Uzbekness

Ozbekchilik: Ozbekkä khas urf-adätlär.
Uzbekness: manners and customs peculiar to an Uzbek.

(Z. M. Mä'rufaw, 1981)

Sharq guli Ozbekistan.
The rose of the East is Uzbekistan.

(Hämraqul Riza, "Third Song from a Panegyric Epic," *Pale Blue River*, 1983)*

I, too, am that land's singer, its beloved,
I praise the magnificent, native Uzbek land [diyar]
. . . O Uzbek native land, Uzbek native land.

(Keldi Qadiraw, 1985)**

In the decades after Soviet authorities founded the Turkistan ASSR in 1918, southern Central Asians lost their remaining conventional forms of sovereignty, and their traditional ideas of community greatly altered. To replace those traditions, they acquired substitutes that, in turn, underwent dilution and neutralization. During that period, Uzbeks, looking to other means for express-

---

* Hämraqul Riza, *Zängari därya. She'rlär* (Tashkent: Ozbekistan LKSM Märkäziy Kamiteti "Yash Gwärdiyä" Näshriyati, 1983), p. 35.
** Keldi Qadiraw, "Ozbek diyari," *Ozbekistan ädäbiyati wä sän'äti*, February 1, 1985, p. 4.

ing and sustaining the sense of group and place instead of relying on the lifeless official songs and emblems assigned to them, endeavored to imbue positions of leadership with the meaning of the nationality.

Understanding that no ethnic aggregation could function if bereft of a unifying human presence at the core, they intended to focus the society's ethics and values on the person of the leader. Moscow's purge trials, which eliminated Uzbekistan's two main indigenous chiefs—Akmal Ikram and Fayzullah Khoja—in the late 1930s and "liquidated" three different Uzbek heads of government succeeding Khoja in the position of chairman, Council of Ministers, as "enemies of the people," intimidated politicians and intellectual leaders at all levels of society. Causing something even more insidious than the paralysis of Uzbekistan's governance and cultural life, political repression struck a severe blow at nationality identity by damaging the delicate ties between Uzbek leaders and the led. Uzbek group identity, up to that time only tenuously developing, virtually ceased between 1938 and 1956 partly because the threatening, embattled existence of a series of CPUz, UzSSR Council of Ministers, and UzSSR Supreme Council Presidium chiefs nearly guaranteed their political and ethnic immobility.[1]

After the Twentieth Congress of the CPSU (1956) stilled the harsh echoes from Stalin, a political-economic system devoid of effective public checks and balances and known for its lack of loyalty among politicians invited abuses in the UzSSR and elsewhere. Central Asians can cite the illustrative case of Yadgar S. Nasriddinova (b. 1920), who became one of the most prominent Soviet Central Asian women in twentieth-century politics. From the 1940s to 1970s she enjoyed an active career in Uzbekistan's and the Soviet Union's top political ranks: beginning in 1956 she held a position in the Central Committee, CPSU; between 1959 and 1970, Nasriddinova sat as chairman, Supreme Council, UzSSR; and from 1970 to 1974, she chaired the Council of Nationalities of the Supreme Council, USSR. As a consequence, she started playing a part in USSR diplomacy. During his visit to the USSR in 1972, President Richard M. Nixon invited her to dinner in the U.S. embassy in Moscow; in April 1974 she received Senator Edward Kennedy in her offices during his visit to the Kremlin (see figure 18.1). Yet when the press issued the uncontested list of nominees for the USSR Supreme Council seats in mid-1974, it passed over her name. Unlike Muhitddinov and Nishanov, also fallen Uzbek leaders whom the authorities pressed into diplomatic service, she remained in the USSR, where she received minor assignments, banished from the UzSSR. That estrangement from her place of origin and a scandal connected with her name caused the editors of the *Uzbek Soviet Encyclopedia* to ignore her birth in Qoqan and her long public and party service in the UzSSR by erasing her entry from their compendium. Without public warning this formidable political leader became a nonentity through the intervention of outsiders.[2]

Figure 18.1 Yadgar S. Nasriddinova, chair, Council of Nationalities, USSR Supreme Council, receives U.S. Senator Edward Kennedy in April 1974. UPI photo.

The rapid turnover after 1937 in CPUz first secretaries made them ineffective in office. The unusually long tenure (more than 24 years) of Sharaf R. Rashidov and his allies brought some much-desired stability to UzSSR politics but also encouraged nepotism and corruption. Before and after Rashidov's death, hostile rumors circulated in Uzbekistan, possibly by secret Soviet agents, that he was a crypto-Tajik who surrounded himself with Tajik appointees. (If so, he had emulated the political behavior of Central Asian chieftains like Yamin ad-Dawla Mahmud of Ghazna [r.998–1030] who, for security, hired outsiders as bodyguards and pitted tribes and ethnic groups against one another.) Whether or not the rumors were true, they reflected a general proclivity to distrust the loyalty and nationality interest of the leader in question. In 1984 and 1985 hundreds of Rashidov's former associates lost their positions, ostensibly for corruption in government and party affairs. A specific accusation—"for shortcomings in his work and for abusing his post to solve housing problems of members of his family"—brought about the removal of Akram R. Khojayew, a member of the Central Committee, CPUz, and deputy chairman of the UzSSR ten years after the political disgrace of Nasriddinova. Analysts conjectured that the purge of Rashidov's associates constituted a political machine's reprisal as much as it did large-scale corruption among public officials. Each, however, had equally bad effects on public opinion in Uzbekistan.

By denigrating the former CPUz first secretary, his rivals, with Russian encouragement, again denied the Uzbeks identity with a prominent contemporary leadership figure from their own society. The death of a true leader devastates the polity, but with self-respect it can recover; the removal of leaders through political maneuvers cloaked in charges of corruption has more far-reaching effects. Such a loss became a matter of indifference to the populace because Soviet political acts attached and detached the leader to or from his/her people without their consent. Even more serious was the harm to the nationality's self-esteem when higher officials accused the co-ethnic leader of venality and dishonesty. Demeaning events like these continued into the mid-1980s and, under the existing system of authoritarian government, continue to hurt the Uzbek nationality's self-image. A harmonious meshing of ethnic interests between political leader and populace simply cannot develop. In retrospect, public statements asserting a pattern of alleged corruption or genuine instability characterized the decades of Uzbekistan's upper Soviet leadership from the 1930s to the 1980s.

Russians and Ukrainians held most positions of power in the hierarchies, whereas Uzbeks sat in many visible seats but had no authority (in this they resembled the Kazak puppet khans placed on the throne of eighteenth-century Khiva by Uzbek tribal politicians). Such an arrangement deprived Uzbeks of the chance to identify with a political organization and leadership of their own.[3]

The continuing debacle in local leadership remained a principal obstacle to Uzbek group cohesion. Soviet political life in Central Asia did not allow Uzbeks to overcome the nineteenth-century legacy of arbitrary rule under Nasrullah Khan and his heirs who, like many subsequent Manghit and Soviet Uzbek leaders, offered conspiratorial, destructive, secretive, venal, antipopular, self-serving, and inhumanly ideological models.

By the 1980s, a new Central Asian leader to match the ideal khan or amir had yet to crystallize in the imagination of Uzbeks or other nationalities in the region. Until some features and symbols of actual sovereignty returned to the Uzbek scene in a voluntary relationship between an Uzbek leader and his own nationality, a vision of the good Uzbek leader was likely to remain elusive. That ambiguity infected all Uzbek works of imagination as, with the likelihood of change in the political conditions seemingly remote, Uzbek creative intellectuals sought substitutes for the unifying presence of a real ethnic leader.

DISSENTERS

Direct action offered one avenue away from cultural and political subordination. In 1957 a group in Uzbekistan organized to protest the lack of independence. Inevitably, the Soviet secret police arrested members of the group and charged one of them, Babur Shakiraw, with Uzbek nationalism and attempting to cross the border (a crime) and flee the country. To avoid injecting political dissent into the proceedings, the formal accusation spoke of "anti-Soviet agitation and propaganda." Shakiraw's human rights activity increased during his eight-year incarceration. In 1974 he and other prisoners complained about working conditions in Vladimir Prison and attempted to extract recognition as political prisoners. His insistence on using the outlawed term "political prisoner" to describe himself earned him fifteen days confinement in a special punishment cell in March 1975, even though past and present versions of the constitution of the USSR guarantee the right to free speech. Within the camps Shakiraw insisted on speaking his native language and refused to address camp or prison officials in Russian. (Prisoners could suffer disciplinary measures for speaking in their own tongues.)[4] During April–July 1977 Shakiraw took part in a 100-day campaign to obtain recognition as a political, rather than a criminal, prisoner, and he and his fellows continued the drive later that year with hunger strikes. Among other things, he wanted to show that the Soviet authorities regularly punished citizens for speaking their minds.[5] Persons in his predicament often resorted to *samizdat* (unofficial publishing) and unauthorized communications to the outside world.

In March 1977, Babur Shakiraw, Nikolai Budulak Sharygin, and others addressed an appeal concerning the Helsinki Accords to President Jimmy Carter that begins, "We, a group of Soviet political prisoners, call upon you to vote for democracy—for every person's right to the unhampered development of his or her individual self." The appeal protests the mistreatment of political prisoners but also raises questions relating to general civil and human rights. The signatories speak about the suppression of religion and protest ethnic discrimination in every form. They object to compulsory ideological indoctrination and to bans on intellectual and creative activity in the prison camps, including the authorities' practice of blocking prisoners' communication from and to the outside world.[6] In early 1980 Soviet officials released Shakiraw from the labor camps, according to information from the International Secretariat of Amnesty International, London. Shakiraw's history shows that Uzbekistan possesses individuals and groups dedicated to democratic principles and ready to act on them.

In addition, after May 1944, the CPSU and the Soviet government indirectly educated many towns and villages of the Uzbek SSR in the field of civil and human rights. Crimean Tatars exiled to Central Asia gradually reconstituted themselves as a community in Uzbekistan, and by 1967 their peaceful protests and organized petitions and appeals had won them exoneration for the false charge of mass treason during World War II made by Stalin's government. The Crimean Tatars continued, despite police methods, mass trials, economic sanctions, and bureaucratic resistance, to demand restitution of their group and individual prerogatives, including the right to live at home in the Crimea.[7]

Uzbekistan's other inhabitants could not have failed to learn about this drive so openly and resolutely carried on by Crimean Tatars, for the exiles had to reach the highest Soviet leadership and overcome the prejudices against Crimean Tatars encouraged by propagandists sent throughout Uzbekistan in 1944 by officials of the region. Written proof that the Uzbek intelligentsia did become aware of the Crimean Tatar effort appeared in a negative fashion. Crimean Tatar spokesmen complained that Uzbek writers in the established Union of Writers of Uzbekistan sided with the regime in Moscow against the Crimean Tatars' push to regain their rights. Mustafa Jemilev, a foremost figure in the Tatar movement, in June 1970 delivered testimony in the courtroom where he and Il'ya Gabay defended themselves against charges of slandering the policies of the USSR in testimony that cited the response from the Union of Writers of Uzbekistan to one of many public appeals sent by the Crimean Tatars to various offices in the USSR. Jemilev said that Uzbek novelist and poet Asqad Mukhtar, the deputy chairman of the Union of Writers of Uzbekistan, as well as author Rahmat Fayziy and Sagdullaev, the secretary of the party organization of the Union of Writers of Uzbekistan, denounced these appeals in a letter to the Committee for State Security (KGB). The letter became a key piece of evidence used against Crimean Tatar leaders by the state prosecutor to incriminate Reshat Bayramaw, a Crimean Tatar activist who distributed copies of the appeals, and resulted in a three-year prison sentence for him. Jemilev ironically commented that the same Uzbek writers who would not support their Crimean Tatar coreligionists and fellow Turkic people in Central Asia would readily write in the press and speak to conferences of foreign Asian and African writers about their solidarity with the drives for national sovereignty and independence of those non-Soviet people.[8]

In that censored society, men such as Shakiraw and Jemilev reveal strong convictions about personal and group rights. Those two went to prison for their beliefs, and their readiness to face repeated prosecution educated many in Uzbekistan about democracy and prepared the ground for greater expectations in the sphere of civil rights. That points toward an intellectual modernity developing in the culture and society. Although most Uzbek men and women may not feel ready for that degree of direct action, they can express their attitudes indirectly through the Central Asian medium of literature. In the Uzbek view, literature sustains group life, and they devote their energies to that form of communicating.

Seeking a remedy for the pervasive ethnic disabilities of the present political and social system, Uzbek writers and other intellectuals again began admiring the natural and man-made beauty of their environment, identifying with their particular version of modern civilization. As always, ambiguities gray the black and white distinctions between politics and aesthetics. Whatever his shortcomings, Sharaf R. Rashidov was more than a durable machine politician, for he prided himself on being widely published and read as an Uzbek author. In his numerous political and fictional writings (in rhetoric the two differed little), Rashidov paid homage to the Russian masters of the USSR and their ideology. In one of his booklets, widely circulated in translation, he included a long section entitled "With the Russian People Forever, Our Elder Brother" that demonstrated his approach to Uzbek-Russian relations: "The greatness of the Russian people is measured, first and foremost, by their heroic achievements over many centuries and by all that they have done for human happiness on earth."⁹ During the Twenty-fifth Congress of the CPSU in February 1976, Rashidov preceded Eduard A. Shevardnadze, then first secretary of the Georgian SSR, in expressing admiration for the leadership qualities of then General Secretary Leonid I. Brezhnev in a recognizable Central Asian sentiment: "The thinkers of the East said: 'When a state is headed by a wise man who loves his people and is concerned about improving his country's lot, this is great happiness for the state and for the people.' [Applause] The Soviet people. . . call [Brezhnev] such a person." First Secretary Rashidov characterized Brezhnev as a man with "supreme modesty, brilliant talents, revolutionary optimism, proletarian solidarity, firm class position, spiritual beauty and personal charm"¹⁰ yet neglected to mention any connection between those leadership qualities and the well-being of the Central Asians and others under the supreme sovereignty.

Rashidov, knowing that the rules of political survival for subordinate, non-Russian leaders in the USSR required repeated expressions of faith in the dominant Russians and their Marxist ideology, paid the necessary, perhaps cynical, tribute to Moscow. Most Uzbeks understood their CPUz first secretary's obligation to take the stance he did in the Soviet system. At Rashidov's funeral in Tashkent on November 2, 1983, many people acknowledged the need, under the circumstances, for such an Uzbek political figure. But, although they perceived Rashidov's extraliterary motives, they could not express great respect for his writing. His endless panegyrics to Russia, then, succeeded temporarily as Sovietwide political devices but failed as indigenous art for the emerging Uzbek nationality. In that crucial regard, the leader's main aesthetic method, his literary animus, could not contribute to a distinctive new Uzbek profile in Central Asia.

Later writers, artistically more self-emancipated and politically less intimidated than First Secretary Rashidov, changed the tone and extended the circumference of their creative environment. Passing beyond the formal signposts embodied in the official identity symbols for the UzSSR, they recaptured reader interest by turning from the routine obeisance to ideology and Russian hegemony to pay lyrical homage to the art and human nature within Uzbekistan, mirroring the most attractive values and hopes of their society, admiring its Uzbekness. By projecting an intellectual, aesthetically stimulating "country of the Uzbeks," the new writers synthesized in literature a vision of their homeland and nationality that might become its first modern transmutation.

POETS

Many wrote about spring, the countryside, or magical moonlight, but the more evocative verse decorated the paths of Central Asians who had left a mark on their world. Asqad Mukhtar (b. 1920) and other establishment poets, along with some editors and teachers, conducted a remarkable effort to develop verse writing in young Uzbeks growing up in the mid-1950s. To those mentors must go credit for increasing the number of women entering the literary field. Those endeavors by senior Uzbeks evidently aimed to compensate for the grievous physical and psychological losses, though it could never replace them, suffered by the culture from the communist party rampage throughout the 1930s and 1940s. In the 1950s and 1960s the main literary journal, *Shärq yulduzi*, introduced scores of new writers to the public in its pages under the headings *Yängi namlär* (New Names), *Yashlär sähifäsi* (Young People's Page), and *She'riyätimizning kenjä äwladi* (Our Poetry's Youngest Generation). To encourage women to enter the field, the journals also reserved pages entitled *Qizlär awazi* (Girls' Voice) or *Qizlär guldästäsi* (Girls' Bouquet of Flowers). This singling out of poets by gender showed that Uzbekistan had not moved into a phase in its cultural development in which women could exercise their rights without mentors or patrons.

Among the many poets appearing in those pages, several began to show up repeatedly. Etibar Akhunawa (b. 1933), from Andijan, had published her poetry in Girls' Voice and *Qizlär ijadi* (Girls' Art) by the time she was 26. Educated in Tashkent's Lenin State University, she held positions in the editorial staff of *Shärq yulduzi* and then on the principal political newspaper of the UzSSR, *Sawet Ozbekistani*. Her verse began appearing in literary journals during the 1960s; in 1961 *Tangdä* (At Daybreak), a collection of her verse, came out, the first of nine booklets of poems, published by 1981. Her earliest published long poem, *Dutar häwasi* (A Dutar's Melody, 1970) continued in the same lyric vein as those of other Uzbek women: lyric verse devoted to nature, the seasons, family, and feelings of love and sadness. A critic commenting about the period said that those young poets of the 1960s earnestly tried to write with fresh ideas and a *yängi gäp* (new voice).[11]

CPUz leaders selected Akhunawa for membership in the party; continuing her role as a social-political activist, in 1977 authorities trusted her to make an extended visit to Canada. In 1980 the Young Communists of Uzbekistan awarded her their prize for literature. A short poem she wrote that same year had the line, "Finishing a panegyric is a thousand times easier than giving a public report" (she chose the resonant Arabic term *mä'ruzä* for "report" rather than the usual Russian *dakläd*, pairing and internally rhyming it in the same line with the Arabic word *qäsidä*, for "panegyric"). She titled another verse written that same year *Anä yurt qoshighi* (Song of the Motherland):

> Motherland,
> Thou art my calligraphy,
> I still have not written [it] at all.
> Thou art my overflowing happiness,
> I have not forgotten this at all.[12]

She also wrote essays on contemporary cultural and social themes. One of them, "If We Dream, Is That Wrong? What Do You Say?" raised the idea that "the creators of the cotton and silk that is being sown and made to grow in our homeland [*yurtimiz*] are women." Yet, she said, they did not have pretty scarves or dresses made out of those fabrics. In the same essay, the writer asserted that working Uzbek women no longer sang lullabies, told fairy stories, or asked their children riddles because of the heavy daily demands of work and housekeeping. But, said essayist Akhunawa, women should not forget these rhymes and songs because riddles and tales help acquaint children with the group's customs and with legendary heroes of the distant past in a crucial transmission of cultural identity. Disrupting that cultural transaction between parent and offspring in familial relations could reflect negatively on the roots of group identity as well.[13] Akhunawa observed, understood, and made public her thoughts about the importance of her sisters' children for the Uzbek future. In this way, the new intellectuals among Uzbek women replaced the casualties of political intrigue like Yadgar Nasriddinova with another kind of strength—maintaining Uzbek cohesion—which may in the long run prove more significant than political position in the contemporary Soviet hierarchy.

A male poet of this new generation, (Abdu)Razzaq Abdurashidaw (b. 1936) completed Tashkent State University's requirements in philology, went into journalism, and had joined both the state-run Union of Writers and the CPUz by the time he was 40. He published his first poetry in 1956, followed by frequent contributions to literary journals over the next two decades. He entitled the initial collection of his strong rhythmic verse *Yol bashidä* (On the Way, 1962, 47 pages, 5,000 copies). In it the young poet sounded the themes of *Olkä* (The Country), "Märghilan," *Anä tupraq* (Dear Soil) along with many other motifs. Although born in Tashkent, he expressed passionate admiration for the tenth-century town of Marghilan, famous for silk weaving of unearthly beauty with a population, at his writing, of about 100,000, mainly Uzbeks. (Note the echo of the earlier nicknaming of Central Asian towns:)

> Silkmaker's town of the Ages,
> Luxuriant, comely Marghilan, like its satin,
>
> . . . .
>
> My Marghilan, my silkmaker's town,
>
> . . . .

Even those who have neither seen nor touched *khanätläs*, (the splendid striped silk fabric), can appreciate Abdurashidaw's rendition.

His bright sensuality yielded to a darker mood when he shifted his attention to the cluster of historic Islamic monuments in Samarkand:

> Registan,
> O age-old plaza!
> How much misery that friendly head of thine saw.
> Thy colors are stains of woe or sprayed blood.
> Is thy stone the head of captive beauties?!
> Forgive me if I
> lacerate thy heart,
> If I recall the past, that instant. . .
> Really I'm thy offspring too, not a stranger,
> For that reason my compassion is for thee, Registan!
>
> . . . .

Abdurashidaw's poetry scored high marks in Uzbek literary criticism, and observers placed him among the young people working hard to achieve artistic mastery. But one critic, reviewing poems published around 1970, took Abdurashidaw to task for the stanza about the Registan: "Such one-sided thought will not bring glory to the poet." Objecting to the writer's seeing the past of Samarkand only negatively, the critic commented, "one must also keep at the center of attention questions like the emergence of great changes in science, culture, and economic life and [have in mind] that the roots of a good many current successes reach into and rest on the past." (In other words, Samarkand's Registan has much greater meaning to Central Asians than conveyed in Abdurashidaw's gloomy one-dimensional treatment.) The critic counselled young writers to avoid the thematic and ideological simplification so frequently encouraged before 1956 and to move on to a modern aesthetic and intellectual complexity in their poetry. But an allegorical nuance in the poet's work might allude to the atrocities perpetrated among the educated by the authorities in Samarkand and elsewhere in the 1920s and 1930s. If so, the writer would resemble those poets of the 1920s who used Aesopian circumlocutions to despair over the destruction of independent Turkistanian culture. In either reading of Abdurashidaw's lines, the poet does identify with the colors, the experiences, and the places of Central Asia. When he turns to the idea of homeland rather than its elegant artifacts, the poetry becomes more universal but less evocative. In his ballad "The Dear Soil," he declares:

> Every nationality has its own desire,
>
> its own song, its own epic,
>
> It has its own place—its own garden
>
> so far, preserved thousands of years.[14]

CULTURAL AND ETHNIC HYBRIDS

Poets of another sort then entered the scene to raise questions about both form and identity of Central Asian verse. Since at least 1961 communist spokesmen all over the USSR had called for an ethnically sublimated individual to embody a unionwide, homogenized Soviet ethnic group. The numbers of such hybrid individuals recognized by the ideologists remain small and include few writers. In Uzbekistan such a rarity is Rahim (Raim) Hakimawich Farhadiy (b. 1942), child of an Uzbek physician and a physiologist mother "born in Russia," evidently a Tatar or Russian. Raim married into the prominent family of Sergei P. Borodin (1905–1974), a popular Russian novelist and onetime member of the literary circle Pereval, and Rauza Ya. Borodina (b. 1922), a journalist and translator of many works into Uyghur and Russian. Raim, following his parents' footsteps, trained in the Samarkand Medical Institute, where his father had long headed the department of pathology, and in 1965 became a doctor. After a brief experience specializing in social hygiene and the organization of public health care and three years of work in the UzSSR Komsomol, Raim began taking advanced literature courses offered by the state-run Union of Soviet Writers in Moscow. He then became assistant to the editor in chief of *Zvezda Vostoka*, the Russian-language and Russian-oriented literary journal issued in Tashkent, a testimony to his fluent command of that language. His father-in-law, Sergei P. Borodin, served as a senior member of that magazine's editorial board.

Raim Farhadiy came from a privileged circle into a situation with many prerogatives.[15] Society often observed that pattern in late twentieth-century Russia but less frequently in Uzbekistan unless the protégé's parentage included Uzbek and Russian, Uzbek and Tatar, or some other outside ethnic group. Only if they held favored status in the early decades of the UzSSR, could pure Uzbek couples transmit some of that privilege to their offspring.

Farhadiy's life and career resembled those of several other younger men from Central Asia whose family background and exposure to Moscow's cultural or educational institutions had modified or loosened the usual close ties with their nationality and who characteristically lived and worked a great deal of the year outside Central Asia. (Raim Farhadiy actively engaged in international youth organizations.) Such Soviet cosmopolitanism emerged from men such as Chingiz Aitmatov from Kirgizstan, Timur Zulfikarov from Tajikistan, and Olzhas Sulaymanov from Kazakhstan. These three and Raim Farhadiy deserve attention because of their ethnic ambivalence as token "new Soviet men" and the writing facility that they frequently demonstrate with the ready cooperation of the CPSU and state publishing houses. They almost invariably compose in Russian and release their literature in that language, although one or two speak some Central Asian language. Certain of Raim Farhadiy's translations from the Uzbek of Uyghun, Ghafur Ghulam, and others into Russian have appeared in print, but he apparently avoids publishing any of his adult work in Uzbek (or Tatar), suggesting that he lacks literary confidence in his Turkic language. When his early poems appeared in an Uzbek-language literary magazine, the editors listed a translator's name alongside. In the children's literature that Dr. Farhadiy has increasingly attempted and published, however, he evidently employs Uzbek.[16] Farhadiy's serious verses are intellectually simple, accessible poems that evoke sensory images and carry out themes of interest to Central Asianists.

His writing, like that of other demi–Central Asians, raises fundamental questions about general literary theory and Soviet nationality policies. Can truly indigenous literature be written in a foreign language? and how does literature composed in a foreign language—written by a native-born author—contribute to the identity of the culture or personality of the writer's putative nationality and region? The answers do not come easily. Aitmatov and Zulfikarov live mainly in Moscow and Sulaymanov has spent many years there. Their lifestyle as outsiders supplements the effects of foreign language choice and family background. Some scholars put these writers into the same category as Russian and Jewish authors who focus on Central Asia in their fiction, which leads to the conclusion that local birth and upbringing may be modified by the Central Asian's acculturation to the Russian literary and social environment. Their linguistic alienation completes the process.[17]

These borderline writers, like many alienated intellectuals or artists given asylum in and writing about other societies, appear to render the signs of Central Asian identity more persistently, perhaps more eagerly than do 100-percent Uzbeks, Kirgiz, or Kazaks. As a result, their works initially seem more Uzbek or Kazak than those of entirely Central Asian authors. One of Dr. Farhadiy's Russian-language poems, "The Samarkand Tint," which evokes his native city's superb palette, illustrates the point:

> About the secret of making a tint
> The ages have lost all memory . . .
> In vain new chemists' firm intent
> To divine the tiles' old sorcery.
>
> On fine days it looks so dismal,
> During rain the tint is gay.
> The wall, like distant littoral,
> Runs smoothly, airily away.
>
> And mutely we stand and look
> At walls, the dome, pale azure.
> Here, from the sky the Master took
> Its magnificent composure.
>
> Like tiny smoke puffs, a pattern.
> A flower and a blue star.
> Those passed by do not return,
> Repeatable, they never are.
>
> In this blueness, no cloud streaks
> The stream's pure radiance.
> But in the figured lines, breaks
> Hide the rifts of existence.
>
> Day long, one tint will difference
> Its shades interminably.
> Features of a fervent countenance
> Now emerge from them indelibly.
>
> Twists, branches, bends,
> Flowers, stars on tall blue planes.

Manifest are the strong hands,
Those thin lines of taut veins.

A Master of Tints, wonderfully alive,
Lived dreaming and grieving,
And, so this tint would still survive,
Infused it with his whole being.

On fine days it looks quite dismal,
During rain the tint is gay.
As bright as things primeval,
Glowing, it does not die away.

(1972–1974) In memory of Sergei P. Borodin.[18]

Dr. Farhadiy's quatrains (in thought, often only paired couplets) show off the artistic wonders of Central Asia, including the power of its medieval designs and colors, seeing them with a visitor's eyes. His conceit of a Master Tintmaker behind those elegant facades in Samarkand harmonizes with his frugal diction, persuasive because it avoids melodrama and excess. His style and theme first appeared in his earlier, Russian-language collection, *Frescoes of Afrasiyab*, in which the 28-year-old poet pays homage to his birthplace by referring to early medieval, pre-Islamic Afrasiyab—Samarkand's predecessor. (In 1965 inside buried rooms at the fortified city of Afrasiyab, archeologists discovered colorful Sogdian wall paintings in bold blue, rust, brown, yellow, and tan frescoes depicting a procession of robed men and women on camels and one elephant. The inscription, a diplomatic note dating from the seventh century A.D., identifies the Chaganian envoy Bur-Zatak and his embassy bringing gifts from the Hunnic ruler Turantash to the potentate of Samarkand.)

Thirty-eight of 116 pages of Dr. Farhadiy's *Frescoes of Afrasiyab* he devotes to Central Asian scenes, history, and ethnographic vignettes such as "Creator of a Jug," "*Läylǎk*: The Stork—Bird of Happiness" (here he uses the Uzbek word for stork), "Ulugh Beg," "Samarkand," "A Falling Minaret" (the leaning minaret of Ulugh Beg's madrassah in Samarkand before engineers righted it), "The Zarafshan," and the like, all of which conveyed abundant local color. But the timing of the booklet made the collection's spontaneity questionable, for the poet dedicated his booklet to the official commemoration of what the sponsors termed the city of Samarkand's 2,500th anniversary in 1969.[19]

What counts most for literary (nationality) group identity in a writer? Dr. Farhadiy demonstrated that a poet produces tone through creative phrasing and expression. Can an outsider (or an insider using the outsiders' tongue) reproduce the tone of a talented Central Asian writing in his native language so well that readers cannot distinguish between them? The limited number of

Frescoes issued (5,000) suggests that, despite the large potential market of Russian speakers in the UzSSR, the publisher felt that this poet would reach a small audience. If the foreigner imitated but could not capture that tone, what are the implications for indigenous ethnic group identity? The answers come down to determining the significance of language and the art of using it. Dr. Farhadiy's case offers inconclusive evidence, for his biography places him partly inside the ethnic Uzbek perimeter but his choice of language medium moves him outside. It complicates the situation further that he understands Uzbek well enough to write simple texts in it and translate from complex ones into a Slavic language, which makes him almost a bilingual writer. (A closer examination of the poems may supply answers.)

Uzbek historians usually avoid grouping the Russian writings of people like Dr. Farhadiy with Uzbek poetry in serious studies or anthologies. Moreover, in their later criticism, they speak about the emergence of a lyricism—an important means of expression in this literature—that excludes foreigners writing about Central Asia. Only a few decades earlier, ideological critics regarded the lyric poem negatively; now not merely had the genre revived but a special mood and method had developed in it that gave writers the opportunity to convey feelings and ideas that politics had stifled between the 1930s and 1950s.

The author of one thoughtful literary history shared many of the perceptions and sensitivities of his generation. Ibrahim Ghafuraw (b. 1937), born and educated in Tashkent, published criticism in *Ozbekistan mädäniyäti* beginning in 1959. He worked in the main state literary publishing house of the UzSSR capital, the Ghafur Ghulam Literature and Art Publishing House, which issued much of the new Uzbek poetry of the 1970s and 1980s. Ghafuraw understood the literary focus of his generation and appreciated the significance of this new lyricism:

> In the lyric meditations [*meditätsiyälär*] of Uzbek poets concerning the place of time as well as of the human being existing in this complex world, the ideas are irrigated with an emotional atmosphere [*ätmasferä*] and a powerful lyricism. Especially in the verses of poets such as Zulfiya, Asqad Mukhtar, Shukrulla, Erkin Wahidaw, Abdulla Aripaw, Gulchehra Nurullayewa, Halima Khudayberdiyewa, Aydin Hajiyewa, M. A'zam, Rauf Parfi, and Erkin Samandar, there is great attention to unbinding the philosophy of the time, to opening up its dramatic content.

Ghafuraw felt that thoughtful, meditative lyrics reveal everything at once, peacefully and smoothly. He described that mood as the calmness of a great, majestic river.[20] The first three names on his list came from the older generation, but seem aesthetically the most defensible selections. Those names following Shukrulla's (b. 1921), then, identify younger poets composing Uzbek verse in the 1980s whose writings speak to readers with a sense of shared values in close group communication. By 1980 poetry, the favorite old genre in Central Asia, reached a literate population of about six million. Twentieth-century publishers tried to meet that demand by issuing Uzbek verse in editions of 25,000 to 100,000 copies. The anomaly of Dr. Farhadiy could not obscure this evidence that most Uzbeks chose to speak, write, and read in their mother language.[21]

The verse of another young poet, Rauf Parfi (b. 1943), who started contributing to Uzbek literature seriously in the 1960s, helps answer the query about whether writing in a foreign language can convey the essence of Uzbek (or any other) literary nationality and suggests a way to understand the importance for Uzbek nationality group awareness of literature written in Russian. Two of Parfi's brief collections—*Subhidäm* (Early Morning), with the young poet Surat Aripaw, and *Äks säda* (Echo)—came out in Uzbek in 5,000 and 10,000 copies, respectively—the usual circulation for books of verse by contemporary individual poets in Uzbekistan. Like his pre–twentieth-century countrymen, Parfi refused to title his poems, enabling readers to approach them without preconceptions. In *Äks säda* the poetry spoke of stark white clouds, pearly downpours, and dawn exploding. He meditated concerning the endless minutes slowing down a young person's life but avoided ethnographic references. In a fantasy of Central Asia his preoccupation is the hypnotic blue gleam reflecting from monuments of the past:

> Today I had a dream. In my dream
> I seemed to stroll in Bukhara.
> Above my head, tall minarets,
> Beneath my feet a rose garden.
>
> I seemed to stroll in Bukhara,
> With me would walk the Sun.
> It melted like a flowing perplexity
> A stone left intact by the ice age.
>
> Above my head tall minarets
> Appeared to gaze enviously.
> The ages momentarily before me
> Flowed like a pale blue flame.
>
> Beneath my feet a rose garden,
> Pale blue burning on and on. . .
> Bukhara, keeping a pale blue rose,
> Captivated me forever.
>
> It parted me from my senses,
> I think I saw my heart. . .

Today I had a dream. In my dream
I seemed to stroll in Bukhara.[22]

Such sensitivity to the shapes and colors in a writer's imagined landscape (homeland?) signaled an identity that delineated a range of sensation through which the poet expressed feelings of attachment to people and location more surely than if he had inserted place names, signs of a "community of economy," or other external or objective factors often ascribed to nationality.

In their verses both Farhadiy and Parfi created shimmering visions of places whose names shine in Uzbek history: Samarkand and Bukhara were simultaneously historic world centers and personal locales. The Russian-language poem of Dr. Farhadiy differs from Parfi's because of the focus on another city but also because Parfi distilled Bukhara's almost fluorescent blue-green into a personal experience, bringing alive his visualization of the old Central Asian civilization. Above all, Parfi's Uzbek lexicon, unlike Dr. Farhadiy's Russian vocabulary and diction, evoked in Uzbek associations and phonetic pulsations for Central Asians that connect ancestral phraseology with the wording of masterpieces out of the heritage or with the intonations of written and oral eloquence. No Russian sentence could carry this same rhythm or representation for a true Uzbek. Dr. Farhadiy could skillfully describe designs and pigment for readers, but no matter how well he perceived the intrinsic web of ethnicity around him, he could not transmogrify or recreate his perception in the foreign language well enough to communicate to an Uzbek audience all the inherited qualities and emotional charge manifested in Uzbek verse.

REGIONAL HETEROGENEITY

These two poets, and many more, elicited the special emanations and hues of definite places, emphasizing the specific over the universal in their vision. Subregionalisms in Uzbek verse might add up to a larger communal self-awareness, but such poetry fragmented Uzbekistan into its numerous parts and then reassembled it into an ethnically undifferentiated (unpartitioned) Central Asian past and perhaps future as well. This late twentieth-century literary regionalism might partly respond to that arid political unit, the UzSSR as a whole. Such localism probably also arose from the difficulty provincial authors had penetrating the privileged ranks of an established literary institution that remained entrenched in the union republic capital and controlled all the arms of the publishing and other critical apparatus. (So tight was this control that branches of the state monopoly publishers issued virtually no books of Uzbek literature in the Uzbek language outside Tashkent. An occasional exception appeared in Tajikistan for its large Uzbek minority—in 1979 equaling almost 40 percent of the Tajik population in the TajSSR.)[23]

Uzbek intellectuals growing up outside Tashkent felt challenged to become like those at the administrative center, which may have contributed to uniformity, perhaps cohesion. Some became too urbanized; others brought to Tashkent the verve and flavor of their neighborhoods, contributing nuances to the overall thought and art of Uzbekistan. One who retained his subregional persona when he came to the UzSSR capital was Jamal Kamal (b. 1938), a complex, interesting young poet and translator from the tiny village of Chitkaran in Shafirkan rayan, Bukhara oblast.

Kamal received his education in Bukhara City, where he went on to teach foreign literature and, as had other modern Uzbek writers, became a journalist, working in the editorial department for the government newspaper *Bukhara häkikäti*. In the 1980s, with his schoolteacher wife and three children, he lived in Tashkent, where academic work attached him to the A. S. Pushkin Institute for Literature of the UzSSR Academy of Science and later to a literary publishing house. Simultaneously, Kamal prepared to take his doctorate while composing his own verse and translating Shakespeare; Avicenna; Aleksandr S. Pushkin; Jalaliddin Rumiy (1207 Balkh–1273 Konya), a Central Asian mystic writing in Farsi; and other renowned authors into Uzbek.[24]

A good poet reveals not only something about his era but much about his mind and heart when he puts his verse before readers. Kamal offered abundant specimens of his language and thought over the decade and a half starting with the appearance of his first collection of poems in 1968 at the age of 30. His prosody, enriched with a classical vocabulary and style reminiscent of the bilingual and trilingual literary circles of old Bukhara, combines the resources of both Farsi and Turki and sometimes Arabic or Urdu, making his poetry and thought attractively complex. But Kamal's verse was also very up-to-date, as his book *Qädäh: Lirikä* (A Toast: Lyric Verse, 1980), issued in 7,000 copies, richly demonstrates. *Qädäh* includes poems such as *Suwäyda* (Inner Heart) which plays on a word in the title that was taken from the vocabulary of Mir Ali Shir Nawaiy and elegantly used to extend some lines by the Farsi poet Shaykh Sa'di (1208–1292).

Kamal repeatedly speaks about his country, his homeland, and his people in developing these fourteen quatrains. In the same small collection he includes the earlier eulogy "Uzbekistan." To celebrate his first twenty years of verse writing, he adds both these poems to a larger volume, *Suwäyda* (1983), a 238-page collection of Kamal's lyric poetry and translations that the publisher issued in 20,000 copies. These verses convey an attachment to his people's milieu. Unlike some of his detached peers, he expressed feelings of admiration for his land, as in the last stanza of "Fakhirä" (1980):

The bitter adversaries who cannot see thee,
Let their eyes go blind, their faces blacken.
Thou wast created by Truth [God], live on, veracious,
O Dear Bukhara—ornament the universe!

Fakhirä (prideworthy, splendid), although no longer current in the Uzbek vocabulary, functioned, as an earlier discussion in this book about town epithets said, as a popular attribute in medieval times for the country of Bukhara. It was typical of Kamal's poetic method to recover such an evocative Arabic loanword from the Chaghatay literary language to link present with past while restoring descriptive nicknaming to his beloved Bukhara. Pride of place anchored the poet in his environment.[25] Kamal and an Uzbek associate accompanied some foreign writers on a tour of Bukhara in the mid-1970s. As they viewed the colorfully decorated halls of Sitarä-i Mahi Khassa, the Bukharan amirs' palace, a young male guide pointed to carvings and decorations, attributing each in turn to "the style of China," "the style of Iran," and so on. One guest asked whether a Bukharan style had developed. The confused guide could not reply. Commented Kamal later: "In reality, it was sufficient to speak about the Bukharan master craftsmen who created these very elegant halls. . . yes, let us learn to say categorically that we ourselves made our own places!"[26]

Praise, discussed in chapter 5, "Ideology and the Literature of Praise," has characterized much of Uzbek rhetoric since 1924. In the first half of the present century writers carefully paid obligatory compliments to the Russian regime, the sole political organization, the supreme ruler, and the mystique of manual labor. Poets like Kamal, born after the mid-1930s and publishing at first mainly in the late 1950s and 1960s, made Central Asian literature of the Soviet period more versatile and credible by focusing on subjects with personal and, by extension, ethnic group meaning. Without relinquishing his creative base in Bukhara, Kamal found the lyrical means to identify with the recently delimited land of the Uzbeks.

Kamal chose the *qäsidä* (panegyric), the form favored by earlier Central Asians to render praise to eminent or powerful leaders, for his ode to Uzbekistan. Technically his panegyric did not entirely emulate the standard Central Asian *qäsidä*s, which lauded their subject in 20 to 200 rapidly traversed couplets (rhyming *aa*, *ba*, *ca*, and so on to the end). Kamal's panegyric consists of eleven six-line stanzas (the stanza's first three and the final line having sixteen syllables apiece, lines four and five, eight). After the first stanza, whose lines rhyme *aaaaaa*, the rhyme is *bbbbba*, *ccccca*, *ddddda*, and so forth, with the same *a* rhyme terminating all the stanzas. That elaborate structure (similar to the medieval *musaddas* strophe) gives the poem a deliberate, fugal quality absent from the rhyming distichs of a customary *qäsidä*. This more complicated form increased the poet's opportunities to add dramatic emphasis to his theme.[27] Poet Kamal uses those possibilities to good effect in the tenth stanza of the panegyric to the Uzbek land:

> Roaming thy rose gardens, when I offer my thought concisely,
> Grandeur, benevolence, supreme generosity are joined to thee
>   intimately.
> The true reason for it all is because thy offspring are a varied bouquet,
> Therefore, thou art ever alluring,
> Thou art a bright, full moon,
> This was such supreme joy for me that I was enthralled by thee!. . .[28]

The traits the poet ascribes to his country correspond to those attributes long regarded in old Central Asian ethical writings as the requisite virtues of a good ruler. The terms of reference in lines four and five reach back in style to a Central Asian panegyric that Rudaki (*ca.* 855–941) had once addressed to a traveling Samanid prince:

> O Bukhara! Be glad, live happily,
> You see, the shah [amir] goes as a guest to thee.
> The Amir is a moon, and Bukhara a sky.
> The moon rises in the sky.
> The Amir is a cypress, and Bukhara a garden,
> The cypress is a requisite for the garden.

A long narrative poem, "Wäräkhshä" (the name of an elegantly decorated pre-Islamic ruin nineteen miles northwest of Bukhara City dating from A.D. 400–900), that Kamal published in the late 1970s critics called "one of the most outstanding of our literary works in the spirit of attachment to the patria. . . It completely expands today's concept of homeland [*wätän*]."[29] The poet's phraseology suited the late twentieth-century situation in a region where nationality has supplanted kingship or dynasty as an identifying framework for life and art. Thus, by assimilating the legacy of the monumental civilization of Central Asia into the modern vision of community, creative artists such as Kamal seem to find both the idiom and the metaphor to communicate a reconstituted group identity to their countrymen and the world in the decades ahead. This careful, intellectual, aesthetic independence suggests that the old belief in the perfectability of rulers could transfer at the right interval to cultural leaders in dependent Uzbekistan. Regenerating a sense of group purpose and future of real Uzbekhood, these cultural leaders demonstrate that tradition, through the sustaining power of literature and its ideas, can influence societies across time.

Central Asia's values continue largely intact, neither shallow and eradicable nor easily mutable, which undercuts the Soviet ideologists' notion that by incessant indoctrination they might form an ethnically sterile character for an Uzbek nationality as it nears the twenty-first century. Central Asians generally, including Uzbeks, continue to reject the suspiciousness, fostered by Russian Marxists, of the outside world and its cultural variants. More time and testimonies will determine whether this segment of Central Asia's corporate identity can become strictly Uzbek or will return to a broader vision. This depends on both popular values and ideas of cultured intellectuals. Nearly all the ethical and cultural evidence affirms that the Central Asian trait of deliberateness has prepared Uzbeks to think and act for the long term.

Uzbeks have time, patience, and a formidable value structure. If a defensive image of the Uzbek universe should push its members strongly inward to the confines of the UzSSR, a monoethnic Uzbekistan might become spiritually solidified. Should Uzbeks continue to turn outward to embrace the larger civilization in which the posterity of Abul Khayr Khan had played a key role for six centuries, a regional Central Asian identity along supraethnic lines could reassert itself, despite the Soviet Russian preference for a unionwide community of superficially self-identified, counterfeit ethnic subgroups oriented to Moscow rather than to their own "city of men," or "mother of cities."

Notes

CHAPTER 1

1. Äbdurräzzaq Sämärqändiy, *Mätlä-i sa'däyn wä mäjmä-i bähräyn* (Tashkent: Ozbekistan SSR "Fän" Näshriyati, 1969), LL231–38, pp. 179–82; Abd-ar-Razzak Samarkandi, "Mesta voskhoda dvukh schastlivykh zvezd i mesta sliiania dvukh morei," in V. G. Tizengauzen, comp., *Sbornik materialov otnosiashchikhsia k istorii Zolotoi Ordy. Izvlecheniia iz persidskikh sochinenii* (Moscow-Leningrad: Izdatel'stvo Akademii Nauk SSSR, 1941), vol. 2, p. 198; Boriway A. Akhmedov, *Gosudarstvo kochevykh uzbekov* (Moscow: Izdatel'stvo "Nauka." Glavnaia Redaktsiia Vostochnoi Literatury, 1965), pp. 45, 51.

2. 'Abd-al-Razzaq, "Matla' al-sa'dayn," (mss., Petrograd University no. 157, LL291a) cited by Vasiliy V. Barthold in "Ulugh-Beg," in V. Minorsky and T. Minorsky, trans., *Four Studies on the History of Central Asia*, 3 vols. (Leiden: E. J. Brill, 1958), vol. 2, pp. 164–65.

3. John Rawls, *A Theory of Justice* (Cambridge, Mass: The Belknap Press of Harvard University Press, 1971), pp. 301–3.

4. Michael Walzer, *Spheres of Justice: A Defense of Pluralism and Equality* (New York: Basic Books, 1983), pp. 17–20, 316–18.

5. Eskandar Beg Monshi, *Tarikh-e 'Alamara-ye 'Abbasi. History of Shah 'Abbas the Great*, 2 vols., trans. Roger M. Savory (Boulder, Colo.: Westview Press, 1978), vol. 1, pp. 90, 92, 94; Mäs'ud bin 'Othman Kohistani, *"Ta'rikh-i äbu'l khäyr khani,"* trans. S. K. Ibragimov (Alma Ata: Izdatel'stvo "Nauka" Kazakhskoi SSR, 1969), LL319b–320a, pp. 151–52.

6. Makhmud ibn Vali, *More tain otnositel'no doblestei blagorodnykh (Geografiia)*, trans. Boriway A. Akhmedov (Tashkent: Izdatel'stvo "Fan" Uzbekskoi SSR, 1977), LL156a–156b, p. 32.

7. Fäzlällah ibn Ruzbihan Isfähaniy, *Mihman namä-yi bukhara* trans. and text R. P. Dzhalilova (Moscow: Izdatel'stvo "Nauka." Glavnaia Redaktsiia Vostochnoi Literatury, 1976), pp. 19–25; LL95b–107a, pp. 122–36; Fadlullah b. Ruzbihan Khunji, *Tarikh-i 'aläm-ara-yi ämini* trans. and abridged by V. Minorsky (London: The Royal Asiatic Society of Great Britain and Ireland, 1957), pp. 1–8; Zähiriddin Muhämmäd Babir, *Babirnamä* (Tashkent: Ozbekistan SSR Fänlär Äkädemiyäsi Näshriyati, 1960), p. 185; Zahiruddin Muhammad Babur Padshah Ghazi, *The Babur-nama in English. (Memoirs of Babur)*, trans. by Annette S. Beveridge (London: Luzac & Co., 1922, repr. 1969), pp. 353–55.

8. Robin M. Williams, Jr., "Change and Stability in Values and Value Systems: A Sociological Perspective," in Milton Rokeach, ed., *Understanding Human Values, Individual and Societal* (New York: The Free Press, 1979), pp. 15–46; Milton Rokeach, *The Nature of Human Values* (New York: The Free Press. Collier Macmillan Publishers, 1973), pp. 3–35.

9. Mullah 'Alim Makhdum Hajji, *Ta'rikh-i turkistan* (Tashkent: Turkistan Giniral Gobirnatorighä Tab' Basmäkhanädä, 1915), pp. 192–93; Sadriddin Ayni, "Amir Nasrullo va askari nizomi," *Ta'rikhi amironi manghitiyai Bukhoro*, 15 vols., in Sadriddin Ayni, *Qulliyat* (Dushanbe: Nashriyoti "Irfon," 1966), vol. 10, p. 37.

10. Mirza 'Abdal'azim Sami, *Ta'rikh-i salatin-i manghitiya (Istoriia mangytskikh gosudarei)*, trans. L. M. Epifanova (Moscow: Izdatel'stvo Vostochnoi Literatury, 1962), L65a, p. 56; Akhmad Donish, *Risolai Ahmadi Donish 'Ta'rikhi saltanati Manghitiya'. (Istoriia mangitskoi dinastii)*, trans. I. A. Nadzhafova (Dushanbe: Izdatel'stvo "Donish," 1967), pp. 38–40; Khanikoff, *Bokhara: Its Amir and Its People*, trans. Clement A. de Bode (London: James Madden, 1845), pp. 305–11.

11. Reinhard Bendix, *Kings or People: Power and the Mandate to Rule* (Berkeley and Los Angeles: University of California Press, 1978), 692 pp.; Jonathan M. Wiener, review essay on Bendix's *Kings or People* in *History and Theory*, no. 1 (February 1981): 68–83.

CHAPTER 2

1. Kai Ka'us ibn Iskandar, *Qabus namä: A Mirror for Princes*, trans. Reuben Levy (London: Cresset Press, 1951), pp. 45–48; David Sellwood et al., *An Introduction to Sasanian Coins* (London: Spink & Sons, Ltd., 1985), pp. 143–44.

2. *The Koran: Interpreted*, trans. A. J. Arberry (Toronto: Macmillan, 1969) sura iii "The House of Imran," p. 76, line 25; Al-Ghazali, *Nasihat al-Muluk: Book of Counsel for Kings*, intro. and trans. F. R. C. Bagley (London: Oxford University Press, 1964), p. 46.

3. Yusuf Khas Hajib, *Qutadghu bilig (Säädätgä yollawchi bilim)* transcribed and translated to Uzbek by Qäyum Kärimaw (Tashkent: Ozbekistan SSR "Fän" Näshriyati, 1971), LL35b–36a, p. 176, lines 806–7; Yusuf Khas Hajib, *Kutadgu Bilig* [Wisdom of Royal Glory: A Turko-Islamic Mirror for Princes] trans. Robert Dankoff (Chicago: University of Chicago Press, 1983).

4. Ghazali, *Nasihat al-Muluk* pp. 1xx–1xxiii, 14, 75.

5. Äbu Bäkr Muhämmäd ibn Jä'fär Närshäkhiy, *Bukhara tärikhi*, trans. Ä. Räsulew (Tashkent: Ozbekistan SSR "Fän" Näshriyati, 1966), L109, p. 81; Narshakhi, *The History of Bukhara* trans. Richard N. Frye (Cambridge, Mass.: Mediaeval Academy of America, 1954), pp. 77, 93.

6. Närshäkhiy, *Bukhara tärikhi*, L109, pp. 81–82; Narshakhi, *The History of Bukhara*, p. 93.

7. Narshakhiy, *Bukhara tärikhi*, L108, p. 81.

8. Abu Nasr al-Farabi, *Mabadi' ara' ahl al-madina al fadila* [Al-Farabi on the Perfect State] revised text and trans. Richard Walzer (Oxford: Clarendon Press, 1985), chap. 15, para. 12, pp. 246–49.

9. Ahmad binni Mahmud Yugnakiy, "Hibatul-haqayiq," in *Ozbek ädäbiyati*, vol. 1 (Tashkent: OzSSR Däwlät Bädiiy Ädäbiyat Näshriyati, 1959), p. 64; Edib Ahmed b. Mahmud Yukneki, *Atebetu'l-Hakayik*, ed. Reshid Rahmeti Arat (Istanbul: Atesh Basimevi, 1951), p. 51.

10. *Ozbek khälq mäqalläri* (Tashkent: OzSSR Däwlät Bädiiy Ädäbiyat Näshriyati, 1960), p. 111; *Ozbek tilining izahli lughäti*, vol. 2, Z. M. Mä'rufaw, ed. (Moscow: "Rus Tili" Näshriyati, 1981), p. 29.

11. Ahmad Yugnaki, *Hibatul-haqayiq*, trans. to Uzbek by K. Mahmudawa (Tashkent: Ghäfur Ghulam namidägi Bädiiy Ädäbiyat Näshriyati, 1971), p. 64, cited in *Ocherki istorii obshchestvenno-filosofskoi mysli v Uzbekistane* (Tashkent: Izdatel'stvo "Fan" Uzbekskoi SSR), p. 155.

12. *Älpamish. Dastan* recited by Fazil Yoldash Oghli, comps. Hadi Zärif, Torä Mirzäyew (Tashkent: Ghäfur Ghulam namidägi Ädäbiyat wä Sän'ät Näshriyati, 1979), pp. 184–85.

13. *Älpamish. Dastan*, pp. 369, 381–82.

14. *Yusuf wä Ahmäd. Jusuf und Ahmed. Ein ozbegisches Volksepos im chiwaer Dialekte* text, trans. H. Vambéry (Budapest: Druck des Franklin-Verein, 1911), LL30–31; Arminius Vambéry, *Sketches of Central Asia* (London: Wm. H. Allen, 1868), p. 348.

15. Muhammad bin Muhammad al-Jabbar al-Utbi, *The Kitab-i-Yamini, Historical Memoirs of the Amir Sabaktagin, and the Sultan Mahmud of Ghazna, Early Conquerors of Hindustan and Founders of the Ghaznavide Dynasty*, trans. James Reynolds (London: Printed for the Oriental Translation Fund of Great Britain and Ireland, 1858), pp. 217–18, 242–43, 447–48.

16. Nizam al-Mulk, *The Book of Government or Rules for Kings* trans. Hubert Darke (London: Routledge & Kegan Paul, 1960), pp. 50, 120; Stanley Lane-Poole, *The Mohammadan Dynasties* (New York: Frederick Ungar, 1965, repr. of 1893 ed.), p. 287.

17. B. Ya. Vladimirtsov, *The Life of Chingis-Khan* (New York: Benjamin Blom, 1930, repr. 1969), pp. 66–71; Abul-Ghazi Bahadur Khan, *Shäjärä-i Turk. Histoire des Mongols et des Tatares* text prepared and trans. by Petr I. Desmaisons, L136; (Amsterdam: Philo Press, 1970, repr. of 1871–1874 ed.).

18. Ahmed ibn Arabshah, '*Aja'ib al-maqdur fi akhbar timur: Tamerlane or Timur the Great Amir* trans. J. H. Sanders (London: 1936, repr. Lahore: Progressive Books, n.d.), pp. 145–46, 296–99, 312; V. V. Barthold, "Ulugh-Beg," in *Four Studies on the History of Central Asia* (Leiden: E. J. Brill, 1958), vol. 2, p. 39.

19. Timour, *Tuzukat-i Timuri: Institutes Political and Military* trans. Major Davy (Oxford: The Clarendon Press, 1783, repr., n.d.), p. 213.

20. Timour, *Tuzukat-i Timuri*, pp. 221, 223.

21. Ibn Arabshah, '*Aja'ib al-maqdur fi akhbar timur*, p. 307.

22. Henry H. Howorth, *History of the Mongols from the 9th to the 19th Century*, part 2, section 2 (London: 1880, repr. New York: Burt Franklin, n.d.), pp. 686–90; Bori A. Akhmedov, *Gosudarstvo kochevykh uzbekov* (Moscow: Izdatel'stvo "Nauka," 1965), pp. 27, 29, 55–56, 131–33, 161–62; Barthold, "Ulugh Beg," in *Four Studies on the History of Central Asia*, vol. 2 (Leiden: E. J. Brill, 1958), pp. 108–9, 165, 171n.

23. Mäs'ud bin 'Othman Kohistani, "Ta'rikh äbu'l khäyr khani," in *Materialy po istorii kazakhskikh khanstv XV–XVIII vekov (Izvlecheniia iz persidskikh i tiurkskikh sochinenii)*, trans. S. K. Ibragimov (Alma Ata: Izdatel'stvo "Nauka" Kazakhskoi SSR, 1969), LL321a, 323a–323b, pp. 153–55, 515–58.

24. Mahmud bin Amir Wali, "Bähr äl-asrar fi mänaqib äl-akhyar," in *Materialy po istorii kazakhskikh khanstv XV–XVIII vekov (Izvlecheniia iz persidskikh i tiurkskikh sochinenii)*, trans. S. K. Ibragimov (Alma Ata: Izdatel'stvo "Nauka" Kazakhskoi SSR, 1969), LL131a–131b, pp. 354–55; Mirza Muhammad Haidar Dughlat, *Tarikh-i rashidi. A History of the Moguls of Central Asia*, trans. E. Denison Ross (London: Sampson Low, Marston and Company, 1898, repr. New York: Praeger Publishers, 1970), pp. 375–77.

25. Mäs'ud bin 'Othman Kohistani, "Ta'rikh äbu'l khäyr khani," L342, p. 170; Shir Muhämmäd bin Amir 'Äwäz biy Mirab balmu'nis, "Firdäws äl-iqbal," L24b, p. 436.

26. Mas'ud ibn Usman Kohistani, "Tarikh-i äbu'l khäyr khani," mss. inv. no. 5392, LL24–5, cited by A. A. Semenov, "K voprosu o proiskhozhdenii i sostave Uzbekov Sheibani Khana," *Trudy Akademii Nauk Tadzhikskoi SSR* 12 (1954):25.

27. Khwand Amir, "Habib-as siyar," vol. 4, p. 134, cited by Bori A. Akhmedov in *Gosudarstvo kochevykh Uzbekov* (Moscow: Izdatel'stvo "Nauka," 1965), p. 145; Kemal ad-Din 'Abd ar-Razzaq ibn Ishaq Samarqandiy, *Matla al-sa'dayn wa majma' al-bahrayn*, mss. (Gos. Publichnaia Biblioteka im. M. E. Saltykova-Shchedrina, Dorn 299; Institut Vostokovedeniia) C442, C443; Leningradskii Gos. Universitet no. 157, extract in *Sbornik materialov otnosiashchikhsia k istorii Zolotoi Ordy*, V. G. Tizengauzen, comp. (Moscow-Leningrad: Izdatel'stvo Akademii Nauk SSSR, 1941), vol. 2, Persian text LL464b, 469b; Russ. trans. p. 201.

28. A. J. E. Bodrogligeti, "Muhammad Shaybani's '*Bahru'l-hudâ*', An Early Sixteenth Century Didactic Qasida in Chaghatay," *Ural-Altaic Yearbook*, no. 54 (1982):1–56.

CHAPTER 3

1. *The Koran Interpreted* trans. Arthur J. Arberry (Toronto: Macmillan Company, 1969), sura II, The Cow, 28, p. 33; *The New English Bible* (New York: Oxford University Press, 1971), Genesis 2, 19–20, p. 3; Mir 'Ali Shir, *Muhakamat al-lughatain* trans. Robert Devereux (Leiden: E. J. Brill, 1966), L1, p. 1; Arthur Jeffery, *A Reader on Islam* ('S-Gravenhage: Mouton, 1962), pp. 401–2, 553–55.

2. Rashid al-Din, *Jami' al-tawarikh. The Successors of Genghis Khan*, trans. John A. Boyle (New York: Columbia University Press, 1971), p. 122; Ahmed ibn Arabshah, *'Aja'ib al-maqdur fi akhbar timur: Tamerlane or Timur the Great Amir*, trans. J. H. Sanders (London, 1936, repr. Lahore: Progressive Books, n.d.), p. 78; Zayn ad-Din Qazvini, *Tärikh-i guzidä* continued from his father's work under the same title, *Sbornik materialov, otnosiashchikhsia k istorii Zolotoi Ordy. Izvlechenie iz persidskikh sochinenii* V. G. Tizengauzen, comp. (Moscow-Leningrad: Izdatel'stvo Akademii Nauk SSSR, 1941), vol. 2, Persian text, pp. 221–22, 226; Russian, pp. 93, 97; also cited by Bori A. Akhmedov, *Gosudarstvo kochevykh Uzbekov* (Moscow: Izdatel'stvo "Nauka" Glavnaia Redaktsiia Vostochnoi Literatury, 1965), p. 13.

3. Akhmedov, *Gosudarstvo kochevykh Uzbekov*, pp. 14–16.

4. Nizamuddin Shami, *Histoire des conquetes de Tamerlan intitutlée Zafar-nama* (Prague: F. Tauer, 1937), cited by Aleksandr A. Semenov, "K voprosu a proiskhozhdenii i sostave Uzbekov Sheibanikhana," in *Trudy Akademii Nauka Tadzhikskoi SSR*, no. 12 (1954), p. 20; V. G. Tizengauzen, comp., *Sbornik materialov*, vol. 2 (1941), pp. 105–25, 155; Akhmedov, *Gosudarstvo kochevykh Uzbekov*, p. 38.

5. Abul Ghazi Bahadur Khan, *Shäjärä-i turk. Histoire des Mongols et des Tatares*, ed. and trans. Petr I. Desmaisons (Saint Petersburg: 1871–1874), repr. (Amsterdam: Philo Press, 1970), L175.

6. Paul Pelliot, *Notes sur l'histoire de la Horde d'Or* (Paris: Librairie d'Amerique et d'Orient, 1949 [title page], 1950 [cover]), pp. 92–94; Arminius Vámbéry, *History of Bokhara. From the Earliest Period down to the Present*, 2d ed. (London: Henry S. King & Co., 1873), p. 245; B. D. Grekov and A. Iu. Iakubovskii, *Zolotaia Orda i ee padenie*, (Moscow: Izdanie Akademii Nauk SSSR, 1950), p. 301; A. Iu. Iakubovskii, *K voprosu ob etnogeneze uzbekskogo naroda* (Tashkent: Izdatel'stvo UzFAN, 1941), p. 3; M. V. Kriukov, "'Liudi', 'nastoiashchie liudi'," in *Etnicheskaia onomastika* (Moscow: Izdatel'stvo "Nauka," 1984), pp. 6–8.

7. Akhmedov, *Gosudarstvo kochevykh uzbekov*, pp. 13–15; René Grousset, *The Empire of the Steppes: A History of Central Asia* trans. Naomi Walford (New Brunswick, New Jersey: Rutgers University Press, 1970), p. 407.

8. Mas'ud ibn Usman Kuhistani, *Tärikh-i äbu'l khäyr khani*, mss. inventory no. 5392, LL7–15, cited by Aleksandr A. Semenov, "K voprosu o proiskhozhdenii i sostave Uzbekov Sheibani-Khana," in *Trudy Akademii Nauk Tadzhikskoi SSR*, vol. 12 (Stalinabad, 1954), p. 24.

9. Sayf al-Din Akhsikenti, *Majmu' at-tawarikh*, mss. LO IVAN SSSR V-667, cited

by T. I. Sultanov, "Opyt analiza traditsionnykh spiskov 92 'plemen ilatiia'," in *Sredniaia Aziia v drevnosti i srednevekov'e (istoriia i kul'tura)* (Moscow: Izdatel'stvo "Nauka." Glavnaia Redaktsiia Vostochnoi Literatury, 1977), pp. 165–76.

10. Mähämmäd Qul Jamrat oghli, "Polkan," in *Shaybani khan dastani* recorded and ed. by Ghazi 'Alim (Samarkand-Tashkent: Ozbekistan Däwlät Näshriyati, 1928), p. 5 (preface); Khanikoff, *Bokhara: Its Amir and Its People* trans. Clement A. De Bode (London: James Madden, 1845), p. 76; Sultanov, "Opyt analiza traditsionnykh spiskov 92 'plemen ilatiia," pp. 167, 171, 174; Ganda Singh, *Ahmad Shah Durrani. Father of Modern Afghanistan* (London: Asia Publishing House, 1959), pp. 15, 25–26, 326; Mahmud bin Amir Wali, "Täwarikh-guzidä-i nusrät namä," in *Materialy po istorii kazakhskikh khanstv XV–XVIII vekov. (Izvlecheniia iz persidskikh i tiurkskikh sochinenii),* trans. S. K. Ibragimov (Alma Ata: Izdatel'stvo "Nauka" Kazakhskoi SSR, 1969) L105a, p. 28.

11. *Ozbekistan SSR tärikhi* vol. 1, book 1 (Tashkent: Ozbekistan SSR Fänlär Äkädemiyäsi Näshriyati, 1956), pp. 411, 413; Mäs'ud bin 'Uthman Kohistani, *Ta'rikh-i äbu'l khayr khani* (written *ca.* 1543), *Materialy po istorii kazakhskikh khanstv XV–XVIII vekov. (Izvlecheniia iz persidskikh i tiurkskikh sochinenii),* rev. and trans. S. K. Ibrahimov (Alma Ata: Izdatel'stvo "Nauka" Kazakhskoi SSR, 1969), pp. 140–71, especially LL312a–312b, 320b–321a; Ibid., (mss. only), L226b, cited by Bori A. Akhmedov, *Gosudarstvo kochevykh Uzbekov,* pp. 50–51; Häfiz-i Tanïsh ibn Mir Muhämmäd Bukhari, *Shäräf namä-yi shakhi* facsimile and trans. M. A. Salahet-dinawa (Moscow: Izdatel'stvo "Nauka." Glavnaia Redaktsiia Vostochnoi Literatury, 1983), LL27b–28a, pp. 76–77; Fazlallah ibn Ruzbihan Isfahaniy, *Mihman namä-i bukhara* (Moscow: Izdatel'stvo "Nauka," LLV, 70a, pp. 93, 117.

12. Mirza Muhammad Haidar, Dughlat, *Tärikh-i räshidi. A History of the Moghuls of Central Asia,* trans. E. Denison Ross (London: Sampson Low, Marston, 1898), repr. (New York: Praeger, 1970), pp. 82, 92, 272–73; Mäsud bin Othman Kohistani, LL325b–326b; V. V. Bartol'd, "Abulkhair," *Sochineniia,* vol 2, book 2 (Moscow: Izdatel'stvo "Nauka," 1964), p. 489.

13. Naghïm Bek Nurmukhammedov, *Qoja Akhmed Yassaui mavzoleyi* (Alma Ata: "Öner" Baspasï, 1980), p. 12; Abd-ar-razzaq as-Samarqandiy, "Matla as-sa'deyn wa majma al-bahrayn," *Sbornik materialov otnosiashchikhsia k istorii Zolotoi Ordy,* comp. V. G. Tizengauzen (Moscow-Leningrad: Izdatel'stvo Akademii Nauk SSSR, 1941), pp. 199–200.

14. Älisher Näwaiy, "Säddi iskändäriy," *Khämsä* (Tashkent: OzSSR Fänlär Äkädemiyäsi Näshriyati, 1958), pp. 1330–34.

15. Zahiriddin Muhammad Babur, *Babar namä,* ed. Annette S. Beveridge (London: Luzac, 1905, repr. 1971), L2b; V. M. Zhirmunskii and Kh. T. Zarifov, *Uzbekskii narodnyi geroicheskii epos* (Moscow: OGIZ. Gosudarstvennoe Izdatel'stvo Khudozhestvennoi Literatury, 1947), p. 70; Älisher Näwaiy, "Färhad wä Shirin," in *Khämsä* (Tashkent: Ozbekistan Fänlär Äkädemiyäsi Näshriyati, 1958), p. 639.

16. Muhämmäd Salih, *Shäybaniynamä* (Tashkent: Ozbekistan SSR Fänlär Äkädemiyäsi Näshriyati, 1961), L211, p. 310.

17. Zahiriddin Muhammad Babur, *Babar namä* (facsimile of Chaghatay mss.), ed.

Annette S. Beveridge (London: Luzac, 1905, repr. 1971), L85a, 204b. Mrs. Beveridge notes the pun in *The Babur-nama in English* (London: Luzac, 1969), p. 325. Babur's scornful remarks about Shah Mansur's homosexuality have been deleted from this passage in Mrs. Beveridge's translation as well as from the Soviet transliteration; See also Zähiriddin Muhämmäd Babir, *Babirnamä* (Tashkent: Ozbekistan SSR Fänlär Äkädemiyäsi Näshriyati, 1960), p. 268.

18. Masud bin Othman Kohistani, "Ta'rikh-i äbulkhäyr khani," *Materialy po istorii kazakhskikh khanstv XV–XVIII vekov (Izvlecheniia iz persidskikh i tiurkskikh sochinenii)*, rev. and trans. S. K. Ibragimov, comps. S. K. Ibragimov et al. (Alma Ata: Izdatel'stvo "Nauka" Kazakhskoi SSR, 1969), LL308b–346b, pp. 140–71; Hafiz Tänish ibn Mir Muhämmäd Bukhariy, *Äbdullänamä (Shäräfnamäyi shahiy)* (Tashkent: Ozbekistan SSR "Fän" Näshriyati, 1969), vol. 2, L158a, p. 123; L190b, p. 203; L198a, p. 220; p. 387.

19. Fazlallah ibn Ruzbihan Isfahaniy, *Mihman namä-yi bukhara* trans. R. P. Dzhalilova (Moscow: Izdatel'stvo "Nauka." Glavnaia Redaktsiia Vostochnoi Literatury, 1976), LL22a, 43a, 95b, pp. 62, 73, 123.

20. Miyan Buzruk, "Ozbek (tä'rikhi tekshirishlär)," in *Mä'arif wä oqutghuchi*, no. 3 (1928), p. 49.

21. Iskandar Munshi, "Tarikh-i alam ara-i abbasi," (extracts) trans. A. A. Romaskevich *Materialy po istorii Turkmen i Turkmenii*, ed. V. V. Struve et al. (Moscow-Leningrad: Izdatel'stvo Akademii Nauk SSSR, 1938), vol. 2, pp. 67–112.

CHAPTER 4

1. Fazlallah ibn Ruzbihan Isfahaniy, *Mihman namä-yi bukhara* trans. R. P. Dzhalilova (Moscow: Izdatel'stvo "Nauka," 1976), L72a, pp. 95, 21–26.

2. "Täwarikh-i guzidä-yi nusrät namä," in *Materialy po istorii kazakhskikh khanstv XV–XVIII vekov. (Izvlecheniia iz persidskikh i tiurkskikh sochinenii)*, trans. A. M. Akramov (Alma Ata: Izdatel'stvo "Nauka" Kazakhskoi SSR, 1969), L66b, p. 17; Mäsud bin Othman Kohistani, "*Tä'rikh-i äbu'l khäyr khani*," LL336b–39a, pp. 168–70.

3. Hasan-i Rumlu, *Ähsänu't täwarikh: A Chronicle of the Early Safawis*, trans. C. N. Seddon (Baroda: Oriental Institute, 1934), section A.H. 906 (A.D. 1500), p. 20f; Zahiriddin Muhammad Bäbar, *Bäbar namä* (London: Luzac, 1905, repr. 1971), LL83a, 84b; Mirza Muhammad Haidar, Dughlat, *Tarikh-i rashidi: A History of the Moghuls of Central Asia*, 2d ed., trans. E. Denison Ross (London: Sampson Low, Marston, 1898), repr. (New York: Praeger, 1970), pp. 82, 272.

4. 'Ala-ad-Din 'Ata-Malik Juvaini, *The History of the World Conqueror*, trans. from the text of Mirza Muhammad Qazvini by John Andrew Boyle, vol. 1 (Manchester: Manchester University Press, 1958), LL58–63, pp. 77–81; B. Ya. Vladimirtsov, *The Life of Chingis Khan* (New York: Benjamin Blom, 1930, repr. 1969), pp. 63–71; B. Ia. Vladimirtsov, *Obshchestvennyi stroi Mongolov. Mongol'skii kochevoi feodalizm* (Leningrad: Izdatel'stvo Akademii Nauk SSSR, 1934), p. 84; *The Secret*

History of the Mongols: For the First Time Done into English out of the Original Tongue and Provided with an Exegetical Commentary, trans. Francis Woodman Cleaves, vol. 1 (Cambridge, Mass.: Harvard University Press, 1982), p. 189, para. 254; Igor de Rachewiltz, "Some Remarks on the Ideological Foundations of Chingis Khan's Empire," in *Papers on Far Eastern History*, no. 7 (March 1973), pp. 23–25; V. V. Barthold, "A Short History of Turkestan," in *Four Studies on the History of Central Asia*, vol. 1, trans. V. Minorsky (Leiden: E. J. Brill, 1956), pp. 32, 47–48.

5. Grousset, pp. 393–94; Boribay A. Akhmedov, *Gosudarstvo kochevykh Uzbekov* (Moscow: Izdatel'stvo "Nauka," 1965), p. 42.

6. Fazlallah ibn Ruzbihan Isfahaniy, *Mihman namä-yi bukhara*, trans. R. P. Dzhalilova (Moscow: Izdatel'stvo "Nauka." Glavnaia Redaktsiia Vostochnoi Literatury, 1976), L70a, p. 93.

7. Ibid., LL74a, 70a, pp. 97, 93.

8. Isfahaniy, *Mihman*, L74b, p. 98.

9. Ibid.

10. Mirza Muhammad Haidar, Dughlat, *Tarikh-i rashidi*, p. 156.

11. P. P. Ivanov, *Ocherki po istorii srednei Azii (XVI-seredina XIX v.)* (Moscow: Izdatel'stvo Vostochnoi Literatury, 1958), p. 44.

12. *Täwarikh-i guzidä—nusrätnamä*, prepared by Ä. M. Äkrämaw (Tashkent: Ozbekistan SSR "Fän" Näshriyati, 1967), L119b, facsimile 263, Arabic p. 267; "Sheibaniada," in *Biblioteka vostochnykh istorikov* vol. 1 (Kazan: Izdavaemaia I. Berezinym, 1849), p. lv; "Täwärikh-i guzidä-i nusrät namä," in *Materialy po istorii kazakhskikh khanstv XV–XVIII vekov (Izvlecheniia iz persidskikh i tiurkskikh sochinenii)* trans. S. K. Ibragimov; comps. S. K. Ibragimov, N. N. Mingulov, K. A. Pishchulina, V. P. Iudin (Alma Ata: Izdatel'stvo "Nauka" Kazakhskoi SSR, 1969), L95a, p. 19.

13. Mahmud ben Amir Vali, "Bähr äl-äsrar fi mänaqib äl-äkhyar," in *Materialy po istorii kazakhskikh khanstv XV–XVIII vekov*, L135a, pp. 361–62.

14. Täwärikh-i guzidä-i nusrät namä," in *Materialy po istorii kazakhskikh khanstv XV–XVIII vekov*, trans. S. K. Ibragimov (Alma Ata: Izdatel'stvo "Nauka," KazSSR, 1969), LL95b, 96a, 96b, 97a, pp. 19–21; p. 496, note 53.

15. Isfahaniy, *Mihman*, L75, p. 98.

16. S. V. Bakhrushin et al., eds., *Istoriia narodov Uzbekistana. Ot obrazovaniia gosudarstva Sheibanidov do velikoi oktiabr'skoi sotsialisticheskoi revoliutsii*, vol. 2 (Tashkent: Izdatel'stvo Akademii Nauk UzSSR, 1947), pp. 28–29; Khwaja Baha al-Din Hasan Nithari Bukhari, *Mudhäkkir-i ähbab (Remembrancer of Friends)*, ed. Syed Muhammad Fazlullah (Hyderabad: The Da'iratu'l-Ma'arif Press at Osmania University, 1969), pp. 14–15, 27; Aleksandr A. Semenov, "Kul'turnyi uroven' pervykh Sheibanidov," *Sovetskoe Vostokovedenie* 3 (1956):53.

17. Isfahaniy, *Mihman*, L75a, p. 98; Mullah Shadi, "Fath namä," in *Materialy po istorii kazakhskikh khanstv XV–XVIII vekov*, trans. S. K. Ibragimov, LL71b–72a, p. 71; Zahiriddin Muhammad Bäbar, *Bäbar-namä*, L22a.

18. Isfahaniy, *Mihman*, L3b, p. 58, 22–23.

19. Kamal ad-Din 'Ali Binai, "Shäybani namä," in *Materialy po istorii kazakhskikh*

khanstv XV–XVIII vekov, trans. S. K. Ibragimov, L7a, pp. 95, 103; Isfahaniy, *Mihman*, LL45b–46a, p. 76.

20. "Täwärikh-i guzidä-i nusrät namä," in *Materialy po istorii kazakhskikh khanstv XV–XVIII vekov*, trans. S. K. Ibragimov, L98a, p. 22.

21. Kamal ad-Din 'Ali Binai, "Shäybani namä," in *Materialy po istorii kazakhskikh khanstv XV–XVIII vekov*, trans. S. K. Ibragimov, L8a, p. 105.

22. E. J. W. Gibb, *A History of Ottoman Poetry*, vol. 1 (London: Luzac, 1900, repr. 1958) pp. 260–69ff.

23. Eugene Schuyler, *Turkistan: Notes of a Journey in Russian Turkistan, Khokand, Bukhara, and Kuldja*, vol. 1 (New York: Scribner, Armstrong, 1877) p. 37.

24. Gibb, *A History of Ottoman Poetry*, vol. 1, pp. 267, 269, 272.

25. Isfahaniy, *Mihman*, LL75a–76a, p. 99.

26. Mukhammed Salikh, *Sheibani-name. Dzhagataiskii tekst*, ed. P. M. Melioranskii (Saint Petersburg: Izdaniia Fakul'teta Vostochnykh Iazykov Imperatorskago S.-Peterburgskago-Universiteta, 1908, L128b, p. 131, line 39.

27. Isfahaniy, *Mihman*, L110a, p. 139; Äbu Bäkr Muhämmäd ibn Jä'fär Narshäkiy, *Bukhara tärikhi*, trans. Ä. Räsulew (Tashkent: Ozbekistan SSR "Fän" Näshriyati, 1966), L91, p. 70; Äbu Bäkr Narshakhi, *The History of Bukhara*, trans. Richard N. Frye (Cambridge, Mass.: The Medieval Academy of America, 1954), chap. 31, p. 93; Fazil Yoldash Oghli, *Älpamish: Dastan*, 2d ed., ed. Hämid Alimjan (Tashkent: Ozbekistan SSR Fänlär Äkädemiyäsi, Näshriyati, 1957), pp. 268–69.

28. Käykawus, *Qabus namä* adapted from Chaghatay to Uzbek by Subutay Dalimaw (Tashkent: "Oqituwchi" Näshriyati, 1968), p. 5; chap. 42, p. 117; Kai Ka'us ibn Iskandar, *Qabus Nama: A Mirror for Princes*, trans. Reuben Levy (London: The Cresset Press, 1951), p. 229.

29. "Täwärikh-i guzidä-yi nusrät namä," in *Materialy po istorii kazakhskikh khanstv XV–XVIII vekov*, trans. S. K. Ibragimov; comps. S. K. Ibragimov et al., LL110a–110b, p. 31; Ibid., L96b, p. 20.

30. Mirza Muhammad Haidar, Dughlat, *Tarikh-i rashidi*, pp. 115, 120, 123, 167, 196.

31. Muhammad Shaybani, "Bähru'l hudâ," from A. J. E. Bodrogligeti, "Muhammad Shaybani's 'Bahru'l-hudâ'," in *Ural-Altaic Yearbook* 54 (1982), LL14v–15r, p. 29, trans. p. 46; Ibid., LL14r–14v, p. 29, trans. p. 46. (The transliteration and English translation are adapted from Professor Bodrogligeti's excellent version.)

32. Ibid., LL6r, line 10, 6v line 3, 6v line 11, p. 24, trans. p. 39; Ibid., L11r, line 11, p. 27, trans. p. 43; Ibid., LL6v line 4, p. 24, 22v line 4, p. 34, trans. pp. 39, 53.

33. Shaybaniy Khan, *Diwan* (Istanbul: Topkapi-Ahmet III Library), mss. no. 2436, LL81b–82a. Dr. Timur Kocaoglu kindly drew this passage to my attention and provided a copy of the text.

34. Shaybaniy Khan, *Diwan*, L81b.

35. Muhammad Shaybaniy, "Bahru'l-hudâ," pp. 21–34; "Qäsidä," in *Ozbek sawet entsiklapediyäsi*, vol. 14 (Tashkent: Ozbek Sawet Entsiklapediyäsi. Bash Redäktsiyä,

1980), p. 41; Abu 'Abdallah Ja'far ibn Muhammad Rudaki Samarqandi, "Madär-i mäy," in E. Denison Ross, "A Qasida by Rudaki," *Journal of the Royal Asiatic Society of Gt. Britain and Ireland* (April 1926): 218–37; Marshall G. S. Hodgson, *The Venture of Islam: Conscience and History in a World Civilization*, vol. 1, *The Classical Age of Islam* (Chicago: The University of Chicago Press, 1974), pp. 458–61.

36. Caterino Zeno, "Travels in Persia," in *A Narrative of Italian Travels in Persia in the Fifteenth and Sixteenth Centuries*, trans. Charles Grey (New York: Burt Franklin, n.d., repr. of The Hakluyt Society, first series, no. 49, 1823), pp. 55–56. Barry Rosen very kindly told me about this source.

37. Nizam al-Mulk, *The Book of Government or Rules for Kings: The Siyasät-namä or Siyar al-Muluk*, trans. Hubert Darke (London: Routledge & Kegan Paul, 1960), pp. 120–21.

38. Stenli Len-Pul', *Musul'manskiia dinastii* trans. and ed. Vasiliy V. Bartol'd (Saint Petersburg: Tipografiia M. M. Stasiulevicha, 1899), pp. 230–31; Abu Dawud Sinan, "Kitab at-tahara," chapter 27, in A. J. Wensinck, *Concordance et Indices de la Tradition Musulmane*, vol. 1 (Leiden: E. J. Brill, Union Académique Internationale, 1936) entry for "*Jaddada*," translation from Arabic courtesy of Prof. Pierre Cachia; 'Abdal Razzaq, "Matla al-sa'dayn," cited by Vasiliy V. Barthold, *Four Studies on the History of Central Asia*, vol. 2, *Ulugh Beg*, trans. V. Minorsky and T. Minorsky (Leiden: E. J. Brill, 1958), p. 113.

39. Ahmad Mahdum Kalla Danish, *Risolai Ahmadi Danish 'ta'rikhi saltanati manghitiya'. Traktat Akhmada Donisha 'Istoriia mangitskoi dinastii'*, trans. I. A. Nadzhafova (Dushanbe: Izdatel'stvo 'Danish', 1967), pp. 22, 26; Äbdurähmani Tale', *Äbulfäyzkhan tärikhi. Istoriia Abulfeiz-khana*, trans. Aleksandr A. Semenov (Tashkent: Izdatel'stvo Akademii Nauk Uzbekskoi SSR, 1959), LL42a–42b, p. 44.

CHAPTER 5

1. al-Ghazali, "Ihya' 'ulum al-din," cited in A. J. Arberry, *Sufism: An Account of the Mystics of Islam* (New York: Harper & Row, 1970), p. 81.

2. A. J. Wensinck, *Concordance et Indices de la Tradition Musulmane*, vol. 1 (Leiden: E. J. Brill, Union Académique Internationale, 1936).

3. Imam Muhammad ibn Isma'il al-Bukhari, *Kitab al-jami al-sahih . . .* (Leiden: E. J. Brill, 1862–1908), vol. 2, Kitab 55, surah 23, p. 193, and Kitab 52, surah 10, p. 151; vol. 4, Kitab 86, surah 44, p. 313, and Kitab 87, surahs 1–2, pp. 314–317; Kitab 78, surah 6, p. 110; Kitab 83, surah 16, p. 269. Elliott Zak, a graduate student at Columbia University, graciously found and provided these references to the Arabic version of the hadiths; Muhammad Salik, "On the Conduct of the Faithful," *Muslims of the Soviet East* 2 (1982):15.

4. *Nehcu'l-feradis*, vol. 1 *Tipkibasim*, intro. János Eckmann (Ankara: Turk Tarih Kurumu Basimevi, 1956), pp. 334–443; *Nehcu'l-feradis: Ushtmakhlarning achuq yoli (cennetlerin achik yolu)*, vol. 2 *Metin*, trans. János Eckmann, prepared by Semih Tezcan and Hamza Zulfikar (n.p.: Turk Dil Kurumu Yayinlari: 518 [1984]), pp. 233–

309; János Eckmann, "Die kiptschakische Literatur," in *Philologiae Turcicae Fundamenta*, vol. 2 (Wiesbaden: Franz Steiner Verlag, 1963), pp. 287–88; al-Ghazali, "Ihya' 'ulum al-din," cited in Arberry, *Sufism*, p. 82. János Eckmann, "Die tschaghataische Literatur," *Philologiae Turcicae Fundamenta* (Wiesbaden: Franz Steiner Verlag, 1965), vol. 2, p. 363; Allessio Bombaci, "The Turkic Literatures. Introductory Notes on the History and Style," ibid., p. XLV; E. J. W. Gibb, *A History of Ottoman Poetry* (London: Luzac and Co., 1900, repr. 1958), vol. 1, p. 108.

5. Shaybaniy, "Bähru'l hudâ," pp. 39, 43, 53; Ibn Qotaïba, *Muqaddimatu kitabi sh-shi'ri wa sh-shu'ra': Introduction au livre de la poésie et des poètes*, trans. and intro. Gaudefroy-Demombynes (Paris: Société d'Édition "Les Belles Lettres," 1947), pp. 13–15.

6. Maulana Sharafuddin 'Ali Yazdi, "Zafar nama," excerpted and trans. by H. M. Elliot, in *Tuzak-i-timuri: The Autobiography of Timur* (Lahore: Sind Sagar Academy, 1974), p. 93.

7. Minorsky, "The Poetry of Shah Isma'il I," *Bulletin of the London School of Oriental and African Studies* 18 (1940–1942): 1006a–1053a; Muhammad Shaybaniy "Bähru'l hudâ," LL11r, 18r.

8. "Travels of a Merchant in Persia, A Narrative of Italian Travels in Persia in the Fifteenth and Sixteenth Centuries," trans. Charles Grey, in *Travels to Tana and Persia* (New York: Burt Franklin, n.d.), p. 207.

9. Muhämmäd Yusuf Munshi, *Tärikh-i muqim khaniy: Mukim khanskaia istoriia*, trans. Aleksandr A. Semenov (Tashkent, Izdatel'stvo Akademii Nauk Uzbekskoi SSR, 1956), LL86a–88b, pp. 154–57; Arminius Vámbéry, *History of Bukhara from the Earliest Period Down to the Present*, 2d ed. (London: Henry S. King, 1873), p. 336.

10. Shir Muhämmäd bin Amir 'Awaz Biy Mirab al-Mu'nis, "Firdäws äl-iqbal," trans. S. K. Ibragimov, in *Materialy po istorii kazakhskikh khanstv XV–XVIII vekov (Izvlecheniia iz persidskikh i tiurkskikh sochinenii)* (Alma Ata: Izdatel'stvo "Nauka" Kazakhskoi SSR, 1969), L35a, p. 458.

11. *Hikmät hazrät khoja ähmäd yässawiy* (Tashkent: Izdanie Molly Kemal Khana, syna Molly Islam Khoja, n.d.), summarized in A. Garritskii, "Iz predisloviia k 'Premudrosti' (*hikmät*) Sheikha Khodzhi Akhmeda Eseviiskogo," in *al-Iskandariyya. Sbornik turkestanskogo Vost. Instituta v chest' Professora A. E. Shmidta* (Tashkent, 1923), pp. 35–36.

12. *Etnograficheskie ocherki uzbekskogo sel'skogo naseleniia* (Moscow: Izdatel'stvo "Nauka," 1969), p. 36; Khanikoff, *Bokhara: Its Amir and Its People*, trans. Clement A. deBode (London: James Madden, 1845), p. 275; H. F. Hofman, *Turkish Literature. A Bio-Bibliographical Survey* vol. 1 (Utrecht: The Library of the University of Utrecht; Under the Auspices of the Royal Asiatic Society of Great Britain and Ireland, 1969), pp. 71–81.

13. Tajäldin Balchighil oghli, trans., *Shärh-i thäbat al-'ajizin. Risalä-i 'äzizä [or, qhäzizä]* (Kazan: Qäzan Univirsititining Tab'khanäsindä Basmä Olinmishdir, A.H. 1275); S. V. Bakhrushin, V. Ia. Nepomnin, and V. A. Shishkin, eds., *Istoriia narodov Uzbekistana*, vol. 2 (Tashkent: Izdatel'stvo AN UzSSR, 1947), p. 96.

14. John P. Brown, *The Darvishes* (Oxford: Oxford University Press, 1927), pp. 139–40; Bakhrushin et al., *Istoriia narodov Uzbekistana*, vol. 2, pp. 47, 325.

15. Mir Muhämmäd Ämin Bukhariy, *Ubäydullänamä*, trans. Aleksandr A. Semenov (Tashkent: Izdatel'stvo Akademii Nauk Uzbekskoi SSR, 1957), LL271a–271b, p. 303; Bakhrushin, *Istoriia narodov Uzbekistana*, vol. 2, p. 95; Jiri Becka, "Tajik Literature from the Sixteenth Century to the Present," in Jan Rypka, *History of Iranian Literature* (Dordrecht, Holland: D. Reidel, 1968), pp. 509–10.

16. Abdul Ghani, *Life and Works of Abdul Qadir Bedil* (Lahore: Publishers United, 1960), p. 122; Becka, "Tajik Literature," pp. 515–17; I. M. Mominov, *Mirzä Bedilning fälsäfiy qäräshläri* (Tashkent: Ozbekistan SSR Fänlär Äkädemiyäsi Näshriyati, 1958), pp. 36–37, 96–98.

17. V. L. Viatkin, "Ferganskii mistik Divana-i-Mashrab," in *äl-Iskändäriyyä. Sbornik turkestanskogo vostochnogo Instituta v chest' Professora A. E. Shmidta* (Tashkent, 1923), pp. 24, 27; "Divana-i-Mashrab," trans. N. S. Lykoshin, *Sredniaia Aziia* 2 (February 1910): 68–69; Jori Qadir and Khaliq Dawut, *Uyghur binakarliq sän'ätidin ornäklär. Examples of Uygur Architectural Art* (Kashgar: Qäshqär Uyghur Näshriyati, 1984), p. 86; Gunnar Jarring, *Return to Kashgar: Central Asian Memoirs in the Present*, Central Asia Book Series, vol. 1 (Durham, N.C.: Duke University Press, 1986), pp. 185–97.

18. Mäshräb, *Tänlängän äsärlär* (Tashkent: Ozbekistan SSR Däwlät Bädiiy Ädäbiyat Näshriyati, 1963), pp. 71–72.

19. Viatkin, "Ferganskii mistik Divana-i-Mäshräb," pp. 29–30; Bukhariy, *Ubäydullänamä*, p. 217.

CHAPTER 6

1. V. V. Radlov, *Opyt slovaria tiurkskikh nariechii*, vol. 1 (Saint Petersburg: Imperatorskaia Akademiia Nauk, 1893), cols. 828–30; Z. M. Mä'rufaw, ed., *Ozbek tilining izahli lughäti*, vol. 2 (Moscow: "Rus Tili" Näshriyati, 1981), p. 445; Lazar Budagov, *Sravnitel'nyi slovar' turetsko-tatarskikh nariechii*, vol. 1 (Saint Petersburg: Tipografiia Imperatorskoi Akademii 1869), pp. 206, 629, vol. 2 (1871), p. 362; Shaykh Sulayman Afandi-yi Bukhari, *Lughat-i chaghatay wa turki-yi 'osmani*, vol. 1 (Istanbul: Mihran Matba'äsi, A.H. 1298 / A.D. 1882), p. 58; *The Koran Interpreted*, trans. Arthur J. Arberry (Toronto: Macmillan, 1969), pp. 271, 273, sura XIII "Thunder," 32, 45.

2. Abd-ar Razzaq as-Samarqandi, "Matla as-sa'dayn wa majma al-bahrayn," in *Sbornik materialov, otnosiashchikhsia k istorii Zolotoi Ordy*, vol. 2, comp. V. G. Tizengauzen, (Moscow-Leningrad: Izdatel'stvo Akademii Nauk, 1941), pp. 196–97; Mirkhwand, "Rauzat as' safa," vol. 6, L423, cited by Bori A. Akhmedov in *Gosudarstvo kochevykh Uzbekov* (Moscow: Izdatel'stvo "Nauka." Glavnaia Redaktsiia Vostochnoi Literatury, 1965), pp. 39, 123.

3. A. Chuloshnikov, "Torgovlia moskovskogo gosudarstva s srednei Aziei v XVI–XVII vekakh," in *Materialy po istorii uzbekskoi, tadzhikskoi i turkmenskoi SSR* (Leningrad: Izdatel'stvo Akademii Nauk SSSR, 1932), part 1, p. 62; Zahiriddin

Muhämmäd Babir, *Babirnamä* (Tashkent, Ozbekistan SSR Fänlär Äkädemiyäsi Näshriyati, 1960) (A.H. 899/A.D. 1494), p. 76.

4. Mirza Muhammad Haidar, Dughlat, *Tarikh-i Rashidi: A History of the Moghuls of Central Asia*, trans. E. Denison Ross (London: Sampson Low, Marston and Co., 1898; repr. New York: Praeger, 1970), pp. 232–33.

5. Mirza Muhammad Haidar, Dughlat, *Tarikh-i Rashidi*, pp. 232–34.

6. Anthony Jenkinson, "The Voyage of Master Anthony Jenkinson, made from the citie of Mosco in Russia, to the citie of Boghar in Bactria, in the yeere 1558: written by himselfe to the Merchants of London of the Moscovie companie," in Richard Hakluyt, *Voyages* (London: J. M. Dent & Sons, Everyman's Library 1907; repr. New York: Dutton, 1962), p. 457.

7. Hakluyt, *Voyages*, p. 460.

8. Polat Säliyif, *Ozbekistan tarïkhï (XV–XIXinchi äsrlär)* (Samarkand-Tashkent: Ozbekistan Däwlät Näshriyatï, 1929), p. 84; Vasiliy V. Barthold, *Istoriia izucheniia Vostoka v Evrope i Rossii*, no. 7 (Leningrad: TsIK SSSR. Leningradskii Institute Zhivykh Vostochnykh Iazykov, 1925), p. 176.

9. Hafiz Tänish ibn Mir Muhämmäd Bukhariy, *Äbdullänamä (Shäräfnamäyi shahiy)* (Tashkent: Ozbekistan SSR "Fän" Näshriyati, 1969), L176a, pp. 167–68; Ibid., L196b, pp. 217–18; Ibid. (1983), part 1, L118b–19a, pp. 254–55; A. Chuloshnikov, "Torgovlia moskovskogo gosudarstva s srednei Aziei v XVI–XVII vekakh," in *Materialy po istorii uzbekskoi, tadzhikskoi i turkmenskoi SSR* (Leningrad: Izdatel'stvo Akademii Nauk SSR, 1932), p. 65.

10. Grigoriy Khilkov, comp., *Sbornik kniazia khilkova* (Saint Petersburg, Br. Panteleevy, 1879), p. 488.

11. Iskandar Munshi, "Tarikh-i alam ara-i Abbasi," trans. A. A. Romaskevich, *Materialy po istorii Turkmen i Turkmenii*, ed. V. V. Struve et al. (Moscow-Leningrad: Izdatel'stvo Akademii Nauk SSSR, 1938), L301, pp. 76–77.

12. Vladimir A. Ulianitskii, "Snosheniia Rossii s sredneiu Azieiu i Indieiu v XVI–XVII vv. Po dokumentam Moskovskago Glavnago Arkhiva Ministerstva Inostrannykh Diel," *Chteniia v Imperatorskom Obshchestvie Istorii i Drevnostei Rossiiskikh pri Moskovskom Universitetie*, book 3 for 1888 (1889), p. 56.

13. Munshi, "Tarikh-i alam ara-i Abbasi," L53a, p. 77.

14. Struve et al., *Materialy po istorii uzbekskoi, tadzhikskoi i turkmenskoi SSR* (Leningrad: Izdatel'stvo Akademii Nauk SSSR, 1932) vyp. 3, part 1 "Torgovlia s moskovskim gosudarstvom i mezhdunarodnoe polozhenie srednei Azii v XVI–XVII vv.," pp. 114, 122–23, 256, 335; S. V. Zhukovskii, *Snosheniia Rossii s Bukharoi i Khivoi za posliednee trekhsotlietie* (Petrograd: Trudy Obshchestva Russkikh Orientalistov, 1915), no. 2, p. 29.

15. Ilyas Nizamiddinaw, "Hindistanning Ozbek elchiläri," *Mehnät wä turmush*, no. 6 (1974), p. 22; Mukhammed Iusuf Munshi, *Mukim khanskaia istoriia*, trans. Aleksandr A. Semenov (Tashkent: Izdatel'stvo Akademii Nauk Uzbekskoi SSR, 1956), L50b, p. 101; L42a, p. 88; pp. 89–92, 97, 139–45, 148; Boriway A. Akhmedov, *Istoriia Balkha (XVI-pervaia polovina XVIII v.)* (Tashkent: Izdatel'stvo "Fan" Uzbekskoi SSR, 1982), pp. 190–92.

16. Abul Ghazi Bahadur Khan, *Shäjärä-i turk. Histoire des Mongols et des Tatares*, ed. and trans. Petr I. Desmaisons (Saint Petersburg, 1871–1874; repr. Amsterdam: Philo Press, 1970), LL326–27.

17. Shir Muhammad bin Amir Awaz Biy Mirab Mu'nis, "Firdaws al-iqbal," trans. S. K. Ibragimov, in *Materialy po istorii kazakhskikh khanstv XV–XVIII vekov (Izvlecheniia iz persidskikh i tiurkskikh sochinenii)* (Alma Ata: Izdatel'stvo "Nauka" Kazakhskoi SSR, 1969), L35a, p. 458.

18. N. I Veselovskii, "Priem v Rossii i otpusk sredneaziatskikh poslov v XVII i XVIII stolietiiakh," *Zhurnal Ministerstva Narodnago Prosvieshcheniia*, part 234 (July 1884), p. 89.

19. Eugene Schuyler, *Peter the Great, Emperor of Russia: A Study of Historical Biography*, vol. 2 (New York, 1884; repr. Russell & Russell, 1967), pp. 196–200.

20. Chingiz Valikhanof et al., *The Russians in Central Asia* (London: Edward Stanford, 1865), pp. 539–40; Michael T. Florinsky, *Russia: A History and an Interpretation*, vol. 1 (New York: Macmillan, 1955), p. 383; S. V. Zhukovskii, *Snosheniia Rossii s Bukharoi i Khivoi za posliednee trekhsotlietie*, no. 2 (Petrograd: Trudy Obshchestva Russkikh Orientalistov, 1915), pp. 45–46.

21. Ibid., pp. 48–49.

22. *A Narrative of the Russian Military Expedition to Khiva Under General Perofski in 1839* (Calcutta: Office of the Superintendent of Government Printing, 1867), p. 10; Zhukovskii, *Snosheniia Rossii s Bukharoi i Khivoi*, pp. 58–59.

23. Shir Muhämmäd bin 'Awaz Biy Mirab al-Mu'nis, *Firdäws al-iqbal*, trans. S. K. Ibragimov, LL35a–35b, 41b; pp. 458–59, 474–75.

24. D. Golosov, "Pokhod v Khivu v 1717 g. otriada, pod nachal'stvom leib-gvardii preobrazhenskago polka Kapitana Kniazia Aleksandra Bekovicha-Cherkasskago," *Voennyi sbornik*, no 10 (1861), supplement no. X, letter no. 7, pp. 360–61.

25. Valikhanof, *The Russians in Central Asia*, p. 540.

26. Shir Muhämmäd bin Ämir 'Awaz Biy Mirab al-Mu'nis, *Firdäws äl-iqbal*, L36a, p. 460; Edward Allworth, "Encounter," in *Central Asia: A Century of Russian Rule* (New York: Columbia University Press, 1967), p. 9.

27. Golosov, "Pokhod v Khivu v 1717 g." letter no. 54, pp. 363–64.

28. S. M. Solov'ev, *Istoriia rossii s drevneishikh vremen*, vols. 17–18, book IX (Moscow: Izdatel'stvo Sotsial'no-Ekonomicheskoi Literatury, 1963), pp. 353–54.

29. S. V. Bakhrushin et al., eds., *Istoriia narodov Uzbekistana*, vol. 2 (Tashkent: Izdatel'stvo AN UzSSR, 1947), p. 130; Abul Ghazi Bahadur Khan, *Shäjärä-i turk*, LL275–76.

30. A. N. Popov, "Snosheniia Rossii s Khivoiu i Bukharoiu pri Petrie Velikom," *Zapiski Imperatorskago Russkago Geograficheskago Obshchestva* 9 (1853), p. 270.

31. Zhukovskii, *Snosheniia Rossii s Bukharoi i Khivoi*, pp. 62–64.

32. Mir Abdoul Kerim Boukhary, *Histoire de l'Asie Centrale*, 1e Série, vols. 1–2, trans. Charles Schefer (Paris: École des Langues Orientales Vivantes, Publications, 1876; repr. Amsterdam: Philo Press, 1970), pp. 101–4; Shir Muhämmäd bin Ämir 'Awaz Biy Mirab äl-Mu'nis, "Firdäws äl-iqbal," L38b, p. 466.

33. Vasiliy V. Barthold, "A Short History of Turkestan," in *Four Studies on the History of Central Asia* trans. V. Minorsky and T. Minorsky (Leiden: E. J. Brill, 1956), pp. 65–66.

CHAPTER 7

1. Yaqut, *Irshad*, vol. 1, L92, in Franz Rosenthal, *A History of Muslim Historiography* (Leiden: E. J. Brill, 1952), p. 43; Franz Rosenthal, "Islamic Historiography," in *International Encyclopedia of the Social Sciences* (New York: Macmillan, 1968), vol. 6, p. 408.

2. Muhammad bin Khavendshah bin Mahmud (Mirkhond), *The Rauzat us-Safa, or Garden of Purity, Containing the Histories of Prophets, Kings, and Khalifs*, trans. E. Rehatsek (London: Royal Asiatic Society. Oriental Translation Fund, New Series I, 1891), pp. 21–31; Alishir Nawaiy, *Mähbub äl-qulub* (Moscow-Leningrad: Izdatel'stvo Akademii Nauk SSSR, 1948), pp. 8–13.

3. Zahiriddin Muhammad Babur, *The Babar-nama. Being the Autobiography of the Emperor Babar. Written in Chaghatay Turkish; now Reproduced in Facsimile*, ed. Annette S. Beveridge (London: Luzac and Co., 1905, repr. 1971), L201.

4. Mirza Muhammad Haidar, Dughlat, *Tarikh-i Rashidi. A History of the Moghuls of Central Asia*, trans. E. Denison Ross (London: Sampson Low, Marston & Co., 1898, repr. New York: Praeger Publishers, 1970), prologue, p. 2; text, p. 129.

5. Abul Ghazi Bahadur Khan, *Shäjärä-i turk. Histoire des Mongols et des Tatares*, ed. Petr I. Desmaisons (Saint Petersburg: 1871–1874, repr. Amsterdam: Philo Press, 1970), Turki text pp. 2–3, 72; Abul Ghazi Bahadur Khan, *The Genealogical History of the Tatars* (London: J. & J. Knapton, J. Darby, A. Bettesworth et al., 1730), vol. 1, pp. xxxi–xxxii.

6. Muhämmäd Yusuf Munshi, *Tärikhi muqim khaniy. Mukim-khanskaia istoriia*, trans. Aleksandr A. Semenov (Tashkent: Izdatel'stvo Akademii Nauk Uzbekskoi SSR, 1956); Mirmuhämmäd Ämin Bukhariy, *Ubäydullänamä. Ubaidulla-name*, trans. Aleksandr A. Semenov (Tashkent: Izdatel'stvo Akademii Nauk Uzbekskoi SSR, 1957), pp. 98–101, LL85b–88a; Äbdurähmani Tale', *Äbulfäyizkhan tärikhi. Istoriia Abulfeizkhana*, trans. Aleksandr A. Semenov (Tashkent: Izdatel'stvo Akademii Nauk, 1959).

7. Mir Abdoul Kerim Boukhary, *Histoire de l'Asie centrale*, trans. Charles Schefer (Paris: Ecole des Langues Orientales Vivantes, Publications, 1ᵉ Série, 1976, repr. Amsterdam: Philo Press, 1970), pp. 171–72; Georges de Meyendorff, *Voyage d'Orenbourg à Boukhara, fait en 1820* (Paris: Librairie Orientale de Dondey-Dupré Père et fils, 1826), p. 197; M. Abduraimov, *Voprosy feodal'nogo zemlevladeniia i feodal'noi renty v pis'makh emira Haidara. Opyt kratkogo issledovaniia istochnika* (Tashkent: Izdatel'stvo Akademii Nauk Uzbekskoi SSR, 1961), pp. 7, 57–58, 103.

8. Khanikoff, *Bokhara: Its Amir and Its People*, trans., Clement A. de Bode (London: James Madden, 1845), p. 294.

9. Aleksandr A. Semenov, "Predislovie," in Mukhammed Iusuf Munshi, *Mukim-*

khanskaia istoriia, trans. Aleksandr A. Semenov (Tashkent: Izdatel'stvo Akademii Nauk Uzbekskoi SSR, 1956), pp. 22–25.

10. R. Kh. Aminova et al., eds., *Istoriia uzbekskoi SSR*, vol. 1, *S drevneishikh vremen do serediny XIX veka* (Tashkent: Izdatel'stvo "FAN" Uzbekskoi SSR, 1967), p. 717; de Meyendorff, *Voyage d'Orenbourg à Boukhara*, pp. 297–99; Franz Rosenthal, "Islamic Historiography," in *International Encyclopedia of the Social Sciences* (New York: Macmillan, 1968), vol. 6, p. 410; Khanikoff, *Bokhara*, p. 281.

11. de Meyendorff, *Voyage d'Orenbourg à Boukhara*, pp. 282, 291; Mirza Shems Bukhari, "Zapiski Mirzy Shemsa Bukhari," in *Uchenyia zapiski izdavaemyia Imperatorskim Kazanskim Universitetom* (Kazan: v Tipografii Universiteta, 1861), book 1, p. 11.

12. "Mr. Moorcroft," *The Asiatic Journal and Monthly Register for British India and Its Dependencies* (May 1826), p. 609; Ibid., (June 1826), p. 712.

13. A. Mukhtarov, "Vvedenie," in Muhammad Hakimkhan, *Muntäkhäb ättäwarikh* (Dushanbe: Akademiyai Fanhai RSS Tojikiston. Instituti Ta'rikhi ba nomi Ahmadi Donish, 1983), pp. 16–19, 21–35; Hajji Muhämmäd Häkimkhan bin Säyyid Mä'sumkhan, *Muntäkhäb ät-täwarikh*, mss. copied A.H. 1294 / A.D. 1877 in Chaghatay, trans. from Tajik, original written *ca.* 1842; *Sobranie sochinenie vostochnykh rukopisei Akademii Nauk Uzbekskoi SSR*, eds. A. Urunbaev and L. M. Epifanova (Tashkent: Izdatel'stvo "Nauka" UzSSR, 1964), vol. 7, pp. 31–33; Hakimkhan, *Muntäkhäb ät-täwarikh*, comp. Ährar Mukhtaraf, mss. completed in Kitab, 1844; facsimile from its author's personal copy published in Dushanbe: Näshriyat-i "Danish," 1985).

14. Ahmad Donish, *Risolai Ahmadi Donish "Ta'rikhi saltanati manghitya". Traktat Akhmada Donisha "Istoriia mangitskoi dinastii"*, trans. I. A. Nadzhafova (Dushanbe: Nashriyati "Donish," 1967), pp. 38–40, 42; Mirza 'Abdal 'Azim Sami, *Tarikh-i salatin-i manghitiya. (Istoriia mangytskikh gosudarei)*, trans. L. M. Epifanova (Moscow: Izdatel'stvo Vostochnoi Literatury, 1962), LL62b–63a, 64b–66b, pp. 52–53, 55–59, Khanikoff, *Bokhara*, pp. 305–6, 310–14; Akhmad Donish, "Rare Events," in *puteshestvie iz Bukhary v Peterburg. Izbrannoe* (n.p.: Tadzhikgosizdat, 1960), p. 107.

15. Nikolai Murav'ev, *Puteshestvie v Turkmeniiu i Khivu v 1819 i 1820 gg* (Moscow: Tipografiia Avgusta Semena, 1822), part I, p. 129, part II, pp. 121–22, 140.

16. Shir Muhämmäd bin Ämir 'Awaz Biy Mirab al-Mu'nis, *Firdäwsäl iqbal*, mss. no. 5364/1, L72b, cited in Quwämiddin Muniraw, *Munis, Agähiy wä Bäyaniyning tärikhiy äsärläri* (Tashkent: Ozbekistan SSR Fänlär Äkädemiyäsi Näshriyati, 1960), pp. 12, 14, 19; Abul Ghazi Bahadur Khan, *Shäjärä-i turk*, L334, p. 357.

17. Agähiy, "Gulshän-i däwlät," OzSSR FÄ Äbu Räyhan Beruniy namidägi Shärqshunaslik Instituti qolyazmälär fandi, inw. no. 7572, LL3b–5a, cited in Muniraw, p. 48.

18. Agähiy, *Riyazud däwlä*, inw. no. 5364/II, L352a, cited in Muniraw, p. 132; Bayaniy, *Shäjäräi kharäzmshahiy*, inw. no. 9596, LL301b–302a, cited in Muniraw, p. 132; James Abbott, *Narrative of a Journey from Heraut to Khiva, Moscow, and St.*

Peterburgh during the late Russian Invasion of Khiva (London: James Madden, 1856), vol. 1, p. 74.

19. Edward Allworth, *Central Asian Publishing and the Rise of Nationalism* (New York: New York Public Library, 1965), pp.10–12; M. Gavrilov, "Neskol'ko slov o sovremennoi literature sartov," *Turkestanskie viedomosti* (1912), no. 18, cited by G. N. Chabrov, "U istokov uzbekskoi poligrafii. (Khivinskaia pridvornaia litografiia 1874–1910)," in *Kniga. Issledovaniia i materialy. Sbornik*, no. IV (Moscow: Izdatel'stvo Vsesoiuznoi Knizhnoi Palaty, 1961), pp. 317–28; Ibid., p. 320; Muhämmäd Yusuf Bäyaniy, "Shäjärä-i khwaräzmshahiy," mss. no. 9596, LL2b–4b, cited in Muniraw, p. 51; "Firuz," "Täbibiy," in *Ozbek ädäbiyati* (Tashkent: OzSSR Däwlät Bädiiy Ädäbiyat Näshriyati, 1960), vol. 4, pp. 143–55.

20. Muniraw, pp. 31–35, 38–49, 50–51, 54, 157–58; S. K. Ibragimov et al., eds., *Materialy po istorii kazakhskikh khanstv XV–XVIII vekov (Izvlecheniia iz persidskikh i tiurkskikh sochinenii)*, trans. S. K. Ibragimov (Alma Ata: Izdatel'stvo "Nauka" Kazakhskoi SSR, 1969), p. 433.

21. I. M. Mominov, *Mirzä Bedilning fälsäfiy qäräshläri* (Tashkent: Ozbekistan SSR Fänlär Äkädemiyäsi Näshriyati, 1958), pp. 36–37, 96–98.

22. Fazil bek Atabek oghli, *Dukchi ishan waqi'äsi. Färghanädä istibdad jälladläri* (Samarkand-Tashkent: Ozbekstan Däwlät Näshriyati, 1927), p. 30; Richard A. Pierce, *Russian Central Asia, 1867–1917: A Study in Colonial Rule* (Berkeley: University of California Press, 1960), p. 226.

CHAPTER 8

1. Mullah 'Alim Makhdum Hajji, *Tä'rikh-i turkistan* (Tashkent: Turkistan Giniräl Gubirnätarighä Tob'ä Basmäkhanädä, 1915), pp. 3–4.

2. Mullah 'Alim Makhdum Hajji, *Tä'rikh-i turkistan*, p. 4. Professor Pierre Cachia kindly rendered the Arabic language sentence into English.

3. Sattar Khan Abdalghafar-oghli, "Vospominaniia Sattar-Khana Abdul-Gafarova," *Turkistan wilayätining gäziti* (1890), reprinted in Nikolai P. Ostroumov, *Sarty. Etnograficheskie materialy* (Tashkent: Tipo-Litografiia S. I. Lakhtina, 1890), pp. 98–119; Ostroumov, *Sarty*, 2d ed. (Tashkent: Tipografiia Gazety "Sredneaziatskaia Zhizn'," 1908), pp. 138–39, 150–51; Edward Allworth, *Uzbek Literary Politics* (The Hague: Mouton & Co., 1964), pp. 27–29; Eugene Schuyler, *Turkistan. Notes of a Journey in Russian Turkistan, Khokand, Bukhara, and Khiva*, vol. 2 (New York: Scribner, Armstrong & Co., 1877), pp. 219–25; Georgiy Safarov, *Kolonial'naia revoliutsiia (opyt Turkestana)* (Moscow: Gosudarstvennoe Izdatel'stvo, 1921), p. 52.

4. Mahmud Khoja, "Tä'rikh wä jaghrafiyyä," *Ayinä*, no. 27 (April 26, 1914):502.

5. Ibid., pp. 502–3; Mazheruddin Siddiqi, *The Qur'anic Concept of History* (Karachi: Central Institute of Islamic Research, 1965), p. 205; *The Koran Interpreted*, Arthur J. Arberry, trans. (Toronto, Ontario: Macmillan, 1969), Sura XVIII:83.

6. Khoja, "Tä'rikh wä jaghrafiyyä," p. 504.

7. Hajji Mu'in, "Milliy tä'rikh haqindä," *Ayinä*, no. 10 (February 28, 1915):258.

8. "Turkistan tä'rikhi keräk," *Ayinä*, no. 38 (July 12, 1914): 898–99.

9. Akhmet Z. Validov, "O sobraniiakh rukopisei v bukharskom khanstve (otchet o komandirovke)," *Zapiski Vostochnago Otdieleniia Imperatorskago Russkago Arkheologicheskago Obshchestva*, vol. 23 for 1915 (1916):245, 248–261; Khoja, "Isma'il beg häzrätläri ilä sohbät," *Ayinä*, no. 49 (September 27, 1914):162–64; *Tärjüman*, no. 1 (1885), cited by Zarif Radzhabov, in *Iz istorii obshchestvenno-politicheskoi mysli tadzhikskogo naroda vo vtoroi polovine XIX i v nachale XX vv.* (Stalinabad: Tadzhikskoe Gosudarstvennoe Izdatel'stvo, 1957), pp. 386–87.

10. "Turkistan tä'rikhi keräk," pp. 899–900; Ähmäd Zäki Välidi, *Turk wä tatar tarikhi*, vol. 1 (Kazan: Millät Elektro-Tipografiia, 1912), pp. 268–69.

11. Khoja, "Tä'rikh wä jaghrafiyyä," p. 504; K. E. Bendrikov, *Ocherki po istorii narodnogo obrazovaniia v Turkestane* (Moscow: Bezbozhnik, 1960), pp. 268, 343, 379.

12. Khoja, "Tä'rikh wä jaghrafiyyä," *Ayinä*, no. 28 (May 3, 1914), pp. 528–29.

13. Ibid.

14. Ostroumov, *Sarty.* (Tashkent: Izdanie Knizhnago Magazina "Bukinist," 1896), p. 140; Ibid. (Tashkent: Tipografiia Gazety "Sredneaziatskaia Zhizn'," 1908), p. 184.

15. M. M. Virskii, ed., *Sbornik materialov dlia statistiki samarkandskoi oblasti, za 1887–1888 gg.*, vol. 1 (Samarkand: Izdanie Samarkandskago Oblastnago Statistiches-kago Komiteta, 1890), p. 291; *Pis'ma Nikolaia Ivanovicha Il'minskago k Ober-Pro-kuroru Sviateishago Sinoda Konstantinu Petrovichu Pobiedonostsevu* (Kazan: Izdanie Redaktsii Pravoslavnago Sobiesiednika, 1895), letter no. 23, February 29, 1884, pp. 74–75, secret letter, February 10, 1884, p. 63.

16. Bendrikov, *Ocherki po istorii narodnogo obrazovaniia v Turkestane*, pp. 140, 253, 256, 259, 261.

17. Ibid., pp. 256–67; A. Samoilovich, "Pervoe tainoe obshchestvo Mlado-Bukhartsev," *Vostok* 1 (1922), p. 97.

18. Serge Zenkovsky, "'Kulturkampf' in Pre-Revolutionary Central Asia," *American Slavic and East European Review* 14 (1955):29; "Abduqadir Shäkuriy," in *Ozbek Sawet entsiklapediyäsi* (Tashkent: Ozbekistan SSR Fänlär Äkädemiyäsi, 1971), vol. 1, p. 41; Tursunqul, "25 yillik pïdagok," *Mä'arif wä oqutghuchi*, no. 4 (1926):28–32; photo of the school children is on p. 29.

19. Ostroumov, *Sarty.* (1908), pp. 244–45.

20. Bendrikov, *Ocherki po istorii narodnogo obrazovaniia v Turkestane*, pp. 259–61; [Graf K. K. Palen], *Otchet po revizii turkestanskago kraia. Uchebnoe dielo* (Saint Petersburg: Senatskaia Tipografiia, 1910), pp. 133–34.

21. [Archive] TsAU UzSSR, f. 47, d. 3493. "Po voprosu o preobrazovanii Up-ravleniia uchebnymi zavedeniiami v uchebnyi okrug," ll. 129–35, 1909, cited in Bendrikov, *Ocherki po istorii narodnogo obrazovania v Turkestane*, pp. 274, 275, 276–78; S. M. Gramenitskii, "Otkrytyi vopros," *Turkestanskie viedomosti*, no. 10

(1909):42; *Ozbekistan SSR tärikhi* (Tashkent: Ozbekistan SSR Fänlär Äkädemiyäsi Näshriyati, 1957), vol. 1, book 2, p. 347.

22. *Ozbekistan SSR tärikhi* (Tashkent: Ozbekistan SSR Fänlär Äkädemiyäsi Näshriyati, 1957), vol. 1, book 2, p. 348; *Istoriia uzbekskoi SSR*, vol. 2 (Tashkent: Izdatel'stvo "Fän" Uzbekskoi SSR, 1967), p. 314.

23. *Sawet ozbekistanining yazuwchiläri* (Tashkent: OzSSR Däwlät Bädiiy Ädäbiyat Näshriyati, 1959), pp. 98, 172–74; Äbdulla Awlaniy, ed., *Ädäbiyat khrestamätiyasi* (Tashkent: Ozdäwnäshr, 1933), pp. 376–77.

24. Munäwwär Qari ibn 'Abduräshid Khan, *Ädib-i thani*, 2d ed. (Tashkent: Ghulamiyä Mätbu'äsidä Chab Awlindi, A.H. 1329/A.D. 1911), pp. 1–17.

25. Munäwwär Qari, *Ädib-i thani*, pp. 9, 11, 18–19.

26. Munäwwär Qari, "Iskändär dhualqärnain," "Hajjaj ilä därwish," in *Ädib-i thani*, pp. 20, 21–30, 41.

27. Munäwwär Qari, *Ädib-i thani*, pp. 42–44.

28. Ibid., p. 2; Mähmud Khojä Bihbudiy, *Pädärkush yakhud (oqumagan balaning hali?)* (Samarkand: Tipo-Litografiia T-va B. Gazarov i N. Sliianov, A.H. 1331/A.D. 1913), p. 19, trans. by Edward Allworth in "Murder as Metaphor in the First Central Asian Drama," *Ural-Altaic Yearbook*, no. 58 (1986):82,95,97.

29. U. B. Bazarov, *Ideinye osnovy tvorchestva Khamzy Khakim-Zade Niiazi* (Tashkent: Izdatel'stvo Akademii Nauk Uzbekskoi SSR, 1960), p. 20; Hamza Hakim Zadä Niyaziy, "Yengil ädäbiyat," in Aleksandr A. Semenov, ed., *Sobranie vostochnykh rukopisei Akademii Nauk Uzbekskoi SSR*, vol. 7 (Tashkent: Izdatel'stvo "Nauka" Uzbekskoi SSR, 1964), p. 261.

30. *Täräqqiy* (November 14, 1906), cited by Zafir Radzhabov, in *Iz istorii obshchestvenno-politicheskoi mysli tadzhikskogo naroda vo vtoroi polovine XIX i v nachale XX vv.* (Stalinabad: Tadzhikskoe Gosudarstvennoe Izdatel'stvo, 1957), p. 392.

31. Edward Allworth, "The Changing Intellectual and Literary Community," in Edward Allworth, ed., *Central Asia, a Century of Russian Rule* (New York: Columbia University Press, 1967), pp. 350–51.

32. Munäwwär Qari, *Hawa'ij-i diniyyä* reproduced under the title *'Äqa'id* (Mecca: M. Moosa Turkistani and Sons, A.H. 1373/A.D. 1953/54), inside front cover; Bendrikov, *Ocherki po istorii narodnogo obrazovaniia v Turkestane*, p. 267.

33. Ibid., p. 268.

34. [Archive] TsAU UzSSR, f47, d. 4757, "Ob otkrytii novometodnykh maktabov," 1. 119, cited in Bendrikov, *Ocherki po istorii narodnogo obrazovaniia v Turkestane*, p. 343.

35. M. F., "Makhmud Khoja Begbudi," *Nauka i prosveshchenie*, no. 1 (Tashkent 1922):23–25; Ertürk, "Mahmud Hoca Behbudi (Oluminin 31 jilligi munasibati blan)," *Millij Türkistan*, no. 66 (March 1950):21–24.

36. Abul Nasir Naji, "Habibim munawwar qari," *Yash turkistan*, no. 55 (1934): 12–14; Jarcek, "Munavvar Qari-Patriot and Reformer (On the occasion of the nine-

teenth anniversary of his martyrdom by the Bolsheviks in the cause of Turkestanian Freedom)," *Millij Türkistan*, no. 76B (December 1951–January 1952):14–17.

37. Edward A. Allworth, "Suppressed Histories of the Jadids in Turkistan and Bukhara," in *Turkestan als historischer Faktor und politische Idee. Festschrift für Baymirza Hayit zu seinem 70. Geburstag 17. Dezember* ed., Erling von Mende (Cologne: Studienverlag, 1988), pp. 33–46.

38. Sädriddin 'Äyniy, *Bukhara inqilabi tä'rikhi uchun materiyallar* (Moscow: SSSR Khälqlarning Märkazi Näshriyati, 1926), pp. 67–68; Faizulla Khodzhaev, "O mlado-Bukhartsakh," *Istorik marksist*, no. 1 (1926):128; Khodzhaev, *K istorii revoliutsii v Bukhare* (Tashkent: Uzbekskoe Gosudarstvennoe Izdatel'stvo, 1926), p. 12; Edward Allworth, "Suppressed Histories of the Jadids in Turkistan and Bukhara," *Turkestan als historischer*, ed. von Mende.

39. *Ozbekistan SSR tärikhi*, vol. 1, book 2, p. 347; Khodzhaev, *K istorii*, p. 15; [Archive], "Po voprosu o preobrazovanii Upravleniia uchebnymi zavedeniiami v uchebnyi okrug." LL129–35, 1909, cited in Bendrikov, *Ocherki po istorii narodnogo obrazovania v Turkestane*, pp. 276–78, 280; Richard A. Pierce, *Russian Central Asia, 1867–1917: A Study in Colonial Rule* (Berkeley: University of California Press, 1960), pp. 88, 307; Khodzhaev, "O mlado-Bukhartsakh," p. 130; Petr G. Galuzo, *Turkestankoloniia* (Tashkent: Gosudarstvennoe Izdatel'stvo UzSSR, 1935), p. 199; *Istoriia Khorezma s dreveishikh vremen do nashikh dnei* (Tashkent: Izdatel'stvo "Fan" Uzbekskoi SSR, 1976), p. 147.

CHAPTER 9

1. *Tujjar* (1907), cited in Zarif Radzhabov, *Iz istorii obshchestvenno-politicheskoi mysli tadzhikskogo naroda vo vtoroi polovine XIX a v nachale XX vv.* (Stalinabad: Tadzhikskoe Gosudarstvennoe Izdatel'stvo, 1957), p. 391; Ziya Sä'id, *Ozbek wäqtli mätbu'ati tä'rikhigä mäteriyällär, 1870–1927* (Tashkent-Samarkand: Ozbekistan Däwlät Näshriyati, 1927), p. 48.

2. Äbdurähmän binni Farman-Quli Rähmät, "'Ilm fa'idasi," *Säda-i Färghanä*, no. 116 (March 21, 1915), cited in Radzhabov, *Iz istorii obshchestvenno-politicheskoi mysli tadzhikskogo naroda*, p. 392.

3. Tursunqul, "25 yillik pidagok," *Mä'arif wä oqutghuchi*, no. 4 (1926):31; Faizulla Khodzhaev, *K istorii revoliutsii v Bukhare* (Tashkent: Uzbekskoe Gosudarstvennoe Izdatel'stvo, 1926), pp. 1–15; *Ozbekistan SSR tärikhi*, vol. 1, book 2 (Tashkent: Ozbekistan SSR Fänlär Äkädemiyasi Näshriyati, 1957), p. 348.

4. Albert Kudsi-Zadeh, *Sayyid Jamal al-Din al-Afghani: An Annotated Bibliography* (Leiden: E. J. Brill, 1970), items 53 (1879), 65 (1881), and 72 (1883), in which the annotator comments on al-Afghani's positions in these reforms of Islam.

5. Mahmud Khoja Behbudiy, ["songrä bulärni misrdän kelgäni"], *Shuhrät* (Tashkent) no. 9 (January 1908), cited in Ziya Sa'id, *Ozbek waqtli mätbu'ati, 1870–1927*, (Samarkand-Tashkent: Ozbekistan Däwlät Näshriyati, 1927), p. 41.

6. Abdalrauf Fiträt, *Munazärä*, trans. Muällim Hajji Mu'in ibn Shukrullah Sämärqändiy (Tashkent: Turkistan Kitabkhanäsi, Tipolitografiia V. M. Il'ina, A.H. 1331/A.D. 1913), 41 pp.; Mahmud Khojä, "Munazärä haqindä," in *Munazärä*, pp. 38–41.

7. Gunnar Jarring, *Some Notes on Eastern Turki (New Uighur) Munazara Literature* (Lund: CWK Gleerup, Scripta Minora, 1981), pp. 5–7; Ergash R. Rustamov, *Uzbekskaia poeziia v pervoi polovine XV veka* (Moscow: Izdatel'stvo Vostochnoi Literatury, 1963), pp. 201–344.

8. Fiträt, *Munazärä*, pp. 5–6.

9. Ibid., p. 8.

10. Fiträt, *Munazärä*, p. 9.

11. Abd-ur-Rauf, *Razskazy indiiskago puteshestvennika*, trans. A. N. Kondrat'ev (Samarkand: Izdanie Makhmud Khoja Bekbudi, Tip-Litografiia Tovarishchestva Gazarov i K. Sliianov, 1913), pp. 17–18, 67–74, 94–95; Äbdälrä'uf, *Bayyanat-i seyyah-i hindi* (Dar al-Khilafät, Istanbul: Hikmat, A.H. 1331/A.D. 1912/13.

12. Fiträt, *Munazärä*, p. 20.

13. Ibid., p. 16.

14. Osman Amin, *Muhammad 'Abduh* (Washington, D. C.: American Council of Learned Societies, 1953), p. 79; Mähmud Khojä, "Hadith-i shärif mushrik goshti häqqindä," *Ayinä*, no. 16 (June 15, 1915):434–39; *äl-Islah* (Tashkent, 1915), cited in Radzhabov, *Iz istorii*, p. 407.

15. *äl-Islah*, no. 4 (February 15, 1916), cited in Alexandre Bennigsen and Chantal Lemercier-Quelquejay, *La Presse et le Mouvement National chez les musulmans de Russie avant 1920* (Paris: Mouton & Co., 1964), p. 165; Mähmud Khojä Behbudiy, in *Turkistan wilayätining gäziti*, no. 23 (June 26,1903), cited in Michel Gavrilov, "Les Corps de Métiers in Asie Centrale et leurs status (Rissala)," *Revue des Études islamiques* (1928):217–18.

16. Mufti Mähmud Khojä bin Bihbud Khojä, "Turkistan idaräsi," *Shora* (Orenburg), no. 23 (1908):722; Radzhabov, *Iz istorii*, p. 406 (Radzhabov omits reference to the source for the direct quotation cited here).

17. Mähmud Khojä Behbudiy, *Pädärkush yakhud oqumagan balaning hali?* (Samarkand: Behbudiy Näshriyati, Tipo-Litografiia Tovarishchestva Gazarov i K. Sliianov, 1913), p. 1.

18. Mamajan Rähmanaw, *Ozbek teätri tärikhi (XVIII äsrdän XX äsr äuwäligächä ozbek teätr mädäniyätining täräqqiyat yolläri)* (Tashkent: Ozbekistan SSR "Fän" Näshriyati, 1968), pp. 413–14.

19. Edward Allworth, "Murder as Metaphor in the First Central Asian Drama," *Ural-Altaic Yearbook*, no. 58 (1986), pp. 65–73, 91.

20. Aleksandr Samoilovich, "Dramaticheskaia literatura Sartov," *Viestnik imperatorskago obshchestva Vostokoviedieniia*, no. 5 (October 1, 1916):77–78, 79–81.

21. Ibid., pp. 81–83; Äbdullah Qadiriy, *Bäkhtsiz kiyaw* (Tashkent: Izdanie Seid Arifdzhanova. Tipografiia Kantseliarii Turkest. Gen.-Gub., 1915), 40 pp.; Hämzä Häkimzädä Niyaziy, *Zähärli häyat yakhud 'ishq qurbanläri. Turkistan mä'ishatindän*

alinmish qiz wä kuyaw faji'asidur (Tashkent: Matbaa-i Ghulamiyä, A.H. 1335/A.D. 1916); Hajji Mu'in ibn Shukrullah, *Eski mäktäb, yängi mäktäb* (Samarkand: n.p., 1916), 48 pp.; Tashpulat T. Tursunov, *Formirovanie sotsialisticheskogo realizma v uzbekskoi dramaturgii* (Tashkent: Izdatel'stvo Akademii Nauk Uzbekskoi SSR, 1963), pp. 14–16.

22. Rähmanaw, *Ozbek teätri tärikhi*, pp. 342–43.

23. Ibid., p. 411.

24. N. Nurdzhanov, *Tadzhikskii narodnyi teatr. Po materialam kuliabskoi oblasti* (Moscow: Izdatel'stvo Akademii Nauk SSSR, 1956), p. 113; *Säda-i Turkistan* (August 23, 1914), cited in Radzhabov, *Iz istorii*, p. 373; "Sämärqänd shähär mäktäbidän," *Ayinä* (May 31, 1914):639; Mu'ällim Z. Muzaffari, "Tiyatir e'lani," *Ayinä*, no. 41 (August 2, 1914), back page; Rähmanaw, *Khamza i uzbekskii teatr* (Tashkent: Gosudarstvennoe Izdatel'stvo Khudozhestvennoi Literatury UzSSR, 1960), p. 47.

25. Sä'id, *Ozbek waqtli mätbo'ati tä'rikhigä materiyallar*, pp. 45–65; Bennigsen and Lemercier-Quelquejay, *La presse*, pp. 162–69, 262–67.

26. Sä'id, *Ozbek waqtli mätbu'ati*, pp. 58–60.

27. Ibid., pp. 36–37, 39, 43.

28. Bähram Beg Dawlät Shah, "Sart mäs'äläsi," *Ayinä*, no. 17 (February 19, 1914):300–301; "Millätni kim islah etar?" *Ayinä*, no. 12 (January 11, 1914):274–75; "Millät, millät, millät," *al-Islah*, no. 16 (September 1, 1915):500–501.

29. Munäwwär Qari ibn 'Abduräshid Khan-oghli, *Ädib-i thani*, 2d ed. (Tashkent: Ghulamiyä Mätbu'äsi, A.H. 1329/A.D. 1911), p. 34; Qari 'Othman ibn Äbdalkhaliq Shashi, *Ta'lim-i äwwäl* (Tashkent: Litografiia Gulam Khasan Arifdzhanova, 1910), p. 38.

CHAPTER 10

1. Michael T. Florinsky, *Russia: A History and an Interpretation* (New York: Macmillan, 1953), pp. 1190, 1199–2000; "Duma wä Turkistan," *Tujjar*, no. 8 (October 9, 1907), cited by A. V. Piaskovskii, in *Revoliutsiia 1905–1907 godov v Turkestane* (Moscow: Izdatel'stvo Akademii Nauk, 1958), p. 552.

2. Mähmud Khojä Behbudiy, in *Khurshid* (October 11, 1906), cited in Yähya G. Ghulamaw, Räshid N. Näbiyew, and Mäwlan G. Wähabaw, *Ozbekistan SSR tärikhi (bir tamlik)* (Tashkent: Ozbekistan SSR Fänlär Äkädemiyäsi Näshriyati, 1958), p. 381.

3. [Archive] TsGIA UzSSR, f. 2, op. 1, d. 291, 1. 152, cited by Tukhtamet Tukhtametov, in *Rossiia i Khiva v kontse XIX—nachale XX v. Pobeda khorezmskoi narodnoi revoliutsii* (Moscow: Izdatel'stvo "Nauka," 1969), p. 67.

4. Sädriddin 'Ayniy, *Bukhara inqilabi tä'rikhi uchun materiyallär* (Moscow: SSSR Khälqlarning Märkäzi Näshriyati, 1926), pp. 72–73.

5. I. M. Muminov, ed., *Istoriia Khorezma s drevneishikh vremen do nashikh dnei* (Tashkent: Izdatel'stvo "Fan" Uzbekskoi SSR, 1976), p. 137.

6. Mamajan Rähmanaw, *Ozbek teätri tärikhi* (Tashkent: Ozbekistan SSR "Fän" Näshriyati, 1968), p. 306.

7. Turkistanli Receb Baysun, *Türkistan millî hareketleri* (Istanbul, 1943 [title page], 1945 [cover]), pp. 18–19; Mo'minjan Muhämmädjan oghli, *Turmish orinishläri (bir mulläbächäning khatirä däftäri)* (Tashkent: Ozbekistan Däwlät Näshriyati, 1926), pp. 311–12; Edward Allworth, "Suppressed Histories of the Jadids in Turkistan and Bukhara," in *Turkestan als historischer Faktor und politische Idee: Festschrift für Baymirza Hayit zu seinem 70. Geburstag, 17 Dezember 1987*, ed. Erling von Mende (Cologne: Studienverlag, 1988), pp. 33–46.

8. *Vosstanie 1916 goda v Srednei Azii i Kazakhstane. Sbornik dokumentov* (Moscow: Izdatel'stvo Akademii Nauk SSSR, 1960), documents nos. 1, 70, 88, 91, 265, 490, 495 (these last two appear to be pure gossip), pp. 25, 122–24, 149–52, 158–60, 395–402, 688–89, 695–96.

9. *Ta'min-i mä'arif-i jämi'ät-i khäyriyäsinin nizamnamä wä khatt-i häräkätidir* (Abode of Happiness [Istanbul]: (Metin) Mätba'äsi A.H. 1327 / A.D. 1909), 8 pp.; for a censored, translated version, see A. Arsharuni and Kh. Gabidullin, *Ocherki panislamizma i pantiurkizma v Rossii* (Moscow: Bezbozhnik, 1931), pp. 133–35; Zeki Velidi Togan, *Bugünkü Türkili (Türkistan) ve yakin Tarihi* (Istanbul: Arkadash, Ibrahim Horoz ve Güven Basimevleri, 1942–47), p. 355; Allworth, ed., *Central Asia, a Century of Russian Rule* (New York: Columbia University Press, 1967), pp. 198–200.

10. Togan, *Bugünkü Türkili*, p. 356; *Ozbekistan SSR tärikhi*, vol. 1, book 2 (Tashkent: Ozbekistan SSR Fänlär Äkädemiyäsi Näshriyati, 1957), p. 431; *Turan* (April 30, 1917), cited in R. Kh. Abdushukurov, *Oktiabr'skaia revoliutsiia, rastsvet uzbekskoi sotsialisticheskoi natsii* (Tashkent: Gosudarstvennoe Izdatel'stvo Uzbekskoi SSR, 1962), p. 62.

11. 'Ayniy, *Bukhara inqilabi*, p. 159.

12. Khodzhaev, *K istorii*, p. 21.

13. Ibid., p. 13; Faizulla Khodzhaev, "O mlado-Bukhartsakh," *Istorik Marksist*, no. 1 (1926):133; Sadriddin Aini, *Vospominaniia* (Moscow-Leningrad: Izdatel'stvo Akademii Nauk SSSR, 1960), pp. 383–84, 415–21, 1037; Allworth, "Intellectual and Literary Changes," in Allworth, ed., *Central Asia*, pp. 78–122; Seymour Becker, *Russia's Protectorates in Central Asia: Bukhara and Khiva, 1865–1924* (Cambridge, Mass.: Harvard University Press, 1968), pp. 244–45, 255.

14. 'Ayniy, *Bukhara inqilabi*, p. 153.

15. Ibid., pp. 164–207; Khodzhaev, "O mlado-Bukhartsakh," pp. 134–37; Personal interviews of Edward Allworth with Ahmad Naim Nusratullabek (Oktem), Keban Hotel, Istanbul, May–June 1968; Khodzhaev, *K istorii*, pp. 24–27.

16. Khodzhaev, "O mlado-Bukhartsakh," p. 135; Khodzhaev, *K istorii*, p. 29.

17. Khodzhaev, "O mlado-Bukhartsakh," p. 130.

18. G. Nepesov, *Iz istorii khorezmskoi revoliutsii, 1920–1924 g.g.* (Tashkent: Gosizdat UzSSR, 1962), pp. 75, 148; Ella R. Christie, *Through Khiva to Golden Samarkand* (London: Seeley, Service & Co., 1925), pp. 104–6.

19. Nepesov, *Iz istorii khorezmskoi revoliutsii*, pp. 77–78.

20. Ibid., p. 78; Muminov, ed., *Istoriia Khorezma*, p. 136; Zarif Radzhabov, *Iz istorii obshchestvennoi mysli tadzhikskogo naroda vo vtoroi polovine XIX i v nachale XX vv.* (Stalinabad: Tadzhikskoe Gosudarstvennoe Izdatel'stvo, 1957), pp. 430–32.

21. Ibid., p. 431; Nepesov, *Iz istorii khorezmskoi revoliutsii*, pp. 78, 81; M. Kh. Aliakberov, "O memuarakh Palvanniiaza Iusupova," *Obshchestvennye nauki v Uzbekistane*, no. 2 (1968):72.

22. *S'ezdy sovetov sovetskikh sotsialisticheskikh respublik. Sbornik dokumentov, 1917–1922 g.g.*, vol. 2 (Moscow: Gosizdat Iuridicheskoi Literatury, 1960), pp. 511–12.

23. K. Mukhammedberdyev, *Kommunisticheskaia Partiia v bor'be za pobedu narodnoi sovetskoi revoliutsii v Khorezme* (Ashkhabad: Turkmenskoe Gosudarstvennoe Izdatel'stvo, 1959), pp. 47–48.

24. *Ocherki istorii kommunisticheskoi partii Turkestana* (Tashkent: Gosizdat Uzbekskoi SSR, 1959), p. 37; M. G. Vakhabov, "O sotsial'noi prirode sredneaziatskogo dzhadidizma i ego evoliutsii v period velikoi oktiabr'skoi revoliutsii," *Istoriia SSSR*, no. 2 (1963):47.

25. Ziya Sä'id, pp. 63-66; M. G. Vakhabov, p. 53.

26. Mustafa Choqay-oghli, "Khoqand Mukhtariyäti haqindä," *Yeni Turkistan*, no. 7 (December 1927):7; Joseph Castagné, "Le Turkestan depuis la Revolution Russe (1917–1921)," *Revue du Monde Musulman*, vol. L (June 1922):46–47.

27. *Svobodnyi Samarkand* (November 9 [21], 1917), cited in Radzhabov, *Iz istorii obshchestvennoi mysli*, p. 432–33; *Hurriyät* (December 22, 1917), cited by A. A. Gordienko in *Obrazovanie turkestanskoi ASSR* (Moscow: "Iuridicheskaia Literatura," 1968), pp. 139–41; Yähya Gh. Ghulamaw, R. N. Näbiyew, and M. Gh. Wähabaw, *Ozbekistan SSR tärikhi (bir tamlik)* (Tashkent: Ozbekistan SSR Fänlär Äkädemiyäsi Näshriyati, 1958), p. 486.

28. Khodzhaev, *K istorii*, pp. 23, 28.

29. Baymirza Hayit, *Turkestan im XX. Jahrhundert* (Darmstadt: C. W. Leske Verlag, 1956), p. 60; Alexander G. Park, *Bolshevism in Turkestan, 1917–1927* (New York: Columbia University Press, 1957), pp. 15–16.

CHAPTER 11

1. Akmal Ikram-oghli, *Ishtirakiyon*, June 11, 1919, cited by Mavlian G. Vakhabov, *Formirovanie uzbekskoi sotsialisticheskoi natsii* (Tashkent: Gosudarstvennoe Izdatel'stvo Uzbekskoi SSR, 1961), p. 316; Faizulla Khodzhaev, *K istorii revoliutsii v Bukhare* (Tashkent: Uzbekskoe Gosudarstvennoe Izdatel'stvo, 1926), p. 67; M. Nemchenko, *Natsional'noe razmezhevanie srednei Azii* (Moscow: Izdanie Litizdata NKID, 1925), p. 19; Mamadzhan Rakhmanov, *Khamza i uzbekskii teatr* (Tashkent: Gosudarstvennoe Izdatel'stvo Khudozhestvennoi Literatury, 1960), p. 176; Tashpulat T. Tursunov, *Formirovanie sotsialisticheskogo realizma v uzbekskoi dramaturgii* (Tashkent: Izdatel'stvo Akademii Nauk Uzbekskoi SSR, 1963), pp. 34–36.

2. Glenda Fraser, "Basmachi," *Central Asian Survey*, no. 1 (1987): 1–73; Helénè Aymen de LaGeard, "The Revolt of the Basmachi According to Red Army Journals (1920–1922)," *Central Asian Survey*, no. 3 (1987):1–35.

3. "Turkistan musulmanlarining ikinchi qoroltayinda berilgän qärarnamä," *Yash Turkistan*, no. 29 (April/Nisan 1932):9–13; Baymirza Hayit, *Turkestan im XX. Jahrhundert* (Darmstadt, C. W. Leske Verlag, 1956), pp. 203–7; Q. Yudakhin, *Ozbek-rus lughäti* (Tashkent: Izdanie Aktsionernogo Obshchestva "Sredazkniga," 1927), p. 616; Z. M. Mä'rufaw, ed., *Ozbek tilining izahli lughäti*, vol. 1 (Moscow: "Rus Tili" Näshriyati, 1981), p. 476.

4. *"Turkistan musulmanlarining ikinchi qoroltayinda berilgän qärarnamä,"* pp. 14–15; Joseph Castagné, *Les Basmatchis* (Paris: Editions Ernest Leroux, 1925), p. 35; Marie Broxup, "The Basmachi," *Central Asian Survey*, no. 1 (July 1983):62–63.

5. M. A. Miropiev, *O polozhenii russkikh inorodtsev* (Saint Petersburg: Synodal'naia Tipografiia, 1901), p. 372; Evgenii D. Polivanov, *Etnograficheskaia kharak-teristika Uzbekov* (Tashkent: Uzbekskoe Gosudarstvennoe Izdatel'stvo, 1926), pp. 14, 16.

6. Ibid., p. 18. Umarjan Ismailov, cited in Allworth, *Uzbek Literary Politics* (The Hague: Mouton & Co., 1964), p. 225; Abai Kunanbaev, *Izbrannoe proizvedenie* (Moscow: OGIZ. Gosizdat Khudozhestvennoi Literatury, 1945), pp. 260–61.

7. V. Ul'ianov (Lenin), Dzhugashvili-Stalin, "Ko vsiem trudiashchimsia musul'manam Rossii i Vostoka," *Gazeta Vremennago Rabochago i Krest'ianskago Pravitel'stva*, no. 17 (November 24 [7 December], 1917):1.

8. Polivanov, *Etnograficheskaia*, p. 18; "Torma isdäligi: Sartuqan," *Mushtum*, no. 11 (September 3, 1924):19.

9. Bolat Saliyif, *Orta asiya tarikhi (11–15inchi 'äsrlär)* (Samarkand-Tashkent: Ozbekistan Däwlät Näshriyati, 1926), p. 113; Polat Säliyif, *Ozbekistan tarikhi (XV–XIXinchi äsrlär)* (Samarkand-Tashkent: Ozbekistan Däwlät Näshriyati, 1929), p. 48; Miyan Buzruk, "Ozbek (tä'rikhi tekshirishlär)," *Mä'arif wä oqutghuchi*, no. 3 (Samarkand 1928):43–44.

10. I. I. Zarubin, *Spisok narodnostei turkestanskogo kraia* (Leningrad: Rossiiskaia Akademiia Nauk. Trudy Komissii po Izucheniiu Plemennogo Sostava Naseleniia Rossii i Sopredel'nykh Stran, 1925), no. 9, pp. 14–16.

11. Ziya Sä'id, *Ozbek waqtli mätbu'ati tä'rikhigä materiyallar.1870–1927* (Tashkent-Samarkand: Ozbekistan Däwlät Näshriyati, 1927), pp. 51–52, 67–70; Alexandr Bennigsen et Chantal Lemercier-Quelquejay, *La presse et le mouvement national chez les Musulmans de Russie avant 1920* (Paris: Mouton & Co., 1964), pp. 164–65, 264–65.

12. Sä'id, *Ozbek waqtli matbu'ati tä'rikhigä materiyallar*, p. 68; *S'ezdy sovetov RSFSR i avtonomnykh respublik RSFSR. Sbornik dokumentov 1917–1922 g.g.*, vol. 1 (Moscow, Gosudarstvennoe Izdatel'stvo "Iuridicheskoi Literatury," 1959), p. 243.

13. *Izvestiia TurkTsIK*, August 27, 1920, cited in Vakhabov *Formirovanie uzbekskoi sotsialisticheskoi natsii*, pp. 324–25; Georgii Safarov, *Kolonial'naia revoliutsiia: opyt Turkestana* (n.p.: Gosudarstvennoe Izdatel'stvo, 1921), pp. 105, 121–25; *Ortä Asiya kammunistik täshkilatlärining tärikhi* (Tashkent: "Ozbekistan" Näshriyati, 1969), p. 768.

14. "Iz deiatel'nosti Turkestanskogo Komissariata po Natsional'nym Delam," *Zhizn' natsional'nostei*, no. 20 (June 1, 1919):4; *S'ezdy sovetov*, pp. 390–91.

15. Yähya Ghulamawich Ghulamaw, Räshid Näbiyewich Näbiyew, and Mäwlan Ghäffarawich Wähabaw, *Ozbekistan SSR tärikhi (bir tamlik)* (Tashkent: Ozbekistan SSR Fänlär Äkädemiyäsi Näshriyati, 1958), pp. 557–58; *Ortä Asiya kammunistik täshkilatlärining tärikhi*, p. 769.

16. *S'ezdy sovetov*, pp. 653–54.

17. Ibid., pp. 466–67; Ghulamaw, Nabiyew, and Wähabaw, *Ozbekistan SSR tärikhi*, p. 558.

18. "Samarqandda tiyatir," *Ayinä*, no. 10 (December 28, 1913):234.

19. *Birinchi olkä ozbek til wä imla qoroltayining chiqarghan qararlari* (Tashkent: Turkistan Jomhoriyäning Däwlät Näshriyati, 1922), pp. 31, 34; Dzh. Baibulatov, *Chagataizm-pantiurkizm v uzbekskoi literature* (Moscow-Tashkent: OGIZ, Sredneaziatskoe Otdelenie, 1932), p. 9.

20. *Birinchi olkä*, p. 42.

21. Ibid., p. 39.

22. Pitrat (Fitrat), Cholpan, Batu, Elbek, *Ozbek yash sha'irläri* (Tashkent: Turkistan Däwlät Näshriyati, 1922), p. 76.

23. Ibid., pp. 58–60, 62–63.

24. *S'ezdy sovetov*, pp. 361–62.

25. Cholpan, "Bakuda shärq qurultayighä kelgandä," in Pitrat, Cholpan, Batu, and Elbek, *Ozbek yash sha'irläri*, p. 40; Allworth, "The Controversial Status of Soviet Asia," in Allworth, *Soviet Asia: Bibliographies: A Compilation of Social Science and Humanities Sources on the Iranian, Mongolian, and Turkic Nationalities; With an Essay on the Soviet Asia Controversy* (New York: Praeger, 1975), pp. xvi–lix; M. Sultan-Galiev, "K ob'iavleniiu Azerbaidzhanskoi sovetskoi respubliki," *Zhizn' natsional'nostei* no. 13 (70), 29 April, 1920, p. 1; Joseph V. Stalin, "Report to the 4th Conference of the Central Committee with Nationality Leaders, June 10, 1923," trans. in R. Schlesinger, ed., *The Nationalities Problem and Soviet Administration* (London: Routledge and Kegan Paul, 1956), p. 71; Fayzulla Khoja, "Bukharadägi rewalyutsiyä wä Ortä Asiyäning milliy chegärälänishi tärikhigä dair," in Khoja, *Tänlängän äsärlär*, vol. 1 (Tashkent: Ozbekistan SSR "Fän" Näshriyati, 1976), p. 299.

26. Darwish [penname for Nadhir Toraqol-uli], "Turkistanda hazirgi siyasi akhwal," *Inqilab*, no. 3 (Tashkent, April 1, 1922):1.

CHAPTER 12

1. 'Abdalrahman Sa'adi, "Chighatay wä ozbek ädäbiyati häm sha'irläri," *Inqilab*, nos. 7/8 (October–November 1922):54.

2. Ghazi Yonis (Yunus), "Qonghir tärikhchilär," *Bilim ochaghi*, nos. 2/3 (May 15, 1923):64–65, 69–70.

3. Nikolai P. Ostroumov, *Sarty. Etnograficheskie materialy. Poslovitsy i zagadki Sartov*, part 3 (Tashkent: Tipo-Litografiia Torg. Doma "F. I. G. Br. Kamenskie," 1895), pp. 5–6.

4. Ziya Sä'id, *Ozbek waqtli mätbu'ati tä'rikhiga matiriyallar 1870–1927* (Tashkent-Samarkand: Ozbekistan Däwlät Näshriyati, 1927), pp. 60–71; Edward Allworth, *Uzbek Literary Politics* (The Hague: Mouton & Co., 1964), pp. 216, 219, 229; Alexandre Bennigsen et Chantal Lemercier-Quelquejay, pp. 262–76.

5. Edward Allworth, *"Bilim ochaghi* 'The Source of Knowledge,' a Nationalistic Periodical from the Turkistan Autonomous Soviet Socialist Republic," *Central Asiatic Journal* 10, no. 1 (March 1965):62.

6. 'Usmankhan, *Turkistan* (September 11, 1922), cited in Ziya Sä'id, pp. 94–95, 96–97.

7. Zähriddin A'lam, *Turkistan* (September 11, 1922), cited in Ziya Sä'id, p. 95.

8. *Ozbekistan SSR tärikhi*, vol. 2 (Tashkent: Ozbekistan SSR Fänlär Äkädemiyäsi Näshriyati, 1958), pp. 228, 231.

9. [Archive] Sergo Ordzhonikidze (to a conference of BPCR leaders), IML TsPA, f. Sredazbiuro TSK VKP(b), d. 31, 1. 40, cited in Mavlon G. Vakhabov, *Formirovanie uzbekskoi sotsialisticheskoi natsii* (Tashkent: Gosudarstvennoe Izdatel'stvo Uzbekskoi SSR, 1961), p. 378.

10. Ibragim M. Muminov, *Istoriia Khorezma s drevneishikh vremen do nashikh dnei* (Tashkent: Izdatel'stvo "FAN" Uzbekskoi SSR, 1976), pp. 171–72; *Bukhara akhbarati* (November 2, 1922), cited in Vakhabov, *Formirovanie uzbekskoi*, p. 380.

11. Fäyzullä Khojäyew, "Bukharadägi rewalyutsiyä wä Ortä Asiyäning milliy-territariäl chegärälänishi tärikhigä dair," in *Tänlängän äsärlär*, vol. 1 (Tashkent: Ozbekistan SSR "FÄN" Näshriyati, 1976), p. 287.

12. A. Zeki Velidi Togan, *Bugünkü Türkili (Turkistan) ve yakin Tarihi*, vol. 1 (Istanbul: Arkadash Ibrahim Horoz ve Güven Basimevleri, 1942–1947), p. 424.

13. Akmal Ikramov, *Izbrannye trudy*, vol. 1 (Tashkent: Izdatel'stvo "Uzbekistan," 1972), pp. 20–21; Mustapha Chokaiev, "Turkestan and the Soviet Regime," *Journal of the Royal Central Asian Society*, no. 18 (1930):414, cited in Alexander G. Park *Bolshevism in Turkestan 1917–1927* (New York: Columbia University Press, 1957), p. 92; Bennigsen et Lemercier-Quelquejay, *Les Mouvements Nationaux chez les Musulmans de Russie: 1. Le "Sultangalievisme" au Tatarstan* (Paris and The Hague: Mouton & Co., 1960), pp. 239–50.

14. Khojäyew (1976), *Tänlängän äsärlär*, pp. 291–92.

15. [Archive] MLI MPA, 62-f., 1-r., 99-d; RKP(b) Märkäziy Kamiteti Ortä Asiya byurasining mäteriälläri; MLI MPA, 62-f., 1-r., 99-d., 26 wäräq, cited in *Ortä Asiya kammunistik täshkilatlärining tärikhi* (Tashkent: "Ozbekistan" Näshriyati, 1969), pp. 777–78.

16. "Färghanä khäbärläri," *Mushtum*, no. 6 (July 25, 1924):11.

17. *Ortä Asiya*, pp. 785–86; Ibragim M. Muminov, ed., *Istoriia uzbekskoi SSR s dreveishikh vremen do nashikh dnei* (Tashkent: Izdatel'stvo "FAN" UzSSR, 1974), pp. 335–36.

18. [Archive] MLI Ozbekistan filiälining pärtiyä ärkhiwi, 60–f., 1-r., 3329-d., 91 wäräq; 3356-d., 26–27-wäräqlär, *Pravda* May 24, 1924, cited in *Ortä Asiya*, p. 795.

19. S. V. Bakhrushin, V. Ia. Nepomnin, and V. A. Shishkin, eds., *Istoriia narodov Uzbekistana*, vol. 2 (Tashkent: Izdatel'stvo AN UzSSR, 1947), p. 131.

20. *Vserossiiskii tsentral'nyi ispolnitel'nyi Komitet XI Sozyva: vtoraia sessia* (Moscow, 1924), pp. 89, 317–19; Park, *Bolshevism in Turkestan*, pp. 94–98.

21. M. A. Nemchenko, *Natsional'noe razmezhevanie srednei Azii* (Moscow: Izdanie Litizdata NKID, 1925), p. 15.

22. [Archive] "(Rezoliutsiia)," TsGA UzSSR, f. 47, op. 1, d. 479-a, 11. 11–12, reproduced in *S'ezdy sovetov soiuznykh i avtonomnykh sovetskikh sotsialisticheskikh respublik srednei Azii. Sbornik dokumentov, 1923–1937 g.g.*, vol. 7 (Moscow, Izdatel'stvo "Iuridicheskaia Literatura," 1965), pp. 72–73; [Archive] Khojayew, "Ozbekistanni täshkil etish mäsäläsigä dair äsasiy qaidälär," MLI MPÄ, f. 62, ap. 1, d. 151, 2-3 wäräqlär, cited in Khojayew, *Tänlängän äsärlär*, vol. 1, pp. 528, 531.

23. Khojayew, "Bukharadägi rewalyutsiyä wä Ortä Asiyaning milliy chegärälänishi tärikhigä dair," *Tänlängän äsärlär*, p. 299.

24. Khojayew, "Birdän-bir toghri yol," *Tänlängän äsärlär*, pp. 384, 387.

25. Khojayew, "Bukharadägi rewalyutsiyä," pp. 292–93.

26. Nemchenko, *Natsional'noe*, p. 4.

27. 'Shaqashuldor', "Milliyät mäs'äläsining chigilini yishalmay qaldukku!," *Mushtum*, no. 22 (December 19, 1924):3.

28. *Mushtum*, no. 9 (September 8, 1924):2; *Mushtum*, no. 11 (October 3, 1924):8; *Mushtum*, no. 17 (November ?, 1924):1.

29. "Uzbekskaia SSR," in *Vsesoiuznaia perepis' naseleniia 1926 goda*, vol. 15 (Moscow: Izdanie TsSU SSSR, 1926), pp. 8–9; I. V. Zakharova, "Material'naia kul'tura Uigurov Sovetskogo Soiuza," in *Sredneaziatskii etnograficheskii sbornik* (Moscow: Izdatel'stvo Akademii Nauk SSSR, 1959), p. 216.

30. Habib T. Tursunov, *Ozbekistan Sawet Satsiälistik Respublikäsining bärpa etilishi* (Tashkent: Ozbekistan SSR Fänlär Äkädemiyäsi Näshriyati, 1958), pp. 144–45; "Postanovlenie XII Vserossiiskogo S'ezda Sovetov ob utverzhdenii razdeleniia Turkestanskoi Avtonomnoi Sovetskoi Sotsialisticheskoi Respublikoi," *Izvestiia TsIK SSSR i VTsIK*, no. 118 (May 26, 1925), cited in *KPSS i sovetskoe pravitel'stvo ob Uzbekistane. Sbornik dokumentov (1925–1970)* (Tashkent: "Ozbekistan," 1972), pp. 13–14.

31. *Ortä Asiya kammunistik täshkilatlärining tärikhi*, pp. 778–79, 801–2; Muminov, ed., *Istoriia uzbekskoi SSR*, p. 335.

32. "Ozbekistan Ijtima'i Shoralär Jumhoriyätining tuzilishi munasäbäti bilän yasaladorghan bäyrämning kunini bilgiläsh häqida," *Oz.I.Sh.J. Ishchi wä Dehqan Hukumätining qanun wä boyroqlarining yighindisi*, no. 53 (December 25, 1925), Article 500, pp. 1896–97; Vladimir Tiurikov, comp., *Letopis' poluveka. Khronika kul'turnoi zhizni Uzbekistana (1924–1974)* (Tashkent: Izdatel'stvo Literatury i Iskusstva imeni Gafura Guliama, 1975), p. 7; P. G. Pod'iachikh, *Naselenie SSSR* (Moscow: Gosudarstvennoe Izdatel'stvo, 1961), pp. 162–82.

33. E. Zel'kina, "Zemel'naia reforma v srednei Azii," *Revoliutsionnyi Vostok*, no. 3

(1927):134, cited in Park, *Bolshevism in Turkestan*, p. 94; Ä. Näbikhojayew and M. Jälalaw, "Tughilish: Ozbekistan Kampärtiyäsi birinchi s'ezdining 60 yilligigä," *Ozbekistan ädäbiyati wä sän'ati*, no. 6 (February 8, 1985):1.

34. Sadriddin Ayniy, *Namunai adabiyoti tajik. 300–1200 hijri* (Samarkand: Chopkhanai Nashriyoti Markazii Khalqii Ittikhadi Jamoli, 1926); Sadriddin Ayni, *Ustod Rudaki. Epokha, zhizn', tvorchestvo* (Moscow: Izdatel'stvo Vostochnoi Literatury, 1959), p. 109.

35. "Ozbekistan Qoshma Ijtima'i Shorlar Jomhoriyati inqilab qomitäsining khitabnamäsi," *Ozbekistan Ijtima'i Shoralar Jomhoriyati Ishchi wä Dehqan Hukumatining Qanun wä Boyroqlarining Yinghindisi*, no. 1 (January 8, 1925):6–7; *Gazety SSSR 1917–1960, Bibliograficheskii spravochnik*, vol. 1 (Moscow: "Kniga," 1970), p. 198.

36. "Turkistan" and "Turkistan Härbiy Akrugi," in *Ozbekistan sawet entsiklapediyäsi*, vol 11 (Tashkent: Ozbekistan Sawet Entsiklapediyäsi, 1978), pp. 367, 381–82.

37. Miyan Buzuk (*sic*, Buzruk), "Ozbek (Tä'rikhi tekshirishlär)," *Mä'arif wä oqutghuchi*, no. 3 (1928):43.

38. Fiträt, *Bedil (bir mäjlisdä)* (Moscow: Millät Ishläri Kämisärligi qashinda "Märkäziy Shärq Näshriyati," 1923 [1924 on cover], p. 9f.

CHAPTER 13

1. "Ozbekistan Ijtima'i Shora Jomhoriyäti hokomätining qärarläri," *Ozbekistan Ijtima'i Shoralar Jomhoriyäti Ishchi wä Dihqan Hokomäti qanon wä boyroqlarining yighindisi*, no. 16 (May 18, 1925), articles 172–73, pp. 551–54; Edgar Knobloch, *Beyond the Oxus: Archeology, Art and Architecture of Central Asia* (London: Ernest Benn, 1972), pp. 145–71.

2. *Ozbekstan Ijtima'i Shoralar Jomhoriyäti Ishchi wä dihqan hokomätining qanon wä boyroqlarining yighindisi*, no. 60 (December 31, 1925):529; Alexander G. Park, *Bolshevism in Turkestan, 1917–1927* (New York: Columbia University Press, 1957), pp. 214–21.

3. V. V. Stasov, "Tron khivinskikh khanov," *Viestnik iziashchnykh iskusstv* 4 (1886):405–9.

4. Stasov, "Tron Khivinskikh Khanov, pp. 409–10; *Mélanges asiatiques* 7 (1876):394; V. V. Struve, A. K. Borovkov, et al., eds., *Materialy po istorii Turkmen i Turkmenii* (Moscow-Leningrad: Izdatel'stvo Akademii Nauk SSSR, 1938), p. 27.

5. Eugene Schuyler, *Turkistan: Notes of a Journey in Russian Turkistan, Khokand, Bukhara, and Kuldja*, vol. 1 (New York: Scribner, Armstrong, 1877), pp. 71–72; Mir-Salikh Bekchurin, "Opisanie mecheti Azreta nakhodiashchiisia v gorodie Turkestanie," *Voennyi sbornik*, no. 8 (August 1866):210–17; Naghïm Bek Nurmukhammedov, *Qoja Akhmed Yässaui mavzoleii* (Alma Ata: "Öner" Baspasï, 1980), pp. 32–37.

6. Andrew D. Kalmykow, *Memoirs of a Russian Diplomat: Outposts of Empire, 1893–1917* (New Haven, Conn.: Yale University Press, 1971), p. 200; Aleksandr A. Semenov, "Nadpis' na mogil'noi plite bukharskogo Emira Shakh Murad Ma'suma

1200–1215/1785–1800 g.g.," in *Epigrafika Vostoka*, vol. 7 (Moscow-Leningrad: Izdatel'stvo Akademii Nauk SSSR, 1953), p. 42, n. 3; A. Iu. Iakubovskii, "Timur (opyt kratkoi kharakteristiki)," *Voprosy istorii*, nos. 8/9 (1946):63; A. Shebunin, "Kuficheskii Koran Imp. SPb. Publichnoi biblioteki," in *Zapiski Vostochnago Otdieleniia Imperatorskago Arkheologicheskago Obshchestva*, vol. 6 for 1891 (Saint Petersburg: Tipografiia Imperatorskoi Akademii Nauk, 1892), pp. 69–74, 122; Joseph Castagné, "Le bolchevisme et l'Islam. Restitution aux musulmans du coran d'Osman," *Revue du Monde musulman*, no. 51 (1922):10; Aleksandr Belenitsky, *Central Asia*, Archaeologia Mundi, trans. James Hogarth (Cleveland, Oh.: World Publishing; Geneva: Nagel Publishers, 1968), pp. 98–99; T. I. Zeimal', *Pamiatniki Kul'tury i Iskusstva Uzbekistana v Gostudarstvennom Ermitazhe* (Tashkent: Izdatel'stvo Literatury i Iskusstva im. Gafura Guliama, 1987) 24 specimens in separate plates.

7. B. A. Antonenko, ed., *Istoriia tadzhikskogo naroda*, vol. 3, book 1 (Moscow: Izdatel'stvo "Nauka," 1964), p. 143; *Ozbekistan ijima'i shoralar jomhoriyäti ishchi wä dihqan hokomätining qanon wä boyroqlarining yighindisi*, no. 25 (July 4, 1925), article 282, pp. 959–60; W. Trembicky, "Flags of Non-Russian Peoples under Soviet Rule," *The Flag Bulletin*, no. 3 (Summer 1969);119–24.

8. Gh. R. Rashidov, "Samarkand—pervaia stolitsa uzbekskoi SSR," *Obshchestvennye nauki v Uzbekistane*, no. 9 (1970):50–55.

9. *Ozbekstan ijima'i shoralar jomhoriyäti ishchi wä dihqan hokomätining qanon wä boyroqlarining yighindisi*, nos. 35/36 (December 16, 1926):673–74, 679–84; *Materialy po raionirovaniiu Uzbekistana. Kratkaia kharakteristika proektiruemykh okrugov i raionov*, vol. 1 (Samarkand: Izdanie TsKR Uz., 1926), pp. 8, 63, 129–39, 148, 155–56, 175, and maps I–XII.

10. "Ozbekstan ijima'i shoralar jomhoriyäti inqilabiy kämitätining mihnätkäshlärgä khitabnamäsi," *Ozbekstan ijima'i shoralar jomhoriyäti inqilab kämititining qärarläri*, no. 1 (January 8, 1925):1–2; "Ishlärni ozbek tilidä yorgozish häm ozbekstan jomhoriyätining inqilabi kämiti khozoridä märkazi yirläshdirish häy'ati wä mähällärdä mozafat yirläshdirish häy'atlari tozolish toghrisida; 31inchi dikabr 1924-inchi yil San 48," *Ozbekstan ijima'i shoralar jomhoriyäti ishchi wä dehqan hokomätining qanon wä boyroqlarining yighindisi*, no. 1, article 22 (January 8, 1925):59–64; Habib T. Tursunov, *Ozbekistan Sawet Satsiälistik Respublikäsining bärpa etilishi* (Tashkent: Ozbekistan SSR Fänlär Äkademiyäsi Näshriyati, 1958), p. 177.

11. P. Rysakov, "Praktika shovinizma i mestnogo natsionalizma," *Revoliutsiia i natsional'nosti*, nos. 8/9 (December 1930):29, 31.

12. Rahim Inaghamof, *Ozbek ziyalilari* (Tashkent: Tipolitografiia no. 1, 1926), p. 30; Mannan Ramiz, "Ziyalilar qurultayining gäldägi wäzifäläri," *Mä'arif wä ogutghuchi*, no. 6 (June 1927):3; I. Stalin, "Politika sovetskoi vlasti po natsional'nomu voprosu v Rossii," *Zhizn' natsional'nostei*, October 10, 1920, p. 1.

13. *Ozbekistan kammonist (balshäwik)lär firqäsining IInchi qurultayi. (1925inchi yil 22–30 noyäbr). Qurultayining hisabi* (Samarkand: Ozb. Kam. (Balshäwiklär) Firqäsi Märkäzqomining Näshri; Tashkent: Ozbekistan Däwlät Näshriyatining Birinchi Basmakhanäsi, 1926), p. 467.

14. *Ozbekstan ijtima'i shoralar jomhoriyäti ishchi wä dihqan hokomätining qanon wä boyroqlarining yighindisi*, no. 25 (October 30, 1926), Article 117, pp. 458–62.

15. "Ozglawlit hozorida ripirtoar ostidän näzarät qiladirghan bash qomitä toghrisidaghi nizamlarni 'ämälga qoyish häqidä," *Ozbekstan ijtima'i shoralar jomhoriyäti ishchi oä dihqan hokomätining qanon oä boyroqlarining yighindisi*, no. 9 (March 7, 1927), article 45, pp. 199–202.

16. "Färghänä ziyalilar qoroltayi nimä dedi?," *Mä'arif wä oqutghuchi*, no. 6 (June 1927):54–55.

17. Sh. Rahimiy, "Ikkinchi shora ziyalilar qurultayi aldida," *Mä'arif wä oqutghuchi*, nos. 9/10 (1927):9; [Mannan Ramiz], "Ortaq ramizning 'ozbekstanda mä'arif yolida qilinadighan näwbätdägi wä'zifälär' degän mä'rozäsi boyincha qurultay tamanidan chiqarilghan qararlar," *Mä'arif wä oqutghuchi*, no. 12 (December 1927):89; Alexander G. Park, *Bolshevism in Turkestan, 1917–1927* (New York: Columbia University Press, 1927), pp. 244–45; *Plan tret'ego goda piatiletki respublik Srednei Azii. (Kontrol'nye tsifry na 1931 god)* (Tashkent: Sredne-Aziatskii Gosplan, 1931), p. 134; *Protokoly i stenograficheskie otchety s'ezdov i konferentsii kommunisticheskoi partii sovetskogo soiuza. Piatnadtsatyi s'ezd VKP(b). Dekabr' 1927 goda. Stenograficheskii otchet*, vol. 1 (Moscow: Gosizdat Politicheskoi Literatury, 1961), p. 168.

18. Aleksandr A. Semenov, "Persidskaia novella o Mir-Ali-Shire 'Nevai'," *Biulleten' SAGU*, no. 13 (1926):177–86; *Mir-Ali-Shir. Sbornik k piatisotletiiu so dnia rozhdeniia* (Leningrad: Izdatel'stvo Akademii Nauk SSSR, 1928), pp. 167–74.

19. S. D. Miliband, *Biobibliograficheskii slovar' sovetskikh Vostokovedov* (Moscow: Glavnaia Redaktsiia Vostochnoi Literatury, 1975), pp. 493–94, 601.

20. Fiträt, "Nawayining fars sha'irlighi häm uning fars diwani toghrisida," *Mä'arif wä oqutghuchi* no. 12 (24) (1926) [pp. unknown]; *Mir-Ali-Shir*, pp. 171–72.

21. Ibid., p. 1.

22. Fiträt, *Eng eski turk ädäbiyati nämunäläri* (Samarkand: Ozbekistan Däwlät Näshriyatining Näshri, Ozbekistan Mätbä'ä Ishläri Tristining Birinchi Mätbä'äsi, 1927); Fiträt, *Ozbek ädäbiyati nämunäläri* (Tashkent-Samarkand, Oznäshr, 1928); Edward Allworth, *Uzbek Literary Politics* (The Hague: Mouton, 1964), p. 53.

23. Rakhmat Madzhidi, "Literatura Uzbekistana," in *Literatura Uzbekistana* (Moscow: Gosudarstvennoe Izdatel'stvo "Khudozhestvennaia Literatura," 1935), p. 22; Allworth, *Uzbek Literary Politics*, pp. 158–62.

24. R. R. Fitrat, Prof. Instituta Iazyka i Literatury Uzbekistana, B. S. Sergeev, Nauchnyi Sotrudnik Gosudarstvennoi Publichnoi Biblioteki Uzbekistana, *Kaziiskie dokumenty XVI veka. Tekst perevod, ukazatel' vstrechaiushchikhsia iuridicheskikh terminov i premechaniia* (Tashkent: Izdatel'stvo Komiteta Nauk UzSSR, 1937), pp. 48–49, 78; Allworth, Chapter 1, *Central Asia, a Century of Russian Rule* (New York: Columbia University Press, 1967), pp. 30–35.

25. *Report of Court Proceedings in the Case of the Anti-Soviet "Bloc of Rights and Trotskyites" Heard Before the Military Collegium of the Supreme Court of the U.S.S.R. Moscow, March 2–13, 1938* (Moscow: People's Commissariat of Justice of the U.S.S.R., 1938), pp. 792, 799; Allworth, *Uzbek Literary Politics*, pp. 78–80.

26. *Rodonachal'nik uzbekskoi literatury. Sbornik statei ob Alishere Navoi* (Tashkent: Izdatel'stvo Uzbekistanskogo Filiala Akademii Nauk SSSR, 1940), pp. 5–10.

27. Allworth, *Uzbek Literary Politics*, pp. 81–86.

28. Käykawus, *Qabusnamä* (Tashkent: "Oqituwchi" Näshriyati, 1968), pp. 11, 27.

29. Boris A. Litvinskii and N. M. Akramov, *Aleksandr A. Semenov* (Moscow: "Nauka," 1971), pp. 159, 163–65; Aleksandr A. Semenov, "Mir Ali Shir Nevai," *Literatura i iskusstvo Uzbekistana*, no. 2 (1938):124–38; Abdurrakhman Saadi, "Navoi kak literaturoved i kritik," *Literatura i iskusstvo Uzbekistana*, no. 2 (?) (1938):88, 96; Satti Khusainov, "Velichaishii uzbekskii poet," *Pravda Vostoka*, September 15, 1938, p. 3.

CHAPTER 14

1. S. P. Tolstov, *Drevniaia kul'tura Uzbekistana* (Tashkent: Izdatel'stvo UzFAR, 1943), pp. 4–5.

2. A. Iu. Iakubovskii, *K voprosu ob etnogeneze uzbekskogo naroda* (Tashkent: Izdatel'stvo UzFAN, 1941), pp. 3–12, 18.

3. Iakubovskii, *K voprosu ob etnogeneze uzbekskogo naroda*, p. 18.

4. Karl H. Menges, "People, Languages and Migrations," in Edward Allworth, ed., *Central Asia, a Century of Russian Rule* (New York: Columbia University Press, 1967), map, p. 71, pp. 377–78; Allworth, *Nationalities of the Soviet East: Publications and Writing Systems* (New York: Columbia University Press, 1971), p. 377.

5. Tolstov, *Drevniaia kul'tura Uzbekistana*, p. 6.

6. Aleksandr A. Semenov, "Obrazovanie uzbekskogo gosudarstva i zavoevanie Uzbekami Maverannakhra," in *Istoriia narodov Uzbekistana*, vol. 2, ed. S. V. Bakhrushin, V. Ia. Nepomnin, and V. A. Shishkin (Tashkent: Izdatel'stvo Akademii Nauk Uzbekskoi SSR, 1947), pp. 22–23.

7. S. E. Malov, "Mir Alisher Navoi v istorii tiurkskikh literatur i iazykov srednei i tsentral'noi Azii," *Izvestiia Akademii Nauk SSSR, Otdelenie literatury i iazyka* vol. 6, book 6 (1947), p. 475.

8. Iakubovskii, *K voprosu ob etnogeneze uzbekskogo naroda*, p. 19.

9. Kamilla V. Trever, Iakubovskii, M. E. Voronets, *Istoriia narodov Uzbekistana*, Iakubovskii, vol. 1, "Predislovie" (Tashkent: Izdatel'stvo AN UzSSR, 1950), p. 8.

10. "Aleksandre Iur'evich Iakubovskii," in B. V. Lunin, comp., *Biobibliograficheskie ocherki o deiateliakh obshchestvennykh nauk Uzbekistana*, vol. 2 (Tashkent: Izdatel'stvo "FAN" Uzbekskoi SSR, 1977), pp. 345–46.

11. Iakubovskii, *K voprosu ob etnogeneze uzbekskogo naroda* (Tashkent: Izdatel'stvo "FAN" UzSSR, 1976).

12. A. Iu. Iakubovskii, "Timur (opyt kratkoi kharakteristiki)," *Voprosy istorii*, nos. 8/9 (1946), p. 71; René Grousset, *The Empire of the Steppes: A History of Central Asia*,

trans. Naomi Walford (New Brunswick, N.J.: Rutgers University Press, 1970), pp. 264–65, 470–71.

13. Zeki Velidi Togan, *Presentation Volume to Professor M. Shafi* (Lahore: 1955), pp. 105–14, cited by V. Minorsky in the foreword to V. V. Barthold, *Four Studies on the History of Central Asia*, vol. 2 (Leiden: E. J. Brill, 1958), pp. viii, 14.

14. Boriway A. Akhmedov, *Gosudarstvo kochevykh Uzbekov* (Moscow: Izdatel'stvo "Nauka," 1965), pp. 15, 38–39; S. V. Bakhrushin et al., eds., *Istoriia narodov Uzbekistana*, vol. 2 (Tashkent: Izdatel'stvo AN UzSSR, 1947), pp. 21–71; S. P. Tolstov, R. N. Nabiev, Ia. G. Gulamov, and V. A. Shishkin, eds., *Istoriia Uzbekskoi SSR*, vol. 1 (Tashkent: Izdatel'stvo Akademii Nauk Uzbekskoi SSR, 1955).

15. A. I. Niiazov, "X plenum TsK KP(b) Uzbekistana. Doklad sekretaria TsK KP(b) Uzbekistana tov. A. I. Niiazova o sostoianii i merakh uluchsheniia ideologicheskoi raboty v respublike," *Pravda Vostoka*, February 24, 1952, pp. 2–4.

16. Ibragim Muminov, *Rol' i mesto Amira Timura v istorii srednei Azii v svete dannykh pis'mennykh istochnikov* (Tashkent: Izdatel'stvo "FAN" UzSSR, 1968) (5,000 copies published in the Russian ed.).

17. A. P. Novosel'tsev, "Ob istoricheskoi otsenke Timura," *Voprosy istorii*, no. 2 (February 1973):3–4, 17–19.

18. Raim Farhadi, "Tamerlan," trans. Edward Allworth with Eugenia Martin, *Granitsy serdtsa. Stikhi raznykh let* (Tashkent: Izdatel'stvo Literatury i Iskusstva imeni Gafura Guliama, 1976), pp. 113–14.

CHAPTER 15

1. *I s'ezd intelligentsii Uzbekistana. 11–13 oktiabria 1956 goda. Stenograficheskii otchet* (Tashkent: Gosudarstvennoe Izdatel'stvo Uzbekskoi SSR, 1957), pp. 3–7, 133.

2. "S'ezd intelligentsii Uzbekistana," *Pravda Vostoka*, October 13, 1956, pp. 1–4.

3. *Ozbekistan SSR tärikhi* (Tashkent: Ozbekistan SSR Fänlär Äkädemiyäsi Näshriyati, 1957), pp. 292–94; Mavlian G. Vakhabov, *Formirovaniia uzbekskoi sotsialisticheskoi natsii* (Tashkent: Gosudarstvennoe Izdatel'stvo Uzbekskoi SSR, 1961), pp. 207–13; "Jädidizm" [notice the Soviet ending on the word], *Ozbekistan sawet entsiklapediyäsi*, vol. 4 (Tashkent: Ozbek Sawet Entsiklapediyäsi. Bash Redäktsiyäsi, 1973), pp. 278–79.

4. *I s'ezd intelligentsii Uzbekistana*, pp. 48–53, 55–57; *Ozbekistan SSR tärikhi* (Tashkent: Ozbekistan SSR Fänlär Äkädemiyäsi Näshriyati, 1958), p. 511.

5. "Doklad mandatnoi komissii s'ezda," *Pravda Vostoka*, October 14, 1956, p. 3; *I s'ezd intelligentsii Uzbekistana*, p. 132; *Itogi vsesoiuznoi perepisi naseleniia 1959 goda. SSSR (svodnyi tom)* (Moscow: Gosstatizdat TsSU SSSR, 1962), p. 206; *Itogi vsesoiuznoi perepisi naseleniia 1959 goda. Uzbekskaia SSR* (Moscow: Gosstatizdat. UsSU SSSR, 1962), p. 126; N. Lenin (V. Ul'ianov), "Zadachi revoliutsionnoi molodezhi," *Sobranie sochineniia*, vol. 4, "Iskra" 1900–1903 g.g. (Moscow-Peterburg: Gosudarstvennoe Izdatel'stvo, 1923), pp. 145–46.

6. "S'ezd intelligentsii Uzbekistana. Prodolzhenie doklada tov. N. A. Mukhitdinova," *Pravda Vostoka*, October 13, 1956, p. 3.

7. "'Zadachi intelligentsii sovetskogo Uzbekistana v osushchestvlenii istoricheskikh reshenii XXI s"ezda KPSS'. Doklad pervogo sekretaria TsK KP Uzbekistana tov. Sh. R. Rashidova na II s"ezde intelligentsii respubliki 11 dekabria 1959 goda," *Pravda Vostoka*, December 12, 1959, p. 4; *Itogi vsesoiuznoi perepisi naseleniia 1959 goda. Uzbekskaia SSR* (Moscow: Gosstatizdat. TsSU SSSR, 1962), p. 138.

8. *II s'ezd intelligentsii Uzbekistana. 11–12 dekabria 1959 goda. Stenograficheskii otchet* (Tashkent: Gosudarstvennoe Izdatel'stvo Uzbekskoi SSR, 1960), pp. 12–13, 25–28, 36–37, 45.

9. "Iz doklada G. S. Sultanova—predsedatel' mandatnoi Komissii vtorogo s"ezda intelligentsii Uzbekistana," *Pravda Vostoka*, December 13, 1959, p. 3; *II s'ezd intelligentsii*, pp. 46, 50–52, 108–9.

10. R. Kh. Aminova, et al., eds., *Istoriia uzbekskoi SSR. S drevneishikh vremen do serediny XIX veka*, vol. 1 (Tashkent: Izdatel'stvo "Fän" Uzbekskoi SSR, 1967), p. 502.

11. Ibid., p. 501.

12. *Ozbekistan Sawet Satsiälistik Respublikäsining mä'muriy-territariäl bolinishi. 1975 yil 1 äprelgächä bolgän mä'lumat* (Tashkent: "Ozbekistan" Näshriyati, 1975), pp. 155–56.

13. *Ozbekistan Sawet Satsiälistik Republikäsining mä'muriy-territariäl bolinishi*, pp. 8, 150–75; *Ozbekistan Sawet Satsiälistik Respublikäsnining mä'muriy-territariäl' bolinishi. 1954 yilning 1 iuuligächä bolgän mä'lumat* (Tashkent: Ozbekistan SSR Aliy Sawetining Prezidiyumi. Infarmätsian-Stätistikä Bolimi, 1954), pp. 10–13.

14. Izzät Sultan, "Iman," *Äsärlär* (Tashkent: Ghäfur Ghulam namidägi Ädäbiyat wä Sän'ät Näshriyati, 1971), pp. 155–208; *Ozbek sawet ädäbiyat tärikhi*, vol. 3, book 2 (Tashkent: Ozbekistan SSR "Fän" Näshriyati, 1972), pp. 331–32; Uyghun, "Dostlär (Orinsiz shubhä)," *Äsärlär*, vol. 5 (Tashkent: Ghäfur Ghulam namidägi Ädäbiyat wä Sän'ät Näshriyati, 1978), pp. 167–222.

15. "Dostlär," pp. 170, 182–83, 199; Aleksandr I. Solzhenitsyn, *The Gulag Archipelago, 1918–1956: An Experiment in Literary Investigation*, vol. 3, books 5–7 (New York: Harper & Row, 1979), pp. 442–43.

16. "Dostlär," pp. 221–22.

17. Yakov Mosheev, "My Recollections of Now Raion: The Status of a Peripheral Theatre in Soviet Tajikistan," *Central Asian Survey*, nos. 2/3 (November 1982–January 1983):121.

18. *Kommunisticheskaia partiia Uzbekistana v tsifrakh (1924–64)* (Tashkent: Izdatel'stvo "Uzbekistana," 1964), p. 68; "Naselenie," *Bol'shaia sovetskaia entsiklopediia. Soiuz Sovetskikh Sotsialistichekikh Respublik*, summary volume (Moscow: Gosudarstvennyi Nauchnyi Institut "Sovetskaia Entsiklopediia," 1947), columns 60, 62.

19. "S'ezd mändät kamissiyäsining daklädini qabul qilädi," *Qizil Ozbekistan*, January 27, 1962, p. 3; "Goremie serdets, silu talanta bogatstvo znanii—velikomu delu kommunizma. II s'ezd intelligentsii Uzbekistana," *Pravda Vostoka*, January 26, 1962,

p. 1; "Ozbekistan intelligentsiyä III s'ezdi. Ortaq Sh. R. Räshidaw daklädi yuzäsidän muzakärälär," *Qizil Ozbekistan*, January 27, 1962, p. 2; "Ozbekistan intelligentsiyä III s'ezdi. Ortaq Sh. R. Räshidaw daklädi yuzäsidän muzakärälär," *Qizil Ozbekistan* (January 28, 1962), pp. 2–3.

20. Akmal Ikramov, *Izbrannye trudy*, vol. 1 (Tashkent: Izdatel'stvo "Uzbekistan," 1972), p. 22; ibid., vol. 2 (1973), pp. 29, 566; "Plenum TsK KP Uzbekistana," *Pravda*, March 15, 1959, p. 3; Grey Hodnett and Val Ogareff, *Leaders of the Soviet Republics. 1955–1972: A Guide to Posts and Occupants* (Canberra: Australian National University, 1973), p. 381; *Sawet Ozbekistanining yazuwchiläri* (Tashkent: OzSSR Däwlät Bädiiy Ädäbiyat Näshriyati, 1959), p. 110.

21. *Sawet Ozbekistanining yazuwchiläri*, pp. 110–11; Shäraf Räshidaw, *Käshmir goshighi. Qissä* (Tashkent: Ghäfur Ghulam namidägi Ädäbiyat wä Sän'ät Näshriyati, 1970), p. 39; Erkin Nasyrov, Raim Farkhadi, and Petr Filippov, *Pisateli sovetskogo Uzbekistana* (Tashkent: Izdatel'stvo Literatury i Iskusstva imeni Gafura Guliama, 1977), pp. 157–58; *Current Soviet Leaders*, vol. 3, no. 1 (Oakville, Ontario, Canada: Mosaic Press, 1976), p. 6; Sharaf Rashidov, *The Banner of Friendship* trans. (Moscow: Progress Publishers, 1969), 214 pp.; Rashidov, *Sobranie sochinenii v piati tomakh*, vol. 4, "Literaturno-kriticheskie stat'i, Vospominaniia. Zrelost' kinopovest,'" trans. (Moscow: "Khudozhestvennaia Literatura," 1980).

22. John Soper, "Shake-up in the Uzbek Literary Elite," *Central Asian Survey*, no. 4 (April 1983): 59, 73, 77.

23. Ergash R. Rustamov, *Uzbekskaia poeziia v pervoi polovine XV veka* (Moscow: Izdatel'stvo Vostochnoi Literatury, 1963), pp. 69–70; Wahid Y. Zahidaw, "Näwaiyning yängi tapilgän äsäri," *Shärq yulduzi*, no. 6 (1957): 127–33.

24. E. E. Bertel's, *Navoi. Opyt tvorcheskoi biografii* (Moscow-Leningrad: Izdatel'stvo Akademii Nauk SSSR, 1948), p. 102.

25. Mutal M. Ermatov, *Etnogenez i formirovanie uzbekskogo naroda* (Tashkent: Izdatel'stvo "Uzbekistan," 1968), pp. 14–15; Aleksandr Iu. Iakubovskii, "Predislovie," in K. V. Trever, A. Iu. Iakubovskii, and M. E. Voronets, eds., *Istoriia narodov Uzbekistana. S drevneishikh vremen do nachala XVI veka*, vol. 1 (Tashkent: Izdatel'stvo Akademii Nauk Uzbekskoi SSR, 1950), p. 8.

CHAPTER 16

1. Edward Allworth, *Central Asian Publishing and the Rise of Nationalism* (New York: New York Public Library, 1965), pp. 10–16.

2. Ian Matley, "Industrialization," in Allworth, ed., *Central Asia: A Century of Russian Rule* (New York: Columbia University Press, 1967), p. 327.

3. *Pechat' SSSR v 1979 godu. Statisticheskii sbornik* (Moscow: "Statistika," 1980), p. 102; *Pechat' SSSR v 1980 godu*, p. 136; *Pechat' SSSR v 1970 godu*, p. 89.

4. "Vsesoiuznaia perepis' naseleniia," *Vestnik statistiki*, no. 9 (1980):61; *Pechat' SSSR v 1979 godu*; *Pechat' SSR v 1980 godu*; *Pechat' SSR v 1981 godu. Statisticheskii*

sbornik (Moscow: "Statistika," 1980), pp. 171–77 ("Finansy i Statistika," 1981), pp. 219–25; 1982, pp. 216–22.

5. *Pechat' SSSR v 1982 godu*, pp. 216–22; *Pechat' SSSR v 1984 godu*, pp. 216–22.

6. *Pechat' SSSR v 1980 godu*, p. 63; *Pechat' SSSR v 1981 godu*, p. 98; *Pechat' SSSR v 1982 godu*, p. 98; *Pechat' SSSR v 1983 godu*, p. 98; *Pechat' SSSR v 1984 godu*, p. 98.

7. *Pechat' SSSR v 1979 godu*, pp. 22–23; *Pechat' SSSR v 1980 godu*, pp. 24–25; *Pechat' SSSR v 1982 godu*, pp. 24–26; *Pechat' SSSR v 1983 godu*, pp. 24–25; *Pechat' SSSR v 1984 godu*, pp. 24–25.

8. *Pechat' SSSR v 1982 godu*, pp. 99–100; *Pechat' SSSR v 1983 godu*, pp. 99–100; *Pechat' SSSR v 1984 godu*, pp. 99–100.

9. *Naselenie SSSR. Po dannym vsesoiuznoi perepisi naseleniia 1979 goda* (Moscow: Izdatel'stvo Politicheskoi Literatury, 1980), p. 23.

10. "Democratic Panslavism" (1849), in Paul W. Blackstock and Bert F. Hoselitz, eds., *Karl Marx and Friedrich Engels, The Russian Menace to Europe. A Collection of Articles, Speeches, Letters and News Dispatches*, (Glencoe, Illinois: Free Press, 1953), p. 70.

11. *Program of the Communist Party of the Soviet Union* (New York: International Publishers, 1963), p. 122; Richard T. DeGeorge, *Soviet Ethics and Morality* (Ann Arbor: University of Michigan Press, 1969), pp. 2, 89, 10.

12. "Programma KPSU," *Vodnyi transport*, March 7, 1986, part 5, p. 6.

13. B. V. Lunin, comp., *Biobibliograficheskie ocherki o deiateliakh obshchestvennykh nauk Uzbekistana*, vol. 2 (Tashkent: Izdatel'stvo "Fan," Uzbekskoi SSR, 1977), p. 301.

14. Said Sh. Shermukhamedov, *O natsional'noi forme sotsialisticheskoi kul'tury uzbekskogo naroda* (Tashkent: Izdatel'stvo Akademii Nauk Uzbekskoi SSR, 1961), pp. 60–71.

15. Ibid., p. 57.

16. Ibid., p. 72.

17. Allworth, "The Search for Group Identity in Turkistan, March 1917–September 1922," *Canadian-American Slavic Studies*, no. 4 (Winter 1983):497–98.

18. M. Häsänaw, comp., "Babalärimiz hikmäti," *Tashkent aqshami*, June 9, 1973, p. 3.

19. Ibid.

20. Ä. Äzimaw, *Sawet kishisining gozälligi* (Tashkent: Ozbekistan KP Märkäziy Kamitetining Näshriyati, 1971), p. 11; *Ocherki istorii obshchestvenno-filosofskoi mysli v Uzbekistane* (Tashkent: Izdatel'stvo "Fan" Uzbekskoi SSR, 1977), pp. 62–63.

21. Äbu Bäkr Muhämmäd ibn Jä'fär Närshäkhiy, *Bukhara tärikhi* (Tashkent: Ozbekistan SSR "Fän" Näshriyati, 1966).

22. *Ocherki istorii obshchestvenno-filosofskoi mysli v Uzbekistane*, p. 155.

23. Äzimaw, *Sawet kishisining gozälligi*, pp. 27–28; Mälik Murädaw and Ghulam Ghäfuraw, "Ädibning ijad yoli. Kitab sähifäläridä," *Oqituwchilar gäzetäsi*, January 4, 1981, p. 4.

24. Äzimaw, *Sawet kishisining gozälligi*, p. 29.

25. Erkin Äzläraw, Äbdugäni Rähimaw, Khäyritdin Äsälaw, and Kärim Khälikber-diyew, *Ozbek tili. Rus mäktäbining 9- wä 10- sinfläri uchun därslik*, 8th ed. (Tashkent: "Oqituwchi," 1982), p. 151.

26. *Ozbek khälq mäqalläri* (Tashkent: OzSSR Däwlät Bädiiy Ädäbiyat Näshriyati, 1960), pp. 105–6.

27. Jämäl Shäräpaw, "Anä qälbi bezawtä," *Ozbekistan ädäbiyati wä sän'äti*, January 4, 1985, pp. 2, 7; Olmäs Jälaläwa, "'Anä qälbi bezawtä,'" *Ozbekistan ädäbiyati wä sän'äti*, January 25, 1985, p. 2; "'Anä qälbi bezawtä,'" *Ozbekistan ädäbiyati wä sän'äti*, February 1, 1985, p. 5; *Ozbekistan ädäbiyati wä sän'äti*, February 15, 1985, p. 5; Mäshräb Babayew, "Bezawtälik. Insan, ailä wä äkhlaq," *Ozbekistan ädäbiyati wä sän'äti*, March 15, 1985, p. 6.

28. N. Khudayqulaw, "Aqibät. (Bolgän waqeä)," *Tashkent aqshami*, December 9, 1981, p. 3; Häsänäli Rustämaw, "Mädäniyät älifbäläri. Mäktäb islahati—däwr täläbi," *Ozbekistan ädäbiyäti wä sän'äti*, January 18, 1985, p. 2; personal conversation between the educator and the author.

29. Gr. Andreev, "Zakulisnyia storony sartskago byta," *Sredniaia Aziia*, no. 5 (1910):114–15.

30. Ibid., pp. 115, 122.

31. John N. Hazard, "Statutory Recognition of Nationality Differences in the USSR," in Allworth, ed., *Soviet Nationality Problems* (New York: Columbia University Press, 1971), pp. 95–96; P. V. Donskoi and P. N. Dudko, "Porochnaia kniga. Rets. na kn.: S. G. Borodai 'Bachchevodstvo v Uzbekistane' Tashkent, 1948," *Izvestiia Akademii Nauk UzSSR*, no. 5 (1954):125–28; Q. Yudakhin, *Ozbik-rus lughäti* (Tashkent: Izdatel'stvo Akts. O-va "Sredazkniga," 1927), p. 81; S. F. Äkabiraw, Z. M. Mä'rufaw, and Ä. T. Khojäkhanaw, eds., *Ozbekchä-ruschä lughät* (Moscow: Kharijiy wä Milliy Lughätlär Däwlät Näshriyati, 1959), p. 57; Z. M. Mä'rufaw, ed., *Ozbek tilining izahli lughäti*, vol. 1 (Moscow: "Rus Tili" Näshriyati, 1981), p. 86.

32. *Nehcu'l-feradis*, vol. 1, *Tipkibasim*, introduction by János Eckmann (Ankara: Turk Tarih Kurumu Basimevi, 1956), pp. 334–443.

33. Älisher Näwaiy, "Sädd-i Iskändäriy," in *Khämsä*, ed., Parsa Shämsiyew (Tash-kent: OzSSR Fänlär Äkädemiyäsi Näshriyati, 1958), p. 1284; Näwa'iy, *Mähbub äl-qulub* (Moscow-Leningrad: Izdatel'stvo Akademii Nauk SSSR, 1948), pp. 8–15; Näwaiy, *Mähbub ul-qulub (Qälblär sewgilisi)* (Tashkent: Ghäfur Ghulam namidägi Ädäbiyat wä Sän'ät Näshriyati, 1983), pp. 15–28.

34. Sh. Äbduräzzäqawä, comp., "Danälär bisatidän. Ädalät," *Oqituwchilär gäzetäsi*, June 27, 1981, p. 4; Ibid., July 11, 1981, p. 4; Adam Smith, *The Theory of Moral Sentiments* (Indianapolis: Liberty Classics, 1982), p. 82; Jämäl Kämal, *Suwäyda. She'rlär* (Tashkent: Ghäfur Ghulam namidägi Ädäbiyat wä Sän'ät Näshriyati, 1983), pp. 15–16, 116–17.

35. Äbduräzzäqawä, comp., "Danälär bisatidän. Hälallik," *Oqituwchilär gäzetäsi*, September 30, 1981, p. 4; Äbduräzzäqawä, comp., "Danälär bisatidän. Häqgoylik," *Oqituwchilär gäzetäsi*, November 4, 1982, p. 4; Äbduräzzäqawä, comp., "Danälär bisatidän. Häqiqät," *Oqituwchilär gäzetäsi*, December 19, 1982, p. 4.

36. *Ozbek sawet ädäbiyati tärikhi*, vol. 3, book 2 (Tashkent: Ozbekistan SSR "Fän"

Näshriyati, 1972), p. 331; Izzät Sultan, *Äsärlär, tort tamlik*, vol. 1, *Drama* (Tashkent: Ghäfur Ghulam namidägi Ädäbiyat wä Sän'ät Näshriyati, 1971), pp. 155–208.

37. N. Nawikawa [mukhbirimiz: interview with Kamil Yäshin], "'Qirq urugh äymaqläshsä . . .' Yazuwchi minbari," *Oqituwchilär gäzetäsi*, May 9, 1981, p. 3; Ramz Babajan, "Ijadiy aktiwlik mäs'uliyati," *Ozbekistan mädäniyati*, February 1, 1980, pp. 2–3.

38. Shäräf R. Räshidaw, *Ozbekistan alimlärining yuksäk burchi* (Tashkent: Ozbekistan KP Märkäziy Kamitetining Näshriyati, 1980), p. 19; Umärjan Ismäilaw (shtätsiz mukhbirimiz), "Burch wa mäs'uliyät. Ämmawiy häräkätgä äyläntirämiz," *Oqituwchilär gäzetäsi*, January 18, 1981, p. 1.

39. Khudäyberdi Tokhtäbayew, "Burch," *Ozbekistan ädäbiyati wä sän'äti*, January 4, 1985, p. 4.

40. S. Toräbekawä (datsent), "Ädäbiy tänqid. Burch wä mäs'uliyät tuyghusi," *Ozbekistan ädäbiyati wä sän'äti*, April 12, 1985, p. 3.

41. Nizämiddin Mähmudaw, "Soz mäs'uliyati," *Ozbekistan ädäbiyati wä sän'äti*, January 18, 1985, p. 3.

42. Lesley-Anne Zullo, "The Status of the Lexicon of Modern Written Uzbek: An Investigation" (M. A. thesis, Columbia University, 1988), pp. 101–3.

43. "Quwanchli yäkunlär, mäs'uliyätli wazifälär," *Ozbekistan ädäbiyati wä sän'äti* (January 4, 1985), pp. 1–2; Nuriddin Shukuraw and Ilham Häsänaw, "Täyänch nuqtä—mehnät, mäharät, mäs'uliyät," Ibid., (January 25, 1985), p. 3; Ibrähim Ghäfuraw, "Birinchi kitab mäs'uliyati," Ibid., (March 8, 1985), p. 5; "Ijadkar bäkhti wä mäs'uliyat," Ibid., (January 18, 1985), p. 3; [Ibid. means article continued in subsequent issues of *Ozbekistan ädäbiyati wä sän'äti*.] *Itogi vsesoiuznoi perepisi naseleniia 1970 goda*, vol. 4 (Moscow: "Statistika," 1973), p. 202.

CHAPTER 17

1. Muhammad Sadiq, *Ädäb-us salihin*, adapted and trans. by N. S. Lykoshin, in *"Khoroshii ton" na Vostokie* (Petrograd: Sklad u V. A. Berezovskago, 1915), pp. 5, 43; V. P. Semenov Tian-Shanskii, ed., *Rossiia. Polnoe geograficheskoe opisanie nashego otechestva*, vol. 19, *Turkestanskii krai* (Saint Petersburg: Izdanie A. F. Devriena, 1913), pp. 393–94.

2. Edward Allworth, visit to Uzbekistan in October–November 1983.

3. Sadiq, *Ädäb-us salihin*, pp. 66–67; Arthur Jeffery, ed., *A Reader on Islam: Passages from Standard Arabic Writings Illustrative of the Beliefs and Practices of Muslims* ('S-Gravenhage, Netherlands: Mouton, 1962), pp. 553–55.

4. Jeffrey, *Reader on Islam*, pp. 553–54; Sadiq, *Ädäb-us salihin*, pp. 78–79.

5. *Sawet Ozbekistanning yazuwchiläri* (Tashkent: OzSSR Däwlät Bädiiy Ädäbiyat Näshriyati, 1959), pp. 186–87; Erkin Nasyrov, Raim Farkhadi, and Petr Filippov, comps., *Pisateli sovetskogo Uzbekistana* (Tashkent: Izdatel'stvo Literatury i Iskusstva imeni Gafura Guliama, 1977), pp. 230, 245–48; *Ozbek she'riyäti äntalagiyäsi. Sawet*

she'riyäti, vol. 5 (Tashkent: Ozbekistan SSR Däwlät Bädiiy Ädäbiyat Näshriyati, 1962), pp. 518–24; N. A. Bondarenko, V. D. Novoprudskii, and Ia. D. Khodzhaev, comps., *Pisateli sovetskogo Uzbekistana* (Tashkent: Izdatel'stvo Literatury i Iskusstva imeni Gafura Guliama, 1984), pp. 461–67.

6. *Ozbekistan Sawet Satsiälistik Respublikäsining mä'muriy-territariäl bolinishi. 1966 yil 1 yänwärgächä bolgän mä'lumat* (Tashkent: "Ozbekistan" Näshriyati, 1966), p. 70.

7. Allworth, *The End of Ethnic Integration in Southern Central Asia* (Washington, D.C.: Kennan Institute for Advanced Russian Studies, Occasional Paper no. 159, 1982).

8. Hafiz-i Tänish ibn Mir Muhämmäd Bukhariy, *Shäräf namäyi shakhi (kniga shakhskoi slavy)* (Moscow: Izdatel'stvo "Nauka." Glavnaia Redaktsiia Vostochnoi Literatury, 1983), part 1, L100b, p. 221; Jämal Kämal, *Suwäyda. She'rlar* (Tashkent: Ghafur Ghulam namidägi Ädäbiyati wä Sän'äti Näshriyati, 1983), p. 83.

9. Zahiriddin Muhammad Babur, *The Babur-nama in English (Memoirs of Babur)* (London: Luzac, 1922, repr. 1969), L181, p. 289, L44b, p. 75; Fazlallah Ruzbihan Isfahaniy, *Mihman namä-i Bukhara* (Moscow: Izdatel'stvo "Nauka." Glavnaia Redaktsiia Vostochnoi Literatury, 1976), L116a, p. 235; Hafiz Tänish ibn Mir Muhämmäd Bukhariy, *Äbdullänamä*, vol. 2 (Tashkent: Ozbekistan SSR "Fän" Näshriyati, 1969), pp. 71, 123, 214, 221, 239; Mir Mukhammed Amin-i Bukharai, *Ubaidulla-name* (Tashkent: Izdatel'stvo AN UzSSR, 1957), pp. 48, 53, 61, 69, 70; Mirzä 'Äbdäl 'Äzim Sami, *Tär'ikh-i salatin-i Mänghitiyä (Istoriia mangytskikh gosudarei)*, trans. L. M. Epifanovna (Moscow: Izdatel'stvo Vostochnoi Literatury, 1962), pp. 106–7; Arminius Vámbéry, *Travels in Central Asia, Being the Account of a Journey from Teheran Across the Turkoman Desert on the Eastern Shore of the Caspian to Khiva, Bukhara, and Samarkand* (New York: Harper & Brothers, 1865), pp. 273, 435; *Ädäbiyatimiz äwtabiagräfiyäsi* (Tashkent: 1973), pp. 279–80, cited in Ilse Laude Cirtautas, *Chrestomathy of Modern Literary Uzbek* (Wiesbaden: Otto Harrassowitz, 1980), p. 50; Kämal, *Suwäyda. She'rlär*, p. 83.

10. Hasan-i Rumlu, *A Chronicle of the Early Safawis, Being the Ahsanu't-Tawarikh*, trans. C. N. Seddon, Gaekwad's Oriental Series LXIX (Baroda: Oriental Institute, 1935), vol. 2, p. 22; *Izvestiia*, April 7, 1925, cited in J. Castagné, "Les Musulmans et la politique des Soviets en Asie Centrale," in *Revue du monde Musulman* (Paris: Éditions Ernest Leroux, 1925), pp. 34–36; Vladimir Tiurikov, *Letopis' poluveka. Khronika kul'turnoi zhizni Uzbekistana (1924–1974)* (Tashkent: Izdatel'stvo Literatury i Iskusstva imeni Gafura Guliama, 1975), p. 16.

11. Fazlallakh ibn Ruzbikhan Isfakhani, *Mikhman-name-ii Bukhara* (Moscow: Izdatel'stvo "Nauka," 1976), L70a, p. 93.

12. Mänsur Äfzälaw, Sabirjan Ibrahimaw, and Säydähmäd Khudaybergänaw, comps., *Ozbek khälq mäqalläri*, 2d ed. (Tashkent: OzSSR Däwlät Bädiiy Ädäbiyat Näshriyati, 1960), pp. 19–20; Ibid., 4th ed. (1978), pp. 19–21; Bärat Bayqabilaw, "Täbärruk tupraq. (Dastandän pärchä)," *Oqituwchilär gäzetäsi*, June 3, 1981, p. 4; Mähkäm Pirnäzäraw; dotsent, "Pärtiyä rejäläri—khälq rejäläri. Burchdarlik tuyghusi," *Oqituwchilär gäzetäsi*, January 15, 1981, p. 2.

13. James Critchlow, "*Vätän* and the Concept of 'Homeland' in the Muslim Soviet Republics, in Chantal Quelquejay-Lemercier et al., eds., *Passé Turco-Tatar. Présent Soviétique. Turco-Tatar Past. Soviet Present* (Paris: Editions Peeters. Editions de l'Ecole des Hautes Etudes, 1986), pp. 481–88.

14. B. A. Antonenko, ed., *Istoriia tadzhikskogo naroda*, vol. 3, book 1 (Moscow: Izdatel'stvo "Nauka," 1964), p. 143; specimens of Bukharan and Khwarazmian paper money from 1921 and USSR notes dated 1983–1985.

15. *Säda-i Färghanä* (1914–1915), cited in Zafir Radzhabov, *Iz istorii obshchestvenno-politicheskoi mysli tadzhikskogo naroda vo vtoroi polovine XIX i v nachale XX vv.* (Stalinabad: Tadzhikskoe Gosudarstvennoe Izdatel'stvo, 1957), p. 405.

16. *Ozbekistan SSR tärikhi*, vol. 2 (Tashkent: Ozbekistan SSR Fänlär Äkädemiyäsi Näshriyati, 1958), p. 611; *Ozbekistan kammonist (balshäwik)lär firqäsining IInchi qurultayi (1925inchi yil, 22–30 noyäbr) Qurultayning hisabi* (Samarkand: Ozb. Kam. (Balshäwiklär) Firqäsi Märkäzqomining Näshri. Tashkent: Ozbikstan Däwlät Näshriyatining Birinchi Basmakhanäsi, 1926); *XX s'ezd kommunisticheskoi partii Uzbekistana. 3–5 fevralia 1981 goda. Stenograficheskii otchet* (Tashkent: "Uzbekistan," 1981), pp. 85–86.

17. *Itogi vsesoiuznoi perepisi naseleniia 1970 goda. Natsional'nyi sostav naseleniia SSSR, soiuznykh i avtonomnykh respublik, kraev, oblastei i natsional'nykh okrugov*, vol. 4 (Moscow: "Statistika," 1973), pp. 20, 202; *Chislennost' i sostav naseleniia SSSR. Po dannym Vsesoiuznoi perepisi naseleniia 1979 goda* (Moscow: Finansy i Statistika, 1984), pp. 71, 110.

18. Dzh. Baibulatov, *Chagataizm-Pantiurkizm v uzbekskoi literature* (Moscow-Tashkent: Ob"edinenie Gosudarstvennykh Izdatel'stv. Sredneaziatskoe Otdelenie, 1932), pp. 35–37; Abdullah Rejeb Baysun, *Türkistan millî hareketleri* (Istanbul: n.p., 1943 [title page], 1945 [cover]), p. 180.

19. Edward J. Lazzerini, "Ismail Bey Gasprinskii (Gaspirali), the Discourse of Modernism, and the Russians," in Allworth, ed., *Tatars of the Crimea. Their Struggle for Survival* (Durham, North Carolina: Central Asia Book Series, Duke University Press, 1988), chap. 6, pp. 149–169.

20. *Ädäbiyat khrestomatïyasi* (Tashkent: Ozdawnäshr, 1933), p. 371; Begäli Qasimaw, "Aq tanglär kuychisi. Äbdüllä Äwlaniy tughilgän kunning 100 yilligigä," *Shärq yulduzi*, no. 8 (1978):217; Fitrat, *Shärq siyasäti*, scribe 'Äbdalqadir Murad (n.p.: Tarqatghuchi [Distributor]): Yash Bukharalilar Qomitasining Näshriyat Shu'bäsi, 1919), p. 45; S. Ayniy, *Qisqächä tärjimäi halim* (Tashkent: OzSSR Däwlät Bädiiy Ädäbiyat Näshriyati, 1960), p. 123; *Sawet Ozbekistanining yazuwchiläri* (Tashkent: OzSSR Däwlät Bädiiy Ädäbiyat Näshriyati, 1959), p. 32; I. M. Muminov, ed., *Istoriia Khorezma. S drevneishikh vremen do nashikh dnei* (Tashkent: Izdatel'stvo "Fan" Uzbekskoi SSR, 1976), p. 22.

21. Konst. Arkhipov, "Sovetskoe pravovoe stroitel'stvo. Bukharskaia Narodnaia Sovetskaia Respublika (Obzor konstitutsii)," *Sovetskoe pravo*, vol. 4 (1923):134–37; Timur Kocaoglu, "The Existence of a Bukharan Nationality in the Recent Past," in Allworth, ed., *The Nationality Question in Soviet Central Asia* (New York: Praeger, 1973), pp. 151–58.

22. *Ozbekistan Ijtima'i Shoralar Jomhoriyäti Ishchi wä Dihqan Hokomätining qanon wä boyroqlarining yighindisi*, no. 24 (August 6, 1927); 647–50, 664–65; *Ozbekistan Ijtima'i Shoralar Jomhoriyätining qanon äsasi (kanstitotsyä)si* (n.p.: Iz-vo pri Upr. Del. SNK UzSSR, n.d. [received by U.S. Library of Congress, 1927]), pp. 16–19, 31–32; *Konstitutsiia (osnovnoi zakon) Uzbekskoi Sovetskoi Sotsialisticheskoi Respubliki* (Samarkand: Izdanie Upravleniia Informatsiei TsIK i SNK UzSSR, 1927), pp. xii–xiii, xx; B. A. Antonenko, ed., *Istoriia tadzhikskogo naroda*, vol. 3, book 1 (Moscow: Izdatel'stvo "Nauka," 1964), pp. 156–57, 216–17.

23. "Sekretari Tsentral'nogo Komiteta KPSS: Nuritdin Akramovich Mukhitdinov," *Izvestiia*, December 22, 1957, p. 1; *Pravda*, February 13, 1968; *Who's Who in the USSR 1965/66* (New York: Scarecrow Press, 1966), p. 571.

24. *Directory of USSR Ministry of Foreign Affairs Officials: A Reference Aid* (Washington, D.C.: Central Intelligence Agency, September 1985), p. 22; *Pravda*, July 12, 1969, p. 3; *Who's Who in the USSR, 1965/66*, p. 600; Rafik N. Nishanov, "USSR for Peace and Security," *Ceylon Daily News*, November 6, 1971, pp. 11–12, includes photo of Nishanov; TASS, August 3, 1985, cited in the *New York Times*, August 4, 1985, p. 11.

25. *Constitution (Fundamental Law) of the Uzbek Soviet Socialist Republic of February 23, 1937, as amended through June 25, 1948* (New York: American Russian Institute, April 1950), p. 6; *Konstitutsiia (osnovnoi zakon) Uzbekskoi Sovetskoi Sotsialisticheskoi Respubliki* (Tashkent: Gosizdat UzSSR, 1961), p. 11; "Ozbekistan Sawet Satsiälistik Respublikäsining Kanstitutsiyäsi (Äsasiy qanuni)," *Sawet Ozbekistani*, April 20, 1978, p. 3; R. Kh. Mukhamedova, *Prezidium Verkhovnogo Soveta Soiuznoi Respubliki* (Tashkent: Izdatel'stvo "Fän" UzSSR, 1980), p. 112; *A.A.P.S.O. in Brief* (leaflet) (Cairo: The Afro-Asian People's Solidarity Organization, 1978), p. 2; R. A. Tuzmukhamedov, *Natsional'nyi suverenitet* (Moscow: Izdatel'stvo Instituta Mezhdunarodnykh Otnoshenii, 1963), p. 59.

26. "Ozbekistan sawet satsiälistik respublikäsining gimni," *Sawet Ozbekistani*, April 20, 1978, p. 1; W. W. Gruzä and A. Ä. Äzizaw, *Ozbek tili. Rus mäktäblärining 9 wä 10-inchi sinfläri uchun oqish kitabi* (Tashkent: OzSSR Däwlät Oquw-Pedägagikä Näshriyati, 1955), p. 129; "Gimn," in *Ozbek sawet entsiklapediyäsi*, vol. 3 (Tashkent: Ozbekistan SSR Fänlär Äkädemiyäsi, 1972), pp. 344–45.

27. H. Tursunaw, M. Akhunawä, and R. Nurullin, "Ozbekistandä tärikh fäning äktuäl problemäläri," *Ozbekistan kammunisti*, no. 6 (June 1977):66–72, 70–71; K. Sh. Shaniiazov, "K voprosu ob uchastii tiurkskikh plemen tsentral'noi Azii i iuzhnoi Sibiri v etnogeneze uzbekskogo naroda," in *Istoriko-kul'turnye kontakty narodov altaiskoi iazykovoi obshchnosti. Tezisy dokladov XXIX sessii postoiannoi mezhdunarodnoi altaisticheskoi konferentsii (PIAC). Tashkent, sentiabr', 1986 g. 1. Istoriia, literatura, iskusstvo* (Moscow: Akademiia Nauk SSSR. Institut Vostokovedeniia, 1986), pp. 70–73.

CHAPTER 18

1. Michael Rywkin, *The Soviet Nationalities Policy and the Communist Party Structure in Uzbekistan. A Study of the Methods of Soviet Russian Control, 1941–1946* (Ph.D. diss., Columbia University, 1960), pp. 57, 173, table 1.

2. *Zasedaniia Verkhovnogo Soveta SSSR, deviatogo sozyva (pervaia sessiia 25–26 iiulia 1974 g. Stenograficheskii otchet)* (Moscow: Izdanie Verkhovnogo Soveta SSSR, 1974), p. 239; *Pravda*, May 23, 1972, p. 4; *Bol'shaia sovetskaia entsiklopediia*, vol. 17 (Moscow: "Sovetskaia Entsiklopediia," 1974), p. 309; *Ozbek sawet entsiklapediyäsi*, vol. 5 (Tashkent: Ozbekistan SSR Fänlär Äkädemiyäsi, 1976), p. 55.

3. John H. Miller, "Cadres Policy in Nationality Areas—Recruitment of CPSU First and Second Secretaries in Non-Russian Republics of the USSR," *Soviet Studies*, no. 1 (January 1977):8–18; Michael Rywkin, "Power and Ethnicity: Party Staffing in Uzbekistan (1941/46, 1957/58)," *Central Asian Survey*, no. 1 (1985):46–48; Rywkin, "Power and Ethnicity (1983/84)," *Central Asian Survey*, no. 1 (1985):5–6, 12–40; Kai Ka'us ibn Iskandar, Prince of Gurgan, *A Mirror for Princes. The Qabus Nama* (1082), trans. Reuben Levy (London: The Cresset Press, 1951), p. 230; Kaykawus, *Qabusnamä*, trans. Agähiy, adapted by Subutay Dalimaw (Tashkent: "Oqituwchi" Näshriyati, 1986), chap. 42.

4. *Prisoners of Conscience in the USSR: Their Treatment and Conditions*, 2d ed. (London: Amnesty International Publications, 1980), p. 101.

5. "Konstitutsiia (osnovnoi zakon) Soiuza Sovetskikh Sotsialisticheskikh Respublik," *Izvestiia*, October 8, 1977, art. 50, p. 4.

6. "Political Prisoners Appeal to President Carter," *A Chronicle of Human Rights in the USSR*, no. 28 (October–December 1977):41–44.

7. Edward Allworth, ed., *Tatars of the Crimea. Their Struggle for Survival*, Central Asia Book Series (Durham, N.C.: Duke University Press, 1988).

8. *Shest' dnei. "Belaia kniga"* (New York: Fond Krym, 1980), pp. 311, 345–47.

9. Sharaf Rashidov, *The Banner of Friendship* (Moscow: Progress Publishers, 1969), p. 57.

10. L. I. Brezhnev, "The Report of the CPSU CC," *Pravda*, February 25, 1976, pp. 2–9, trans. in *Current Soviet Policies*, vol. 7 (Columbus, Ohio: American Association for the Advancement of Slavic Studies, 1976), p. 25; Eduard A. Shevardnadze, *Pravda*, February 27, 1976, pp. 2–3, trans. in *Current Soviet Policies*, vol. 7, p. 54; Sharaf R. Rashidov, *Pravda*, February 27, 1976, p. 2, trans. in *Current Soviet Policies*, vol. 7, p. 52.

11. "Qizlär awazi," *Shärq yulduzi*, no. 3 (1959):88–89; "Qizlär ijadi," *Sharq yulduzi*, no. 3 (1963); E'tibar Akhunawä, "Dutar häwasi. Dastan," *Shärq yulduzi*, no. 8 (1970):3–8; N. A. Bondarenko et al., eds., *Pisateli sovetskogo Uzbekistana. Spravochnik* (Tashkent: Izdatel'stvo Literatury i Iskusstva imeni Gafura Guliama, 1984), p. 65; Mukärrämä Murädawä, "Shäbnäm," *Shärq yulduzi*, no. 1 (1971): 227–28.

12. E'tibar Akhunawä, *Men tangni uyghatdim. She'rlär wä dastan* (Tashkent: Ghäfur Ghulam namidägi Ädäbiyat wä Sän'ät Näshriyati, 1980), pp. 141, 4.

13. Akhunawä, "Arzu qilsäk, yamanmi? Siz nimä deysiz?" *Sawet Ozbekistan*, May 14, 1985, cited by Räna Habib, in unpublished article, "Gäp ozbek päkhtäsi häqidä," (1985), p. 1; Räna Habib, in an unpublished article, "Negä ozbek äyalläri ällä äytmäydilär?"

14. Ishäq R. Mulläjanaw, *Ozbekistan ähalisi*. (Tashkent: "Ozbekistan" Näshriyati, 1974), p. 128; Räzzaq Äbduräshidaw, *Yol bashidä*. *She'rlär* (Tashkent: OzSSR Däwlät Bädiiy Ädäbiyat Näshriyati, 1962), pp. 11, 38; Räzzaq Äbduräshidaw, *Qälbim qolingdä* (Tashkent: Ozbekistan LKSM Märkäziy Kamiteti "Yash Gwärdiyä" Näshriyati, 1970), pp. 5–6; Ähmädjan Eshanqulaw, "Umidbäkhsh ahänglär," *Shärq yulduzi*, no. 2 (1972):218–19.

15. Farkhadi, *Freski Afrasiaba*. *Stikhi i poema* (Tashkent: Izdatel'stvo Khudozhestvennoi Literatury imeni Gafura Guliama, 1970), p. 115; Erkin Nasyrov, Raim Farkhadi, and Petr Filippov, comps., *Pisateli sovetskogo Uzbekistana. Bibliograficheskii spravochnik* (Tashkent: Izdatel'stvo Literatury i Iskusstva imeni Gafura Guliama, 1977), p. 204.

16. Rähim Färhädiy, trans. Atäyar, "Hämzä," *Shärq yulduzi*, no. 1 (1971):103–4; Färhädiy, trans. Atäyar, "Tuyabab," *Sharq yulduzi*, no. 6 (1971):163; Nasyrov et al., *Pisateli sovetskogo Uzbekistana*, p. 204.

17. Comments made by Professor Michael Zand during a discussion about literature and nationality identity at the Conference on Central Asia: The Decades Ahead, Munich, Germany, August 20, 1985.

18. Raim Kh. Farkhadi, "Samarkandskaia kraska," in *Ballada o sedoi vesne*, trans. Edward Allworth, with Rose Raskin (Moscow: "Molodaia Gvardiia," 1977), pp. 96–97.

19. Farkhadi, *Freski Afrasiyab*, pp. 5–38; I. M. Muminov et al., ed. *Istoriia Samarkanda*, vol. 1 (Tashkent: Izdatel'stvo "FAN" Uzbekskoi SSR, 1969), pp. 133–38, plates between 128–29 and between 144–45.

20. Ibrahim Ghäfuraw, *She'riyät—izlänish demäk*. *Ädäbiy-tänqidiy acherk* (Tashkent: Ghäfur Ghulam namidägi Ädäbiyat wä Sän'ät Näshriyati, 1984), pp. 208–9; Allworth, *Uzbek Literary Politics* (The Hague: Mouton, 1964), pp. 92, 102.

21. *Chislennost' i sostav naseleniia SSSR. Po dannym Vsesoiuznoi perepisi naseleniia 1979 goda* (Moscow: Finansy i Statistiki, 1984), p. 110.

22. Räuf Pärfi, "Bukun bir tush kordim," *Shärq yulduzi*, no. 1 (1966):140–41, revised trans. Allworth 1985–86; Allworth, "An Old Mood Returns to Central Asian Literature," *Literature East and West*, no. 2 (1967):150–51.

23. *Chislennost' i sostav naseleniia*, p. 132.

24. *Ozbekistan sawet satsiälistik respublikäsining mä'muriy-territariäl bolinishi. 1966 yil 1 yänwärgächä bolgän mä'lumat* (Tashkent: "Ozbekistan" Näshriyati, 1966), p. 32; Nasyrov, Farkhadi, and Filippov, *Pisateli sovetskogo Uzbekistana*, p. 83; Äbu Äli ibn Sina, *She'riyät*, ed. and trans. Jämal Kämal (Tashkent: Ghäfur Ghulam namidägi Ädäbiyat wä Sän'ät Näshriyati, 1980); Conversations with the author of this book, 1983, 1985, in Tashkent.

25. Kämal, *Qädäh. Lirikä* (Tashkent: Ghäfur Ghulam namidägi Ädäbiyat wä Sän'ät Näshriyati, 1980), pp. 68–70, 160–62; Pärsä Shämsiyew, and Sabirjan Ibrahimaw, comps., *Näwaiy äsärläri lughäti. Älisher Näwaiy äsärlärining on besh tamligigä ilawä* (Tashkent: Ghäfur Ghulam namidägi Ädäbiyat wä Sän'ät Näshriyati, 1972), p. 573.

26. Kämal, *Suwäyda. She'rlär* (Tashkent: Ghafur Ghulam namidägi Ädäbiyat wä

Sän'ät Näshriyati, 1983), p. 83; Kämal and Tashpolät Ähmäd, "Shärqning buyuk ällamäsi. Ibn Sina wätänida," *Ozbekistan mädäniyäti*, March 11, 1980, p. 2; For contemporary color photographs of Bukharan palace architecture, consult Robert H. Allshouse, ed., *Photographs for the Tsar. The Pioneering Color Photography of Sergei Mikhailovich Prokudin Gorskii* (New York: The Dial Press, 1980), pp. 181–83.

27. Alessio Bombaci, "The Turkic Literatures. Introductory Notes on the History and Style," *Philologiae Turcicae Fundamenta*, vol. 2 (Wiesbaden: Franz Steiner Verlag, 1965), p. L.

28. "*Qäsidä*," in *Ozbek sawet entsiklapediyäsi*, vol. 14 (Tashkent: Ozbek Sawet Entsiklapediyäsi. Bash Redäktsiyä, 1980), p. 41; Kämal, *Suwäyda. She'rlär*, pp. 195–96.

29. Evgenii E. Bertel's, *Izbrannye trudy. Istoriia persidsko-tadzhikskoi literatury* (Moscow: Izdatel'stvo Vostochnoi Literatury, 1960), p. 134; Aleksandr Belenitsky, *Central Asia*, trans. James Hogarth (Cleveland: World Publishing, 1968), pp. 142–54, plates 139–41; Kämal, *Dastanlär* (Tashkent: Ghäfur Ghulam namidägi Ädäbiyat wä Sän'ät Näshriyati, 1979); Ghäffar Mominaw and Äbdulla Mätyaqubaw, "Dastan-lärdä häyat tälqini," *Ozbekistan mädäniyäti*, January 8, 1980, p. 3.

Bibliography

The following list includes separate publications cited in this study as well as some additional entries relevant to the chapters. Central Asian and other Middle Eastern names appear in English alphabetical order according to last names rather than first names.

Abbott, James. *Narrative of a Journey from Heraut to Khiva, Moscow, and St. Peterburgh during the late Russian Invasion of Khiva*. Vol. 1. London: James Madden, 1856.

Äbdälrä'uf. *Bäyanat-i seyyah-i hindi*. Dar al-Khilafät [Istanbul]: Hikmat, A.H. 1331/A.D. 1912/13. *See also* Abd-ur-rauf and Firät.

Abduraimov, M. *Voprosy feodal'nogo zemlevladeniia i feodal'noi renty v pis'makh emira Haidara. Opyt kratkogo issledovaniia istochnika.* Tashkent: Izdatel'stvo Akademii Nauk Uzbekskoi SSR, 1961.

Äbduräshidaw, Räzzaq. *Qälbim qolingdä*. Tashkent: Ozbekistan LKSM Märkäziy Kamiteti "Yash Gwärdiyä" Näshriyati, 1970.

——. *Yol bashidä. She'rlär*. Tashkent: OzSSR Däwlät Bädiiy Ädäbiyat Näshriyati, 1962.

Abd-ur-Rauf. *Razskazy indiiskago puteshestvennika*. Translated by A. N. Kondrat'ev. Samarkand: Izdanie Makhmud Khoja Bekbudi, Tip-Litografiia Tovarishchestva Gazarov i K. Sliianov, 1913.

Abdushukurov, R. Kh. *Oktiabr'skaia revoliutsiia, rastsvet uzbekskoi sotsialisticheskoi natsii*. Tashkent: Gosudarstvennoe Izdatel'stvo Uzbekskoi SSR, 1962.

Äfzälaw, M., et al., comps. *Ozbek khälq mäqalläri*. Tashkent: OzSSR Däwlät Bädiiy Ädäbiyat Näshriyati, 1960.

Aini, Sadriddin. *Ustod Rudaki. Epokha, zhizn', tvorchestvo.* Moscow: Izdatel'stvo Vostochnoi Literatury, 1959. *See also* Ayni and Ayniy.

———. *Vospominaniia.* Translated by Anna Rozenfel'd. Moscow-Leningrad: Izdatel'stvo Akademii Nauk SSSR, 1960.

Äkabirov, S. F., et al., eds. *Ozbekchä-ruschä lughät. Uzbeksko-russkii slovar'.* Moscow: Kharijiy wä Milliy Lughätlär Däwlät Näshriyati, 1959.

Akhmedov, Boriway A. *Gosudarstvo kochevykh Uzbekov.* Moscow: Izdatel'stvo "Nauka." Glavnaia Redaktsiia Vostochnoi Literatury, 1965.

———. *Istoriia Balkha (XVI-pervaia polovina XVIII v.).* Tashkent: Izdatel'stvo "Fan" Uzbekskoi SSR, 1982.

Akhunawä, E'tibar. *Men Tangni uyghatdim. She'rlär wä dastan.* Tashkent: Ghäfur Ghulam namidägi Ädäbiyat wä Sän'ät Näshriyati, 1980.

Alimaw, Ä. *Sawet kishisining gozälligi.* Tashkent: Ozbekistan KP Märkäziy Kamitetining Näshriyati, 1971.

'Ali Shir, Mir. *Muhakamat al-lughatain.* Translated by Robert Devereux. Leiden: E. J. Brill, 1966. *See also* Mir Ali Shir, and Nawaiy or Navoi.

Allshouse, Robert H., ed. *Photographs for the Tsar. The Pioneering Color Photography of Sergei Mikhailovich Prokudin-Gorskii.* New York: Dial Press, 1980.

Allworth, Edward. *Central Asian Publishing and the Rise of Nationalism.* New York: New York Public Library, 1965.

———. *The End of Ethnic Integration in Southern Central Asia.* Occasional Paper 159. Washington, D.C.: The Wilson Center, Kennan Institute for Advanced Russian Studies, 1982.

———. *Soviet Asia: Bibliographies . . . With an Essay on the Soviet Asia Controversy.* New York: Praeger Publishers, 1975.

———. *Uzbek Literary Politics.* The Hague: Mouton and Company, 1964.

Allworth, Edward, ed. and coauthor. *Central Asia: A Century of Russian Rule.* New York: Columbia University Press, 1967.

———. *Central Asia: 120 Years of Russian Rule.* Durham, N.C.: Central Asia Book Series, Duke University Press, 1989.

———. *Soviet Nationality Problems.* New York: Columbia University Press, 1971.

———. *Tatars of the Crimea. Their Struggle for Survival.* Durham, N.C.: Central Asia Book Series, Duke University Press, 1988.

Älpamish. Dastan. 2d edition. Edited by Hämid Alimjan. Tashkent: Ozbekistan SSR Fänlär Äkädemiyäsi, 1957.

———. Recited by Fazil Yoldash Oghli; compiled by Hadi Zärif, and Torä Mirzäew. Tashkent: Ghäfur Ghulam namidägi Ädäbiyat wä Sän'ät Näshriyati, 1979.

Amin, Osman. *Muhammad 'Abduh.* Washington, D.C.: American Council of Learned Societies, 1953.

Aminova, R. Kh., et al., eds. *Istoriia uzbekskoi SSR.* Vol. 1. Tashkent: Izdatel'stvo "FAN" Uzbekskoi SSR, 1967.

Antonenko, B. A., ed. *Istoriia tadzhikskogo naroda.* Vol. 2, book 1. Moscow: Izdatel'stvo "Nauka," 1964.

Arabshah, Ahmed ibn. *'Aja'ib al-magdur fi akhbar timur. Tamerlane or Timur the Great Amir.* Translated by J. H. Sanders. Lahore: Progressive Books, n.d., reprint of 1936 edition.

Arberry, A. J. *Sufism. An Account of the Mystics of Islam.* New York: Harper and Row, 1970.

Arsharuni, A., and Kh. Gabidullin. *Ocherki panislamizma i pantiurkizma v Rossii.* Moscow: Bezbozhnik, 1931.

Atabek-oghli, Fazil bek. *Dukchi ishan waqi'äsi (Färghanädä istibdad jälladläri).* Samarkand-Tashkent: Ozbekstan Däwlät Näshriyati, 1927.

Atkin, Muriel. *The Subtlest Battle.* Philadelphia: Foreign Policy Research Institute, 1989.

Awlaniy, Äbdulla, ed. *Ädäbiyat khrestamätïyasï.* Tashkent: Ozdäwnäshr, 1933.

Ayni, Sadriddin. *Qulliyat.* Vols. 1–10. Dushanbe: Nashriyoti "Irfon," 1966.

'Äyniy, Sädriddin. *Bukhara inqilabi tärikhi uchun materiyallar.* Moscow: SSSR Khälqlarning Märkazi Näshriyati, 1926.

———. *Namuna-i adabiyot-i tajik. 300–1200 hijri.* Samarkand: Chopkhanai Nashriyati Markazii Khalqii Ittikhadi Jamoli, 1926.

———. *Qisqächä tärjimäi halim.* Tashkent: OzSSR Däwlät Bädiiy Ädäbiyat Näshriyati, 1960. See also Aini.

Äzläraw, Erkin, et al. *Ozbek tili. Rus mäktäbining 9- wä 10-sinfläri uchun därslik.* 8th ed. Tashkent: "Oqituwchi," 1982.

Bäbar, Zahiriddin Muhammad. *Bäbar namä.* London: Luzac and Company, 1905, reprinted 1971.

Babir, Zähiriddin Muhämmäd. *Babirnamä.* Tashkent: Ozbekistan SSR Fänlär Äkädemiyäsi Näshriyati, 1960.

Babur, Zahiruddin Muhammad Padshah Ghazi. *The Babur-nama in English (Memoirs of Babur).* Translated by Annette S. Beveridge. London: Luzac and Company, 1922, reprinted 1969.

Bâdemji, Ali, *1917–1934 Türkistan Milli istiklâl Hareketi ve Enver Pasha.* Vol. 7. Istanbul: Kutlugh Yayinlari, 1975.

Baibulatov, Dzh. *Chagataizm-pantiurkizm v uzbekskoi literature.* Moscow-Tashkent: OGIZ, Sredneaziatskoe Otdelenie, 1932.

Bakhrushin, S. V., et al., eds. *Istoriia narodov Uzbekistana ot obrazovaniia gosudarstva Sheibanidov do velikoi oktiabr'skoi sotsialisticheskoi revoliutsii.* Vols. 1–2. Tashkent: Izdatel'stvo Akademii Nauk UzSSR, 1947, 1951.

Bäqa, Muhämmäd Yusuf al-Munshi ibn Khojä. *Tadhkirä-i muqim khaniy.* Translated by Joseph Senkowski. St. Petersburg: Imprimerie de l'Académie Impériale des Sciences, 1824.

Barthold, Vasiliy V. *Four Studies on the History of Central Asia*. Vol 1. Translated by V. Minorsky and T. Minorsky. Leiden: E. J. Brill, 1958.

———. *Istoriia izucheniia Vostoka v Evrope i Rossii*. Leningrad: TsIK SSSR. Leningradskii Institute Zhivykh Vostochnykh Iazykov, No. 7, 1925.

Bartol'd, V. V. *Sochineniia*. Vols. 1–10. Moscow: Izdatel'stvo "Nauka," 1963–69.

Baysun, Turkistanli Rejeb. *Türkistan millî hareketleri*. Istanbul: N.p., [title page] 1943, [cover] 1945.

Bazarov, U. B. *Ideinye osnovy tvorchestva Khamzy Khakim-Zade Niiazi*. Tashkent: Izdatel'stvo Akademii Nauk Uzbekskoi SSR, 1960.

Becker, Seymour. *Russia's Protectorates in Central Asia: Bukhara and Khiva, 1865–1924*. Cambridge, Mass.: Harvard University Press, 1968.

Behbudiy, Mahmud Khoja. See Bihbudiy, Mähmud Khojä.

Belenitsky, Aleksandr. "Central Asia" in *Archaeologia Mundi*. Translated by James Hogarth. Cleveland, Ohio: World Publishing Company; Geneva: Nagel Publishers, 1968.

Bendix, Reinhard. *Kings or People. Power and the Mandate to Rule*. Berkeley and Los Angeles: University of California Press, 1978.

Bendrikov, K. E. *Ocherki po istorii narodnogo obrazovaniia v Turkestane*. Moscow: Bezbozhnik, 1960.

Bennigsen, Alexandre, and Lemercier-Quelquejay, Chantal. *La Presse et le Mouvement National chez les Musulmans de Russie avant 1920*. Paris: Mouton and Company, 1964.

———. *Les Mouvements Nationaux chez les Musulmans de Russie: 1. Le "Sultangalievisme" au Tatarstan*. Paris and The Hague: Mouton and Company, 1960.

———. *Le soufi et le commissaire. Les conféries musulmanes en URSS*. Paris: Éditions du Seuil, 1986.

Bertel's, Yevgenii E. *Izbrannye trudy. Istoriia persidsko-tadzhikskoi literatury*. Moscow: Izdatel'stvo Vostochnoi Literatury, 1960.

———. *Navoi. Opyt tvorcheskoi biografii*. Moscow-Leningrad: Izdatel'stvo Akademii Nauk SSSR, 1948.

Biblioteka vostochnykh istorikov. Kazan: Izdavaemaia I. Berezinym, 1849.

Bihbudiy, Mähmud Khojä. *Pädärkush yakhud (oqumagan balaning hali?)*. Samarkand: Tipo-Litografiia T-va B. Gazarov i N. Sliianov, A.H. 1331/A.D. 1913.

Biobibliograficheskie ocherki o deiateliakh obshchestvennykh nauk Uzbekistana. Vols. 1–2. Compiled by B. V. Lunin. Tashkent: Izdatel'stvo "FAN" Uzbekskoi SSR, 1977.

Birinchi olkä ozbek til wä imla qoroltayining chiqarghan qararlari. Tashkent: Turkistan Jomhoriyätining Däwlät Näshriyati, 1922.

Bodrogligeti, Andras J. E. *Khalis' Story of Ibrahim: A Central Asian Islamic Work in Late Chagatay Turkic*. Leiden: E. J. Brill, 1974.

Bondarenko, N. A., Novoprudskii, V. D., and Khodzhaev, Ia. D., comps. *Pisateli sovetskogo Uzbekistana. Spravochnik*. Tashkent: Izdatel'stvo Literatury i Iskusstva imeni Gafura Guliama, 1984.

Boukhary, Mir Abdoul Kerim. *Histoire de l'Asie Centrale.* Vols. 1–2. Translated by Charles Schefer. Paris: École des Langues Orientales Vivantes, Publications, 1e série, 1876; reprinted Amsterdam: Philo Press, 1970.

Brown, John P. *The Dervishes.* Oxford, England: Oxford University Press, 1927.

Budagov, Lazar. *Sravnitel'nyi slovar' turetsko-tatarskikh nariechii.* Vols. 1–2. St. Petersburg: Tipografiia Imperatorskoi Akademii Nauk, 1869.

Bukhari, Häfiz-i Tanïsh ibn Mir Muhämmäd. *Shäräf namä-yi shakhi.* Vol. 1. Facsimile and translation by M. A. Salahetdinawa. Moscow: Izdatel'stvo "Nauka." Glavnaia Redaktsiia Vostochnoi Literatury, 1983.

al-Bukhari, Imam Muhammad ibn Isma'il. *Kitab al-jami al-sahih.* Vols. 1–4. Leiden: E. J. Brill, 1862–1908.

Bukhari, Khwaja Baha al-Din Hasan Nithari. *Mudhäkkir-i ähbab. ("Remembrancer of Friends").* Edited by Syed Muhammad Fazlullah. Hyderabad: Da'iratu'l-Ma'arif Press, Osmania University, 1969.

Bukhari, Shaykh Sulayman Afandi-yi. *Lughat-i chaghatay wa turki-yi 'osmani.* Istanbul: Mihran Matba'äsi, A.H. 1298/A.D. 1882.

Bukhariy, Hafiz Tänish ibn Mir Muhämmäd. *Äbdullänamä (Shäräfnamäyi shahiy).* Vol. 2. Tashkent: Ozbekistan SSR "Fän" Näshriyati, 1969. *See also* Bukhari, Häfiz-i Tanïsh.

Bukhariy, Mir Muhämmäd Ämin. *Ubäydullänamä.* Translated by Aleksandr A. Semenov. Tashkent: Izdatel'stvo Akademii Nauk Uzbekskoi SSR, 1957.

Castagné. *Les Basmatchis.* Paris: Editions Ernest Leroux, 1925.

Chadwick, Nora K., and Zhirmunsky, Victor. *Oral Epics of Central Asia.* Cambridge, England: University Press, 1969.

Christie, Ella R. *Through Khiva to Golden Samarkand.* London: Seeley, Service and Company, 1925.

Cirtautas, Ilse Laude. *Chrestomathy of Modern Literary Uzbek.* Wiesbaden: Otto Harrassowitz, 1980.

Constitution (Fundamental Law) of the Uzbek Soviet Socialist Republic of February 23, 1937 as amended through June 25, 1948. New York: American Russian Institute, April 1950.

Current Soviet Leaders. Vol. 3. Oakville, Ontario, Canada: Mosaic Press, 1976.

Danish. *See* Donish.

DeGeorge, Richard T. *Soviet Ethics and Morality.* Ann Arbor: University of Michigan Press, 1969.

D'Encausse, Hélène Carrère. *Réforme et révolution chez les Musulmans de l'empire russe. Bukhara 1867–1924.* Paris: Librairie Armand Colin, 1966.

Directory of USSR Ministry of Foreign Affairs Officials. A Reference Aid. Washington, D.C.: Central Intelligence Agency, September 1985.

Dokumenty k istorii agrarnykh otnoshenii v bukharskom khanstve. Translated by O. D. Chekhovich. Tashkent: Izdatel'stvo Akademii Nauk UzSSR, 1954.

Donish, Ahmad Mahdum Kalla. *Risola-i Ahmad-i Donish 'Ta'rikh-i saltanati Manghitiya'. (Istorii mangitskoi dinastii).* Translated by I. A. Nadzhafova. Dushanbe: Izdatel'stvo "Donish," 1967.

———. *Puteshestvie iz Bukhary v Peterburg. Izbrannoe.* N.p.: Tadzhikgosizdat, 1960.

XX s'ezd kommunisticheskoi partii Uzbekistana. 3–5 fevralia 1981 goda. Stenograficheskii otchet. Tashkent: "Uzbekistan," 1981.

[Dughlat, Mirza Muhammad Haidar]. *Tarikh-i rashidi. A History of the Moguls of Central Asia.* Translated by E. Denison Ross. London: Sampson Low, Marston and Company, 1898; reprinted New York: Praeger Publishers, 1970.

Ermatov, Mutal M. *Etnogenez i formirovanie uzbekskogo naroda.* Tashkent: Izdatel'stvo "Uzbekistan," 1968.

Etnicheskaia onomastika. Moscow: Izdatel'stvo "Nauka," 1984.

Etnograficheskie ocherki uzbekskogo sel'skogo naseleniia. Moscow: Izdatel'stvo "Nauka," 1969.

al-Farabi, Abu Nasr. *Mabadi' ara' ahl al-madina al fadila. Al-Farabi on the Perfect State.* Text prepared and translated by Richard Walzer. Oxford, England: Clarendon Press, 1985.

Farkhadi, Raim. *Ballada o sedoi vesne.* Moscow: "Molodaia Gvardia," 1977.

———. *Freski Afrasiaba. Stikhi i poema.* Tashkent: Izdatel'stvo Khudozhestvennoi Literatury imeni Gafura Guliama, 1970.

———. *Granitsy serdtsa. Stikhi raznykh let.* Tashkent: Izdatel'stvo Literatury i Iskusstva imeni Gafura Guliama, 1976.

Ferrier, J. P. *History of the Afghans.* Translated by William Jesse. London: John Murray, 1858.

Fiträt. *Bedil (bir mäjlisdä).* Moscow: Millät Ishläri Kämisärligi Qashinda "Märkäziy Shärq Näshriyati," [title page] 1923 [cover], 1924.

———. *Eng eski turk ädäbiyati nämunäläri.* Samarkand: Ozbekistan Däwlät Näshriyatining Näshri, Ozbekistan Mätbä'ä Ishläri Tristining Birinchi Mätbä'äsi, 1927.

———. *Munazärä.* Translated to Turki by Muällim Hajji Mu'in ibn Shukrullah Sämärqändiy. Tashkent: Turkistan Kitabkhanäsi, Tipolitografiia V. M. Il'ina, A.H. 1331/A.D. 1913.

———. *Ozbek ädäbiyati nämunäläri.* Tashkent-Samarkand: Oznäshr, 1928.

———. *Shärq siyasäti.* N.p.: Tarqatghuchi: Yash Bukharalilar Qomitasining Näshriyat Shu'bäsi, 1919.

——— and B. S. Sergeev, *Kaziiskie dokumenty XVI veka. Tekst perevod, ukazatel' vstrechaiushchikhsia iuridicheskikh terminov i primechaniia.* Tashkent: Izdatel'stvo Komiteta Nauk UzSSR, 1937.

Pitrat [Fiträt], Cholpan, Batu, Elbek. *Ozbek yash sha'irläri*. Tashkent: Turkistan Däwlät Näshriyati, 1922. *See also* Äbdälrä'uf and Abd-ur-Rauf.

Florinsky, Michael T. *Russia: A History and an Interpretation*. Vols. 1–2. New York: The Macmillan Company, 1955, 1953.

Frye, Richard N. *Bukhara. The Medieval Achievement*. Norman: University of Oklahoma Press, 1965.

Galuzo, Petr G. *Turkestan-koloniia*. Tashkent: Gosudarstvennoe Izdatel'stvo UzSSR, 1935.

Gazety SSSR 1917–1960, Bibliograficheskii spravochnik. Vol. 1. Moscow: "Kniga," 1970.

Ghäfuraw, Ibrahim. *She'riyät—izlänish demäk. Ädäbiy-tänqidiy acherk*. Tashkent: Ghäfur Ghulam namidägi Ädäbiyat wä Sän'ät Näshriyati, 1984.

Ghani, Abdul. *Life and Works of Abdul Qadir Bedil*. Lahore: Publishers United, 1960.

al-Ghazali, *Nasihat al-Muluk: Book of Counsel for Kings*. Translated by F. R. C. Bagley. London: Oxford University Press, 1964.

Ghulamaw, Yähya G., Näbiyew, Räshid N., and Wähabaw, Mäwlan G. *Ozbekistan SSR tärikhi (bir tamlik)*. Tashkent: Ozbekistan SSR Fänlär Äkädemiyäsi Näshriyati, 1958.

Gibb, E. J. W. *A History of Ottoman Poetry*. Vols. 1–6. London: Luzac and Company, 1900, reprinted 1958.

Gordienko, A. A. *Obrazovanie turkestanskoi ASSR*. Moscow: "Iuridicheskaia Literatura," 1968.

Grekov, B. D., and Iakubovskii, A. Iu. *Zolotaia Orda i ee padenie*. Moscow: Izdatel'stvo Akademii Nauk SSSR, 1950.

Grousset, René. *The Empire of the Steppes: A History of Central Asia*. Translated by Naomi Walford. New Brunswick, New Jersey: Rutgers University Press, 1970.

Gruzä, W. W., and Äzizaw, A. Ä. *Ozbek tili. Rus mäktäblärining 9- wä 10-inchi sinfläri uchun oqish kitabi*. Tashkent: OzSSR Däwlät Oquw-Pedägagikä Näshriyati, 1955.

Hajib, Yusuf Khas. *Qutadghu bilig (Säadätgä yollawchi bilim)*. Translated to Uzbek by Qäyum Kärimaw. Tashkent: Ozbekistan SSR "Fän" Näshriyati, 1971.

Hajib, Yusuf Khass. *Wisdom of Royal Glory (Kutadqu Bilig). A Turko-Islamic Mirror for Princes*. Translated by Robert Dankoff. Chicago: University of Chicago Press, 1983.

Hajji, Mullah 'Alim Makhdum. *Ta'rikh-i turkistan*. Tashkent: Turkistan Giniral Gobirnatorighä Tab' Basmäkhanädä, 1915.

Hakimkhan, Muhammad. *Muntäkhäb ät-täwarikh*. Dushanbe: Akademiyai Fanhai RSS Tojikistan. Instituti Ta'rikhi ba nomi Ahmadi Donish, 1983.

———. *Muntäkhäb ät-täwarikh*. Vol. 2. Dushanbe: Näshriyat-i "Danish," 1985.

Häkimkhan bin Säyyid Mä'sumkhan, Hajji Muhämmäd. *Muntäkhäb ät-täwarikh* (1843), mss. No. 5019; 594; copied 1877. (Listed in catalogue *Sobranie sochineniia vostochnykh rukopisei Akademii Nauk Uzbekskoi SSR*, vol. 7. Tashkent: Izdatel'stvo "Nauka" UzSSR, 1964, pp. 31–33.)

Hakluyt, Richard. *Voyages*. London: J. M. Dent and Sons, Everyman's Library, 1907; reprinted New York: Dutton, 1962.

Hanway, Jonas. *The Revolutions of Persia: Containing the Reign of Shah Sultan Hussein, with the Invasion of the Afghans, and the Reigns of Sultan Mir Maghmud and his Successor Sultan Ashreff*. Vol. 1. London: n.p., 1753.

Hayit, Baymirza. *Islam and Turkestan under Russian Rule*. Istanbul: Can Matbaa, 1987.

———. *Turkestan im XX. Jahrhundert*. Darmstadt: C. W. Leske Verlag, 1956.

———. *Türkistanda Öldürülen Türk Shairleri. Mazlum Türklerin Hayatindan Parchalar*. Ankara: Kardesh Matbaasi, 1971.

Hodnett, Grey, and Ogareff, Val. *Leaders of the Soviet Republics. 1955–1972. A Guide to Posts and Occupants*. Canberra: Department of Political Science, Research School of Social Sciences, The Australian National University, 1973.

Hofman, H. F. *Turkish Literature. A Bio-Bibliographical Survey*. Vols. 1–2. Utrecht: The Library of the University of Utrecht under the Auspices of the Royal Asiatic Society of Great Britain and Ireland, 1969.

Howorth, Henry H. *History of the Mongols from the 9th to the 19th Century*. Vols. 1–5. New York: Burt Franklin, n.d., reprint of the 1880 edition.

Hudud al-Alam. The Regions of the World. A Persian Geography, 372 A.H.–982 A.D. Translated and annotated by V. Minorsky. London: Luzac and Company for the Trustees of the E. J. W. Gibb Memorial, 1970.

Iakubovskii, A. Iu. *K voprosu ob etnogeneze uzbekskogo naroda*. Tashkent: Izdatel'stvo UzFAN, 1941.

Ibn Sina. *See* Sina.

Ibragimov, S. K., et al., comps. *Materialy po istorii kazakhskikh khanstv XV–XVIII vekov. (Izvlecheniia iz persidskikh i tiurkskikh sochinenii)*. Alma Ata: Izdatel'stvo "Nauka" Kazakskoi SSR, 1969.

Ikramov, Akmal. *Izbrannye trudy*. Tashkent: Izdatel'stvo "Uzbekistan," 1972.

Inaghamof, Rahim. *Ozbek ziyalilari*. Tashkent: Tipolitografiia Number 1, 1926.

Isfähaniy, Fäzlällah ibn Ruzbihan. *Mihman namä-yi bukhara*. Text prepared and translated by R. P. Dzhalilova. Moscow: Izdatel'stvo "Nauka." Glavnaia Redaktsiia Vostochnoi Literatury, 1976. *See also* Khunji.

Iskandar, Kai Ka'us ibn. *Qabus namä. A Mirror for Princes*. Translated by Reuben Levy. London: The Cresset Press, 1951.

al-Iskandariyya. Sbornik turkestanskogo Vost. Instituta v chest' professora A. E. Shmidta. Tashkent, 1923.

Istoriko-kul'turnye kontakty narodov altaiskoi iazykovoi obshchnosti. Tezisy dokladov XXIX sessii postoiannoi mezhdunarodnoi altaisticheskoi konferentsii (PIAC). Tashkent, sentiabr', 1986 g. 1. Istoriia, literatura, iskusstvo. Moscow: Akademiia Nauk

SSSR. Institut Vostokovedeniia, Institut Iazykoznaniia, Vsesoiuznaia Assotsiatsiia Vostokovedov; Akademiia Nauk Uzbekskoi SSR Institut Iazyka i Literatury im. A. S. Pushkina, 1986.

Itogi vsesoiuznoi perepisi naseleniia 1959 goda. SSSR (svodnyi tom). Moscow: Gosstatizdat TsSU SSSR, 1962.

Itogi vsesoiuznoi perepisi naseleniia 1959 goda. Uzbekskaia SSR. Moscow: Gosstatizdat. TsSU SSSR, 1962.

Itogi vsesoiuznoi perepisi naseleniia 1970 goda. Vol. 4. Moscow: "Statistika," 1973.

Ivanov, P. P. *Ocherki po istorii srednei Azii (XVI-seredina XIX v.)*. Moscow: Izdatel'stvo Vostochnoi Literatury, 1958.

————. *Vosstanie Kitai-Kipchakov v Bukharskom Khanstve, 1821–1825. Istochniki i opyt ikh issledovaniia*. Moscow-Leningrad: Izdatel'stvo Akademii Nauk SSSR, 1937.

Jarring, Gunnar. *Return to Kashgar. Central Asian Memoirs in the Present*. Vol. 1. Central Asia Book Series. Durham: Duke University Press, 1986.

————. *Some Notes on Eastern Turki (New Uigur) Munazara Literature*. Lund: CWK Gleerup, Scripta Minora, 1981.

Jeffery, Arthur. *A Reader on Islam*. 'S-Gravenhage: Mouton and Company, 1962.

Juvaini, 'Ala-ad-Din 'Ata-Malik. *The History of the World Conqueror*. Translated by John Andrew Boyle from the text of Mirza Muhammad Qazvini. Vols. 1–2. Manchester, England: Manchester University Press, 1958.

KPSS i sovetskoe pravitel'stvo ob Uzbekistane. Sbornik dokumentov (1925–1970). Tashkent: "Ozbekistan," 1972.

Kalmykow, Andrew D. *Memoirs of a Russian Diplomat. Outposts of the Empire, 1893–1917*. New Haven, Conn.: Yale University Press, 1971.

Kämal, Jämal. *Dastanlär*. Tashkent: Ghäfur Ghulam namidägi Ädäbiyat wä Sän'ät Näshriyati, 1979.

————. *Qädäh. Lirikä*. Tashkent: Ghäfur Ghulam namidägi Ädäbiyat wä Sän'ät Näshriyati, 1980.

————. *Suwäyda. She'rlär*. Tashkent: Ghäfur Ghulam namidägi Ädäbiyat wä Sän'ät Näshriyati, 1983.

Käykawus. *Qabus namä*. Adapted from Chaghatay translation by Agahiy to Uzbek by Subutay Dalimaw. Tashkent: "Oqituwchi" Näshriyati, 1968. *See also* Iskandar, Kai Ka'us ibn.

Khalid-Oghli, Imam Qurban 'Ali Hajji. *Täwärikh-i khamsä'*. Kazan: "Örnäk" Matbä'äsi, 1910.

Khan, Abul Ghazi Bhadur. *Shäjärä-i Turk. Histoire des Mongols et des Tatares*. Text and translation prepared by Petr I. Desmaisons. St. Leonards, England: Ad Orientem; Amsterdam: Philo Press, 1970, reprint of the 1871–1874 edition.

————. *The Genealogical History of the Tatars*. Vol. 1. London: J. and J. Knapton, J. Darby, A. Bettesworth, et al., 1730.

Khan, Émir Said Alim. *La Voix de la Boukharie Opprimée.* Vols. 1–2. (Tajik and French) Paris: Librairie Orientale et Américaine, 1929.

Khan, Munäwwär Qari ibn 'Abduräshid. *Ädib-i thani.* 2d ed. Tashkent: Ghulamiyä Mätbu'äsi, A.H. 1329/A.D. 1911.

Khanikoff, *Bokhara: Its Amir and Its People.* Translated by Clement A. de Bode. London: James Madden, 1845.

Khilkov, Grigoriy, comp. *Sbornik kniazia khilkova.* St. Petersburg: Br. Panteleevy, 1879.

Khodzhaev, Faizulla. *K istorii revoliutsii v Bukhare.* Tashkent: Uzbekskoe Gosudarstvennoe Izdatel'stvo, 1926.

Khojäyew, Fäyzullä. *Tänlängän äsärlär.* Vol. 1. Tashkent: Ozbekistan SSR "Fän" Näshriyati, 1976.

Khunji, Fadlullah b. Ruzbihan. *Tarikh-i 'aläm-ara-yi ämini.* Translated and abridged by V. Minorsky. London: The Royal Asiatic Society of Great Britain and Ireland, 1957.

Knobloch, Edgar. *Beyond the Oxus. Archeology, Art and Architecture of Central Asia.* London: Ernest Benn, 1972.

Kommunisticheskaia partiia Uzbekistana v tsifrakh (1924–64). Tashkent: Izdatel'stvo "Uzbekistana," 1964.

Konstitutsiia (osnovnoi zakon) Uzbekskoi Sovetskoi Sotsialisticheskoi Respubliki. Samarkand: Izdanie Upravleniia Informatsiei TsIK i SNK UzSSR, 1927.

Konstitutsiia (osnovnoi zakon) Uzbekskoi Sovetskoi Sotsialisticheskoi Respubliki. Tashkent: Gosizdat UzSSR, 1961.

The Koran. Interpreted. Translated by A. J. Arberry. Toronto: The Macmillan Company, 1969.

Kudsi-Zadeh, A. Albert. *Sayyid Jamal al-Din al-Afghani. An Annotated Bibliography.* Leiden: E. J. Brill, 1970.

Kunanbaev, Abai. *Izbrannoe proizvedenie.* Moscow: OGIZ. Gosizdat Khudozhestvennoi Literatury, 1945.

Lane-Poole, Stanley. *The Mohammadan Dynasties.* New York: Frederick Ungar Publishing Company, 1965, reprint of the 1893 edition.

Len-Pul', Stenli. *Musul'manskiia dinastii.* Edited and translated by Vasiliy V. Bartol'd. St. Petersburg: Tipografiia M. M. Stasiulevicha, 1899.

Litvinskii, Boris A., and Akramov, N. M. *Aleksandr A. Semenov.* Moscow: "Nauka," 1971.

Lockhart, Laurence. *Nadir Shah. A Critical Study Based Mainly on Contemporary Sources.* London: Luzac and Company, 1938.

Lubin, Nancy. *Labour and Nationality in Central Asia: An Uneasy Compromise.* London: Macmillan, 1984.

Malcolm, John. *The History of Persia from the Most Early Period to the Present Time.* London: John Murray, 1829.

Mä'rufaw, Z. M., ed. *Ozbek tilining izahli lughäti.* Vols. 1–2. Moscow: "Rus Tili Näshriyati, 1981.

[Marx, Karl, and Engels, Friedrich]. *Karl Marx and Friedrich Engels, The Russian Menace to Europe. A Collection of Articles, Speeches, Letters and News Dispatches.* Edited by Paul W. Blackstock and Bert F. Hoselitz. Glencoe, Ill.: The Free Press, 1953.

Mäshräb. *Tänlängän äsärlär.* Tashkent: Ozbekistan SSR Däwlät Bädiiy Ädäbiyat Näshriyati, 1963.

Materialy po istorii Ura-Tiube. Sbornik aktov XVII–XIX vv. Moscow: Izdatel'stvo Vostochnoi Literatury, 1963.

Materialy po istorii Uzbekistana. Tashkent: Izdatel'stvo Akademii Nauk Uzbekskoi SSR, 1963.

Materialy po istorii uzbekskoi, tadzhikskoi i turkmenskoi SSR. Leningrad: Izdatel'stvo Akademii Nauk SSSR, 1932.

Materialy po raionirovaniiu Uzbekistana. Kratkaia kharakteristika proektiruemykh okrugov i raionov. Samarkand: Izdanie TsKR Uz., 1926.

Medlin, William K., et al. *Education and Development in Central Asia. A Case Study on Social Change in Uzbekistan.* Leiden: E. J. Brill, 1971.

Meyendorff, Georges de. *Voyage d'Orenbourg à Boukhara, fait en 1820.* Paris: Librairie Orientale de Dondey-Dupré Père et fils, 1826.

Miliband, S. D. *Biobibliograficheskii slovar' sovetskikh Vostokovedov.* Moscow: Glavnaia Redaktsiia Vostochnoi Literatury, 1975.

Mir-Ali-Shir. Sbornik k piatisotletiiu so dnia rozhdeniia. Leningrad: Izdatel'stvo Akademii Nauk SSSR, 1928.

Mirkhond [Mirkhwand], Muhammad bin Khavendshah bin Mahmud. *The Rauzat us-Safa, or Garden of Purity, Containing the Histories of Prophets, Kings, and Khalifs.* Vol. 1. Translated by E. Rehatsek. Oriental Translation Fund, new series. London: Royal Asiatic Society, 1891.

Miropiev, M. A. *O polozhenii russkikh inorodtsev.* St. Petersburg: Synodal'naia Tipografiia, 1901.

Mominaw, I. M. *Mirzä Bedilning fälsäfiy qäräshläri.* Tashkent: Ozbekistan SSR Fänlär Äkädemiyäsi Näshriyati, 1958. *See also* Muminov, Ibragim M.

Monshi, Eskandar Beg. *Tarikh-e 'Alamara-ye 'Abbasi. History of Shah 'Abbas the Great.* Vols. 1–2. Translated by Roger M. Savory. Boulder, Colo.: Westview Press, 1978.

Muhämmädjan-oghli, Mo'minjan. *Turmish orinishläri (bir mulläbächäning khatirä däftäri).* Tashkent: Ozbekistan Däwlät Näshriyati, 1926.

Mukhamedova, R. Kh. *Prezidium Verkhovnogo Soveta Soiuznoi Respubliki.* Tashkent: Izdatel'stvo "FAN" UzSSR, 1980.

Mukhammedberdyev, K. *Kommunisticheskaia Partiia v bor'be za pobedu narodnoi sovetskoi revoliutsii v Khorezme.* Ashkhabad: Turkmenskoe Gosudarstvennoe Izdatel'stvo, 1959.

al-Mulk, Nizam. *The Book of Government or Rules for Kings.* Translated by Hubert Darke. London: Routledge and Kegan Paul, 1960.

Mulläjanaw, Ishäq R. *Ozbekistan ähalisi.* Tashkent: Ozbekistan Näshriyati, 1974.

Muminov, Ibragim M., ed. *Istoriia Khorezma. S drevneishikh vremen do nashikh dnei.* Tashkent: Izdatel'stvo "Fan" UzSSR, 1976.

———. *Rol' i mesto Amira Timura v istorii srednei Azii v svete dannykh pis'mennykh istochnikov.* Tashkent: Izdatel'stvo "FAN" UzSSR, 1968.

———. *Istoriia uzbekskoi SSR s drevneishikh vremen do nashikh dnei.* Tashkent: Izdatel'stvo "FAN" UzSSR, 1974.

———, et al., eds. *Istoriia Samarkanda.* Tashkent: Izdatel'stvo "FAN" Uzbekskoi SSR, 1969.

Munawwar Qari. *See* Khan and Qari.

Munirov, Quwämiddin. *Munis, Agähiy wä Bäyaniyning tärikhiy äsärläri.* Tashkent: Ozbekistan SSR Fänlär Äkädemiyäsi Näshriyati, 1960.

Mu'nis, Shir Muhämmäd bin Ämir 'Awaz Biy Mirab Khwaräzmiy. *Firdäws äl-iqbal,* mss. No. TY 82, Istanbul Üniversitesi Kütübhanesi, copied A.H. 1296/A.D. 1878/79; this copy includes a continuation of Mu'nis's history by his nephew Agahiy.

———. *Firdäws äl-iqbal.* Ed. Yuri Bregel. Leiden: E. J. Brill, 1983, 1988, 2 vols.

Munshi, Muhämmäd Yusuf. *Tärikh-i muqim khaniy. Mukim khanskaia istoriia.* Translated by Aleksandr A. Semenov. Tashkent: Izdatel'stvo Akademii Nauk Uzbekskoi SSR, 1956.

al-Munshi. *See* Bäqa.

Murav'ev, Nikolai. *Puteshestvie v Turkmeniiu i Khivu v 1819 i 1820 gg.* Moscow: Tipografiia Avgusta Semena, 1822.

Nahju'l-feradis. Vol. 1, *Tipkibasim.* Introduction and text prepared by János Eckmann. Ankara: Turk Tarih Kurumu Basimevi, 1956.

Nahju'l-feradis. Ushtmakhlarning achuq yoli (jennetlerin achik yolu). Part transliterated by János Eckmann, prepared for publication by Semih Tezjan and Hamza Zulfikar, N.p.: Turk Dil Kurumu Yayinlari No. 518 [1984].

A Narrative of the Russian Military Expedition to Khiva under General Perofski in 1839. Calcutta: Office of the Superintendent of Government Printing, 1867.

Narshakhi. *The History of Bukhara.* Translated by Richard N. Frye. Cambridge, Mass.: The Medieval Academy of America, 1954.

Närshäkhiy, Äbu Bäkr Muhämmäd Jä'fär. *Bukhara tärikhi.* Translated into Uzbek by Ä. Räsulew. Tashkent: Ozbekistan SSR "Fän" Näshriyati, 1966.

Naselenie SSSR. Po dannym vsesoiuznoi perepisi naseleniia 1979 goda. Moscow: Izdatel'stvo Politicheskoi Literatury, 1980.

Näsir, Muhämmäd Mahdi ibn Muhämmäd. *"Jähan kushäy." Histoire de Nader Chah, connu sous le nom de Thahmas Kuli Khan, Empereur de Perse.* Translated by William Jones. London: P. Elmsly, 1770.

Nasyrov, Erkin; Farkhadi, Raim; and Filippov, Petr. *Pisateli sovetskogo Uzbekistana.* Tashkent: Izdatel'stvo Literatury i Iskusstva imeni Gafura Guliama, 1977.

Näwaiy, Älisher. *Khämsä.* Tashkent: OzSSR Fänlär Äkädemiyäsi Näshriyati, 1958.

———. *Mähbub äl-qulub.* Moscow-Leningrad: Izdatel'stvo Akademii Nauk SSSR, 1948.

———. *Mähbub ul-qulub (Qälblär sewgilisi).* Tashkent: Ghäfur Ghulam namidägi Ädäbiyat wä Sän'ät Näshriyati, 1983. *See also* 'Ali Shir, Mir, and Navoi, Alisher.

Nemchenko, M. *Natsional'noe razmezhevanie srednei Azii.* Moscow: Izdanie Litizdata NKID, 1925.

Nepesov, G. *Iz istorii khorezmskoi revoliutsii, 1920–1924 g.g.* Tashkent: Gosizdat UzSSR, 1962.

Niyaziy, Hämzä Häkimzadä. *Zähärli häyat yakhud 'ishq qurbanläri. Turkistan mä'ishat-indän alinmish qiz wä kuyaw faji'asidur.* Tashkent: Matbaa-i Ghulamiyä, A.H. 1335/A.D. 1916.

Nurdzhanov, N. *Tadzhikskii narodnyi teatr. Po materialam kuliabskoi oblasti.* Moscow: Izdatel'stvo Akademii Nauk SSSR, 1956.

Nurmukhammedov, Naghïm Bek. *Qoja Akhmed Yassaui mavzoleyi.* Alma Ata: "Öner" Baspasï, 1980.

Ocherki istorii obshchestvenno-filosofskoi mysli v Uzbekistane. Tashkent: Izdatel'stvo "Fan" Uzbekskoi SSR, 1977.

Ortä Asiya kammunistik täshkilatlärining tärikhi. Tashkent: "Ozbekistan" Näshriyati, 1969.

Ostroumov, Nikolai P. *Sarty. Etnograficheskie materialy.* 1st ed. Tashkent: Tipo-Litografiia S. I. Lakhtina, 1890.

———. *Sarty. Etnograficheskie materialy.* Tashkent: Izdanie Knizhnago Magazina "Bukinist," 1896.

———. *Sarty. Etnograficheskie materialy.* 2d ed. Tashkent: Tipografiia Gazety "Sredneaziatskaia Zhizn'," 1908.

———. *Sarty. Etnograficheskie materialy. Poslovitsy i zagadki Sartov.* Tashkent: Tipo-Litografiia Torg. Doma "F. I. G. Br. Kamenskie," 1895.

Ozbek ädäbiyati. Vol. 1. Tashkent: OzSSR Däwlät Bädiiy Ädäbiyat Näshriyati, 1959.

Ozbekistan kammonist (balshäwik)lär firqäsining IInchi qurultayi. (1925inchi yil 22–30 noyäbr). Qurultayining hisabi. Samarkand: Ozb. Kam. (Balshäwiklär) Firqäsi Märkäzqomining Näshri; Tashkent: Ozbekistan Däwlät Näshriyatining Birinchi Basmakhanäsi, 1926.

Ozbekistan SSR tärikhi. Vols. 1–2. Tashkent: Ozbekistan SSR Fänlär Äkädemiyäsi Näshriyati, 1956–1958.

Ozbekistan Sawet Satsiälistik Respubliräsining mä'muriy-territariäl bolinishi. 1966 yil 1 yänwärgächä bolgän mä'lumat. Tashkent: "Ozbekistan" Näshriyati, 1966.

Ozbekistan Sawet Satsiälistik Respubliräsining mä'muriy-territariäl bolinishi. 1954 yilning 1 iyuligächä bolgän mä'lumat. Tashkent: Ozbekistan SSR Aliy Sawetining Prezidiyumi. Infarmätsian-Stätistikä Bolimi, 1954.

Ozbekistan Sawet Satsiälistik Respublikäsining mä'muriy-territariäl bolinish. 1975 yil 1 äprelgächä bolgän mä'lumat. Tashkent: "Ozbekistan" Näshriyati, 1975.

Ozbek sawet ädäbiyat tärikhi. Vol. 3, book 2. Tashkent: Ozbekistan SSR "Fän" Näshriyati, 1972.

Ozbek she'riyäti äntalagiyäsi. Sawet she'riyäti. Tashkent: Ozbekistan SSR Däwlät Bädiiy Ädäbiyat Näshriyati, 1962.

[Palen, Graf K. K.]. *Otchet po revizii turkestanskago kraia: Uchebnoe dielo.* Saint Petersburg: Senatskaia Tipografiia, 1910.

Park, Alexander G. *Bolshevism in Turkestan, 1917–1927.* New York: Columbia University Press, 1957.

Pelliot, Paul. *Notes sur l'histoire de la Horde d'Or.* Paris: Librairie d'Amerique et d'Orient, [title page] 1949, [cover] 1950.

I [Pervyi] s'ezd intelligentsii Uzbekistana. 11–13 oktiabria 1956 goda. Stenograficheskii otchet. Tashkent: Gosudarstvennoe Izdatel'stvo Uzbekskoi SSR, 1957.

Piaskovskii, A. V. *Revoliutsiia 1905–1907 godov v Turkestane.* Moscow: Izdatel'stvo Akademii Nauk, 1958.

Pierce, Richard A. *Russian Central Asia, 1867–1917: A Study in Colonial Rule.* Berkeley: University of California Press, 1960.

Pis'ma Nikolaia Ivanovicha Il'minskago k Ober-Prokuroru Sviatieishago Sinoda Konstantinu Petrovichu Pobiedonostsevu. Kazan: Izdanie Redaktsii Pravoslavnago Sobesiednika, 1895.

Plan tret'ego goda piatiletki respublik Srednei Azii. (Kontrol'nye tsifry na 1931 god). Tashkent: Sredne-Aziatskii Gosplan, 1931.

Pod'iachikh, P. G. *Naselenie SSSR.* Moscow: Gosudarstvennoe Izdatel'stvo, 1961.

Polivanov, Evgenii D. *Etnograficheskaia kharakteristika Uzbekov.* Tashkent: Uzbekskoe Gosudarstvennoe Izdatel'stvo, 1926.

"Polkan," Mähämmäd Qul Jamrat-oghli. *Shaybani khan dastani.* Recorded and edited by Ghazi 'Alim. Samarkand-Tashkent: Ozbekistan Däwlät Näshriyati, 1928.

Prisoners of Conscience in the USSR: Their Treatment and Conditions. 2d ed. London: Amnesty International Publications, April 1980.

Program of the Communist Party of the Soviet Union. New York: International Publishers, 1963.

Protokoly i stenograficheskie otchety s'ezdov i konferentsii kommunisticheskoi partii sovetskogo soiuza. Piatnadtsatyi s'ezd VKP(b). Dekabr' 1927 goda. Stenograficheskii otchet. Moscow: Gosizdat Politicheskoi Literatury, 1961.

Pulatov, Timur. *The Life Story of a Naughty Boy from Bukhara.* Translated by Dudley Hagen. Moscow: Raduga Publishers, 1983.

Qabus nama. See Kaykawus.

Qadir, Jori, and Dawut, Khaliq. *Uyghur binakarliq sän'ätidin ornäklär. Examples of Uyghur Architectural Art.* Kashgar: Qäshqär Uyghur Näshriyati, 1984.

Qadiriy, Äbdullah. *Bäkhtsiz kiyaw.* Tashkent: Izdanie Seid Arifdzhanova. Tipografiia Kantseliarii Turkest. Gen.-Gub., 1915.

Qari, Munäwwär. *Hawa'ij-i diniyyä.* Reprinted as *'Äqa'id.* Mecca: M. Moosa Turkistani and Sons, A.H. 1373/ A.D. 1953–54. *See also* Khan, Munäwwär Qari ibn 'Abduräshid.

Quelquejay-Lemercier, Chantal, et al., eds. *Passé Turco-Tatar, Présent Soviétique. Turco-Tatar Past, Soviet Present.* Paris: Éditions Peeters. Éditions de l'École des Hautes Études, 1986.

Radlov, V. V. *Opyt slovaria tiurkskikh nariechii.* Vols. 1–8. St. Petersburg: Imperatorskaia Akademiia Nauk, 1893, reprint.

Radzhabov, Zarif. *Iz istorii obshchestvenno-politicheskoi mysli tadzhikskogo naroda vo vtoroi polovine XIX i v nachale XX vv.* Stalinabad: Tadzhikskoe Gosudarstvennoe Izdatel'stvo, 1957.

Rähmanaw, Mamajan. *Ozbek teätri tärikhi (XVIII äsrdän XX äsr äwwäligächä ozbek teätr mädäniyätining täräqqiyat yolläri).* Tashkent: Ozbekistan SSR "Fän" Näshriyati, 1968.

Rahmanov, Mamadzhan. *Khamza i uzbekskii teatr.* Tashkent: Gosudarstvennoe Izdatel'stvo Khudozhestvennoi Literatury UzSSR, 1960.

Räshidaw, Shäraf. *Käshmir qoshighi. Qissä.* Tashkent: Ghäfur Ghulam namidägi Ädäbiyat wä Sän'ät Näshriyati, 1970.

———. *Ozbekistan alimlärining yuksäk burchi.* Tashkent: Ozbekistan KP Märkäziy Kamitetining Näshriyati, 1980.

Rashidov, Sharaf. *The Banner of Friendship.* Moscow: Progress Publishers, 1969.

———. *Sobranie sochinenii v piati tomakh.* Vol. 4. Moscow: "Khudozhestvennaia Literatura," 1980.

Rawls, John. *A Theory of Justice.* Cambridge, Mass.: The Belknap Press of Harvard University Press, 1971.

Reis, Sidi ali. *The Travels and Adventures of the Turkish Admiral, Sidi Ali Reis in India, Afghanistan, Central Asia, and Persia, during the years 1553–1556.* Translated by Arminius Vámbéry. London: Luzac and Company, 1899.

Report of Court Proceedings in the Case of the Anti-Soviet "Bloc of Rights and Trotskyites" Heard Before the Military Collegium of the Supreme Court of the U.S.S.R. Moscow, March 2–13, 1938. Moscow: People's Commissariat of Justice of the U.S.S.R., 1938.

Riza, Hämraqul. *Zängari därya. She'rlär.* Tashkent: Uzbekistan LKSM Märkäziy Kamiteti "Yash Gwärdiyä" Näshriyati, 1983.

Rodonachal'nik uzbekskoi literatury. Sbornik statei ob Alishere Navoi. Tashkent: Izdatel'stvo Uzbekistanskogo Filiala Akademii Nauk SSSR, 1940.

Rokeach, Milton. *The Nature of Human Values.* New York: The Free Press, Collier Macmillan Publishers, 1973.

Rosenthal, Franz. *A History of Muslim Historiography.* Leiden: E. J. Brill, 1952.

Rozi, Sher 'Äli, comp. *Ozbäk maqallari.* Moscow: SSSR Khälqlarining Märkäz Näshriyati, 1926.

Rumlu, Hasan-i. *Ähsänu't täwarikh. A Chronicle of the Early Safawis.* Vols. 1–2. Text and translation prepared by C. N. Seddan. Baroda, India: Oriental Institute, 1934.

Rumer, Boris. *Soviet Central Asia—"A Tragic Experiment."* Boston: Unwin Hyman, 1989.

Rustamov, Ergash R. *Uzbekskaia poeziia v pervoi polovine XV veka.* Moscow: Izdatel'stvo Vostochnoi Literatury, 1963.

Rypka, Jan. *History of Iranian Literature.* Dordrecht, Holland: D. Reidel Publishing Company, 1968.

Rywkin, Michael. *Moscow's Muslim Challenge. Soviet Central Asia.* Armonk, New York: M. E. Sharpe, Inc., 1982.

Rywkin, Michael. *The Soviet Nationalities Policy and the Communist Party Structure in Uzbekistan. A Study of the Methods of Soviet Russian Control, 1941–1946.* Ph.D. dissertation, Columbia University, 1960.

Sadiq, Muhammad. *Ädäb-us salihin.* Adapted and translated by N. S. Lykoshin as *"Khoroshii ton" na Vostokie.* Petrograd: Sklad u V. A. Berezovskago, 1915.

Safarov, Georgiy. *Kolonial'naia revoliutsiia (opyt Turkestana).* Moscow: Gosudarstvennoe Izdatel'stvo, 1921.

Sä'id, Ziya. *Ozbek wäqtli mätbu'ati tä'rikhigä mäteriyällär, 1870–1927.* Tashkent-Samarkand: Ozbekistan Däwlät Näshriyati, 1927.

Said Alim Khan. *See* Khan.

Salih, Muhämmäd. *Shäybaniynamä.* Tashkent: Ozbekistan SSR Fänlär Äkädemiyäsi Näshriyati, 1961.

Salikh, Mukhammed. *Sheibani-name. Dzhagataiskii text.* No. 27. Edited by P. M. Melioranskii. St. Petersburg: Izdaniia Fakul'teta Vostochnykh Iazykov Imperatorskago S.-Peterburgskago Universiteta, 1908.

Säliyif, Polat. *Ozbekistan tarïkhï (XV–XIXinchi äsrlär).* Samarkand-Tashkent: Ozbekistan Däwlät Näshriyati, 1929.

Sämärqändiy, Äbdurräzzaq. *Mätlä-i sa'däyn wä mäjmä-i bähräyn.* Tashkent: Ozbekistan SSR "Fän" Näshriyati, 1969.

Sami, Mirza 'Abdal'azim. *Ta'rikhi-i salatin-i manghitiya (Istoriia mangytskikh gosudarei).* Translated by L. M. Epifanova. Moscow: Izdatel'stvo Vostochnoi Literatury, 1962.

Sawet ozbekistanining yazuwchiläri. Tashkent: OzSSR Däwlät Bädiiy Ädäbiyat Näshriyati, 1959.

Schlesinger, R., ed. *The Nationalities Problem and Soviet Administration.* London: Routledge and Kegan Paul, 1956.

Schuyler, Eugene. *Peter the Great, Emperor of Russia: A Study of Historical Biography.* Vols. 1–2. New York, 1884, reprinted by Russell and Russell, 1967.

————. *Turkistan. Notes of a Journey in Russian Turkistan, Khokand, Bukhara, and Kuldja.* Vols. 1–2. New York: Scribner, Armstrong and Company, 1877.

The Secret History of the Mongols. Translated by Francis Woodman Cleaves. Vols. 1–2. Cambridge, Mass.: Harvard University Press, 1982.

S'ezdy sovetov sovetskikh sotsialisticheskikh respublik. Sbornik dokumentov, 1917–1922 g.g. Vols. 1–2. Moscow: Gosizdat Iuridicheskoi Literatury, 1960.

Shami, Nizamuddin. *Histoire des conquetes de Tamerlan intitulée Zafar-nama.* Prague: F. Tauer, 1937.

Shämsiyew, Pärsä, and Ibrahimaw, Sabirjan, comps. *Näwaiy äsärläri lughäti. Älisher Näwaiy äsärlärining on besh tamligigä ilawä.* Tashkent: Ghäfur Ghulam namidägi Ädäbiyat wä Sän'ät Näshriyati, 1972.

Shashi, Qari 'Othman ibn Äbdalkhaliq. *Ta'lim-i äwwäl.* Tashkent: Litografiia Gulam Khasan Arifdzhanova, 1910.

Shaybaniy-Khan. *Diwan.* Mss. no. 2436. Istanbul: Topkapi-Ahmet III Library.

Shermukhamedov, Said Sh. *O natsional'noi forme sotsialisticheskoi kul'tury uzbekskogo naroda.* Tashkent: Izdatel'stvo Akademii Nauk Uzbekskoi SSR, 1961.

Shest' dnei. "Belaia kniga." Sudebnyi protsess Il'i Gabaia i Mustafy Dzhemileva. Vol. 2. New York: Fond Krym, 1980.

Shukrullah, Hajji Mu'in ibn. *Eski mäktäb, yängi mäktäb.* Samarkand: n.p., 1916.

Siddiqi, Mazheruddin. *The Qur'anic Concept of History.* Karachi: Central Institute of Islamic Research, 1965.

Sina, Äbu Äli ibn. *She'riyät.* Translated by Jämal Kämal. Tashkent: Ghäfur Ghulam namidägi Ädäbiyat wä Sän'ät Näshriyati, 1980.

Singh, Ganda. *Ahmad Shah Durrani. Father of Modern Afghanistan.* London: Asia Publishing House, 1959.

Smith, Adam. *The Theory of Moral Sentiments.* The Glasgow Edition of the Works and Correspondence of Adam Smith, 1982. New York: Oxford University Press. Reprinted by Liberty Classics, Indianapolis.

Sobranie vostochnykh rukopisei Akademii Nauk Uzbekskoi SSR. Vol. 7. Tashkent: Izdatel'stvo "Nauka" Uzbekskoi SSR, 1964.

Solov'ev, S. M. *Istoriia rossii s drevneishikh vremen.* Vols. 17–18. Moscow: Izdatel'stvo Sotsial'no-Ekonomicheskoi Literatury, 1963.

Solzhenitsyn, Aleksandr I. *The Gulag Archipelago, 1918–1956. An Experiment in Literary Investigation.* Vol. 3, books 5–7. New York: Harper and Row Publishers, 1979.

Sredneaziatskii etnograficheskii sbornik. Moscow: Izdatel'stvo Akademii Nauk SSSR, 1959.

Sredniaia Aziia v drevnosti i srednevekov'e (istoriia i kul'tura). Moscow: Izdatel'stvo "Nauka." Glavnaia Redaktsiia Vostochnoi Literatury, 1977.

Steensgard, Niels. *The Asian Trade Revolution of the Seventeenth Century. The East.* Chicago: University of Chicago Press, 1974.

Struve, V. V., ed. *Materialy po istorii Turkmen i Turkmenii*. Vols. 1–2. Moscow-Leningrad: Izdatel'stvo Akademii Nauk SSSR, 1938.

[Sufi Allah Yar]. *Shärh-i thäbat al-'ajizin. Risalä-i 'äzizä [or, ghäzizä]*. Translation and commentary by Tajäldin Balchighil oghli. Kazan: Qäzan Univirsititining Tab'khanäsi, A.H. 1275.

Sultan, Izzat. *Äsärlär. Tort tamlik*. Vol. 1, *Drama*. Tashkent: Ghäfur Ghulam namidägi Ädäbiyat wä Sän'ät Näshriyati, 1971.

Tale', Äbdurähmani. *Äbulfäyzkhan tärikhi. Istoriia Abulfeizkhana*. Translated by Aleksandr A. Semenov. Tashkent: Izdatel'stvo Akademii Nauk Uzbekskoi SSR, 1959.

Ta'min-i mä'arif-i jämi'ät-i khäyriyäsinin nizamnamä wä khatt-i häräkätidir. Dar al-Säadät [Abode of Happiness—Istanbul]: (metin) Mätba'äsindä Tab Olinmishdir, A.H. 1327/A.D. 1909.

Täwarikh-i guzidä—nusrätnamä. Text prepared by Ä. M. Äkrämaw. Tashkent: Ozbekistan SSR "Fän" Näshriyati, 1967.

Tian-Shanskii Semenov, V. P., ed. *Rossiia. Polnoe geograficheskoe opisanie nashego otechestva*. St. Petersburg: Izdanie A. F. Devriena, 1913, volume 19 "Turkestanskii Krai."

Timour. *Tuzukat-i Timuri. Institutes Political and Military*. Translated by Major Davy. Oxford, England: The Clarendon Press, 1783, reprinted n.d.

[Timur]. *Tuzak-i-Timuri. The Autobiography of Timur*. Translated by H. M. Elliot and edited by John Dowson. Lahore: Sind Sagar Academy; reprint Publ. M. Masood, 1974.

Tiurikov, Vladimir, comp. *Letopis' poluveka. Khronika kul'turnoi zhizni Uzbekistana (1924–1974)*. Tashkent: Izdatel'stvo Literatury i Iskusstva imeni Gafura Guliama, 1975.

Tizengauzen, V. G., comp. *Sbornik materialov otnosiashchikhsia k istorii Zolotoi Ordy. Izvlecheniia iz persidskikh sochinenii*. Vols. 1–2. Moscow-Leningrad: Izdatel'stvo Akademii Nauk SSSR, 1941.

Togan, Zeki Velidi. *Bugünkü Türkili (Türkistan) ve yakin Tarihi*. Istanbul: Arkadash, Ibrahim Horoz ve Güven Basimevleri, 1942–1947.

———. *Presentation Volume to Professor M. Shafi*. Lahore: 1955, cited by V. Minorsky in the foreword to Barthold, *Four Studies* . . . , volume 2. *See above*.

Tolstov, S. P. *Drevniaia kul'tura Uzbekistana*. Tashkent: Izdatelstvo UzFAN, 1943.

Travels to Tana and Persia. New York: Burt Franklin, n.d.; reprinted from The Hakluyt Society, first series, No. 159, MCDDDLXXIII.

Trever, Kamilla V.; Iakubovskii, Aleksandr Iu.; and Voronets, M. E. *Istoriia narodov Uzbekistana*. Vol. 1. Tashkent: Izdatel'stvo AN UzSSR, 1950.

Trudy dvadtsat piatogo mezhdunarodnogo kongressa Vostokovedov, Moskva 9–16 avgusta, 1960. Moscow: Izdatel'stvo Vostochnoi Literatury, 1963.

Tukhtametov, Tukhtamet. *Rossiia i Khiva v kontse XIX—nachale XX v. Pobeda khorezmskoi narodnoi revoliutsii*. Moscow: Izdatel'stvo "Nauka," 1969.

Tursunaw, Häbib T. *Ozbekistan Sawet Satsiälistik Respublikäsining bärpa etilishi*. Tashkent: Ozbekistan SSR Fänlär Äkädemiyäsi Näshriyati, 1958.

Tursunov, Tashpulat T. *Formirovanie Sotsialisticheskogo realizma v uzbekskoi dramaturgii*. Tashkent: Izdatel'stvo Akademii Nauk Uzbekskoi SSR, 1963.

Tuzmukhamedov, R. A. *Natsional'nyi suverenitet*. Moscow: Izdatel'stvo Instituta Mezhdunarodnykh Otnoshenii, 1963.

al-Utbi, Muhammad bin Muhammad al-Jabbar. *The Kitab-i-Yamini, Historical Memoirs of the Amir Sabaktagin, and the Sultan Mahmud of Ghazna*. Translated by James Reynolds. London: Printed for the Oriental Translation Fund of Great Britain and Ireland, 1858.

Uyghun. *Äsärlär*. Vol. 5. Tashkent: Ghäfur Ghulam namidägi Ädäbiyat wä Sän'ät Näshriyati, 1978.

Vakhabov, Mavlian G. *Formirovanie uzbekskoi sotsialisticheskoi natsii*. Tashkent: Gosudarstvennoe Izdatel'stvo Uzbekskoi SSR, 1961.

Valikhanov, Chingiz, et al. *The Russians in Central Asia*. London: Edward Stanford, 1865.

Vámbéry, Arminius. *History of Bokhara. From the Earliest Period Down to the Present*. 2d ed. London: Henry S. King and Company, 1873.

————. *Chagataische Sprachstudien*. Leipzig, 1867; reprinted Amsterdam: Philo Press, 1975.

————. *Sketches of Central Asia*. London: Wm. H. Allen and Company, 1868.

————. *Travels in Central Asia. Being the Account of a Journey from Teheran Across the Turkoman Desert on the Eastern Shore of the Caspian to Khiva, Bokhara, and Samarkand*. New York: Harper and Brothers, 1865.

Virskii, M. M., ed. *Sbornik materialov dlia statistiki samarkandskoi oblasti, za. 1887–1888 gg.* Samarkand: Izdanie Samarkandskago Oblastnago Statisticheskago Komiteta, 1890.

Vladimirtsov, B. Ya. *The Life of Chingis-Khan*. New York: Benjamin Blom, 1930, reprinted 1969.

————. *Obshchestvennyi stroi Mongolov. Mongol'skii kochevoi feodalizm*. Leningrad: Izdatel'stvo Akademii Nauk SSSR, 1934.

Vosstanie 1916 goda v Srednei Azii i Kazakhstane. Sbornik dokumentov. Moscow: Izdatel'stvo Akademii Nauk SSSR, 1960.

Vserossiiskii tsentral'nyi ispolnitel'nyi Komitet XI Sozyva: vtoraia sessia. Moscow, n.p., 1924.

Vsesoiuznaia perepis' naseleniia 1926 goda. "Uzbekskaia SSR." Vol. 15. Moscow: Izdanie TsSU SSSR, 1926.

II [Vtoroi] s'ezd intelligentsii Uzbekistana. 11–12 dekabria 1959 goda. Stenograficheskii otchet. Tashkent: Gosudarstvennoe Izdatel'stvo Uzbekskoi SSR, 1960.

Walzer, Michael. *Spheres of Justice: A Defense of Pluralism and Equality.* New York: Basic Books, 1983.

Wensinck, A. J. *Concordance et Indices de la Tradition Musulmane.* Vol. 1. Leiden: E. J. Brill, Union Académique Internationale, 1936.

Who's Who in the USSR 1965/66. New York: Scarecrow Press, 1966.

Wimbush, S. Enders, and Bennigsen, Alexandre A. *Muslim National Communism in the Soviet Union: A Revolutionary Strategy for the Colonial World.* Chicago: University of Chicago Press, 1980.

Yudakhin, Q. *Ozbek-rus lughäti.* Tashkent: Izdanie Aktsionernogo Obshchestva "Sredazkniga," 1927.

Yugnaki, Ähmäd. *Hibatul-haqayiq.* Translated into Uzbek by K. Mahmudawa. Tashkent: Ghäfur Ghulam namidägi Bädiiy Ädäbiyat Näshriyati, 1971.

Yukneki, Edib Ahmed b. Mahmud. *Atebetu'l-Hakayik.* Edited by Reshid Rahmeti Arat. Istanbul: Atesh Basimevi, 1951.

Yusuf wä Ahmäd. Jusuf und Ahmed. Ein ozbegisches Volksepos im chiwaer Dialekte. Text and translation prepared by H. Vámbéry. Budapest: Druck des Franklin-Verein, 1911.

Zarubin, I. I. *Spisok narodnostei turkestanskogo kraia.* Leningrad: Rossiiskaia Akademiia Nauk. Trudy Komissii po Izucheniiu Plemennogo Sostava Naseleniia Rossii i Sopredel'nykh Stran, 1925.

Zasedaniia Verkhovnogo Soveta SSSR, deviatogo sozyva (pervaia sessiia) 25–26 iiulia 1974 g. Stenograficheskii otchet. Moscow: Izdanie Verkhovnogo Soveta SSSR, 1974.

Zhukovskii, S. V. Snosheniia Rossii s Bukharoi i Khivoi za posliednee trekhsotlietie. Petrograd: Trudy Obshchestva Russkikh Orientalistov, Number 2, 1915.

Index